The Joan Palevsky  Imprint in Classical Literature

In honor of beloved Virgil—

"O degli altri poeti onore e lume . . ."

—Dante, *Inferno*

The publisher gratefully acknowledges the generous contribution to this book provided by Joan Palevsky.

Imperial Ideology and Provincial Loyalty in the Roman Empire

CLASSICS AND CONTEMPORARY THOUGHT

Edited by Thomas Habinek

Imperial Ideology and Provincial Loyalty in the Roman Empire

Clifford Ando

UNIVERSITY OF CALIFORNIA PRESS
Berkeley   Los Angeles   London

University of California Press
Berkeley and Los Angeles, California
University of California Press, Ltd.
London, England
© 2000 by the Regents of the University of California

Library of Congress Cataloging-in-Publication Data
Ando, Clifford, 1969–
    Imperial ideology and provincial loyalty in the Roman Empire / Clifford
Ando.
       p.   cm. — (Classics and contemporary thought ; 6)
    Includes bibliographical references and index.
    ISBN 0-520-22067-6 (alk. paper)
    1. Rome—History—Empire, 30 B.C.–476 A.D.—Influence.   2. Alle-
giance—Rome.   3. Rome—Provinces—Administration.   4. Rome—Cultural policy—Influence.   5. Political stability—Rome.   I. Title.   II. Series.
DG59.A2 A64   2000
937′.06—dc21   99-041499
                                                    CIP

Manufactured in the United States of America
09 08 07 06 05 04 03 02 01 00
10 9 8 7 6 5 4 3 2 1

Albert Ando
patri optimo

fecisti patriam diversis gentibus unam
—RUTILIUS NAMATIANUS *DE REDITU SUO* 1.63

CONTENTS

ILLUSTRATIONS

PREFACE AND ACKNOWLEDGMENTS

The stability of the Roman empire requires substantial and specific explanation. What induced the quietude and then the obedience of her subjects? Roman military power might explain the lack of protests and revolts among provincials, but it cannot account for their gradual Romanization, especially if we designate by that term the absorption and local application of the forms and structures of Roman political and legal thought. Greeks proved no less permeable to Roman influence in those spheres of activity than did the populations of Gaul, Spain, or North Africa; our answer to the question posed above must, therefore, confront the translation of symbolic forms across cultures at different stages of literacy, urbanization, and technological development. As a process that transformed the empire from an *imperium,* a collection of conquered provinces, into a *patria,* a focus for the patriotic loyalties of its subjects, Romanization thus defined cannot be measured through the spread of Roman artifacts, nor can it be disproved by the ubiquitous evidence of persistent local cultures. The study of Roman interaction with provincials at the local level likewise suggests that the internal stability of the empire relied not on Roman power alone, but on a slowly realized consensus regarding Rome's right to maintain social order and to establish a normative political culture.

In this essay I argue that the official discourse of the imperial government, and the principles of legitimation to which it gave voice, found a ready audience in the polyglot population of the Roman provinces. I analyze the nature and appeal of that discourse on two levels. First, recognizing that complex systems of belief can be neither scripted nor imposed, I seek to articulate both Rome's invocation of its subjects' obedience and their justifications for participating in their own subjugation. Second, although I focus on the tropes and arguments through which Greeks and Romans discussed these issues, I construct my argument in a contemporary idiom, drawing above all on the work of Max Weber and his successors, Pierre Bourdieu and Jürgen Habermas not least among them.

I suggest that provincials internalized imperial ideology during the long periods of tranquillity that characterized the first and second centuries A.D. and, therefore, that the empire survived its crises because of what had been achieved in times of peace. Nevertheless, it would be difficult to overestimate the impression left by Rome's initial incursions in any given area. The extraordinary swiftness of Roman conquest played no small role in preparing an enthusiastic audience for imperial propaganda. Many populations around the Mediterranean attributed Roman victories to their gods' desertion of themselves and alliance with the Romans.

In point of fact, the governors and administrators who followed Roman arms into new provinces were often irresponsible and frequently corrupt. Yet the seemingly inexhaustible forces that Romans hurled against each other in the middle of the first century B.C. can only have reinforced provincials' impression of Roman power, as surely as they urged that the object of those contests was the rulership of the world. Although Augustus defined his power and his position differently before different constituencies, his charismatic appeal everywhere ultimately derived from his success in war. He burnished that appeal through his ability to guarantee to all security in their persons and their property. It was thus through the charismatic figure of Augustus, and then through the charismatic office he endowed, that provincials first began to conceive for themselves a role as participants in rather than subjects of Roman imperial power.

For example, Augustus claimed responsibility for all victories won by Roman arms under his *auspicia.* Yet provincials probably had little interest in Roman sacral law. Over time, however, both at Rome and elsewhere, such claims suggested that emperors had access to powers and potentialities beyond the mortal. More important, emperors sought to profit from their victories through *aurum coronarium,* an ad hoc levy that required provincials to display gratitude for imperial benefactions. (Those skeptical of the systems of mass communication then prevailing should note that this institution produced revenue only if emperors notified municipalities of their recent deeds.) In asking for provincials' gratitude, emperors had also to universalize the benefits of their actions. That is to say, they had to describe their actions as advantageous not simply to Rome or to Roman citizens, but to all residents of the empire. That rhetoric—designed, no doubt, to fill the coffers of Rome—unintentionally privileged a definition of the Roman community based not on citizenship but on residence, not on legal status but on a shared relationship with the emperor of the world.

The regular functioning of the imperial bureaucracy likewise observed a putative division between citizens and aliens. But the rituals it enforced, such as the census or the annual oaths of loyalty, similarly could direct attention away from differences in legal status and toward the equivalence of all as subjects of a higher power. Pliny swore his oath to Trajan at the same time and in the same place as did the Bithynians. Again, Augustus had offered himself as guarantor of the rationality of his administration: his charismatic power promised that his representatives would obey and enforce Rome's published laws and that provincials could appeal the decisions of any administrator to that individual's superintendent. Residents and communities throughout the empire displayed their faith in such promises and in the truth value of Roman documents by learning to manipulate Roman regulations in their favor, by using Roman authorities to adjudicate local disputes, and above all, by constructing personal and institutional histories from the data supplied by notarized records of their interactions with the central power.

Imperial Ideology and Provincial Loyalty in the Roman Empire argues for similar unifying and universalizing tendencies in the distribution of imperial art and monuments, in the creation of a shared calendar and history through imperial cult, and in Rome's desire to found her actions on the *consensus* of her citizens and subjects. Imperial ideology emerges here as the product of a complex conversation between center and periphery. I do not, however, insist upon the existence of some unitary imperial culture. Rather, acknowledging that a society's illusions are often the most interesting and potent aspects of its reality, I seek to demonstrate that residents of the empire believed in the universality of certain political ceremonies and of the foundational beliefs that such ceremonies expressed. By contextualizing this intellectual and cultural shift in the everyday, this work narrates a profound and widespread redefinition, not simply of the role and nature of government, but of individuals' relations with each other, their localities, and the larger community of their empire.

Five years ago I began with a question: Why did the empire last so long? I name this work an essay because it does no more than sketch the path to an answer. Experts will see how cursory are its treatments and summaries of complex issues and long-standing problems. Some topics elsewhere deemed essential to imperial history may startle by their absence. It would be churlish now to apologize for what this book is not. I beg a single indulgence. I know as well as anyone how meager is the documentation I have provided, of both ancient evidence and modern scholarship. It was once fuller: at one time the notes contained the text of all literature cited and the bibliography of modern works stretched to some twenty-seven hundred items. But that material filled the notes with more words than were in the text and, I came to understand, brought the argument no closer to proof. It also rendered publication impossible.

The Social Science and Research Council of Canada provided a grant to aid research on this work, as did the James H. Zumberge Faculty Research and Innovation Fund at the University of Southern California, while the libraries and interlibrary loan staffs at the University of Michigan, York University, the University of Toronto, and the University of Southern California made that research possible.

Conversations with David Potter about the usurpation of status symbols and with Bruce Frier about Weber shaped this work when it was in the planning stages. Later, Hal Drake and one anonymous reader provided generous reports for the University of California Press. Tom Habinek's series has proved a congenial home. Andy Meadows provided valuable assistance acquiring the illustrations. Dennis Kehoe, Pete O'Neill, and David Smith read individual chapters and offered invaluable instruction on matters great and small. Ann Hanson read the entire manuscript with characteristic thoroughness and taught me all the little that I know about Roman administration. As editor, Kate Toll rescued this work when it had been rejected elsewhere and has overseen its progress with all conceivable professionalism and courtesy. Cindy Fulton has managed the book's production, and Paul Psoinos has edited its text, with exceptional care.

To borrow another's language, as advisor and friend Sabine MacCormack illuminated this work and my life *probitate mentis, moribus, studiis simul.* Finally, if anyone has, Jessica made this work possible and asked nothing in return. I doubt she can have known how much one could spend on photocopies and filing cabinets. This book is mean compensation for all that they have given me.

ABBREVIATIONS

Abbreviations of journal titles are those found in *L'Année Philologique,* with a few small and easily deciphered variations. Papyrological corpora and series are denoted by the abbreviations in J. F. Oates et al., *Checklist of editions of Greek and Latin papyri, ostraca, and tablets.* The fourth edition of that work was published as *BASP* Supplement 7 (1992); I have followed the edition revised as of 10 June 1999 and published at http://odyssey.lib.duke.edu/ papyrus/texts/clist.html. Abbreviations of titles of ancient works generally follow those in *LSJ, OLD, Blaise-Chirat,* or *Lampe;* they are also expanded in the Index Locorum.

AbhBay	*Abhandlungen der Bayerischen Akademie der Wissenschaften, phil.-hist. Abteilung*
AbhGött	*Abhandlungen der Akademie der Wissenschaften in Göttingen, phil.-hist. Klasse*
AbhHeid	*Abhandlungen der Heidelberger Akademie der Wissenschaften, phil.-hist. Klasse*
AbhMainz	*Abhandlungen der geistes- und sozialwissenschaftlichen Klasse der Akademie der Wissenschaften und der Literatur in Mainz*
AÉ	*L'Année Épigraphique*
AJ	F. Abbott and A. C. Johnson, *Municipal administration in the roman empire* (Princeton, 1926)
AJA	*American Journal of Archaeology*
AJP	*American Journal of Philology*
ANRW	*Aufstieg und Niedergang der römischen Welt* (Berlin, 1972–)
Archiv	*Archiv für Papyrusforschung und verwandte Gebiete*
ASP	*American Studies in Papyrology*
BAGB	*Bulletin de l'Association Guillaume Budé*
BAR	British Archaeological Reports

BASP	*Bulletin of the American Society of Papyrologists*
BCH	*Bulletin de Correspondance Hellénique*
BÉFAR	Bibliothèque de l'École Française d'Athènes et de Rome
BGU	*Aegyptische Urkunden aus den Königlichen* [later *Staatlichen*] *Museen zu Berlin, griechische Urkunden*
BHAC	*Bonner Historia-Augusta Colloquium*
BICS	*Bulletin of the Institute of Classical Studies, London*
BKT	*Berliner Klassikertexte*
BL	*Berichtigungsliste der griechischen Papyrusurkunden aus Ägypten*
Blaise-Chirat	A. Blaise and H. Chirat, eds., *Dictionnaire latin-français des auteurs chrétiens* (Turnhout, 1954)
BMC	*Coins of the Roman Empire in the British Museum* (London, 1923–)
BMCR	*Bryn Mawr Classical Review*
ByzF	*Byzantinische Forschungen*
BZ	*Byzantinische Zeitschrift*
C. Iust.	*Corpus iuris civilis*, vol. 2, ed. P. Krueger, *Codex Iustinianus* (Berlin, 1929)
C. Th.	T. Mommsen, ed., *Codex Theodosianus*, vol. 1, pars posterior, *Theodosiani libri XVI cum Constitutionibus Sirmondinis* (Berlin, 1905)
CAH	*The Cambridge ancient history*
CAH²	*The Cambridge ancient history*, 2d edition
Cahiers Glotz	*Cahiers du Centre Gustave Glotz*
CÉFR	Collection de l'École Française de Rome
Chron. min.	T. Mommsen, ed., *Chronica minora saec. IV. V. VI. VII.*, 3 vols. (Berlin, 1892–1898)
CIG	A. Boeckh, ed., *Corpus inscriptionum Graecarum* (Berlin, 1828–1877)
CIL	*Corpus inscriptionum Latinarum* (Berlin, 1863–)
ClassAnt	*Classical Antiquity*
Const. Sirm.	T. Mommsen, ed., *Codex Theodosianus*, vol. 1, pars posterior, *Theodosiani libri XVI cum Constitutionibus Sirmondinis* (Berlin, 1905)
CP	*Classical Philology*
CPG	M. Geerard, ed., *Clavis patrum Graecorum* (Turnhout, 1974–1987)
CPJud.	V. A. Tcherikover, A. Fuks, and M. Stern, eds., *Corpus Papyrorum Judaicarum* (Cambridge, 1957–1964)
CPL	R. Cavenaile, ed., *Corpus papyrorum Latinorum* (Wiesbaden, 1958)
CPR	*Corpus papyrorum Raineri*
CQ	*Classical Quarterly*
CRAI	*Comptes Rendus de l'Académie des Inscriptions et Belles Lettres*
DOP	*Dumbarton Oaks Papers*
Ed. Iust.	*Iustiniani XIII Edicta quae vocantur*, in *Corpus iuris civilis*, vol. 3, ed. R. Schoell and W. Kroll., *Novellae* (Berlin, 1963)
EJ	V. Ehrenberg and A. H. M. Jones, *Documents illustrating the reigns of Augustus and Tiberius*, 2d ed., revised (Oxford, 1976)
EntrHardt	*Entretiens*, Fondation Hardt pour l'Étude de l'Antiquité Classique
FGrH	F. Jacoby, ed., *Die Fragmente der griechischen Historiker* (Leiden 1923–)
FHG	K. Müller, ed., *Fragmenta historicorum graecorum* (Paris, 1851–1885)

FIRA	S. Riccobono et al., eds., *Fontes iuris Romani antejustiniani* (Rome, 1940–1941)
Gibbon	E. Gibbon, *The history of the decline and fall of the Roman empire*, ed. D. Womersley (London, 1994)
GRBS	*Greek, Roman and Byzantine Studies*
HGM	L. Dindorf, ed., *Historici Graeci minores* (Leipzig, 1870–1871)
HSCP	*Harvard Studies in Classical Philology*
HThR	*Harvard Theological Review*
HZ	*Historische Zeitschrift*
I. Cret.	M. Guarducci, ed., *Inscriptiones Creticae* (Rome, 1935–1950)
I. Didyma	A. Rehm and R. Harder, eds., *Die Inschriften von Didyma* (Berlin, 1958)
I. Ephesus	*Die Inschriften von Ephesus* (Bonn, 1979–)
IBM	*The collection of ancient Greek inscriptions in the British Museum*
ICS	*Illinois Classical Studies*
IG	*Inscriptiones Graecae* (Berlin, 1873–)
IGBulg	G. Mikhailov, ed., *Inscriptiones Graecae in Bulgaria repertae* (Serdica, 1956–)
IGLS	L. Jalabert, R. Mouterde, et al., eds., *Inscriptions grecques et latines de la Syrie* (Paris, 1929–)
IGRR	R. Cagnat et al., eds., *Inscriptiones Graecae ad res Romanas pertinentes* (Paris, 1901–1927)
ILS	H. Dessau, ed., *Inscriptiones Latinae selectae* (Berlin, 1892–1916)
Inscr. Ital.	*Inscriptiones Italiae* (Rome, 1931–)
Integration	*Rome et l'intégration de l'empire, 44 av. J.-C.–260 ap. J.-C. Tome 1,* F. Jacques and J. Scheid, *Les structures de l'empire romain* (Paris, 1990); tome 2, C. Lepelley, ed., *Approches régionales de haut-empire romain* (Paris, 1998)
IRT	J. M. Reynolds and J. B. Ward-Perkins, *Inscriptions of Roman Tripolitania* (Rome, 1952)
JbAC	*Jahrbuch für Antike und Christentum*
JDAI	*Jahrbuch des Deutschen Archäologischen Instituts*
JEA	*Journal of Egyptian Archaeology*
JECS	*Journal of Early Christian Studies*
JHS	*Journal of Hellenic Studies*
JJP	*Journal of Juristic Papyrology*
JNG	*Jahrbuch für Numismatik und Geldgeschichte*
JÖAI	*Jahreshefte der Österreichischen Archäologischen Instituts*
JQR	*Jewish Quarterly Review*
JRA	*Journal of Roman Archaeology*
JRS	*Journal of Roman Studies*
JThS	*Journal of Theological Studies*
Lampe	G. W. H. Lampe, *A patristic Greek lexicon* (Oxford, 1968)
LSJ	H. G. Liddell, R. Scott, and H. S. Jones, eds., *A Greek-English lexicon*, 9th ed. (Oxford, 1968)
MAAR	*Memoirs of the American Academy in Rome*
Malcovati[5]	E. Malcovati, ed., *Imperatoris Caesaris Augusti operum fragmenta*, 5th ed. (Turin, 1969)

MAMA	*Monumenta Asiae Minoris Antiqua*
MC	L. Mitteis and U. Wilcken, *Grundzüge und Chrestomathie der Papyruskunde*, Bd. II, *Juristischer Teil*, Hälfte II, *Chrestomathie* (Leipzig, 1912)
MDAI(I)	*Mitteilungen des Deutschen Archäologischen Instituts, Abteilung Istanbul*
MDAI(M)	*Mitteilungen des Deutschen Archäologischen Instituts, Abteilung Madrid*
MDAI(R)	*Mitteilungen des Deutschen Archäologischen Instituts, Römische Abteilung*
MÉFR	*Mélanges de l'École Française de Rome (Antiquité)*
MH	*Museum Helveticum*
Mommsen, *GS*	T. Mommsen, *Gesammelte Schriften* (Bonn, 1905–1913)
MRR	T. R. S. Broughton, *The magistrates of the Roman Republic* (New York and Atlanta, 1951–1986)
MW	M. McCrum and A. G. Woodhead, eds., *Select documents of the principates of the Flavian emperors* (Cambridge, 1961)
N. Th.	*Novellae Theodosii*, in T. Mommsen and P. Krueger, eds., *Codex Theodosianus*, vol. 2, *Leges Novellae ad Theodosianum pertinentes* (Berlin, 1905)
NHLL	*Nouvelle histoire de la littérature latine* (Turnhout, 1993–)
NumChron	*Numismatic Chronicle*
OGIS	W. Dittenberger, *Orientis Graeci inscriptiones selectae* (Leipzig, 1903)
OLD	P. G. W. Glare, ed., *Oxford Latin dictionary* (Oxford, 1968–1982)
ORF[3]	E. Malcovati, ed., *Oratorum Romanorum fragmenta liberae Rei Publicae*, 3d ed. (Turin, 1967)
P. Amh.	B. P. Grenfell and A. S. Hunt, eds., *The Amherst papyri* (London, 1900–1901)
P. Apokrimata	W. L. Westermann and A. A. Schiller, eds., *Apokrimata: Decisions of Septimius Severus on legal matters* (New York, 1954)
P. Babatha	See *P. Yadin*
P. Berlin	Berlin papyri
P. Cair. Isid.	A. E. R. Boak and H. C. Youtie, eds. *The archive of Aurelius Isidorus in the Egyptian Museum, Cairo, and the University of Michigan* (Ann Arbor, 1960)
P. Cair. Masp.	J. Masparo, ed., *Papyrus grecs d'époque byzantine. Catalogue général des antiquités égyptiennes du Musée du Caire* (Cairo, 1911–1916)
P. Coll. Youtie	A. E. Hanson, ed., *Collectanea papyrologica: Texts published in honor of H. C. Youtie* (Bonn, 1976)
P. Columbia	Columbia papyri
P. Corn.	W. Westermann and C. J. Kraemer, Jr., eds., *Greek papyri in the library of Cornell University* (New York, 1926)
P. Euphrates	Euphrates papyri (see Feissel and Gascou 1995)
P. Fam. Tebt.	B. A. van Groningen ed., *A family archive from Tebtunis* (Leiden, 1950)
P. Fay.	B. P. Grenfell, A. S. Hunt, and D. G. Hogarth, eds., *Fayum towns and their papyri* (London, 1900)
P. Flor.	*Papiri greco-egizii, Papiri fiorentini*

P. Fouad	A. Bataille et al., eds., *Les papyrus Fouad* (Cairo, 1939)
P. Giss.	O. Eger, E. Kornemann, and P. M. Meyer, eds., *Griechische Papyri im Museum des oberhessischen Geschichtsvereins zu Giessen* (Leipzig, 1910–1912)
P. Got.	H. Frisk, ed., *Papyrus grecs de la Bibliothèque municipale de Gothembourg* (Gothenburg, 1929)
P. Hamburg	*Griechische Papyrusurkunden der Hamburger Staats- und Universitätsbibliothek*
P. Heidelberg	*Veröffentlichungen aus der Heidelberger Papyrussammlung*
P. Iand.	*Papyri Iandanae*
P. Köln	*Kölner Papyri*
P. Lond.	*Greek papyri in the British Museum*
P. Mich.	*Michigan papyri*
P. Oslo	*Papyri Osloenses*
P. Oxy.	*The Oxyrhynchus papyri*
P. Panop. Beatty	T. C. Skeat, ed., *Papyri from Panopolis in the Chester Beatty Library, Dublin* (Dublin, 1964)
P. Petaus	U. Hagedorn, D. Hagedorn, L. C. Youtie, and H. C. Youtie, eds., *Das Archiv des Petaus* (Cologne, 1969)
P. Phil.	J. Scherer, ed., *Papyrus de Philadelphie* (Cairo, 1947)
P. Ryl.	*Catalogue of the Greek and Latin papyri in the John Rylands Library, Manchester*
P. Stras.	*Griechische Papyrus der Kaiserlichen Universitäts- und Landesbibliothek zu Strassburg*
P. Tebt.	*The Tebtunis papyri*
P. Vindob.	Vienna papyri
P. Würz.	*Mitteilungen aus der Würzburger Papyrussammlung*
P. XV Congr.	*Actes du XVe Congrès international de papyrologie, Brussels 1979* [*Pap. Brux. 16–19*]
P. Yadin	N. Lewis, ed., *The documents from the Bar Kochba period in the Cave of Letters: Greek papyri* (Jerusalem, 1989)
P. Yale	*Yale papyri in the Beinecke Rare Book and Manuscript Library*
Pan. Lat.	*Panegyrici Latini*
Pap. Brux.	*Papyrologica Bruxellensia* (Brussels 1962–)
PBA	*Proceedings of the British Academy*
PBSR	*Papers of the British School at Rome*
PCPhS	*Proceedings of the Cambridge Philological Society*
PEQ	*Palestine Exploration Quarterly*
Peter, *HRR*	H. Peter, *Historicorum Romanorum reliquiae* (Leipzig, 1906–1914)
PG	*Patrologia cursus completus, Series Graeca*
PIR	*Prosopographia imperii Romani*
PL	*Patrologia cursus completus, Series Latina*
PLRE	A. H. M. Jones, J. R. Martindale, and J. Morris, eds., *The prosopography of the later Roman empire*, vol. 1, A.D. 260–395 (Cambridge, 1971)
PSI	*Papiri greci e latini: Pubblicazioni della Società italiana per la ricerca dei papiri greci e latini in Egitto*

RPhil	*Revue de Philologie*
RAC	*Reallexicon für Antike und Christentum* (Stuttgart, 1950–)
RE	*Realencyclopädie der classischen Altertumswissenschaft*
RÉL	*Revue des Études Latines*
RevArch	*Revue Archéologique*
RevHist	*Revue Historique*
RHDFE	*Revue Historique de Droit Français et Étranger*
RhM	*Rheinisches Museum*
RIB	R. G. Collingwood and R. P. Wright, *The Roman inscriptions of Britain*, vol. 1, *Inscriptions on stone* (Oxford, 1965)
RIC	*Roman imperial coinage* (London, 1923–)
RIDA	*Revue Internationale des Droits de l'Antiquité*
RMR	R. O. Fink, *Roman military records on papyrus* (Cleveland, 1971)
Robert, *Hellenica*	L. Robert, *Hellenica: Recueil d'épigraphie de numismatique et d'antiquités grecques* (Limoges, 1940–1965)
Robert, *OMS*	L. Robert, *Opera minora selecta* (Amsterdam, 1969–1990)
RPC	A. Burnett, A. M. Amandry, and P. P. Ripollès, *Roman provincial coinage*, vol. 1 (in 2 parts), *From the death of Caesar to the death of Vitellius* (London and Paris, 1992)
RS	M. Crawford, ed., *Roman statutes* (London, 1996)
SB	*Sammelbuch griechischen Urkunden aus Ägypten*
SC de Cn. Pisone patre	*Senatus consultum de Cn. Pisone patre* (see Eck, Caballos, and Fernández 1996)
SEG	*Supplementum Epigraphicum Graecum*
Sel. pap.	A. S. Hunt and C. C. Edgar, eds., *Select papyri* (Cambridge, 1932)
Sherk, *MDRW*	R. K. Sherk, *The municipal decrees of the Roman West*. Arethusa Monographs, 2 (Buffalo, 1970)
Sherk, *RDGE*	R. K. Sherk, *Roman documents from the Greek East* (Baltimore, 1969)
SIG	W. Dittenberger, ed., *Sylloge inscriptionum Graecarum*, 3d ed. (Leipzig, 1915–1921)
SitzBay	*Sitzungsberichte der Bayerischen Akademie der Wissenschaften, phil.-hist. Klasse*
SitzHeid	*Sitzungsberichte der Heidelberger Akademie der Wissenschaften, phil.-hist. Klasse*
Smallwood, *Gaius*	E. M. Smallwood, ed., *Documents illustrating the principates of Gaius, Claudius and Nero* (Cambridge, 1967)
Smallwood, *Nerva*	E. M. Smallwood, ed., *Documents illustrating the principates of Nerva, Trajan and Hadrian* (Cambridge, 1966)
SO	*Symbolae Osloenses*
StCl	*Studii Clasice*
StudGoth	Studia Graeca et Latina Gothoburgensia
Studia Pontica	J. G. C. Anderson, F. Cumont, and H. Grégoire, eds., *Studia Pontica* (Brussels, 1903–1910)
Syme, *RP*	R. Syme, *Roman papers* (Oxford, 1979–1991)

TAPA	*Transactions of the American Philological Association*
TAPhS	*Transactions of the American Philosophical Society*
Theb. ostr.	A. H. Gardiner, H. Thompson, and J. G. Milne, eds., *Theban ostraca* (London, 1913)
WC	L. Mitteis and U. Wilcken, *Grundzüge und Chrestomathie der Papyruskunde*, Bd. I, *Historischer Teil*, Hälfte II, *Chrestomathie* (Leipzig, 1912)
WS	*Wiener Studien*
WZRostock	*Wissenschaftliche Zeitschrift der Universität Rostock*
YCS	*Yale Classical Studies*
ZKG	*Zeitschrift für Kirchengeschichte*
ZPE	*Zeitschrift für Papyrologie und Epigraphik*
ZSavRom	*Zeitschrift der Savigny-Stiftung für Rechtsgeschichte, romanistische Abteilung*

CHAPTER ONE

Introduction

Communis Patria

We take the Roman empire for granted. As an agglomeration of territories and ethnic groups conquered in swift and bloody wars—and the swiftness of that conquest continues to defy historical explanation—the empire possessed an internal stability that ought to elicit considerable surprise. Instead, we treat its longevity as inevitable; historians from Flavio Biondo to Otto Seeck and beyond have set their sights on its ultimate decline and fall, rather than on its remarkable tenure. Studies of resistance and insurrection abound, but they invariably reinforce our view of the empire's history as one of actively appreciative prosperity, punctuated only rarely by purely local disturbances.[1]

The most important exception to this tradition is, paradoxically, its most famous exponent, Edward Gibbon, whose *History* remains the greatest work on its topic. While conducting research in the fall of 1773, Gibbon penned a brief essay that he later published as the closing chapter of the *History*'s third volume.[2] Although titled "General observations on the fall of the Roman empire in the West," the chapter immediately directs attention away from its avowed topic: "The rise of a city, which swelled into an empire, may deserve, as a singular prodigy, the reflection of a philosophic mind. But the decline of Rome was the natural and inevitable effect of immoderate greatness. Prosperity ripened the principle of decay; the causes of destruction multiplied with the extent of conquest; and as soon as time or accident had

---

1. For evidence and analysis of revolts see Dyson 1971 and 1975, Pekáry 1987, and Goodman 1991, with the important caveats in Alföldy 1989. Pekáry and Goodman draw rather different conclusions from their data than do I.

2. Craddock 1989, 8.

removed the artificial supports, the stupendous fabric yielded to the pressure of its own weight. The story of its ruin is simple and obvious; and instead of inquiring why the Roman empire was destroyed, we should rather be surprised that it had subsisted so long."[3]

Historians of Rome's decline, like those of late antiquity, have long studied Gibbon's topic without addressing his question. The praises of Rome have been catalogued, but their motivation remains unexplored; the fall of Rome seemingly can be explained without knowing how it reached the heights whence it fell; "the boundaries of the classical world" are delineated, but their genesis, apparently, is self-evident.[4] Those who have investigated with brilliance and insight the haunting power exercised by cultural memories of "eternal Rome" have rarely asked why Egyptians or Greeks or Gauls felt that "the most brilliant light of all the earth had been extinguished" or that "in one city the whole world had perished" when the "head of the Roman empire" was cut off.[5] We can no longer afford such innocence. Neither the exercise of power nor obedience to empires remains unproblematic. Gibbon's question requires an answer.

If Gibbon saw that it is longevity and not caducity that demands inquiry and explanation, why did he entitle his study *The history of the decline and fall of the Roman empire?* Did he come to believe that the story of the empire's ruin was neither simple nor obvious? If so, why did he publish the unaltered text of the "General observations" in 1781, since it seems to contest the value of his great undertaking?

Gibbon presents a similar paradox in the *History*'s first volume. Readers in 1776 cannot have known that five more volumes would follow over the next dozen years, and yet they may have been surprised to learn of Septimius Severus that "posterity, who experienced the fatal effects of his maxims and example, justly considered him as the principal author of the decline of the Roman empire."[6] If our first instinct is to look backward over what we have read, to understand what Severus had done to justify this verdict, we should also look forward. An empire that on Gibbon's reckoning survived twelve hundred years after Severus had planted the seeds of its decline was

---

3. Gibbon "General observations" (2.509).

4. Essays on Rome's "fall" abound; the metaphor scarcely requires documentation. Provincial praise of Rome: Gernentz 1918. "The boundaries of the classical world" in A.D. 200: Brown 1971, 11.

5. Jerome *In Ezechielem* 1 *pr.;* cf. 3 *pr.* (*Quis crederet ut totius orbis exstructa victoriis Roma corrueret, ut ipsa suis populis et mater fieret et sepulcrum, ut tota Orientis Aegypti, Africae littora olim dominatricis urbis, servorum et ancillarum numero complerentur. . . . ?*), 7 *pr.* and 8 *pr.* On memories of *Roma aeterna* see Klingner 1927; Dölger 1937; Bréhier 1949, 11–14; Courcelle 1964; Paschoud 1967; Fuhrmann 1968; Klein 1986.

6. Gibbon chapter 5 (1.148).

indeed remarkable, and historians of that empire must surely consider the forces that sustained it, even as they narrate the unfolding of those events that encompassed its ruin.

Viewed from this perspective, the antithesis between stability and decline, between longevity and loss, begins to dissolve. To identify the causes of Rome's destruction, Gibbon had to demonstrate that the empire had been susceptible to them. His work thus intertwines an exposition of the empire's artificial supports with the story of their removal. The exposition of those supports is less explicit than we might have wished because the history of stability does not lend itself to narrative, and narrative was Gibbon's chosen tool. Gibbon therefore began only when "the Roman monarchy, having attained its full strength and maturity, began to verge towards its decline."[7]

In point of fact, Gibbon combined diachronic and synchronic exposition, both within and across chapters, so artfully as to escape the conscious awareness of his readers. Many happily remember that he begins "in the second century of the Christian Æra," when "the empire of Rome comprehended the fairest part of the earth, and the most civilized portion of mankind."[8] But his diachronic analysis begins only in his fourth chapter, and his preceding chapters themselves locate the origins of "the system of the Imperial government" in the reign of Augustus: it is in the institutions of Augustus that Gibbon sought the supports that Severus was to overthrow at the end of the second century.[9]

Gibbon began with the insight that the empire, although acquired and ultimately dissolved through force, had not been sustained by it. Unlike other ancient monarchies, in which Gibbon saw "despotism in the centre, and weakness in the extremities," Rome did not control—indeed, could not have controlled—its provinces by stationing a garrison in every city.[10] According to Gibbon's calculations, a premodern economy could not have sustained such a body of nonproductive manpower as would fill those garrisons.[11] What made the policing of the Roman empire unique, and ren-

---

7. Gibbon "Preface" (1.1).

8. Gibbon chapter 1 (1.31).

9. Gibbon would later regret beginning his narrative with the death of Marcus. In the margin of his own copy of volume 1 he wrote: "Should I not have given the *history* of that fortunate period which was interposed between two Iron ages? Should I not have deduced the decline of the Empire from the civil Wars, that ensued after the fall of Nero, or even from the tyranny which succeeded the reign of Augustus? Alas! I should: but of what avail is this tardy knowledge? Where error is irretrievable, repentance is useless" (Gibbon 1972, 338).

10. Gibbon chapter 2 (1.70).

11. Gibbon chapter 5 (1.127); cf. chapter 9 (1.237), arguing that only complex societies can sustain artistic forms of intellectual endeavor.

dered its political culture uniquely homogeneous, was the fact that control through coercion was in some profound sense unnecessary. Citing with approval the speech of Agrippa in Josephus's *Jewish War,* Gibbon argued that Roman magistrates had seldom "required the aid of a military force" because "the vanquished nations, blended into one great people, resigned the hope, nay even the wish, of resuming their independence, and scarcely considered their own existence as distinct from the existence of Rome."[12]

Gibbon pursued this insight on two fronts, one ideological and one cultural. First, Gibbon recognized that individual emperors and even the "Imperial system" could face challenges from within the governing class, especially from the men who superintended the legions on the emperor's behalf. To explain the lack of such challenges in the first two centuries, he maintained that Augustus and his successors identified civilian corporate bodies as the final repositories of authority in the state in order to persuade potential usurpers that neither assassination nor revolts would earn the throne.[13] Guilty of murder or treason, the usurper would have had to watch the Senate nominate and the people elect a man whose first official act would be gratefully to execute his benefactor. It had been this constitutional "distance" between military and civilian authority that saved, as their proximity would later damn, the feeble or truculent men whom fate placed on the throne.[14] Gibbon thus considered a stable succession one essential measure of the empire's stability. To adopt this measure is, however, not to ask why cities or legions or senators devoted their energies to promoting particular candidates for the rulership of the world rather than to contesting the system that assigned such power to a single—a single *Roman*—individual. The legitimacy of the "system of the Imperial government," in all its extent, is presupposed, in the eighteenth as in the second century.

Second, Gibbon argued that the Romans had offered citizenship as a reward for those who adopted Roman culture. Gibbon did not inquire too deeply whether or why provincials would have wanted Roman citizenship; he understood that it brought important legal privileges and protections, and perhaps he regarded these as sufficient enticement. What is more serious, he posited the existence of a Roman culture that was, if not homogeneous, at least distinct from some notional provincial cultures. On this understanding, not only did individuals move from one culture to the other as though changing their cloaks—itself a dominant ancient metaphor for cultural bilingualism—but Roman culture remained static, impervious to in-

---

12. Gibbon chapter 2 (1.70).
13. Gibbon chapter 3.
14. Cf. Gibbon chapters 3 and 4 on Tiberius, Caligula, Claudius, Nero, Vitellius, Domitian, and Commodus (1.104, 117, and 120).

fluences brought by provincials from their former lives.[15] Cultures were one thing; their participants, another.

These arguments beg many questions. Gibbon saw some of them, but I shall leave his answers to one side for the moment. Today we cannot avoid several problems that Gibbon's chronological parameters neatly excluded, in particular those arising from Roman conquest. Processes of acculturation were preceded by acts of annexation. What made Roman power persuasive or even attractive to the populations of the provinces? What rendered provincial cultures permeable to Roman paradigms for the legitimate exercise of government? In short, what induced quietude rather than rebellion?

To answer these questions we must first understand that provincial obedience to Roman domination was an ideological construct, its realization dependent on many people's sharing a complex of beliefs that sanctioned a peculiarly Roman notion of social order. In Part 1 of this work I examine this problem from two perspectives. Chapter 2 considers the intersection between ancient experience and modern theories of domination and ideology. Although this book shares with traditional ideology criticism the goal of exposing the ideological work accomplished by the particular voices of imperial culture, it simultaneously draws from Weber a concern for the origins of provincial obedience. Emphasizing the flexibility of doxic systems, I shall argue that the Roman state successfully invoked the obedience of its subjects by appealing to several principles of legitimation concurrently. Particular constituencies responded to those principles whose validity they were predisposed to accept. It was, therefore, Rome that supplied the initial articulation of the values to which residents of the empire oriented themselves as members of its community, and it was the belief that others shared those values that legitimized Rome's representation of social order. Acquiescence and, ultimately, loyalty to Rome thus required recognition that the Roman construction of society, in relations between provinces, cities, individuals, emperors, and empire, adequately mapped the collective value commitments of its residents.

On this understanding, provincial obedience to Roman domination must be explained by revealing the mechanisms that rendered its particular apportioning of wealth and power morally palatable to those whom it seemingly disadvantaged. The Roman government could not have achieved this ideological revolution unless, at some level, both its official discourse and the apparatus that it imposed satisfied and, indeed, deliberately responded to the needs of those it governed. We should, however, be wary of identifying the needs of the population, both economic and psychological, with those of their Roman overlords. What is more, the needs of provincials were

15. Seneca *Controversiae* 9.3.13; cf. Suetonius *Augustus* 98.3 and Pliny *Ep.* 4.11.3.

neither identical nor even articulated in the same fashion in different parts of the empire: the specific historical forces that generated them arose in local dynamics. Likewise, the Roman government pursued its own immediate goals largely without regard for the long-term effects that its actions had on the mentality of provincial populations.

Modern scholars of empire tend to read promises to maintain social order with suspicion. We must not allow anachronistic cynicism to cloud our vision. As Chapter 3 demonstrates, many around the Mediterranean regarded Roman success in war as evidence that their own gods had sanctioned Roman conquest. Similarly, there is abundant evidence that populations around the empire, particularly in the Greek East, recognized and appreciated the political and economic stability with which the imperial government endowed daily life. Such people tended to view Romans' exercise of coercive force as legitimate and to concede Rome the right to impose a particular jural-political order. We must therefore separate provincials' occasional reactions to particular impositions or individuals from their acknowledgment that the imperial government had the right, indeed, the responsibility, to maintain its normative order. Such an acknowledgment was, moreover, at some level uncontroversial: no ancient writer disputed that a complex society could endure only if compliance with its laws and mores was binding.[16] What was new under the empire was the transference of that responsibility, in some measure, from the local community to the larger community of the empire.

At the same time, the Romans came to regard the arts of government as their special skill and boasted of this both at home and abroad. When provincials took up this refrain, they did so most often by congratulating Rome for having unified the world. The end of the first century A.D. thus witnessed a gradual convergence in rhetoric about Rome and her provinces and about citizens and subjects, producing varied descriptions of the empire as a single community, united by the city of Rome, its emperor, and the common interests of its people.

We could ascribe the motivation for provincial iterations of Roman propaganda solely to self-interest. But the mere existence of that propaganda raises another possibility. The Roman government devoted enormous resources to communicating with its subjects. Part 2 of this book explores the mechanisms, aims, and effects of these communicative actions. The Romans brought to the governance of their empire a set of theories developed in their own political life, and they somewhat counterintuitively adapted these to the governing of provincial aliens. As Romans had sought to found the order of Roman society on *consensus,* a unanimous intersubjective

16. Cf. Parsons 1971, 15.

agreement about social, religious, and political norms, so under the empire the Roman government encouraged its subjects to play an active role in empowering their rulers. Above all, they sought expressions of *consensus*, realized through religious and political rituals whose content could be preserved in documentary form. In so doing, Romans surrendered their notions of social order to the constructive and deconstructive powers of provincial discourse.

Rome's desire for *consensus* thus opened a conceptual and discursive space for provincials and Romans alike to negotiate the veracity of Roman propaganda and the rationality of Roman administration. Chapter 4 follows Jürgen Habermas in treating the communicative practices of imperial Rome as doubly contingent: utterances, whether rhetorical or imperative, could be successful only when their auditors assented to their inherent validity claims. On the one hand, because Rome claimed to govern rationally—because Rome claimed to dominate legitimately—Rome had to justify its demands upon provincials and, when challenged, had to redeem its justifications through discourse and not through force. For example, the government affirmed the legal validity of texts produced by its bureaucracy by first copying and then checking them (*describere et recognoscere*), a process that concretized its claims on its subjects, even as texts authenticated or notarized in this fashion provided those subjects with a tool with which to manipulate the organs of their government. Provincials, on the other hand, acknowledged the truth content of Roman official documents in several ways, but above all by using those documents to construct histories of themselves, their institutions, and their empire.

The exchange of official, authenticated documents produced an atmosphere in which collectivities throughout the empire competed in their expressions of loyalty. Chapter 5 considers this culture of loyalism in detail. For example, documents invoking *consensus* rarely claimed to represent the will of the entire world; rather, they purported to represent the will of particular groups. By describing those groups, such documents also interpellated them as discrete collectivities. Their loyalties thus divided, these collectivities had no basis for united action and, instead, competed in expressions of fealty to the prevailing order. To take but one famous example, at the close of the trial of Gnaeus Piso, not only did the Senate thank the equestrian order and the plebs as though these were standing corporate bodies, but it published its thanks in every major city and every legionary camp in the empire. Such expressions of loyalty created a burden on parallel corporations to do the same.

Not all communication was written, or even verbal. Chapters 6 and 7 consider the ideological import of processes of government and official works of art. Chapter 6 investigates three social dramas that implicitly or explicitly invoked and expressed the *consensus* of provincials. First, the Roman government asked its subjects to be grateful for its efforts on their behalf. Specifically, Roman emperors advertised their military victories anywhere to provincials everywhere and requested in return both verbal and financial expressions of gratitude. Such monies officially took the form of gold for an honorary crown. To make this irregular levy regularly remunerative, the Romans had both to distribute news widely and to universalize the benefits of their victories. That is, they had to describe benefits of immediate relevance to particular groups as somehow relevant to all, regardless of location or legal rank. In thus narrating their actions, the Romans' propaganda was not only universalizing but unifying, as well.

Second, Roman leaders turn out paradoxically to have needed the support of provincials most desperately when undertaking military action. Accounts of usurpations occasionally reveal or carefully elide the efforts taken by legionary commanders and would-be emperors to secure the good will of the regions through which they needed to pass. Third, populations around the empire adopted, and the Romans encouraged, acclamation, a ritual for the expression of *consensus*. Through rhythmic, unisonal chanting, populations recognized the legitimacy of officials, gave thanks for benefactions, or even signaled their displeasure. Insofar as acclamations were perforce unanimous, they necessarily expressed *consensus*. Thus, while specific contingencies might elicit acclamations from a given community, the content and the nature of those acclamations implied their potential iteration across the empire, and thus invoked imagined visions of the empire as a unified community.

Chapter 7 turns to the concrete symbols of Roman power, arguing that they possessed both immediate and long-term relevance. While the government produced coins whose types and legends spoke to the issues of the day, the users of those coins need not have understood those issues in their every detail; nor can we demonstrate that they did so. Instead, ancient testimony proves that people used imperial coins because they believed in their purity and universal currency. That faith was itself founded upon the belief that the emperor personally supervised the coinage and guaranteed its currency. Imperial portraits were likewise generated by individual emperors, or at least depicted individual emperors, but collections of imperial statues concretized a narrative of imperial history as the succession of charismatic individuals. Harmonizing with other ideological forces that depicted the imperial succession in dynastic terms, such collections urged that their viewers shared a past with any others who might view the same or similar portrait groups. Roman milestones and military standards similarly operated on multiple levels, identifying a point in space or a single legion among many, while suggesting the totalities of which those were particulars. The diffusion of such symbols throughout the empire gave to its inhabitants a universal symbolic language that operated across linguistic boundaries; today we recognize their influence not only on Greeks, but among those speaking Egyptian or Syriac, Punic or Palmyrene.

Part 3 turns from the pragmatics and theory of communicative action to the creative accomplishments of imperial ideology. We have already implicitly raised the problem this section seeks to address, for in referring to unifying tendencies in imperial propaganda we have begged a complex question: Unified around what? As we have seen, Gibbon himself raised this problem when he argued that "the vanquished nations, blended into one great people, resigned the hope, nay even the wish, of resuming their independence, and scarcely considered their own existence as distinct from the existence of Rome." But even in the second century, as Gibbon knew and contemporaries must have known, the residents of the empire shared neither language nor dress, neither climate nor cuisine. What can have united all those inside the empire and simultaneously distinguished them from those outside it?

Gibbon constructed his response to this question by drawing on classical social theory. He understood societies to be established through a form of social contract and to be maintained by individuals' willingness to subordinate personal desires to the regulation of the laws. According to Gibbon, "that public virtue which among the ancients was denominated patriotism, is derived from a strong sense of our own interest in the preservation and prosperity of the free government of which we are members."[17] From this understanding of legitimate orders, Gibbon argued that the "fairest portion of mankind" had been "united by laws, and adorned by arts."[18]

In thus privileging law as a force for socialization, Gibbon relied primarily on Cicero,[19] whose most rigorous attempt to distinguish societies and differentiate social orders comes in his *Republic*. In Book 6 of that work, Scipio Africanus announces that "nothing that happens on earth is so pleasing to that chief god who rules the entire world as the assemblies and gatherings of men united by the rule of law, which are called communities."[20] Cicero's fifth-century commentator Macrobius responded favorably to this defini-

---

17. Gibbon chapter 1 (1.39). See also chapter 9 (1.240): "Civil governments, in their first institutions, are voluntary associations for mutual defence. To obtain the desired end, it is absolutely necessary, that each individual should conceive himself obliged to submit his private opinion and actions, to the judgment of the greater number of his associates."

18. Gibbon chapter 2 (1.56); cf. chapter 1 (1.31): "The gentle, but powerful influence of laws and manners had gradually cemented the union of the provinces."

19. Gibbon's library contained several editions of the works of Rousseau and Locke, but he cites those authors only in the second volume and beyond.

20. Cicero *Rep.* 6.13.2: *nihil est enim illi principi deo qui omnem mundum regit, quod quidem in terris fiat, acceptius quam concilia coetusque hominum iure sociati, quae civitates appellantur.* See also

tion. "What could be more deliberate or more guarded than Cicero's definition of the term 'communities'? He wrote that 'the assemblies and gatherings of men united by the rule of law are called communities.' Indeed, there
have been bands of slaves and gladiators, and these were assemblies and
gatherings, but they were not united by the rule of law. That multitude
alone is righteous whose every man consents in obedience to its laws."[21] In
the same era Augustine alluded to this definition when he asked, "Who is so
blind of thought that he does not see how valuable is that social order that
constrains even sinners within the bonds of some limited earthly peace?"[22]

When Cicero spoke of "communities" (*civitates*), he implicitly raised the
problem of membership that would become fundamental to Gibbon's conception of societies and governments. Indeed, when one seeks to circumscribe the sense of community that obtained in the Roman empire of the
second century, the spread of Roman citizenship may seem an obvious
route of inquiry. But citizenship *as explanation* must remain an illusory fan-
tasy, destined to collapse under the weight of the phenomena for which its
champions intend it to account. A conquering power can grant all manner
of legal rights to its subjects without winning their allegiance; conversely,
long-standing legal aliens can feel and display patriotism as strongly and
publicly as any citizen. Citizenship's inability to engender loyalty was, in fact,
a topic of debate even in the ancient world, and that debate became particularly acute after the Social War, for two related reasons. First, some of the
newly enfranchised had recently fought against Rome on behalf of some
other polity, and, second, many citizens now lived so far from Rome that
they might never see their *patria*.

Cicero explored the emotive aspects of this problem at the opening of
Book 2 of *De legibus*. Cicero has referred to the land in which they walk as
his *patria*, which elicits a question from Atticus: "Have you then two *patriae*?
Or is our *communis patria* the only one? Unless, that is, you think that Cato's
fatherland was not Rome, but Tusculum?" To which Cicero responds (in a
passage replete with textual problems): "Absolutely I think that both he and
all other municipal men have two *patriae*: one by birth, and one by citizenship. . . . Thus we consider as our *patria* both the place where we were born
and that place by which we are adopted. But that *patria* must be preeminent
in our affection in which the name *res publica* signifies the common citizenship of us all. For her it is our duty to die; to her we ought to give our entire

---

Rep. 1.39, quoted in Chapter 2 at n. 147, as well as *Leg. Man.* 41, *Off.* 1.124, and *Clu.* 146, whose
climax is quoted in Chapter 10 at n. 2.

21. Macrobius *Comm.* 1.8.13, closing with *illa autem sola iusta est multitudo, cuius universitas
in legum consentit obsequium.*

22. Augustine *Gen. litt.* 9.9.14. Augustine elsewhere discussed Cicero *Rep.* 6.13.2 in detail;
see *Civ.* 2.21 and 19.21, and cf. *Lib. arbitrio* 1.5.11, 1.6.15, and *Serm. Dolbeau* 23.7.

selves, and on her altar we ought to place and to dedicate, as it were, all that we possess."[23]

Cicero thus urged that political loyalties need not stand in conflict with each other. Although the next sentence survives only in mutilated form, it seems clear that Cicero concluded this section by urging that loyalty to the *communis patria* must take precedence over that to any other political collectivity. In the hierarchy of allegiances outlined by Cicero, loyalty toward Rome occupied a superordinate position: her laws and her culture provided the normative fabric that would, to borrow the phrase of Rutilius Namatianus, "create from distinct and separate nations a single fatherland."[24] Himself a *novus homo*, Cicero appreciated the possibility that an individual could be a member of several social and political collectivities at the same time. Each of these subgroups—Cicero's family, his municipality, the Senate, the people of Rome—had different criteria for membership, which divided and differentiated his circle of acquaintances. Indeed, it was precisely this segmentation of his world that gave Rome its power: as the *communis patria* it united all those groups and all their members, assigning to each his proper place.[25]

Gibbon was too percipient an observer of men to believe that emperors conferred civility with citizenship. He saw citizenship as a reward that induced many to assimilate to Roman customs. Gibbon therefore argued that Caracalla had brought this process of acculturation to a halt when, in A.D. 212, he cavalierly distributed citizenship to all residents of the empire with a stroke of his pen.[26] Nevertheless, so long as citizenship had, at some implicit level, rewarded efforts to become Roman or even to identify with Roman interests, its possession could be relied upon to induce individuals to identify shared concerns with widely disparate, polyglot participants in their political reality, purely on the basis of their common citizenship.[27]

Gibbon thus neatly avoided the simplicity in Cicero's processual argument. Where Gibbon divorced acculturation from legal ranks and the contingencies that determined them, Cicero assumed an organic connection between social institutions intended to express the normative values of the social order, on the one hand, and the motivational mechanisms for obedience to that order, on the other. And yet Cicero's seductive assumption can direct our attention to rather different consequences that seemingly follow upon definitions of citizenship and thus to problems that Gibbon's reliance

23. Cicero *Leg.* 2.5. On Cicero's thought regarding patriotism and the competing claims of Rome and Arpinum see Hammond 1951 and esp. Bonjour 1975, 169–178 and 218–234.
24. Rutilius Namatianus *Red.* 1.63.
25. Cf. Parsons 1971, 13–14, on role pluralism.
26. Gibbon chapter 7 (1.212), and cf. chapter 6 (1.186).
27. Cf. B. Anderson 1983, 15–16.

on classical theory will have obscured. For example, membership in modern states requires citizenship, and therefore arguments about the role of government in society can proceed from legalistic definitions of membership. Thus a modern state posits a conceptual boundary between citizens and aliens, and it places demands on its citizens because it has responsibility for their corporate good. It justifies those demands by advertising the benefits that it directs back to its citizens, and citizens' claims upon the state for its benefits are legitimated by their legal status.

The manifest circularity of these propositions reveals the source of the great durability shown by entrenched conceptualizations of community.[28] The intersecting, almost redundant claims of the government seduce by their varied appeals, and the auditor who assents to one tenet imperceptibly makes the accompanying edifice his own. But the Roman empire divided the population of the world differently, into citizens, noncitizen residents of the empire, and barbarian nonresidents who might yet be conquered. The delineation of the boundary between citizen and alien remained the prerogative of the Roman state, and a history of that boundary might provide one perspective on the history of the foundation and formation of the Roman community. Histories of the foundation and formation of the community, conversely, could articulate alternative criteria of communal membership.

It is, therefore, ironic and yet intelligible that provincials' reception of Roman propaganda about victory in war provides the best medium through which to investigate their attempts to contest the state's boundary between citizens and aliens. In their celebrations of martial virtue, the Romans paraded representations of the "rivers, mountains, and provinces" involved in the military action. They also displayed captives in appropriate native costume, forcing them to assume postures suggestive of defeat and humiliation. When such captives were not available, as when Diocletian and Maximian restored the wives, sisters, and children of the Great King to their lord, their likenesses would do.[29] Chapter 8 suggests that provincials as early as the reign of Augustus began to propose their own models for the Roman community, ones in which the distinction between citizens and aliens yielded to that between those within and those outside the empire. They did so in the iconographic language supplied by Roman triumphal art.

This desire on the part of aliens to identify themselves as Roman reveals once again the poverty of citizenship as a path of inquiry. Viewing oneself as Roman must have required allowing others that conceit and therefore must have posited the empire itself as a united and unified community. Yet

28. Cf. Bourdieu 1977, 164–165, and 1990, 54–56 and 129–130.
29. Gibbon chapter 13 (1.383–384), with a neat piece of detective work in n. 87.

the one commonality among Rome's disparate provincials, beyond the name "Roman," was precisely the government that denied them official use of that name.[30] As Chapter 9 explains, resident aliens, who shared the government with citizens as with each other, chose instead to view themselves as Roman, and to view other residents as equally Roman, because of the perceived universality of the political rituals that regularly reconstituted them as a community. By concentrating on the forms through which power was concretized and communal membership was enacted, we can shift the parameters of our inquiry away from constitutional niceties and toward the ideas and ritual enactment of those ideas that shaped self-definitions in the provinces.

As we shall see, provincials who sought to identify themselves as Romans but who acknowledged the differential legal ranks imposed by Rome discovered a unifying tendency in the administrative rituals of Roman government. The swearing of loyalty oaths, the filing of a census return, the payment of taxes, and the procuratorial assize: these actions were simultaneously the field in which the ideological paradigms of the ruling order were acted out and the site in which those paradigms were most passionately contested.

Paradoxically, the appropriation of Roman forms for the construction of provincial identities took place in urban centers constructed or refurbished, often through official patronage, in order to promote the uninterrupted transfer of local wealth to Rome.[31] And yet, whatever the Romans' motivation, the circulation produced by imperially sponsored or subsidized building was not without real benefits to local populations. If, as Gibbon saw, "even the majestic ruins that are still scattered over Italy and the provinces, would be sufficient to prove, that those countries were once the seat of a polite and powerful empire," he was doubly correct to point out that "the provinces would soon have been exhausted of their wealth, if the manufactures and commerce of luxury had not insensibly restored to the industrious subjects, the sums which were exacted from them by the arms and authority of Rome. As long as the circulation was confined within the bounds of the empire, it impressed the political machine with a new degree of activity, and its consequences, sometimes beneficial, could never become pernicious."[32]

If we concentrated solely on material-social relations, then we might conclude that the symbolic capital generated in this economy merely legitimated an asymmetrical order that it both concealed and reproduced.[33] But

---

30. Cf. Ando 1999.
31. See Wiseman at *CAH*[2] IX 390.
32. Gibbon chapter 2 (1.70 and 80–81).
33. Cf. Bourdieu 1977, 196, and esp. 1990, 123–125.

Gibbon, seeking to understand the abortive acculturation of the provinces, rightly turned his attention elsewhere. He insisted instead that private contributions to the refurbishing of civic spaces along Roman lines revealed both the deep penetration of Roman paradigms for civic life and the accessibility of Roman paradigms to manipulation by non-Romans.[34] Local embracing of Roman classicism thus endowed public spaces and public buildings with new significance and simultaneously altered the meanings of the Roman administrative rituals conducted in them. When Gibbon wrote that "all the provinces of the empire, were embellished by the same liberal spirit of public magnificence, and were filled with amphitheatres, theatres, temples, porticos, triumphal arches, baths, and aqueducts, all variously conducive to the health, the devotion, and the pleasures of the meanest citizen," he spoke too loosely.[35] For these structures offered their benefits not just to citizens, but to all residents of the empire. As one modern study of Roman urbanism has concluded, "the message, the subject of the narrative, was about membership, about commonality—human membership in the community, and the community's in the larger whole. It was not a statement about unity but about an essential quality upon which unity depended."[36]

Of course, Roman imperial culture did not exist only in cities, nor can its spread be assessed by merely quantifying urbanization. Yet there can be no doubt that Rome administered through cities and consequently brought urbanization in all areas of the Mediterranean to new heights.[37] The Christian Tertullian, writing in the late second and early third centuries, usually praised Rome only to damn her, yet even he acknowledged that humanity had advanced to new levels of material prosperity under the empire:[38]

> Clearly the world itself is manifestly every day better cultivated and better arranged than it was formerly. Everything is accessible, everything is known, everything is for sale everywhere. Delightful farms have erased once desolate wastelands, fields have subdued forests, herds have routed the wild beasts, deserts are sown, rocks broken, and swamps drained: there are now more cities than there were even houses once. Islands are no longer dreadful, nor do reefs terrify. Everywhere are houses, everywhere people, everywhere the commonwealth, everywhere life.

Tertullian, of course, warned that this prosperity of "the arrogant human race" would be subject to remedial pruning, but it suffices for now merely

---

34. Gibbon chapter 2 (1.70–74).
35. Gibbon chapter 2 (1.74).
36. MacDonald 1986, 269.
37. On the mechanics of governing through cities, see Stahl 1978 and Jacques at *Integration* 1.219–289.
38. Tertullian *Anima* 30; cf. Aristides *Or.* 26.94.

to note his identification of the world with the Roman state, and the state with the material prosperity created through Roman power. In the particular urbanism of the Roman empire, every forum became a speculum for that other Forum; each city, a representation of the City. The improvements in quality of life brought by these urban centers thus reflected to Rome's credit. The slow desertion of the classical city in late antiquity may have been due, in part, to Christian withdrawal from this world, and it was, in part, a response to the financial and personal duties incumbent on the curial class. But Rome, ironically, made that desertion possible by lowering the place such cities held in the hearts of men. The idea of Rome even held off the realization that Rome herself had fallen. There can be no other explanation for affirming within Justinian's *Digest,* more than a century after the sack of Rome, the *sententia* of Modestinus, "Rome is the *communis patria* of us all."[39]

39. Modestinus at *Dig.* 50.1.33: *Roma communis nostra patria est.*

PART ONE

Ancient and Modern Contexts

CHAPTER TWO

Ideology in the Roman Empire

No date identifies that moment when Rome ceased to rule her subjects through coercion and began to rely on their good will; no event marked the transformation of her empire from an aggregate of ethnic groups into a *communis patria*. The history of that transformation cannot seek certainties. The provincial population of the empire was probably never unanimous in its appreciation of Rome, nor would all residents of the empire have agreed on every detail of their shared culture. The existence of the *communis patria* relied not on any genuine identity between the patriotic sentiments of its members, but on their faith in the existence of such an identity. The components of that faith were manifold, but they all began with, indeed, were predicated upon, the universality of Rome and her emperors: for these were the men who provided and participated in the symbolic representation of *Romanitas*, who wrote and featured in the *res gestae populi Romani*, and who defined and defended the *orbis Romanus*.

The attempt to identify the shared concerns of the citizens of the empire—to distinguish, as it were, what was "Roman" about the Roman empire,[1] or what criteria were assumed to define those who belonged and to exclude those who did not—makes a strong claim for the existence of a Roman imperial ideology. This claim may arouse controversy, for it stands in

---

1. Brunt 1990, 269, states that "what was specifically Latin in the common civilization of the empire made little impact in the east." I suggest that too little effort has been devoted to defining "what was specifically" Roman "in the common civilization of the empire." Compare Amory 1997, 5: "What did the word 'Roman' mean to the millions of inhabitants of the Mediterranean littoral and its hinterland?" Amory's brief answer is rather different than my own.

contradiction to two fundamental tenets of modern scholarship on ideology: first, that the spread of an ideology was, like nationalism itself, dependent upon the existence of systems of mass communication;[2] and second, that an ideology—at least from a Marxist perspective—is an omnihistorical reality, existing primarily to propagate the working class's submission to the rules of the established order.[3] Ideology thus operates effectively because even its critics are *"always already* subjects, and as such constantly practice the rituals of ideological recognition."[4]

Writing on ideology at this level has provoked trenchant criticisms. First, in its focus on class, such writing results in two critical forms of myopia. On the one hand, by concentrating on the subjugation of the proletariat, it can suggest that members of the bourgeoisie were not similarly situated within a social totality, indeed, within the same social totality. On the other hand, by taking the fact of asymmetrical power relations for granted, historical inquiries often end merely by describing beliefs or texts as ideological, as though exposing them as such would in itself reveal their appeal and their enduring power.[5] Second, ideological discourse thus conceived presumes an untenable theory of subjectivity. On this view, ideological systems simply maintain themselves in accordance with functional imperatives, while social actors become cultural puppets, whose capacity for intention is circumscribed by plays of *différence* and whose statements bear no necessary referential relation to any existing state of affairs.[6]

2. See Thompson 1990, 1–3; on nationalism, see B. Anderson 1983, 38–47.

3. Althusser 1970, 132–133 and 161, on which see Barrett 1991, 19–22, and cf. Thompson 1990, 33–44 and esp. 37–40. Marx himself recognized that ideology was a historical phenomenon, insofar as it must evolve to meet new contradictions in the structure of objective social relations (Larrain 1979, 48–49), and thus Marx insisted that ideology, like religion, must be studied first at the level of material social relations (ibid., 48–49 and 178–179). For Marx, the mere existence of *an* ideology, as a feature of man's subliminal understanding of social relations which might otherwise appear asymmetrical to his consciousness, is, however, guaranteed by emergence of classes (see, for example, McCarney 1980, 95).

4. Althusser 1970, 172–173; emphasis in original.

5. Cf. Jameson 1981.

6. The most famous exposition of ideological analysis in these terms is Foucault 1972. Foucault, of course, resisted attempts to align his work with ideology critique, but his arguments on this issue were largely untenable (McCarthy 1993, 47, and cf. 56–57). Honneth 1991, 105–148, provides a rigorous philosophical critique of Foucault's semiological structuralism; for a critique of Foucault's theories of power, see Kögler 1990. Foucault seems later to have recognized that his early theory of discourse could not form the basis of historical inquiry (see, e.g., Foucault 1980, 100–101). For a more positive analysis of Foucault's contribution to the theory of ideology, see Barrett 1991, 123–156 and esp. 134–141. Note, however, that Marxist scholars had already developed powerful critiques of epistemological definitions of ideology—for a particularly rigorous development of these themes, see McCarney 1980, 80–99; and Rossi-Landi has long sought, from a semiotic perspective, to redirect philosophical reflection away from ideology as such, and toward its manifestation as a set of privileged discourses (1990, 62–

Although Pierre Bourdieu has sought to distance his own theory of *habitus* and *doxa* from Marxist theories of ideology, and from the work of Louis Althusser in particular,[7] we may adduce his work to break down the assumptions that have constrained Marxist inquiry into the ancient world. Bourdieu seeks, *inter alia*, to explain the ability of established social orders to maintain themselves; in doing so, he focuses his attention on societies whose structures embody permanent hierarchies of wealth and power. Bourdieu escapes the boundaries of Marxist thought not least because his inquiry reaches so far beyond the level of politics and economics, and he signals his departure from their inquiries in his rejection of their vocabulary and in his coinages of *habitus* and *doxa*. Nevertheless, like Althusser and Foucault, Bourdieu cautions against the objectivist fallacy inherent in any attempt to fix a synoptic diagram of a doxic system like Roman imperial ideology.[8] An ideology, like Bourdieu's habitus, is embedded in history: individuals in Bourdieu's societies, like those in the world of Althusser, are always already subject to a system of thought that systematically directs their attention away from the arbitrariness of the hierarchies obtaining in their society.[9]

Similarly, it has been the task of Weber and his successors to explain how an individual within such a system can be led to misrecognize the objective conditions of his existence: that is to say, how the status of being always already subject to an ideology is maintained in time. To adopt the phraseology of Clifford Geertz, it was precisely Weber's attempt "to write a sociology of culture and a social psychology in a single set of sentences" that gave his "work its orchestral complexity and harmonic depth."[10] To overcome ideology critique's reductive view of subjectivity, we must integrate the study of ideology with a model of socialization. This integration has achieved its most rigorous form in Jürgen Habermas's writings on the lifeworld.[11] Drawing on Piaget's theories of development, Habermas argues that socialization is inherent in cognitive development: the decentering of egocentric understandings of the world is part and parcel of developing an intuitive appreciation for the understanding, the normative expectations, of some other. On this basis, Habermas argues that "every action oriented to reaching understanding can be conceived as part of a cooperative process of interpretation aiming at situation definitions that are intersubjectively recognized."[12] In

71 and 297–335). Marxist literary critics have also long emphasized a non-Althusserian, historicist approach to the study of ideology: see in particular Jameson 1988, 1.62 and 140–141.

   7. Bourdieu 1977, 188.

   8. Bourdieu 1990, 7–11.

   9. Bourdieu 1977, 164–169.

   10. Geertz 1983, 121.

   11. Habermas 1984, 69–74, and 1987, 119–152. For an aggressive critique of this theory, see J. Alexander 1991, 52 and 63–65.

   12. Habermas 1979, 69–94, and, more briefly, *idem* 1984, 69–70.

other words, Habermas insists that "speaking and acting subjects know how to achieve, accomplish, perform, and produce a variety of things without explicitly adverting to, or being able to give an explicit account of, the structures, rules, criteria, schemata, and the like on which their performances rely."[13] Habermas calls the shared social world of such actors their "lifeworld," a body of knowledge and beliefs that stores the interpretive work of previous generations even as it permits those interpretations to be placed in question and subjected to critical revision.[14]

By grounding his communications theory on such a model of socialization, Habermas succeeds in breaking down the historical fallacy—one by no means limited to Marxists—of viewing classes and other collective actors as agents in history and as subscribers to particular ideologies. His approach allows us to view such groups as constructed through intersubjective relations, between subjects who succeed in reasoning with each other. Collective actors can thus be described as communicating with each other once we have understood, and continually remember, that the identity of social groups is itself fragile and merely the product of processes of socialization carried out between individuals.[15] Simultaneously, it is the continued functioning of individuals within cultural systems that both legitimates those systems and provides for their continuance. Socialization thus conceived has a central place in the maintenance of the lifeworld: just as it instructs individuals in the boundaries and rules of that world, so it cloaks some central core of that world's values with normative legitimacy. Insofar as these values are shared and are subconsciously or semiconsciously assumed to be shared, they provide a stable, indeed, a valid, foundation for communication as a process for reaching intersubjective understanding. As Thomas McCarthy writes, it is then the aim of "rational reconstruction" "to render explicit what underlies such practically mastered, pretheoretical know-how, the tacit knowledge that represents the subject's competence in a given domain," and to acquire "explicit knowledge of the 'deep' structures and rules, the mastery of which is implicit in the competence of a subject to generate meaningful symbolic configurations."[16] At some level, of course, it lies in the nature of such rules and values, in their essence as foundations for lifeworlds, that they should remain unarticulated. Thus, if processes of communication necessarily, if only implicitly, open the lifeworld to criticism and revision, the need to function within a collectivity will urge individuals subconsciously to criticize and to revise only so much, only so far.

13. McCarthy 1993, 130–131.
14. Habermas 1984, 70–71.
15. On this aspect of Habermas's theory, see Honneth 1991, 269–276.
16. McCarthy 1993, 130–131.

Bourdieu, too, following Victor Turner, emphasizes the bounded flexibility of ideologies, whatever their names. He insists, therefore, that it is unnecessary to posit individual subjects mindlessly misrecognizing the fact of their subjugation to an arbitrary social order. Rather, a habitus, or an ideology, is a system of belief that channels rather than stifles creativity: habitus is generative.[17] Roman imperial ideology need not, therefore, have been monolithic or even universal: rather, "official language, particularly the system of concepts by means of which the members of a given group provide themselves with a representation of their social relations (e.g., the lineage model or the vocabulary of honor), sanctions and imposes what it states, tacitly laying down the dividing line between the thinkable and unthinkable, thereby contributing towards the maintenance of the symbolic order from which it draws its authority."[18] The emperors and governing class at Rome did not have to provide their world with Scripture, but merely with a system of concepts that could shape, and in so doing slowly unite, the cultural scripts of their subjects. What were the basic features of the generative grammar dictated by Rome to its provincial audiences?

At a superficial level, the Roman imperial government advertised to its subjects the existence of a shared history and a common political theology: the history was that of Rome in the era of her empire, and the one constant in the religious firmament was the emperor.[19] Official expressions of this ideology thus concentrated attention on the figure of the emperor. In a recent essay Ludwig Koenen has explicated the "Janus-like character" of the Ptolemaic kings; rather than concentrating on the different ways the Ptolemies presented themselves to their Greek and Egyptian subjects, however, Koenen focuses on the complex translation of Egyptian ideas into terms which made the pharaonic character of Ptolemaic kingship palatable to Greeks.[20] In this way, the Ptolemaic kings made important strides toward creating a common culture—albeit unique to their kingdom—by using their own position as the common reference point for the different ethnic

17. See V. Turner 1974, 17, and Bourdieu 1977, 20–21 and 78, and 1990, 54–55. For a Marxist perspective on the boundaries of ideological consciousness, see Jameson 1981, 47–49.

18. Bourdieu 1977, 21.

19. In a resolutely polytheistic world, the imperial cult within a generation "became the most widespread of all cults," "a pillar of the new order in every Roman city in the West" (Zanker 1988, 297 and 304). Chapter 9 proposes that the imperial cult offers direct refutation of the recent assertion that "no pagan seriously dreamed of bringing all humankind to give worship in one body to one deity" (Goodman 1994, 32). For a broader conception of the theological justifications for empire, see Dölger 1932 and Enßlin 1943 and 1954. On the complications this ideology posed for the Christian proponents of empire, see Batiffol 1913a, Peterson 1935, Kantorowicz 1963, and Beskow 1962.

20. Koenen 1993.

groups under their control. The Roman emperor came to fill a similar function: the desire at all levels of the population to see stability in the history of
the empire was expressed first and foremost by the fiction of dynastic continuity on the throne that became so prevalent in the second century; and
virtually every pagan religion made room for the emperor in its pantheon—or, rather, allowed its practitioners to accommodate the extraordinary power of the emperor in their individual theologies.[21]

The unification of the empire may have been a goal of some emperors,
but modern scholars would describe this as a method of an ideology and not
its ultimate purpose, however latent that purpose may have been. A regime's ideology makes explicit the particular principles of legitimation to
which it appeals, and to the extent that the regime is successful the ideology gives voice to the foundational beliefs on which an individual subject's
normative commitment to the social order is based.[22] To quote Marx: "Every
child knows that a social formation which did not reproduce the conditions
of production at the same time as it produced would not last a year."[23] On
those terms, we can describe the function of ideology as "to efface the domination intrinsic to power in order to present the latter at the level of appearance under two different aspects: on the one hand, as the legitimate
rights of sovereignty, and on the other, as the legal obligation to obey it."[24]
Ideology then operates by constructing and conveying meaning in whatever
available forms of signification "within a system of domination in such a way
as to sanction its continuance"—"to establish and sustain relations of power
which are systematically asymmetrical."[25]

An ideology thus represents in various forms the Janus-faced nature of
domination: we may regard as ideological those symbolic phenomena generated by individuals in order to represent their imagined relationship to
the "real conditions of their existence,"[26] as well as patently official claims
to the inherent validity of whatever legitimating principle serves as the war-
rant for an official action.[27] Such a legitimating principle ultimately derives
its historical importance from its acceptance by the subjects of the regime
which invokes it. Max Weber gave this fact a classic formulation in his
definition of domination:[28]

21. Cf. Price at *CAH*[2] X 841–847, stressing that provincial municipalities "responded to"
rather than "replicated" Roman religious practices, which were not "designed to be copied."

22. For the phrasing I am indebted to Kronman 1983, 37.

23. Marx to Kugelmann, 11 July 1868 (*Selected correspondence* [Moscow, 1955], 209),
quoted in Althusser 1970, 127.

24. Foucault 1980, 95.

25. Giddens 1983, 19; Thompson 1990, 6–7 and 56.

26. Althusser 1970, 162; cf. Larrain 1979, 45–47.

27. Kronman 1983, 39. Cf. Chapter 4, "Habermas and Rome."

28. Weber 1978, 946; italics in original.

Domination [which Weber has also called *authoritarian power of command*] will thus mean the situation in which the manifested will (*command*) of the *ruler* or rulers is meant to influence the conduct of one or more others (*the ruled*) and actually does influence it in such a way that their conduct to a socially relevant degree occurs as if the ruled had made the content of the command the maxim of their conduct for its very own sake. Looked upon from the other end, this situation will be called *obedience.*

Weber himself acknowledged the awkwardness of his definition; he argued, however, that "the merely external fact of the order being obeyed is not sufficient to signal domination" in his sense: "We cannot overlook the meaning of the fact that the command is accepted as a 'valid' norm."[29] Weber thus analyzed and classified his three ideal types of legitimate domination with an eye toward "both the organization that implements and the beliefs that sustain a given system."[30]

Weber himself repeatedly emphasized that he designed his "pure types" as tools for sociological inquiry and not as descriptive categories; indeed, he often stated that "the composition of the beliefs" that sustained any particular system of domination was rarely simple and that his types were therefore almost never to be found in their pure form.[31] Weber's types may nevertheless prove useful to the present project in the attempt to distinguish the different principles of legitimation to which the emperor appealed in his relations with the different constituencies he solicited for support: the army, the civilian bureaucracy, the Senate, the population of the provinces, and the city of Rome.[32] This list is, of course, excessively schematic, and not every emperor satisfied each of these groups. Although some emperors survived for a long time while alienating one constituency—Caracalla displeased the city of Rome, and the Senate never really warmed to Hadrian—most successful emperors presented themselves in a fashion that kept the peace between themselves and their audiences, and among the audiences themselves. We must also remember that particular groups were predisposed to obey—and even to demand—specific claims to authority.

With these cautions in mind, we may begin with the hypotheses that the Senate understood the emperor's rule to be based on rational grounds, that the army stressed the traditional nature of his power, and that the population of the provinces viewed him as a charismatic figure in Weber's sense.[33]

29. Weber 1978, 946; see also 263.
30. Bendix 1960, 293–294.
31. Weber 1978, 246, 263, and 1161; cf. Kronman 1983, 7.
32. Cf. Josephus *Bell. Iud.* 7.65–67, canvassing the sentiments in Italy upon the return of Vespasian: he divides the population between Senate, people, and army.
33. For quick definitions of these terms, see Weber 1978, 215, but analysis of these types is the subject of 212–251 and 941–1211.

Figure 1. Nero supervises his second *congiarium*. Aes from the mint of Rome. *BMC* I, Nero no. 141.

We must not adhere too rigidly to this schema in our interpretation of either the conceptual underpinnings of imperial ideology or the rituals and forms of Roman political life. Rather, by looking for the flexibility in imperial ideology and in the government's self-presentation, we can understand why Theodor Mommsen saw a dyarchy at the heart of imperial government and Fergus Millar saw a passive-reactive bureaucracy dominated by the figure of the emperor: that is what they were intended to see. For example, Neronian issues from the mints at Rome and Lyons depict the emperor distributing largesse: the superhuman figure of the emperor sits high on a platform, while a representative citizen receives his *tessera* (Fig. 1). Although the two most common types do depict the attendants who actually performed the distribution, the chief roles are reserved for the emperor and his client. The direct relation between the two, symbolized in some types by personified Liberalitas, is made concrete by either the gazes they exchange or their mutual extension of hands toward each other; those hands never meet, but they obviate the need for individuals to acknowledge or depict the bureaucratic apparatus that made the system work.[34]

This assertion does not require the conclusion that those scholars were unable to see through Roman propaganda to some elusive substance that lay underneath. On the contrary: a society's illusions are often the most interesting aspects of its reality. In work devoted to analyzing the development of Roman imperial illusions, Jean Béranger has shown with admirable clarity that the political vocabulary popularized in Augustan documents resonated with both Roman military terminology and Latin political philosophy: in its concision, its rigor, and, paradoxically, its generality, Augustan diction thus appealed simultaneously to soldiers and intellectuals.[35] Roman

34. *BMC* I, Nero nos. 138–141 and 308–310, or *RIC* I², Nero nos. 151–162, 394, 434, 435, 501–506, and 576. On these coins see Brilliant 1963, 76–77.

35. Béranger 1975, 153–163.

political rituals were similarly notable for what they left unspoken. Individuals therefore possessed considerable latitude in construing the ideological thrust of particular behaviors. For example, the use of adoption to designate a successor appealed on one level to those who interpreted the Principate as a legal institution: after all, the bureaucracy had started out as the personal *familia* of a single man, and, as such, it had to be willed by the emperor to his successor, although in practice its fate was never in doubt.[36] To the extent that adoption announced a specific heir to the charisma of the current emperor, it also might appeal to those who wished to see dynastic succession at the heart of imperial rule; even if the designated successor then required the acclamation of his subjects, this need should not distract from the charismatic power that accrued to the adopted heir from the mere fact of his designation.[37] Without doubt few if any people assigned their loyalties through a single principle of legitimation, but nothing about a Roman adoption precluded an individual from viewing it from many perspectives simultaneously.

Although Weber gave a privileged position to legal-rational authority,[38] he wrote a particularly rigorous and penetrating analysis of charismatic authority.[39] He based this analysis on the insight that charismatic authority in its pure form can exist only *"in statu nascendi.* It cannot remain stable, but becomes either traditionalized or rationalized, or a combination of both."[40] Charismatic authority possesses the inherent flaw that its holder cannot have a true heir precisely because of his own exceptional nature, quite apart from the possibility that patent failure in any endeavor may be interpreted as evidence that one's charisma is no longer genuine.[41] Weber proposed three possible scenarios for the routinization of charisma:[42]

> From a unique gift of grace charisma may be transformed into a quality that is either (a) transferable or (b) personally acquirable or (c) attached to the incumbent of an office or to an institutional structure regardless of the persons involved. We are justified in still speaking of charisma in this impersonal sense only because there always remains an extraordinary quality which is

36. On these terms, the year 68 must have marked a turning point in the Principate: even if Gaius had not designated an heir, Roman law would have provided for the succession of his property within his family. In 68 there were no more Julio-Claudian men, and the *familia Caesaris* could have dissolved. I know of no essay treating this problem directly, but see Béranger 1977, 353–366, and Levick 1986, 190–195.

37. Weber 1978, 1124–25; Béranger 1975, 137–152, 263, and 281–299.

38. Kronman 1983, 50–52.

39. Weber 1978, 241–270 and 1111–1157; cf. Bendix 1960, 298–328.

40. Weber 1978, 246; cf. 1121–1123.

41. Weber 1978, 242 and 263.

42. Weber 1978, 1135.

not accessible to everyone and which typically overshadows the charismatic subjects.

The remainder of this chapter focuses on the charismatic nature of the imperial office. Yet we should linger for a moment on different perspectives raised by Weber's formulation, and above all on the transference from Augustus to his Republican magistracies of a charismatic power that transformed the substance but not the surface of those institutions.[43]

Scholarship on the Augustan principate has often foundered on a modern dichotomy between constitutional and extraconstitutional interpretations of the offices and influence of the *princeps*, drawing support for their mutual, rigid opposition from some supposed binarism in Roman thought between *imperium* and *auctoritas*.[44] Jean Béranger long ago demonstrated the falsehood of such binarisms: the coexistence of Republic and monarchy is everywhere attested, explicitly and implicitly, both in documentary and in literary texts.[45] Likewise, the notional sovereignty of the *populus Romanus* remained integral to imperial ideology and received expression in the continued holding of elections through the early third century.[46] Béranger tried to shift scholars' attention instead toward what we might call institutionalized forms of juridical liminality within Roman politics and Augustan propaganda, to the actions Augustus undertook as a private citizen and to the scope already available under the Republic for differentiation between institutions and magistrates on the basis of differential forms and grades of *auctoritas*.[47]

Institutionalization lacks in theory and abstract discourse the force it acquires in practice. Ancient narratives fail to direct our attention to this issue precisely because their authors systematically misrecognized the arbitrary, constitutional underpinnings of the charismatic office that ruled their world. In political and juridical life in particular, legal texts and constitutional arguments objectify and consecrate the structure of power relations

43. For a clearheaded analysis of Weber's writings on the institutionalization of charisma, see S. N. Eisenstadt's introduction to Weber 1968, esp. xviii–xxxviii.

44. Cf. Kienast 1982a, 366–370. J. A. Crook, drawing on Hopkins 1978, has provided one of the best summaries of the problem, but nevertheless concludes that the modern scholar must choose a basis for the Principate: "There is no compatibility between the two pictures, and no compromise will accomodate both; it is necessary to choose" (*CAH*[2] X 113–123 at 119).

45. Béranger 1975, 259, citing evidence in n. 3, and cf. Judge 1974. For a late instance see Dio 56.43.4. See also Béranger 1977, demonstrating that *imperium* changed its semantic range in the early Principate. Forced by Augustus to retain its traditional meaning in very untraditional times, *imperium* came to signify all manner of extraconstitutional powers.

46. Béranger 1975, 209–242 and 261, and cf. Chapter 5 at nn. 115 and 137.

47. Béranger 1953, 114–131, and 1975, 243–258.

among the groups and the classes that are themselves produced and organized through the functioning of those mechanisms.[48] Through the language of abstraction, such texts legitimate the principles immanent in the practices and structures of the societies they purport to regulate. In the formulation of Pierre Bourdieu,[49]

> The objectification accomplished by . . . all forms of credentials is inseparable from the objectification which the law guarantees by defining *permanent positions* which are distinct from the biological individuals holding them, and may be occupied by agents who are biologically different but interchangeable in terms of the qualifications required. Once this state is established, relations of power and domination no longer exist directly between individuals; they are set up in pure objectivity between institutions, i.e. between socially guaranteed qualifications and socially defined positions, and through them, between the social mechanisms which produce and guarantee both the social value of the qualifications and the positions and also the distribution of these social attributes, among biological individuals.

As we shall see, provincials' tacit and often unconscious recognition of the legitimacy of Roman government, within certain spheres of operation, was qualitatively similar to the contests among senators and *viri militares* for the throne of the empire: by playing their respective games according to the rules of imperial ideology, each group shifted the topic of public discourse from the legitimacy of the empire to the legitimacy of specific emperors and magistrates.[50]

The first emperor of Rome, Julius Caesar, clearly derived much of his authority from charismatic achievements, and in his early years Augustus advertised in every way possible his belief that he had inherited his adoptive father's charisma.[51] Augustus, however, ultimately desired to disguise his domination behind a Republican guise; his ability to repudiate his ties to Julius Caesar and the triumviral era, ironically, came to him only because he acquired a transcendent charismatic status in his own right: it was expressed in his first years in power in his arrogation of the praenomen Imperator.[52]

---

48. Bourdieu 1990, 132; cf. *idem* 1977, 187–189.

49. Bourdieu 1977, 187–188; cf. *idem* 1977, 78, *idem* 1990, 10 and 56.

50. Cf. Bourdieu 1977, 164–168.

51. Weinstock 1971. See Fronto *Ep. ad Verum* 2.1.8: *Postquam res p. a magistratibus annuis ad C. Caesarem et mox ad Augustum tralata est.*

52. On the repudiation of Caesar, see Syme 1939, 316–317, who overstates the swiftness with which such an ideological shift could take place: Julius Caesar as divine parent continues to play a role in Augustan victoriousness into the late 20s (Gagé 1930b, 3, and 1932, 67–69). On Augustus's nomenclature see T. Mommsen 1887, 2.2.763–786, von Premerstein 1937, 250–260, and Syme, *RP* 1.361–377, esp. 370–372. Taeger 1960 discusses imperial cult as a channel for popular recognition of the charisma of the imperial office.

As victoriousness proved a foundation of Augustus's claim to exceptional status, so it became the unique prerogative of the emperor.

Augustus bequeathed more than his name to the office that he had created: his legacy simultaneously attached a degree of charisma to that office and demanded charismatic appeal from its occupant.[53] The various constituencies of the empire expressed their approval for—indeed, senators and soldiers alike believed that they themselves alone selected—an emperor by their unanimous acclamation. Nor was anything less than unanimity acceptable: a totality less one could not express *consensus*. In Weber's eyes, a regime based on a charismatic claim to power demanded no less: "Since the effectiveness of charisma rests on the faith of the ruled, their approval of the designated successor is indispensable. . . . In its essence [the ceremonial election of a new monarch] was something completely different, namely, the recognition or acknowledgment of a qualification older than the election, hence of a charisma, acceptance of which its bearer was in fact entitled to demand. In principle, therefore, a majority decision was at first not possible, for a minority, no matter how small, might be right in its recognition of a genuine charisma, just as the largest majority might be in error."[54] A Roman obsessed with the legal basis of the Principate could also justify the need for election by *consensus:* how else but unanimously could the *populus Romanus* transfer all its *imperium et potestas* to him and into him?[55] Few men possessed the prestige at the moment when they ascended the throne to silence a disgruntled but respected minority. On the other hand, the successful emperor was, by virtue of his success, unique, and he could claim the acclamation of his subjects as his right. So, for example, emperors could rarely afford to indict someone for attempting to usurp the throne. To do so was tantamount to exposing the arbitrariness of one's own power; better to call such men brigands, public enemies, disturbers of the public calm.[56] Likewise, the failure by members of a suspicious cult to acknowledge and acclaim such a ruler constituted not only treason, but a religious offense as well.[57]

---

53. Tacitus *Hist.* 1.32.1 reflects cynically on the charismatic power of the imperial office: *neque illis iudicium aut veritas, quippe eodem die diversa pari certamine postulaturis, sed tradito more quemcumque principem adulandi licentia adclamationum et studiis inanibus.*

54. Weber 1978, 1125–1126.

55. Ulpian at *Dig.* 1.4.1 *pr.: Quod principi placuit, legis habet vigorem: utpote cum lege regia, quae de imperio eius lata est, populus ei et in eum omne suum imperium et potestatem conferat.* On the legal importance of the *populus* in imperial ideology see Millar 1988, and cf. *idem* 1989.

56. See *SHA Pesc.* 1.1 and *Quad. tyr.* 2.1–2, as well as Ammianus 26.6.13.

57. See Bendix 1960, 305–306, or Kronman 1983, 45. Note Cyprian's sleight of hand in defending his episcopate: by insisting that those who challenge his authority in fact contest the *iudicium Dei et Christi*, Cyprian implicitly transforms his election by acclamation into mere human recognition of a prior divine selection (*Ep.* 66.1; cf. *Ep.* 55.8.3).

For example, a Roman would probably have justified the persecution of Christians by reference to past religious legislation: the Senate had for centuries protected the *res publica* from infection by foreign cults that might prevent proper *concordia* between the state and its gods. The need for *consensus* in such legislation, and the metaphors for the state through which it was expressed, remain entirely compatible with Weber's model of charismatic leadership. Since the Roman emperor was himself a fixture of the state pantheon and mediated between the *populus Romanus* and the divine, he could no more function without the support of religious *consensus* than could the state when poisoned by the Bacchanalia. In that respect the religious functions of the imperial office operated in harmony with Republican conceptions of the state religion and aided in cloaking the office with respectability.[58]

The evolution of Augustus's name into the title for the office that he created advertised both the source and the existence of the charismatic power attaching to that position.[59] Weber drew his examples of charismatic offices from the Catholic church—in its concept of *character indelebilis* "we encounter the most radical form of depersonalization of charisma and of its transformation into a qualification that is inherent in everybody who has become a member of the office hierarchy through a magic act, and that sanctifies official acts"[60]—but that should merely serve as a salutary reminder of the religious authority that the name Augustus signified. We might well suspect, therefore, that Dio's comment regarding the titulature for the imperial office, that "the use of the titles 'Caesar' and 'Augustus' confers on the emperors no power distinct to the individual; the one displays in particular the continuity in their line, while the other the brilliance of the office," severely underestimates what authority the mere holding of the office gave to its occupant.[61]

We might with profit allow Dio's observation to sidetrack us for a moment, in order to pursue the implications of this titulature a bit further. Nothing illustrates the multiple influences that shaped the evolution and

58. On Roman religious legislation, see Chapter 9, "The Discovery of Roman Religion."

59. Augustus himself had understood that his name would be used thus: *Quas ob res triumphus ei [sc. Tiberio] decretus est multique et magni honores. Censuerunt etiam quidam ut Pannonicus, alii ut Invictus, nonnulli ut Pius cognominaretur. Sed de cognomine intercessit Augustus, eo contentum repromittens, quod se defuncto suscepturus esset* (Suetonius *Tiberius* 17.1–2). See also Ovid *Fasti* 1.615–616, referring to Tiberius as *tanti cognominis heres*, and cf. Plutarch *Otho* 3.1. On the dynastic implications of Augustan titulature see T. Mommsen 1887, 2.2.818–822 and 1139–1143.

60. Weber 1978, 1141.

61. Dio 53.18.2: ἡ γὰρ δὴ τοῦ Καίσαρος ἥ τε τοῦ Αὐγούστου πρόσρησις δύναμιν μὲν οὐδεμίαν αὐτοῖς οἰκείαν προστίθησι, δηλοῖ δ' ἄλλως τὸ μὲν τὴν τοῦ γένους σφῶν διαδόχην, τὸ δὲ τὴν τοῦ ἀξιώματος λαμπρότητα. Contrast Ovid *Fasti* 1.608: *hic socium summo cum Iove nomen habet.*

reception of imperial ideology so well as an examination of attitudes toward dynastic succession in the early Principate. I can attempt only a few comments here, but the issue will run through the rest of this book like a leitmotiv. Despite Augustus's efforts to present his position in traditional terms, no one at Rome maintained any illusions as to its extraconstitutional nature: what mattered to the upper classes was the conciliatory, even deferential, tone with which he cloaked his power. The deference achieved its most characteristic expression in relations between Augustus and the Senate. Just as Augustus flattered that body that it remained the final repository of authority in the state, so it reciprocated by granting him all that he desired.[62] This stance required official propaganda to find an inoffensive term to describe Augustus's position within the commonwealth; eventually it settled on *statio* ("station").[63] Tragedies within his family repeatedly forced Augustus to confront the further problem that his constitutional fiction did not, indeed could not, provide an explicit mechanism to oversee the succession.[64] He eventually settled on two different approaches, to appeal to different, no doubt overlapping, audiences. First, he arranged for Tiberius to hold an equal share in his own constitutional powers: thus, in a very real sense, Tiberius was already an emperor before the death of Augustus.[65] Second, in A.D. 4 he adopted the forty-six-year-old Tiberius as his son.[66] Tiberius's refusal to accept all the honors previously held by Augustus caused confusion

62. On relations between emperor and Senate see Chapter 5.

63. See Béranger 1953, 184–186. For Augustus's own usage see Suetonius *Augustus* 28.2 and Gellius 15.7.3. See also *BMC* I, Augustus nos. 91–94; Ovid *Tristia* 2.219–220; *SC de Cn. Pisone patre* 128–130; Valerius Maximus 5.6 *pr.*, and cf. 3.2 *ext.* 3; Velleius 2.91.2, 2.124.2, and 2.131.1–2; Suetonius *Claudius* 38.3; Pliny *Pan.* 7.3 and 86.3; Tacitus *Dial.* 17.3; Antoninus Pius at Fronto *Ep. ad Ant. Pium* 6; Tertullian *Apol.* 11.9; *SHA Commodus* 1.8 and *Clodius Albinus* 2.3; Eutropius 9.27.1; and Ammianus 15.8.14.

64. Stuart Jones at *CAH* X 151–158; Syme 1939, 419–439. "In elective monarchies, the vacancy of the throne is a moment big with danger and mischief. The Roman emperors, desirous to spare the legions that interval of suspense, and the temptation of an irregular choice, invested their designated successor with so large a share of present power, as should enable him, after their decease, to assume the remainder, without suffering the empire to perceive the change of masters" (Gibbon chapter 3 [1.98]).

65. See, among many studies, Brunt 1977, 97–98. Velleius explicitly acknowledged, through words he put in the mouth of Augustus, that Tiberius held equal powers with Augustus, but that did not prevent the moment of the succession from being fraught with tension (2.123.2–124.2; cf. Ando 1997, 297–298). For later literary reflections on this process of transferring power, see Philostratus *Vit. Apoll.* 6.30, on Titus (Ἀναρρηθεὶς δὲ αὐτοκράτωρ ἐν τῇ Ῥώμῃ καὶ ἀριστείων ἀξιωθεὶς τούτων, ἀπῄει μὲν ἰσομοιρήσων τῆς ἀρχῆς τῷ πατρί) and Pliny *Pan.* 8.6 on Trajan's promotion: first son and Caesar, later *imperator* and *consors tribuniciae potestatis*.

66. The *fasti Amiternini* report the date as 26 June (*CIL* I, p. 323 = *EJ* p. 49), but Velleius as 27 June (2.103, a paragraph with several textual problems in its reporting of numbers: see Woodman's note *ad loc.*). Cf. Suetonius *Tiberius* 23.

and discomfort in the Senate, not least because his acceptance would have flattered the Senate that the honors were its to give. His refusal of the name *Augustus* by itself left contemporaries without a form of address that advertised his uniqueness and justified their obsequience.[67] Tiberius's evident disdain for the charade did not deter the Senate: it continued to insist on drafting and passing a *lex de imperio,* otherwise known as a *lex regia,* at the start of each new reign into the third century.[68]

So persistent was this official emphasis on superficially nondynastic sources of legitimacy, particularly at Rome, that Elias Bickermann argued *principes* of the first century founded their legitimacy on the consensus of the ruled and on the existence of a *lex regia,* rather than on the consecrated status of their immediate predecessors and fathers.[69] Although he was certainly correct to identify this rhetoric as a strand within imperial propaganda, the audience for such legal niceties was a peculiarly Roman one, and its use at Rome did not preclude the employment of dynastic arguments there and elsewhere. Despite the passage of such a law, the Julio-Claudian emperors clearly derived their authority from Augustus: his charisma retained force after his death above all through its incarnation as a divinity, Victoria Augusti.[70] In the provinces, moreover, and in the barracks, constitutional debates and *leges de imperio* meant little in this period: in such localities the belief that dynastic continuity would ensure the continuation of the benefits of the Augustan age was expressed above all through vows on behalf of the Augustan, or divine, house.[71] Even at Rome, different audiences continued to respond to different forms of legitimation: after the death of Nero, Otho allowed the plebs to address him as Nero, and he even adopted Nero as his cognomen on official documents, before the disapprobation of the governing class deterred him from this practice.[72]

---

67. On *Augustus* as a title for the office, see Suetonius *Tiberius* 17.2 (quoted above in n. 59).

68. See Brunt 1977; cf. Ulpian at *Dig.* 1.4.1 *pr.* (quoted above in n. 55), Dio 53.18.4–5, and *SHA Alex. Sev.* 8.1.

69. Bickermann 1929, 28–31.

70. See Chapter 8, "Augustus and Victory."

71. See Rose 1997a for provincial galleries honoring the *domus divina.* For some remarkable examples, see Reynolds 1986, 112, on the statues of Aeneas and Anchises in the Sebasteum at Aphrodisias; cf. *EJ* no. 96, from Thespiae, or *P. Lond.* 1912 (*Sel. pap.* 212.28–34), in which Alexandria asks Claudius for permission to make his birthday a holiday and to erect a gallery of portraits of his household. Cf. Edmondson 1997, 99 and 101–105, discussing the integration of *diva Augusta* into the cult for *divus Augustus* in Lusitania. On oaths and related texts, see Philo *Flacc.* 49 and 81, on the differential piety shown by the Jews and Flaccus εἰς τὸν Σεβαστὸν οἶκον, or the oaths from Gangra (*EJ* no. 315), Nicoclia (*EJ* no. 105*), and Assus (Smallwood, *Gaius* no. 33). References to the house or to the Augusti in dedications simply explode under Claudius (*RIB* 91; West 1931, no. 68; *IGRR* IV 584; Smallwood, *Gaius* no. 135, from four corners of the empire).

72. Plutarch *Otho* 3.1–2.

Bickermann was partially misled by the redundancy of the adoption. Why should Augustus have observed such legal and constitutional niceties if the niceties were not, in fact, substantive? In the crises of the late 20s B.C., Augustus had learned from the plebs how greatly they relied upon his personal guarantee of social order.[73] Augustus had to designate a successor, and adoption allowed him to establish a multigenerational succession that included minors while sharing constitutional authority only with those next in line. By designating successors through adoption, Augustus developed a multivalent system for concretizing the transfer of charisma between generations. This had the unfortunate consequence of marking males as either successors to the throne or candidates for elimination.[74] We can trace the dynastic plans of the Julio-Claudians in many ways—not least in the language with which communities around the empire celebrated imperial children—but no evidence is quite so chilling as the exclusion of relatives from the family mausoleum.[75] Over the next century, adoption took on an importance all its own, precisely because it could designate males outside the emperor's family. We can measure its growing importance not simply in references to adoption in the year 68, but in references before and after that year to the emperor's *providentia*, his providence.[76] The emperor displayed that quality above all in his taking thought for the stability of the empire after his death, and that act had its most concrete realization in the designation of a successor. As with other terms and concepts in Augustan ideology, *providentia* was multifaceted: Tiberius and later Julio-Claudians could speak with gratitude of the *providentia* of their predecessors and of the Senate. Yet it was the end of that dynasty that forced a crystallization of this concept and its language: it was up to Titus and Domitian to articulate clearly the role of Augustus in the succession and to assimilate to his paradigm the actions of their father.[77]

After the civil wars of 68, Vespasian and his sons initially tried to distance themselves from their predecessors and to assert the existence of a charismatic appeal of their own, although they did so using the forms and language consecrated by Augustan practice.[78] The Flavian municipal laws, for

73. Syme 1939, 331–348; Yavetz 1969, 26; Kienast 1982a, 84–99.
74. Béranger 1975, 139–140.
75. On those excluded from the mausoleum of Augustus see Panciera 1994, 80–84. On altars to Gaius and Lucius around the empire, see Gros 1988. The language of *AÉ* 1992, 1597, is characteristically dynastic: Ὁ δᾶμος Νέρωνα Κλαύδιον Δροῦσον τὸν αὑτοῦ πάτρωνα καὶ εὐεργέταν διὰ προγόνων, θεοῖς.
76. On *providentia* see Nock 1972, 264–265, and Baynes 1935, 83.
77. Béranger 1975, 338–341.
78. Tacitus *Hist.* 4.73: *ceterum libertas et speciosa nomina praetexuntur; nec quisquam alienum servitium et dominationem sibi concupivit ut non eadem ista vocabula usurparet.* Thus Vespasian, de-

example, ignore all earlier emperors except for the two who received consecration.[79] In this Vespasian clearly sought to establish the credentials of his own family as a dynasty: like Augustus he elevated his son to a share in the imperial power and celebrated that act abundantly on his coins.[80] Popular dislike for the chaos of the civil wars certainly aided them in this effort, but there were at least three problems with the Flavian position. First, however much Vespasian wished to establish a dynasty with an independent claim to the throne, the collocation in his nomenclature of Caesar and Augustus would inevitably remind all who saw it, as Dio recognized, of the man and the family that first occupied the throne. Second, it was impossible for the administration to ignore the *acta* of previous emperors, whether they had been consecrated or not. The *Tabula Banasitana,* a bronze tablet from Mauretania in the reign of Commodus, provides clear recognition of this latter fact: the leader of a Mauretanian tribe had requested a grant of citizenship for several members of his family, and an imperial freedman, Asclepiodotus, provided him with an authenticated copy of the relevant documents. The documents, it is guaranteed, were "copied and verified from the record of those granted Roman citizenship by the divine Augustus and Tiberius Caesar Augustus and Gaius Caesar and the divine Claudius and Nero and Galba and the divine Augusti Vespasian and Titus and Domitian Caesar and the divine Augusti Nerva and Trajan Parthicus and Trajan Hadrian and Hadrian Antoninus Pius and Verus. . . . Asclepiodotus the freedman produced the file."[81] Asclepiodotus verified the document in front of twelve witnesses, whose signatures followed and were reproduced on the bronze tablet. Though the first editors seized upon the absence of Otho and Vitellius to suggest that the compilation of citizenship records dates from the reign of Vespasian, who refused to recognize his two predecessors, it is most unlikely—as Sherwin-White recognized—that there was no need for an accurate record of these data before 69, and equally unlikely that such a compilation could have been made from previously scattered docu-

---

siring the Senate's cooperation, allowed it to define his powers, and they were those of his predecessors. Cf. Gagé 1931a, 37–41.

79. See, for example, *lex municipii Salpensani* (*ILS* 6088), XXV and XXVI, or *lex municipii Malacitani* (*ILS* 6089), LIX, or *lex Irnitana,* LXXIII. The general instructions about refraining from public business on certain days *per venerationem domus Augustae* (*lex Irnitana,* LXXXXII) presumes, since it specifies no dates, the existence of an official calendar of recognized dates (after the fashion of the *Feriale Duranum*).

80. Mattingly, *BMC* II, xxxv and xliii.

81. *Editio princeps* in Seston and Euzennat 1971; the text is reproduced in Sherwin-White 1973b. See ll. 22–26: *Descriptum et recognitum ex commentario civitate romana donatorum divi Aug. et Ti. Caesaris Aug. et C. Caesaris et divi Claudi et Neronis et Galbae et divorum Aug. Vespasiani et Titi et Caesaris Domitiani et divorum Aug. Ner[v]ae et Trai(i)ani Parthici et Trai(i)ani Hadriani et Hadriani Antonini Pii et Veri . . . quem protuli Asclepiodotus lib(ertus).*

ments as late as that year.[82] Although this document dates from the end of the second century, the administrative need for continuity to which it testifies must have existed earlier.[83]

The third problem facing the Flavians was the conservatism inherent in the *statio principis* as a charismatic office: denouncing all one's predecessors might well cheapen the aura of the office itself. Conversely, *pietas* toward a select group of predecessors could validate one's credentials as *capax imperii*.[84] Thus, while the civil war still hung in the balance in 69 Domitian denounced the desecration of the portraits of Galba but allowed those of Otho and Vitellius to be destroyed.[85] After three years on the throne Vespasian seems to have advertised his rule as, in some fashion, directly continuous with that of Augustus: in A.D. 74 he celebrated the one-hundredth anniversary of the creation of the title *Augustus* with a coin imitating a victory coin of Augustus.[86] He had already revived two specifically Augustan bronze types in A.D. 71.[87] Although Vespasian subsequently restored several Julio-Claudian types, it remained for Titus to issue a set of restored coins in bronze, carefully selected from the issues of his predecessors: Augustus, Tiberius, Claudius, and Galba are so honored, while Caligula, Nero, Otho, and Vitellius are not.[88] Titus clearly rejected deification as the criterion for membership in his honor roll. The selection instead relied on popular historical memory to suggest, implicitly, the qualities to which Titus aspired; at the same time, it shaped popular history by labeling some emperors as worthy of honor. Flavian reluctance to allow deification alone to dictate imperial history finds reflection in the titulature of priesthood in the imperial cult throughout this period: Flavian priesthoods, even within the same province, possess the titles "priest of the *Augusti*," "priest of the *divi Augusti*," and "priest of the *divi Augusti* and the *Augusti*" indiscriminately.[89]

There were, thus, pragmatic as well as ideological reasons urging emperors in the late first and second century to fashion stronger links with their

82. Seston and Euzennat 1971, 481–482; Sherwin-White 1973b, 90–91. For Egyptian knowledge of Roman politics in 68–70 as reflected in contemporary dating formulas, see Hanson 1982, 56–57.

83. On such *commentarii civitate donatorum*, see Nicolet 1991, 132–133, discussing Cicero *Ep. ad fam.* 13.36.1. Von Premerstein did not devote space to these *commentarii* as such, but cf. col. 733 on *commentarii censorii* (*RE* s.v. *commentarii*).

84. Grant 1950, with the summary of his conclusions at 169–171; Béranger 1975, 263; MacCormack 1981, 93–106.

85. See Chapter 7 at n. 153.

86. Mattingly, *BMC* II, xxxviii.

87. Mattingly, *BMC* II, xlix.

88. Mattingly, *BMC* II, lxxv–lxxviii.

89. Fishwick 1970, *passim*, but esp. 301–303 and 306–307, and *idem* 1994, 130–131. Cf. Edmondson 1997, 104–105, on priestly titles in Lusitania.

predecessors. By the reign of Trajan, a century and more of imperial rule had taught even the Senate at Rome to praise adoption as a system for designating a successor: thus Pliny not only spoke at length on the issue in his *Panegyric*, but also in writing to Trajan referred to Nerva always as the emperor's divine father.[90] Trajan probably despised the weakness of Nerva, however much it had served him; in his replies to Pliny, Trajan therefore eschews any language that would claim a familial relationship with earlier emperors: he cites the established rule of the *principes* and refers to Augustus only as "the divine Augustus."[91] We get a rather different picture of Trajan's lineage in the poem that Hadrian wrote for his adoptive father, to accompany a dedication that emperor made to Zeus Casius: "Trajan, the descendant of Aeneas, has dedicated to Zeus Casius these marvels, from the king of men to the king of gods."[92]

As Hadrian stressed the genealogical connection between Trajan and Aeneas and between Trajan and Augustus, so he evidently laid great stress on his descent from Trajan, to judge from an extraordinary papyrus preserved in Heptacomia, the capital of the Egyptian nome Apollonites. The text was evidently performed at a celebration of the consecration of Trajan. In it Apollo said: "I have come to you, people, to proclaim the new emperor Hadrian, whom all things gladly serve because of his virtue and the *genius* of his divine father."[93] This emphasis harmonizes with the message of contemporary coins, which advertised the adoption in both iconography and legend.[94] The role of Apollo in this political drama also adduced the possibility of divine selection, a theme that became prevalent at Rome in supposedly sycophantic texts under Domitian and, as so often, in straightforward texts under Trajan.[95] The announcement of Hadrian's accession

90. See, for example, *Pan.* 8.6, and *Ep.* 10.8.1 (*Cum divus pater tuus, domine . . .*).

91. At Pliny *Ep.* 10.7 and 84. His "descent" from Nerva continued to appear in his official titulature; alas, to my knowledge there are no moments in extant texts where Trajan must refer to Nerva in the body of his letter.

92. *Anth. Pal.* 6.332; Arrian confirms the attribution and quotes several lines (*Parthica* fr. 36).

93. *P. Giss.* 3, edited with helpful notes by Kornemann; see ll. 2–6: [2]ἥκω σοι, ὦ δῆμ[ε], | [3]οὐκ ἄγνωστος Φοῖβος θεὸς ἄνα-|[4]κτα καινὸν Ἀδριανὸν ἀγγελῶ[ν], | [5]ὧι πάντα δοῦλα [δι'] ἀρετὴν κ[αὶ] | [6]πατρὸς τύχην θεοῦ χαίροντες. On this text see also den Boer 1975 and MacCormack 1981, 105 n. 55.

94. *BMC* III, Hadrian nos. 1–51, with varying images but all with legends referring to Hadrian and DIVUS TRAIANUS as his father. Compare *BMC* III, p. 124 no. *, an aureus pf Trajan with a laureate Trajan on obverse, with the legend IMPERATOR CAESAR NERVA TRAIANUS OPTIMUS AUGUSTUS GERMANICUS DACICUS, and a laureate Hadrian on reverse, with the legend HADRIANO TRAIANO CAESARI.

95. On Domitian, see Statius *Silvae* 4.3, and cf. 3.52. Under Trajan, see Pliny *Pan.* 8.3 and 10.4, as well as Tacitus *Hist.* 1.15.1: *nunc me deorum hominumque consensu ad imperium vocatum.* On continuities in style and substance between Domitian and Trajan see Waters 1969. Com-

incited the customary embassies from the cities of the empire; in responding to that from Astypalaea, Hadrian thanked its citizens for their pleasure at his succession to the "ancestral office."[96] It was "ancestral" not simply by virtue of its age, but also because of the idealized continuity that linked its occupants from dynasty to dynasty.

Hadrian seems to have imposed this new emphasis on deification on his bureaucracy and on provincial celebrations of imperial cult. His departure from the criteria adopted by Titus gave public sanction to the Senate as *the* authority in determining the honors for dead emperors. Individuals participating in administrative rituals could now swear by the *genius* of the reigning emperor and the *numina divorum Augustorum.*[97] Evidence from the federal cult of the Three Gauls suggests that "with the accession of Hadrian, the emphasis of official policy abruptly turned to the worship of emperors and Imperial ladies who had been officially deified."[98] Epigraphical records of the celebration of imperial holidays—the birthdays and dates of accession of *divi*—also explode in frequency in the Antonine period.[99] Nor did the Antonine emperors allow cities to avoid paying honors to former emperors: when the *gerousia* of Ephesus asked permission to recast damaged statues of former emperors into images of Marcus Aurelius and Lucius Verus, not only did the emperors refuse, but they also offered advice on how local officials might yet assign the proper name to each statue.[100] Indeed, in A.D. 147/148, the prefect of Egypt, M. Petronius Honoratus, published an edict sanctioning the celebration of games in honor of Livia and another *divus* or *diva.*[101] The Antonine age must therefore have witnessed an increased rate of as-

---

pare Dio 73.2, describing Roman crowds parodying acclamations for Commodus after his death. On divine election at Rome in the second and third centuries, see Nock 1972, 252–270; Baynes 1935, 83; Charlesworth 1936, 114–122, and 1937, 117–118; and Fears 1977. Seneca had, of course, allowed Apollo to proclaim Nero (*Apocol.* 4).

96. Smallwood, *Nerva* no 449a (*IGRR* IV 1031C = Oliver 1989, no. 64), ll. 7–9: ἐκ τοῦ ψηφίσμα[τος ὑμῶν] | [ἔμαθον] ὅπως ἥσθητε διαδεξαμέν[ου ἐμοῦ] | [τὴν πατ]ρῴαν ἀρχήν.

97. E.g., *CPL* 159 (*AÉ* 1937, 112), a birth certificate from A.D. 127.

98. Fishwick 1978, 36–39 at 36–37; cf. *idem* 1994, 131.

99. See Snyder 1940, *passim*. It remained possible for the worship of a particular emperor to lapse in popularity—sometimes worship remained only as long as official enthusiasm and disappeared with official disapprobation: see Oliver 1949 and Gilliam 1969. On the other hand, honors for popular emperors could continue for centuries: Prudentius lists Augustus among the pagan gods of Rome without batting an eye (Fishwick 1990b). There exists a considerable bibliography on the survival—indeed, the waxing—of imperial cult in the Christian empire: among many studies see Batiffol 1920; Bréhier 1920; Karayannopulos 1956; Bowersock 1982; and *idem* 1986, 299 and 302–303.

100. *I. Ephesus* 25 (Oliver 1989, no. 170). Cf. Magie 1950, 855–860, on the *gerousia* of Ephesus, and Pekáry 1985, 38–39.

101. *P. Oxy.* XVII 2105.

similation of local civic calendars to one another, in a process already visible in Flavian municipal laws.[102] Truly there now were *fasti imperii Romani!*[103]

The articulation of dynastic claims to legitimacy seems thus to have reached maturity in the reign of Hadrian: it was probably in his reign that work began on the Temple of the Divi in Rome, which honored all consecrated emperors, and the priesthood bearing his name, the *sodalis Hadrianalis*, may have been associated with the rites performed there.[104] The stability and concord of the Antonine house, then, provided time for all to familiarize themselves with the language appropriate to the fiction: thus Fronto, when writing to Marcus or Lucius Verus, referred to the other emperor as "your brother," and, when writing to Marcus, described Trajan, Hadrian, and Antoninus as his great-grandfather, grandfather, and father, respectively; similarly, Marcus and Verus referred to each other as "my brother" in their letters to Fronto.[105] No Antonine emperor ever claimed direct descent from Augustus, but it was not beyond the imagination of a Greek to claim that ancestry for them: when Melito of Sardis attempted to teach Marcus about Christianity, he dated the flowering of his religion to the reign of Augustus, "your ancestor."[106]

Chapter 6 will treat the propaganda of Septimius Severus during the years following his accession in considerable detail. Here it suffices merely to observe that his claims of descent from Marcus found their most concrete expression when his sons interred his ashes in the Antonine mausoleum.[107] Alexander Severus still appealed to direct ancestry from the Antonine house in his public utterances, referring to Trajan and Marcus Aurelius as "my ancestors," and elsewhere to "my father Antoninus, my grandfather Severus, and my more remote ancestors."[108] The author of the *Historia Au-*

---

102. See *lex Irnitana* 31, 90, and 92, noting that some days are holidays *propter venerationem domus Augustae*. On renaming months see Scott 1931a, Hanson 1984a, and now *P. Oxy.* LV 3780. On the reorganization of calendars around the Roman new year see Hanson 1989, 439; on similar reorganizations around the birthday of Augustus see Laffi 1967 and Hodot 1982, 175–176.

103. Cf. Mitchell 1993, 1.113.

104. For the temple, see Wissowa 1912, 347, or Nock 1972, 215. For the priesthood, see *ILS* 1117, 1128, 1137, 1141 (and 1142), 1174, and 1192. It can be no accident that the priesthood is so well attested among the lieutenants of Severus.

105. See Fronto *De Feriis Alsiensibus* 3.5, *Princ. hist.* 1.1, and *Ep. ad Antoninum* 3.3.

106. Melito fr. 1*, 7 (Eusebius *Hist. eccl.* 4.26.7): κατὰ τὴν Αὐγούστου τοῦ σοῦ προγόνου μεγάλην ἀρχήν.

107. Dio 76.15.4; cf. Herodian 3.15.7 and 4.1.4. See Richard 1966a; Richard 1966b and 1978 discuss Julio-Claudian and Flavian practices on analogy with the dynastic symbolism in Antonine and Severan funerals.

108. On Severus Alexander, see Oliver 1989, no. 275 (*Sel. pap.* 216), col. II, ll. 3–4: ἐν οἷς Τραιανόν τε καὶ Μᾶρκον, τοὺς ἐμαυτοῦ προγόνους αὐτοκράτορά(ς τ)ε μάλιστα δὴ θαυμάσαι

gusta allowed Alexander to remark on the power of such titulature before the Senate: "I see, Conscript Fathers, what leads you to urge us to assume this name also. The first Augustus is the first *auctor* of this empire, and to his name we all succeed, either by some adoption or by hereditary right." Someday, Alexander prayed, his achievements might allow his own name to be associated with the titulature of the office, to be awarded by judgment of the Senate.[109] By the mid-third century it became common simply to parade the images of the *divi* at ceremonies, as if the direct links between emperors were self-evident and their guarantee of the empire's eternal victory unquestioned.[110]

The types of evidence thus far cited—citizenship records, festival pageants, coins, imperial portraits—as well as the political rituals and concepts thus far adumbrated played roles within a multidimensional mosaic that honored both emperor and government, not least by advertising their centrality to Roman *Religionspolitik*. Each was a symbol of the continuity and history of the empire. Each also issues a salutary reminder to us that we little understand the broad range of significance each carried in its context. Indeed, our concentration on the person of the emperor in this chapter risks submerging other strands within imperial propaganda: Roman claims to legitimate rule did not end with the charismatic authority of the emperor. Rome also universalized the benefits of her achievements; that is to say, she represented "institutional arrangements which [served] the interests of some individuals . . . as serving the interests of all."[111] In this way Roman ideology marked a huge advance beyond the claims of traditional Hellenistic euergetism—though that, too, played a role in imperial public relations. For example, Roman emperors boasted to provincial cities across the empire about military victories won against barbarians on distant borders in terms that demanded and received reciprocal expressions of gratitude from those cities.[112] Starting in particular with the reign of Hadrian, the imperial administration also explicitly advertised an ideology of unification. This ideology constructed the empire as an all-embracing collective by minimizing differences in culture and class and emphasizing the similarity of each individual's relationship to the emperor and especially the all-inclusive

---

ἀξίους γεγενημένους. Cf. no. 277b (*BGU* 1074), l. 8: Ὅσα θεῷ Ἀντωνείνῳ πατρὶ ἐμῷ καὶ θεῷ (Σε)ουήρῳ πάππῳ μου καὶ τοῖς ἄνωθεν προγόνοις ἐκρίθη.

109. *SHA Alex. Sev.* 7–11, and esp. 10.3–4 and 11.

110. On the development of the emperor as guarantor of the empire's eternity see Instinsky 1942, esp. 345–355. For the third century, on the coinage of Decius, see Chapter 7, "Decius and the *Divi*," and on the *divi* and Aurelian, see Chapter 7 at nn. 262–263.

111. Thompson 1990, 61–62.

112. On *aurum coronarium* see Chapter 6, "*Aurum Coronarium.*"

benefits of Roman rule.[113] Hadrian's ideological breakthrough became possible, however, because the concrete testimonials to Roman rule—milestones, imperial portraits, military standards, holidays—had long diffused throughout the empire and endowed its inhabitants with a shared symbolic language through which Hadrian and his successors could disseminate their revolutionary geography.[114]

Although this book adopts the propaganda of the imperial government as a starting point for its inquiry, we should not for that reason forget that most of the work of iterating and reiterating the state ideology took place not at the level of explicit state publication but in the day-to-day lives of the population, both in their contact with branches of the imperial administration and most particularly in their encounters with those private institutions that had a stake in the status quo.[115] Foucault has exhorted scholars to the study of ideology at this level: "In other words, rather than ask ourselves how the sovereign appears to us in his lofty isolation, we should try to discover how it is that subjects are gradually, progressively, really and materially constituted through a multiplicity of organisms, forces, energies, materials, desires, thoughts, etc."[116] Althusser called the institutions that perform this task "ideological state apparatuses," and saw at the root of their effectiveness their apparent diversity:[117] "If the ideological state apparatuses 'function' massively and predominantly by ideology, what unifies their diversity is precisely this functioning, insofar as the ideology by which they function is always in fact unified, despite its diversity and its contradictions, *beneath the ruling ideology*, which is the ideology of 'the ruling class.' . . . The ideological state apparatuses are multiple, distinct, 'relatively autonomous' and capable of providing an objective field to contradictions."[118] Rome's success in administering so large an empire with such stability testifies above all to her success in securing the good will of local commercial, political, and religious institutions.

Daily exposure to the ubiquitous symbolic representations of Roman ideology could not fail to have a profound influence on Greek intellectual life. Centuries of domination slowly erased cultural memories of other systems

---

113. It was Hadrian's work that made it possible for the *koinon* of Lycia to thank Antoninus Pius because πάσας εὐεργετῶν τὰς ἐπαρχείας παρέχει δικαιοσύνην εἶναι τοῖς πᾶσι αὐτῶν ἀνθρώποις (*IGRR* III 704 = Oliver 1989, no. 136, ll. 14–15).

114. On "unification" as a *modus operandi* of ideology, see Thompson 1990, 64. On the particular power of nonverbal sign systems, see Rossi-Landi 1990, 68–69.

115. Cf. Althusser 1970, 144.

116. Foucault 1980, 97; cf. Giddens 1983, 20; B. Anderson 1983, 38–39; and Jameson 1988, 2.54.

117. Althusser 1970, 143.

118. Althusser 1970, 146, 149; emphasis in original.

of government that had once been potential, if unrealistic, alternatives to Roman rule.[119] The passage of time thus created conceptual boundaries for the Graeco-Roman ideological consciousness. That these boundaries were unconscious does not diminish their relevance as "nodal points" within contemporary cultural documents: indeed, they were implicit above all in texts which attempted to revise or repress them.[120] These nodal points established the boundary of the doxa, between those things that can be the subject of public discourse and those that cannot. It was, moreover, individuals' consensual commitment to a particular normative order that drew this boundary and directed attention away from its own arbitrariness.[121] We find one reflection of the Greek world's long exposure to the daily onslaught of Roman images in the metaphors and analogies drawn in theological texts. Pagan and Christian monotheists frequently needed to describe the relations which existed between God and the minor supernatural powers that filled the world. It was natural for a Latin writer like Tertullian to draw an analogy with the terminology and representatives of imperial domination:[122]

> Now, suppose [the demons whom pagans regard as gods] to be gods; but you concede, do you not, on the basis of common consent, that there is a god, more sublime and more potent, *princeps*, as it were, of the universe, of absolute *maiestas?* For that is how most men apportion divinity; they hold that the *imperium* of supreme control rests with one, the various functions of divinity among many. . . . So they hold that his procurators and prefects and governors [*et procurantes et praefectos et praesides*] should be respected equally with him.

On the other hand, Tertullian could also argue that the mere existence of a divine bureaucracy, as it were, ought not prevent one from understanding God's rule over the world as a *singulare et unicum imperium:*[123]

> Indeed, I say that no dominion [*dominatio*] is so completely that of a single individual, so singular, in a word so monarchical, that it cannot be administered through other persons closely connected with it, whom the dominion itself

---

119. For example, the government established by the Italians during the Social War imitated Roman coins and had a senate of five hundred members, two consuls, and twelve praetors (Strabo 5.4.2; cf. Brunt 1988, 112). On the evolution of Greek political thought under the empire see Ando 1999.

120. Jameson 1981, 47–49.

121. Bourdieu 1977, 167–168.

122. Tertullian *Apol.* 24.3 (trans. Glover, adapted). On the *summus deus* and the *dii minores,* see *Pan. Lat.* IX(12).2.4–5 and Arnobius *Adversus nationes* 1.25–27 and 2.2–3, with Ando 1996, 188–189. Ancient arguments for a terrestrial monarchy, citing the analogous governance of heaven, were, of course, common in East and West. See, for example, Tertullian *Apol.* 24.4 Athenagoras *Leg.* 18.2, and Herodian 4.5.7, as well as Baynes 1933 and 1946b, 140.

123. Tertullian *Adv. Praxean* 3.2–5.

has assigned as its agents [*officiales*]. If there is a son to him whose monarchy it is, the monarchy itself is not immediately divided, nor does it cease to be a monarchy if the son is taken up as a participant [*particeps*] in it. . . . Therefore, although the divine monarchy is administered through so many legions and armies of angels [*tot legiones et exercitus angelorum*], . . . it does not cease to be the monarchy of a single God. . . . Do you really think that they who are the limbs, tokens, and instruments, the very power and the whole sum of his monarchy [*membra et pignora et instrumenta et ipsam vim ac totum censum monarchiae*], are also its undoing?

Western authors drew such analogies between the earthly and heavenly kingdoms above all when describing the ceremonial appropriate for honoring Christ the King.[124] For a Greek, like the author of the Aristotelian treatise *De mundo,* even in the second century the preeminent cultural paradigm for the court of a despot remained the Great King of Persia: the Supreme God acts in the world through lesser powers, just as the Great King ruled all of Asia through generals and satraps and kings, themselves the slaves of the Great King:[125]

Now we must suppose that the majesty of the Great King falls short of the majesty of the god who rules the cosmos by as much as the difference between the king and the poorest and weakest creature in the world, so that if it was beneath the dignity of Xerxes to appear himself to be the actual executor of all things, to carry out his wishes himself and to administer the empire by personal supervision, it would be still more unbecoming for God.

When Apuleius in the West translated this text into Latin, he retained the references to the Persian kings but adopted throughout Roman terms for their subordinates.[126] Within a century the situation in the East had assimilated to that in the West: even for a Christian author prior to the conversion of Constantine, Roman law on *maiestas* could provide raw material suitably familiar to his audience for use in the explication of Scripture.[127] In the sixth century Christian writers in Constantinople knew precisely which

124. See Fontaine 1971 and Dufraigne 1994, 329–455. On artistic representations of Christ's advent in the West see Kantorowicz 1965, 37–75, L'Orange 1955, and Holum and Vikan 1979.

125. [Aristotle] *De mundo* 397b9–398b28 at 398b1–7 (trans. after Furley). See also Aristides 43.18 and Celsus as quoted in Origen *Cels.* 8.35, both writing in the third quarter of the second century, as well as Maximus of Tyre *Or.* 11.12.

126. Apuleius *De mundo* 25–26, writing not only of *militiae principes et curiae proceres et urbium ac domorum rectores,* but also of the king's *dispensatores pecuniae, quaestores vectigalium, tribunos aerarios,* and many others.

127. Methodius *De resurrectione* 2.24.1, on which see Price 1984b, 203, and below , Chapter 7, "The Power of Imperial Portraits." See also [Aristides] *Or.* 35.24, speaking of the emperor: οἰόμενος δεῖν τὸν ὡς ἀληθῶς βασιλέα τῷ τῶν ὅλων ἀπεικάσθαι Βασιλεῖ κατά τε τὴν φιλανθρωπίαν καὶ τὴν πρόνοιαν ἁπάντων τῶν ἀρχομένων.

court represented the epitome of earthly power: that of the Roman emperor. Leontius, like Romanus or Proclus of Constantinople,[128] compared and contrasted the entrance of Christ into Jerusalem on Palm Sunday with the familiar spectacle of an imperial *adventus:*[129]

> Truly that crowd recognized a royal entrance. Just as in present times when a king of the world has gone out to do battle with a usurper, and when he returns from the victory all the citizens of his city meet him carrying flowers, weaving songs of praise, throwing eulogies before him instead of roses . . .
>
> How did the crowd recognize the Lord as king? He wasn't wearing a wordly crown; he wasn't clad in purple; he didn't bring a multitude of soldiers with him; horses and chariots inlaid with gold didn't go in procession before him; he didn't ride in a chariot with the royal purple trappings.

The allusions within the homilies of Leontius fascinate all the more because he clearly occupied a relatively low social position: he described only those imperial ceremonies that one could see on the streets of the city. Mark the Deacon, the biographer of Porphyry, bishop of Gaza, occupied a similar position: to him, the dignitaries who processed for the baptism of Theodosius, the son of Arcadius, shone like stars on earth.[130] We might note that in the centuries after Roman rule fell in the West the culture there lost control over the details of its history: the author of the *Constitutum Constantini* seems to have thought that Constantine, like the Great King, ruled through satraps.[131] No citizen of the New Rome on the Bosporus would have made that error.

I have twice contrasted the Roman principate with Ptolemaic or Hellenistic kingship. The comparison is illuminating on several levels. First, a Hellenistic monarch *was* the state: no Greek ever addressed Antiochus or Antigonus or Seleucus as "King of the Greeks," or "King of the Seleucid Kingdom," or even "King of the Greeks who live in Asia": it was characteristically Roman to insist that a king must be king of something.[132] Second,

128. On Romanus *Cantica* 16, see Topping 1977; on Proclus of Constantinople, see *PG* 65.773C; on the assimilation of imperial imagery in depictions of Christ's advent by Christian artists in the East, see Grabar 1968, 44–45.

129. Leontius *Homilies* 3.18–22, 61–66 (trans. Allen and Datema, slightly modified). For further allusions to the trappings of the imperial office in Leontius see 2.131–136 (the cloak of a *triumphator*), 2.147–152 (another list: white horses, carriages inlaid with gold, a troop of bodyguards—bodyguards are also mentioned at 3.9 and 8.113—and a procession of dignitaries), 3.70–96 (continuing 3.61–66), 10.451–456 (a usurper fashions a crown, wears purple, acquires soldiers for a bodyguard, and builds camps, to which compare 4.5 and 10.32–33), and cf. 5.198–203 (God as ἀγωνοθέτης).

130. Marcus Diaconus *Vita Porph.* 47.

131. *Constitutum Constantini* 19.

132. See, for example, Livy 29.12.14, on those who signed the peace of Phoenice. Contrast Polybius 22.7–8: kings are identified by name: (ὁ βασιλεὺς Πτολεμαῖος, Εὐμένης,

Hellenistic monarchs tended to live in an agonistic relationship with their fellow kings and with their predecessors.[133] Roman *principes,* as Ammianus notes, were servants of the *res publica:* though Rome "has entrusted the management of her inheritance to the Caesars, as to her children," it is Rome who is regarded as mistress and queen throughout the world; her glory guarantees respect for the Senate and the name of the Roman people, while the *princeps* must restrain his behavior out of respect for the dignity of the imperial office.[134] This theme finds its most vivid expression in those moments when Rome is depicted addressing an emperor: if these passages were intended to honor the emperor, they nevertheless implied the priority of Rome herself as the repository of authority.[135] In this they harmonized with a traditional coin type which depicted Roma seated in a position of superiority while the emperor stood: sometimes they held hands; sometimes the emperor offered her a Victory—many permutations were possible.[136] Thus loyalty to the imperial office was a vehicle for, indeed, the primary expression of, loyalty to the state. But loyalty to an individual emperor did not subsume loyalty to Rome herself, and it was possible under the empire for a usurper, or even the Senate, to argue that the loyalty to Rome occasionally stood in contradiction to personal loyalty to the occupant of the throne. In a Weberian sense, we may distinguish between loyalty toward a charismatic office and personal loyalty to the holder of that office: in the so-called crisis of the third century, for instance, failure in war was understood to signal the unworthiness of the current emperor and not any inherent flaw in the system that had produced both him and the centuries of peace that had preceded.[137] Competition between individuals for the throne thus enhanced the legitimacy of the imperial system by implicitly recognizing debate over who would occupy the throne as the only legitimate topic for public discourse.

Σελεῦκος, etc.), and private individuals by nationality (Νικόδημος ὁ Ἠλεῖος, Ἀπολλωνίδας ὁ Σικυώνιος, Κάσσανδρος Αἰγινήτης).

133. This is not to say that emperors didn't compete to distinguish their achievements: witness the peculiar claims made in *Pan. Lat.* II(10).7.2 regarding the achievements of Maximian.

134. Ammianus 14.6.5–6, and cf. 25.10.15. On these passages and the issues they raise, see Straub 1939, 198–200, and Matthews 1989, 231–252.

135. See Ammianus 20.5.10 (on the *genius publicus*). Cf. *Pan. Lat.* VI(7).10.5–11.4; Symmachus *Rel.* 3.9, Pacatus at *Pan. Lat.* XII(2).11.3–7 (on which see Lippold 1968, 240–241), Corippus *In laudem Iustini Augusti minoris* 1.288–290 (with Av. Cameron's note *ad loc.*). Cf. Callu 1960; Béranger 1975, 411–427; and MacCormack 1975b.

136. See MacCormack 1975b, 141 n. 3, and 1981, 178 n. 81. Variations on these types certainly occur as early as Trajan: Bellinger and Berlincourt 1962.

137. As with losses by Republican generals (on which see Rosenstein 1990), hindsight always revealed omens signaling the illegitimacy of a failed emperor's charisma and his corresponding loss of divine favor. For example from the early and late empire, see Suetonius *Nero* 39.1 or *Otho* 8.3, or Ammianus 25.10.3 or 30.5.16–19.

Nothing embodies the many and contradictory levels of Roman ideology better than the titulature and political vocabulary of the Principate. The use of *princeps,* with its implications of constitutionality, suggested that the emperor was at one level the most important man among many.[138] Benedict Anderson was wrong to regard such an ideology as specifically modern, but he was correct in assessing its dangers for the ruler: "If Kaiser Wilhelm II cast himself as 'No. 1 German,' he implicitly conceded that he was *one among many of the same kind as himself,* that he had a representative function, and therefore could, in principle, be a *traitor* to his fellow-Germans (something inconceivable in the dynasty's heyday. Traitor to whom or to what?)."[139] Greek authors reveal the purely Roman nature of this ideology—meaning an imagined representation of the real distribution of power in society— when they scoff at this pretense: whether one addresses him as *imperator, princeps,* or Augustus, he is simply a king.[140]

Even at Rome, of course, the emperor could not maintain his fictional equality for long; the mystique of his office was too religious in nature for that. The image of the emperor as "one among many of the same kind as himself" was ultimately supplanted by a much more powerful and longer-lasting image, that of an emperor over many who were equal in their subordination to him. The power of this rhetoric lay in its seduction of the provincial population: to use Althusser's term, it interpellated individuals as concrete subjects and encouraged them to view other provincials as well as imperial officials as similarly concrete subjects. In effect, to adapt Althusser's critique of Christian ideology, this aspect of imperial ideology sought to "obtain from [its subjects] the recognition that they really do occupy the place it designates for them as theirs in the world," with the implicit condition "there can only be such a multitude of possible subjects on the absolute condition that there is a Unique, Absolute, *other subject,* i.e. [the emperor]."[141] Emperors drew on this special relationship between themselves and each of their subjects not only when they guaranteed on their own authority the fair review of any appeal from below, but in particular when they explicitly reminded the provincial populations that local imperial officials could be held accountable for their actions.[142] Ironically, imperial

---

138. See Syme 1939, 313–330 at 311–312, and Brunt and Moore on Augustus, *Res gestae* 13.

139. B. Anderson 1983, 82; emphasis in original.

140. Appian *praef.* 22–23. See also Dio 53.17–18 and John Lydus *Mag.* 1.4 and 2.2. On Greek names for the Roman emperor, see Wifstrand 1939; for the period beyond Wifstrand's essay, see Rösch 1978.

141. Althusser 1970, 173, 178.

142. The reception of this ideology finds its most interesting expression in the ready adoption by Greeks of the concept of emperor as "father," a concept altogether absent from Hellenistic kingship. Chapter 9 explores this theme in further detail.

ideology therefore guaranteed the fairness of its administration—an administration that personified the hallmarks of Weber's legal-rational bureaucracy as no other European empire, ancient or modern[143]—by appeal to the singular, even superhuman status of its highest official.

As an inquiry into the reception and currency of certain strands in political thought in the imperial period, this book offers a twofold attack on *Quellenforschung:* first, because modern scholarship on ancient historiography has devoted too little effort to the sources of information available to the authors of contemporary history under the Principate; and second, because the change in metaphoric language discussed above suggests more than a change in the realia of the authors' lives: the centuries that separated them had witnessed a profound social evolution, such that new paradigms—providing new sources of metaphor—had replaced the old. A concomitant reorientation of the culture's historical self-awareness had taken place. Ideas that had been expressed by Greeks before they came into contact with Rome, and that we may be tempted to identify as "Greek," were for contemporaries so thoroughly identified with what they considered Roman that they considered such ideas Roman in origin; and it is that belief, and not the ultimate origin of any particular strand of political philosophy, that will have precedence here.[144] Of course not every strand of political philosophy sent down from on high provided new paradigms and organizing metaphors. Provincials absorbed and iterated those ideas that they wished their overlords to endorse, embody, and express. Above all, provincials exploited ideological tropes that gave them leverage over *civiles principes.*[145]

Though we shall move far beyond the parameters of ancient political thought in the remainder of this work, we should not lose sight of the concepts through which a Greek or a Roman might have described the unity of the Roman world. Political philosophers did not consider the unification of the world prior to Alexander the Great, and he left no writings to explain his conciliatory gestures toward his Persian subjects. Later generations were therefore free to imagine that Alexander himself had desired that "one set of customs should rule all men" and that "all should look to one rule of law as toward a common light."[146] Though the words which I translate as "cus-

---

143. Weber 1978, 218–219: he requires specific spheres of competence, a hierarchy with right of appeal and statement of grievances, rules governing the conduct of officials, and especially the recording of all acts, decisions, and rules in writing, "even in cases where oral discussion is the rule or is even mandatory."

144. As they considered themselves Roman: cf. the instructive reproach by Nicephorus Phocas in 968, to Liutprand of Cremona: *vos non Romani, sed Langobardi estis* (Liutprand *Leg.* 182.24).

145. See Ahl 1984, on the related "art of safe criticism."

146. Plutarch *Fort. Alex.* 330D: εἰ δὲ μὴ ταχέως ὁ δεῦρο καταπέμψας τὴν Ἀλεξάνδρου ψυχὴν ἀνεκαλέσατο δαίμων, εἰς ἂν νόμος ἅπαντας ἀνθρώπους διῳκεῖτο καὶ πρὸς ἓν δίκαιον ὡς πρός

toms" and "rule of law" certainly subsume the concept of a single legal system, they imply a great deal more. Cicero draws on a similar ambiguity in Latin in his definition of a political society: "A commonwealth is the property of a people; but a *populus* is not every crowd of men, gathered in whatever fashion, but a crowd united by common interest and consensual commitment to a particular normative order."[147] By the end of the second century Christians seized upon this strand in imperial thought and used it in apologetic literature to justify their patriotism: divine providence had ordained that Augustus should found the Roman empire at the same time that Christ was born; it was therefore God's will that the Roman empire should unite the world to prepare it for conversion to Christianity.[148] The spread of Roman law, and of Roman respect for the rule of law, thus lent to daily life a reassuring and stable predictability. This promise of social order, and above all the rhetoric in which it was conveyed and discussed, appealed directly to the self-interest of provincials. To place the entire world beneath the rule of law, to inculcate men in the habits of peace: such were the burdens laid upon Rome which, at the prodding of her subjects, she at long last took up. They will serve as our beginning and our goal in explaining the evolution of the empire into a "singular and perfect coalition of its members."[149]

κοινὸν ἐπέβλεπον φῶς. On such interpretations of Alexander's behavior, see Tarn 1948, 399–449.

147. Cicero *Rep.* 1.39.1: '*Est igitur' inquit Africanus 'res publica res populi, populus autem non omnis hominum coetus quoquo modo congregatus, sed coetus multitudinis iuris consensu et utilitatis communione sociatus.*'

148. See Melito of Sardis *Apol.* fr. 1 (Eusebius *Hist. eccl.* 4.26.7–11); Tertullian *Apol.* 32.1 and *Nat.* 2.17.18–19; Cyprian *Ep.* 55.4, arguing that the dissemination of Christian literature requires the empire; Origen *Cels.* 2.30 (and cf. 8.72, where Origen and Celsus debate the possibility of uniting the world under a single νόμος); Eusebius *Triak.* 4.2 and 16.5–8; Eusebius *Demonstratio* 3.7.29–31; Lactantius *Inst.* 7.15.11 and 25.6–8; Gregory Naz. *De vita sua* 562–572; John Chrysostom *Homiliae in Sanctum Matthaeum Evangelistam* 8.4 (*PG* 57 col. 87) and *Homilia in diem natalem d. n. Jesu Christi* 2 (*PG* 49.1 col. 353); Augustine *Ep.* 138.3.17 and *Civ.* 18.22 and 27 (but cf. also *Ep.* 93.22 and 199.46–48); Orosius 6.1.5–9; and Prudentius *Symm.* 2.608–622. See Baynes at *CAH* XII 660–661, T. E. Mommsen 1959, 339–340, and Paschoud 1967.

149. Gibbon "General observations" (2.513).

CHAPTER THREE

The Roman Achievement in Ancient Thought

In October 417, Rutilius Namatianus left Rome for his ancestral hall: the fields of Gaul summoned home their native son.[1] He bid a tearful farewell to the city, the fairest queen of her world, and for the sin of his departure he offered in atonement a speech of praise: "You have made from distinct and separate nations a single fatherland: it has benefited those who knew not laws, to be captured by your conquering sway; and by giving to the conquered a share in your law, you have made a city of what was once a world."[2] Rutilius gauged Rome's achievement looking back over four centuries of imperial history. From the opposite perspective Vergil expressed a very similar conception of Rome's *propriae artes:* "Remember, Roman, to rule the nations with your dominion—these will be your arts—to crown peace with rule of law, to spare the defeated, and to conquer the proud."[3] In uttering

---

1. *Red.* 1.20: *indigenamque suum Gallica rura vocant.* For the date, see A. D. E. Cameron 1967, expanding upon Courcelle 1964, 104–111.

2. *Red.* 1.63–66: *fecisti patriam diversis gentibus unam: / profuit iniustis te dominante capi; / dumque offers victis proprii consortia iuris, / urbem fecisti quod prius orbis erat.* Cf. Claudian *Cons. Stil.* 3.130–181, esp. 150–159 (quoted below at n. 73). On Rome as *urbs domina* or *domina rerum,* see Gernentz 1918, 125–127, to whose catalogue should be added Prudentius *Symm.* 1.427–432; Eusebius *Triak.* 9.8 (τῇ βασιλευούσῃ πόλει); *Expositio totius mundi* 54 (*Campania . . . et ipsa sibi sufficiens et cellarium regnanti Romae*); and *I. Cret.* IV 316, honoring Praetextatus as τὸν λαμπρότατον ἀπὸ ἐπάρχων τῆς βασιλευούσης Ῥώμης. See also A. Alföldi 1947, J. Toynbee 1947 and 1953, and cf. Christ 1938 and Georgacas 1947.

3. *Aeneid* 6.851–853. To this passage compare Cicero *Tusc.* 1.1.2, on which see n. 25 below, and Pomponius Mela 1.41 (*Orae sic habitantur ad nostrum maxime ritum moratis cultoribus, nisi quod quidam linguis differunt et cultu deum quos patrios servant ac patrio more venerantur*) and 65. Vergil's language found many imitators, among whom see esp. Prudentius *Symm.* 1.455–457, lamenting that Rome, *quae domitis leges ac iura dedisti gentibus, instituens, magnus qua tenditur orbis, armorum morumque feros mansuescere ritus,* should cling to barbarous superstition.

these sentiments Vergil and Rutilius participate in a long-standing ancient tradition of reflection on the nature and effects of Roman rule. Indeed, the similarity of these sentiments and their fame have rendered their truth self-evident even as they have obscured their import. In what sense can we—in what sense did they—imagine that governance through law could unite an empire?

In ancient and modern thought, the nature of the Roman achievement has been indissolubly linked with investigations of Roman influence: Rome succeeded insofar as provincials took on a Roman lifestyle. To this extent, investigators have likewise divided their attention between East and West. Indeed, in his remarks Vergil contrasts Roman *artes* with those of Greece, and so we may leave open the possibility that he saw Rome imposing the rule of law on her eastern conquests. But there can be no doubt that the dominant view, both Greek and Roman, of the relationship between their cultures is best summed up by Horace: "Conquered Greece conquers the wild victor and introduces her arts into rustic Latium."[4] Modern surveys of intellectual life in the late Republic and under Augustus wholeheartedly endorse his generalization.[5] Under the circumstances we might well conclude that Rome had little to offer the Hellene, and therefore that "[Romanization] is chiefly a word which describes what subsequently happened in certain areas of the western empire, and what did not happen in the East."[6]

Such a view must rest, however, on a rather constrained, albeit traditional, view of what constitutes Romanization, one that assumes that Romanization takes place among less civilized peoples: the process consists largely in providing the infrastructure—and therefore, it is presumed, also the impulse—for urbanization.[7] Necessary consequences, as it seems, are the monetarization of the economy, an increase in the population, and heavier exploitation of natural resources.[8] With such a model in mind, one is bound to be disappointed by the changes wrought in the East; and yet, it is easily argued, no one should have expected Pliny in Bithynia to be-

4. *Ep.* 2.1.156–157; cf. Cicero *Brutus* 73.254 (*Quo enim uno vincebamur a victa Graecia, id aut eruptum illis est aut certe nobis cum illis communicatum*) and Ovid *Fasti* 3.101–102 (*nondum tradiderat victas victoribus artes Graecia, facundum sed male forte genus*).

5. See Rawson 1985, 320; cf. Bowersock 1965, 73–84 and 122–139.

6. Bowersock 1965, 72; cf. Sartre 1991, 502, and Rawson at *CAH*[2] IX 447. Brunt 1990, 269, speaks for many when he asserts: "By contrast, where Greek was already the language of culture, of government, and of inter-regional trade, the Romans carried further the process of Hellenization."

7. See, for example, Raven 1993, 64–78 and 100–121; Mitchell 1993, 1.198–226. Recent work on Romanization has developed new paths of inquiry without necessarily producing new results. Recent literature with full bibliographies includes Freeman 1993, D. Mattingly 1997, Alcock 1997, and Woolf 1998.

8. Mocsy 1970, 7; Hopkins 1980, 102–103.

have like Agricola in Britain, encouraging *homines dispersi ac rudes* "to build temples, marketplaces, and homes"; there was no need, presumably, for a Roman to teach a Greek *eloquentia.*[9] This does not mean that Rome did not greatly affect the material welfare of her eastern provinces; indeed, it must now be conceded—as it was in antiquity—that "all the Greek cities [rose] up under [Rome's] leadership. . . . The coasts and interiors have been filled with cities, some newly founded, others increased under and by [her]."[10]

This renaissance can be charted in any number of ways: by the sheer number of foundations in the eastern provinces, both new cities and old, which were then renamed or, at least, adopted a new or second "founder";[11] by the increase in the number of cities that issued their own coins;[12] by the scale and scope of renovations and new construction;[13] and finally by the renewal of old festivals and the foundation of new ones: the innumerable Sebasteia that crowded the landscape and the calendar in the first centuries of our era.[14] The efflorescence of Greek civic life almost always bore the stamp of Roman approval and had, in any event, been made possible by the peace imposed by Roman power. As Dionysius of Halicar-

---

9. Tacitus *Agr.* 21.1–2; cf. Florus 2.33.59–60. There were, of course, limitations to what such a policy could achieve. Brunt 1990, 268, thus announces: "Whatever its purposes, the government could do no more than encourage a process which, with no system of public education, it lacked the means to impose. Provincials Romanized themselves." Millett 1990 and Woolf 1998 follow and develop this model. Cf. Branigan 1991, 103: "The important point is that substantial parts of the native population of Britain can be seen to be adopting Roman patterns of behavior and belief which, in most cases at least, can have offered no immediate material benefits. I suggest, then, that in so far as we can begin to discern human behaviour and human attitudes from the mute testimony of archaeological evidence, it suggests that in a distant province like Britain, there were many people—not just a handful—who thought like the Romans, perhaps thought of themselves as Romans, and who viewed the Roman way of life as, on the whole, beneficial to them and worth emulating."

10. Aelius Aristides *Or.* 26.94 (trans. Oliver). See also Tertullian *Anima* 30, quoted in Chapter 1 at n. 38. For a different point of view, see the mid-second-century Rabbis Judah bar Ilai, Yose ben Halafta, and Simeon bar Yohia, preserved in the Babylonian Talmud: Judah begins, "How splendid are the works of this people! They have built marketplaces, baths, and bridges." To which Simeon responds: "Everything they have made, they have made only for themselves: marketplaces, for whores; baths, to wallow in; bridges, to levy tolls" (de Lange 1978, 268; on the dating of the interlocutors, see Stemberger 1996, 76).

11. See A. H. M. Jones 1971, index (b), s.v. "Imperial foundations"; Mitchell 1993, 1.80–98.

12. Cf. Magie 1950, 472–473; Harl 1987; Millar 1993b, 256–257: "Relevant criteria for defining a 'Greek city' would be . . . the capacity to mint coins bearing the name of the community. . . . The most explicit symbols of a city's identity and status were its coins."

13. See MacDonald 1982 and 1986. Urbanization is discussed province by province in the regional surveys provided by *CAH*[2] X and *Integration* 2.

14. Cf. Magie 1950, index s.v. "Festivals and Contests"; Mitchell 1993, 1.217–225. There could be links between all these phenomena: cities issued coins to advertise their loyalty. See, on coins of Ephesus advertising its Hadrianeia, Robert, *Hellenica* 7.84.

nassus wrote when commending the renaissance of stylistic purity in contemporary rhetoric: "I think that the cause and origin of this great revolution [i.e., this return to the purities of classical rhetoric] has been the conquest of the world by Rome, who has thus made every city focus its attention upon her. Her leaders are chosen on merit and administer the state according to the highest principles. They are thoroughly cultured and in the highest degree discerning, so that under their ordering influence the sensible section of the population has increased its power and the foolish have been compelled to behave sensibly."[15] Cities carefully advertised their civic identity in ways that acknowledged their position within a greater whole: local issues, for example, rapidly devolved into denominations readily convertible to Roman currency—and many such issues bore the portrait of Augustus as the seal and sign of their allegiance.[16] In thus concentrating our attention on the impact of Roman rule on civic space and the rhythms of urban life, we may better appreciate both the immediate and the long-term cultural impact of Roman conquest.[17]

The vision of Romanization thus obtained from the eastern provinces also harmonizes more closely with Roman writings on the normal course of conquest. In our eagerness to chart the urbanization of western Europe we have failed to ask whether Romans conquered new territory with the explicit purpose of altering the indigenous culture, to say nothing of adding the indigenous population to the *populus Romanus*. Did they expect Gauls and Spaniards to assimilate to Roman mores and, more important, did they expect provincials in Greece and Spain to have the same experience of Roman imperialism? In our search for answers we may begin with Roman myths about the foundation of Rome itself. For the many and varied legends of the foundation of Rome agree on at least two details: Rome's original population had been heterogeneous, to say the least, and it had established and maintained itself in its early years through warfare.[18]

15. Dionysius Hal. *Orat. vett.* 1.3 (trans. Usher), on which see Gabba 1982 and 1984, and Hidber 1996, 75–81 and 117–123.

16. On provincial denominations see Howgego 1985, 52–60; *RPC* I 26–37; and Kroll 1997. On portraits of Augustus see Grant 1946, 328–344 and 463–470; Howgego 1995, 84; and *RPC* I 38–51. Cf. Millar 1984, 53–54, on the novelties of scale and uniformity in the cults established for Augustus in this period.

17. On the role of imperial cult in reshaping urban life see Price 1984b; Gros 1988; Alcock 1993, 181–199; and Mitchell 1993, 1.100–117. On Roman influence on urbanism in the early empire see Chapter 8 at nn. 134–139.

18. On foundation legends see the classic treatment by Bickermann 1952, and cf. Curty 1995. For recent treatments of the Roman foundation story, see Gruen 1992, 6–51, and Wiseman 1995. These treatments generally do not deal with the most controversial versions of the story—controversial to the Romans, that is—in which Aeneas was allowed to escape Troy in exchange for his having betrayed the city to the Greeks: see Dionysius Hal. *Ant. Rom.* 1.46.2–

Turning to the most influential narratives of the foundation legend, we find both Livy and Vergil attempting to explain why Aeneas shed his own ethnic identity and adopted another's. Livy viewed this change as purely political: Aeneas, in a dangerous situation, about to fight against an enemy more closely related to his allies than he was, offered to take his allies' name as his own.[19] According to the *Aeneid,* the Roman people sprang forth from the ashes of a civil war: *tanton placuit concurrere motu, Iuppiter, aeterna gentis in pace futuras?* Though Aeneas won the battle against Turnus and his Italian allies, the Trojans did not absorb the Latins. Rather, Troy and Trojan would disappear, and the Romans, born from Italian stock, became powerful through Italian virtue.[20] Vergil, of course, did not narrate the process of reconciliation, but he alluded to the aftermath of this war in the curse of Dido at the end of Book 4 and especially in the conversation between Jupiter and Juno in Book 12. Servius, reacting to the former passage, knew that this outcome contradicted normal expectations about conquest in war: "*Unjust peace*: As I wrote above, because one's language, customs, and name—which the conqueror is accustomed to impose—are lost, as Juno demands in Book 12."[21] Servius confronted the same issue in explicating the opening of Book 1, where Vergil asserted that his poem would narrate the origin of the *genus Latinum:*[22]

> The Latins therefore descend not only from the Trojans, but also from the Aborigines. This, moreover, is the true explanation. We know that the conquered take on the name of their conquerors. Therefore, after the victory of Aeneas, the name "Latin" could have disappeared. But, wishing to earn the good will of the Latins, Aeneas not only allowed them to retain the name "Latin" but even imposed it on the Trojans. Rightly, therefore, does Vergil assign to him the power to have allowed that name to perish. Wherefore Vergil himself depicts Juno in Book 12 asking that the name "Latin" not perish. Likewise, we read in the curse of Dido [the request] that Aeneas pass his life under the terms of an unjust peace, for that peace is unjust in which he who conquers loses his name.

According to this model, the Romans ought not to have existed under that name at all, nor ought the rulers of Italy to have spoken Latin. Operating under a similar set of expectations, when Augustine complained that dif-

---

1.48 (but esp. 1.48.3–4), Porphyrio on Horace *Carmen saeculare* 41, Tertullian *Nat.* 2.9.12–18, Servius on *Aen.* 1.242 and 647, Dares 37–44, and *Origo gentis Romanae* 9.2.

19. Livy 1.2.4–5.

20. Vergil *Aeneid* 6.756–757 and 12.827–829. On Vergil's politics of identity see Toll 1991 and 1997.

21. Servius on *Aen.* 4.618: *PACIS INIQUAE ut supra* [1.6] *diximus, propter perditam linguam, habitum, nomen, quae solet victor imponere, sicut in duodecimo postulat Iuno.*

22. Servius on *Aen.* 1.6; cf. Vergil *G.* 4.559–562.

ferences in language created conflict between communities, he anticipated the counterargument that Rome had imposed not only her yoke but also her language on those whom she had conquered and had thus promoted peace between men. "That is true enough," he lamented, "but can that achievement be compared to the number and magnitude of the wars, to the vastness of the slaughter, or to the sheer outpouring of human blood by which it was gained?"[23]

Stepping back and approaching the problem from another direction, we might note that the *immensa Romanae pacis maiestas* impressed Aelius Aristides particularly because internecine strife had been an unfortunate constant in Greek life, one that no previous hegemony had dispelled.[24] Aristides therefore readily conceded the claim of Vergil: "For if [the knowledge of how to rule] had existed [before your time], it would have existed among the Hellenes, who distinguished themselves for skill very greatly in the other arts, you will admit. But this knowledge is both a discovery of your own and to other men an importation from you."[25] The attitude of Plutarch had been no different:[26]

> While the mightiest powers and dominions among men were being driven about as Fortune willed, and were continuing to collide with one another because no one held supreme power—though all wished to hold it—, the continuous movement, drift, and change of all peoples remained without remedy,

23. Augustine *Civ.* 19.7. That Roman conquest was brutal qualified but did not negate the benefits of her rule: *Ne multis morer, condita est civitas Roma velut altera Babylon et velut prioris filia Babylonis, per quam Deo placuit orbem debellare terrarum et in unam societatem rei publicae legumque perductum longe lateque pacere* (*Civ.* 18.22).

24. Pliny *Nat.* 27.2–3, and cf. 14.2. Note that Pliny views the empire as allowing free commerce between all regions of the world, whereas Aelius Aristides argues that the empire brings all its goods to the city of Rome (*Or.* 26.11, and cf. Plutarch *Fort. Rom.* 325E). Gernentz 1918, 137–143, collects additional passages on these themes. On ancient literature critical of Roman economic exploitation see Bauckham 1991. See also Tertullian *Anima* 30, quoted in Chapter 1 at n. 38, as well as the passages listed in Chapter 9, nn. 44 and 238.

25. *Or.* 26.51 (trans. Oliver, adapted). Klein 1981 provides a convenient biography of Aristides. Bleicken rightly identifies the governance of the empire as central to Aristides' panegyric and analyzes two strands within his thought on *das römische Herrschaftsprinzip*, namely *Reichsverwaltung* and *Bürgerrechtspolitik* (1966, 234–247). To this passage compare Cicero *Tusc.* 1.1.2 and Dionysius Hal. *Ant. Rom.* 1.3.1–5, and cf. Gernentz 1918, 129–145 and esp. 129–137. In this context we might note that Polybius 6.2.3 attributed the Romans' conquest of the world directly to their particular form of government: the most important benefit of his history is τὸ γνῶναι καὶ μαθεῖν πῶς καὶ τίνι γένει πολιτείας ἐπικρατηθέντα σχεδὸν πάντα τὰ κατὰ τὴν οἰκουμένην ... ὑπὸ μίαν ἀρχὴν τὴν Ῥωμαίων ἔπεσεν. Even if Cornell 1991, 61, is correct to fault Greek authors for "starting from the premise that Rome was a city-state of the Greek type, and that its institutions should be analyzed accordingly," the point is not so significant as he suggests: Romans, too, wrote of the Roman empire as if it were still just a city. (See below, n. 83.)

26. *Fort. Rom.* 317B–C (trans. Babbitt), on which see C. Jones 1971, 70, 101.

until such a time as Rome acquired strength and growth . . . and thus the affairs of this vast empire gained stability and security, since the supreme government, which never knew reverse, was brought within an orderly and single cycle of peace.

Already in the age of Augustus it was possible for Dionysius of Halicarnassus to argue that not a single nation disputed Rome's universal hegemony or her rule over itself: indeed, his Greek audience would learn from his history not to chafe at Roman rule, "which is established according to reason, for it is a law of nature, one common to all men, which the passage of time will not destroy, that the strong shall always rule over the weak."[27] In writing the preface to his history of the Roman rise to power, Appian delivered a comparable verdict on the history of the Hellenistic Greeks:[28]

> Their contests were waged not so much for the sake of acquisition of empire as out of mutual rivalry, and the most glorious of them were fought in defense of Greek freedom against the aggression of foreign powers. . . . In short, Greek power, although passionately contentious for hegemony, never advanced securely beyond the boundaries of Greece; and although the Greeks were marvelous at keeping their country unenslaved and undefeated for a long period, they seem to me, at any rate, from the time of Philip son of Amyntas and Alexander son of Philip to have acted shamefully and in a fashion most unworthy of themselves.

Herodian offered a similar judgment as an explanatory aside when describing the factional strife that erupted in eastern cities during the war between Niger and Severus: "This is an ancient condition among the Greeks, who exhausted Greece by always quarreling with each other and desiring to destroy those who seemed to be preeminent."[29] Herodian's comment suggests that Greek cities continued for some time to exhaust themselves in petty rivalries, of which fact some Greeks remained painfully aware.[30]

This particular accomplishment—that of creating and enforcing a peace—also impressed some Jews, another group with a predilection for

27. Dionysius Hal. *Ant. Rom.* 1.3.5 and 5.2. On Dionysius as Augustan intellectual, see Gabba 1991.

28. Appian *praef.* 30–31.

29. Herodian 3.2.8.

30. E.g., Cassius Dio 52.37.9–10, and cf. 52.30.6. See also Dio Chrysostom *Or.* 38–41, with Magie 1950, 635–636, and C. Jones 1978, 83–94; and Pausanias 7.17.4 on the freedom granted by Nero and withdrawn by Vespasian, with C. Jones 1971, 18, and Habicht 1985, 123. Brunt 1990, 79, provides a substantial catalogue of data on "the mutual rivalry of cities." To his evidence should surely be added boasts like that of the Ephesians, that their city was ἡ πρώτη καὶ μεγίστη μητρόπολις τῆς Ἀσίας (*SIG* 867; a shortened version of this slogan appears on many of that city's coins). On this theme see also Robert 1977; Sartre 1991, 190–198; and Haensch 1997, index III 7 s.v. "Rivalität anderer Städte mit dem Statthaltersitz."

self-destruction. Almost three decades after the Jewish revolt, Josephus argued that *stasis* within and between Jewish communities, as much as crimes by Roman magistrates, had kindled the revolts in Judaea under Nero.[31] Two pieces of Rabbinic lore excerpted in the Sefer Ha-Aggadah comment directly on this topic:[32]

> R. Simeon ben Lakish said: The words "Behold, it was . . . good" (Gen. 1:31) apply to the kingdom of Heaven. The full statement, "Behold, it was very good" applies to the Roman Empire. But how can the Roman Empire be described as "very good"? What a baffling statement! Well, the empire merits such designation because it exacts justice for human beings.

And again:[33]

> "And Thou makest man as the fishes of the sea" (Hab. 1:14). As among the fishes of the sea, the greater swallow the smaller, so it is with humankind: were it not for fear of government, the stronger would swallow the weaker. This is indeed what we have been taught: R. Hanina, deputy high priest, used to say: Pray for the well-being of the [Roman] government—but for fear of it, men would swallow one another alive.

Such appeals to the value of the Roman empire speak all the louder for the casual nature of their introduction into a discourse otherwise concerned with the elucidation of Scripture. Christians, too, likened Rome to a force that restrained men's natural tendencies toward self-destruction. Irenaeus of Lyons, for example, argued from Paul that God empowered the rulers of this world: as men no longer feared God, they should at least fear each

---

31. He conveys this more strongly in his autobiography (17–413 *passim*) than in *Bellum Iudaicum;* in the latter narrative Josephus argues that conflict between Jewish leaders sapped Jewish strength. Note *Vit.* 100, where Josephus pleads that the Romans expect the Jewish factions to destroy each other.

32. Sefer Ha-Aggadah 5.91 (trans. Braude), excerpted from the Genesis Rabbah (94:9). Simeon should probably be dated to the middle of the third century; Genesis Rabbah was compiled in Palestine sometime after 400 (Stemberger 1996, 86 and 279–280). As de Lange 1978, 258–260, argues, "for the Jews it was axiomatic that historical events affecting them bore the mark of divine intervention." Thus Jews had already begun to cede divine favor to Rome as early as Pompey's conquest of the East.

33. Sefer Ha-Aggadah 5.92 (trans. Braude), excerpted from the Genesis Rabbah (9:13). Compare the more negative assessment offered by two passages from the Palestinian Talmud (translated in Lieberman 1946a, 348–349): "Here is the policy of the wicked government which begrudges a man his money. 'This one is rich: let us appoint him magistrate [ἄρχων]; this one is rich: let us appoint him councilor [βουλευτής]'"; and "Like this thorn of which you disengage yourself here and it entangles you there, so the wicked Esau [i.e. Rome] molests you continuously: 'Bring your capitation tax, the public taxes [τὰ δημόσια], the *annona!*' If he [says that he] has not [the money], [Esau] fines him, robs him, and imposes penalties upon him." The first story is attributed to Johannan ben Zakkai in the first century A.D.; the second is found in a portion of the Pesiqta Rabbati attributed to R. Tanhuma bar Abba, of the fifth generation of Amoraim, from the fourth century (Stemberger 1996, 96 and 299).

other. Nor, he argued, should men revolt against unjust magistrates; God will deal with them. "Thus this earthly empire was established not by the Devil, who is never at rest and who does not want even the pagans to live in peace, but by God for the benefit of the gentiles, so that men, fearing the empire of men, might not devour each other like fish but might, through the establishment of laws, reject the multifarious wickedness of the pagans."[34] We might note in passing that such had been the immediate reaction of the Greeks to the arrival of Augustus, even if all he really did was bring the civil wars to a close. The *koinon* of Asia nevertheless declared him a "savior, one who stopped war and arranged peace."[35] Greeks also reacted by coining new words to describe those pragmatic enough to appreciate the benefits conferred by that savior: an edict connected with honors voted by the *koinon,* from a text in Halicarnassus, records the actions of a Greek citizen of Rome, Gaius Julius M....., a high priest (of the imperial cult), φιλοκαίσαρος.[36]

Greeks had long been impressed by Rome's generous policy with citizenship, and Aristides was no exception.[37] Roman citizenship, he wrote, recognized no physical boundaries, and its spread created a "common republic of the world under the single best ruler and governor, in which everyone comes, as it were, into a common agora."[38] Romans, too, recognized the important role that the sharing of political rights had played in securing her empire in Italy:[39]

34. Irenaeus *Adv. haereses* 5.24.2.

35. *EJ* no. 98, tablet b, ll. 35–36 (*OGIS* 458): σωτῆρα . . . τὸν παύσαντα μὲν πόλεμον, κοσμήσοντα [δὲ εἰρήνην]. This document was to be distributed to the members of the *koinon,* and fragments have been found in Priene, Apamea, Eumenea, and Dorylaeum. Similar wording was adopted by the people of Myra in Lycia: θεὸν Σεβαστὸν θεοῦ υἱὸ[ν] Καίσαρα αὐτοκράτορα γῆς καὶ θαλάσσης, τὸν εὐεργέτ[ην] καὶ σωτῆρα τοῦ σύνπαντος κόσμου, Μυρέων ὁ δῆμος (*EJ* no. 72; cf. no. 88 to Tiberius). On the honors decreed to Augustus in this period, see Syme 1939, 473–474. On the titles *pacator orbis* and εἰρηνοποιὸς τῆς οἰκουμένης, see A. Alföldi 1935, 36; Robert, *OMS* V 654; and see Chapter 8 at n. 246.

36. *EJ* no. 98a, ll. 42–43. This text antedates by a decade the earliest attested use of this word in *LSJ.* The parallel term, φιλοσέβαστος, is current also from the reign of Augustus (*SIG* 804 [Cos, A.D. 1]; cf. West 1931, no. 15 [Corinth, ca. A.D. 32]).

37. See the letter of Philip V to Larisa (*SIG* 543 = *IG* IX.2 517); cf. Dionysius Hal. *Ant. Rom.* 2.16–17 and 4.22.2–4. For later references see Gernentz 1918, 133–135. To his list add Libanius *Or.* 30.5: καὶ μετὰ τῆς τῶν θεῶν τουτωνὶ συμμαχίας ἐπιόντες Ῥωμαῖοι τοῖς ἐναντίοις μαχόμενοί τε ἐνίκων καὶ νενικηκότες βελτίω τοῖς ἡττημένοις τοῦ πρὸ τῆς ἥττης τὸν ἐπ᾽ αὐτῇ χρόνον ἐποίουν φόβους τε ἀφελόντες καὶ πολιτείας τῆς αὐτῶν μεταδόντες.

38. *Or.* 26.60: (καὶ οὔτε θάλαττα διείργει τὸ μὴ εἶναι πολίτην οὔτε πλῆθος τῆς ἐν μέσῳ χώρας. . . . ξένος δ᾽ οὐδεὶς ὅστις ἀρχῆς ἢ πίστεως ἄξιος,) ἀλλὰ καθέστηκε κοινὴ τῆς γῆς δημοκρατία ὑφ᾽ ἑνὶ τῷ ἀρίστῳ ἄρχοντι καὶ κοσμητῇ καὶ πάντες ὥσπερ εἰς κοινὴν ἀγορὰν συνίασι τευξόμενοι τῆς ἀξίας ἕκαστοι.

39. Cicero *Balb.* 13.31. Among other passages see esp. the speech of Camillus in Livy 8.13.16, on which see Brunt 1971, 539 n. 1.

Without any doubt it was Romulus, the principal founder of this city, who played the greatest role in laying the foundation of our empire and in advancing the name of the Roman people, when he showed in his treaty with the Sabines that this community ought to be augmented by receiving even our enemies; on his authority and by that example there has been no interruption by our ancestors in the dispensing and spread of citizenship. Thus many from Latium, the Tusculans, the Lanuvians, and whole nations of every sort have been received into our polity, from the Sabines, the Volsci, and the Hernici . . .

Of course, by the time Rome became heavily involved in the East, Romans no longer tended to grant citizenship to communities en masse, but rather dispensed it as a reward for, and inducement to, loyalty among those in a position to promote stability. Not surprisingly, on this topic Aristides focused attention on the Roman practice of governing individual cities by acquiring the cooperation of their best men. He was, therefore, quick to overlook the difficulties which Greek cities faced, when, for instance, the Roman citizens among them sought to avoid local courts: "Many in each city are your fellow-citizens no less than of their own kinsmen. . . . There is no need for garrisons to hold their citadels, but the men of greatest standing and influence in every city guard their fatherlands for you."[40] Lest anyone conclude that Aristides here subtly criticized the quislings who cooperated with the Roman overlords, let them first read Plutarch's "Precepts of statecraft": "Not only should the statesman show himself and his native city blameless toward [the Romans], but he should also have a friend among the men of high office, as a firm bulwark of his administration; for the Romans themselves are most eager to promote the political interests of their friends; and it is a fine thing, too, to seize the benefits of friendship with our leaders . . . in order to benefit the public welfare."[41] Romans now ruled the world, and Greeks who wished to serve their cities could do so better by placating rather than antagonizing them.[42]

That the Romans had a policy of using citizenship and other inducements to invite the cooperation of their subjects may be confirmed on two levels. First, it had been a truism of Roman imperialism even under the Republic that "an empire remains powerful so long as its subjects rejoice in it."[43] Sallust, in a move laden with irony, allows Sulla to voice the sentiment

40. *Or.* 26.64 (trans. Oliver). See also Josephus *Bell. Iud.* 2.331–332: Florus negotiates with τούς τε ἀρχιερεῖς καὶ τὴν βουλήν· τῶν δὲ πάντα περὶ ἀσφαλείας καὶ τοῦ μηδὲν νεωτερίσειν ὑποσχομένων, εἰ μίαν αὐτοῖς καταλείποι σπεῖραν. On this incident see Rajak 1991, 127.

41. *Prae. ger. reip.* 814C. Cf. Dio Chrysostom *Or.* 31.111: obviously the Romans preferred that their subjects be "free and honorable" rather than that they should "rule over slaves."

42. See C. Jones 1971; Gabba 1984; Eckstein 1985, 1990, and 1995, 8–27 and 194–236; Erskine 1990, 181–204; Stern 1987; and Shaw 1995.

43. Livy 8.13.16: *Certe id firmissimum longe imperium est quo oboedientes gaudent.* Cf. Cicero *Verr.* 2.3.14 and *Leg. Man.* 41. Tacitus did not approve that Caratacus was joined by those *qui pacem*

in a speech to Bocchus: "Even from the beginnings of their empire the Roman people have preferred to acquire friends rather than slaves, thinking it
safer to rule by good will rather than by force."[44] Second, Romans freely admitted that they focused their attention on acquiring the good will of local
elites. Long before the crisis of the Social War, Cato the Elder had combined these themes in his attack on Quintus Minucius Thermus. Insulting
the leaders of Rome's allies was in itself against Roman self-interest; humil-
iating them in front of their subjects compounded that error tenfold: "What
of our alliance? Where was the loyalty of our ancestors?"[45] In the generation
before Augustus, Cicero had congratulated his brother Quintus for ensuring
that "the government of the communities is in the hands of their leading
citizens."[46] Writing of an earlier age, Livy argued that "everyone agreed that
in the cities the *principes* and all the noblest men were for an alliance with
Rome and rejoiced in the status quo, while the common mass and those displeased with their circumstances desired a revolution."[47] A century and a
half later, Pausanias recalled that, in the aftermath of the destruction of
Corinth and the reduction of Greece into the province of Achaea, L. Mum-
mius "put an end to the democracies and established magistracies on the
basis of property assessments."[48] That such had been imperial practice—at
least in the judgment of Dio—is clear from the advice voiced by Maecenas
in his famous debate with Agrippa in Book 52:[49]

> In the place of [those dismissed from the Senate], enroll the noblest, the best,
> and the richest, selecting not only from Italy but also from allied and subject
> peoples; for these you may regard as a multitude of assistants, and you will
> place the chief men from all the nations in security. These nations, having no
> famous leader, will not try to change things, and the leading men among each
> group will love you because they have a share with you in the empire.

Dio was fully conscious of his double heritage, Greek and Roman, but his political loyalties lay with Rome, and his political ideals were formed by hers.
In this he was unexceptional.[50]

---

nostram metuebant (*Ann.* 12.33). On this aspect of Roman thought see Hammond 1948, 118–
120.

44. Sallust *Iug.* 102.6.
45. *ORF*[3] Cato fr. 58 (Gellius 10.3.17).
46. *Ep. ad Quint. fratrem* 1.1.25 (trans. Shackleton Bailey).
47. Livy 35.34.3.
48. Pausanias 7.16.6. On these events see de Ste. Croix 1981, sections V.iii and VI.iv.
49. Dio 52.19.2–3.
50. Cf. the generalization offered by Brunt 1990, 273: "I have never been able to discover
that the promotion of leading provincials had any effect on Roman policy, or on the ideas of
emperor, senators, or Equites. They were apparently uncritical of the established order."

Let us return to Cicero's formulation of the loyalties that contended within the hearts of Italians promoted to Roman citizenship:[51]

> *Atticus:* Have you then two *patriae?* Or is our *communis patria* the only one? Unless, that is, you think that Cato's fatherland was not Rome, but Tusculum?
>
> *Marcus:* Absolutely I think that both he and all other municipal men have two *patriae:* one by birth, and one by citizenship. . . . Thus we consider as our *patria* both the place where we were born and that place by which we are adopted. But that *patria* must be preeminent in our affection in which the name *res publica* signifies the common citizenship of us all. For her it is our duty to die; to her we ought to give our entire selves, and on her altar we ought to place and to dedicate, as it were, all that we possess.

Can a case be made that Cicero spoke not only for himself, but also for other Italians and, indeed, for other provincials? We should, of course, be chary of romanticizing "Italian aims at the time of the Social War": the rebels before their rebellion had demanded only representation to go with taxation, "political unity and equality within the structure of the Roman state."[52] Similar methodological pitfalls lie before scholars working on the Greek East. The increasing sophistication of narratives for the co-optation of the governing class in the East, the hard-won achievement of the last half-century, is now under attack by those who wish to view first-century Greeks through twentieth-century postcolonial eyes.[53] All evidence suggests that Greeks experienced power and assessed claims to legitimate domination in ways profoundly different than did the subjects of early modern empires. Even without that distraction, however, the dynamics of civic life, especially in relations between men who sought close contact with Rome and those who didn't, remain elusive.[54] Nevertheless, some general trends can be described without controversy.

51. Cicero *Leg.* 2.5.

52. Brunt 1988, 93–143 at 113.

53. To measure the achievements of the last half-century, compare the figures tabulated in Hammond 1957 with the catalogue compiled by Halfmann 1979. For discursive treatments of these issues see Bowersock 1965; A. H. M. Jones 1974, 90–113; Syme, *RP* 2.566–581 and *RP* 4.1–20. For a more large-scale survey see Sartre 1991. For further review of recent work see Ando 1999.

54. Compare Oliver 1979, who stresses the use some made of their Roman citizenship to avoid local liturgies (cf. Plutarch *Prae. ger. reip.* 815A), with Eck 1980, who seeks evidence for just the opposite: members of senatorial families who also held municipal magistracies and priesthoods. To a certain extent a resolution to these approaches is provided by chronology: Augustus himself furnishes ample testimony in support of Oliver in the Cyrene Edicts (esp. no. III of 7/6 B.C. = *EJ* no. 311, no. III, to which we should compare the letter which he sent to Rhosus, Tarsus, and Seleucia, *EJ* no. 301, esp. II.8). And certainly from the time of Hadrian, the issue becomes anachronistic: individual opposition to particular emperors or to imperial cult there may have been, but the empire was simply a fact of life (C. Jones 1971, 119–132).

In their initial attempts to structure the eastern provinces, Romans generally dissolved the federations of Greek cities that had become so prevalent in the third and second centuries B.C., and not unreasonably: the Achaean League had served to focus anti-Roman sentiment in the mid-second century, and hence its defeat endowed the new province with its name.[55] They also imposed new systems of legal and social stratification on some provincial populations—the best-attested system is, not surprisingly, that in Egypt—and elsewhere forbade individuals from holding citizenship in more than one city at a time.[56] But Augustus and his successors were attempting to govern a vast empire with a small bureaucracy,[57] and the exploitation of preexisting leagues answered this aim.[58] Much the same desire for administrative efficiency must have lain behind the ranking of cities into "smaller, bigger, and biggest,"[59] and also behind the ranking of communities in different classes, with smaller ones attached to the nearest *civitas*.[60] These measures had the additional advantage that they directed loyalties and patriotic sentiments away from the individual polis and toward a larger community.

For example, we know from Strabo that the Romans established assize

55. Pausanias 7.16.10.

56. On the new status system in Egypt see Chapter 9 at n. 75. On the *lex Pompeia* see Sherwin-White 1966 on Pliny 10.114.1. Although Dio confirms that Pompey's arrangements still obtained in many respects, the restrictions on dual or multiple citizenship clearly fell into abeyance by the end of the first century (Dio 37.20.2, with Mitchell 1984, 123; and cf. Ruggini 1976).

57. Hopkins 1980, 121; and see Luttwak 1976, 17–19, on Rome's "economy of force." Burton 1993 and Peachin 1996 analyze particular consequences of Rome's attempt to govern with so few personnel. We can easily sympathize with the claim of Augustus reported by Plutarch: when Augustus learned that Alexander had been depressed because he had already conquered the world, "he marveled that Alexander had not considered it the greater task to set in order his dominion than simply to have acquired his hegemony" (*Reg. et imp. apoth.* 207D).

58. J. Keil at *CAH* XI 557; Magie 1950, 530ff., on the annexation of Lycia-Pamphylia; Bowersock 1965, 91–93, and Sartre 1991, 207–211, on the Κοινὸν τῶν Ἐλευθερολακώνων and on the Achaean League and the κοινά which it subsequently absorbed; Bowersock 1965, 97–98, on the Thessalian League; Habicht 1975 and Sartre 1991, 258–263, on the organization of the province of Asia; and Sartre 1991, 339–340 on Syria, contrasting the situation there with that which prevailed in Arabia.

59. Antoninus Pius to the province of Asia at *Digest* 27.1.6.2. Cf. Athenagoras *Leg.* 1.2 (αἱ δὲ πόλεις πρὸς ἀξίαν τῆς ἴσης μετέχουσι τιμῆς) and *AJ* no. 100.

60. See Jacques at *Integration* 1.219–250. Cf. *AJ* pp. 10–20, with documents nos. 151 (*ILS* 6090) and 154 (*ILS* 6091, with Chastagnol 1981); compare *CIL* IX 2165. Note the punishment meted out by Severus to Byzantium and Antioch: πᾶσά τε ἡ πόλις (τὸ Βυζάντιον) κατεσκάφη, καὶ θεάτρων τε καὶ λουτρῶν παντός τε κόσμου καὶ τιμῆς ἀφαιρεθὲν τὸ βυζάντιον κώμη δουλεύειν Περινθίοις δῶρον ἐδόθη, ὥσπερ καὶ Ἀντιόχεια Λαοδικεῦσιν (Herodian 3.6.9; cf. Ulpian at *Dig.* 50.15.1.3), and the wish that the *Historia Augusta* attributes to Hadrian: *Antiochenses inter haec ita odio habuit, ut Syriam a Phoenice separare voluerit, ne tot civitatum metropolis Antiochia diceretur* (*Hadr.* 14.1).

districts and provincial boundaries without any regard for previously existing political or ethnic divisions.[61] In promoting the imperial cult in Asia Minor, the Romans distributed priesthoods according to these assize districts,
ignoring, once again, earlier boundaries between political and ethnic collectivities, and the same policy appears to have obtained in Syria, Cyrenaïca,
and Galatia. In many areas the Romans assigned responsibility for maintenance of the cult and election of its chief priests to *koina,* councils com-
prised, once again, of cities that lay within political boundaries as Rome had
determined them.[62] Various policies and movements thus came together to
provide a method for provincials simultaneously to display their loyalty and
to situate themselves within a new conceptualization of geographic space.

By the early second century Hadrian understood Greeks to be suffi-
ciently comfortable with their status within the empire to establish a new
league dedicated to the celebration of Hellenic culture.[63] Hadrian could
have derived that understanding from viewing the celebrations endowed at
Ephesus by C. Vibius Salutaris in A.D. 104, which "consciously framed the
Roman presence within the institutional, historical and sacral structures of
the city."[64] In a similar vein, Greek cities in the Antonine period now focused their rivalries on claiming positions of priority in the esteem of their
overlords and in displays of loyalty: Ephesus, for example, referred to itself
as "the first and greatest metropolis of Asia, twice temple warden of the Augusti, and lover of Augustus."[65] This process is already visible in the mid-first
century in an honorific inscription from Aphrodisias. The council and the
people pay tribute to Tiberius Claudius Diogenes: in doing so, they list first,
in positions of priority, not his direct benefactions to Aphrodisias itself, but
his holding of the high priesthood of Asia and his position of sebastophant,
the equivalent of a *flamen Augusti.*[66] Rome thus promoted a reorganization
of political, administrative, and conceptual boundaries throughout the

61. Strabo 13.4.12, on Asia Minor; cf. 12.3.6 and 12, with Lassère 1982, 891–894, and
Mitchell 1993, 1.87–93. On Roman reorganization of political boundaries in the East see
Sartre 1991, 109–116, and the exemplary introductions to each region in *RPC* 1.

62. On Asia Minor see Robert, *Hellenica* 7.206–238; Habicht 1975; Sartre 1995, 189–207;
and Nicolet 1996, 10–18. On Cyrenaïca see Reynolds 1978. On Syria see *AÉ* 1976, 678: *Bulletin Épigraphique* 1976, 718; and Millar 1984, 54. On Galatia see Mitchell 1993, 1.100–103
and 107–113. See now Haensch 1997, index III 2.

63. Spawforth and Walker 1985 and 1986; C. Jones 1996; Birley 1997, 217–220.

64. Rogers 1991. The quotation is from 142–143.

65. *SIG* 867, col. b, ll. 1–4, from A.D. 160. On similar boasts by Nicaea and Nicomedia see
Robert 1977, who analyzes in detail the schemes those cities undertook in order to win the use
of such titles.

66. Reynolds 1981, no. 4, l. 1. For a later assessment of the esteem in which Rome held
priests of the imperial cult, see Philostratus *Soph.* 612–613.

East, in a fashion that redirected hearts and minds away from the centrality of individual cities and toward herself as the city of the empire.

For that is ultimately where Aelius Aristides, in imagining a common agora, and Rutilius Namatianus, with his contrast between *urbs* and *orbis*, concentrated their praise of Rome: the empire, by distributing citizenship throughout the land, by having one ruler who was also the final, single judge, became, in essence, a single polis.[67] Like a city, Rome, too, had constructed a grand set of walls—only hers surrounded the entire empire and were constructed beyond the "outermost circle of the civilized world."[68] Themistius appealed to the same idea in the speech he delivered before Valens and the Senate of Constantinople in the winter of 366, congratulating that emperor for suppressing the revolt of Procopius in a less bloody fashion than he might have done: like a physician attending to the sick part of a single body, he should not punish what can become better—namely the regions that supported Procopius—but should regard the empire as a unified whole, as a single City of the Romans (οὕτω καὶ τῆς ἀρχῆς μιᾶς οὔσης τῆς ὅλης Ῥωμαίων ὥσπερ πόλεως).[69] All these images coalesced in Prudentius's panegyric to Rome's achievement, although he gave all credit for her accomplishment to his God:[70]

> To curb this madness God taught nations everywhere to bow their heads beneath the same laws and [taught] all to become Roman. . . . A common law made them equals, bound them by a single name, and brought them, though conquered, into bonds of brotherhood. We live in every conceivable region scarcely different than if a single city and fatherland enclosed fellow citizens with a single wall and we all gathered at our ancestral hearth. Distant regions and shores divided by the sea now come together *per vadimonia* [i.e., in legal matters] to a single and common forum; now for commerce and crafts to a crowded market; now for marriage to the right to marry a foreign spouse, for a single progeny is born by mixed blood from two different races.

Earlier Christians provided ample testimony to Rome's success in creating a single community within the empire when they described the unification of

---

67. On this theme in Greek political theory under the empire see Ando 1999.

68. *Or.* 26.80–81. Of course, the "wall" turns out to be the army (84), but that makes the analogy no less telling. The notion that the Roman empire encompassed the civilized world had a long currency: it was essential to Polybius, else his history would not have been "universal" (cf. Walbank 1948). But it acquired a special resonance in the age of Caesar (Plutarch *Caesar* 23.3 and 58.7) and in Caesarian propaganda (Weinstock 1971, 40–53). See Gernentz 1918, 103–124—even by his standards a wonderful collection of material—and Nicolet 1991, 29–47.

69. Themistius *Or.* 7.94c–d.

70. Prudentius *Symm.* 2.602–604, 608–618.

the world as a prolegomenon to the establishment of the kingdom of God: for many, it was a task so remarkable that it could have been accomplished only with God's blessing.[71]

Christian belief on this issue was nothing new. Polybius was but one Greek among many who saw in the rise of Rome the operation of Fortune and the necessity of nature.[72] According to Josephus, Agrippa advised the Jews not to count on the aid of God: "For this, too, is arranged on the side of the Romans. For without God's favor so great an empire could not have arisen."[73] Josephus subsequently portrays himself urging his countrymen that it is "God, then, God himself who with the Romans brings the cleansing fire for his temple and destroys this city, which is burdened with so many pollutions."[74] He also depicts several Romans, but most notably Titus, reflecting on the role of the Jewish God in the Romans' success: "'We fought with God as our ally,' he said, 'and it was God who threw the Jews down from these fortifications. For what could the hands or machines of men have achieved against these towers?'"[75] When Josephus later wrote his *Autobiography*, he asserted that his own status as Pharisee priest and prophet had enabled him to foresee the end of the war, and he confirmed in the *Jewish antiquities* that Daniel had foretold the rise of the Roman empire and that the realization of Daniel's prophecies proved the direct governance of the universe by God.[76] The Babylonian Talmud preserves an anecdote from the next generation, describing a conversation between Rabbi Yose ben Kisma and Hananiah ben Teradion. The former advised the latter to leave aside his hotheaded ways: "Do you not realize that it is Heaven who has ordained this nation to rule? For even though they have laid waste his home, burnt down his temple, slain his saints, and persecuted his servants, still their empire is firmly established."[77]

These men did not endorse unquestioning subservience to Roman authority, nor would a Roman despotism matched by provincial servility have produced the testimonials so conspicuous in imperial literature. Rather, these beliefs acquired special force when combined with the stated aims of

71. See Chapter 2 at n. 169, and cf. Chapter 9, "How Did One Join the Roman Community?"

72. Polybius 1.4.4 and 6.9.12–13; on these passages see Walbank 1972, 63–64. Cf. Woolf 1998, 231: "That sense that the destruction of the Druids and the victory of Rome demonstrated the inadequacy of ancestral cults and accepted wisdom may well have been most widely felt in Gallic society."

73. Josephus *Bell. Iud.* 2.390; cf. *Vit.* 17–19 and 60.

74. Josephus *Bell. Iud.* 6.110.

75. Josephus *Bell. Iud.* 6.411.

76. Josephus *Vita* 17–19 and *Ant. Iud.* 10.276–281; Shaw 1995, 362 and 367.

77. B. 'Abod. Zar. 18a, trans. in de Lange 1978, 268. For the date of this conversation see Stemberger 1996, 74.

those Romans who sought not simply to rule and to profit, but to govern and govern well. Pliny was quite explicit that Rome's mission was the creation of a single *patria* for her citizens: she was "the nurse and mother of all lands, chosen by the *numen* of the gods to make heaven itself brighter, to join together scattered empires, to soften customs, to unite in discourse the wild, discordant tongues of so many peoples by an exchange of language, and to give humanity to man; briefly, to become the single native land of all the peoples in the world."[78] By the fourth century this mission had, according to Claudian, been achieved; by birth a Greek from Alexandria in Egypt, he knew well what the unification of the world had meant to his career: "[Rome] alone received the conquered to her bosom and cherished the human race with a common name, in the fashion of a mother, not of an empress; and she called "citizens" those whom she subdued and bound with her far-reaching and pious embrace. To her pacifying customs we owe everything: . . . that we are all of us one race."[79] The emperor Julian asserted with equal boldness that men, no matter where they were born, become citizens "by participating in Rome's constitution, by adopting our customs, and by using our laws."[80] Such was a necessary, if theoretical, consequence of the extension of citizenship when combined with the Roman notion—one shared intermittently by prodemocratic Greeks—that the state was nothing more than the sum of its citizen body.[81]

Such a positive definition of Rome's achievement presumes that, for each individual, citizenship was an important feature of his self-identification, but the mere granting of citizenship did not guarantee that its possessor would esteem his new *patria* thus. Such an object might be achieved in the first instance in purely pragmatic terms. Roman citizenship, asserted Tacitus, was once a rare gift, one given only as a reward for virtue.[82] Its very existence, he claimed, ought to create a unity of interests, even if only of self-interest, among all who hold it: "Eight hundred years' good fortune and discipline have created this structure [the *imperium Romanum*], which can-

---

78. Pliny *Nat.* 3.39: *breviterque una cunctarum gentium in toto orbe patria fieret.*

79. Claudian *Cons. Stil.* 3.150–155, 159. On Claudian's origin, see A. D. E. Cameron 1970, 2–3 and 6–7. On the similar career of Harpocration, an Egyptian who learned Latin in order to praise Romans in their own tongue, see Browne 1975 and 1977.

80. Julian *Or.* 1.4. On the role of law in defining the Roman community see Chapter 9, "How Did One Join the Roman Community?"

81. See Cicero *Rep.* 1.39.1 and 6.13.2. Hence Republican definitions of *maiestas* center on crimes against the *dignitas* of the *populus Romanus:* e.g., *Maiestatem is minuit qui ea tollit ex quibus rebus civitatis amplitudo constat* (*Rhet. ad Her.* 2.12.17). See also *Rhet. ad Her.* 4.25.35; Cicero *Inv.* 2.17.53; Tacitus *Ann.* 1.72.2; and Valerius Maximus 8.15 *ext.* 1. Thus, too, the analysis offered by Ulpian at *Dig.* 1.4.1.1 (quoted in Chapter 2 at n. 55). On *consensus* and imperial power see von Premerstein 1937, 62–65, and below, Chapters 5 and 6.

82. *Ann.* 3.40.1.

not be overthrown without the destruction of those who would overthrow it. . . . Accordingly love and cherish this peace and our city, which both parties—conquered and conquerors—enjoy with equal rights. Let the evidence of both outcomes teach you not to prefer rebellion with ruin to obedience with security."[83] Such an assertion of a unity of self-interest removed Roman imperialism of the Principate qualitatively from, for example, the ideologies of empire represented in the classical historians of Greece.[84] Of course, Rome was not alone among the empires of the ancient world in praying for, and boasting of, the eternity of her rule.[85] Rather, Roman propaganda of the Principate promoted and allowed considerable advances in the universalization of that message. Tacitus here participated in that trend, giving that ideal a very practical application: if the stability of Rome determined the health and wealth of her subjects, they ought not rebel, if only for their own sake. *Sapientes* in the provinces, no less than those at Rome, were expected to know the difference between *libertas* and *licentia*.[86]

The complex of ideas outlined in this chapter coalesced in a powerful and peculiarly ancient dynamic. Briefly put, belief in divine sanction for Roman conquest inevitably endowed the ideal of an eternal empire with a certain currency. The acceptance of this ideal had the practical outcome of debasing the ideals of rebellion, freedom, and self-determination. The simple suggestion of Dionysius, that the strong always rule over the weak, became substantially more palatable when Greeks or Jews, like Polybius or Josephus, could suggest that their respective gods, or even nature itself, had brought Roman rule about. We must remember that public power, concretized in recognized forms of domination and social action, is not inherently noxious, nor could the Roman empire have survived on might alone. Rather, its long-term health, like that of any social system, depended on its consensual validity.[87]

Indeed, it is in attitudes to the exercise of public power that the ancient experience of imperialism differs most strongly from the early modern world. This divergence creates almost insurmountable obstacles to the profitable comparison of ancient and modern empires, and few attempts in

83. *Hist.* 4.74.3–4: *proinde pacem et urbem, quam victi victoresque eodem iure obtinemus, amate colite.* This use of *urbem,* which Heubner, Chilver, and Townend suggest is "without parallel" (in their notes *ad loc.*), suggests that Romans no less than Greeks continued to conceptualize Rome in the traditional terms of a polis (*contra* Cornell; see above, n. 25).

84. On Hellenistic and Roman philosophies of empire see A. Alföldi 1935, 216–224, and Ando 1999, section II.

85. See Instinsky 1942. For a catalog of invocations of *Roma aeterna,* see Gernentz 1918, 40–46.

86. On Tacitus's distinction between these terms see Chapter 5 at n. 100.

87. Weber 1978, 212–213; cf. Giddens 1984, 330–332, and Habermas 1984, 190.

that field have escaped those hazards.[88] It is arrogance born of luxury that leads us to equate civilization and barbarism, or to patronize subject populations with deterministic ideologies of rebellion. Doing so can only lead to profound errors in understanding the past. Illusory and deceptive continuities between the ancient and modern worlds are partially to blame for contemporary desires to view Rome with twentieth-century eyes. But the Romans knew the seductive power exercised by material prosperity. Whether adorning cities with marble, leading clean water from distant hills, or elevating martial splendor to new heights, the Romans spoke a universal language.[89] The immediately intelligible attractions of Roman urbanism, like the idiom of the Roman triumph, found receptive audiences throughout Mediterranean world.

Individuals and groups participating in such belief systems would have received Roman claims to possess special skill in ruling over others very differently than we might expect. Propaganda is not necessarily rendered persuasive through the exercise of coercive force, nor by the potential thereof. Like all forms of communication, the validity claims of propaganda are open to criticism.[90] But the manifest success of Rome in and of itself gave that propaganda considerable empirical validity. Nor ought we necessarily regard the rhetoric of Romans and provincials with suspicion. "The sincerity of a text has nothing to do with its historicity. What matters is that the words were spoken, that they possessed meaning, that they contribute to the reconstruction of a historical situation. The pretext of 'the common-place' does not dispense with the necessity of inquiry. What is the 'topos' if not the expression, however banal, of a great truth?"[91]

Simultaneously, the conscious if unspoken awareness that one's own ethnic group had failed at self-governance or even merely at self-preservation must have led individuals to search for stability. To the extent that the divine order sanctioned Roman conquest, so far might one proceed—from the premises that the strong shall rule over the weak and that Romans govern well—to a belief that the Roman empire as institution of government and instrument of providence had both the right and the responsibility to maintain social order. That ultimate belief collapsed and obscured the arbitrariness of Roman domination and urged, by daily exposure and converse, the slow acceptance of the mechanisms of Roman governance as objective and institutional. The bureaucracy of Rome, its demands, its sym-

---

88. E.g., Webster and Cooper 1996 or D. Mattingly 1997.

89. Frontinus *Aquis* 2.119: *ad tutelam ductuum sicut promiseram divertemus, rem enixiore cura dignam, cum magnitudinis Romani imperii vel praecipuum sit indicium.*

90. Habermas 1984, 397–399.

91. Béranger 1975, 166; cf. Simon 1994, 2.

bols, and its taxes, thus acquired "the opacity and permanence of things and escaped the grasp of individual consciousness and power."[92]

To understand the force of that belief in the ancient world we must get past our own misgivings about the nature of social order. For Weber, the routinization of charismatic power in and through institutions succeeded or failed on their ability to orient the goal-directed actions of different individuals: that is, to create *consensus* regarding the legitimacy of the social structures that govern individual purposive actions.[93] As S. N. Eisenstadt has argued, to appreciate Weber's insight we must understand that in egocentric calculations of utility the quest for and conception of symbolic order, of the "good society," plays a very important role.[94] Thus, individuals seeking security for their persons and their property might well look to Rome, for she claimed to provide precisely that thing that other societies had not been able to provide for themselves. As the gods had overseen and tacitly approved Roman conquest, so the search for social order created a convergence between the desires of provincials and the publicized aims of Rome. Velleius Paterculus, a Roman proud of his Italian roots, preferred to see human agency at the heart of this historic change: it was Augustus who had ensured that "personal security returned to men, and to each confidence in the ownership of his possessions."[95]

The identification by Aelius Aristides, Plutarch, and Tacitus of shared interests between citizen and subject under the empire thus spoke to a much deeper and ultimately ineffable current in their political consciousness.[96] That unity of self-interest would find natural expression in the inclusive franchise of the Roman state. Aristides, for one, commended the Roman practice of using merit alone as a criterion for citizenship: "Dividing into two groups all those in your empire—by which I mean the entire *oecumene*—you have everywhere appointed to citizenship or even to kinship all the more accomplished, the better-born, and the more influential."[97] For Aristides, the world of individual city-states with their own policies and desires had been submerged within a new mental geography that constructed the world out of Romans and non-Romans. What is more, Roman policy embraced both its citizens and all noncitizens, who could aspire to achieve

---

92. Bourdieu 1977, 184.

93. For a trenchant analysis of Weber's thought on this issue, particularly on paths of inquiry he did not take, see Habermas 1984, 143–271, esp. 216–222, and J. Alexander 1991, 56–58.

94. Eisenstadt at Weber 1968, xli; cf. Habermas 1984, 101.

95. Velleius 2.89.2–4 at 4: *Rediit . . . securitas hominibus, certa cuique rerum suarum possessio.*

96. See above at nn. 40, 41, and 83.

97. *Or.* 26.59. See also 26.60, quoted above in n. 38.

a higher status because Rome granted that opportunity to all.[98] As a consequence, Rome became to her empire what another city was to its surrounding territory: Rome was the *communis patria* of the world.[99]

Aristides has crossed the boundary to which I alluded above: good
Greeks, he suggests, identify themselves as good Romans. Again, Aristides
has an ally in the Maecenas of Cassius Dio, who urged Augustus to open the
consulate to the new senators from the East, so that they might devote
themselves to Rome as to their own possessions: "I say that a share in the
government ought to be given to all citizens: then, having an equal share in
it, they might become our faithful allies, as if they were living in some single
polis of us all, believing this city to be their city and regarding their possessions as its fields and villages."[100] That this sentiment was once voiced concerning Alexandria does not diminish the possibility that Aristides and Dio,
like Claudian, regarded it as the ideal toward which Rome's rulers had directed her.[101] We can see the effect of this ideology in Lucian's work when
he refers to Rome, *sacrosanctam istam civitatem,* simply as "the City."[102] At one
level such metaphors arose from the Greek tendency to divide the world
into Greeks and barbarians,[103] and on that level their usage must reflect the
Greeks' desire to lump themselves together with Romans as common participants in a single ethnic and political reality. Yet these metaphors accomplished that desire through a wholly Greek attempt to envision the residents
of the empire as the inhabitants of a single city. On these terms, the erro-
neous definition of *pomerium* given in the *Suda*—"*Pomerium:* A miniature

98. Bleicken 1966, 246–247; Ando 1999.

99. Aristides *Or.* 26.61: ὅπερ δὲ πόλις τοῖς αὑτῆς ὁρίοις καὶ χώραις ἐστίν, τοῦθ' ἥδε ἡ πόλις
τῆς πάσης οἰκουμένης, ὥσπερ αὐτῆς χώρας ἄστυ κοινὸν ἀποδεδειγμένη. Such is the interpretation of ἄστυ κοινόν given by Sherwin-White 1973a, 259, who argues that many of the ideas
in this passage are "demonstrably Roman." Oliver 1953, 928, disagrees and proposes reasonable Greek antecedents for the phrase. Such *Quellenforschung* hardly advances our understanding of the text: the idea was current from at least the reign of Claudius in Roman thought
and propaganda, and that is the way it would have been read. See Modestinus at *Dig.* 27.1.6.11
and Callistratus at *Dig.* 43.22.18. For the identification of Rome and emperor, see Herodian
1.6.5 (ἐκεί τε ἡ Ῥώμη, ὅπου ποτ᾽ ἂν ὁ βασιλεὺς ᾖ).

100. Dio 52.19.6.

101. Written of Alexandria in *BKT* VII 13 (*P. Berlin* 13045), ll. 28–31; cf. *Archiv* 7.240.

102. Eg. *Nigrinos* 2; cf. C. Jones 1986, 85 n. 31; J. Bompaire, in his Budé edition, translates
ἡ πόλις in these instances with a capitalized *la Ville.* Certainly this form of reference is suitable
for dating formulas: *Numquam enim ab urbis ortu* (Ammianus 25.9.9). The Latin quotation is
from Apuleius *Met.* 11.26. Millar 1977, 277 and n. 11, observes of letters from Constantine to
the city of Rome that though they are "addressed in formal style almost exactly as if to a provincial city," "there remains the significant difference that the name of Rome does not have to be
given."

103. Palm 1959, 56–62, 75–76, and 82–83; cf. Vogt 1967, 8–9, and Brunt 1990, 473–
477.

representation of a city wall"—may be unraveled.[104] To be sure, the compiler could have thought the *pomerium* to be some sort of wall. But why use a representation of a wall around a city that had a real one? Perhaps because the wall which the *pomerium* represented was the imaginary wall around the borders of the empire, through which the community of the empire became coextensive with the territory of its polis.

104. *Suda* Π 2178: Πωμήριον: τὸ τοῦ τείχους εἰκόνισμα.

PART TWO

Consensus and Communication

CHAPTER FOUR

The Communicative Actions of the Roman Government

HABERMAS AND ROME

In A.D. 245 a group of men from Beth Phouraia, a village in the vicinity of Appadana, itself a town some miles north of Dura Europus along the Euphrates, came to Antioch to petition the governor to solve a dispute in their village. Fate has preserved a copy of their petition, along with its subscription; it was first published in 1989, was republished in 1995, and is now officially designated *P. Euphrates* 1:[1]

[1] In the consulship of Imperator Caesar Marcus Julius Philippus Augustus and Maesius Tittianus, five days before the Kalends of September, in the year 293 [of Antioch], on 28 Loos, at Antioch, colony and metropolis, in the Baths of Hadrian:

[3] To Julius Priscus, *perfectissimus* prefect of Mesopotamia, exercising proconsular power, from Archodes son of Phallaios, Philotas son of Nisraiabos, Vorodes son of Sumisbarachos, and Abezautas son of Abediardas, from the imperial village Beth Phouraia, the one near Appadana:

[5] Having a dispute with our fellow villagers, Lord, concerning land and other things, we came here to plead our case before Your Goodness and, after we attended your tribunal for eight months, our case was introduced, as Your Greatness remembers, on the ninth day before the Kalends of September—the day just passed. You, Our Benefactor, having heard part of the case, decided that you would render judgment when, blessedly, you would be in the area.

---

1. First publication in Feissel and Gascou 1989; revised text and commentary in *idem* 1995. On the office occupied by Julius Priscus, the prefect addressed in this petition, see Peachin 1996, 176–179.

[10] Since, therefore, the case has not thus far obtained resolution, and our fellow villagers are trying to expel us from the lands on which we reside and to force the issue before judgment, and since the divine constitutions, which you more than all others know and venerate [αἱ θεῖαι διατάξεις, ἅς τε πρὸ πάντων γνωρίζων προσκυνεῖς], ordain that those finding themselves in possession of goods should remain so until judgment, for this reason we have fled to you and we ask you to command by your subscription [δι' ὑπογραφῆς σου] that Claudius Ariston, *vir egregius,* procurator in the area of Appadana, who superintends the diocese, should preserve everything unharmed and should forbid the use of force before your blessed visit to the region, when, obtaining our desire, we will be able to render Your Fortune our eternal thanks.

[17] I, Aurelius Archodes son of Phallaios have submitted the petition, and on behalf of the others, too.

[19] Subscription of Julius Priscus, *perfectissimus* prefect of Mesopotamia, exercising proconsular power: Ariston, *vir egregius,* will examine your petition.

[22] I have read. 209.

[23] Petition of Archodes son of Phallaios and Philotas son of Nisraiabos.

What does it mean that a purely local dispute with fellow villagers brought these men many miles from home, to one of the centers of the eastern provinces? Their trip from Beth Phouraia to Antioch, far outside the orbit of Appadana, may have been the longest of their lives. Why did they not use indigenous systems of resolving disputes? Why did they think that Julius Priscus would care about their problems? In short, why turn to Rome?

To this question we can tentatively provide a weak and a strong answer. The weak answer is that Archodes and Philotas had been the losers at the local level and turned to Julius Priscus out of sheer cynicism. They had no faith in his justice but hoped merely that he would render a judgment in their favor, for whatever reason. This is a possibility—one, moreover, that we cannot disprove and should not discount. Nevertheless, such cynicism can scarcely account for the tens of thousands of individuals and groups that turned to Rome for justice in the first centuries of this era.[2]

The strong answer allows that the villagers of Beth Phouraia, like millions of others around the Mediterranean, had assented to Rome's right to impose a particular jural-political order on her empire. To do so, they must have acceded to that strand in imperial propaganda that argued the Romans should earn support in the provinces by governing with provincial in-

---

2. Peachin 1996 discusses the Roman government's response to the thousands who turned to Rome for justice in the first three centuries of this era. Burton 1993 similarly argues that procurators assumed a greater and greater portfolio largely in response to provincials' desire to have their disputes adjudicated by a, or any, Roman official. On the number of cases heard at provincial assizes see Haensch 1994, 487 and 493–494. On the use of Roman legal institutions by women and slaves, see Huchthausen 1974a, 1974b, 1975, and 1976.

terests in mind, above all by publishing the law and enforcing it on their subjects and themselves. But how could the agents of Rome have persuaded the villagers of the sincerity of such propaganda? Indeed, how can we construe the ordinances of an imperialist power as persuasive in the first place?

What we require is a model of social action in general, and of communicative action in particular, that reveals what promises the Romans made when they published their laws, letters, and regulations. After all, relations between emperor and governor, and between governor and procurator, and between procurator and villagers, were all conducted through language, whether written or spoken: something about what the Romans said made the villagers think it worth their while to say something back.

Jürgen Habermas has supplied just such a model in his theory of communicative action.[3] Habermas sought to construct a model of society that could obviate a binarism in contemporary social theory, especially in English and American scholarship, between Hobbes and Locke: that is, between viewing as either sustainable or unsound a normative consensus that results from purposive-rational considerations alone.[4] He thus confronted and ultimately denied the legitimacy of the choice set forth above, between sheer cynicism toward, and consensual commitment to, the Romans' way of doing things. Stressing that "concepts of social action are distinguished according to how they specify the coordination among the goal-directed actions of different participants," Habermas urged that all dominant theories presupposed a "teleological structure of action, inasmuch as the capacity for goal-setting and goal-directed action is ascribed to actors, as well as an interest in carrying out their plans of action."[5]

Habermas responded to this impasse by arguing that communication itself, as a process for reaching understanding and consensus, is doubly contingent, in that successful communication of any sort requires participants to reach a mutual or intersubjective agreement concerning the validity of an utterance.[6] According to this view, speech acts implicitly or explicitly make claims regarding their intelligibility, propositional content, and justifiability, and the sincerity of the speaker.[7] "In these validity claims communication theory can locate a gentle but obstinate, a never silent though seldom redeemed claim to reason."[8] That claim exposes all speakers to

---

3. Habermas 1984 and 1987. Habermas 1979, 1–68, was his first statement of the communications theory at the heart of these volumes and remains useful. Habermas 1991, 231–238, describes the stages by which he developed the theory.

4. Habermas 1987, 210–234.

5. Habermas 1984, 101.

6. Habermas 1987, 120.

7. Habermas 1979, 50–68, and *idem* 1984, 286–309.

8. Habermas 1979, 97.

challenge in any one of the above areas, in response to which they must redeem their claim through discourse. Although Habermas himself encompassed an extraordinary scope of interaction within his theory, we may restrict our attention to two strands within his work, his development of Weber's concept of order and his articulation of the place of imperatives within the theory of communicative action.

When studying the stabilization of social systems, Max Weber argued that social actions could be oriented around one of four basic considerations: habit, custom, self-interest, or legitimate order. According to his exposition, the existence of an order depends on the orientation of social actions toward determinable maxims, and social orders are most stable when based on individuals' belief that the order is binding.[9] As a matter of theory, Weber analyzed two systems for guaranteeing the legitimacy of an order. The guarantee could be subjective and based on the affectual, value-rational, or religious considerations of individual participants, or it could be external, insofar as noncompliance would result in sanction by the group or by those officially designated to enforce compliance.[10] Although Weber seems to have recognized that survival instinct cannot by itself explain individual assent to the binding force of a culture's normative order, he later drew on his theoretical guarantees to distinguish between "ideal" legal orders and "real economic conduct." In lived realities, he argued, law as a determinant of human conduct should be defined by its empirical validity, such that the orientation of actions could result merely from accommodation to a coercive apparatus.[11]

Weber would thus seem to allow our weak explanation for provincials' recourse to Rome. And yet, Roman coercion was, more often than not, a mere conceptual possibility, and cannot account for the attractiveness of Roman courts in settling local disputes, particularly in regions that had well-developed legal systems.[12] For Habermas, this view of orientation toward a legal order cannot explain the stability of those societies in which such orders obtain. On this definition, individuals could be forced to negotiate between false polarities of self-interest and survival, and societies could construct value systems incongruent with action orientations.[13] If either of those situations came to pass, the legal order would be incapable of meeting criticism based on validity claims, since its values would not correspond to the normative order it purported to sustain. Habermas surmounted this

---

9. Weber 1978, 29–31.
10. Weber 1978, 33–36.
11. Weber 1978, 312–313.
12. On the interaction between local and Roman legal systems see Mitteis 1891. On the diffusion of Roman law see Crawford 1988.
13. Habermas 1987, 233.

impasse by positing that orders based on subjective recognition of their legitimacy ultimately rely upon their consensual validity. That is to say, individuals undertake and shape their social actions in order to respond to norms of action, *both* because they themselves recognize those norms as binding *and* because they know that other participants in their society feel an equal obligation to recognize those norms.[14]

For a society like that of Rome, which believed that its legitimacy as a normative order and, indeed, its good relations with the divine derived directly from the *consensus* of its participants, communication as a process for reaching understanding was of the utmost importance.[15] Indeed, the Roman empire achieves its unique status among world empires in no small part through its gradual extension of government by *consensus* formation to all its subjects. In doing so, it had to create, adopt, or extend the institutions of communicative practice throughout its territory.[16] Thus Romans believed that the maintenance of their society depended upon a communicative practice that had to satisfy certain conditions of rationality—although it was in the first instance Rome that defined those conditions. Yet that practice exposed the conditions themselves to question: their validity came to rest not on the power of Rome to assert them, but upon the integrative work of Roman and provincial who together coordinated their social actions through criticizable validity claims.[17]

Let us explore this notion of validity claim in that genre of utterance in which it plays its most subtle role, the imperative. For it is precisely Rome's monopoly over coercive force that has hindered our ability to understand both the willingness of Romans and provincials to form *consensus* through dialogue and the extent to which Romans felt their society rested upon such *consensus*. Habermas divided imperatives into two pure types. The first, the so-called simple imperative, depends on conditions of sanction: "With his imperative, the speaker raises a claim to power, to which the hearer, if he accepts, yields. It belongs to the meaning of an imperative that the speaker harbors a grounded expectation that his claim to power will carry." It does not matter whether the sanction is positive or negative, that is, whether the speaker wishes to threaten or to entice: "So long as the speaker does not appeal to the validity of norms, it makes no difference whether the potential for sanction is grounded *de jure* or *de facto*."[18]

The second type is the normatively authorized imperative. When uttering such a command, the speaker grounds the validity of his command not

14. Habermas 1984, 190.
15. See Chapter 2 at nn. 54–55 and Chapter 9, "The Discovery of Roman Religion."
16. Cf. Habermas 1987, 262.
17. Habermas 1984, 397–399.
18. Habermas 1984, 300 and 301, and cf. *idem* 1991, 239.

merely upon his contingent will and ability to enforce it, but upon a power to command that has been granted to him by the consensual commitment of others, including the hearer. But each time a speaker utters a command grounded upon that consensual commitment, he makes a validity claim, in varying degrees of explicitness, about the order that sanctions officials to maintain its normative script, about the legitimacy of the particular process that designated him the agent of that order, and about his interpretation of the normative script itself.[19] Validity claims can be rejected or defended, but those actions require dialogue; to resort to brute force would be to destroy the veil of objectivity that rationality grants to relations of domination.

The auditor of a normatively authorized imperative may well be subject to external sanction, but the long-term maintenance of the system depends on the intersubjective recognition of the normative validity claim of the order and its agent. To adopt the phrasing of Habermas, the magistrates of Rome did not coerce the subjects of the empire; rather, they "rationally motivated" them, because magistrates assumed both that their commands satisfied the conditions of rationality imposed by the ideology of Roman government and that they could discursively redeem their imperatives by elaborating on their truth content and expounding on their normative justification.[20]

The villagers of Beth Phouraia were not alone, but their experience can function as a heuristic key only if we can establish that many will have attained similar familiarity with Roman rules and Roman procedures, rudimentary as it was. Disseminating such knowledge will have required the existence and consistent use of systems of mass communication. In the study of premodern empires, the burden of proving the existence of such systems, of revealing their mechanics and of documenting provincial reception of their products, is especially heavy. To that end, this chapter speaks to the fact of communication. We can investigate, for example, the distribution of documents by the government at Rome, as well as its injunctions upon local governments to display and store those documents. These might seem mere issues of mechanics, but that is not the case. As we have seen, by sending out such regulations, the government raised a claim about its sincerity. It can have expected individuals to abide by those regulations only if it made allowances for the practical difficulties faced by residents of the empire in even learning of the existence, to say nothing of the content, of Roman texts. Did Rome account for the slow rates of travel and the varying levels of illiteracy that obtained in its empire?

Although this chapter addresses the fact of communication rather than

---

19. Habermas 1984, 301, and 1987, 121; cf. Bourdieu 1977, 187–189, and 1990, 132.
20. Habermas 1984, 302.

the content of communiqués, awareness alone of the government's efforts to distribute information accomplished considerable ideological work. Scholars in other disciplines have argued that the full exploitation of literacy within a hierarchical bureaucracy can in itself shape popular perceptions not simply of the role of writing in daily life but of the proper functioning of government as well.[21] Chapter 9 will argue that the emperors of Rome portrayed their governance as rational and will pursue the consequences of that ideological stance in greater detail. At this time we may offer the limited conclusion that widespread cognizance of the existence of such rules, even in the absence of secure knowledge about them, itself cemented provincials' faith in the rationality of imperial administration. That faith manifested itself in the collection and exploitation of private copies of imperial documents, in individuals' use of their own census returns, of imperial rescripts, and of records of past civil and criminal cases. People collected such documents not simply to protect themselves against unwarranted actions by the government, but because they believed that such documents in fact gave them power over the agents of the government and, in certain contexts, over their rivals in court. The texts under study in this chapter thus originated in, and in some fashion represent, a normative reality governing the social actions of ruler and ruled.

Studying communicative action in these terms reminds us that the government of Rome did not exist as an autonomous political and military institution, either in Italy or in the ancient Mediterranean world more generally. On the contrary, we have already seen that the myriad cultures of the Mediterranean were often, albeit for reasons complex and disparate, predisposed to receive favorably Roman claims to a certain level of moral and political agency, as both author and guarantor of social and political stability. That accommodation to Roman rule could not, in an ancient context, have existed in a solely political sphere, as though the ancient mind recognized even the possibility of separating political and religious affairs. Such accommodation therefore rendered individual cultures permeable to Roman influences in other sites, as Romans and provincials sought a mutual understanding about the role and function of government. All this took centuries to achieve, but Roman imperial culture ultimately both developed from and contributed to the institutionalization of a jural-political order based upon the consensual value commitments of both Romans and provincials.

The experience of Archodes son of Phallaios and Philotas son of Nisraiabos can only have reinforced their impression of the catholicity of Roman government and the uniformity of its regulations. Thus they have dated

---

21. Hariman 1995, 141–176; cf. Frier 1985, 285–286, as well as Chapter 2 at n. 143.

their petition by the dating systems of Rome and Antioch. But their experience in the cogs of the Roman judicial system was not a happy one. As they indicate to Julius Priscus, with considerable bitterness, they waited eight months before their case was heard, and then Priscus refused to render a decision. Four days later they petitioned Priscus again and offered him an alternative, that he should order Claudius Ariston merely to maintain the status quo until Priscus himself could render a decision.

This petition, too, obtained an unsatisfactory resolution. Priscus ordered Ariston not to act but to examine their petition. Archodes and his friends returned from Antioch with some power over Ariston—they may well have come to Antioch only after Ariston himself had refused to act—and they now possessed evidence that their petition had been read and duly entered into the archives of the empire to whose abstract power and authority they had turned and whose concrete mechanisms they had now seen.

In fact, it was presumably *seeing* that led them to file their second petition. As they themselves said, they attended the prefect's tribunal for eight months. In that time, they had probably seen judgments rendered, and they had certainly watched and interpreted the behavior of Priscus himself. Above all, they had seen him perform *proskynesis* before imperial documents. If they had come to Antioch hoping to accrue greater authority from its magistrate, they now understood the most characteristically Roman feature of Roman administration, its rationality. As Priscus had power over Ariston, so others had power over Priscus, and they could now appeal to him, citing his own behavior and several unnamed and unquoted imperial constitutions, on the basis of their shared status as subjects of a higher power.

NOTARIZED DOCUMENTS AND LOCAL ARCHIVES

The mechanics of the bureaucracy that distributed official documents remain opaque. It seems fairly certain that imperial archives under the Principate were housed at Rome and there all originals remained; it seems equally certain that governors in the provinces worked without proper archives until the second century.[22] Officially made and legally valid copies of imperial documents could be sent to the interested parties, in the case of municipalities or branches of government, or to the local administrative center to be posted, in the case of individuals; all private individuals were

22. On the distribution of documents, the essential secondary literature begins with Wilcken 1920 and 1930. Haensch 1992 and 1994 canvass the sources and assess the bibliography with rigor. On the reception and use of official documents see Chapter 9, "The Faith of Fifty Million People." On archives at Rome, see Corbier 1974, Bats 1994, Coudry 1994, Moatti 1993 and 1994, and Moreau 1994.

then free to make their own copies of whichever subscriptions they wished.[23] This official, authenticated copy would be prefaced by a formula recording the date on which the copy was made, the clerk who supervised its production, the names of the witnesses who verified its authenticity, and sometimes a note on the location of the document within the original archive; the official copy would also carry the seals of the witnesses. What makes our present task so difficult is that there was no fixed practice regarding the recopying of these administrative protocols. The documents cited throughout this chapter and throughout this book as a whole therefore preserve or describe some evidence or aspects of the process by which copies were made, authenticated, distributed, and received, but they do so in ways that reflect local circumstances.

Yet their very status as copies dramatically increases their value as evidence for our project. The mere existence of such documents provides powerful testimony to provincials' awareness of the procedures of the imperial bureaucracy and to their desire to exploit its rules for their own purposes. In addition, multiple attempts to record the authenticity of the copy, however different in practice, further testify to the extent of provincials' belief that manipulation of the Roman government required playing by its rules. A necessary corollary to such an attempt is the belief that the Roman government would itself play by those rules. The widespread unofficial use of a technical term for "authenticated" (*authenticus*) copy instantiates the perspective of both sides: the government's desire to achieve order through documentation and provincials' familiarity with that desire.[24]

The government at Rome exploited every opportunity to send documents to the provinces, whether to a single city, to the cities of a single province, or to the provinces in general. Although the sheer abundance of Roman texts is striking, we must also marvel at the continuity of certain strands within Roman self-presentation throughout the period of Roman rule. Above all, the government at Rome always paraded its wish that its words should come to the attention of all its subjects. The earliest surviving record of the wording with which the government expressed this desire is in a law of 100 B.C. regulating certain aspects of provincial administration. The text survives in two copies, both translated into Greek and neither complete, one from Delphi and one from Cnidus. Perhaps the most astonishing fea-

---

23. Examples of private copies of *subscriptiones* will be cited and discussed in Chapter 9; for the principle, see Wilcken 1920, 14–27; W. Williams 1980, 288; Haensch 1992, 261–262; and Feissel and Gascou 1995, 76–77.

24. Cf. Nicolet 1994, 152, who cautions us not to be misled by the chaotic appearance of surviving texts: the sheer numbers of surviving documents, and the frequency with which they cite other official texts, prove that Romans and provincials navigated their system with an ease that eludes us.

ture of this text's survival is the existence of a copy at Delphi at all, for the law contains no clause requiring Delphi to receive or to preserve the text. The Senate demanded publication only in the province of Asia:[25]

> The praetor to the province of Asia, to whom the province of Asia shall have fallen in the consulship of Gaius Marius and Lucius Valerius, is to send letters to the people and states and to the kings written down above and likewise to those to whom the consul shall think it proper to write, according to this statute. . . . And he is to see, insofar as it be possible, that whatever letters he sends according to this statute, to whomever he sends them, be delivered according to this statute, and that according to the customs of those to whom letters may be sent according to this statute, the letters, engraved on a bronze tablet, or, if not, either on a marble slab or even on a whitened board, be openly published in the cities in a sanctuary or agora, in such a way that the people shall be able to read them properly from ground level.[26]

The Senate required that the next governor send copies of the relevant documents to the communities concerned. This was regular practice, and was commonly specified in *senatus consulta*.[27] The copies here discussed could have been made at the same time as the final version of the *senatus consultum* was fixed, when the document was deposited in the *Aerarium Saturni;* it was there received by the urban quaestor, and it was his action that acknowledged its receipt into law.[28]

---

25. Hassall, Crawford, and Reynolds 1974, 197–200.

26. *RS* no. 12: Delphi copy, column B, ll. 20–26. I have adapted the translation of its editors in that work.

27. Cf. Frederiksen 1965, 184–187. See the treaty with Cibyra, *post* 189 B.C. (*OGIS* 762), the treaty between Rome and Epidauros of 114 B.C. (*IG* IV² 1.63), the *Senatus consultum de Astypalaeensibus* of 105 B.C. (Sherk, *RDGE* no. 16A), and the treaty with Thyrreum of 94 B.C. (*SIG* 732). From Pergamum there survives a resolution of the βουλή, on the process there observed to engrave and publish documents which have arrived from Rome (*SIG* 694, of 129 B.C.). For practice under the empire, in this as in all things more regular, see Haensch 1992, 249.

28. Mere posting of a text inscribed on bronze did not make law; that is a mistaken deduction (e.g., Williamson 1987, 167–168) from the complaint of Cicero that Antony had posted forged texts that the Roman people had assumed were legal (*Phil.* 1.26; cf. *Leg.* 3.46, with Rawson 1991, 145–146). But Cicero knew correct procedure: Antony used bribery to induce others to swear falsely that they had witnessed the fixing of the texts and then *senatus consulta* that the Senate had never passed were deposited in the *aerarium* (*Phil.* 5.12). Cf. Livy 3.55.13 and Plutarch *Cato minor* 17.3 with Bonnefond-Coudry 1989, 554–573, and Coudry 1994, 67. Under the empire veterans obtained copies of their grants of citizenship (*diplomata*) from the officially inscribed copy in Rome. (Extant diplomas have been edited by Nesselauf in *CIL* XVI; see his commentary on pp. 196–197 of that volume.) These documents assert that they have been "copied and checked" from bronze texts mounted at specific locations in the city of Rome. The *Tabula Banasitana* proves, however, that *commentarii civitate donatorum* for nonmilitary personnel were maintained in archives. Military diplomas cannot, therefore, support the claim that mere inscription on bronze legitimated a text.

Rome did not take it upon herself to produce and distribute copies throughout every village and hamlet in the empire. Rather, as in so many areas of provincial administration, Rome relied on the local governments in larger cities to carry out its wishes both within their walls and, at the very least, to bring its wishes to the attention of the smaller communities within their *territoria*. This practice is already clearly visible in documents from the late Republic. Note, for example, the elaborate instructions given by one Roman governor to the *conventus* of the province of Asia:[29]

> For these reasons I have written to the *koinon* of the Greeks, to you, to Ephe-
> sus, Tralles, Alabanda, Mylasa, Smyrna, Pergamum, Sardis, and Adramyttium,
> in order that each of you might dispatch [copies of this letter] to the cities in
> your own judiciary district and see to it that the letter is engraved on a pilaster
> of white stone in the most conspicuous place, so that justice might be estab-
> lished for all time uniformly for all the province, and in order that all other
> cities and peoples might do the same thing among themselves, and that they
> might deposit [a copy of this letter] in the archives of the Nomophylakia and
> the Chrematisteria. Do not ask why I wrote in Greek, since it was my intention
> that nothing contrary to the interpretation of my letter could possibly be in
> your mind.

Under the Principate, this process became much more uniform, and not simply for the provinces under the emperor's control. The evolution of this process began with Caesar's institution of the *acta*, in that the state there-after made public, in an official capacity, a record of the verbal processes from meetings of the organs of government.[30] Augustus may have ended the posting of the *acta senatus*, but the bureaucracy under his control placed an ever-increasing emphasis on precision in the recording of official utter-ances. Under the Principate, the validity of documents corresponded with their accuracy.[31]

It was, of course, true as a matter of politics at Rome that Augustus had agreed to divide the administration of the provinces between his legates and officials assigned through traditional sortition, and in his public utterances Augustus honored that agreement. In doing so, however, he chose language

29. Sherk, *RDGE* no. 52, ll. 42–57 (copy from Miletus: *AJ* no. 22); a more fragmentary copy is known from Priene. Both Sherk and Robert (*Hellenica* 7:227) incline toward a date of 51/50 B.C. Trans. Sherk, with slight changes.

30. Bats 1994, 20; White 1997 takes a rather more limited view than most about the con-tent and distribution of the *acta*.

31. Haensch 1992, 217, argues from the regulations on the falsifying of records that the government at Rome correlated the legitimacy of records directly with their integrity and ac-curacy; cf. Coudry 1994, 74–76.

that emphasized throughout his agency in all matters. This language is all the more striking in documents distributed to public provinces like Cyrene:[32]

> Imperator Caesar Augustus, pontifex maximus, holding the tribunician power for the nineteenth time, writes: That *senatus consultum* which was passed when C. Calvisius and L. Passienus were consuls, with me present and participating in the writing, and which pertains to the security of the allies of the Roman people, I decided to send to the provinces, appending to it my covering letter, in order that it be known to all in our care. From this it will be clear to all those who inhabit the provinces how much care I and the Senate take that none of our subjects suffer any wrong or exaction.

Although Augustus attributed to the Senate an equal concern for the welfare of the provincials, provincials had no reason to respect that claim: the Senate and senators had administered them—badly—for a century. On the other hand, people throughout the provinces clearly hoped that Augustus's promises did herald a change in the nature of Roman administration and, in thanking him for his efforts, sought to make those promises a reality. Cassius Dio explicitly approved of Augustus's interference in "senatorial" provinces already during his tour of the East in 21/20 B.C.—"he cared for them as if they were his own"—and provincials at the time happily regarded such documents as emanating from the *princeps* alone.[33]

Although Rome continually asked local communities to preserve copies of all documents within their archives, recipients could and frequently did ask for copies of documents relevant to their status after, and sometimes long after, the documents' initial enactment. The magistrates in these communities clearly expected Rome to have preserved a copy, and, more important, they believed it possible and even appropriate to ask Rome to abide by the content of the document, else they would not need the copy. For example, in 39 B.C. Aphrodisias sent an ambassador to Rome on just such a mission, requesting, among other things, copies of four separate documents. In response they received a letter from Octavian with the copies attached:[34]

32. Oliver 1989, no. 12, ll. 72–82 (Sherk, *RDGE* no. 31 = *EJ* no. 311). Trans. Oliver, with revisions. For the constitutional significance of this letter and the edicts that accompanied it, see L. Wenger 1942. Though I do not believe that the institutionalization of *auctoritas* as a quality of the *princeps* went nearly as far as von Premerstein suggested (1937, 176 and 218–223), he was quite right to stress its usefulness in dialogue with a Senate unhappy about the emperor's exercise of *imperium* within the *pomerium* and especially within the walls of the Curia.

33. Dio 54.7.4–5. Compare Tacitus *Ann.* 1.2.2: *neque provinciae illum rerum statum abnuebant, suspecto senatus populique imperio ob certamina potentium et avaritiam magistratuum, invalido legum auxilio, quae vi ambitu postremo pecunia turbabantur.* On provincial understandings of the settlement of 27 B.C. see Millar 1984 and Lintott 1993, 114.

34. Reynolds 1982, no. 6, ll. 14–16, 23–32, 46–53 (trans. Reynolds).

Solon son of Demetrius, your ambassador, . . . has urged us to send to you from the public records [ἐκ τῶν δημοσίων δέλτων] these copies of the edict, the *senatus consultum*, the treaty, and the law that relate to you. . . . The copies of the privileges that relate to you are these that are subjoined; I wish you to register them among your public records. Letters of Caesar . . .

Aphrodisias then inscribed the text of the Senate's decree with exceptional care, preserving the protocols describing its location within the senatorial archives as well as the original request made for its publication: [35]

In the consulship [of C. Calvisius C. f. and L. Marcius] L. f.; from the record of decrees referred to the Senate, file [?one, pages four], five, six, seven, eight, nine; and in the quaestorian files of the year when M. Marti[. .] were urban [quaestors], file one. . . . .

And it is agreed by the Senate . . . that [the consuls] should have this decree of the Senate [engraved] . . . on bronze tablets [and set up in the Temple of Jupiter], in Rome, on the Capitol; [and that they should arrange that other] tablets [be displayed] at Aphrodisias in the sanctuary of [Aphrodite] and in the [?market place(s) of the Plarasans and Aphrodisians, ?where they are clearly visible] . . .

Although the precise system of organization used in the Senate's archives remains unknown (Were the records broken down into monthly subdivisions? Were imperial and quaestorian archives organized on the same principles?),[36] it nevertheless seems clear that the official copies were made and certified from the archives, when available, rather than from the bronze copies that were posted publicly in Rome.[37] This is the implication of the protocols in the *senatus consultum* of 44 B.C. on the privileges of the Jews, the inscribed text of which was viewed and copied by Josephus more than a century later:[38]

35. Reynolds 1982, no. 8, ll. 1–3, 82, 90–93 (trans. Reynolds, slightly revised).

36. Cf. Reynolds 1982, 65–66, and Coudry 1994, *passim* and esp. 67–68. The more abundant records of Roman Egypt reveal that military archives organized documents by type and date: a private copy of a veteran's *epikrisis* was explicitly labeled as extracted "from the roll of examinations bearing the outside title: Examinations of Longaeus Rufus, late prefect, conducted by Allius Hermolaus, tribune of Legion II Traiana Fortis, from Epeiph 24 to Thoth 29 of the 26th year of Aurelius Commodus Antoninus Caesar" (*Sel. pap.* 315). Birth certificates were similarly catalogued according to the date on which they were filed: see Schulz 1942, 88, on the *kalendarium*. The daybooks of procurators and other Roman officials in Egypt were organized first by month, then by day: see Wilcken 1894, 97–98 and 104–109. See also on the *procurator ab ephemeride*, below in n. 60.

37. But compare the contemporary epistle from Augustus to Rhosus, in Syria (*EJ* no. 301), ll. 5–6, where Octavian specifies that the exemplar of the attached document was a stele on the Capitol.

38. Josephus *Ant. Iud.* 14.219 and 221 (trans. Marcus, modified).

Decree of the Senate, copied from the Treasury, from the public records of the quaestors, Quintus Rutilius and Quintus Cornelius being urban quaestors, from the first page of the second file. . . . As for the decision concerning the Jews rendered by Gaius Caesar with the concurrence of the Senate, which there was not time to have registered in the Treasury, we wish this matter disposed of in accordance with the decision of the consuls Publius Dolabella and Marcus Antonius; we also order that these documents be recorded on tablets and brought to the urban quaestors, and that they take care to have them inscribed on diptychs.

Josephus cited this document amidst a long series of Roman texts. He justified the length of his quotations by referring to popular skepticism regarding honors granted to the Jews by kings of Persia and Macedon. The writings of those kings, he lamented, were no longer extant. "But the decrees of the Romans are stored in public places in the cities and even now are engraved on bronze tablets on the Capitol."[39] Josephus also recalled that Julius Caesar gave a copy of his text on bronze to the Jews of Alexandria. On the other hand, we cannot know precisely on what medium Aphrodisias preserved the texts that they received from Octavian in 39 B.C. What is clear is that they heeded the suggestion that they preserve those texts and that they subsequently preserved copies of other documents relating to their relations with Rome. They so esteemed them—whether for their legal value or as monuments of civic history—that they inscribed them anew on an archive wall in the early third century.[40]

The production of official copies required the imperial bureaucracy to employ innumerable scribes, and the administrative protocols within surviving texts confirm their presence. Indeed, few things testify to the literacy of the Roman administration so well as the sheer abundance and variety of *scribae* employed in its bureaucracy—working no doubt in the equally abundant and variegated *tabularia*.[41] The satirist Lucian undoubtedly did not keep minutes himself, but he expected his audience to agree with him that the supervising of judicial records was a lofty responsibility:[42]

If you should consider the matter, I would seem to you to hold not the least responsibility for the governance of Egypt: the introduction of cases to the court, the arrangement of their proceedings, and the recording of absolutely

39. Josephus *Ant. Iud.* 14.188.

40. Reynolds 1982, 33–37, and cf. below, "Local Archives and Local History."

41. See the indexes in Dessau, *ILS* 3.1.433–434 for *scribae* and 435–436 for *tabularia*. On *tabularia* in particular, see the superb articles by Sachers, *RE* s.vv. *tabularium* and *tabularius*. On scribes in Roman life, see A. H. M. Jones 1960, 151–175; Badian 1989; Purcell 1983; and Teitler 1985. Texts published since these studies reveal the existence of a college of scribes, of limited duration (*AÉ* 1991, 114–115).

42. Lucian *Apol.* 12.

everything that is done and said. It was my job to give order to the speeches of
the lawyers, to preserve the judgments of the magistrate as clearly and accurately as possible, with the greatest rectitude, and to deliver those same to the
public records to be stored for all time.

The literacy and activity of the Roman administration impressed its subjects,
not least in the sheer magnitude of its interest in their daily lives. The Babylonian Talmud preserves an anecdote capitalizing on that impression, an
episode all the more valuable for the importance of literacy in the culture
that produced it:[43]

> The sages said in the name of Rav: If all the seas were ink, all reeds were pen,
> all skies parchment, and all men scribes, they would be unable to set down the
> full scope of the Roman government's concerns. And the proof? The verse,
> said R. Mesharsheya, "Like the heaven for height, and the earth for depth, so
> is the heart of kings unfathomable" [Prov. 25:3].

The author of the *Historia Augusta* also presumed upon his readers' acquaintance with the government's obsessive documentation and, above all,
upon their awareness of authentication as a guarantor of a document's
truth value:[44]

> There exists a letter written by the Divine Claudius while he was still a private
> citizen, in which he thanks Regilianus, the general of Illyricum, because Il-
> lyricum had been recovered while all things were collapsing through the sloth
> of Gallienus. I think that this letter, which I have found among authenticated
> records, ought to be quoted, for it was an official document [*quam ego repertam
> in authenticis inserendam putavi, fuit enim publica*].

The letter, of course, is a fabrication, but its exploitation of official terminology speaks tellingly regarding what its author took for granted about his
audience.

Readers of the *Historia Augusta* probably learned about the process of
authentication by participating in administrative rituals or by acting as witnesses for friends, but they could also have done so by reading the formulaic language that certified the legitimacy of public copies and recorded the

43. Babylonian Talmud Shabbat 11a, excerpted in Sefer Ha-Aggadah 5.93 (trans. Braude).
Compare Sifre §354 (Hammer 1986, 371): "*For they shall suck the abundance of the seas* [Deut.
33:19]: Two take away abundantly and give abundantly, and these are the sea and the government. The sea gives abundantly and takes away abundantly. The government gives abundantly
and takes away abundantly." Sifre was compiled in the late third century; this chapter springs
from a haggadic section attributed to the "school of Ishmael" (Stemberger 1996, 247–250 and
272–273).

44. *SHA Tyr. trig.* 10.9. Cf. von Premerstein, *RE* s.v. *commentarii*, cols. 751–752.

location of their exemplars. This language also suggests something of the magnitude of the task undertaken by imperial scribes:[45]

> Copied and approved in the consulship of Imperator Otho Caesar Augustus on 18 March, from the file of the proconsul Lucius Helvius Agrippa, which Gnaeus Egnatius Fuscus, the quaestor's scribe, produced, in which was written what is written below—table 5, sections 8, 9, and 10: . . .

The precise meaning carried by "approved" (*recognitum:* approved, checked, inspected) in this document seems clear: the quaestorial scribe brought forth a file from the official records of the proconsul of Sardinia. The copy made from that file required and received "approval," proof that its contents had been checked against the original.

The lack of regularity in the recording of administrative protocols can lead to confusion when the same terms appear elsewhere in slightly different contexts, not least in direct copies of imperial responses. For instance, in 139 Sextilius Acutianus petitioned the emperor Antoninus Pius to obtain a copy of a rescript of Hadrian, and that copy was ultimately inscribed in Smyrna in Latin:[46]

> [Latin] Imperator Caesar T. Aelius Hadrianus Antoninus Augustus Pius, to Sextilius Acutianus. I permit you to obtain a copy of the judgment of my deified father, whatever it was he stated as his judgment. I have signed. I have approved it. 19th. Completed 8 April, in Rome, when Caesar Antoninus and Praesens were consuls, both for the second time. [Greek] Sealed in Rome on 5 May, when Imperator Caesar T. Aelius Hadrianus Antoninus and Gaius Bruttius Praesens were consuls, both for the second time. Present were [7 names]. [Latin] Stasimus and Dapenus: produce, according to procedure, the judgment or decision.

The Greek in the midst of this text is clearly formula devised at Smyrna, at the time of its inscription, to describe the process of authentication for future interested parties.[47] But a description of that part of the process of authentication does not suffice as a description of the physical document that was returned to Smyrna. Who wrote each part of the authenticated copy? Who "approved it"? The use of "I have approved it" (*recog*[*novi*]), without some notation that it was written in a different hand, suggests that the emperor who signed the original also approved the copy; but it seems very unlikely that the emperor inspected each document, and for that reason Dessau restored *recog*(*novit*), "he approved it." That is certainly possible, but

---

45. *ILS* 5947, ll. 1–4. This text was inscribed in Sardinia, and it was probably in archives there (cf. *ILS* 2359), rather than at Rome, that this text's exemplar was housed.

46. *ILS* 338, ll. 4–7, 10.

47. W. Williams 1986, 185.

unnecessary. (Cf. *CIL* III 12336, below at n. 50.) In view of the use of "approved" in *ILS* 5947 (see at n. 45), it seems likely that this document was approved by the same secretary, *a libellis*, who numbered the rescript for entry into the archives—the same person who directed the clerks Stasimus and Dapenus to produce the copy.[48]

However difficult it is for us to recover the precise details of the authentication process, each attempt by contemporaries to record those details further substantiates the claim here advanced, namely, that individuals and institutions under the empire regarded the fact of their copy's authentication as worthy of permanent record, not least because its authentication substantiated the legal claims they founded upon it. Another way to certify a document's authenticity was to do just what the clerk in Smyrna did not do: to describe the document as a physical object, rather than to produce a precise visual representation of it. That was the method followed by the *coloni* on the imperial estate *Saltus Burunitanus* in Africa: [49]

> Imperator Caesar Marcus Aurelius Commodus Antoninus Augustus Sarmaticus Germanicus Maximus to Lurius Lucullus and on behalf of others. [Contents of rescript.] And in a second hand: I have signed it. I have approved it. A copy of the letter of the procurator of equestrian rank: . . . In accordance with the sacred subscription of our lord, the most sacred emperor . . . [5 lines erased]. In another hand: We hope that you live very happily. Farewell. Delivered on 12 September in Carthage. Happily completed and dedicated on 15 May in the consulship of Aurelianus and Cornelianus, under the care of Gaius Julius Pelops, son of Salaputus, *magister.*

The villagers of Scaptopara, in Thrace, adopted a combination of these two approaches:[50]

> *Bona Fortuna.* In the consulship of Fulvius Pius and Pontus Proculus, on 16 December, this copy was made and authenticated from the file of petitions and rescripts by our lord Imperator Caesar M. Antonius Gordianus Pius Felix Augustus, namely of those [petitions and rescripts] posted in Rome in the portico of the Baths of Trajan, in the very words which are written below. . . .

---

48. That is also the suggestion of Sherwin-White 1973b, 90, discussing the *Tabula Banasitana.* Cf. Wilcken 1920, 28–29; W. Williams 1980, 290 n. 13; Palazzolo 1977, 53–58; Haensch 1992, 262; and Feissel and Gascou 1995, 68 and 77–80. Feissel and Gascou rightly ask whether the situations obtaining with imperial and procuratorial documents must be analogous. An equally serious question is whether the same practice governed the recording of such protocols from document to document, from region to region, and over time. Cf. below on *P. Oxy.* I 34 (at nn. 63 and 200).

49. *ILS* 6870, col. IV, ll. 1–3, 9–10, 12–13, 23–29 (trans. adapted from Kehoe 1988, 68).

50. *CIL* III 12336 (*SIG* 888). Compare the wording of *P. Oxy.* XVII 2131 (A.D. 207), ll. 2–5 (on which see Chapter 9 at n. 172).

Imperator Caesar M. Antonius Gordianus Pius Felix Augustus . . . I have signed. I have approved. Seals.

The note "In another hand" in the petition to Commodus obviously attempts to describe the appearance of the imperial response and may be intended to suggest that the emperor himself dictated the rescript and signed it, *rescripsi,* with his own hands.[51] Indeed, Diocletian and Maximian ordained in 292 that only authenticated and original rescripts, subscribed by their own hands, and not copies of them, should be entered into the archives.[52] That ruling applied only to documents originating with the emperor, but it points to a need that must have existed long before, namely for local awareness of the location of a copy's exemplar. Thus private individuals frequently copied official documents for personal use, without authentication.[53] Yet these often record the whereabouts of their originals, suggesting once again that their owners recognized the power that accrued from official notarization. In A.D. 103, a Latin letter from the prefect of Egypt was copied by a scribe for an individual; the official clerk of the cohort then notarized that copy: "[This letter] was received on 24 February in year 6 of our emperor Trajan, through Priscus the *singularis.* I, Avidius Arrianus, adjutant of the Third Cohort of the Ituraeans, state that the original letter is in the *tabularium* of the cohort."[54] Finally, the word "seals" in the petition inscribed at Scaptopara (at n. 50) must have been intended to assure the reader of the published copy that the original carried the seals of the witnesses to its authentication.[55]

LOCAL ARCHIVES AND LOCAL HISTORY

We have seen that the central government, beginning at least in the late Republic, urged local municipalities to retain a documentary history of their relations with Rome in their own archives. For cities in the East, epigraphical texts existed, and still exist, in relative abundance: these cities did not have to be told what an archive was. Decades and centuries of Roman rule

51. On imperial involvement in the writing and signing of correspondence see Ammianus 15.1.3 and the bizarre tale at Marcus Diaconus *Vita Porph.* 49–51, and cf. Millar 1977, 220–222 and 251; Reynolds 1982, 47–48; Corcoran 1996, 146 n. 99; and esp. Youtie 1975b, 211–212. For the protocols with which officials signed and dated documents, see Wilcken 1920, 28–29, largely followed by J. Thomas 1983, 28–29, and Feissel and Gascou 1995, 79–80; for a slightly different theory see Haensch 1992, 262.

52. *C. Iust.* 1.23.3; cf. *C. Th.* 1.3.1.

53. Cf. Feissel and Gascou 1995, 77.

54. *Sel. pap.* 421 (*P. Oxy.* VII 1022; A.D. 103), ll. 24–31. The word *authenticus* passes into Greek (αὐθεντικός) in this meaning from Roman usage.

55. For preserved seals see *BGU* III 970 (*MC* 242) and *BGU* XI 2061, and cf. Vandorpe 1995.

nevertheless changed the conceptual role that documentary texts played in constituting the cities' sense of identity. We can observe this process most clearly in communities in whose development Rome and Roman documents played a formative role. For example, the Senate published a series of documents to honor Germanicus and the other children of the *domus divina,* for which our sole surviving documentary evidence springs from copies inscribed by, or simply published in, municipalities in the West. These texts occasionally indicate that they represent merely one in a long series of texts received and recorded by the city: for example, the decree of Pisa concerning honors for Lucius Caesar announces that the city will inscribe the present as well as past decrees.[56] Although municipal texts on stone do not observe any greater consistency in the preservation of administrative protocols than do epigraphical records of imperial documents, surviving evidence nevertheless allows us to conclude that, by the early second century, municipal archives functioned on patterns analogous to—and no doubt patterned on—state archives at Rome.[57] This is certainly suggested by the contents and diction of the municipal law imposed on Tarentum, a Greek city, at its incorporation as a municipality during the last decades of the Republic.[58]

When a Roman magistrate or an imperial secretary sent a document across the Mediterranean, the recipient had a heavy burden of proof when challenged on the authenticity of his copy: the original could lie hundreds of miles and many months away. Within the territory of a municipality that burden must have been much smaller. Nevertheless, occasional diligence or perversity induced a local scribe to quote the administrative protocols from the heading of an official document. This may account for the particularly detailed heading of an inscription from Caere. The text in question recorded an act of the town council, voted on 13 April 114, acknowledging the generosity of one Ulpius Vesbinus, an imperial freedman:[59]

> Copied and checked in the portico of the Temple of Mars from the *commentarium* that Cuperius Hostilianus ordered to be produced by T. Rustius Lysiponus, scribe, in which was written what is written below: When L. Publi-

56. Pisa: *ILS* 139, ll. 27–31 (*EJ* no. 68). For early references to the *domus*, see *Tabula Siarensis,* frag. I (*RS* 37; frag. [a]), l. 10; *SC de Cn. Pisone patre,* ll. 162–163; *EJ* no. 135 (*CRAI* 1913, 680); *EJ* no. 137 (*CIL* XIII 4635), as well as *IGRR* IV 1608, ll. 9–10 ([ἐπεὶ δέ]ον πρὸς τὸν σεβαστὸν οἶκον εὐσε-|[βείας]). See now Knibbe, Engelmann, and Iplikcioglu 1993, publishing inscriptions from Ephesus, nos. 2, from the hand of Tiberius (πρός τε τὸν ἐμὸν πατέρα καὶ τὸν οἶκον ἡμῶν ἅπαντα), and 4 and 5, both probably written by Germanicus (πρὸς σύμπαντα τὸν οἶκον ἡμῶν and πρὸς τὸν οἶκον ἡμῶν).

57. See von Premerstein, *RE* s.v. *commentarii,* cols. 745–757, and Preisigke 1917.

58. *Lex municipii Tarentini, ILS* 6086; see esp. ll. 7–20 and 39–42.

59. *ILS* 5918a, ll. 4–9 (*FIRA* III 113 = Smallwood, *Nerva* no. 475).

lius Celsus and C. Clodius Crispinus were consuls, the former for the second time, on the Ides of April, when M. Pontius Celsus was dictator and C. Suetonius Claudianus was the aedile for judicial matters and prefect of the treasury. The daily record book[60] of the municipality of Caere, page 27, section 6: . . . Then, on the first column of the next page, . . . Then, on the first column of page [2]8, . . .

Note first that the municipality dated, and without doubt had long dated, events by the consuls at Rome. As Italians the Caeretans had long since come to orient their sense of historical time around the rhythms of the Roman state, but this practice would spread across the Mediterranean world.[61] Second, the town carefully followed the same procedure that we have observed in Rome: the only text that could function as an exemplar for the inscribed copy was not one produced by the decurions at the time of their vote, but rather the one that had been properly deposited in their municipal *tabularium.*[62]

An edict of Flavius Titianus, prefect of Egypt in A.D. 127, proves conclusively that the organizational structure of the innumerable local archives of Roman Egypt was determined from the top:[63]

> The accountants up to now in the Catalogue, called secretaries according to the old usage, shall tally up the agreements, including the names of the nomographoi and parties, the [index?] number of the documents, and the types of contracts, and they shall deposit them in both libraries. Those called copyists shall, whenever they examine the so-called composite roll for deposition, make marginal notations if there has been anything expunged or anything different added; and they shall deposit a copy on a separate sheet in both libraries—for I command that there shall obtain in the rest of Egypt as well the procedure now followed in the Arsinoïte and [.....]polite nomes. They shall also add the page numbers and the names of the parties. Likewise, those

---

60. The equivalent within the imperial administration was probably maintained by the little-attested *procurator ab ephemeride* (*ILS* 1575); the connection between this official and the enigmatic *commentarii diurni* (Suetonius *Augustus* 64.2) remains to my knowledge unexplored beyond the brief treatment in Peter 1897, 1.350–351. Suetonius believed that Augustus attached great value to chronological accuracy and that the emperor recorded on his letters the hour of the day or night at which they were written (*Augustus* 50). It would be rash to see any continuity in this position between the first and sixth centuries, so I simply mention that John Lydus devoted some time to the secretaries who keep the *regesta* (which he derives from *res gestae*) and *cottidiana*, the daily record books, for the imperial chancery: *Mag.* 20.

61. Compare the self-conscious references to Roman dating at *Acta Apollonii* 7, *Acta Pionii* 23, and Marcus Diaconus *Vita Porph.* 34; cf. Haensch 1997, 705–707.

62. Sherk, *MDRW* 65–66.

63. *P. Oxy.* I 34, verso, col. I l. 7–col. II l. 2 (A.D. 127). Translation after Pierce 1968, 77. For the archives of Roman Egypt, Pierce 1968 and Cockle 1984 are fundamental. See also n. 200 below.

called secretaries of the Bureau of Examination of the officiating chief justices
shall do the same and shall deposit every five days.

The edict of Titianus was preceded by an order of Mettius Rufus in A.D. 89,
which was concerned with the validity and accuracy of property returns and
which therefore ordered the keepers of local archives to ensure that their
records were revised every five years.[64]

Local communities were always particularly anxious to preserve communications relevant to their own status. Cities collected such documents
primarily through embassies sent after the accession of a new emperor was
announced.[65] Papyri preserve some responses from emperors to such embassies,[66] and a recent accession provided the pretext for many of the
embassies described in the *Acta Alexandrinorum*.[67] Such embassies brought
the emperor a "gift"—gold for his crown[68]—and listed for the emperor the
specifics of their legal status in relation to the imperial administration. The
emperor responded with a brief letter confirming their status; most of
the letters preserved on the archive wall at Aphrodisias are of this genre.[69]
The form of this diplomatic ritual, iterated throughout the empire on innumerable pretexts, played an important role in distributing information
between the emperor and his subjects. More subtly, its content helped to inculcate an awareness of Rome's desire for *consensus:* magistrates in cities like
Aphrodisias throughout the empire would learn to promise their support
only if the emperor's subordinates would distribute his benefactions in proportion to their enthusiasm for his rule. Chapters 5 and 6 will explore this
economy of diplomatic exchange in greater detail. The value of the texts
generated through this diplomacy did not end with the next embassy and
the next letter. On the contrary: not only did each letter prove valuable in
the next round of negotiations with the central power, but the aggregate
data in an archive of such letters contained and displayed one perspective
on the histories of Aphrodisias and the empire, and of imperial concern for
that community. The lists of emperors in the *Tabula Banasitana* and *lex de imperio Vespasiani* sprang from very different contexts, and supplied different

---

64. *P. Oxy.* II 237, translated and discussed by Cockle 1984, 115.

65. See *P. Oxy.* LV 3781, from 25 August 117, an announcement of the accession of
Hadrian. The editors of that text provide a list of surviving announcements: *P. Oxy.* VII 1021
(*WC* 113), 17 November 54, for Nero; *SB* XII 10991, A.D. 175, for Avidius Cassius; *BGU* II 646
(*WC* 490), 6 March 193, for Pertinax; *SB* I 421, A.D. 226, for Maximus Caesar; *P. Oxy.* LI 3607,
A.D. 238, for Gordian I and II. On the form of such diplomacy see Millar 1977, 410–418.

66. The editors of *P. Oxy.* LV 3781 list *SB* VI 9528, from Vespasian, and *SB* X 10295, from
Avidius Cassius. The list could be expanded: cf. *P. Oxy.* XLII 3022, from Trajan.

67. See *P. Oxy.* XXV 2435 and XLII 3021–3022, with the editors' introductions.

68. See Chapter 6, "*Aurum Coronarium.*"

69. See Reynolds 1982, 107–113, and see esp. letters 17, 18, 20, and 25.

data, but they no less than the Aphrodisian archive wall provided a narrative of imperial history and boasted of the respect that Romans would pay to similarly documented precedents from their shared past.[70]

Cities, of course, did not exist in isolation, but it did not necessarily follow from the mere fact of empire that cities would use imperial communications with other municipalities to assess or to establish their own status. That action required a conviction both that the imperial government had a conceptual framework within which to judge cities individually and in relation to each other, and that such a framework possessed validity from reign to reign.[71] The archive wall from Aphrodisias confirms that the Aphrodisians, at least, held such a conviction: three of the documents from that wall are addressed to other cities: a letter from Octavian to Ephesus, a subscript by Octavian to a petition from Samos, and a subscript from Trajan to Smyrna.[72] At about the same time that J. Reynolds published the texts on the archive wall at Aphrodisias, R. G. Goodchild edited a similar archive in Cyrene. It, too, contains several documents, albeit ranging over a smaller chronological period, which attest to the status of the city and to imperial fondness for it. For example, the first document is a letter from Hadrian that simply forwarded, on his own initiative, as it seems, a copy of the reply he made to an appeal from a rival city: "The archon of the Panhellion has already had occasion to write to me concerning your claim. . . . I wrote back what I thought, and for you I sent a copy of the relevant reply [which my friend(?) Salvius] Carus, *clarissimus*, the proconsul, [will give to you]."[73] Similar archives undoubtedly existed elsewhere. Possible additional examples include the archive wall at Ephesus, with texts dating from Actium to the early 30s A.D.;[74] the walls of the Potamoneum at Mytilene, which initially included only texts relating to Potamon, but the city may have added others arising from its dealings with Rome;[75] the collection of epistles from Hadrian at Astypalaea, inscribed on the same stone as a response from Augustus to the Cnidians and a letter from Hadrian to, perhaps, the Rhodians (the stones have been reused in several locations)[76]; the letters that passed between Hadrian, his proconsul Avidius Quietus, and his procurator Hesperus on the temple lands at Aezani[77]; the collection of letters from Hadrian,

---

70. On the *Tabula Banasitana* see Chapter 2 at n. 72; on the *lex de imperio Vespasiani* see Chapter 5, "The Senate as *Socius Laborum*."

71. See Chapter 3 at nn. 17–19.

72. Reynolds 1982, documents 12, 13, and 14.

73. Oliver 1989, no. 120, on which see Reynolds 1978. Trans. Oliver, modified.

74. Knibbe, Engelmann, and Iplikcioglu 1993.

75. On Potamon and his archive see Parker 1991.

76. Oliver 1989, nos. 6, 64–68.

77. *MAMA* Ix, P1–4.

Antoninus Pius, Marcus Aurelius, and Lucius Verus at Coronea[78]; and the large collection of letters from Marcus, Marcus and Commodus, and Commodus alone that survives in eighteen fragments in the Athenian agora.[79] It is not known how copies of documents addressed to one city ended up in the archive of another, although it is clear that on occasion the emperor could explicitly order the addressee to furnish such a copy.[80] During Pliny's tenure in Bithynia, he wrote to Trajan many times quoting or referring to the rescripts and letters of earlier emperors: all these documents were presented to Pliny by the parties before him in support of their petitions.[81] Pliny's attempts to confirm the legitimacy of documents by comparing them with the originals at Rome corroborates our certainty that he did not travel with duplicates of all documents relevant to all matters in Bithynia. More important, those attempts harmonize closely with the spirit that drove Rome to ask municipalities to store copies of documents and that drove those municipalities to record the administrative protocols from Roman documents. All those parties, like Pliny, wished to ensure that such texts were both genuine and correct.[82] Eventually proconsular governors could come to rely on the *tabularia* of their provinces: these are attested in Alpes Cottiae, Asia, Dacia, Dalmatia, Egypt, Galatia, Gallia Celtica, Gallia Narbonensis, Hispania Tarraconensis, Illyricum, Lusitania, Mauretania, Noricum, Numidia, Pannonia Superior, Sardinia, and Syria.[83]

Tabularia advertised and recorded one perspective on the history of the empire as a whole, as well as a history of its relations with its constituent communities. It was a peculiarly Roman perspective. Yet we need not assume that the mere existence of a record house altered well-established patterns of communal memory nor that the slow spread of a Roman institutional historiography could in itself reshape prevalent local models of communal life. We must keep in mind that Spaniards in Baetica did not look down on isolated outposts in the plains but on vibrant communities

---

78. Oliver 1989, nos. 108–118.

79. Oliver 1989, nos. 193–203.

80. Augustus to the Rhosians, *EJ* no. 301, ll. 6–8; cf. Haensch 1992, 449.

81. See especially *Ep.* 10.31.4 and 10.79.5, with Sherwin-White's notes *ad loc.*, and Haensch 1992, 254–263.

82. For example, *Ep.* 10.65.3: *Recitabatur autem apud me edictum, quod dicebatur divi Augusti ad Andaniam pertinens . . .* [many other documents are named], *quae ideo tibi non misi, quia et parum emendata et quaedam non certae fidei videbantur, et quia vera et emendata in scriniis tuis esse credebam;* on which see Palazzolo 1977, 46–52. On legislation concerning the accuracy of copies, see above at nn. 63–64 and below in n. 200. On the value of spurious documents, see Chapter 9 at nn. 203–206.

83. Evidence in Sachers, *RE* s.v. *tabularium*, cols. 1967–1968. See now Haensch 1992 and Robert 1994, 105–106.

like Urso where, long before the Flavian municipal laws, Spaniards could have learned about Roman political and religious institutions, about *IIviri*, and scribes, and lictors; about *librarii;* about *haruspices* and togas; about provisions for *ludi scaenici* and, most particularly, about the correspondence between the seating at such spectacles and the proper ordering of society; and about the swearing of oaths by magistrates *per Iovem deosque Penates* and the recording of those oaths *in tabulas publicas* by the *scriba publicus.*[84]

NEW LEGISLATION AND INDIVIDUAL LIABILITY

We have thus far examined the evidence for the state's desire to make information of every kind accessible to the residents of the empire. We have seen that this held true for announcements of news, broadly defined, as well as for administrative ordinances. How can we be sure that anyone learned of or from these publications? I have argued that the act of dissemination in itself carried an expectation that people would read published texts and, moreover, that Rome cannot have placed this burden on provincials without incurring certain implicit obligations. Above all, Roman claims to good governance demanded that Rome do everything in its power to aid provincials in meeting its demands. We have already seen that communities could only aid themselves by responding to the announcement of the accession of a new emperor; in fact, the institution of *aurum coronarium* obligated communities to respond not only to accession announcements but also to the news of a recent imperial victory.[85] Extant evidence suggests that the government had similar expectations for the reception of its administrative regulations and legal texts. Given the logistical difficulties to be surmounted by individual residents in attempting to learn new regulations, a demand from Rome that its subjects comply with its regulations from the

---

84. *Lex Ursonensis, ILS* 6087: see LXII, LXX and LXXI, LXXXI, CXXV–CXXVII. On the role of colonies see Cicero *Font.* 13: *Est in eadem provincia Narbo Martius, colonia nostrorum civium, specula populi Romani ac propugnaculum istis ipsis nationibus oppositum et obiectum.* On the role of governors in maintaining class distinctions, see Pliny *Ep.* 9.5.3: *A quo vitio tu longe recessisti, scio, sed temperare mihi non possum quominus laudem similis monenti, quod eum modum tenes ut discrimina ordinum dignitatumque custodias; quae si confusa turbata permixta sunt, nihil est ipsa aequalitate inaequalius.* On colonies as images of Rome before a provincial audience see Edmondson 1990. On maintaining status distinctions in the seating at amphitheaters and other spectacles see Kolendo 1981 and Zanker 1988, 324–328. See also MacCormack 1981, 21, on Livy 5.23.2: Romans wrote as though populations naturally sorted themselves by gender and rank, even when pouring from the gates upon the arrival of a dignitary. On the collapse of classical expressions of rank and class through ceremonial see Jussen 1998, esp. 108–122.

85. See Chapter 6, *"Aurum Coronarium."*

date of their publication would have been wholly unrealistic; and the impracticality of that demand might have suggested that it existed for appearance's sake alone. But the truth is rather different, indeed. Roman magistrates acknowledged that new information did not spread instantaneously through a population, and they made careful provisions for that fact.

Bronze and marble had certain advantages as media for textual publication, foremost among which were their longevity and the aura of legitimacy with which they cloaked their contents.[86] But not every text required such treatment: the action of the local senate at Pisa (see at n. 56) indicates at the very least that the town had not previously inscribed on bronze or marble earlier news bulletins about Lucius Caesar. The local senate may have judged other media more suitable, not least for the speed with which they could be exploited.[87] Whitened boards and papyrus, for example, lent themselves to promulgating texts rapidly throughout an area, especially when the text had to be on display only for a limited time, after which people could be expected to review its contents in an archive. For this was how the government normally proceeded: it held the people accountable for the terms of a new ordinance only after it had been posted publicly for thirty days. That initial copy might appear on perishable wood, but the text would exist for consultation thereafter in *tabularia publica*.[88] To this end new legislation sometimes carried the provision that its text should be promulgated in every city at a specific time, regardless of when any given city's officials received the text: the author presumably wished the entire province to be held uniformly accountable after a certain date.[89]

The Roman government thus shifted significant responsibility for the wide dissemination of its texts onto itself. This cannot have disguised completely the burden that its legislation placed upon its subjects, but it nevertheless must have represented an enormous ideological shift. Roman officials consequently insisted on assigning obligations both to themselves as authors and to their subjects as audience members: they should publish with care and dispatch, and their subjects should read promptly and carefully. Extant regulations from Roman municipalities demonstrate that this

---

86. See below at nn. 220–223.

87. On the media of publication used by the imperial government see Riepl 1913, 335–345 and 364–371; and L. Wenger 1953, 54–102. Bowman 1991, 128, rightly emphasizes that the "discovery [of the Vindolanda tablets] underlines the crucial importance of establishing a typology of writing materials and their uses. These leaf tablets must have been cheap (or free) and easy to make. They completely undermine the argument that writing materials were available only to the well-to-do."

88. Von Schwind 1940, 59–63, 84–89; L. Wenger 1953, 55–59 but esp. 58–59.

89. Wörrle 1975, no. 1, ll. 43–45.

rule obtained in criminal and administrative proceedings,[90] while the jurist Ulpian reveals that it also obtained in civil cases:[91]

> By "public notice" we mean one written in clear letters, posted in such a way that it may be read properly from ground level, in front of an inn, for example, or in front of a place of business—not in a hidden place, but in the open. Should it be written in Greek, or in Latin? I think that depends on the location, lest someone be able to plead ignorance of the letters. Certainly, if someone should say that he didn't understand the letters or did not see what was posted, when many did read and the notice was publicly posted, then he will not be heard.

The Gospel of John provides rather dramatic confirmation of Rome's concern that local populations understand such signs: Pilate posted a placard beneath the cross of Christ, with "Jesus of Nazareth, King of the Jews," written in Hebrew, Greek, and Latin.[92] The penetration of these policies and their justifications into the imaginative world of provincial populations can be seen, for instance, in their use in the Midrash for the elucidation of Scripture:[93]

> R. Eleazar said: "Although the Torah was revealed on Mt. Sinai, Israel was not punished for its transgression until it was promulgated to them in the Tent of Meeting. It was like an edict [διάταγμα] that had been written and sealed and brought to the city, but in respect whereof the inhabitants of the city are not bound until it has been promulgated to them in a public place [δημοσίᾳ] of the city."

We should not fail to notice that R. Eleazar has drawn this analogy not simply with Roman practice, but with the reasoning behind it: it would not be fair to hold the inhabitants of a city liable for the contents of a law from the time when it was drafted; once, however, it has been properly promulgated, the burden of responsibility falls upon their shoulders.

The practice of fixing a grace period during which people could become acquainted with the text of a new statute was, in fact, already in place in the

90. E.g., the *IIviri* of the *municipium Irnitanum* must allow thirty days between the announcing that new decurions are required and taking action on that announcement (*lex Irnitana*, XXXI).

91. Ulpian at *Dig.* 14.3.11.3. Cf. Agathias 5.4.2, on the death of Anatolius: ὅτι τε αἱ γραπταὶ σανίδες ἐκεῖναι καὶ τὰ ῥάκη τὰ ὑποπόρφυρα ἐς τόδε αὐτῷ ἀπετελεύτησαν, ἃ δὴ πολλὰ τοῖς τῶν εὐδαιμόνων οἴκοις θαμὰ ἐπέβαλλε, τὴν ἐς βασιλέα εὔνοιαν προϊσχόμενος, καὶ ταύτῃ ἅπαντα ἐσφετερίζετο.

92. John 19:19-20.

93. *Shir Hashirim Rabba* to Cant. 2:3, a sixth-century compilation from numerous earlier sources, translated in Liebermann 1962, 200-201.

early second century B.C., when the Senate saw fit to forbid the secret and organized worship of Bacchus: [94]

> [The Senate thought it proper] that you proclaim these orders in a public meeting for no less than three market days (24 days); [95] and, in order that you may know the judgment of the Senate, it was as follows: "They have decreed that, if there is anyone who acts contrary to this decree, which is written above, then capital charges must be laid against them." And [the Senate thought it proper] that you should inscribe this on a bronze tablet, and that you command it to be posted wherever it can most easily be read.

Eventually the increasing complexity of the Roman state led the government to abandon the use of potentially contestable or variable criteria—the span between market days—and to adopt a fixed term. The association between market days and the publication of new ordinances had by this time become fixed in the Roman imagination. When, therefore, Roman antiquarians conducted their researches into the history of the calendar, at least one writer identified the needs of the government as the moving force behind the creation of market days in the first place. The grammarian Macrobius, writing in the early fifth century A.D., quoted this passage from one Rutilius: [96]

> Rutilius writes that the Romans instituted market days so that farmers might work in the fields for eight days, but on the ninth, leaving the country, they might come to Rome to the market and learn about the laws, and so that plebiscites and senatorial decrees might be brought before a larger number of people, since these documents, once posted for twenty-four days, might easily become known to one and all. Whence also arose the custom that laws should be promulgated for twenty-four days.

Though probably incorrect, this etiology testifies precisely to the ideologically inspired desire of the government to publish, and of the people to read, official texts.

Once established, thirty days remained the customary time period for any such legislative activity within the purview of the Roman administration across the breadth of the empire. See, for example, the edict of L. Antistius Rusticus, legate of Domitian, to the citizens of Pisidian Antioch, on actions to be taken during a famine: [97]

---

94. *ILS* 18, ll. 22–27. The formula which appears at the top of the *SC de Bacchanalibus* confirms nicely how conservative Roman political institutions were: *senatus consulta* were witnessed and deposited with the same formula two centuries later (*SC de Cn. Pisone patre* 1–4).

95. On the precise length of a *nundinum* see T. Mommsen 1887, 3.1.375–377.

96. Macrobius *Sat.* 1.16.34–35.

97. *MW* no. 464, col. 2, ll. 1–19 (*AJ* no. 65a). But cf. *P. Amh.* II 85, an application to lease land belonging to orphaned children. The exegete who received the application must post the

Since the *duoviri* and decurions of the most outstanding colony of Antioch have written to me that, because of the harshness of the winter, the price of grain has shot up; and since they seek that the plebs should have the opportunity to buy [grain], let all those who are citizens or inhabitants of the colony of Antioch declare before the *duoviri* of the colony, within thirty days of the day when this edict of mine is posted, how much grain each has, and in what place.

The development of such administrative matters in the late empire frequently remains slightly beyond our grasp, because the editors of the Codes systematically purged such protocols from their texts.[98] We therefore know the motivation for Theodosius's law of 18 August 390 only because contemporary sources connect that law to its inspiration: Theodosius had ordered in anger that the army should slaughter whoever responded to a specious announcement of games in the circus at Thessalonica and was then forced by private guilt and public disapprobation to ordain curbs on his own temper. In the future, his own ministers were not to exact any severe punishment pronounced by the emperor until thirty days had passed.[99] If thirty days was law in some contexts and conventional in others, that span could be extended: announcing a new punishment for harboring deserters, Arcadius and Honorius allowed four months from its date of publication before people would be held liable to its conditions.[100] Occasionally even the truncated texts of the Codes preserve evidence for this desire that official texts be available to the public, and the appearance of instructions for the distribution and publication of laws in the unexpurgated texts known as the *Sirmondian constitutions* and in the *Novels* affirms their status as a regular, perhaps a universal, feature of imperial legislation: "For the rest, O Florentius, dearest and most beloved Father, let Your Illustrious and Magnificent Authority, to whom it is beloved and familiar to please the emperors, bring it about through posted edicts that the decrees of Our August Majesty come to the knowledge of all peoples and of every province."[101] The texts of these laws passed into the Codes from imperial archives, but all were explicitly is-

---

lease for ten days, lest an objection be brought; *P. Amh.* II 86 contains similar language regarding potential objections but no ordinance regarding the posting of the proposed lease.

98. On the editing of these texts, see Seeck 1919, Honoré 1979 and 1986, and Corcoran 1996, 13–18.

99. *C. Th.* 9.40.13. On the massacre, see Ambrose *Ep.* 51, Paulinus *Vit. Ambr.* 24, Rufinus *Hist.* 11.18, Sozomen 7.25.1–7, and Theodoret 5.17.1–18.19. Rufinus, Sozomen, and Theodoret all connect the law to the massacre.

100. *C. Th.* 7.18.9 *pr.*

101. *N. Th.* 1.8. Compare *C. Th.* 8.4.26, 8.5.6, 8.7.10, and 9.38.9, as well as *N. Th.* 2.3, 3.10, 4.3, 5.1.5, 5.2.2, 5.3.2, 7.1.3, 7.2.3, 7.3.2, 7.4.10, 8.3, 9.5, 10.1.5, 11.4, 12.3, 14.9, 15.2.4, 16.9, 17.1.5, 17.2.7, etc. Elsewhere see *Const. Sirm.* 9.

sued to the empire as a whole. What evidence exists to suggest that this concern for distribution had any effect? And what good would "posted edicts" do in a world of low literacy?

TO READ OR TO HEAR THE LAW

All these documents raise a problem that can be analyzed but not definitively solved: Was the imperial government realistic in its expectation that posting written texts, in however many places, would result in their contents' coming "speedily to the knowledge of all"? Extant evidence does not suggest that many in the cities could have read complex texts, and literacy was undoubtedly lower in smaller communities.[102] This investigation aligns itself with, and tends to support, those who emphasize that a small number of literate individuals could go a long way.[103] All those who take this position are indebted to a series of distinguished articles by H. C. Youtie, in which he discussed the mechanics by which the semiliterate and illiterate (the ὀλιγο-γράμματοι and ἀγράμματοι) functioned in a society that frequently demanded literacy from a vast portion of its members.[104] Above all, Youtie was right to maintain that the imperial government did not expect that its subjects—or all its officials—would be literate: rather, it demanded that they have access to a literate person. In the last instance, this could be a scribe in the bureaucracy itself.[105]

The government's acknowledgment of the logistical difficulties faced by its subjects in fact extended to include the problem of literacy, in two ways: first, the government insisted that published materials should be legible; second, it probably required that all such texts be recited at least once at the time of their posting. This official action took place regardless of whether private individuals subsequently read a posted edict for the benefit of friends or strangers. Documents cited in this chapter—the governor's letter to the *koinon* of Asia (at n. 29), Augustus's edict on the Jews (at n. 146), and the prefect of Egypt's edict on banditry (at n. 186)—amply testify to the provisions made concerning the location of publication: "in the most conspicuous place," where "conspicuous" must imply "to the most people," the *celeberrumo loco* of the *Tabula Siarensis* and the *Senatus consultum de Cn. Pisone patre*.[106] Elsewhere—restored in the *senatus consultum* on Aphrodisias (at

---

102. Harris 1989, esp. 206–221, on civic and political uses of literacy.
103. See Hanson 1991 and Hopkins 1991a.
104. Youtie 1971a, 1971b, 1975a, and 1975b.
105. Youtie 1975a, *passim*, and esp. 218–219. On Petaus the illiterate *komogrammateus* see Hanson 1991, 170–175.
106. *Tabula Siarensis:* see *RS* 37, frag. (b), col. II, l. 27. *SC de Cn. Pisone patre:* see l. 171.

n. 35), the *senatus consultum de Bacchanalibus* (at n. 94), the edict of Alexander Severus (at n. 151)—this requirement is specified through language requiring publication "in a place [clearly or most] visible [to those who wish to read]," where "visible" must imply the provision elsewhere made explicit, "to those standing [in a normal position]": "at ground level" in the law on praetorian provinces from Delphi (at n. 26), in Claudius's edict on the Jews (at n. 148), and in Ulpian's regulations regarding legal notices (at n. 91).[107]

All these injunctions acquire greater potency from at least the middle of the first century, when the government will have designated certain locations for the publishing of new laws and the populace will have become accustomed to finding them there. For example, when Lusius Geta, the prefect of Egypt, forwarded a warning on illegal exactions from priests to Claudius Lysanius, *strategus* of the Arsinoïte nome, he urged that official to post his edict "in the customary places"; the existence of such a place presumed a long history of regular publication. That place was usually the local temple of the imperial cult.[108] For instance, an unpublished Hadrianic inscription from Asia Minor cited its text "from the wall of published petitions,"[109] and Archodes son of Phallaios and Philotas son of Nisraiabos not only reminded Priscus where they had met him—the Baths of Hadrian—but also noted where they would later receive their answer, on its "wall of published petitions."[110] The rhythms and quirks of Roman administration thus cooperated with imperial construction projects to refashion provincials' urban and mental landscapes, ultimately redefining for them not only the appearance of a legitimate city, but also the perceived function of a city and a government in their daily lives.

We do not often find explicit instructions that the writing itself must be clear; indeed, the Roman government has been charged with publishing documents on bronze in spite of the fact that, or even because, they would then be difficult to read.[111] But that injunction was sometimes given—for

---

107. These provisions subsequently appear in municipal documents: in the reign of Antoninus Pius, the town of Tergeste decreed a statue for its patron, L. Fabius Severius, *in celeberrima fori nostri parte* (*ILS* 6680, l. 61); similarly, the town of Brundisium ordered the erection of a statue for the daughter of its patron, L. Clodius Pollio, *frequentissimo loco* (*AÉ* 1910, 203); the *curia* at Cales instructed its *IVviri* to inscribe the letter of the town patron L. Vitrasius Silvester *celeber(rumo) loco u(nde) d(e) p(lano) r(ecte) l(egi) p(ossit). C(ensuerunt) c(uncti)* (*CIL* X 4643, ll. 28–29); the arch voted for Gaius Caesar at Pisa was to be erected *celeberrimo coloniae nostrae loco* (*EJ* no. 69, l. 34).

108. Smallwood, *Gaius* no. 383 (*AJ* no. 164 = *OGIS* 664), ll. 1–6, quoted below in n. 180. Cf. Kunderewicz 1961. In the last instance, individuals attempted to validate their petitions by citing the locations at which they were submitted: see *CPR* XVIIA no. 18, in which the petitioner records that he encountered the *strategus* at a particular city gate.

109. Bowersock 1991, 339 n. 6.

110. *P. Euphr.* 1, l. 2, in Feissel and Gascou 1995, 71.

111. Williamson 1987, 162–164.

example, in the prefect of Egypt's edict on divination (at n. 186)—and some parallels exist: in A.D. 49 Cn. Vergilius Capito forwarded an edict to a local *strategus* on exactions and bid him "swiftly post it in the metropolis of the nome . . . in clear and legible letters, so that [his] words might be manifest to all."[112] That the letters had to be clear had, after all, been the general rule for "public notices" as defined by Ulpian (at n. 91). Indeed, the phrase adopted by Ulpian, "whence it may be read properly from ground level" (*unde de plano recte legi possit*), in which "properly" (*recte*) may well have reflected a concern for the legibility of the writing, became so standard a provision by the late Republic that it could be abbreviated at least as early as the *Tabula Heracleensis* in the 40s B.C.[113] Edicts and notices of actions in civil suits are posted and preserved with different aims, of course: laws must be available to interested parties indefinitely, whereas Ulpian's documents must be available to all for a finite period.

Similar in this regard to Ulpian's texts are documents relating to elections, which had to be available to all until the election. Thus, for example, the *Tabula Hebana* required that the whitened boards featuring the names of candidates for election be placed in a location where they could be most conveniently read.[114] This provision then passed into the Flavian municipal charters that governed local elections, charging electoral officials with responsibility for publishing the names of all candidates "in such a way that they can be read properly from ground level."[115] The same charters held that the *IIvir* in charge of letting out public contracts for the collection of municipal taxes, for example, not only had to enter all the information pertaining to such leases into the *tabulas communes* but also had to display such data for the entire period in which he held office "in such a way that they can be read properly from ground level."[116] That the legibility of such texts was important, and not simply the location of their publication, is implied by some negative evidence: when Gaius was pestered by the people because he had imposed new taxes without first publishing their requirements, he responded by publishing the law "in the tiniest letters and in the most inaccessible location, such that no one was able to make a copy."[117] Finally, it should be noted that many smaller corporate bodies relied on written

---

112. *AJ* no. 163 (*OGIS* 665), ll. 8–13. The inscription is unfortunately damaged at precisely these lines.

113. *Tabula Heracleensis* = *RS* 24 (*AJ* no. 24 = *ILS* 6085), ll. 13–16.

114. *Tabula Hebana* = *RS* 37–38 (*EJ* no. 94a), ll. 20–21.

115. *Lex municipii Malacitani* (*ILS* 6089), chapter LI; translation by Crawford at *JRS* 76, 188.

116. *Lex municipii Malacitani* (*ILS* 6089), chapter LXIII; *lex Irnitana*, (Chapter LXIII) on tablet VIIB (at *JRS* 76, 190).

117. Suetonius *Gaius* 41.1. Compare Tacitus *Ann.* 2.14.3, on Claudius's interest in the orthography of public documents.

posters to spread information: when Aurelius Eudaimon, the *prytanis* of Oxyrhynchus, wished to convene an ad hoc meeting of the local senate of Oxyrhynchus, he presumed that posting a written announcement on the day of the meeting would give its members sufficient notice.[118]

The *Senatus consultum de Bacchanalibus* required not only that local communities inscribe the law in bronze but also that it be read aloud on three separate occasions. (See at n. 94.) Such a requirement does not survive in all such texts, but parallels may be found. In the *senatus consultum* that accompanied the treaty between Rome and Astypalaea, the Senate asked not only that an inscribed copy of the treaty be set up in a crowded public place but also that the text of the treaty be read aloud in the Astypalaean assembly every year.[119] Much more impressive and thorough injunctions were imposed on the publication of the *lex Tarentina*, which may or may not be identified with the *lex Glaucia* of 101/100 B.C., though in its text much is conjectural:[120]

> Let the praetor *peregrinus* see to it that copies of this law are given to the ambassadors of all the allies of Latin status, of foreign nations, and of friendly kings, if they wish [to have copies], and let him see to it that this law is read aloud every sixth months of each year in the assembly and before the Senate. Let the quaestor in charge of the *aerarium* take care that a bronze tablet inscribed with this law in clear letters be placed in the Forum where it can be read properly from ground level. When the tablet has been placed thus, let all the magistrates see to it that the tablet is not torn down nor receives any damage from one who would consult it or approach it to copy it or touch it for another reason.

The reasons for such measures are not far to seek. The authors wished to conciliate Rome's allies by advertising the Roman government's desire to prosecute extortionate magistrates: new magistrates, therefore, heard the law read aloud and swore an oath to abide by it, and, even more important, copies of the law were made available to all those who would benefit by its implementation.[121]

---

118. *P. Oxy.* XII 1412, ll. 14–16.

119. Sherk *RDGE* no. 16 (*IGRR* IV 1028), ll. 12–15.

120. Much depends on the length of line. Not all is as dark as the brackets in recent editions suggest: extensive parallels for phrases in this text may be found in the better-preserved portions of the *lex Acilia repetundarum* (*FIRA* I 7 = *RS* 1) and in the *Tabula Bantina* (*FIRA* I 6 = *RS* 7). I here adopt the text and adapt the translation in Lintott 1982. J. S. Richardson has taken issue with Lintott, arguing primarily against the possibility of line lengths as long as necessary for Lintott's restorations (at *RS* 8), but he argues by assertion alone (e.g., "it is clear that"). Furthermore, I cannot agree with his confidence in restoring *nomina* in the missing portion of l. 12, and on that much else depends. Bibliography and sources for Glaucia's praetorship are surveyed in *MRR* 1.571–572, 1.574–575, and 3.196.

121. On this aspect of Republican legislation see Sherwin-White 1982, 21.

Cicero confirmed that this practice survived in the late Republic when, in his dialogue *De finibus,* he attacked an Epicurean because he saw a fundamental conflict of interest between that man's philosophy and the demands of service to the state: [122]

> In return for what, when soon you enter into office and ascend to address the assembly—for you will have to announce the rule you intend to observe in administering justice, and, perchance, if it should seem good to you, you can say something about your forbears and yourself, in accordance with ancestral custom—what, I say, would it take for you to confess that you will do everything in that magistracy with an eye toward pleasure, and that you have done nothing in life except in pursuit of pleasure?

Cicero elsewhere referred to the recitation of legislation, both in draft and in the form passed by the assembly. For example, he described in *De officiis* the dishonorable actions of Marius Gratidianus: while that man was praetor, he and his colleagues and the tribunes of the plebs cooperated in drafting an edict on currency, and they agreed to gather in the afternoon to ascend the Rostra. As they parted company, Gratidianus went straight to the Rostra and "alone announced what had been composed in cooperation." [123] The decision by these men to appear together on the Rostra implies the belief that this mode of publication both was established and garnered considerable attention; Cicero's comment, that Gratidianus by his action became dear to the multitude as no one else, confirms this.

To this evidence we may compare Herodian's description of the advertising campaign mounted for Severus's celebration of the Secular Games: [124]

> At that time occurred those ceremonies that were called the Secular Games, when people heard that three generations had elapsed since they had last been celebrated. So heralds traveled throughout Rome and Italy, summoning all the people to come and attend games the like of which they had never seen before and would not see again.

Herodian emphasized that Severus directed his invitation not simply to the population of Rome, but to that of Italy generally, although we are free to doubt that many undertook the journey. [125] But the important fact for us, as, no doubt, for Severus and his audience, is simply that he asked them to come. An ancient college of priests, the *quindecimviri sacris faciundis,* over-

122. Cicero *Fin.* 2.22.74.

123. Cicero *Off.* 3.80.

124. Herodian 3.8.10 (trans. Whittaker).

125. Cf. Josephus on the announcement of the triple triumph of Vespasian, Titus, and Domitian in 70 at *Bell. Iud.* 7.122: προδιασαφηθείσης δὲ τῆς ἡμέρας ἐφ' ἧς ἔμελλεν ἡ πομπὴ γενήσεσθαι τῶν ἐπινικίων, οὐδεὶς οἴκοι καταλέλειπτο τῆς ἀμέτρου πληθύος ἐν τῇ πόλει.

saw the preparations for these games and even arranged for their efforts to be immortalized in a record book, the *Commentarium de ludis saecularibus,* much of whose text survives on bronze to the present day.[126] It describes the announcement as follows:[127]

> These men were chosen by lot, and on the same day an edict was published in these words: Imperator Caesar, son of the divine Marcus Antoninus Pius Germanicus Sarmaticus, brother of the divine Commodus, grandson of the divine Antoninus Pius, great-grandson of the divine Hadrian, descendant of the divine Trajan Parthicus and of the divine Nerva, L. Septimius Severus Pius Pertinax Augustus Arabicus Adiabenicus Parthicus Maximus, pontifex maximus, holding the tribunician power for the twelfth year, saluted *imperator* eleven times, three times consul, *pater patriae,* and [M. Aurelius Antoninus and L. Septimius Geta], together with the other *quindecimviri sacris faciundis,* declare: We command that the seventh Secular Games be celebrated.

The elaborate roll call of Severus's ancestry and titulature transformed the announcement into something far more significant than an advertisement for a party at Rome. It also offered a biography of Severus, in the form of a catalogue of the enemies of Rome defeated at his hands, as well as a portrait of the stability of one family upon the imperial throne.

By the late empire the mechanics of the imperial administration had become familiar features of everyday life. In the high empire, therefore, the promulgation of an edict was not generally an occasion worthy of mention in the historical record. But we should not on that account assume that the arrival of a new text was an insignificant moment, for, even as *adoratio* became the standard way of greeting an emperor,[128] so it became the standard way to meet the physical representatives of him and his *imperium:* his image,[129] his standards,[130] and his edicts. We find clear attestation of such behaviors in the empire as early as the reign of Hadrian. For example, in an extract from a proceeding in Egypt before the local *commentariensis,* the magistrate himself, one Julius Theon, rendered his judgment by bowing both literally and figuratively before the rescripts of Trajan and Hadrian: "There is no need to inquire into possession, as we are bound to respect and to venerate the rescripts of the deified Trajan and our lord Hadrian Caesar

---

126. Scheid 1994 relates the epigraphic impulse exhibited on this occasion to the archival obsessions of other Roman priestly colleges.

127. *Commentarium* at Pighi 1965, 147; see col. II, ll. 14–18. This edict was followed by others over the next several months, and preceded by one whose text is almost entirely lost (see col. I, ll. 54–57ª; col. III, ll. 25–32; col. Vª, ll. 33–36; col. VIIIª, ll. 5–13).

128. A. Alföldi 1934, 45–64, and cf. Avery 1940.

129. A. Alföldi 1934, 64–73; cf. Chapter 7, "The Arrival of Roman Portraits."

130. *ILS* 986; cf. Chapter 7, "*Signa* of Rome, *Signa* of Power."

Augustus that have been cited."[131] Something of this sort probably lies behind the honor paid by Hadrian of Tyre to the tablet sent by Commodus on which was written his promotion to *ab epistulis Graecis:* Hadrian "invoked the Muses, as was his wont, prostrated himself before the imperial tablets, and breathed out his soul over them, thus making of that honor his funeral shroud."[132]

Hadrian's veneration of the letter from Commodus recalls the strategy adopted by the villagers of Beth Phouraia. Their appeal to the "sacred constitutions, which you esteem above all else and before which you prostrate yourself," must have been based on autopsy.[133] Like so many others, the villagers had fixed their gaze on the behavior of those in power. Some years later, the tenants of land belonging to a temple of Zeus in Baetocaece, a Syrian village far to the west of Beth Phouraia, wrote to the emperors Valerian and Gallienus to confirm the privileges of their temple. They later inscribed both Valerian's response and the documents that they had quoted in their original petition. They closed their archive with the solemn pronouncement that they had inscribed "the rescripts that are venerated by all" as a testimony to the piety of the emperors toward their god and his sanctuary.[134] By the early fourth century, such behavior is the subject of casual reference. In 313, Anulinus, the proconsul of Africa, informed Constantine of his recent efforts to secure peace between Donatists and the orthodox. He opened his letter by referring to the instructions he had recently received from Constantine: "Having received and venerated the heavenly letters of your Majesty . . ."[135]

Christians had a special interest in the arrival of edicts. Both Lactantius and Eusebius describe the posting of the first edict of persecution at Nicomedia, and the reaction of the man who pulled down and tore up the text.[136] This same moment may well be described in a Midrashic text, from Esther Rabba, in which a parable is drawn to explicate Jeremiah 36:23:[137]

> *Like a king who sent letters* [γραφαί] *to every city.* In every city, when the king's letters arrived, the people embraced and kissed them, rose to their feet, un-

---

131. *P. Tebt.* II 286, ll. 21–24: περὶ γὰρ τῆς νομῆς οὐδὲν ζητεῖν δεόμεθα προσκυνεῖν ὀφείλοντες τὰς ἀναγνωσθείσας τοῦ θεοῦ Τραιανοῦ καὶ τοῦ κυρίου ἡμῶν Ἀδριανοῦ Καίσαρος Σεβαστοῦ ἀποφάσεις.

132. Philostratus *Soph.* 590 (trans. Wright, modified).

133. *P. Euphr.* 1, l. 12: αἱ θεῖαι διατάξεις, ἅς τε πρὸ πάντων γνωρίζων προσκυνεῖς.

134. *IGLS* VII 4028(E), ll. 40–43.

135. *Relatio Anulinis proconsuli* at *Gesta Conlationis Carthaginiensis anno 411*, 3.216. Augustine quotes this text at *Ep.* 88.2; it is also reprinted as von Soden 1913, no. 10.

136. Lactantius *Mort. pers.* 13; Eusebius *Hist. eccl.* 8.5.

137. Trans. Lieberman 1944, 8, who draws the connection between this text and the episode described by Lactantius and Eusebius. The Midrash Esther can be dated ca. 500 and draws on earlier material (Stemberger 1996, 318–319).

covered their heads and read them in fear, in awe, in trembling and in trepidation. But when they arrived at the king's own city, the people read them, tore them, and burnt them.

It is tempting to see "the king's own city" as a reference to Nicomedia, but surely the value of the analogy to the rabbi lay in the contrast between the exception—the disrespect shown by Jehoiakim to the word of the Lord, and by the Christian to the imperial edict—and the familiar, prevailing pattern of behavior: the *adoratio* of texts authored by the Divine Hand, and the complete attention given to their contents.[138]

This behavior served a similar function twice more in the Midrash: at Vayykra Rabba 27.6, R. Isaac is described as saying, "Like a king who sent out his orders to a city. What did the people do? They rose to their feet, uncovered their heads, and read it in awe, fear, trembling, and trepidation."[139] R. Berechia relates the same parable in *Pesiqta de R. Kahana* 77a. Both men wrote under Diocletian. But the value of the familiar in explicating texts and providing paradigms did not change over time. A century later John Chrysostom exploited his congregation's familiarity with this ceremonial behavior when he advised them to show the same respect at the recitation of the Bible as at the reading of βασιλικὰ γράμματα:[140]

> Therefore let us listen to what is read today: strain for me your mental powers and, shaking off all laziness and secular concerns, pay attention to what is said. For divine laws are brought down from heaven for our salvation. When imperial documents are read aloud, there is a great calm, and all commotion and uproar disappear; everyone pricks up their ears and longs to hear whatever the imperial letters reveal; and great danger attends whoever should make a momentary disturbance and break the concentration of the listeners. Here all the more it is necessary to stand in fear and trembling, to maintain a deep silence, and to avoid any disturbance in the explanations, so that you can understand what is said, and so that the king of heaven, receiving our obedience, might think us worthy of great gifts.

Finally, in a more private moment, Basil of Caesarea flattered his friend Candidianus, then governor of Cappadocia: "When I took your letter in my hand, I experienced something worth hearing. I paid honor to it, as if it were making a state announcement; and, just as I broke the seal of wax, I feared to look on it, as no accused Spartan ever feared to look on a Laconian dispatch."[141]

---

138. On the *divina manu* that signed the text preserved on the Brigetio Tablet (*FIRA* I 93), see Corcoran 1996, 146, and cf. Millar 1977, 251.
139. Translation in Lieberman 1944, 7.
140. *Hom. in cap. II Gen.* 14.2 (*PG* 53.112). Cf. *idem, Homil. in Matth.* 19.9, quoted in Chapter 6 at n. 32.
141. Basil *Ep.* 3.1.

THE DISTRIBUTION AND RECEPTION OF OFFICIAL DOCUMENTS

We have already examined the process by which the Roman government guaranteed the accuracy of a notarized document, as well as the value that provincials came to place on preserving some trace of that notarization. The documents considered thus far have frequently required such a guarantee because they had some import within a particular legal context, and the party to which they were addressed had some investment in advertising the status of the text. Not all documents required such guarantees, nor were all Roman documents addressed to the parties to a particular dispute. In fact the emperor often addressed whole provinces or the entire empire. Scholars have traditionally differentiated such documents by labeling them edicts of "local" or "universal" application,[142] but such distinctions rapidly broke down when imperial utterances of any sort began to pass for law. As Ulpian wrote early in the third century, "[Because the people have transferred their *imperium et potestas* to the emperor], whatever the emperor has determined by a letter or subscript or has decreed on judicial investigation or has pronounced in an interlocutory matter, or has prescribed by an edict, is undoubtedly a law."[143] A particularly egregious example of this extension of applicability is the response of Alexander Severus to the *koinon* of Bithynia, to a question on appeals, quoted by Paul in his *Responsorum libri xxiii* and excerpted from that source into the *Digest,* and preserved also in two roughly contemporary copies from Oxyrhynchus.[144]

Evidence for the mechanisms and institutions of publication under the empire does not, as a rule, survive, and this fact has led some to doubt the existence of any formal procedure during this period.[145] Yet even a skeptical reading of extant texts reveals abundant evidence of authors' desire to disseminate and recipients' desire to record publications of every kind. Among documents already quoted, the Fifth Cyrene Edict and the *Senatus consultum de Cn. Pisone patre* exist because some local institution saw fit to create a monument out of a text addressed not specifically to its needs but to the needs of a larger community. Further evidence of this kind is not hard to find; it exists from every corner of the empire and from every period.

We should recall that emperors left the task of inscribing a text to its recipient and likewise remember that only a small portion of imperial publications required preservation in a permanent medium. Every surviving im-

---

142. E.g., W. Williams 1975, 43–45, listing documents of each type; cf. Corcoran 1996, 2.

143. See Ulpian at *Dig.* 1.4.1.1 (quoted in Chapter 5 at n. 112). On the contrast between theory and practice in imperial law courts regarding the precedential power of rescripts to private individuals, see Corcoran 1996, 48–54.

144. Paul at *Dig.* 49.1.25; *P. Oxy.* XVII 2104 and XLIII 3106.

145. Talbert 1984, 306.

perial document therefore offers further proof that someone was listening when the emperor spoke. Augustus, for example, responded to an offering of honors from the Jewish people (τὸ ἔθνος τὸ τῶν Ἰουδαίων) with a decree permitting them to practice their ancestral rites and protecting their synagogues from theft. He then ordered the publication of his decree in the province of Asia: [146]

> "As for the resolution that was offered to me by them, on behalf of my piety toward all men and on behalf of Gaius Marcius Censorinus, I order it and this edict to be set up in the most conspicuous [part of the temple] assigned to me by the *koinon* of Asia in Pergamum." This was inscribed on a pillar in the Temple of Caesar.

We possess this text not simply because Augustus ordered it to be published on his temple, but also because Josephus found it inscribed there and copied it. In other words, an individual of a subsequent generation thought an earlier imperial epistle relevant to the reconstruction of his past and, therefore, a constituent part of his present. Strife between the Jews and local populations in the East continued, and Claudius was forced to issue several letters to various parties on their status. [147] He addressed one such letter to the empire as a whole: [148]

> I want the magistrates of the poleis and the colonies and the municipalities, both those within Italy and outside it, and the kings and dynasts through their individual representatives, to have this my edict inscribed and kept on exhibition no less than thirty days, such that it can be easily read from ground level.

Claudius gave explicit instructions for the publication of his edict and, once again, Josephus transcribed the text and thus preserved it for posterity.

Rescripts to inquiries from private individuals or private organizations did not require elaborate provisions for their distribution; they would simply be posted at Rome or at the Sebasteum in a city near the emperor: "I, Imperator Caesar Vespasianus, have signed [this rescript] and ordered it to be posted on a whitened board. It was published in year 6, in the month Loos, on the Capitol, on the sixth day before the Kalends of January." [149] In this case, Vespasian required only promulgation on a whitened board. A local group of physicians spent their own money to have it inscribed. They must also have been responsible for the final sentence, which attempts to record—for a local audience—the circumstances of its original publica-

---

146. Josephus *Ant. Iud.* 16.165.
147. The topic is briefly surveyed by Feldman 1993, 96–98.
148. Josephus *Ant. Iud.* 19.291.
149. *MW* no. 458, ll. 17–20 (*FIRA* I 73).

tion. The use of both local and Roman dating systems again speaks to both its origin and its audience. The physicians also paid to inscribe a subsequent rescript of Domitian alongside this text. Furthermore, Vespasian's diction suggests that this document was a rescript and not an edict, and therefore of "local" rather than "universal" application. Indeed, the Severan jurist Arcadius Charisius cited it as a rescript a century and a half later. Its citation by Charisius and its inclusion in the *Digest*, however, betray the paradox: even if it was originally a rescript, it quickly acquired the force of an edict of "universal application."[150] Of course some documents were unambiguously intended for the empire as a whole; such was the case with an edict of Alexander Severus, greeting the empire upon his accession: "Let it be a concern for the magistrates of each city to set up copies of this my edict in public where they will be most visible to those who wish to read."[151] By this proclamation Alexander no doubt hoped to create good will at the start of his reign. It may be compared to the extant edicts proclaiming the accession of a new emperor, and, like them, it no doubt achieved wide currency in its day. We do not know what circumstances led to its being recopied a century after its promulgation, but this much is certain: someone must have found this text relevant to contemporary life.

Given the number of extant inscriptions from the Roman empire,[152] we might well be disappointed at the relative lack of multiple copies of such edicts or letters of universal application. Under the circumstances, it is helpful to recall the observation of Stephen Mitchell, on the occasion of his publication of Maximinus's edict on the Christians, in a text from Pisidian Colbasa: "It is salutary to reflect, given a general preoccupation with the importance of original documentary sources in ancient history, that the central episodes within the most important event in the history of the Roman empire, namely its conversion to Christianity, would not only be unintelligible but quite probably imperceptible without the survival of literary evidence."[153] We might well, therefore, express surprise at the opposite phenomenon, at just how many documents are known from several copies, particularly when we combine the evidence of surviving inscriptions with literary attestation of the existence of further publication.[154] To the law on provincial administration known from Delphi and Cnidus and the letter to the *conventus* of Asia mentioned above,[155] we can presently add the dossier

---

150. Arcadius Charisius at *Dig.* 50.4.18.30, and many other examples could be cited.

151. *Sel. pap.* 216 (*P. Fay.* 20), col. 2, ll. 21–23.

152. See MacMullen 1982 and 1990, 8–12.

153. Mitchell 1988, 106.

154. A few of these examples are cited by Eck 1993, 190.

155. The law on provincial administration above at n. 33; letter to the *conventus* of Asia (Sherk, *RDGE* no. 52) above at n. 37.

of documents that includes the letter of 9 B.C. from Paulus Fabius Maximus to the *koinon* of Asia, known from fragments at Priene, Apamea, Eumenea, Dorylaeum, and Maeonia;[156] the *Res gestae* of Augustus, known from three copies in Galatia but known from literary sources to have been inscribed in Rome as well;[157] the *senatus consultum* specifying the honors for Germanicus Caesar, recorded on the *Tabula Siarensis* and *Tabula Hebana* (named for the cities in Baetica and Etruria where they were found);[158] the *Senatus consultum de C. Pisone patre*, of which six copies have been found in Spain;[159] the reply of Claudius to the Dionysiac artists, preserved on two papyri from Egypt;[160] Hadrian's letter to the Achaean League, in copies from Athens and Olympia;[161] Hadrian's edict on a tax moratorium in Egypt in A.D. 136, known from three papyri, two from Philadelphia and one from the Fayum;[162] the two different parts of the dossier surrounding the senatorial debate on expenditures for gladiatorial displays, of which the *oratio* of the emperor himself is preserved at Sardis, while a bronze tablet at Italica, in Baetica, preserves the speech of a senator in the debate which followed;[163] the Severan rescript on the privileges of senators, now known from copies at Paros, Satala, Phrygian Pentapolis, Ancyra, Ephesus, Alexandria in the Troad, and Pisidian Antioch;[164] a pair of Severan rescripts, both famous because their extant copies record different dates of promulgation for largely identical texts (the copies of one rescript are of unknown provenance; the copies of the other, on *cessio bonorum*, were discovered at Oxyrhynchus);[165] another Severan edict declaring so-called mutual security illegal, preserved on two papyri;[166] the so-called Second Edict of Caracalla, preserved in the well-known *P. Giss.* 40 and in a fragmentary copy from Oxyrhynchus, and mentioned in both Justinianic corpora;[167] the letter of Alexander Severus to the

---

156. Sherk, *RDGE* no. 65.

157. In Galatia at Ancyra, Apollonia, and Antioch: Brunt and Moore 1967, 1–2; Suetonius *Augustus* 101.4: *altero indicem rerum a se gestarum, quem vellet incidi in aeneis tabulis, quae ante mausoleum statuerentur.* That it was inscribed at Rome is confirmed by the text itself: *rerum gestarum . . . incisarum in duabus aheneis pilis, quae su[n]t Romae positae, exemplum sub[i]ectum (EJ* p. 2).

158. For the *Tabula Siarensis* and *Tabula Hebana* see now *RS* 37–38.

159. Eck 1993, 190–191, or Eck, Caballos, and Fernández 1996, 1–6; cf. Tacitus *Ann.* 3.17.4–19.2.

160. *BGU* IV 1074 (of A.D. 275) and *P. Oxy.* XXVII 2476 (of A.D. 288).

161. Oliver 1989, no. 78A–B.

162. Smallwood, *Nerva* no. 462 = Oliver 1989, nos. 88A–C.

163. Oliver and Palmer 1955.

164. Robert 1987, 128–133; C. Jones 1984.

165. *BGU* I 267 and *P. Stras.* I 22; *P. Oxy.* XII 1405 and XLIII 3105.

166. *P. Mich.* IX 529, verso, 39–53 (*SB* XIV 11863), and *P. Flor.* 382.

167. *P. Giss.* 40, col. ii, ll. 1–15 = *P. Oxy.* XXXVI 2755; mentioned by Ulpian at *Digest* 50.2.3.1 and quoted in *C. Iust.* 10.61(59).

koinon of Bithynia, quoted by Paul and excerpted into the *Digest*, and preserved in two copies from Oxyrhynchus;[168] the many copies of Diocletian's Price Edict;[169] the first persecution edict, posted at Nicomedia on 24 February 303;[170] Constantine and Galerius's edict on accusations, extant fragments of which survive in Latin in Tlos in Lycia and in Greek in Athens;[171] the text published by S. Mitchell from Colbasa, mentioned above, of which Eusebius read and translated another copy in Tyre, and a further copy of which is extant in Arycanda in Lycia;[172] Constantine's edict *De accusationibus*, cited in the Theodosian Code and known from fragments in Lyttus, Sinope, Tlos in Lycia, Pergamum, and Padua;[173] and finally clause 24 of edict 13 of Justinian, extant in a copy on papyrus from Oxyrhynchus and preserved in the corpus of his edicts.[174] The existence of these copies is all the more striking when we consider that all the edicts of universal application listed by W. Williams in 1975 were known from single copies, though his list is constrained by the rigidity of his definitions.[175] This list can be dramatically enlarged by adding the vast numbers of private copies of official documents preserved on papyrus: citations from the Praetor's Edict, for instance, prove that Roman legal documents of various types were accessible in some form to the general public.[176]

Occasionally emperors intended particular texts for broad distribution and wide application within a single province. In that case current evidence suggests that they sent the text to the provincial governor, who then forwarded the document to the people's attention, explicitly attributing its content to the emperor himself.[177] A relatively early example is preserved

168. *Digest* 49.1.25; *P. Oxy.* XVII 2104 and XLIII 3106.

169. Lauffer 1971, Chaniotis and Preuss 1990, and Corcoran 1996, 205–233.

170. See Corcoran 1996, 179–180.

171. *CIL* III 12134; *IG* II² 1121 (*CIG* 356).

172. Mitchell 1988 (*AÉ* 1988, 1046).

173. *C. Th.* 9.5.1 (*C. Iust.* 9.8.3). For the epigraphical evidence see Habicht and Kussmaul 1986 or Corcoran 1996, 190. There is considerable controversy regarding the date and authorship of this text: by Licinius on 1 January 314 or Constantine in 320—Habicht and Kussmaul cite earlier studies (138)—but the answer does not affect the text's relevance here.

174. *Ed. Iust.* 13.24 and *P. Oxy.* LXIII 4400.

175. W. Williams 1975, 44.

176. See *P. Yadin* 28–30, with Goodman 1991a, 170–172.

177. Of course, governors could freely publish texts within their own provinces. On governor's *mandata* and their publication see Finkelstein 1934; Sherwin-White 1966, on Pliny *Ep.* 10.22.1; and Potter 1996a. These *mandata* were not themselves usually published, but rather shaped the individual governor's edict, which was published. As always, a counterexample is available: see Marcianus at *Dig.* 48.3.6.1 (*Sed et caput mandatorum exstat, quod divus Pius, cum provinciae praeerat, sub edicto proposuit, ut . . .*). But at least one person brought a case before Pliny and based his case explicitly on Trajan's *mandata* (*Ep.* 10.110.1), and it may be that the person whose case Corbulo judged on Cos appealed to Augustus because he knew that Corbulo's *mandata* required that such appeals be heard (*IGRR* IV 1044 = *AÉ* 1974, 629; on which see Bur-

from Pisidia, in an ordinance intended to protect the provincials from irresponsible agents of the government: [178]

> Sextus Sotidius Strabo Libuscidianus, *legatus pro praetore* of Tiberius Caesar Augustus, says: It is the most unjust thing of all for me to tighten up by my own edict that which the Augusti, one the greatest of gods, the other the greatest of emperors, have taken the utmost care to prevent, namely that no one should make use of carts without payment. However, since the indiscipline of certain people requires an immediate punishment, I have set up in the individual towns and villages a register [*formula*] of those services that I judge ought to be provided, with the intention of having it observed, or, if it shall be neglected, of enforcing it not only with my own power, but with the majesty of the best of princes, from whom I received instructions concerning these matters.

Although Libuscidianus took responsibility for the *formula,* he buttressed his own authority with that of his *princeps.* Governors could also simply forward to the attention of the people the emperor's own words. For example, an embassy from Alexandria to Claudius received a direct response from Claudius himself: [179]

> Lucius Aemilius Rectus proclaims: Since all the city, because of its size, was not able to be present at the reading of the most sacred and most beneficent letter to the city, I considered it necessary to post the letter, so that each one of you, reading it man by man, might marvel at the majesty of our god Caesar and have gratitude for his good will toward the city. Year 2 of Tiberius Claudius Caesar Augustus Germanicus Imperator, the 14th of the month New Augustus.

Aemilius Rectus followed good Roman practice and arranged for the letter of Claudius to be read aloud, but, acknowledging that not all could be present and desiring nevertheless that all should know the text, he had a copy

---

ton 1976). Indeed, Lucian writes as if the general features of these instructions were well known: οὐχὶ καὶ ἐν τῷ τῶν ἐντολῶν βιβλίῳ ὃ ἀεὶ παρὰ βασιλέως λαμβάνετε, τοῦτο πρῶτον ὑμῖν ἐστι παράγγελμα, τῆς ὑγιείας τῆς ὑμετέρας αὐτῶν ἐπιμελεῖσθαι (*Pro lapsu* 13); I believe that, in every instance in which *mandata* were inscribed, they were commands issued to cover specific problems, and not general instructions such as might have been issued to all legates: see *IGLS* V 1998, ll. 1–5 (*SEG* XVII 755) and *CIL* III 7086 (*IGRR* IV 336). See also, for example, the edict of Quintus Veranius on public records in Lycia, from the reign of Claudius: Τοῦτο τὸ ἐπ[ίκρι]-|[44]μα καθ᾽ ὅλην ἐπαρ[χεία]ν ἣν πεπίστευμαι οἱ ἔνεδροι το[ῦ] | [45] Ἀρτεμει[σίου μηνὸς ἄρχον]τες ἀναγραψάτωσαν (M. Wörrle 1975, no. 1, ll. 43–45). Consider, too, the epigram written by Antipater of Thessalonica for Gaius Caesar during his tour of the East, advising the prince πατρῴων δ᾽ ἄρξαι ἀπ᾽ ἐντολέων (*Anth. Pal.* 9.297).

178. Text and translation in Mitchell 1976, 107–109; here, ll. 1–7, 26–31. On self-policing in the Roman administration, see Chapter 9, "The Emperor and His Subordinates."

179. *Sel. pap.* 212 (*P. Lond.* 1912 = Oliver 1989, no. 19 = *CPJud.* 153), ll. 1–13.

posted; this would have had the concomitant effect of establishing the text's legality. He obviously presumed that the local population contained enough literate individuals to spread the news to all interested parties.[180]

The standard charter issued at the incorporation of municipalities in the Flavian period displayed a similar concern for making information accessible to the public, especially information regarding legal procedure. Such provisions are particularly notable given the tendency in ancient political thought to associate publication of the laws with the evolution of a government toward democracy or, at least, equity:[181]

> Rubric. That magistrates should have in public the *album* of the person who holds the province and should administer justice according to it. Whatever edicts or *formulae* for trials or *sponsiones* . . . or interdicts the person who governs the province has displayed in the province, whichever of them relate to the jurisdiction of that magistrate who is in charge of the administration of justice in the Municipality of Flavium Irnitanum, he is to have them all displayed and published in the *municipium* in his magistracy every day, for the greater part of the day, such that they may be properly read from ground level.[182]

We have already seen that Bithynians approached Pliny and quoted earlier imperial rescripts in their legal briefs. Pliny also recorded that some provincials read and heeded the instructions in his provincial edict. The Christians, for example, famously claimed that they ceased to hold their feasts after learning that Pliny had forbidden such gatherings in his edict, and provincials in Egypt often quoted prefectural edicts in court.[183]

The problem faced by Strabo Libuscidianus did not go away: persons associated with the government continued to requisition supplies and animals illegally. Emperors and governors continually exhorted people to obey such requests only when accompanied by the appropriate *diplomata:* such was the admonition of Germanicus on the occasion of his visit to Egypt in A.D. 19, of L. Aemilius Rectus in 42, of Domitian in the *mandata* he gave to Claudius Athenodorus, as also of M. Petronius Mamertinus, prefect of Egypt

---

180. Compare the wording in the roughly contemporary edict of Lusius Geta on the immunity of priests (A.D. 54), Smallwood, *Gaius* no. 383 (*AJ* no. 165 = *OGIS* 664 = *IGRR* I 1118) ll. 1–6: [1]Λούσιος [Γέτας] Κλαυδίῳ Λυσα | [2]νίαι στρατηγῷ Ἀρσινοείτου | [3]χαίρειν. Τὸ ὑπογεγραμμένον | [4]ἔκθεμα πρόθες ἐν οἷς καθήκει | [5]τοῦ νομοῦ τόποις, ἵνα πάντες | [6](ε)ἰδῶσι τὰ ὑπ' ἐμοῦ κελευόμενα.

181. See, e.g., Livy 9.46.

182. *Lex Irnitana* tablet IXb, ll. 28–37. See González 1986, containing a translation by M. Crawford (used here, with minor alterations). Two other Flavian municipal laws survive, though neither is complete: the *leges municipiorum Salpensani et Malcitani* (*ILS* 6088 and 6089).

183. See Pliny *Ep.* 10.96.7. On prefectural edicts from Egypt, fifty-nine of which are attested or quoted by provincials, see Katzoff 1980.

from 133 to 137.[184] The prefect Julius Saturninus tried a slightly different approach when he responded to complaints from villagers in Syria:[185]

> Julius Saturninus to the citizens of Phaene, chief village of the district of Tracho, greetings. If someone, whether soldier or civilian, billets himself with you by force, write to me and you will receive redress. For you do not owe any contribution to visitors, and, since you have a hostel, you cannot be forced to receive visitors in your homes. Post this letter of mine in the open in your chief village, lest anyone make the excuse that he acted in ignorance.

Saturninus has confirmed the principle suggested above: ignorance of the law may be used as an excuse, but not if the written text of the law is commonly available. Saturninus directed his injunction against imperial officials and soldiers who were a bit too eager in their activities. The prefects of Egypt sometimes faced the opposite problem, namely local officials who did not enforce existing statutes against illegal magic practices or banditry:[186]

> Let each of you take care that a copy of this letter is displayed publicly in the district capitals and in every village in clear and easily legible writing on a whitened board, and let him continually make inquiry and, if he finds any person behaving contrary to the prohibitions, let him send him in bonds to my court.

To close this survey, I present a letter of the prefect of Egypt, forwarding an edict of the tetrarchs on taxation:[187]

> [1] Aurelius Optatus, the most eminent prefect of Egypt, says: Our most provident emperors Diocletian and Maximian, the Augusti, and Constantius and Maximian, the most noble Caesars . . . [7] Thus it is possible for all to know the amount levied on each aroura . . . [8] from the imperial edict which has been published and the schedule attached thereto, to which I have prefixed for public display copies of this edict of mine. . . . [13] For it is fitting that each person discharge most zealously the full burden of loyalty . . . [14] The magistrates and presidents of the councils of each city have been ordered to dispatch to each village or place whatsoever a copy both of the imperial edict together with the schedule and also [a copy] of this [edict of mine] as well, to the end that the munificence of our emperors and Caesars may come as speedily as possible to the knowledge of all.

---

184. Germanicus: *Sel. pap.* 211. Aemilius Rectus: *AJ* no. 162 (*WC* no. 439). Domitian: *IGLS* V 1998 (*MW* no. 466 = *SEG* XVII 755), ll. 17–19, 21–23. Mamertinus: *Sel. pap.* 221.

185. *AJ* no. 113 (*IGRR* III 1119 = *OGIS* 609).

186. *P. Coll. Youtie* 30, ll. 12–18 (*P. Yale* inv. 299; reedited with translation in Rea 1977 and again in N. Lewis 1995, 315–327). On the stipulation regarding the legibility of the writing, see also *OGIS* 665 (above at n. 112). Cf. *Sel. pap.* 224, ll. 17–20 (*P. Oxy.* XII 1408).

187. *P. Cair. Isid.* 1, ll. 1–3, 7, 8–10, 13, 14–18.

Notable again are the injunctions laid upon the local institutions of government to ensure the proper publication of these documents, as is the description of the purpose of publication, which, in echoing the rhetoric of the *Novels,* suggests that we have finally arrived in the late Empire.[188]

FINDING HISTORY IN THE FILING CABINET

In A.D. 357, following Julian's resounding victory over the allied kings of the Alamanni at the battle of Strasbourg, the senior emperor, Constantius, tried to claim responsibility for the victory. In so doing he drew the ire of Ammianus Marcellinus, then an imperial officer stationed in Syria and, in his retirement, the author of a distinguished history:[189]

> Puffed up by the grandiloquence of his flatterers, at that time and subsequently Constantius arrogantly told many lies in his published edicts, often writing that he alone had fought and conquered and raised up the suppliant kings of nations, although he had not even been present for the deeds. If, for example, a general acted bravely against the Persians while Constantius was in Italy, with no mention of the general anywhere in the long text he would send out laureled letters to the detriment of the provinces, suggesting with odious boasting that he had fought in the front ranks.[190] Finally, there are extant his own utterances, deposited in the public record houses, [in which . . . extolling himself to the sky . . .].

To this we may compare Ammianus's address to those who would criticize his account of the treason trials at Rome:[191]

> Although I imagine that some readers of this history will by detailed scrutiny notice and complain that this happened first, and not that, or that things which they themselves witnessed have been passed over, satisfaction must be made only to this extent: not everything that transpires among squalid people is worthy of narration, nor, if that were required, would even the array of information from the public record houses themselves suffice.

The specific context and content of these remarks will be addressed later,[192] though here we may mention the testimony of Themistius, from earlier in 357, concerning the abundance of "laureled letters" sent to Con-

---

188. The style and Latinity of imperial legislation underwent profound changes in the late third and early fourth centuries. Among many studies, see Vernay 1913, Mohrmann 1946, Wieacker 1955, and Vidén 1984.

189. Ammianus 16.12.69–70. The lacuna in the final sentence (27 letters in V and 12 letters in E) most likely does not affect the overall content of the passage.

190. Compare Dio 75.2.3–4 on the boasting of Severus.

191. Ammianus 28.1.15.

192. See Chapter 6, "*Aurum Coronarium.*"

stantinople by Constantius.[193] However much they annoyed Ammianus, such letters had a long history: some had heralded the ascension of the *optimus princeps*.[194] At present it is sufficient to note that three assumptions underlie Ammianus's remarks: first, that imperial edicts and letters contained information useful to the construction of a historical narrative, even if that information could not always be trusted; second, that public record houses existed and contained detailed records, among which were copies of past imperial edicts and letters; and third, that historians could and should exploit such material in their work. The Theodosian Code corroborates a limited version of the first point, demonstrating that imperial archives existed in several major cities and that they retained the texts of imperial documents for at least a century.[195]

We need not believe that the government had the needs of an Ammianus foremost in its mind. Rather, it sought in the first instance to justify and to contextualize the content of the document at hand: a new tax, a census, the announcement of a victory, a birth in the imperial household. Each new piece of information formed part of the larger history of the imperial commonwealth. Imperial guardianship of the empire, though expressed through specific acts of generosity or battles on particular borders, became a benefit for all through a process of universalization, while a barrage of images in everyday life endowed the residents of the empire with a shared iconographic language through which they could share their emperor. Similarly, the harmless, almost imperceptible accumulation of data in administrative texts created a sense of inevitable continuity at the heart of the empire: just as the government both distributed and honored legal documents, so each text originated with an emperor who succeeded to his predecessor's obligations even as he succeeded to his powers. Just as a historical narrative can tell the story of, and so can construct, a community, so an awareness of a shared history is constitutive of one. Within this model each document becomes a piece in a mosaic whose overall pattern did not require articulation and which, in all probability, lay just outside the conscious awareness of those whose world it circumscribed and depicted. Documents that interpellated individuals as concrete subjects of emperor and empire added another page to the history of each such individual as a subject. In-

---

193. Themistius *Or.* 4.58a, and cf. 53d, delivered on January 1, 357.

194. Pliny *Pan.* 8.2. Cf. Pliny *Nat.* 15.133: [*Laurus*] *Romanis praecipue laetitiae victoriarumque nuntia additur litteris et militum lanceis pilisque, fasces imperatorum decorat;* Livy believed the custom to be very old indeed (5.28.13). The use of laurel rapidly became an imperial prerogative, though Tacitus suggests that Agricola as legate could have sent laureled letters to Rome (*Agric.* 18.6).

195. Seeck 1919, chapter 1, supported by Matthews 1993, 31–41, and C. Kelly 1994, 162–166.

dividuals' pasts, like that of their empire, became directly continuous with their presents, and their immediate identity a function of their past relations with the imperial government.

This chapter has focused mainly on the distribution of administrative and legal texts, whose content presumably offered sufficient cause for their publication. That is, these documents did not exist purely to distribute news, although, as the complaint of Ammianus warns us, rigid criteria did not separate news bulletins and legal texts. We cannot determine the genre of text to which Paullus Fabius Persicus referred, but during the reign of Claudius he warned the cities of Asia that they were draining their resources by starting new priesthoods "as often as cheerful news arrived from Rome."[196] I close this chapter by reflecting on the evolution of individuals' historical self-awareness. As the Roman government forced provincials to redefine their relations with each other, with their cities, and with their physical environment, so its documents and its diction will have effected shifts in the legal and conceptual terminology through which individual identity was described and delimited. Chapter 9 will investigate the interpellation of individual subjects in the rituals conducted by the government and its magistrates. Here we can step beyond the assessment of local, administrative responses to Roman texts by investigating contemporary awareness of the government's role in distributing news about the events in its large empire, and then by considering the changes this awareness brought to the construction of historical narratives.

If writing contemporary history in the ancient world was difficult, the modern study of the practice has pitfalls of its own.[197] Seeking, perhaps unconsciously, to avoid the problem, modern students of imperial historiography explain the unanimity of the later traditions by constructing literary genealogies; but the very unanimity of that tradition urges us to reconsider the sources available to the first literary historians of the period.[198] In what follows, we must also cast our net beyond the literary historians, to men like the author of the Thirteenth Sibylline Oracle and the anonymous writer who, in Oxyrhynchus in the mid-third century, tried to compile a list of em-

196. *SEG* IV 516 (Smallwood, *Gaius* no. 380), col. IV, ll. 11–15 at 11–12: ὁσάκις τε γὰρ ἂν ἀπὸ τῆς Ῥώμης ἱλαρωτέρα ἔλθῃ ἀγγελία. See also *SEG* XXIII 206, from Messene, ll. 20–21, on which see Chapter 5 at n. 6.

197. Peter 1897, 1.159–271, provides the only full-scale analysis. His treatment has been bettered for some specialized topics (eg. by Stein 1930a and 1930b), but no one else has attempted anything on such scale: Fornara 1983, 47–90 and esp. 56–61 and 67–76, is too cursory. Avenarius 1956 contains much valuable information on ancient theory.

198. See Millar 1964, 121: "The question [of how Dio obtained information] is of some importance, for while criticism of ancient historians has tended to concentrate on the analysis of how they used written sources, the fact that in each case *some* writer must have been the first to record a given period has at times almost been forgotten" (emphasis in original).

perors on the back of a scrap of papyrus: he could figure out roughly how many years had passed since Augustus, but he was unsure how many years some had ruled, and some more ephemeral presences got lost.[199] If men like Herodian relied on imperial epistles to inform them about events on the frontiers, men like the author of *P. Oxy.* I 35 could learn about past rulers of their world from documents as simple as a land register.[200]

Modern writers, suspicious of monarchs as of empires, view the Roman government's role in the dissemination of news with profound cynicism and hope to find similar hostility in ancient authors. In doing so they have privileged the quality of information over its mere existence as a subject of analysis. But it was largely thanks to the Roman government that the vast majority of the population of the Mediterranean world received information about their world an order of magnitude greater in quantity and quality than it ever had before, or would again before the dawn of the modern era. Certainly people could not rely on private correspondence to bring the news. Indeed, we can never overestimate the difficulty faced by the men and women of antiquity in merely communicating, to say nothing of acquiring information on specific topics. Typical of letter writing in antiquity in general are sentences by one Apollinarius, an Egyptian who journeyed to Italy to join the imperial fleet, writing home to his mother: "From Cyrene, having found a man going toward you, I thought it necessary to write"; or "and, if I find someone [to carry my letters], I will write to you."[201] The situation for men of wealth was no different: all had to rely on the good will of pri-

---

199. The Thirteenth Sibylline Oracle: Olmstead 1942, Lieberman 1946b, and Potter 1990. *P. Oxy.* I 35: Gaius is somehow omitted, but his years (four) are assigned to Claudius. Galba has also fallen out; and in the late second century the author becomes confused, listing Commodus, Severus, Antoninus (Caracalla), Alexander (Severus), Maximinus, Gordian (singular), Philip, Decius. All those missing are definitely attested in contemporaneous dating formulas in Egypt. (Cf. Rathbone 1986.) The author also simply avoided the very real difficulty caused by inconsiderate emperors who died in the middle of a consular year (also a problem for those tried to write *annales* under a monarchy: Ando 1997). A. E. Hanson has suggested to me that *P. Oxy.* I 35 may have a bureaucratic origin, citing the counting difficulty with the years for Claudius (δ instead of ιδ as an error of sight) and comparing the problems presented by the spelling of Γαίηος in *P. Oxy.* LV 3780, l. 7, a copy of a list of the new month names instituted under Caligula.

200. See, for instance, the register in the archive of Petaus (*P. Petaus* 127): the history of a parcel of land is detailed, each event in that history being dated by regnal year (Domitian, Nerva, Trajan are mentioned in order). Regulations regarding the accuracy of property records in local archives were very strict: see Wörrle 1975, no. 1, from Myra in Pisidia in the reign of Claudius, with superb commentary; *P. Oxy.* II 237 (*Sel. pap.* 219), from A.D. 89, on which see Cockle 1984; *P. Fam. Tebt.* 15 and 24, from the reign of Trajan; *P. Oxy.* I 34, from A.D. 127; and Oliver 1989, no. 186, from Pisidia in the second century. For regulations at Rome, see Haensch 1992, 217 and 230–231, and Moreau 1994.

201. *P. Mich.* VIII 401, ll. 5–7; ibid. 402, ll. 13–14.

vate individuals, sometimes with unfortunate results.[202] Libanius apologized to Hyperechius for a delay in his correspondence because those who had volunteered to carry his letters were unsuitable.[203] A letter from Themistius to Libanius was delayed when the party to whom Libanius had entrusted it gave it to someone else.[204] And the possibility that a letter from Augustine to Jerome got routed through Rome accidentally, and was there copied and distributed, before a copy—and not the original—reached Jerome, was all too real for both men.[205] Although the practice was illegal, soldiers exploited the imperial post for private letters, suggesting once again that private means were irregular and unreliable.[206]

We have no basis for an empirical assessment of the reliability and speed of private mail in antiquity. Documents generated by the imperial bureaucracy do, however, provide some data; and, in view of the government's monopoly over systems of mass communication, its difficulties must have been compounded manifold for private individuals. The most recent surveys of these data were compiled by A. H. M. Jones and R. Duncan-Jones, although neither attempted a study on the scale of that conducted by W. Riepl, who was himself indebted to that judicious compiler of evidence, L. Friedlaender.[207] Jones collected the data from the approximately fifty constitutions for which there survives a record not only of the time and place where they were signed by the emperor but also of the time and place where they were received. Edicts could easily take four or more months to reach Africa from the East, and Jones's evidence yields a minimum of one month for travel between Illyricum and Rome. Duncan-Jones analyzed dated papyri for the last appearance of deceased emperors on documents and the first appearance of the names of new emperors. His study is thus particularly useful, because the new administration, as it were, usually wanted to be the one spreading the news of its accession. As evidence for this desire we may invoke the preserved proclamations of the accessions of Nero and Pertinax, as well as the descriptions of letter-writing activity in historical accounts of usurpations.[208]

202. On the means by which Cicero acquired news when away from Rome, see White 1997. On Symmachus and the bearers of his letters, see Matthews 1974, 63, 80–81.

203. Libanius *Ep.* 704, to Hyperechius 1 (Seeck 1906, 182–183).

204. *Ep.* 66 (Norman no. 52).

205. Augustine to Jerome: *Ep.* 67; Jerome to Augustine, at Augustine *Ep.* 68. The letter in question is *Ep.* 40: that letter, we should note, was itself written because an earlier one from Augustine to Jerome was never delivered (*Ep.* 40.v.8). On their correspondence at this time, see J. Kelly 1975, 217–220.

206. See Youtie 1976, on *P. Mich.* III 203.

207. A. H. M. Jones 1964, 402–403; Duncan-Jones 1990, 7–29; Riepl 1913, part III: "Mittel und Schnelligkeit der Nachrichtenbeförderung"; Friedlaender 1922, 1.333–342.

208. See *Sel. pap.* 235 (*P. Oxy.* 1021), ordaining a public celebration and advertising the divine lineage of the Julio-Claudian house; and *Sel. pap.* 222 (*BGU* 646), explicitly distributing

Duncan-Jones surmised that news of an emperor's death took almost two months to reach Egypt when he died in Italy, and from 50 to 100 percent longer when he died elsewhere.[209] Jones understated the problem when he wrote that "despite the very heavy outlay on the *cursus velox,* communication between the *comitatus* and the outlying authorities was not strikingly rapid."[210]

Classical historians distinguished between the writing of ancient and contemporary history primarily through the nature of the research that each required. This remained true from a historiographical perspective, quite apart from complaints that partisanship and self-interest made writing the truth under a monarchy difficult.[211] To put it briefly, the writing of ancient history required that the author read older literary histories and perform *onerosa collatio,* while research on contemporary history demanded first and foremost the interrogation of eyewitnesses.[212] "Contemporary" meant within living memory: thus Polybius began his history in 220 because he could still find eyewitnesses among the previous generation whom he could question about the events of that time.[213] In his theoretical musings on historiography, Polybius maintained that the proper writing of history demanded three things: the study of written memoirs and a comparison of their contents, a survey of matters geographical, and experience concern-

---

information so that everyone—presumably around the empire—will celebrate for the same length of time on the same days. See further Tacitus *Hist.* 2.86.4, on the activities of Antonius Primus, *serendae in alios invidiae artifex,* and 2.98.1. The author of the *Historia Augusta,* most attuned to matters of political behavior, concocted letters that the Senate dispatched *ad omnes provincias,* exhorting the fall of Maximinus (*Max.* 15.3–16.7). On the letter-writing activities of Julian and Procopius, see Chapter 6, "The Slow Journey of Eutherius," and Chapter 7 at n. 83; and cf. MacMullen 1990, 198–203.

209. Such news almost undoubtedly reached Alexandria first, and we have no evidence for the dates when the news arrived there. The evidence suggests that the time lag between the arrival of news in Alexandria and its first attestation elsewhere could be substantial (Duncan-Jones 1990, table 3), although it could also travel much more quickly (ibid. 8 nn. 4, 5).

210. A. H. M. Jones 1964, 402.

211. Tacitus *Ann.* 1.1.2 is a *locus classicus.* See also Pliny on choosing a time period for his own history: *Vetera et scripta aliis? Parata inquisitio, sed onerosa collatio. Intacta et nova? Graves offensae levis gratia* (5.8.12–13; cf. 9.27.2, on the recitation of a *verissimum librum*)—though I would tend to align Pliny's worries at 5.8 more with his experience at 9.27, and less with the admonition of Tacitus, than does Sherwin-White (in his note on 5.8.12). Josephus turned the topos on its head in his reproach to Justus: by waiting until Vespasian and Titus were dead, the latter has been able to pass off a fictional version of events (*Vita* 359). Not that emperors were unaware of the issue, as Augustus made clear to Horace, in an anecdote later quoted by Suetonius: *An vereris ne apud posteros infame tibi sit, quod videaris familiaris nobis esse?* See also Horace, *Carm.* 2.1.1–9 and, more distantly, Juvenal 1.160–161.

212. For the phrase, see Pliny *Ep.* 5.8.12 (quoted above in n. 211); cf. Lucian *Hist. conscr.* 47. To the parallels quoted by Avenarius 1956, 77–79, add Eunapius *Hist.* fr. 30.

213. Polybius 4.2.2.

ing political events.[214] He discussed documentary sources only rarely, but his criticism of Timaeus for "discovering inscriptions on the backs of buildings and lists of *proxeni* on the jambs of temples" was hypocritical: Polybius privileged a document in the Rhodian prytaneum over conflicting literary sources, and he boasted that, regarding the number of Hannibal's troops, he had been able to attain a level of accuracy that even the organizer of the expedition would have envied—precisely because he discovered a bronze tablet drawn up by Hannibal himself, "in every way a reliable source."[215]

In his estimation of Hannibal's inscription, Polybius indulged a typically Roman fondness for bronze.[216] Earlier we saw both that the bronze records on the Capitol were not intended to be the only official archive of the Roman state, and that under the Republic the existence of a text on bronze was not by itself sufficient to make it law. There can be no doubt, however, that bronze tablets were more permanent than texts preserved on boards, and that this fact was recognized in antiquity. As Constantine wrote in A.D. 337: "In order that this law be maintained by perpetual observance, we command that this law be inscribed on bronze tablets and in that form published."[217] Under Tiberius the Senate established a commission, on the recommendation of the emperor himself, to recopy faded and decaying records: they presumably were charged with the conservation of such records as were preserved on perishable media, in this case almost undoubtedly wooden tablets.[218] Only the greatest of conflagrations could destroy bronze records, such as the fire which raged during the battle for Rome in A.D. 69; it was the task afterwards of some unlucky senators to hunt down copies of the three thousand *senatus consulta* and *plebiscita* that had hung on the Capitol.[219]

There can be no doubt why Vespasian made the effort to restore the tablets: three thousand such records would have made the Capitol a strikingly visible monument to the history of the Roman people, "a most ancient and beautiful proof of empire." Indeed, Romans had long associated the use of bronze with the actions of their government and had asked others to

214. Polybius 12.25ᶜ.1.

215. Polybius 16.15.8, and compare 3.33.17–18.

216. Cf. Beard, at Reynolds, Beard, and Roueché 1986, 143, as well as Corbier 1987, 39–43.

217. *C. Th.* 12.4.2; cf. Pliny *Nat.* 34.99.

218. Dio 57.16.2. The nature of the commission and its duration are debated: two *curatores tabulariorum publicorum* are attested under Claudius. See T. Mommsen 1887, 2.1.558–559; Hammond 1938; Corbier 1974, 676–677; and Coudry 1994, 75.

219. Suetonius *Vespasian* 8.5 (cf. 10), and Tacitus *Hist.* 4.40.1–2. As Chilver and Townend point out (in their note *ad loc.*), the discrepancies between the accounts in Suetonius and Tacitus probably arose because the emperor had sent a long list of instructions which Domitian read aloud and from which each author gives a selection.

do the same. When under the Republic they sent documents to other cities, they frequently specified a preference for bronze as the medium of publication.[220] The Senate clearly wished viewers to associate the magnificence of such texts with their city: it thus regularly commanded that the bronze tablet be attached to the local temple to, or statue of, Dea Roma[221] — a practice maintained in the early years of the Principate by asking that such documents be associated with the temples to Augustus.[222] Pliny testified with eloquent indignation to the power of such epigraphic texts when he complained that the honors voted to Pallas by the Senate were inscribed on bronze and attached to a public monument, "as if they were an ancient treaty, as if they were a sacred law."[223]

To Pliny's complaint we should compare the request put by the citizens of Antioch to Titus, on his journey from Jerusalem to Rome in A.D. 70. Relations between Greeks and Jews at Antioch had been difficult for some time, and the Antiochenes attempted to use the occasion of the Jewish revolt as leverage against the Jewish population in their midst.[224] The Antiochenes took heart from the triumphal parades that Titus staged in each major city as he passed through Syria: mimicking the forms and displays of a Roman triumph, he marked his Jewish captives as defeated enemies of Rome.[225] The Antiochenes naturally wished to associate the Jews at Antioch with the other members of their race. Titus met with the population in the theater and there refused their request to expel the Jews from their city. They petitioned him a second time: if he would not expel the Jews, he should at least remove "the bronze tablets on which were inscribed the rights of the Jews."[226] The request reveals the Antiochenes' multilayered assent to the rules and ideals of Roman government: they acknowledged their duty to obey the ordinances of the Roman government, and they believed that those ordinances remained in effect so long as they were preserved in the fashion in which Rome had arranged their formal publication.

Polybius obviously distinguished between literary histories and the autobiographical memoirs of individuals; the comparison of such accounts might lead to the truth, but these documents had no claim to the scope or

220. Frederiksen 1965, 184–185; cf. the provisions in the *lex de provinciis praetoriis* (quoted above at n. 26) and the *SC de Mytilenaeis* (Sherk, *RDGE* 26), col. c, ll. 22–26.
221. E.g., *OGIS* 762; Sherk, *RDGE* no. 16. On provincial temples to Rome see Mellor 1975.
222. E.g., Augustus on the Jews at Josephus *Ant. Iud.* 16.165 (quoted above at n. 146).
223. *Ep.* 8.6.14.
224. Josephus *Bell. Iud.* 7.41–62.
225. Josephus *Bell. Iud.* 7.96, on which see Chapter 7 at n. 228.
226. Josephus *Bell. Iud.* 7.110: τὰς γὰρ χαλκᾶς ἠξίουν δέλτους ἀνελεῖν αὐτόν, ἐν αἷς γέγραπται τὰ δικαιώματα τῶν Ἰουδαίων. The tenants of the Saltus Burunitanus refer to laws on bronze as authoritative, to be acknowledged and known by everyone, everywhere (*ILS* 6870).

the freedom from bias that must characterize historical inquiry. Members of the imperial court and imperial family continued to produce such "pamphlet literature"—to use Hermann Peter's term—and their products profoundly influenced contemporary politics and later historiography. Three and a half centuries after Polybius, Cassius Dio discussed how Rome's transition from republic to monarchy had affected historiography. Under the Republic, he argued, all matters were brought before the Senate and the people, even when they occurred far away:[227] "Because of this, everyone learned of them and many wrote about them, and, in spite of the many sources of bias, the truth about matters can be found in the works of those who wrote about them, and in some fashion in the public records:"[228]

But after this time more and more business was hidden and began to be transacted in secret, and even if something was made public [δημοσιευθείη], it was distrusted as being unprovable [ἀνεξέλεγκτα].[229] For everything is suspected of having been said or done in accordance with the plans of those perpetually in power and those who have influence with them. And therefore, many things are trumpeted about that never happened; and many things that certainly happened are unknown; and everything, so to speak, is publicized in some way different from how it happened. The sheer size of the empire, and the number of things going on, render accuracy concerning them extremely difficult. There are so many events in Rome and in her territory—including the continual and almost daily fights against her enemies—that no one other than those involved easily acquires clear knowledge concerning them. . . . Therefore I will describe all events that must be mentioned, as they were publicized, whether it was really so or in some way different.

Historians have made much of this passage, as though Cassius Dio had personal experience with life in the Republic.[230] In reality Dio had access to the same sources as Polybius. But both Polybius and Dio expected, and did not

---

227. A paraphrase of 53.19.2. Herodian made analogous complaints about contemporary historiography (at 1.1.2 and esp. 2.15.7). English idiom cannot capture the bitter brevity of Tacitus: *inscitia rei publicae ut alienae* (*Hist.* 1.1.1). Note that Suetonius presumed that Augustus established the *cursus publicus* in order for news to be brought to Rome (*Augustus* 49.3, on which see T. Mommsen 1887, 2.2.1029–1031; and Eck 1979, 88–110, discussing Caesar *BC* 3.101).

228. Dio 53.19.3–6.

229. Compare Herodian 7.1.8: ἡ μὲν τῆς διαβολῆς φήμη τοιαύτη ἐγένετο, εἴτε ἀληθὴς ὑπάρξασα εἴτε ὑπὸ τοῦ Μαξιμίνου συσκευασθεῖσα· ἀκριβὲς δὲ εἰπεῖν οὐ ῥᾴδιον, ἐπεὶ ἔμενεν ἀνεξέλεγκτος. Tacitus allowed Sallustius Crispus to reflect on this problem from the monarch's perspective: *Sallustius Crispus . . . monuit Liviam, ne arcana domus, ne consilia amicorum, ministeria militum vulgarentur, neve Tiberius vim principatus resolveret cuncta ad senatum vocando: eam condicionem esse imperandi, ut non aliter ratio constet quam si uni reddatur* (*Ann.* 1.6.3).

230. For more successful readings see Syme 1958, 365–366; Millar 1964, 37–38; and Rubin 1975, 421–422.

disparage, bias in personal memoirs in a democratic age. The change lay not in the public's freedom of access to information, but in its greater expectations of the imperial government: Dio is indignant because the emperor was *not* a Republican politician and therefore ought to tell the truth. The same expectation gripped other historians of the empire. Herodian, for example, once quipped that "the deeds of a king cannot be concealed," only to confess later that he could not discover whether the dispatches of Maximinus were true or false.[231] Late in the fourth century, when Eunapius could no longer simply crib the letters of Julian and the memoirs of Oribasius, he was forced to do some research on his own. Then he too discovered how difficult it was to obtain information: "It was impossible for me, though I acted quite diligently, to investigate fully and to learn about the deeds and character of Gratian, for these things were concealed in the palace with exceptional zeal."[232] He also complained bitterly about the difficulty in learning anything about events in the West: the great distance made reports late and useless; few soldiers or officials had access to information, and they related it with bias anyhow; and merchants had nothing to offer.[233] The result, he concluded, was that he—like Dio—could offer a reasonable account, but he also knew that he had no basis by which to assess its truthfulness.

Literary histories reached their audience—and it was a limited one—slowly, at some remove from the events they described. Not so public oratory. The direct supplying of information to panegyrists remains a controversial subject that economies of scale do not permit me to enter here.[234] I merely offer a few observations. First, *commentarii* as a genre had a long history in Rome, deriving their authority as sources for historians from their putative status as reports submitted by magistrates when leaving office.[235]

231. Herodian 4.11.9, on which see Peter 1897, 1.362–364. Whittaker comments that the *sententia* is "apparently adapted from a line of poetry" (in his note *ad loc.*). Compare 7.1.8 (quoted above in n. 229). Dio reported similar difficulties in the Senate regarding the truth content of letters from Trajan and Severus (68.29.1–3 and 75.7.3).

232. *Hist.* fr. 50.

233. *Hist.* fr. 66.2.

234. For recent treatments with full bibliographies see Portmann 1988 and Nixon and Rodgers 1994, 26–33 and *passim*.

235. Von Premerstein, *RE* s.v. *commentarius*, cols. 731–737, 757–759. See, for example, Cicero's reaction to Caesar's *commentarii: Tum Brutus: . . . Compluris autem legi atque etiam commentarios, quos idem scripsit rerum suarum. Valde quidem, inquam, probandos; nudi enim sunt, recti et venusti, omni ornatu orationis tamquam veste detracta. Sed dum voluit alios habere parata, unde sumerent qui vellent scribere historiam, ineptis gratum fortasse fecit, qui illa volent calamistris inurere: sanos quidem homines a scribendo deterruit; nihil est enim in historia pura et inlustri brevitate dulcius (Brut.* 75.262; cf. *Ep. ad Att.* 1.19.10). See also Lucian *Hist. conscr.* 16: ἄλλος δέ τις αὐτῶν ὑπόμνημα τῶν γεγονότων γυμνὸν συναγαγὼν ἐν γραφῇ κομιδῇ πεζὸν καὶ χαμαιπετές, οἷον καὶ στρατιώτης ἄν . . . τὰ καθ' ἡμέραν ὑπογραφόμενος συνέθηκεν. Compare Eunapius on the *hypomnemata* of Oribasius (fr. 15). Pliny the Elder used the *commentarii* of Corbulo in writing his history, and

Second, we should not expect that every panegyric, on every occasion, "*announce*[*d*] imperial programmes and policies."[236] It remains possible, however, to identify political expedients that drove the content of even the least contemporary of panegyrics, that of Nazarius in Rome in 321, whose information is so often targeted as out of date.[237] Nazarius concentrated primarily on Constantine's rescue of Rome from the tyrant Maxentius a decade earlier and did so, one might argue, to remind the senators of the debt they owed to Constantine at a time when he was already preparing to leave Rome at his back and march on Licinius.

Students of the Latin panegyrics have, as whole, neglected evidence from the Greek East, although the great Greek orators of that age—Himerius, Themistius, and Libanius—have bequeathed to us a corpus that dwarfs the Latin one. Himerius described the function of the orator in service of the *gubernator imperii* as that of a mediator, conveying the needs of the people to their emperor and explaining the edicts of the emperor to his people.[238] In addition to his speeches, we possess from Libanius a vast corpus of letters, some of which discuss his public career. His letters reveal, for example, that he expected emperors and imperial officials to supply him with raw material for his panegyrics: he wrote to Julian and Rufinus requesting information well ahead of drafting his texts.[239] Of course, such news need not come only through official channels: for example, Libanius solicited *commentarii* from one Philagrius, an officer in Julian's army:[240]

> I suppose that you look down on me, since you have recorded the story of the campaign and know that sophists will have to approach you when they want to refer to its events; for I am told that you examine and put into writing every particular, the nature of the localities, the dimensions of cities, height of fortresses, width of rivers, and all successes and reverses. . . . As for my feelings about what you have written, they are as follows: I will no more ask you to read

---

supplemented his information with *commentarii* by a certain Licinius Mucianus (Peter, *HRR* 2.101–107) and by Marius Celsus (on the history of Pliny see Syme 1958, 297, and Townend 1964, 473–474; on Marius Celsus in particular, see Syme 1958, app. 32). Tacitus was able to supplement Pliny for the year 69 with the testimony of the tribune Vipstanus Messalla (*Hist.* 3.25.2; see Syme 1958, 172, 177, and 180), and in writing the *Agricola* may well have used the *commentarii* of Suetonius Paulinus (Peter, *HRR* 2.101). Lucius Verus supplied to Fronto material from his own correspondence and directed his generals Avidius Cassius and Martius Verus to write *commentarii*, which he would forward to Fronto (*Ep. ad Verum imperatorem* 2.3.1).

236. Nixon 1983, 91; cf. Warmington 1974.

237. E.g., by Nixon 1983, 91–93; cf. MacCormack 1975a, 167, and Nixon and Rodgers 1994, 29.

238. *Or.* 14.28–30.

239. See *Epp.* 760 and 1106.

240. *Ep.* 1434.2, 4 (trans. Norman, modified).

them than you ask me to lend you my ears. You will inform me of the bare facts; I will dress them in the robes of rhetoric.

In other letters he told Julian that he intended to attach a copy of the emperor's letter to the published text of a panegyric, and he elsewhere referred repeatedly to the arrival in Antioch of news regarding Julian's campaign.[241] In promising to append Julian's letter to his own panegyric, Libanius draws our attention to a vast, unexplored means by which such information could pass to other cities: that is, through the distribution of panegyrics. Libanius, for example, reported that a panegyric by Themistius had been distributed around Antioch,[242] and the Gallic orator Pacatus explicitly boasted that his panegyric would inform ranks of *literati:* "Distant cities will flock to me; every pen will receive from me the story of your exploits in due order; from me poetry will get its themes; from me history will derive its credibility." In short, Pacatus will equip those whose texts will be read in subsequent generations.[243]

Reliance on official documents for information ultimately shaped the development of historiography under the empire. It did so in ways that have struck earlier scholars as unexpected. Thus Eusebius has often received credit for introducing the explicit quotation of proceedings and legislation into historiographical writing.[244] His innovation is simply one of scale. As we have seen, Polybius quoted freely from documentary texts, as did Livy— and where Livy did not have the actual text, he simply fabricated its content in the style of Republican legislation.[245] In this practice Polybius and Livy put their faith in documentary texts, as revealing *one* truth about the past. As the bureaucracy of Rome invaded the mechanics of daily life, it became possible to view interactions with that bureaucracy as at least one narrative of the past, a narrative that subsequent generations could construct out of the government's own notarized records. Eusebius thus simply followed the martyrologists in viewing the history of his institution as the history of its interaction with the government of Rome. Nor were Christians innovators in that respect, either: the pagan *Acta Alexandrinorum,* whether in its early or its late recensions—that is, whether close to or distant from the form of the dry records of proceedings from which they all ultimately derive—had established the currency of such a historical self-awareness. Certainly within Eusebius's lifetime the scribes charged with recording such proceedings

241. See *Epp.* 758.4, 802, 1220.8, 1402, 1426, and 1434.

242. *Ep.* 818.

243. *Pan. Lat.* XII(2).47.6 (trans. Nixon and Rodgers).

244. Momigliano 1963, 88–91. Among recent studies see Av. Cameron 1983, Chestnut 1986, and Barnes 1989, esp. 97, 110–114.

245. See *RS* I p. 29.

had the Greek title "official writers of the *commentarii*" (e.g.,'Ολύμπιος κομενταρήσιος ὀφφικιάλιος ἐξέδωκα τὰ ὑπομνήματα), in wording that betrays the title's Roman origin.[246]

In fact, earlier Christian Latin writers had universally assented to the truth value of imperial documents. Tertullian, for example, insisted that *cognitiones* before Pontius Pilate—that is, oral proceedings conducted through rapid-fire exchange (*stipulatio*) and recorded verbatim—had rendered a truthful account of the missionary work of Christ to Tiberius and the Senate at Rome.[247] About a decade later, if we believe the chronology of Eusebius, on the other side of the empire, Apollonius of Ephesus wrote a treatise denouncing Montanism. Having attacked briefly one Alexander for pretending to be a Christian, Apollonius reminded his audience, should it wish to know more, that it had the "public archives of Asia" at its disposal.[248] Similarly, Cyprian and his fellow bishops regarded as conclusive the testimony of Martialis of Emerita that had been recorded in a proceeding before a ducenarian procurator.[249] At approximately the same time, Dionysius of Alexandria wrote an account of the trials conducted in Alexandria by Aemilianus. Having begun his account on his own authority, he then validated his narrative by quoting directly from the *acta* recorded at his trial.[250] At almost the same time, in Smyrna, in Asia Minor, the priest Pionius was arrested and put on trial at the arrival of the proconsul Julius Proculus Quintilianus. The preserved narrative of his martyrdom, like the more sophisticated account by Dionysius, makes specific reference to the *commentarii* recorded by stenographers during the proceedings.[251] In fact, the acts of the Christian martyrs everywhere preserve, both implicitly and explicitly, the testimony of official proceedings, as well as testimonials to the accuracy of those proceedings.[252]

---

246. See *P. Oxy.* X 1204.25–26.

247. Tertullian *Apol.* 5.2 and 21.24, and cf. *Coron.* 1.

248. Apollonius at Eusebius *Hist. eccl.* 5.18.9: καὶ οἱ θέλοντες μαθεῖν τὰ κατ' αὐτὸν ἔχουσιν τὸ τῆς Ἀσίας δημόσιον ἀρχεῖον.

249. Cyprian *Ep.* 67.6: *actis etiam publice habitis apud procuratorem ducenarium obtemperasse se idololatriae et Christum negasse contestatus sit.* See also *Ep.* 77.2, in which several disciples praise Cyprian for having shown what they ought to say *apud praesidem . . . prior apud acta proconsulis pronuntiasti.* See also Pontius *Vita Cypriani* 11.1: *et quid sacerdos Dei proconsule interrogante responderit, sunt acta quae referant.*

250. Dionysius of Alexandria at Eusebius *Hist. eccl.* 7.11.6: Αὐτῶν δὲ ἐπακούσατε τῶν ἀμφοτέρων λεχθέντων ὡς ὑπεμνηματίσθη.

251. *Acta Pionii* 19.1, on which see Robert 1994, 105–107.

252. Cf. Wilcken 1894; von Premerstein, *RE* s.v. *cognitio;* and Bisbee 1988, with full bibliography. J. Geffcken argued with characteristic forcefulness against the historicity of the martyr acts and, therefore, against their derivation from official *commentarii* (1906, and cf. 1910), but he represents a distinct minority opinion on this issue. See also Chapter 9 at nn. 113–116 and "The Faith of Fifty Million People."

Eusebius, of course, acknowledged that he based portions of his history on martyrologies that he himself had edited, but he did not explicitly defend that practice or the content of those works.[253] Much later in life Eusebius drafted, then reworked, a text that became a biography of Constantine. The rewriting process involved, among other things, the insertion of verbatim quotations of official documents.[254] At the first such quotation, Eusebius justified his practice on several grounds:[255]

> It seems to me advisable to insert the text of the letter here, since it is related to the present topic, so that it might survive in the interest of history and be protected for our posterity, and also so that the quotation of the edict might confirm the truth of my narrative. The text is quoted from an authenticated copy of the imperial edict preserved in my possession, on which the personal subscription, by Constantine's right hand, signifies its testimony to the trustworthiness of my speech like some sort of seal.

Eusebius offered the text as the guarantor of the truth of his narrative, and in turn guaranteed the reliability of that text by reference to its status as an authenticated copy. He thus located its truth value in the administrative processes of the imperial government, which both produced authenticated documents and honored their contents. In this Eusebius acted no differently than the author of the *Historia Augusta,* although the latter cheated his audience's faith in such documents with a fabrication.[256] Eusebius, of course, wrote in earnest. In his faith in authenticated documents as carriers of true knowledge about history, Eusebius thus wrote not as a Christian, but as a Roman.

---

253. *Hist. eccl.* 5 *pr.* 2.

254. On the genuineness of Eusebius's citations see A. H. M. Jones 1974, 257–262. On the writing of the *Vita Constantini* see Barnes 1989. As an introduction to Eusebius and his view of Constantine, Baynes 1931 remains unsurpassed.

255. Eusebius *Vit. Const.* 2.23.

256. *SHA Tyr. trig.* 10.9.

CHAPTER FIVE

Consensus in Theory and Practice

ROMAN EMPERORS AND PUBLIC OPINION

Authenticated texts defined relations between peripheral entities and the central power on a continuum that included a vast but definable set of fellow participants in the community of the empire; they did so by concretizing discrete moments in a historical narrative in which local collectivities of every sort were slowly subsumed within a greater whole. Indeed, the very existence of those texts constituted a peculiar and uniquely powerful form of propaganda.[1] We need not assume, however, that the emperors of Rome dispatched them with an eye on their cumulative effect. On the contrary: their authors focused their attention firmly on the issue of the moment, whether it was a recent imperial victory or an act of the emperor's benevolent foresight. As we shall see, the arrival of such texts demanded a response, an expression of the community's consensual and unanimous commitment to the order established, embodied, and maintained by these texts and their authors. Romans called this consensual commitment *consensus*.[2] The reality of its unanimity need not concern us here; in so large an empire, in which communication was so difficult, our interest must be in people's belief in that unanimity.

Emperors possessed various means to achieve and give formal expression to *consensus*, each suited to carry a distinct message to a different audience. An autobiography, for example, achieved its ideological work at a different speed, before a different audience, than did the announcement that a

---

1. See Chapter 4, "Habermas and Rome."

2. As Instinsky 1940 has emphasized, Romans regarded *consensus* as perforce universal and unanimous.

prince of the *domus divina* had assumed the *toga virilis*. The disparate messages of imperial propaganda—superficially distracting in their numbers and diversity—ultimately reinforced one another through their shared articulation of the legitimating principles of emperor and empire. We must understand the nature of these messages both in their myriad forms and in their universal, and universalizing, appeal. Above all, we must appreciate that no communication between center and periphery existed in isolation: benefactions demanded thanks, and, as each local collectivity advertised its loyalty and gratitude, so each placed a burden on other, parallel collectivities to do the same. Our inquiry, therefore, has to place each text within a concrete historical situation to see how it invoked its audience's obedience to the ruling order.

The cities of Asia, for example, whose expenditures "as often as cheerful news arrived from Rome" Paullus Fabius Persicus sought to restrain, could be considered parallel collectivities.[3] We are, of course, in no position to assess the sincerity of those cities or of their citizens. But their actions are intelligible on a variety of levels. Roman power had, of course, restricted the autonomy of Greek cities throughout the East, and in so doing had constrained the scope for action in the traditional rivalry of cities.[4] Where cities could compete—indeed, where the fact of Roman power required them to compete—was in the contest for Roman esteem: a contest conducted through behavior and language, and drawing upon sentiments and aspirations, that were themselves long familiar. If, prior to the coming of Rome, Ephesus had boasted its preeminence in Asia, in the late first century A.D. it measured and advertised its preeminence by the tokens of Roman favor. Ephesus won by adapting its traditional ambitions to a new political reality, in which Ephesus and Ephesian history flourished in the orbit of a higher power.[5]

The actions of Publius Cornelius Scipio in the first decade of this era probably inspired the type of excess that provoked Persicus. As quaestor in Achaea with propraetorian authority in A.D. 2, Scipio learned that Gaius Caesar had escaped injury while fighting barbarians "for the salvation of all men" (ὑπὲρ τᾶς ἀνθρώπων πάντων σωτηρίας). "Overjoyed at this excellent news" (ὑπερχαρὴς ὢν ἐπὶ ταῖς ἀρίσταις ἀγγελίαις), he instructed everyone to wear wreaths and to take a holiday; he himself performed sacrifices and

---

3. On Fabius Persicus and his action see Chapter 4 at n. 196.
4. See Chapter 3 at nn. 28–30.
5. On Ephesus and the imperial cult in particular, see Friesen 1993; on the accommodation of Ephesian past and Roman present in civic space and cult, see Rogers 1991. Cf. Walker 1997: under Roman rule, cities in the East developed their agoras simultaneously in two ways, as centers for religious activity, in which the emperor and his family were deeply implicated, and as repositories for the monuments and memory of the city's legendary past.

financed theatrical celebrations "to rival those of the past."[6] The city of Messene honored Scipio for his enthusiasm and his expenditure, and we can easily understand the city's action in traditional terms and thus construe its decree as Scipio's reward for his generous funding of a festival.[7] But the currents of meaning run still deeper, because no one can have failed to know that Scipio was inspired by news concerning Roman victories over distant enemies or that the festival was dedicated to that most manifest god, the emperor Augustus. Lucius Sestius, the imperial legate in Spain immediately following Augustus's campaigns there, sent a similar message to the Astyreans when he dedicated three altars to the name of Augustus on the local shoreline: these "distinguished a previously unremarkable territory."[8] Like the villagers of Beth Phouraia, the citizens of Messene must have watched Roman magistrates with care. Like Julius Priscus, Scipio wielded great power within his province—and Messene's honorific decree testifies to its citizens' awareness of his power. But his lavish display of loyalty, resembling so closely the veneration of imperial edicts, may have revealed to his viewers something of the distance that separated Scipio from his master, a distance so vast that it encouraged the Messenians to follow his example even as it erased the distance between Scipio and themselves.[9]

Insofar as these cities found themselves iterating the principles of the ruling order, we might be tempted to regard them as ideological state apparatuses. But the application of that term would not explain their actions; as we have seen, the personification of institutions and collectivities involves historical fallacies on multiple levels. Rather, the actions of individuals, as of cities, become intelligible once their relations to existing forms of action are rendered transparent. Thus, for example, the concentration of power, first in Rome, and later in the person of the *princeps*, shifted the standards by which power and esteem were measured, but did not require cities or individuals to abandon their desire for either, as it did not fundamentally alter the means by which those goals might be attained. What the city of Messene made clear, in honoring Scipio for honoring Gaius, was that the new standards were obedience to, indeed enthusiasm for, the emperor of Rome. Messene, Ephesus, and hundreds of other cities now watched for news from Rome and used it as justification for expressing their obedience more eloquently or more extravagantly than their neighbors. As with individuals juggling commitments to varied intersecting collectivities, so the in-

---

6. *SEG* XXIII 206.

7. For this type of reading, see Lendon 1997, 176–236.

8. Pomponius Mela 3.13; cf. Pliny *Nat.* 4.111.

9. Compare the sentiment of M. Terentius: *non est nostrum aestimare, quem supra ceteros et quibus de causis extollas: tibi summum rerum indicium di dedere, nobis obsequii gloria relicta est* (Tacitus *Ann.* 6.8.4).

cessant rhythms of communicative action distracted the cities of Asia from recognizing common interest against Rome. Instead, they viewed each other in the first instance as united only in competition for the benefactions of their common master. When Messene thus honored Scipio, or Ephesus advertised its centrality to imperial cult, it had already surrendered to the culture of loyalism that became the most characteristic feature of political life in the Roman world.[10]

The insinuation of new meanings into traditional diplomatic forms took time, and its success in the Roman empire rested in large measure on the person and longevity of Augustus. We have been cautioned not to overemphasize the originality of eastern reactions to Actium: Greek cities knew how to greet the new ruler of the world.[11] But if the format of these exchanges was familiar, their ideological content changed profoundly during the Augustan period. From his arrival in Rome following the murder of his adoptive father, Augustus had sought the loyalty of Caesar's clientele on the basis of his status as son and heir. The next few years witnessed several redefinitions of his constitutional position and the universalization of his clientele, even as the site and source of his unique appeal—his charisma—shifted from his status as *divi filius* to his own person.[12] That shift had profound consequences. No one disputed the charisma of Caesar, and thus Octavian's strength, however derivative, remained inviolable. The charisma of Augustus, on the other hand, required continual validation, and he exploited the mechanics of Hellenistic diplomacy to create opportunities for his subjects to affirm his appeal: Augustus informed provincials of his accomplishments and family affairs, and he expected them to respond with displays of unanimous support. Augustus, of course, did not lack the approval of his subjects, and that allowed an easy solution: he could leave it to them "to devise formulations of acceptance." The principles that legitimized Augustus and the Augustan system were thus, in large measure, the creation of those whom Augustus had ostensibly disenfranchised, and "a product of tacit collusion."[13] The readiness of his contemporaries to acknowledge his greatness allowed the development and routinization of these vehicles of *consensus* to pass unnoticed. Each iteration of this process encouraged provincials to reestablish their relationship with their emperor, to reenact their acknowledgment of his unique charisma, and thus to flatter themselves that their perception of that charisma had played a role in em-

---

10. For the phrase and much instruction on this topic, I am indebted to Rowe 1997.

11. Millar 1984, 37–38.

12. For three different approaches to this complex process, see Gagé 1936, Grant 1946, and Taeger 1960, 89–225.

13. Cf. Syme 1986, 441.

powering him in the first place. And if the active *consensus* of the ruled empowered the ruler, so the regular affirmation of that *consensus* sustained their subjugation.

The easy commerce of classical rhetoric and the stability of the Augustan regime mask the dangers with which the system itself was fraught. In any such dance, one party can lose the beat, and the ballet, to the outside observer at once intricate and effortless, will devolve into an obvious and graceless burlesque. As Pierre Bourdieu has remarked about the tempo of ritual gift exchange, "the passage from the highest probability to absolute certainty is a qualitative leap which is not proportionate to the numerical gap."[14] Augustus would discover, for example, that he could not simply display his adopted heir Gaius to the eastern provinces: the rituals of diplomatic exchange allowed the cities of the East to select their own candidate, and many chose Tiberius, the Hellenist scion of the Claudian line.[15]

The communicative actions that sustained and spread this culture of loyalism did far more than create and advertise *consensus*. Documents invoking *consensus* rarely claimed to represent the will of the entire world; rather, they purported to represent the will of particular groups. In so doing, these documents created rifts within the general population, divided its loyalties, and allowed it to express its unity only when expressing its commitment to the established order.[16] The drawing of new political boundaries in the East is thus mirrored by the division and distraction of populations within cities. This process is, of course, most visible at Rome. The creation of *consensus* there required skill in the manipulation of both message and medium. Communicating with a select body of highly educated and privileged men in the Senate required different skills, different media, and a different message than did interacting with plebeians at Rome, with Italy at large, or with provincial populations. Adopting a mental geography like that of *principes* at Rome, we shall watch information spread in concentric circles away from Rome, noting at each stage how invoking other parties' *consensus* creates pressure for further parties to do the same. Each party to these communicative actions thus competed to claim its own special responsibility for upholding the normative script.

Two events from the late second and early third centuries illustrate well the distinctions drawn by emperors between their various constituencies. For example, educated men of the governing class, not least among them authors of political oratory and contemporary history, needed information

14. Bourdieu 1977, 9. Compare Schechner 1987, 10: "Human performance is paradoxical, a practiced fixedness founded on pure contingency."
15. Bowersock 1984.
16. Cf. Nock 1972, 354, and Ostrow 1990, 368–373 and 376–377.

to give order to their works and their worlds. Most emperors also understood how to use information to shape the contours of political loyalties around the empire. They were, therefore, only too happy to supply products of the imperial pen. This was especially true in moments of crisis, when men challenged each other for the throne or when seemingly unhappy circumstances required an appropriate explanation. This is certainly how Aurelius Victor construed the events that followed the murder of Geta:[17]

> But [Severus's] children, as if under orders to make war on each other, immediately suffered a falling out. Thus Geta, whose name came from his paternal grandfather, was beset and died because his brother was offended by his more moderate nature. This victory was made more shameful by the death of Papinian, at least in the eyes of eager scholars of the past, since they maintain that he was in charge of Caracalla's secretariat at the time and was ordered, as is customary [*uti mos est*], to compose as quickly as possible a news release intended for Rome. In his grief over Geta, Papinian is said to have responded that it was scarcely so easy to disguise parricide as it was to commit it, and for this reason he was killed.

The *Historia Augusta* contains a similar version of this story, along with a further lament for Papinian, that "sanctuary of law and treasure house of jurisprudence."[18]

Caracalla cannot have expected Papinian's prose to reach and directly affect the populace at large. Like Nero after the murder of Agrippina, Caracalla required the literary efforts of a Seneca in conjunction with myriad messages of contrition and justification. Caracalla could easily have learned these techniques from his father, Severus, who exploited all possible avenues of self-advertisement in times both good and bad: "After the good fortune of his victory [over the Parthians in the winter of A.D. 197/198], Severus dispatched a report to the Senate and the people, making much of his achievements, and ordering that his battles and victories should be painted and publicly exhibited."[19] The desire of Severus to communicate with the people was natural: throughout the Principate the emperor maintained a special relationship with the plebs at Rome.[20] In the early third century this relationship required no explanation, and Herodian, who provided this report on the activities of Severus, has merely noted that an emperor employed different media, in part presuming upon different levels of literacy, when communicating with several hundred senators than he did when boasting before thousands of plebeians.

17. Aurelius Victor *Hist.* 20.32–33.
18. *SHA Severus* 21.8 (trans. Magie); cf. *Carac.* 8.4–8.
19. Herodian 3.9.12 (trans. Whittaker).
20. Yavetz 1969; cf. A. D. E. Cameron 1976, 157–192; Wallace-Hadrill 1990, 164–165, and Griffin 1991.

Emperors continued to address different messages to different, overlapping audiences throughout the history of the empire. Indeed, to the extent that the Principate created and fostered stability in municipalities throughout Italy and the Mediterranean world, credit is largely due to the ability of Augustus and his heirs to establish close rapports with different sectors of the population, and with the population at large.[21] In time there would come emperors who passed their entire reigns without seeing Rome; in time other capitals would arise. But Rome remained conceptually important, and, *if* her prestige waned in the third century, the foundation of Constantinople may only have emphasized the unique stature of the true City.[22] In writing the history of Roman imperial cult, as of the development of Byzantine political theology, scholars have traditionally emphasized the influence of Hellenistic practice and thought on the ceremonial and ideology of the Roman imperial office.[23] The effect of these trends has been a general neglect of the continuity of the peculiarly Roman idiom that informed the dialogue between the *princeps* and his fellow Roman citizens.[24]

For example, paintings of the sort ordered by Severus traditionally formed part of a Roman triumph.[25] Severus thus exploited a conventional medium within a uniquely Roman ceremony because he understood the need to inform Rome about his activities in spite of his inability to be in Rome himself. This same need existed for usurpers: as soon as someone tried to become emperor somewhere other than at Rome, he needed to inform the urban population, of all ranks, about his efforts. In armed competition for the throne, candidates zealously displayed to Rome their respect for the City and its populace, or risked their rivals' staking the better claim for its favors.[26] Paradoxically, therefore, claiming the throne from somewhere other than Rome obligated the claimant to behave as if he were at Rome, lest Rome fear a new tyrant from the East. Herodian felt certain that such had been the aim of Gordian following his acclamation:[27]

21. See Chapter 2 at n. 160; cf. Versnel 1980; D'Arms 1981, 121–148; Campbell 1984; and Eck 1993, 201.

22. MacCormack 1975a, 142–143, and 1981, 39–41. See also Bréhier 1915, Beck 1980, and Dagron 1984, 48–76.

23. On imperial cult see Cerfaux and Tondriau 1956, 277. This position provides the foundation for "political" interpretations of imperial cult, which stress the role of cult in diplomatic relations between Greeks and their Roman emperor: see Habicht 1970, and cf. Charlesworth 1935 and Bowersock 1965, 112–121, and *idem* 1982a. On Byzantine political theology see Dagron 1996, citing earlier work; on its Hellenistic antecedents see Walbank at *CAH*² VII.1 62–100.

24. Two notable exceptions are Béranger 1953 and MacCormack 1981; cf. McCormick 1986, 1–34.

25. Chapter 7, "The Art of Victory."

26. Cf. Chapter 6 at nn. 40–45 on the activities of Niger and Severus.

27. Herodian 7.6.1–2.

For a few days Gordian remained at Thysdrus, where the events had taken place, by this time with the title and style of emperor. Then he left Thysdrus and marched to Carthage, the largest and most heavily populated city, as Gordian knew, so that he could act exactly as if he were in Rome. That city is next after Rome in wealth, population, and size, though there is rivalry for second place between it and Alexandria in Egypt. With him went the whole imperial escort, the soldiers stationed there and the tallest young men in the city acting like the bodyguard in Rome. The fasces were garlanded with laurel, a sign that distinguishes an emperor from an ordinary man, and fire was carried before him in procession, so that for a short time the city of Carthage was a kind of replica of Rome in its prosperous appearance.

This behavior, though directed in large measure at an audience at Rome, had the additional and salutary effect of creating "Roman" audiences in urban centers throughout the empire. There also existed a tendency among Roman officials, whether emperors or governors, to behave everywhere as if at Rome, because that is what they knew; and continual exposure to the instruments of Roman power thus created a population familiar with, and ready to interpret, the symbols of its authority.

AUGUSTUS AS AUGUSTAN AUTHOR

In his influence on contemporary literature and his efforts as an author, as in so many other areas of imperial life, Augustus proved both paradigm and nonpareil.[28] His *Res gestae* has generated an enormous scholarly bibliography, not least for a deceptive stylistic simplicity that masks profound debts to Ciceronian diction and rhythm—learned, perhaps, from close readings of his father's *Commentarii*.[29] Nevertheless, the *Res gestae* misleads by its very omnipresence in modern scholarship, for Augustus was alone among Roman emperors in writing such a document to boast of his successes after death: others staked less comprehensive, but more immediate, claims on the historiographical record.[30] Augustus also had many other and more subtle devices in his arsenal. Three such devices—his autobiography of 22 B.C., his epistles to provinces, and his inventories of the state—may stand for all, exposing their differing claims to authority, their artful exploitation of Re-

28. On Augustus and Augustan culture, Syme 1939, 459–475, is classic. *Idem* 1986, 64–81 and 439–454, are remarkable for their concision and insight. For more discursive treatments, see White 1993, 110–205, or Galinsky 1996, the banality of his essay on *auctoritas* notwithstanding. The absence of Augustus as an author from J. D. Thomas's survey of Julio-Claudian literature surprises, given that emperors generally, and Augustus in particular, demonstrably had what Thomas denies to Horace and Seneca, "even [a] slight chance of exercising serious influence on the society to which they belonged" (*CAH*[2] X 905–929 at 929).

29. Béranger 1975, 245.

30. Peter 1897, 1.372–377, surveys the production of "pamphlet-literature" by emperors and the imperial court.

publican antecedents, and their varied effects on contemporary perceptions of Rome, its emperor, and its geography. We may emerge less overwhelmed by the *Res gestae*, but we acquire thereby greater esteem for the influence wielded by emperors in their own time.

Augustus had anticipated the *Res gestae* with at least two autobiographical essays. One of those was a much more substantial document, an autobiography in thirteen books. According to Suetonius, it described his life down to the conclusion of the Cantabrian War.[31] That description masks its real purpose: an apologia in a period marked by several crises, both personal and public. Augustus had returned from Spain in the spring of 24 B.C. in ill health. At Rome he encountered problems that even the devoted diligence of modern scholarship has not disentangled. Augustus had attempted to settle his constitutional position within the Roman state in 27 B.C. and had departed shortly thereafter for Gaul and Spain. He no doubt hoped that his absence would allow a slow accommodation to his continued hegemony while avoiding the friction that his exercise of power at Rome might engender.[32] Yet despite his aims, he had created a frightened and dangerously sycophantic Senate. After Augustus departed Rome, the actions of his friend and prefect of Egypt, Cornelius Gallus, forced him to renounce their friendship in a formal letter to the Senate.[33] That body received his missive as a call to action: it indicted Gallus on many charges, voting unanimously that he should be convicted in the courts, that his property should be given to Augustus, and that the Senate should make a sacrifice of oxen.[34] When Gallus committed suicide and spared the regime an embarrassing prosecution, Augustus could afford to lament that he alone was not permitted to be angry with his friends.[35]

Augustus had left the city in 27 while occupying the consulate, and he

---

31. Suetonius *Augustus* 85.1. Fragments and testimonia collected in Malcovati[5] and in Peter, *HRR* 2.54–64. On its content, aims, and date, Blumenthal 1913 and 1914 remain essential.

32. On the settlement of 27 see Brunt and Moore 1967, 8–12; Kienast 1982a, 71–84; or Crook at *CAH*[2] X 78–79.

33. Jerome places the event in the fall of 27: *Cornelius Gallus Foroiuliensis poeta, a quo primum Aegyptum rectam supra diximus, XLIII aetatis suae anno propria se manu interficit.* Syme 1939, 309–310, surveys the sources; the subsequent bibliography is vast. For the formal ending of a friendship before the Senate compare Tacitus *Ann.* 3.12.2 and 6.29.2; Suetonius *Augustus* 66.1–2 and *Gramm.* 16.1–2; and Dio 53.23.4–7; and see Bauman 1974, 109–113. On the activities of Gallus in Egypt see Koenen and Thompson 1984 and Raaflaub and Samons 1990.

34. Dio 53.24.6–7. The sacrifice, probably for the *salus,* or in gratitude for the *providentia,* of Augustus, suggests that Gallus was regarded as a *hostis publicus* and charged with *maiestas.* (Cf. *EJ* nos. 51 and 52: dedications after the execution of Sejanus.) On this use of *maiestas,* which requires a conceptual identification of Rome and emperor, see Chapter 3 at n. 81, Chapter 7 at nn. 58–61 and 127–135, and Chapter 9, "The Discovery of Roman Religion."

35. Suetonius *Augustus* 66.2.

continued in that office throughout his stay in Gaul and his campaigns in Spain. He had also arranged the appointment of Marcus Valerius Messalla Corvinus as the first *praefectus urbi;* Corvinus held the office for six days and laid it down, pleading ignorance of the function of the office or, more pointedly, that it was an unconstitutional magistracy.[36] Corvinus may have sensed a trap: as a representative of Augustus, he would diminish the authority of the other consul—Statilius Taurus, who was still present in Rome—while lending the dignity of his name to a constitutional novelty. Augustus suffered from ill health throughout his peregrinations and returned in that condition in 24. Soon afterward, Aulus Terentius Varro Murena, the consul-designate, died prior to assuming office.[37] Very shortly thereafter, the dead man's brother by adoption, Lucius Licinius Varro Murena, conspired against Augustus. L. Varro Murena may have been legate in Syria at this time, in command of an army, or the commander may simply have been another relative. The sources preclude certainty.[38] In any event the machinery of the state was set in motion against the conspirators Fannius Caepio and Lucius Varro Murena: "Destroyed on the authority of the state, they suffered at the hands of the law what they had wished to accomplish by violence."[39] The state of the *fasti* has permitted cynical reflection on the power of Augustus to control contemporary record keeping; in any event, "the credit of the government was not enhanced by the fate of Murena and Caepio."[40]

To review these events in order: Augustus lost a consul-designate; having substituted Gnaeus Piso for Varro Murena, he himself fell sick and learned of widespread expectations that he appoint a successor. He did not. He delivered his signet ring to Agrippa, and to Piso a list of the forces and revenues of the state.[41] When he recovered, he laid down the consulate and redefined his powers.[42] He then learned of the conspiracy and had to kill two prominent men—presumably on a charge of *maiestas*.[43] Augustus was

---

36. Tacitus *Ann.* 6.11.3, and Jerome *Chron.* s.a. 26: *Messala Corvinus primus praefectus urbi factus sexto die magistratu se abdicavit incivilem potestatem esse contestans.* For the date see Syme 1939, 403, and *idem* 1986, 212. For concise analysis of the episode see Gibbon chapter 17 (1.611–612).

37. Kienast 1982a, 86–87, reviews the facts and cites earlier scholarship, among which Swan 1966 and Sumner 1978 remain valuable.

38. Dio 53.25 and Velleius 2.91, with Woodman's note *ad locum.* Josephus mentions the legate in Syria but calls him simply Varro (*Bell. Iud.* 1.398; *Ant. Iud.* 15.345). See Syme 1939, 333–336, and *idem* 1986, 40 and 387–393.

39. Velleius 2.91.2.

40. Syme 1986, 393.

41. Dio 53.30.1–2.

42. Brunt and Moore 1967, 10–16, or Kienast 1982a, 87–92.

43. If that is what Velleius means by *publica auctoritate* (2.91.2). That interpretation is strongly supported by the public *supplicatio* voted "as if for a victory" (Dio 54.3.8, on which see Freyburger 1978).

no fool. The conspiracy between the Caesarian Varro Murena and the Republican Caepio bore an unmistakable resemblance to the unlikely bedfellows who had freed the state from the dictatorship of Caesar. The popular belief that he would name a successor revealed the cause of the conspirators' dissatisfaction, and in the voting at the conspirators' trial—in absentia—some senators voted for acquittal.[44] Augustus therefore entered the Senate and tried to read his will, to show that he had named no successor in it, either.[45]

Augustus recognized the need for corrective measures. His long absence from the city had not had the effect that he desired. He now penned his autobiography to remind people of the reasons for their gratitude and their loyalty. In it Augustus emerges as obsessed with the issues that preoccupied his triumviral propaganda: he expatiated at length on the origins of his family, and in that context on his special relationship to Venus; nor did he forget to recall the comet that had carried his father's spirit to be received among the *numina* of the immortal gods.[46] Against the glories of Caesar, Augustus set the treason of Antony: that man, he wrote, had ordered his legions to watch over Cleopatra and to obey her nod and her command.[47] There can then be no doubt wherein lay Vergil's inspiration for his panegyric to Augustus, at the close of his *ecphrasis* of the shield:[48]

Here Augustus Caesar leads Italy into battle,
with senators and people and gods of hearth and state;
he stands on the lofty stern; his joyful temples
blow forth twin flames; on his crest shines his father's star.[49]

. . . .

Antony stands opposite, with barbarian aid and sundry arms,
a conqueror from the nations of the East and the Red Sea;
he drags with him Egypt and eastern men and furthest Bactra;
and his Egyptian wife—ah, unspeakable crime!—follows after.

44. Dio 54.3.5–6.
45. Dio 53.31.1. If Gagé 1982, 620, is right to trust Plutarch, *Comp. Demosth. cum Cic.* 3, that Augustus addressed the autobiography to Maecenas and Agrippa, the preface may have explained his position to his most public friends and most likely heirs.
46. The Julian family: Peter, *HRR* fr. 1 (Malcovati[5] fr. III = Suetonius *Augustus* 2 [compare 94]). The comet: Peter, *HRR* frr. 4 (Malcovati[5] fr. VI = Pliny *Nat.* 2.92–93) and 5 (Malcovati[5] fr. VII = Servius at *Buc.* 9.46).
47. The duty to avenge Caesar: Nicolaus of Damascus fr. 28; cf. Horace *Carm.* 1.2.41–44. Antony and Cleopatra: Peter, *HRR* fr. 14 (Malcovati[5] fr. XVI = Servius at *Aen.* 8.696). Malcovati compares Servius at *Aen.* 8.678. Augustus also produced a full narrative of the Perusine War, including speeches that Appian found difficult to render in Greek (*Civ.* 5.191).
48. Vergil *Aen.* 8.678–681, 685–688. Servius thought that Augustus did, in fact, have the star depicted on his helmet (at *Aen.* 8.681).
49. Cf. Horace *Carm.* 1.12.46–48.

The repeated invocations of Caesar were surely intended to recall the promised passage of Caesar's charisma to Caesar's heir, and the narrative itself will surely have proved that this promise had been fulfilled.

At the same time, Augustus could scarcely afford to found a dynasty on competence, even extraordinary competence, in fulfillment of *pietas.* Caesar may have become a god, but he had also overthrown the Republic. The autobiography therefore also expounded at length Augustus's own achievements, and in particular on his successes during his recent campaigns in Spain. Augustus attempted thereby to establish his own, independent claim to that charisma whose sign and seal was victory in war. It is thus in the historiographic record of his Spanish campaigns that we can detect the autobiography's most pervasive influence.[50] When Augustus returned from the campaigns of 25, he advertised the end of the war: he was acclaimed *imperator* and closed the Temple of Janus.[51] But the war in Spain was hardly over, and, embarrassed by the subsequent successes of his legates in Spain, Augustus directed the Senate to award a triumph to Agrippa and declined for himself a further acclamation as *imperator.*[52] It may safely be assumed that the autobiography matched the symbolism of the closing of Janus: when he ended it with the Cantabrian War, we may infer that Augustus asserted the end of that war as well, and so all contemporary and near-contemporary sources loyally proclaimed. Velleius closed his description thus: "These, therefore, were the provinces, so extensive, so populous, and so warlike, that Caesar Augustus brought to such a condition of peace fifty years ago that, although they had never before been free of serious wars, under the governorship of C. Antistius and later P. Silius and then others, they were free even of brigandage."[53] Precise parallels in syntactical structure with panegyrics both contemporary and later confirm the suspicion that flattery, and not necessarily the truth, was the aim of history writing here, though it is no doubt also true that accurate information about conditions in Spain was hard to come by.[54] And Velleius was not alone in hailing the subjugation of the province. Horace greeted Augustus on his return as a new Hercules, and references in the extant portion of Livy's history suggest that he, too, believed or at least cooperated: Spain was the first of the continental provinces to be entered by the Romans, but the last to be subdued; that hap-

---

50. On these campaigns see Syme, *RP* 2.825–854 and *RP* 5.648–660, or Alföldy at *CAH²* X 449–455.

51. Orosius 6.21.11, very likely relying ultimately on Livy (so Syme, *RP* 5.649, and Arnaud-Lindet in her edition, appendix IV). See also Dio 53.26.1 and 5.

52. Dio 54.11.6; Barnes 1974, 21.

53. Velleius 2.90.4.

54. See Woodman *ad loc.*, citing Cicero *Leg. Man.* 31 and *Pan. Lat.* IV(8).13.1.

pened only in Livy's day, under the leadership and auspices of Augustus Caesar.[55]

Subsequent imperial autobiographies fall into roughly two categories, for which Augustus supplied useful precedents and which we may categorize as apologetic or boastful.[56] Yet we must recognize that even a brief text like the *Res gestae* of Augustus had a limited audience: inscribed on sheets of bronze and attached to his temples, it accomplished the majority of its ideological work not through its content as such, but through its magnificence as a physical monument to the achievements of his reign and thus, ultimately, as a bulwark of support for his heirs.[57]

Multivolume autobiographies reached a limited, educated audience, and they reached that audience slowly. Augustus wrote his autobiography to explain his position, his *statio,* to the governing class, with an eye to posterity. Augustus also needed to address broader audiences at Rome, in Italy, and in the provinces. For that task there were mechanisms already in place, or now being formalized, for the distribution of legal and administrative ordinances. Augustus exploited the attention given to such documents by attaching to them his own letters and addresses. For example, in the last decade of the first century B.C. Augustus and the Senate responded to several embassies from the cities of Cyrenaïca, requesting official clarification regarding the functioning and jurisdiction of local courts. In 5 B.C. Augustus himself forwarded a decree of the Senate on these matters to Cyrene and all the provinces, over which he affixed a cover letter:[58]

> Imperator Caesar Augustus, pontifex maximus, holding the tribunician power for the nineteenth time, writes: The *senatus consultum* passed when C. Calvisius and L. Passienus were consuls, with me present and participating in the writing, that pertains to the security of the allies of the Roman people, I decided

---

55. Horace *Carm.* 3.14.1–4; Livy 28.12.12, and cf. 1.19.3. See also Strabo 3.3.8, with Lassère 1982, 881–884, discussing Strabo's reading of Augustus's *Res gestae.*

56. Tiberius's *commentarius* explained his relations with Sejanus: Suetonius *Tiberius* 61. Vespasian, Titus, and Trajan wrote *commentarii* on their wars, supplying raw material for panegyrists and historians: Josephus *Vita* 341 and 358 and *Contra Apionem* 1.10; Priscian *Inst.* 6.13. Hadrian must have written soon after his accession, as the last secure fragment concerns the execution of the four consulars in the winter of 117/118 (*SHA Hadr.* 7.1–2), the arguments of Bollansée 1994 notwithstanding. Falsifying references to Hadrian's autobiography have confused attempts to collect the fragments of that work (see, e.g., *SHA Hadr.* 14.5–6, 16.1, *Quad. tyr.* 7.6, and Dio 69.11.2). Severus wrote an apologia for his involvement in two civil wars: *SHA Clod. Alb.* 10.1–2, and see Dio 74.3.1 and 75.7.3 and Herodian 2.9.3–4. For literature and further data on emperors through Hadrian see R. Lewis 1993.

57. Cf. Bowie 1970, 206.

58. Oliver 1989, no. 12, ll. 72–82 (Sherk, *RDGE* no. 31 = *EJ* no. 311); trans. Sherk, modified.

to send to the provinces, with my covering letter appended, in order that it be known to all in our care. From this it will be clear to all those who inhabit the provinces how much care I and the Senate take that none of our subjects suffer any wrong or exaction.

Similar documents from the early Principate survive only rarely.[59] We have, however, already seen that Ammianus Marcellinus regarded the publication of news and propaganda in the heading of a law as unremarkable.[60] Later still, the historian Agathias observed that the emperor Justinian used the publication of his *Novels* as a pretext for boasting about his recent victories.[61] Despite the interest of contemporaries, these ideologically charged letters and prefaces survived by the slimmest of threads. Late antique collections of legislation preserve unedited texts from three brief periods in the empire's history.[62] Alas, regardless of the condition in which early legislation reached the late empire, Theodosius and Justinian intended their compilations to have statutory force and thus commanded that texts be purged of prefaces, incongruities, and any "senseless copiousness of words."[63]

Augustus's letter to the provinces can be distinguished from his autobiographical essays on grounds other than genre. Augustus did not seek charismatic recognition from provincials in the same way; he ruled them because he ruled Rome. Nor will provincials have cared terribly much whether Augustus had been motivated by filial piety or naked ambition. On the other hand, they may well have wanted to know the intentions and regulations of the Roman government. The letter to Cyrene thus did not disguise the fact of Roman rule, nor did it justify the process by which that rule was acquired. It did, however, invoke certain principles of governance. In particular, Romans had long advertised their government's desire that its officials should govern justly—that is, for the common good of all participants in their political community, regardless of legal status. Sallust had allowed Sulla to give eloquent phrasing to this sentiment in a speech before Bocchus—"To the Roman people it seemed better, already from the beginning of their em-

---

59. Benner 1975, ix–xi, lists those that survive. The documents reprinted by Malcovati as public letters to provinces or provincial cities are, in fact, responses to petitions or other forms of correspondence.

60. Ammianus 16.12.69, quoted in Chapter 4 at n. 190.

61. Agathias 5.2.4, referring to *Nov.* 1 *praef.*

62. From the Tetrarchic period in the *Collatio legum Mosaicarum et Romanarum;* from the reign of Theodosius II in the *Constitutiones Sirmondianae*—laws from his reign constitute half the collection—and in the Western collections of his so-called *leges novellae;* and from the reign of Justinian in the private collections of his *leges novellae.*

63. Statutory force: *N. Th.* 1.3 (cf. *De Iustiniano codice confirmando* 3). For the rules regarding the editing of texts see *C. Th.* 1.1.5, to which compare *C. Th.* 1.1.6.1 and *De novo codice conponendo* 2.

pire, to seek friends rather than slaves, since they thought it safer to rule by consent than by force"—and Cicero likewise urged his brother Quintus, when instructing him on the proper deportment of a provincial magistrate: "I, for one, believe that those who rule over others must render all decisions such that those who are in their power might be as happy as possible. . . . Therefore I urge you, with all your heart and mind, to pursue the course that you have followed until now: love those whom the Senate and people of Rome have entrusted to your faith and power, protect them with every means at your disposal, and desire their ultimate happiness."[64] We should not impute creativity to the Romans where none is due: Plato had, many centuries earlier, stressed the pedagogical value of persuasive preambles to laws.[65] Nevertheless, under the Principate the persuasive force of imperial rhetoric sprang from a very different and more intricate source than the benevolence of Plato's despots, namely an ideology that stressed the active role of the ruled in empowering the ruler. What is more, the invocation of these principles will necessarily have exposed Augustus and the Senate to criticism based on the validity claims inherent in their communication.

To understand the subtle appeal to this ideology in the letter to Cyrene, we can learn its nuances from its clearer exposition in the *Res gestae*. In the narrative of his own rise to power, Augustus is never the agent: the Senate adlected him and gave him *imperium;* it ordered him to act in concert with the consuls lest the *res publica* suffer any harm; the people made him a consul.[66] Thus he can describe the settlement of 27 B.C. as transferring back to the discretion of the Senate and people of Rome that power which the people, by universal consent (*per consensum universorum*), had surrendered to him.[67] Augustus had once expressed the desire that it might fall to him "to establish the *res publica* safe and secure on its foundation and to earn from that deed the profit that he sought, to be called the author of the best

64. Sallust *Iug.* 102.6; Cicero *Ep. ad Q. fratrem* 1.1.24, 27; and cf. Livy 8.13.16 (discussed in Chapter 3, n. 39).

65. *Leg.* 718B–723D; cf. Benner 1975, 1–4. For a third-century Greek formulation of the Roman emperor's achievement in these terms, see [Aristides] *Or.* 35.30–32.

66. *Res gestae* 1.2–4. The grammatical structure may be indebted to Cicero *Arch.* 21: *Populus enim Romanus aperuit Lucullo imperante Pontum et regiis quondam opibus et ipsa natura et regione vallatum, populi Romani exercitus eodem duce non maxima manu innumerabilis Armeniorum copias fudit, populi Romani laus est urbem amicissimam Cyzicenorum eiusdem consilio ex omni impetu regio atque totius belli ore ac faucibus ereptam esse atque servatam; nostra semper feretur et praedicabitur L. Lucullo dimicante,* cum interfectis ducibus depressa hostium classis est, incredibilis apud Tenedum pugna illa navalis, *nostra* sunt tropaea, *nostra* monumenta, *nostri* triumphi. *Quae quorum ingeniis efferuntur, ab eis populi Romani fama celebratur.*

67. *Res gestae* 34.1, and cf. 6.1. Velleius described the awarding of the title *Augustus* in similar fashion: *quod cognomen illi viro ⟨divino⟩ Planci sententia consensus universi senatus populique Romani indidit* (2.91.1).

state of public affairs and, when dying, to keep with him the hope that the foundation of the *res publica* that he will have laid would remain in its proper place."[68] In 16 B.C., in the aftermath of Augustus's celebration of the *ludi saeculares*, the *monetalis* L. Mescinius Rufus thought it prudently sycophantic to proclaim that desire a reality: "To Jupiter Optimus Maximus the Senate and people of Rome have taken a vow for the health of Imperator Caesar, because through him the *res publica* is in a more prosperous and tranquil condition." On the obverse Rufus insisted that this opinion was shared by all: "To Imperator Caesar Augustus, by unanimous *consensus* and decree of the Senate."[69] The importance of *consensus* is nowhere more clear than in its many appearances in the contrived sequence of events leading up to Augustus's reluctant acceptance of the title *pater patriae:* "The whole body of citizens by sudden, unanimous *consensus* offered him the title of *pater patriae.*" When Augustus refused, Messalla Corvinus spoke in the Senate: "The Senate, in *consensus* with the people of Rome, salutes you as *pater patriae.*" Crying, Augustus responded: "Having realized the object of my prayers, Conscript Fathers, for what am I now to pray to the immortal gods, other than that it be permitted to me to retain this your *consensus* until the end of my life?"[70]

Such language—"I was summoned to the throne by the *consensus* of gods and men"—became the common refrain of loyal subjects and *principes* alike, especially those with an unsteady grip on the throne.[71] It also provided the ideological backdrop for that most characteristic behavior of the would-be *princeps:* the refusal of power.[72] As J. Béranger so astutely pointed out, the theatrical refusal elicited from the people an expression of their *consensus*— a stylized expression of *libertas*—and thus forced them actively to consent to his rule.[73] It was precisely this universal *consensus* that separated the *auctori-*

---

68. Suetonius *Augustus* 28.2.

69. *EJ* no. 35 (*BMC* I, Augustus no. 160).

70. Suetonius *Augustus* 58.1–2. Compare Ovid *Fasti* 2.126–128, attributing agency to *plebs, curia,* and *eques.*

71. See Valerius Maximus *praef.;* Velleius 2.124.2; [Seneca] *Octavia* 485–488; Tacitus *Hist.* 1.15, 1.30, 1.38.1, 1.90.2; Pliny *Pan.* 10.1–2, 54.2, and 58.2; Herodian 7.6.3 (on which see Whittaker *ad loc.:* this is "the only occasion on which H. uses the word συμπνία, which exactly translates the Latin *consensus*"). See also the self-conscious appeal to this ideology by Claudius at Tacitus *Ann.* 12.5.2: if the whole country desires that he should enter into an incestuous marriage, Claudius the "citizen" will yield to *consensus.* See A. Alföldi 1935, 44, and Béranger 1953, 154–156, and *idem,* 1975, 175–179. Instinsky 1940, 275, cautions against placing too much value on the appeals to *consensus* in the years after Nero; he regards such appeals as analogous to the language used by Pliny—as motivated by a reaction to the despotism of Nero and Domitian. The fact that for some this language was self-consciously ideological does not lessen its import.

72. Béranger 1953, 137–169, and *idem* 1975, 165–190.

73. Béranger 1953, 149–150; cf. *idem* 1975, 175.

tas of the *princeps* from the *imperium* of the magistrate.[74] In constitutional terms this fact found expression in the emperor's tribunician power—the *summi fastigii vocabulum*[75]—but in the long run this title did not seize the imagination of the citizens of the empire outside Rome itself. The disjuncture between the legal trappings and the charismatic basis for Augustus's position in turn created the need to find language that could describe the *princeps* and his office in a manner that disguised his power. Over the course of the Principate, certain political behaviors evolved into ritual expressions of *consensus*, of which the most important—because most public and most often repeated—was the imperial arrival, or *adventus*. See, for example, Herodian's description of the treatment of Pescennius Niger at Antioch:[76]

> After Niger had spoken, the entire army and the assembled crowd immediately acclaimed him *imperator* and addressed him as Augustus. Having cloaked him in the imperial purple and provided the other tokens of imperial dignity fashioned from makeshift materials, with ceremonial torches leading the way they conducted Niger to the temples of Antioch and then installed him in his house, which, since they regarded it no longer as a private dwelling but as an imperial palace, they decorated with all the insignia of the imperial office.

Ideological constraints shaped Herodian's narrative throughout: the "makeshift materials," for example, suggested to a Roman audience that the acclamation had been a spontaneous expression of the will of the people.[77] The particular ceremony practiced at Antioch resembled nothing so closely as a Roman triumph and shows to what extent, at the end of the second century, the emperor exhibited himself as a *triumphator perpetuus*, as well as the extent to which provincial populations—like those who honored Gordian in Carthage—were prepared to interpret and even to participate in characteristically Roman political rituals.

The reluctant *princeps*, once forced to the throne, continued to rely on the *consensus* of the people: chosen by them to govern the state, by their own

---

74. Instinsky 1940, 271. Cf. Béranger 1953, 114–131, who rightly stressed, against von Premerstein, the extraconstitutional nature of this *auctoritas* ("L'*auctoritas* inaugurait le régime de la personnalité"): it is an eloquent indication of the distance that separated the Flavian era from the Republic that the *lex de imperio Vespasiani* can mention the emperor's *auctoritas* along with his *iussus mandatusve* (*ILS* 244, l. 7, on which see Brunt 1977, 144). Béranger 1977 analyzes the evolution in the semantic field of *imperium* in similar terms, showing a subtle shift from strictly constitutional to more suggestive and descriptive meanings that followed on increasing grants of *imperium maius* to Pompey and his successors. It was that assocation of *imperium* with control over the totality of Roman territory that allowed *imperium* to become a geographical term, describing the *territorium* over which the Roman people and their *imperatores* exercised control.

75. Tacitus *Ann.* 3.56.2. Cf. Syme 1939, 336; Yavetz 1969; and Eder 1990, 109–111.

76. Herodian 2.8.6 (trans. Whittaker, modified).

77. Compare Ammianus 20.4.17–18, on the elevation of Julian to the rank of Augustus.

declaration he acted not for himself, but *rei publicae causa*.[78] The *princeps* drew on this authority again when he admonished the people to obey the laws and regulations of Roman government: the people, like their emperor, must discipline themselves for the good of all. Both parties thus acknowledged their own unique roles in the maintenance of social order. The people endowed the emperor with their *imperium,* in exchange for which he undertook a burden, the guardianship of the state. In that he was motivated solely by a concern for the public good.[79] Although this language was initially directed primarily at a Roman audience, even under Augustus it was possible for someone—albeit a Roman citizen—to envisage the conquered nations as eager to accept the stability of Roman rule:[80]

> Thus I sang of tending fields and flocks,
> and of trees, while great Caesar near deep Euphrates
> did thunder in war and in welcome supremacy
> gave statutes among the nations and scaled the path to heaven.

Ultimately this ideology, through the political practices that it animated, inspired a sense of geographic and political unity among the subjects of the empire. It succeeded because it was based on a common relationship between the subjects and their emperor and thus could operate even in the absence of a shared language or universal citizenship.[81]

Let us return to texts sent to Cyrene, and in particular to the letter from Augustus that introduced them all. Their purpose was manifold, reaching far beyond the clarification of the inquiry to which Augustus and the Senate ostensibly responded. They advertised anew one strand within traditional Roman ideology of empire, correlating the stability of the empire with the honesty of its representatives. By associating Augustus and the Senate as equal partners in their promulgation, the letters transformed this idea from a self-congratulatory ideal to a principle of legitimation, whose obligatory force redounded upon its authors: as this ideal was guaranteed by the charismatic authority of Augustus, so a failure to realize it would diminish that authority. Similarly, Augustus eschewed the opportunity to issue these letters on his own. By expressing his concern for the proper implementation of the ordinances, Augustus conceded final authority over the empire to Rome itself: he became agent of the *res publica* rather than the state incarnate. It is far too easy for us to miss this distinction and to see Augustus as the monarch who ended democracy at Rome. But Caesar had al-

---

78. Béranger 1953, 169–175. Compare the phrasing of the *lex de imperio Vespasiani* (*ILS* 244), ll. 15 (*ex republica*) and 18–19 (*Utique quaecumque ex usu reipublicae maiestate divinarum humanarum publicarum privatarumque rerum esse censebit*).

79. Béranger 1953, 169–217, and *idem* 1975, 185–186.

80. Vergil *G.* 4.559–562 (trans. Mackail, modified).

81. See Chapter 9, "How Did One Join the Roman Community?"

most claimed that title, and he died for his efforts. The gulf that separated Augustus from Julius Caesar, so small in actual power as in the modern imagination, must have gaped wide in Roman political consciousness.

Finally, Augustus and his staff generated a series of documents that rehearsed and described the state of the empire: its staff, territory, and finances. Their seemingly impersonal rationality imbued them with peculiar persuasive force, one altogether different from that possessed by an autobiography or epistle. The impression these left on contemporaries' self-awareness and on the historiographic record is obscure and has been little explored. In order to begin with explicit testimony, we must turn first to the documents that Augustus deposited with the Vestal Virgins in the final years of his life:[82]

> The Vestals now brought forward the will of Augustus, which he had deposited with them, together with three further rolls, similarly sealed. . . . Of these three rolls, one contained instructions for his funeral; the second a list of his accomplishments, which he wished to have inscribed on bronze tablets and placed before his mausoleum; and the third contained a *breviarium* of the whole empire: how many soldiers were on active duty everywhere, how much money was in the *aerarium* and the *fisci,* and how great were the outstanding debts in taxes. He added the names of freedmen and slaves from whom an explanation could be demanded.

Augustus apparently added to the *breviarium* advice on the governance of the empire: most famously, he warned the Romans not to extend the boundaries of the empire, but he also gave instructions to Tiberius on managing the elections in the *comitia.*[83] Dio's description of these documents is largely in harmony with that of Suetonius, although Dio considered the instructions for Tiberius to have been the subject of a separate, fourth roll.[84] Dio's description, to which we will return several times, is worth quoting in full:[85]

---

82. Suetonius *Augustus* 101.1, 4.

83. Velleius 2.124.3; Tacitus *Agr.* 13.1–2 and *Ann.* 1.11.4.

84. Dio 56.32–33. Suetonius and Tacitus are probably correct; Dio has presumably confused contemporary or posthumous collections of Augustus's sayings and letters, on which see Suetonius *Augustus* 89.2. Vegetius may have possessed one such collection on military matters (1.8, cf. 1.27), and Suetonius possessed a corpus of letters from Augustus to Tiberius (Suetonius *Tiberius* 21) and probably a separate collection of letters between Augustus and Horace (cited in his *V. Horati*). It is, of course, possible that Tiberius attributed to Augustus all manner of instructions and that a collection of these was later thought to have been written as a collection by Augustus himself (Ober 1981, and cf. Brunt 1984, 425 n. 5). What Syme, *RP* 5.673, saw as a restriction may thus have become for Tiberius a source of strength. It is not unlikely that Tiberius himself collected Augustan *praecepta* in an independent *volumen*, given his attitude toward Augustan precedents (cf. Ovid *Pont.* 4.13.25–32; Strabo 6.4.2; Suetonius *Tiberius* 22; Tacitus *Ann.* 1.6.1, 1.77.3, 4.37.3, and *Agr.* 13.1–2).

85. Dio 56.33.1–3, 5–6. To Dio's insistence that Augustus obeyed his own strictures on territorial expansion compare Strabo on Augustus's policy against the Germans (7.1.4), Nicolaus

These things were revealed by his will; it was accompanied by four rolls, which Drusus read aloud. In the first were written instructions for his funeral; in the second all the deeds that he accomplished, which he ordered to be inscribed on bronze tablets placed before his mausoleum; the third contained an account of military matters, an account of public revenues and expenditures, the amount of money in the treasuries, and other things of this sort relating to the empire; the fourth book contained instructions and injunctions for Tiberius and the populace: especially that they should not free too many slaves, lest they fill the city with an indiscriminate mob [ἄλλας τε καὶ ὅπως μήτ' ἀπελευθερῶσι πολλούς, ἵνα μὴ παντοδαποῦ ὄχλου τὴν πόλιν πληρώσωσι], and that they not enroll a great many to citizenship, in order that there be a substantial distinction between themselves and their subjects [μήτ' αὖ ἐς τὴνπολιτείαν συχνοὺς ἐσγράφωσιν, ἵνα πολὺ τὸ διάφορον αὐτοῖς πρὸς τοὺς ὑπηκόους ᾖ]. . . . He also gave them the advice that they be satisfied with their present condition and that they ought never desire to increase the empire further: he said that it would be difficult to guard under those circumstances, and they would therefore be in danger of losing what they had. Indeed, he himself always observed this rule, not only in word but also in deed; when it was in his power to take possession of much barbarian territory, he had not desired it.

Disregarding for the moment the precise nature of the "instructions and injunctions," the *breviarium totius imperii* made available and, presumably, rendered comprehensible a considerable range of information about the empire. This text had distant analogues under the Republic, namely the *breviaria* that were the natural by-products of the organization of new provinces. Unlike the document produced by Augustus, individual commissions will have generated these on an ad hoc basis.[86] Furthermore, the *breviarium* of Augustus must have possessed far greater coherence, not least because it was generated by a single unified staff largely from reports made by other *liberti* or *legati Augusti*.[87] The first such comprehensive document was also generated by Augustus, when his health, which had been poor for more than a year, took a turn for the worse in 23 B.C.:[88]

---

of Damascus on Rome's defensive posture under Augustus (*FGrH* 90 fr. 125), and Dio's own remarks on Augustus's arrangements in the East in 21/20 B.C. (54.9.1).

86. Cf. Nicolet 1991, 181, and *idem*, 1994, 149–150, on Cicero *Leg.* 3.41. These *breviaria*, too, exercised a considerable influence on contemporaries' mental geographies: cf. Shaw 1981, Christol 1994, Moatti 1994, Nicolet 1994, and Isaac 1996. Sherwin-White's narrative for the formation of the province of Asia suggests, despite his misgivings, that the Romans applied considerable geographic knowledge in their decision about what territory to keep and what to give away (1984, 89–91). On Roman geography see also Dilke 1971, Sherk 1974, and, most creatively, Syme, *RP* 6.372–397.

87. Note that Augustus refers all inquiries concerning the contents of the *breviarium* to his *liberti servique* (Suetonius *Augustus* 101).

88. Suetonius *Augustus* 28.1; cf. Dio 53.30.1–2.

He twice thought of restoring the *res publica;* first, immediately after defeating Antony . . . , and again in the weariness of a long illness, when he went so far as to summon the magistrates and Senate to his house and submitted an account of the general condition of the empire [*rationarium imperii*].

The imperial bureaucracy continued to churn out such documents, if we can trust the testimony of Suetonius, echoed by Dio, that Gaius published the accounts of the empire (*rationes imperii*) that Augustus had been accustomed to publish but whose publication had been interrupted by Tiberius.[89] Regarding this possibility we should, however, observe two cautions: first, that Suetonius may be generalizing the two known instances (i.e., at *Augustus* 28.1 and 101.4) into an Augustan practice; and second, that both narratives credit Gaius with publishing information exclusively about public finance and not, for example, about the disposition of the legions.[90]

Such a *breviarium* carried all the more ideological weight under Augustus because it was written by a man who, it was asserted, had "by his deeds brought the entire world [*orbis terrarum*] under the empire of the Roman people."[91] The *Res gestae,* recited at the same session of the Senate as his will, detailed in a "factual exposé of great sobriety"[92] the conquests, diplomatic and military, by which Augustus brought the world to the static condition described and preserved in the *breviarium.* His advice not to extend the borders of the empire would only have strengthened the impression that Augustus had bequeathed to the Romans an empire that was of itself complete and that had reached the natural limits of its territorial expansion. Augustus gave this ideological boast monumental form in the so-called Golden Milestone: when he was appointed commissioner for roads (*curator viarum*) around Rome in 20 B.C., Augustus set up a milestone at the top of the Forum, near the Temple of Saturn, which marked the starting point of all the roads

89. Suetonius *Gaius* 16.1, and cf. Dio 59.9.4. It is quite possible that Dio used Suetonius: Millar 1964, 85–87, is noncommittal on this issue, but there may have been a Greek translation of Suetonius. That would explain the existence of an entry on Suetonius in the *Suda,* an encyclopedia not much concerned with Latin letters (s.v. Τράγκυλλος, T 895). This sort of *breviarium,* that is, a *rationarium imperii,* came to constitute an independent genre of bureaucratic publication (Ando 1993, 421). This can explain the difference between the *Breviarium* of Festus and those of Aurelius Victor and Eutropius, despite the claims of Festus's editors that all three men wrote in the same genre (Eadie, pp. 10–20; Arnaud-Lindet, p. V n. 1; cf. Malcovati 1942, 39–41). For the nonbureaucratic meaning of the word, see Seneca *Ep.* 39.1. It is in any event obvious, whatever the truth regarding the regular publication of these documents, that Tiberius had access to such information and made it available to the Senate: in A.D. 23 he did so in person (Tacitus *Ann.* 4.4.2–3).

90. Cf. Hanson 1981, 352–353, on Egyptian evidence for tax reform under Gaius.

91. The assertion that heads the *Res gestae: rerum gestarum divi Augusti, quibus orbem terrarum imperio populi Romani subiecit (EJ* p. 2, ll. 1–2)—on which see Nicolet 1991, 15–24.

92. Nicolet 1991, 17.

in Italy and, by extension, the empire.[93] He then established a series of imperial appointments to oversee the maintenance of old roads and the building of new ones.[94] Augustus's *breviarium* and its successors, and the impulse that they both expressed and fulfilled—to describe, to render knowable, and therefore to circumscribe, the empire as a whole—had a profound effect on later historiography: their influence has been detected on Strabo, Velleius, Josephus, Pliny the Elder, Tacitus, Appian, Dio, and Eusebius.[95] It must also lie behind the structure of the *Breviarium* of Festus and the *Expositio totius mundi et gentium;* a similar bureaucratic mind-set clearly designed the *Notitia dignitatum.* Such efforts to represent the empire's forces and extent perhaps achieved their most public form in an Antonine monument at Rome which listed all the empire's legions by name, in geographical order, starting with Britain and running clockwise around the Mediterranean.[96]

We would be grievously shortsighted if we privileged texts, and especially texts addressed from *principes* to subjects, as unique carriers of ideological content in the ancient world. Even on the most generous estimation of ancient levels of literacy, Augustus must have exercised considerably wider influence on popular understanding of contemporary events through his manipulation of visual media.[97] He also exploited or revived existing religious institutions, or invented new ones, in order to promote a particular vision of Roman history and Roman religion.[98] The Senate's condemnation of Cornelius Gallus suggests yet another avenue of research, namely the willingness of the governing class to secure their status in the new regime by using their control over some organs of the state to sanction the prevailing order.

THE SENATE AS *SOCIUS LABORUM*

It is altogether too easy, in an age of democracies, to criticize the subjects of monarchies as sycophantic, and in that way to misinterpret the economy of

93. For the location of the *milliarium aureum,* see Pliny *Nat.* 3.66, Suetonius *Otho* 6.2, and Tacitus *Hist.* 1.27.2. For its connection with the roads of Italy, see Plutarch *Galba* 24.4. For its placement by Augustus see Dio 54.8.4.

94. Eck 1979, 25–79.

95. Nicolet 1991, 181–183, and *idem* 1994, and Isaac 1996. On Tacitus see Koestermann on *Ann.* 4.5.1, though why commentators presume that Tacitus here repeats the *breviarium* of Augustus and not the survey recited by Tiberius and presumably recorded in the *acta senatus,* I do not know. (See *Ann.* 4.4.2–3.)

96. *ILS* 2288. As Dessau notes, the text was emended under Marcus and Severus to include legions formed under those emperors.

97. Zanker 1988.

98. Suetonius *Augustus* 31: Augustus assumed control over *res divinae,* the calendar, revived ancient rites; *proximum a dis immortalibus* he celebrated earlier *duces, qui imperium p. R. ex minimo maximum reddidissent.* On these topics see Frier 1979, Bowersock 1990, Y. Thomas 1996, Wallace-Hadrill 1997.

flattery that facilitated exchanges between emperor and Senate. Neither *principes* nor Senate could rule alone—or so they told each other and the world. Emperors required the cooperation of the class from which they themselves had sprung. And, to paraphrase the Senate's decree regarding Gnaeus Piso, senators knew that the safety of the empire had been placed in the guardianship of the House of Augustus.[99] Even Tacitus, no lover of autocracy, and no lover of excessive *libertas,* either, saw that the needs of the *res publica* required a measure of *obsequium ac modestia.*[100] It must have been easy, especially under a good emperor, to believe that loyalty to Rome might profitably be manifested in loyalty toward the man to whom the *populus Romanus* had given their sovereignty. *Civiles principes* and pragmatic senators understood what each had at stake in their relations. The emperor might outshine any given senator, but he treated the Senate as an institution with studied and constitutional deference, and the Senate thanked him with its imprimatur.

The studious courtesy and deference affected by emperor and Senate emerges most clearly in their correspondence. Indeed, for its immediate effects upon the emperor's relations with the governing class, his correspondence with the Senate constituted an important genre of literary activity in its own right.[101] But we shall see that both parties addressed a far wider audience when they addressed each other. As Gibbon argued, Augustus promoted the Senate's public prestige to protect his position from men with mere military distinction. So long as Augustus honored the Senate's authority, it would take more than mere legionaries to remove him or his family from the throne. The Senate, however, knew the frailty of its own position—or learned of it in 41: it was better to have an emperor controlling the armies than to have the soldiers choosing emperors.[102]

It would be difficult to overestimate the volume of correspondence exchanged and business conducted by emperor and Senate.[103] Emperors wrote to the Senate, as they did to the empire at large, about their victories over their common enemies. But they also wrote to update the Senate on their activities and to request that particular actions be taken, and it is these letters that reveal most clearly the solicitous choreography that governed their exchanges. Augustus, for example, wrote to the Senate from the East to boast of his success in recovering the standards from Phraates, but also to keep that body abreast of his arrangements of territorial matters: "These

---

99. *SC de Cn. Pisone patre* ll. 162–163: *cum scirent salutem imperi nostri in eius domus custodia posita(m) esse{t}.*
100. Tacitus *Agr.* 42.4 and *Dial.* 36.2 and 40.2; cf. Baynes 1935, 82.
101. Talbert 1984, 230–231.
102. See Gibbon chapter 3. The Senate in A.D. 41: see Josephus *Ant. Iud.* 19.223–273.
103. On the Senate in government under the Principate see Brunt 1984 and Talbert 1984.

things happened in the City. Augustus administered the subject territory according to the customs of the Romans, but he allowed allied territories to be governed according to their ancestral fashion. He did not think it proper to add any land to the former category or to take possession of any of the latter; rather, he held that they ought to be satisfied with the status quo: all this he enjoined upon the Senate in writing."[104] Cassius Dio's account of the accession of Hadrian reveals the frequency with which the Senate received letters from absent *principes:* his father told him that "the death of Trajan was concealed for several days, in order that the adoption [of Hadrian] might be publicized. This was made clear by his letters to the Senate, because these were signed not by Trajan, but by Plotina, which task she had not previously performed."[105] Dio's father clearly expected, and Dio had no reason to question, that a good emperor would communicate with the Senate several times a week. Dio also mentioned and often quoted the letters of Caracalla and Macrinus that were recited in the Senate during his time in Rome.[106]

The deference of the imperial Senate convinced scholars for years that it had lost some legislative power in the restoration of the "ancient and hallowed form of the Republic."[107] It is, of course, true that under the Principate major legislation either originated with, or required the approval of, the emperor, but even under the Republic a *senatus consultum* had had merely advisory authority and, at least in theory, had required the sanction of the popular assembly to achieve the force of law.[108] It should therefore occasion no surprise that the Senate felt it necessary to consult the emperor before taking action. When the topic of sumptuary legislation reappeared in A.D. 22, the aediles, unwilling to enforce the law solely on their own authority, consulted the Senate, and the Senate referred the entire matter to Tiberius.[109] Nevertheless, the jurists of the Principate were unanimous that *senatus consulta* had the force of law.[110] Pomponius, for example, explained that necessity gave the care of the *res publica* to the Senate because it had become too difficult for the plebs to assemble, and in this way resolutions of the Senate acquired the force of statutes.[111] As a matter of constitutional law

104. Dio 54.9.1.

105. Dio 69.3–4.

106. Millar 1964, 22, cites Dio 77.20, 78.1.4–5, 78.16.2–17.4 and 37.5. See also 72.15.5 from Commodus; 77.18.2, 22.3, and 78.8.3 from Caracalla; and 79.4.4 from Macrinus.

107. Velleius 2.89.3.

108. T. Mommsen 1887, 2.2.914, 3.2.997–999, and 1237–1239.

109. Tacitus *Ann.* 3.52.2. Compare the debate in 63 on honors voted to governors in provincial assemblies at *Ann.* 15.22.1.

110. T. Mommsen 1887, 1238 n. 4, citing Gaius *Inst.* 1.4. On Gaius see Zulueta 1953 *ad loc.,* together with Ulpian at *Dig.* 1.3.9 (*Non ambigitur senatum ius facere posse*), Pomponius at *Dig.* 1.2.12 and 43.12.2, and Papinian at *Dig.* 1.1.7. Cf. Talbert 1984, 432.

111. Pomponius at *Dig.* 1.2.9.

this can hardly be correct, though it is pragmatic: mechanisms of the city-state did not suffice for the new entity that was Rome. Rather, *senatus consulta* drew their authority from the approval of the emperor: his utterances automatically had the force of law, and his approval of the text of a resolution rendered it binding.[112] Nothing so well illustrates the Senate's desire that its utterances be in harmony with those of the *princeps* as the circular argument in the *Senatus consultum Velleianum*. Faced with edicts by Augustus and Claudius that seemed to iterate the content of laws already on the books, the Senate enacted a further *senatus consultum,* urging that "the Senate thinks that those who are approached to make a judgment on these matters will act rightly and appropriately if they make an effort to preserve the will of the Senate on these matters."[113]

The existence of an emperor therefore had the unexpected consequence of raising the constitutional prestige of the Senate by guaranteeing that its resolutions would pass directly and unchallenged into law. As we have stressed, a *civilis princeps* needed the Senate almost as much as it needed him: from that body came the vast majority of the holders of higher offices, and its members also constituted a captive audience of the most influential and wealthy men in their respective communities. Under the right circumstances, each party cultivated the other: the emperor, rather than act on his own initiative, asked for the approval of the Senate before he took action; and the Senate both gave its consent to his actions and, on special occasions, continued to write and to publish *senatus consulta* on its own. The jurist Papinian once ended an argument with the rhetorical flourish "Did not our great emperors so propose and the Senate thus decree?"[114] The latter action was the natural consequence of the former.

The advertisement of *consensus* accomplished through the observance of propriety in these matters deserves emphasis all the more because the emperor had no constitutional obligation to consult the Senate whatsoever. What is more, this was true because of powers that the Senate itself granted

---

112. The role of the emperor's approval: Brunt 1977, 112; cf. Talbert 1984, 433. The force of imperial utterances: T. Mommsen 1887, 2.2.876–877, citing Gaius *Inst.* 1.5 (*Constitutio principis est quod imperator decreto vel edicto vel epistula constituit; nec umquam dubitatum est quin id legis vicem optineat, cum ipse imperator per legem imperium accipiat*) and Ulpian at *Dig.* 1.4.1.1–2 (*Quod principi placuit, legis habet vigorem: utpote cum lege regia, quae de imperio eius lata est, populus ei et in eum omne suum imperium et potestatem conferat. Quodcumque igitur imperator per epistulam et subscriptionem statuit vel cognoscens decrevit vel de plano interlocutus est vel edicto praecepit, legem esse constat. Haec sunt quas volgo constitutiones appellamus*).

113. *Dig.* 16.1.2.1 (Talbert 1984, 442 no. 53). The Senate announces its quandary in the opening of the text: *tametsi ante videtur ita ius dictum esse*.

114. Papinian at *Frag. Vat.* 294.2. Compare Tacitus *Agr.* 40.1: *Igitur triumphalia ornamenta et illustris statuae honorem et quidquid pro triumpho datur, multo verborum honore cumulata, decerni in senatu iubet*.

to the emperor, quite independent from the laws, duly passed by the *comitia,* that granted the emperor his Republican powers and titles.[115] The sixth clause (the so-called discretionary clause) of the *lex de imperio Vespasiani* had legalized the autocratic power of the emperor: "And [on the motion of the Senate the people decree] that whatever [Vespasian] decides will be in accordance with the advantage of the *res publica* and with the *maiestas* of things divine and human, public and private, he shall have the right and power so to act and to do."[116] The search for the motivation that might induce the Senate to subscribe to autocracy has led to some desperate readings of this text; the best answer probably lies in the Senate's desire to win the good will of the de facto monarch "by an unlimited expression of confidence in his wisdom and benevolence."[117] This clause exposes the lie of the second and third of the extant clauses:[118]

> [II] And [the Senate decrees] that he shall be permitted to summon the Senate, to put forward a *relatio* or to submit one to the Senate in writing,[119] and to make senatorial decrees through referral and a vote, just as permission was given to the deified Augustus,[120] to Tiberius Julius Caesar Augustus, and to Tiberius Claudius Caesar Augustus Germanicus; [III] and [the Senate decrees] that, when in accordance with his wish or *auctoritas* or order or command or in his presence a meeting of the Senate is held, the authority of all

115. We do not possess comparable data for Vespasian's early days in Rome, but the *Acta fratrum Arvalium* makes it clear that Otho was granted consular *imperium*, tribunician power, etc., on separate days by separate laws brought before the *comitia* (Henzen p. XCII–XCIII; *ILS* 241):

[41] *VII kalendas Februarias . . .* [44] *ob comitia consularia imperatoris . . .*

[46] *III kalendas Februarias . . .* [49] *ob vota nuncupata pro salute imperatoris . . .*

[58] *pridie kalendas Martias. . . .* [60-61] *ob comitia tribuniciae potestatis imperatoris . . .*

[68] *nonas Martias . . .* [70] *ob comitia sacerdotiorum imperatoris . . .*

[72] *VII idus Martias . . .* [73] *ob comitia pontificatus maximi Othonis Augusti . . .*

This documentary record contradicts the impression given by Tacitus that Otho received tribunician power, the title *Augustus* and all honors of the *princeps* through a single motion (*Hist.* 1.47.1). There is no need to suppose, given the chronological layers visible in the text, that the *lex de imperio Vespasiani* was in any way driven by a *new* impetus to define the office of emperor, or that it was designed to create "a legal substitute for the *auctoritas*" that Vespasian lacked (Last at *CAH* XI 408): *auctoritas* could not be conferred by *lex*. Note that the author of the *Historia Augusta* suggested that the Senate's conferring all the powers of the Principate upon Alexander Severus in a single day was an innovation (*Alex. Sev.* 8.1). On such data about *leges regiae* in the *acta* see Scheid 1992.

116. *Lex de imperio Vespasiani* (*ILS* 244 = *RS* 39), ll. 18–20.

117. Thus the conclusion by Brunt to a brilliant argument (1977, 115).

118. *Lex de imperio Vespasiani* (*ILS* 244), ll. 3–9.

119. On the interpretation of line 3, *facere*, "to put forward," and *remittere*, "to submit in writing," see Talbert 1984, 167 n. 37.

120. For the granting of this power see Dio 53.32.5.

transactions shall be maintained and be observed, just as if that meeting of the Senate had been called and held in accordance with a law.

If the sixth clause seeks to maintain the fiction that the Senate could write a law empowering an autocrat and was vested with the authority to choose him, the second and third clauses promote the fiction that the emperor *ought* to act through legislation, and that he *ought* to bring such legislation before the Senate, by removing as many parliamentary obstacles to his doing so as possible.[121]

Of course, like so many fictions, this polite constitutionality worked because both sides had something at stake in maintaining it. Valuable light is shed on the lived reality of this mode of interaction in its maturity by the letter of Marcus Aurelius and Commodus to the Milesians in 177:[122]

> Having read your letter concerning the contest, we considered it our duty to address the sacred Senate in order that it might grant you what you were asking. It was necessary to address it also concerning several other matters. Since it did not ratify each of the proposals individually, but a *senatus consultum* was passed concerning everything we said that day in common and collectively, the section of the speech relevant to your request has been attached to this reply for your information.

Marcus had probably been approached by several petitioners, and among them was the Milesian embassy, requesting a change in the status of the city's Didymeia. As a *civilis princeps*, when in Rome he consulted his partners in government, the senators, on any such request from a city in a public province. Marcus presented all these matters to the Senate in a single *relatio*. (That is, he made a single motion on all these matters, in but one speech.) Although the emperor's *relatio* was in theory subject to discussion, the fact that the Senate voted on several topics en masse suggests that its role was to display its gratitude at being consulted by responding with an enthusiastic and favorable vote.[123] In this case Miletus received not only a letter from the em-

---

121. On imperial involvement in the legislative activity of the Senate, see O'Brien-Moore, *RE* suppl. VI, s.v. *senatus*, cols. 766–800, and Talbert 1984, 163–184.

122. Oliver 1989, no. 192, ll. 12–20 (*AÉ* 1977, 801; trans. Oliver, modified). This letter was followed by a Latin extract, now damaged, of Marcus's oration to the Senate.

123. Under the Republic there were rare occasions on which several matters were raised in a single *relatio* (T. Mommsen 1887, 3.2.954–955), but members had the right to demand that each part of a *sententia* be subject to a separate vote, as Seneca later recalled (*Ep.* 21.9). In the *Aes Italicense,* the senator says that he will make an exception by *not* discussing the emperor's points in a single *sententia* (ll. 27–28; Oliver and Palmer 1955, 331). A senator, perhaps the emperor Claudius, once rebuked the Senate for eschewing its duty to debate the issue at hand (*CPL* 236, col. III, ll. 17–22 = *BGU* II 611 = Smallwood, *Gaius* no. 367): "For it is extremely unfitting, Conscript Fathers, to the high dignity of this order that at this meeting one man only, the consul designate, should make a speech—and that copied exactly from the proposals of the consuls—while the rest utter one word only, 'Agreed,' and then after leaving the House re-

peror but also the relevant extract from his *relatio* to the Senate, followed, no doubt, by a record of the Senate's vote on this matter. Miletus inscribed all these texts in the languages in which they received them; the text of the *relatio* is, alas, now quite damaged.[124]

It is possible to interpret the existence of this letter as evidence for the gradual replacement of *senatus consulta* by imperial orations as the vehicle of choice for the promulgation of law.[125] There is a sense in which the trend is genuine: the citation by jurists of imperial *orationes* as such implicitly acknowledged that the Senate would vote in favor of an imperial *relatio* as a matter of course.[126] Amidst all the juristic citations of imperial *orationes*, however, in only one instance does the jurist specifically record that the emperor spoke somewhere other than before the Senate, a speech delivered by Marcus Aurelius in 168 in the camp of the Praetorian Guard on the legal rights of veterans.[127] Though this fact confirms what was already known from other sources, that collections of imperial orations existed apart from the *acta senatus*,[128] such an interpretation conceals the more obvious reading of the data, that all other imperial *orationes* either are explicitly described as having been delivered in the Senate or must be presumed to have been delivered there, whether by the emperor in person or by another reading his letter. Although it is possible that some of these *orationes* were delivered as *sententiae*, opinions, during the course of *interrogatio*, or formal debate following the proposal of a motion,[129] it is much more likely that the vast majority of attested *orationes* were delivered as *relationes*, put forward by the emperor in accordance with the powers granted to him by the *lex* that conferred his *imperium*, as was the case with the *oratio* of Marcus Aurelius from 177.[130] Marcus presumably could have answered the Milesians by rescript:

---

mark 'There, we've given our opinion'" (trans. Charlesworth at *CAH* X 698). The author of the two fragmentary speeches on this papyrus was long assumed to be the emperor Claudius. Millar 1977, 350 n. 59, questioned the identification; Talbert 1984, 499–500, argues cogently in favor of the traditional answer.

124. *Editio princeps*, with photographs and excellent commentary, in Herrmann 1975.

125. Herrmann 1975, 163–166; cf. the catalogue of *senatus consulta* and imperial orations in Talbert 1984, 438–458.

126. See, for example, the wording of Ulpian at *Dig.* 27.9.1.1.

127. Ulpian at *Frag. Vat.* 195: *tunc enim secundum orationem divi Marci, quam in castris praetoris recitavit Paulo iterum et Aproniano conss. VIII id. Ian.,* . . .

128. See von Premerstein, *RE* s.v. *commentarii*, cols. 737–741. While it remained customary to begin each year swearing an oath to honor the deeds of Augustus, Claudius ended the practice of opening each month by reading select speeches of Augustus and Tiberius: see Dio 60.10.2.

129. Emperors retained the right, even when acting as private individuals, to offer their opinion at any time in the course of the *interrogatio*, and they often exercised this right (Talbert 1984, 263 n. 7).

130. See clauses II and III of the *lex de imperio Vespasiani*, quoted above (at n. 118).

his insistence in his covering letter that the enclosed text received the approval of the Senate urges that we reconsider whether the growing predominance of the imperial *oratio* necessarily and exclusively came at the expense of the prestige of the Roman Senate.

We must above all beware of assuming that Marcus addressed a single audience when he chose to handle the Milesians' request in this fashion. He first flattered the Senate with his observance of constitutional niceties. It is not necessary to suppose that the Milesians were greatly interested in just how Marcus arrived at the answer that he returned to them, but they cannot have failed to notice that his answer took the form of an address to the Senate: the transmission and inscribing of the text in Latin immediately distinguished it from his cover letter, as did the change, when referring to the Milesians, from second to third person between the letter and the extract from the *oratio*.[131] The state of the text allows no certainty on this question, but it is an easy assumption that the Latin text closed with a record of the Senate's vote on the *relatio:* that was the normal procedure with *senatus consulta,* and the pleasant fiction of issuing the text of the *oratio* rather than a rescript would ring far more hollow if proper protocol were not observed.[132] It is tempting to imagine that the text recorded not simply the fact of a unanimous vote, but also the formal acclamations that announced popular approval of a *sententia* and suggested to the president that he bring the matter to a vote.[133] The publication of what was, in essence, an imperial rescript in the form of a senatorial document therefore advertised to its recipients the *consensus* with which the leading men of the empire supported their *princeps*. It had the additional, if accidental, effect of

131. Compare the set of texts inscribed at Pergamum, on the establishment of that city's Diiphileia Traianeia: first, a fragment of a letter from the proconsul in Greek; second, the text of a *senatus consultum* in Latin; third, a heading announcing a quotation from the *mandata* of Trajan, in Greek; fourth, the quotation, in Latin; and fifth, a letter from Trajan to the city, in Greek (*CIL* III 7086, with valuable commentary by Mommsen = *IGRR* IV 336 = *AJ* no. 73).

132. See, for example, the *SC de Cn. Pisone patre* ll. 172–173 (on which see Eck 1993, 203, or Eck, Caballos, and Fernández 1996, 270), or *Tabula Siarensis* (*RS* 37), frag. B, col. II, ll. 30–31.

133. See Pliny *Ep.* 3.4.4. Tacitus plays on the expectation that such approval would normally carry the day when he denounces the weakness of those consuls who refused to allow a vote on a *sententia* of Thrasea Paetus (*Ann.* 15.22). Compare the remarks of the senator whose speech is recorded on the *Aes Italicense*, prior to his formal remarks on the emperor's *oratio:* "Therefore, when your advice is so good and its objects so salutary, what other 'first opinion' can there be for me to give than that which all individually feel and express in an acclamation of the whole group from the bottom of their hearts?" (ll. 21–22; trans. Oliver and Palmer 1955, 341). In general, outbursts in the Senate were quite frequent, and certainly not always favorable (Talbert 1984, 267). *Pace* Sherwin-White 1966 on Pliny *Ep.* 6.19.3, acclamation is never recorded as the substitute for a formal vote under the Principate. On acclamations in the Senate for the emperor, see Hirschfeld 1913, 682–702; A. Alföldi 1934, 82–83; Staehelin 1944; Baldwin 1981; and Talbert 1984, 297–302.

bringing to the population at large a vague awareness of the procedures and formalities of the Roman Senate.[134]

THE IMPOSING FAÇADE OF SENATORIAL SUPPORT

The wording of the *lex de imperio Vespasiani* thus takes its place in a continuous exchange of flatteries between emperor and Senate, in which the former consented to receive the latter's stamp of approval and so created an opportunity for that august body to display its loyalty and its power.[135] This economy used a currency of anachronistic legalities that, it is easily argued, was not recognized and therefore not honored by populations outside the narrow confines of the ruling elite. The immediate impact of the documents generated by emperor and Senate lay not in provincials' appreciation for their constitutional propriety, but rather in their representation of the Senate's *consensus:* its recognition, couched in its own peculiar idiom, of the emperor's charismatic authority. As we have seen, both parties in this economy stood to gain from the advertisement of their partnership before the wider audience of their Mediterranean empire. The dissemination of documents generated by their interaction then placed an obligation on similar corporate bodies to respond in kind. This promoted the fragmentation of the population into multiple political and religious collectivities, even as it reconstituted them through their shared consent to the imperial order. And, within this larger system, honor accrued to the Senate not simply from being consulted by the emperor, but also from the leadership it displayed in declaring its loyalty.

The Senate took advantage of this honor from the foundation of the Principate, and the mechanics through which it did so emerge with particular clarity in the documents published after the death of Germanicus in October of A.D. 19. To appreciate their import we must first understand the basic features of the process which generated them. For that process the actions of the Senate after the death of Augustus provide a paradigm. The Senate met and voted to Augustus and to Livia extravagant honors. Dio suggests that these had already been approved by both Tiberius and his mother; he adds that other men proposed further honors: the Senate sent a written description of these to Tiberius in order that he might choose those that he wished to have passed into law.[136] In this period *senatus con-*

134. Cf. Chapter 9 at nn. 210–212.

135. "The imposing façade of Senatorial support" is Wellesley's translation from Tacitus *Hist.* 1.76.2: *longinquae provinciae et quidquid armorum mari dirimitur penes Othonem manebat, non partium studio, sed erat grande momentum in nomine urbis et praetexto senatus, et occupaverat animos prior auditus.*

136. Dio 56.46.1–47.1.

sulta, other than those that recorded the decision of the Senate in a trial, still required a vote of the people to become law: this was true of the *leges* that granted imperial powers to Otho and also of the *senatus consultum* that is recorded on the *Tabula Siarensis*.[137] As that tablet reveals, the *Senatus consultum de honoribus Germanici Caesaris* explicitly described its position within this process:[138]

> [In order to preserve the memory of Germanicus Caesar,] who ought never have died, [it has pleased the Senate to conduct a debate about the] due honors of Germanicus Caesar, [. . . and concerning] that matter, on the advice of Tiberius Caesar Augustus, our *princeps*, [. . . it has pleased the Senate] that a list of the opinions [*sententiae*] expressed in that discussion be made for [Tiberius Caesar Augustus . . . so that] Tiberius might select, from the honors which the Senate has urged be passed, those which he and Augusta and Drusus Caesar and the mother of Germanicus Caesar [. . .] think it would be suitable to adopt. Concerning this matter the Senate has decreed as follows . . .

The *Senatus consultum de Cn. Pisone patre,* on the other hand, is the final document produced by the Senate after extended debate concerning the punishment of Gnaeus Piso and his adherents. The description of the proceedings of the Senate in the *Annales* of Tacitus matches the information provided by the *senatus consultum,* and behind it we can detect, once again, the generation through debate of a list of punishments, the selection from them by Tiberius, and the production of the final text on which the Senate then voted.

Tiberius presided at these sessions and brought the *relatio* that asked the Senate to consider the punishment appropriate to the defendants: the consul, Aurelius Cotta, gave the first *sententia*.[139] Once various punishments had been proposed, Tiberius altered or rejected some of them.[140] Tacitus clearly intended his description of Tiberius's response, with its imperfect subjunctives appropriate to the hortatory nature of *senatus consulta,* to give some impression of the formal, legalistic language through which each side masked its deference and its power. The *senatus consultum* preserved traces of this

---

137. On Otho see above in n. 115. Cf. *Tabula Siarensis* (*RS* 37), frag. B, col. II, ll. 27–30. The text of the law subsequently brought before the people is preserved in numerous fragments (*RS* 38). The same process undoubtedly governed the drafting and publication of honors for Drusus; the texts generated by that event are attested on a tablet from Ilici, in Spain (*EJ* no. 94b). When Augustus claimed that his initial moral legislation was passed *per tribuniciam potestatem,* he specified that he himself brought *leges* before the people (*Res gestae* 6.2). Under pressure to reduce the severity of his early measures, Augustus allowed passage of the *lex Papia Poppaea,* but on the motion of the consuls (Dio 56.10.3). He either did not want publicly to retreat, or he appreciated that the Senate had resented his earlier usurpation of its prerogative.

138. *Tabula Siarensis* (*RS* 37), frag. (a), ll. 1–6.

139. Tacitus *Ann.* 3.17.4; cf. *SC de Cn. Pisone patre* ll. 4–8.

140. Tacitus *Ann.* 3.18.1.

process, too.[141] Most important, after the formal close of the text with the record of the number of senators present for the vote, came, first, the announcement that the *senatus consultum* was made solely in response to the *relatio* of Tiberius Caesar and, second, the subscription, as it were, of Tiberius himself: "I, Tiberius Caesar Augustus, holding tribunician power for the twenty-second year, wrote with my own hand: I wish this *senatus consultum,* which was passed on my *relatio* on the fourth day before the Ides of December while Cotta and Messalla were consuls, and which was written on thirteen tablets by the hand of Aulus, my quaestor, to be recorded in the public archives."[142] The *Tabula Siarensis* and *senatus consultum* on Gnaeus Piso thus reveal that the publication of the *senatus consultum* in addition to the *lex* passed by the *comitia* was redundant and legally unnecessary. It must, therefore, have been deliberate and had value *only* as propaganda. The acknowledgment, at the opening of the *Tabula Siarensis,* that these honors would be subject to moderation by Tiberius advertised the loyalty and *consensus* of the Senate in devising these honors as loudly as it did the subsequent *moderatio* and *indulgentia* of the *princeps* in refusing to accept the most extravagant of them.[143]

Relatively few texts of *senatus consulta* survive in the provinces, but proportionately fewer still survive in Rome. We do, however, possess substantial evidence that decrees of the Senate were published and received throughout the early Principate. The evidence is twofold. First, extant municipal decrees sometimes incorporate the wording of the *senatus consultum* to which the municipality responds. As G. Rowe points out, the phrase *qui ibi iure dicundo praerunt* ("those who have jurisidiction *there* [*ibi*]"), in the midst of the decree of Pisa proposing honors for the dead Lucius Caesar, must be excerpted from a senatorial decree. As he notes, a Pisan drafter would have written "those who have jurisdiction *at Pisa,*" and he cites that more appropriate language from the almost contemporaneous decree of Pisa for Gaius Caesar.[144] What he calls "universalizing *ibi*" appears in several extant copies of *senatus consulta.*

The second source of evidence for the publication of *senatus consulta* in the early Principate is the municipal *fasti,* the calendars of municipalities in Italy.[145] Some preserve rather substantial records of senatorial decrees; the *fasti Amiternini,* for example, note the trial and conviction of M. Libo Drusus

---

141. Cf. Eck, Caballos, and Fernández 1996, 134–139.

142. *SC de Cn. Pisone patre* ll. 173–176; cf. Eck 1993, 203, and esp. Eck, Caballos, and Fernández 1996, 272–278.

143. Compare the deeply ironic judgment of Tacitus, writing of false displays of *libertas* (*Ann.* 1.8.4): *ea sola species adulandi superat.*

144. Rowe 1997, 118, discussing *ILS* 139 and 140.

145. *Inscr. Ital.* XIII.3.559–560; cf. Rowe 1997, 70–71.

on 13 September, A.D. 16. But most of the evidence concerns holidays prescribed by the Senate, and the records themselves display the honor paid by
that body to the emperor of the world. Imperial victories, even the safe return of the emperor from a journey, occasioned senatorial thanksgiving, as
did the restoration of the Republic.[146] But lesser deeds also merited notice.
The *fasti Verulani*, for example, record that a *senatus consultum* ordained a
holiday on 16 January in A.D. 10 because the Temple of Concord had been
dedicated on that day. Such records must have arrived with great regularity
under Augustus—the *fasti Caeretani* record the dedication of the Ara Pacis
by abbreviating almost every word except the name of the altar itself—and
the surviving testimony of the *fasti* opens a fascinating window on the rather
terse boast of Augustus in his *Res gestae* that he restored eighty-two temples
in the city of Rome.[147] He didn't need to name the temples in that work;
every resident of Italy may well have had a holiday when the announcement
of a new dedication came to town.

    Senatus consulta represent a relatively late stage in the production of leg-
islation: after the debate and vote in the Senate, only one step remained: to
form a committee that would supervise the wording and writing of an official copy and the depositing of that copy in the archives.[148] As we have seen,
it was entirely understandable that the written text of an imperial *oratio*
could eventually become an acceptable substitute for a redundant *senatus
consultum*. Under the circumstances we should emphasize those few precious pieces of evidence that attest to the independent circulation of extracts from senatorial debates prior to the formulation of a final *senatus consultum*.[149] Of the three most famous such texts, the first chronologically
preserves extracts from two speeches made before the Senate during the
reign of Claudius: the first speech concerns the age of *reciperatores*, and the

---

    146. The restoration of the Republic: *fasti Praenestini* for 13 January 27 B.C. Cf. Ovid *Fasti*
1.587–590.
    147. *Fasti Verulani: fer. ex s. c. quod eo die aedis [Con]cordiae in foro dedic. est.* Compare *fasti
Caeretani, fer. ex s. c. q. e. d. ara Pacis Aug. d.;* Augustus *Res gestae* 20.
    148. The list of the men "present at the writing" stood in the heading of official copies:
Sherk lists extant copies in Greek translations of Roman documents (*RDGE* p. 14). For Roman
practice see T. Mommsen 1887, 3.2.1007–1008. The Senate observed this practice as early as
its decree against the Bacchanalia (*ILS* 18, l. 2). The *SC de Cn. Pisone patre* preserves the formula in full (ll. 1–4); compare the *senatus consultum* of A.D. 19 on the participation of upper-
class Romans in public spectacles (Levick 1983, 98). Local senates all over Italy, Spain, Gaul,
and Africa then imitated both the procedure and the formula: see Sherk, *MDRW* nos. 2, 4, 9,
15, 20, 21, 26, 27, 29–32, 33–36, 42, 44–49, 52, 55, 57, 59, and 61. On formal procedures in
the Roman Senate and other corporate bodies, see L. Wenger 1953, 388–395, who generally
excludes from consideration non-Roman religious groups. (E.g., he does not mention the famous Iobacchoi inscription, *SIG* 1109.)
    149. For extant extracts, see Talbert 1988 and Coudry 1994, 77–81.

second proposes measures to hasten criminal trials.[150] Even though the author of these speeches cannot be positively identified—Claudius is still the most likely candidate—it is relatively certain that the second speech is either a magistrate's *relatio* or the *sententia prima*.[151] Since the speech rebukes the Senate for its habit of not debating extensively, but rather assenting immediately to the *sententia prima*, it would make little sense to have circulated its text after the fashion of the *oratio* of Marcus Aurelius discussed above, since to do so would only have advertised the very weakness that Claudius urged the Senate to overcome. Other speeches by Claudius survive, most notably one on extending citizenship to select members of peregrine communities in Gaul, and the text of that speech probably came from the *acta senatus* (as the two just noted above probably did also), for it has been proposed that the bronze tablets preserve an interjection in the middle of that speech.[152]

The senatorial debate on Gallic aristocrats' expenditures for gladiatorial displays has drawn our attention before.[153] The extant fragments, arising from different points in the debate, exist on different media from two different provinces: a portion of the imperial *oratio* is preserved on a marble slab from Sardis, in Asia, and a large section of the *sententia prima* by an unknown senator is preserved on a single bronze tablet from Italica, in Baetica. The beginning and the end of the latter speech are lost. The significance of the locations where the fragments were found cannot be overemphasized: if the issue at hand was of general interest to wealthy citizens throughout the empire, the preserved paragraphs concern themselves quite specifically with Gaul and, at a single moment, with Italy.[154] The minutes of this session must therefore have been published to the empire at the request of the emperor or the Senate; and, given that the extant texts are preserved on different media, it seems likely that the text was dispatched from Rome on a perishable medium and inscribed locally.

We owe the preservation of the third major verbatim extract of contem-

---

150. *CPL* 236 (Smallwood, *Gaius* no. 367); cf. Levick 1990, 97.

151. Despite the assertions to the contrary by Talbert 1984, 499, the rebuke to the Senate for not debating measures more extensively is general in application and need not be taken to refer to the discussion that preceded it during this meeting: the present infinitives (col. III, ll. 20 and 21) certainly suggest this.

152. Mommsen, *GS* 8.506, regarded the odd paragraph at col. II, ll. 20–22, as the text of an interruption by a senator; Dessau (*ILS* 212, n. 4) left the point without comment, though he separated this paragraph from the main text by dashes (he also omitted to mark the line break between *conscriptis* and *quo tendat;* cf. *CIL* XIII 1668). Oliver and Palmer 1955, 323, accepted Mommsen's view; *contra,* see, implicitly, Syme 1958, 318, and Talbert 1984, 265.

153. See above at nn. 123 and 133, and Chapter 4 n. 163.

154. See *Marmor Sardianum,* frag. 1, col. 1, l. 2, and frag. 1, col. 2, ll. 12–13; cf. *Aes Italicense,* l. 14, ll. 42–43, and l. 56. See Oliver and Palmer 1955, 321.

porary *commentarii* to special circumstances. In 203 Septimius Severus, a man of particular, if peculiar, piety, had begun arrangements for the celebration of the seventh Secular Games.[155] Sometime in the summer of 203 Manilius Fuscus, the *magister* of the college of *Quindecimviri sacris faciundis*, read before the Senate the prepared text of a *relatio* asking that body to sanction the celebration of the games and the use of public monies to fund them: it was the task of the senators, amidst the general prosperity of the human race, to give thanks for present goods and to look after hopes for the future.[156] Calpurnius Maximus, *vir consularis* and *XVvir*, gave the *sententia prima*, reading from his notepad; to the proposals dealing with the specifics of the celebration he added the suggestion that a permanent record of these events be carved in marble, at public expense;[157] Calpurnius Maximus may well have been rewarded for his role in these proceedings with the ordinary consulate for 207.[158] The surviving text of the *commentarium* amply testifies to the passage of his proposal and to the accuracy of the records available to its compilers, though its inscription undoubtedly came about because of the special interest of the college and of its most prominent member, the emperor Septimius Severus. When complete it occupied at least nine marble slabs, with an average line length of approximately 190 letters and a total of some four hundred lines of text, yielding a text about five times the length of the *Res gestae* of Augustus.[159] The men who prepared its text for inscribing worked from documentary sources. It was, as its title, *commentarium*, suggests, a dry and detailed record of proceedings, composed by quoting documentary records and original texts: the *relatio* of Manilius Fuscus, the *sententia prima* of Calpurnius Maximus, the *edicta* of the *XVviri*, the *epistulae* of the emperors to the *XVviri*, and a long series of prayers and formulas for religious observances.

The preservation of these three documents suggests that the *acta senatus* were both extensive and, at least occasionally, broadly distributed. Currently available evidence does not permit strong conclusions about their form or about the mechanisms that existed to distribute them.[160] One possibility immediately suggests itself: they could have been published in the newspaper.[161] The history of the *acta diurna* is, alas, equally obscure. Sueto-

---

155. Pighi 1965; see Chapter 4 at nn. 136–137.

156. *Relatio XVvirorum ad senatum* (Pighi 1965, 142), col. I, ll. 21–22. The name of the month is missing from the date at col. I, l. 5: the gap of six letters can be filled to provide a date in March, May, June, or July.

157. *Sententia Calpurni Maximi* (Pighi 1965, 143–144), col. I, ll. 30–31, 47–48.

158. *Apro et Maximo coss.* for A.D. 207 suggested by *ILS* 1499, 4778, and 9119.

159. Pighi 1965, 137–139.

160. Talbert 1984, 303–334.

161. On the *acta diurna*, also known as the *acta publica*, see Kubitschek, *RE* s.v. *acta*, cols. 287–295; Hirschfeld 1913, 682–688; and Riepl 1913, 380–410. White 1997 treats the late

nius reported that Julius Caesar instigated regular publication of the *acta senatus* during his consulate in 59 B.C. We do not know precisely what form their publication took, whether they were published in the *acta diurna,* or even whether the Senate had stenographers capable of recording proceedings verbatim at this time.[162] Nevertheless, Cicero's frequent references to the *acta* confirm that Caesar's innovation became common practice, at least for a while:[163] "The various speeches made in the Senate are in the abstract of city news [*commentarium rerum urbanarum*]. Pick out the worthwhile items for yourself. You can pass over a lot, such as who was hissed at the games and the quantity of funerals and other nonsense. Most things in it are of use."[164] Caesar had, of course, brought his measure as part of a political program, and it served him by publicizing the opposition of certain senators to popular legislation. Its novelty, however, lay in its recording and publishing of verbal processes from meetings of the organs of government, and its long-term effect lay in changing popular attitudes regarding the validity of texts.[165]

Although Augustus ended the regular publication of the *acta senatus,* the *acta publica* continued to exist, and their bailiwick probably expanded over time.[166] More than a century later Tacitus sneered at the journal and implied that its contents were beneath the notice of a Roman historian. He may have done so because it served the emperors as a useful tool for self-advertisement: certainly his immediate comment was directed against reporting on Nero's amphitheater, and Suetonius was able to recover from it the published, if not the true, place of Caligula's birth.[167] It has also plausibly been suggested that the reports of victorious generals would have been circulated in some form through this medium.[168] We can be certain that Claudius, for one, took an interest in the journal, for Suetonius saw examples of the Claudian alphabet "in many books, in the *acta diurna,* and in inscriptions on buildings."[169] On the other hand, Tacitus also depicted Cossutianus Capito attempting to incite Nero against Thrasea Paetus by warning the emperor that reports of the Stoic senator's "treasonous" behavior

---

Republican *acta publica* and proposes that these were published in only the most restricted sense.

162. For evidence and bibliography see Bats 1994.

163. See Kubitschek, *RE* s.v. *acta,* col. 290, or Riepl 1913, 380–384. See Suetonius *Caesar* 20.1, and Cicero *Ep. ad fam.* 8.11.4, 12.23.2, and 12.28.3.

164. *Ep. ad fam.* 8.11.4 (trans. Shackleton Bailey).

165. Bats 1994; Coudry 1994, 67 and 74–77.

166. Suetonius *Augustus* 36.

167. Tacitus *Ann.* 13.31.1; Suetonius *Gaius* 8.1–2, on which see Kubitschek, *RE* s.v. *acta,* col. 293.

168. Syme 1958, 297, esp. n. 6.

169. Suetonius *Claudius* 41.3, and cf. Tacitus *Ann.* 11.14.3. *SHA Comm.* 15.4 claims that Commodus insisted that the *acta* should report his deeds in full.

were distributed "throughout the provinces and throughout the army" by the *diurna populi Romani,* which certainly suggests that some information, however potentially embarrassing to the emperor, was occasionally published without being censored.[170]

Ceasing automatic publication of the *acta senatus* did, in part, shift attention toward the imperial house, insofar as emperors could use the *acta diurna* to broadcast news about themselves and the *domus divina.* Ceasing publication did not, however, end careful recording of the *acta senatus.* On the contrary, as early as the reign of Tiberius there existed an official, appointed by the emperor, who supervised the recording of senatorial proceedings, and we have already seen that references to and quotations from the *acta senatus* reflect a high degree of diligence and rigor in their compilation.[171] Those references and quotations suggest that emperors and Senate understood the value of publicizing their harmony and solidarity in pursuit of just and fair governance of their empire.

Tacitus's condemnation of the contents of the *acta* is in any event likely to have been disingenuous. Pliny certainly believed that Tacitus read the *acta* regularly: when writing to Tacitus about his exploits in a trial before the Senate, he apologized for supplying information made redundant by the account of the trial published in the *acta publica.*[172] Pliny explicitly connected the value of the *acta* to emperor and Senate in his speech of thanks to Trajan and the Senate on his election to the consulship in A.D. 100:[173]

> But why bother to assemble all these details? As if I could keep in mind or cover in a speech all that you, Conscript Fathers, have decided to publish in the *acta publica* and to inscribe on bronze, lest it pass into oblivion. Previously it was customary only for the speeches of emperors to be commended to eternity by records of this kind, while our acclamations were restricted by the walls of the Senate House, for these were such that neither Senate nor *princeps* could take pride in them. Today our acclamations go forth to the world and to posterity both for the good of the state and in the interest of its dignity, first, so that all the world could be summoned as an active witness to our loyalty; second, to demonstrate that we venture to judge both good and bad rulers, and not only after their deaths.

Pliny understood the ideological function of Trajan's act in the same terms in which we have interpreted the *lex de imperio Vespasiani:* Trajan had allowed

---

170. Tacitus *Ann.* 16.22.3.

171. See Hirschfeld 1913, 689–690. For known secretaries *ab actis senatus* see Coudry 1994, 95–102.

172. Pliny *Ep.* 7.33.3. Compare his letter to Julius Valerianus: when the Senate asked the emperor to clarify the punishment for filing specious lawsuits, *pauci dies, et liber principis severus et tamen moderatus: leges ipsum; est in publicis actis* (5.13.8).

173. Pliny *Pan.* 75.1–3.

the Senate to believe or to pretend that its recognition of his authority endowed him with legitimacy. The Senate responded with a ritual expression of its *consensus,* an acclamation. The publication of the *acta senatus* therefore redounded, in manifold ways, to the glory of both parties. Pliny also acknowledged the ease with which bad *principes* could abuse their control over the mechanisms of publication: since the behavior of the Senate under bad rulers was the same as its deportment under *civiles principes,* even if its motivations were radically different, Domitian no less than Trajan could have "allowed" the publication of its acclamations as an advertisement of its unanimous commitment to his rule.

The prestige of the Senate thus emerged under the Principate considerably enhanced, and it retained that status through the Antonine period. Gibbon rightly saw the value of the Senate in checking the ambitions of the military men, but its value to emperors extended far beyond legionary camps, as the distribution of its texts makes abundantly clear. Augustus and Tiberius further enhanced the Senate's prestige by allowing prosecution on charges of *maiestas* against those who slandered its members. "In these ways and also in the acquisition of new functions, judicial, legislative and electoral, the senate became grander to outward view, just when it was losing that *auctoritas* by which it had previously exercised a genuine control over the state in normal conditions." [174] We can, of course, attempt to assess reactions to senatorial publications in municipalities around the empire, but we should also note one extraordinary measure of the Senate's enhanced prestige: it was only under the empire that the Greek cities of Asia founded cults to the Senate, honoring it on civic coins and appointing priests to administer its worship. [175]

LOCAL REACTIONS TO EVENTS IN THE LIFE OF THE EMPEROR

The arrival of bulletins from Rome elicited responses from municipal and provincial institutions at many levels. Many chose to send embassies to Rome or to the emperor immediately. For example, after the death of Lucius Caesar at Massilia on his way to Spain, on 20 August, A.D. 2, the Senate at Rome passed a *senatus consultum* concerning the honors to be bestowed upon him. [176] The colony at Pisa learned of his death very shortly thereafter, either through the distribution of that decree after the fashion of the *Senatus consultum de honoribus Germanici Caesaris* and *Senatus consultum de Cn. Pisone patre,* or through an immediate announcement in the *acta diurna.*

174. Brunt 1984, 424.

175. Erskine 1997.

176. The existence of this *senatus consultum* is guaranteed by its citation in a resolution of *colonia Iulia Pisana* (*EJ* no. 68, l. 33).

The decurions gathered in the city's Augusteum and passed a set of honors for Lucius Caesar on 19 September: it was also decreed that the town should send an embassy to Augustus to convey its sympathy.[177] Pisa had the unfortunate task of responding to another death in the imperial family two years later, that of Gaius Caesar, who died in Lycia on 21 February.[178] That news reached Pisa on 2 April. Although the colony had no magistrates in office at that time, it organized an immediate response, lest there be a delay in the embassy that would convey to Augustus the measures passed at Pisa "through the *consensus* of all the orders."[179]

But an embassy was only one possible response. Some chose to establish festivals or simply to hold a celebration whenever fortune smiled on the imperial house. Under Claudius, as we have seen, Paullus Fabius Persicus, as governor of Asia, wrote to the *koinon* of the province cautioning cities not to drain their resources by establishing new priesthoods "as often as good news arrived from Rome."[180] This good news could concern any member of the imperial house: Sardis established a holiday and sent ambassadors to congratulate Augustus when Gaius Caesar assumed the *toga virilis* in 5 B.C.; Augustus responded with a letter of thanks that survives to this day.[181] The domestic crises of the next few years, signaled by the retirement of Tiberius and the campaigns of Gaius, aroused a series of complex reactions in the East, where cities jostled to back the right candidate for the rulership of the world.[182] Two and half decades later the future emperor Nero reached manhood: the date was recorded by the *fasti* at Ostia

177. *ILS* 139 (*EJ* no. 68).

178. Although the date is variously reported, as *VIIII* or *VII k. Mart.*, the preponderance of evidence is for the 21st: the *fasti Gabini*, the *fasti Cuprenses*, and the decree at Pisa (*ILS* 140 = *EJ* no. 69) vs. the *fasti anni Verulani*: see *EJ* pp. 39 and 47.

179. *ILS* 140 = *EJ* no. 69. For the arrival of the news, see ll. 7, 12. On the lack of magistrates, see ll. 5–6. For the embassy to Augustus, see ll. 42–47. For the expression of *consensus* see ll. 51–54: [51]*placere conscriptis quae a. d. IIII nonas Apriles,* | [52]*qu[ae Sex.] Aelio Cato C. Sentio Saturnino cos. fuerunt, facta acta con-*|[53]*st[ituta] sunt per consensum omnium ordinum, ea omnia ita fieri agi ha-*|[54]*be[ri.* The *Tabula Siarensis*, the *Annales* of Tacitus and the *SC de Cn. Pisone patre* all refer to the *consensus* of the orders inspired by the cathartic emotions aroused by the death of their prince. A substantial bibliography has now developed on this issue in these texts: see Seston 1962; Versnel 1980; Eck 1995; Nicolet 1995; Eck, Caballos, and Fernández 1996, 247–254; and Rowe 1997. For such embassies at Rome see Dio 58.2.8: πρέσβεις τε ἰδίᾳ μὲν ἡ γερουσία ἰδίᾳ δὲ οἱ ἱππῆς τό τε πλῆθος ἔκ τε τῶν δημάρχων καὶ ἐκ τῶν ἀλοϱανόμων τῶν σφετέρων πρὸς ἀμφοτέρους αὐτοὺς ἔπεμπον, καὶ εὔχοντο ὑπὲρ ἀμφοῖν ὁμοῖως καὶ ἔθυον, τήν τε τύχην αὐτῶν ὤμνυσαν.

180. *SEG* IV 516 (Smallwood, *Gaius* no. 380), col. IV, ll. 11–15: ὁσάκις τε γὰρ ἂν ἀπὸ τῆς Ῥώμης ἱλαρωτέρα ἔλθη ἀγγελία.

181. For the embassy see *EJ* no. 99, I; the letter of Augustus is Sherk, *RDGE* no. 68. Notices about birthdays and the like abound in the *fasti*.

182. On events at Rome see Syme, *RP* 3.912–936, and for reactions in the East see Bowersock 1984.

and the event duly noted by Tacitus, who probably acquired the information from the *acta*.[183] The people of Sardis had probably perused the newspapers from Rome.

We must remember that we owe our knowledge of these events, and hundreds of others like them, to records that someone or some institution in the provinces thought worthy of permanent preservation. Yet these texts reveal but one facet of these events: not only did the texts continue to accomplish their work long after the events in question, but the texts were often preserved through contingencies little related to the events they describe. For example, we can document the embassy from Sardis to Augustus only because the people of Sardis later chose to honor one Menogenes son of Isidorus, who happened to serve on that mission.[184] Yet regardless of their decision to honor him, the embassy and even more the festival must have interrupted the rhythms of civic life in Sardis and focused the attention of all on their relations with, and on the lives of, their distant Roman overlords. Nor should we forget that political and religious groups did not require the wealth or resources of a city to display their *consensus* to Rome. One of the sins of Flaccus, we are told, was that he both forbade the Jews to send an embassy to Gaius on that emperor's accession, and also deliberately failed to forward the text of the Jews' letter, though he had promised to send it on to Rome.[185] The Jews of Alexandria likewise closed their places of business in sympathetic mourning at the death of Drusilla. Philo's emphasis on that act suggests not only that the Jews acted in immediate response to news from abroad, but that they sent an embassy or letter to Rome to offer their condolences.[186]

As the inscribing of the senatorial *acta* at Italica and Sardis suggests, the range of information distributed to the empire went far beyond major events within the *domus divina*.[187] The official version of the downfall of Se-

---

183. *EJ* p. 41 s.a. A.D. 20; Tacitus *Ann.* 3.29.1

184. See Talbert 1988, 146–147, on possible uses for an extract from the *acta senatus* in Egypt: "If there was any specific future purpose intended, use on an honorary inscription to be erected somewhere does seem one possibility. We might recall in this connection that . . . the relatives of the distinguished consular Ti. Plautius Silvanus Aelianus were able to cite verbatim on his funeral monument part of Vespasian's *oratio* in the senate when he was awarded *ornamenta triumphalia* [*Insc. Ital.* IV.1.125 (*ILS* 986), ll. 32–35]."

185. Philo *Flacc.* 97–102 (cf. *Leg.* 247). Pliny undertook to forward the annual greetings of Byzantium to Trajan in order to spare that city the expense of the embassy (*Ep.* 10.43). On refusing to allow such embassies see Box 1939 on Philo *Flacc.* 97, Sherwin-White on Pliny *Ep.* 10.43, or Smallwood 1970 on Philo *Leg.* 239–247.

186. Philo *Flacc.* 56.

187. Cf. Millar 1984, 51, on *AÉ* 1973, no. 501, a Latin text from the colony of Alexander Troas: "We should not treat as banal the fact that a Latin inscription from the north-west corner of Turkey should recall specific actions on the part of three different members of the imperial house." Cf. Hanson 1984a: some residents of Philadelphia "indulged in emperor-watch-

janus depicted his conviction at the hands of the Senate as the suppression of a public enemy who had been plotting a revolution.[188] Sejanus was executed on 18 October, A.D. 31. Within a year that event had been commemorated around the empire. First, in the town of Interamna, in Umbria, Faustus Titius Liberalis, *sevir Augustalis*—a priest of the imperial cult—for the second time, erected at his own expense a dedication "to the eternal Augustan safety and to the public liberty of the Roman people," "to the *genius* of his municipality," and "to the providence of Tiberius Caesar Augustus, born for the eternity of the Roman name, upon the removal of that most pernicious enemy of the Roman people."[189] At Gortyn, in Crete, the proconsular governor P. Viriasius Naso erected a monument to the "*numen* and foresight of Tiberius Caesar Augustus and the Senate, in memory of that day which was the fifteenth before the Kalends of November [i.e., 18 October]."[190] An inscription from this period in Corinth commemorates one Callicratea, a priestess for life of "Augustan providence and the public safety."[191] The colony at Corinth may have been guilty of the zealous and expensive patriotism that Paullus Fabius Persicus sought to suppress, that of establishing a new cult to express *consensus* in the support of emperor and empire on the arrival of good news from Rome. And very near this inscription was found another, on behalf of the safety of Tiberius, dedicated by P. Licinius Atticus Philosebastus, at his own expense: this text uses a rare abbreviation, *s(ua) p(ecunia) f(aciendum) c(uravit)*—but so did that erected by Faustus Titius Liberalis in Umbria.[192] Finally, it is just possible that a dedication to Olympian Zeus at Gerasa, "for the safety of the Augusti and the concord of his city" by a certain Zabdion son of Aristomachus, a priest of Tiberius Caesar, was also inspired by the preservation of Tiberius from the *hostis publicus*.[193]

---

ing"; the city renamed one month after Augustus, another after Tiberius, and another after Gaius. Hanson notes that Philadelphia designated as Γάϊος not the month in which Gaius was born, but that month in which fell his *dies imperii*. "To draw some tentative conclusions: the Caligulan month-names seem to have been introduced in stages, with Γάϊος claiming the premier position. This, in turn, suggests an on-going dialogue between enthusiastic provincials in Alexandria, and their emperor in Rome, not substantially different from the exchange between Claudius and the Alexandrians, when the latter are proffering honors."

188. Suetonius *Tiberius* 65.1.
189. *ILS* 157 (*EJ* no. 51).
190. *ILS* 158 (*EJ* no. 52).
191. West 1931, no. 110.
192. West 1931, no. 15. *ILS* 157 contains the only use of *s. p. f. c.* in that collection.
193. Welles 1938, no. 2: ¹Ἀγαθῆι Τύχηι. Διὶ Ὀλυμπίῳ | ²ὑπὲρ τῆς τῶν Σεβαστῶν σω-| ³τηρίας καὶ τῆς τοῦ δήμου ὁμ-| ⁴ονοίας Ζαβδίων Ἀριστομάχου | ⁵ἱερασάμενος Τιβερίου Καίσαρος | ⁶το(ῦ) επ' ἔτους ἐπέδωκεν ἐκ των | ⁷ἰδίων εἰς τὴν οἰκοδομὴν του ἱερ-| ⁸οῦ δραχμὰς χιλίας εὐσεβείας | ⁹ἕνεκεν. The reading of the date, επ' = A.D. 22/23, is very insecure, and the photograph is awful (plate XCVb). We could correct to εϙ', which would provide the nec-

The suppression of the Pisonian conspiracy also became the occasion for empirewide celebrations. Tacitus provides the fullest narrative of these events, though there can be no doubt that he exploited every opportunity for pathos and irony in the sordid tale.[194] Among other things, Nero summoned the Senate and awarded triumphal honors to Petronius Turpilianus and Cocceius Nerva: this action presumably required the passage of a *senatus consultum,* and would in any event have been advertised in the *acta publica.*[195] He also published an edict for the people containing an official version of the events: it included the evidence against, and confessions of, the condemned.[196] Leonidas of Alexandria, a poet resident in Rome from at least A.D. 64 through A.D. 70, memorialized the celebrations that took place at Rome: "A hundred ox-killing axes drew blood from the willing necks of bulls on the altars of Heavenly Zeus."[197] At some point in the year following the conspiracy Lucius Titinius Glaucus Lucretianus, a priest of Rome and Augustus with a long career of service in the army and a strong history of patronage to his chosen home, fulfilled a vow made during the previous year for the safety of the emperor.[198] That vow, undertaken while on service in the Balearics, he now fulfilled with the dedication of a monument. The vow had presumably been compelled by the danger posed to the *princeps* by the Pisonian conspiracy, news of which reached the emperor's legate at his island outpost. It should come as no surprise that this loyal soldier made the dedication in the year after the suppression of the conspiracy: he no doubt wanted his clients to form an audience to his piety; and, after all, the Arval Brethren were still making sacrifices in 66 "because the plots of wicked men had been detected."[199]

---

essary Gerasene date. The possible sources of error in the transcription of Latin dates (e.g., *trib. pot. xxxiv*) in such a locale were legion: the first texts from Gerasa that correctly transcribe an imperial date come from the reign of Trajan (Welles 1938, no. 252 [in Latin] and no. 56 [in Greek]).

194. Woodman 1993.

195. A few inscriptions under the Principate record the passage of a *senatus consultum* awarding triumphal honors: M. Ulpius Traianus, the father of the emperor and legate of Titus, was honored with *ornamen[t]is ex s(enatus) c(onsulto)* (*ILS* 8970; cf. Bowersock 1973, 134–135). Two texts from the reign of Trajan provide clear evidence for this process: *Huic senatus auctore imp. Traiano Aug. Germanico Dacico triumphalia ornament. decrevit statuamq. pecun. public. ponend. censuit* (*ILS* 1022; cf. *ILS* 1023). See further Talbert 1984, 362–363, esp. n. 11.

196. Tacitus *Ann.* 15.73.1: *Sed Nero vocato senatu, oratione inter patres habita, edictum apud populum et conlata in libros indicia confessionesque damnatorum adiunxit.*

197. *Anth. Pal.* 9.352. Leonidas wrote poems for Poppaea Sabina and Vespasian (*Anth. Pal.* 9.355 and 349) and may well have been in Rome to deliver them.

198. *ILS* 233 (Smallwood, *Gaius* no. 149). Lucretianus had dedicated another monument, to Poppaea and Nero, in 62/63 (*ILS* 8902).

199. Sometime after 11 January 66, the Arval Brethren subscribed to a vow *ob detecta nefariorum consilia* (Henzen, p. LXXXI, frag. c, ll. 1–3 = Smallwood, *Gaius* no. 25). This vow

The existence of so many texts responding to specific events constitutes a powerful body of evidence in its own right. As so often, there is a danger of overemphasizing the importance of actions taken in response to crises. Demonstrating the work achieved by gratitude for peace is more laborious and more rewarding. Throughout the Julio-Claudian period, the mint at Rome struck bronze coins stamped s(ENATUS) c(ONSULTO). The practice began in 19 B.C., when the Roman mint resumed coining bronze. Why did this mark appear only on issues in bronze? Did it point to a division between senatorial control over the minting of bronze and imperial control over issues in precious metals? Perhaps it indicated senatorial endorsement of the legends on these coins?[200] Aase Bay's argument, that Augustus and the moneyers introduced a new system of bronze coinage in that year, and that the mark SENATUS CONSULTO designated the Senate as the issuing authority and marked the coins as legal tender, seems correct.[201] The coinage thus conforms to the ideology promoted through the publication of *senatus con-sulta*. But it seems unlikely that users of these coins will have distinguished between type and legend on the one hand, and legitimacy as legal tender on the other. So, provincials in particular, not familiar with the function of the sc mark on Republican coinage, will surely have interpreted the mark on Augustan bronze as indicating the Senate's approval of the whole coin: its weight, its purity, its type, and its legend. This simplest of messages, in the most intelligible medium, then found imitators around the empire, as the leagues of Asia, Cyprus, and Crete, and innumerable municipalities, confirmed their awarding of honors to Augustus on their issues, often using similar formulas. The *koinon* of Asia even did so in Latin.[202]

In its displays of *consensus,* the Senate thus set an example followed by corporate bodies and individuals throughout the empire. These publicly renewed their own commitment to the emperor and sent evidence of that renewal to the court. In its own way, the continuous stream of embassies between center and periphery itself reminded provincials of the favorable conditions for trade and travel that featured so regularly in panegyrics of Rome and her ruler.[203] But cities were not constrained to advertise their *consensus* only to the emperor: they could emulate the Senate also in seeking a wider audience. For example, when the city of Mytilene established a festival in honor of Augustus, it sent out copies of its decree, to be published on wooden boards or marble tablets, to the most outstanding cities of the

---

was then fulfilled sometime after 19 June (Henzen, p. LXXXIV, ll. 20–24 = Smallwood, *Gaius* no. 26).

200. Kraft 1962, reviewing earlier bibliography.
201. Bay 1972.
202. Sutherland 1976, 16–17, and *RPC* 1.1.380–381 on nos. 2227–2235.
203. See Chapter 3 at n. 24 and Chapter 9 at n. 238.

empire: to the Temple of Augustus dedicated by the *koinon* of Asia at Pergamum, to Actium, Brundisium, Tarraco, Massilia, and Syrian Antioch.[204] Given the rarity of the abbreviation employed by Faustus Titius Liberalis and P. Licinius Atticus Philosebastus in their dedications after the execution of Sejanus, we should perhaps leave open the possibility that each imitated a more widely distributed text whose model display of *consensus* provided a guide for his own articulation of personal loyalty and gratitude.

204. *IGRR* IV 39, dated between 27 and 11 B.C. At least two names are missing from the list (col. a, ll. 11–14). Mytilene also asked permission to publish the decree on the Capitol (col. b, ll. 18–23).

CHAPTER SIX

The Creation of *Consensus*

Rome invoked and sought *consensus* through means more disparate than communicative actions. We turn first to *aurum coronarium,* a tax that was more than a tax: rather, this was at heart an irregular levy, a putatively spontaneous response to the arrival of good news. The Romans asked provincials everywhere to rejoice in and give thanks for benefactions anywhere. In doing so, they relied on an ideology of *consensus,* a belief in the unanimity of sentiment and aspirations among all members of a given community. The universalizing tendencies of Roman propaganda thus had their origin in an ideological belief grounded in the political realities of city-states and not of empires. We shall then discover how the ideological work accomplished in times of peace ensured the empire's ultimate navigation of moments of crisis. Temporary instability on the throne allowed competing claims upon the loyalty of provincial populations. In narrating such crises, ancient historians adopted rather than explored, exploited rather than explained, the tropes of imperial propaganda. Finally, we shall examine briefly the use of acclamations to express *consensus* and, in particular, the slow trend toward recording and publicizing acclamations. Each of these rather different political rituals strongly suggests that the Roman government could achieve *consensus,* as it defined that concept, only by developing and exploiting sophisticated mechanisms for the distribution of information.

AURUM CORONARIUM

All was not voluntary in the practice of diplomacy under the Roman empire, nor was all news joyous. Moments of tragedy, like the death of Gaius Caesar, no doubt continued to elicit sympathetic reactions from cities both large and small. Nevertheless, the primary motivation for such interactions was the arrival of good news: the succession of an emperor or the adoption of an heir, a victory over an enemy of the *res publica*, or the gift of some benefaction to the citizens of empire. As we have already seen, cities responded properly by delivering to the imperial court some articulation of their unanimous thanks. In response to particular types of news, cities could also send the emperor a gift as a token of their appreciation. The empire institutionalized this practice as a tax, but its ideology, echoed by the cities themselves, continued to identify the monies in question as voluntarily given rather than forcibly exacted: it was, on this reasoning, gold with which to fashion a crown, and from this ideology it acquired its name, *aurum coronarium*, "gold for crowns."[1] Although we can choose to understand it as a tax, doing so would obscure the rhetoric with which each side cloaked its role in this script: the emperor universalized actions whose benefits may have been purely regional in scope, while provincials thanked him by accepting the assertion that benefits for some were, in fact, benefits for all.

We must also be clear that the cities of the empire were not required simply to pay the emperor and then thank him for that privilege. The ideology and form of the institution specifically provided them with benefits, too. A late third-century rhetorical handbook drew attention to this in its instructions for writing a "speech when delivering *aurum coronarium*": "After this again add: 'Therefore our city crowns you, paying its debt of gratitude for the benefits we receive every day, and at the same time begging and pleading with you, made confident by your humanity to the whole world, that she will not fail in anything she seeks.' Then ask for the decree to be read."[2] "The decree" is the decree of the city that accompanied the gift of gold. This manual expected its students to be quite explicit before the emperor: if cities played their role in the elaborate fiction of disguising the power to tax, then emperors could be expected to receive favorably any reasonable request that followed that expression of *consensus*.

The chance to speak before the emperor could benefit the ambassador as well as his city:[3]

> After Julian had been proclaimed Augustus embassies came to him from everywhere, and many gold crowns were brought to him from the provinces. On that occasion the inhabitants of Ionia had all their requests granted both large and small, and the Lydians achieved more than they had sought. The

---

1. The only treatments of any significance are Klauser 1944 and Bowman 1967. Kubitschek's *RE* article s.v. *aurum coronarium* is uncharacteristically cursory.

2. Menander Rhetor, Treatise II, XII, Περὶ Στεφανωτικοῦ (Russell and Wilson 178–180; trans. after Russell and Wilson).

3. Eunapius *Hist.* fr. 24 (*Exc. de legationibus* 3; trans. Blockley).

latters' envoy was the rhetor Eunapius, and he was so successful with his embassy that, at the emperor's command, he also spoke on behalf of a contentious lawsuit and won that, too. Moreover, Piso from Clazomenae won fame for his speech.

The orator who spoke before Constantine on the fifth anniversary of his accession, on 25 July 311, put this advice into practice: having thanked Constantine for past benefactions, he paused before asking the emperor for further relief for his city: "Of your own accord," he reminded Constantine, "you deigned to invite us to approach your divinity, of your own accord you deigned to address us, you were the one to ask us what help we needed."[4] It was typical of Julian's anachronistic sense of imperial deportment that he attempted to take the ideology of the tax literally and therefore advertised that he had made it voluntary.[5]

The gift of gold to a king for an anniversary or holiday had a long history in the East.[6] In the Roman Republic, of course, there were no kings, and therefore no imperial anniversaries or accessions: it seems that Rome's first encounters with the practice of giving gold came in its interactions with the cities of the East. In 187 B.C. Marcus Fulvius Nobilior finally settled the war in Greece and was presented with a crown of 150 talents, with which he built a temple of Hercules and the Muses, and in the same year Cn. Manlius Vulso finished the war with the Gauls in Asia and triumphed, displaying, among other things, 212 gold crowns.[7] Romans therefore associated such gifts of gold with military victories, and more specifically with the triumph: a commander was entitled to fashion a crown for his head if he received such gold as a gift; if he was not awarded a triumph, he could not accept the gold.[8] Though none of these early "gifts" of gold should in any way be considered totally voluntary, we may nevertheless consider exceptional Caesar's acceptance of such crowns from cities in Italy on his return in 47 B.C., which Dio quite rightly regarded as a sham.[9]

When Rome finally did acquire a monarch, both Greeks and Romans understood the rituals that governed his arrival at the rulership of the world. After the battle of Actium, Augustus—then still called Octavian—traveled through Asia Minor. At some point in the last four months of 31 B.C.

---

4. *Pan. Lat.* VIII(5).9.1 (trans. Nixon and Rodgers).

5. *C. Th.* 12.13.1.

6. Klauser 1944, 130–138.

7. M. Fulvius Nobilior: Polybius 21.30.10 (additional sources in *MRR* 1.369). Cn. Manlius Vulso: Livy 39.7.

8. Gellius 5.6.5–7 and Servius at *Aen.* 8.721. For the conditions imposed on accepting the gold, see Cicero *Pis.* 37.90, with Nisbet's note *ad locum*. The *Historia Augusta* insists that it remained customary to display such crowns when holding a triumph (*Aurel.* 34.3).

9. Dio 52.50.1–3.

he stopped in Ephesus. There he met with ambassadors from Rhosus, a small city on the coast of Syria. They brought him a crown, the loyalty of their fellow citizens, and a request to preserve the privileges of their city. Augustus responded with praise for Rhosus, for its ambassadors, and for the outstanding services to him performed by its citizen Seleucus. The grateful recipients inscribed this letter on stone. Fergus Millar has written aptly that Augustus's "words reflect a relationship which must have been formed at the same moment with scores, perhaps hundreds, of other Greek cities. . . . Ephesus had thus been for a moment the political focus of the Graeco-Roman world, and no one there could have been unaware that power had just changed hands."[10]

We have already seen that the imperial administration sent out notices to the provinces at the accession of a new *princeps*.[11] The city of Astypalaea dutifully responded to the announcement of Hadrian's accession by sending an embassy, which returned to Astypalaea with a letter from the emperor: "Imperator Caesar Hadrian Augustus, son of the god Trajan Parthicus, grandson of the god Nerva, pontifex maximus, holding tribunician power, consul for the second time, to the magistrates and council and people of Astypalaea, greetings: I learned both from your ambassador, Petronius Heraco, and from your decree how delighted you were with my succession to the ancestral office."[12] At his succession Hadrian apparently relieved Italy of the payment of gold, but only reduced the amount for the provinces.[13] Alas, Astypalaea was unable to assemble even the lesser sum, and sent another embassy to Hadrian, presumably asking to be excused from any payments at all; only the top of his response on that occasion has been preserved.[14] That the offering of *aurum coronarium* had become, in essence, a fixed if irregular tax is virtually proven by Hadrian's ability to reduce it by an empirewide measure, presumably by some fraction of an assessed, known quantity. This was certainly true by the time of Valentinian and Valens, who confirmed that *curi-*

10. Millar 1984, 37–38, discussing *IGLS* III 718 (Sherk, *RDGE* no. 58.iii).
11. See Chapter 4 n. 165. In addition to the papyri cited there, see *SIG* 797 (*IGRR* IV 251 = Smallwood, *Gaius* no. 33), a decree from Assus in the Troad, sending an embassy to Gaius following his accession, or *IG* VII 2711 (Oliver 1989, no. 18; the imperial epistle alone is reproduced as *ILS* 8792 = Smallwood, *Gaius* no. 361), which preserves a dossier relating to an embassy sent by the so-called All-Hellenic League to Gaius to congratulate him on his succession. The response by Gaius is preserved in ll. 21–42. See also Mitford 1991, 191: Sebastopolis "was quick to pay homage to new emperors," making dedications to Trajan, Aelius Caesar, and Marcus Aurelius in the years of their accession.
12. Oliver 1989, no. 64 (*IGRR* IV 1031c = *AJ* no. 75 = Smallwood, *Nerva* no. 449a).
13. *SHA Hadr.* 6.5.
14. Oliver 1989, no. 65 (*SIG* 832 = *IGRR* IV 1032 = *AJ* no. 76 = Smallwood, *Nerva* no. 499b).

ales must contribute to the *aurum coronarium* in proportion to their worth.[15] Nevertheless, in his description of an embassy to Valentinian at precisely this moment, Ammianus confirms that the traditional ideology of *aurum coronarium* still obtained: the ambassadors, named Severus and Flaccianus, were charged to bring gold statues of Victory to the emperor and to use the opportunity of their presentation to complain about the condition of their province.[16] If the monies were a tax, surely the emperor would rather have received them in coin. The sums involved were vast: Libanius said that such joy accompanied the announcement of Julian's elevation that cities sent a thousand or two thousand staters, and sometimes more.[17] Although several extant receipts for payment of this tax suggest that it was assessed on the basis of landownership, the rates vary; at the very least we must concede that the amount assessed per aroura may have been flexible.[18] What the extant receipts do in any event reveal is the existence of an official devoted to the collection of this tax, the πράκτωρ στεφανικῶν.[19]

The variety of occasions on which towns sent *aurum coronarium* to the emperor is astounding; it was clearly an important source of revenue.[20] Augustus boasted that he received such monies not only in response to his triumphs, but also whenever he was acclaimed *imperator*.[21] The appearance of a successor in any form was also greeted in this way: Peter Chrysologus, bishop of Ravenna in the mid-fifth century, explained the journey of the Magi to his congregation by reference to everyday practice: "Public offerings are always prepared at the birth of a king."[22] It is perhaps significant that the author of the *Historia Augusta* described Antoninus Pius as remitting the *aurum coronarium* offered on the occasion of his adoption, rather than at his

---

15. *C. Th.* 12.13.3. See also below at n. 25 on Symmachus *Ep.* 2.57.

16. Ammianus 28.6.7.

17. Libanius *Or.* 18.193, on which see A. H. M. Jones 1964, 430.

18. Bowman 1967, 61, compares *P. Oxy.* XII 1441, revealing a ratio of 29 drachmas on $3\frac{5}{8}$ arourae, with *Theb. ostr.* 96, 4 drachmas on $\frac{1}{6}$ aroura.

19. Bowman 1967, 60. See *P. Oxy.* XII 1441, l. 4, and ibid. 1522, l. 3.

20. *P. Oxy.* XIV 1659 preserves a record of the sums collected in the Oxyrhynchite nome for the payment of the *aurum coronarium* during a five-day period under Elagabalus, during which a total of 12 talents and 5,890 drachmas was paid. As the editors note, many of the extant receipts record small, regular payments (cf. Bowman 1967, 61–62); they therefore suggest that the total payment for this year for the Oxyrhynchite nome alone may have been as high as 950 talents. Compare *P. Oxy.* XII 1413, ll. 25–27, minutes of the town council at Oxyrhynchus during the reign of Aurelian, which record a motion to add 12 more talents to a "crown" already under preparation for the emperor. Pliny mentions several spectacular payments: for his triumph over Britain, Claudius received from Hispania Citerior a crown of 7,000 pounds, and from Gallia Comata one of 9,000 pounds (*Nat.* 33.54).

21. *Res gestae* 21.3.

22. Peter Chrysologus *Serm.* 102.6.

succession.[23] And yet, if gold had been paid on the occasion of someone's elevation to the rank of Caesar, more was nevertheless owed if he was subsequently raised to the rank of Augustus. On the occasion of his elevation to Augustus on 13 March 222, Alexander Severus wrote to the provinces to announce his remission of *aurum coronarium;* at the same time, he apologized that the condition of the treasury forced him to continue in his demand for any such contributions that had not yet been paid in response to his adoption in June of the previous year.[24] The anniversaries of accessions also became excuses for levying the tax: as urban prefect, Symmachus had to draft the *relatio* that accompanied the Senate's contribution of 1,600 pounds of gold on the tenth anniversary of the accession of Valentinian.[25] Similarly, when Constantius II celebrated his *vicennalia* in Rome in 357, the Senate at Constantinople sent Themistius to Rome to deliver a speech and their gift of gold.[26] In the system of exchange that governed relations between city and empire, it is a matter of some irony that Cyrene had to send a gift of *aurum coronarium* to Arcadius, and promise a further donation, in an effort to obtain temporary relief from taxation.[27]

One feature of this scheme cannot be overemphasized: the monies paid toward *aurum coronarium* could become a significant source of revenue only if the emperor informed the provinces of the benefactions for which they were to display gratitude. According to a late expression of the reasoning behind the institution, the illustrious victories of the soldiers, the slaughter of enemies, and imperial triumphs brought joy to the provincials, and news of these events "should be disseminated throughout all the world."[28] An emperor could receive congratulatory gifts for his accession only once. If he wished to generate income by this means, he would have to earn it: that is to say, he had to win battles against the enemies of the state. Under the Republic gold had been given by newly conquered peoples to Roman magistrates for their displays of *clementia*, frequently at the drafting of a treaty. The

23. *SHA Ant. Pius* 4.10.

24. *Sel. pap.* 216 (*P. Fay.* 20), col. 2, ll. 5–13, at ll. 7–8 and 11–12.

25. Symmachus *Rel.* 13. Symmachus elsewhere confirms that the size of a city's "contribution" was, at least occasionally, assessed by the central administration (*Ep.* 2.57.2).

26. On this embassy and the oration written for it (*Or.* 3) see Dagron 1968, 205–212, and Vanderspoel 1995, 101–104. See also Themistius *Or.* 14.181d–182a from 379, on the crowns of gold and good will that the city of Constantine owes to Theodosius for his victories over the Goths.

27. Synesius was the ambassador for Cyrene on this occasion; his official speech has not survived. The *De regno,* long thought to be the *stephanotikos logos,* is a much more aggressive and confrontational text, aimed at a very specific audience, under the guise of being the earlier speech. On Cyrene's gifts and her request, see *De regno* 3. For these events in the life of Synesius, see A. D. E. Cameron, Long, and Sherry 1993, 103–142.

28. *C. Th.* 8.11.3, a law of Valentinian, Valens, and Gratian of A.D. 369.

imposition of this tax under the Principate implied a different ideology altogether: the provinces were expected to participate in the joy of the empire as a whole at the military successes of its emperor.[29] The evolution of this institution therefore reflected another stage in the gradual development of a definition of the world that divided it between those inside and outside the Roman empire.[30]

That this tax indeed operated through the exchange of information for money is suggested by the complaint of Ammianus that Constantius's boasting about his victories in laureled letters caused harm to the provinces.[31] A decade after Ammianus published his *Res gestae,* John Chrysostom delivered a series of homilies on the Gospel of Matthew. As Chrysostom elsewhere suggested to his congregation that they ought to listen respectfully to Scripture as they did to new legislation, so he now again spoke of imperial pronouncements: [32]

> We do not offer to the laws of God calm attention equivalent to the silence that audiences in the theater show to imperial letters. When such letters are read aloud in that place, consuls and prefects and the Senate and people all stand upright, listening with calm attention to what is spoken. And if amidst that profound calm someone should suddenly jump and shout, showing, as it were, insolence toward the emperor himself, he would suffer a capital punishment. But in this place, when letters from heaven are read aloud, there is constant turmoil everywhere. But the One sending these letters is much greater than the emperor, and his assembly is more august, for it contains not only men but angels, too. And the triumphs that these letters announce are much more awe-inspiring than the triumphs announced by letters here on earth.

Cassius Dio displayed a similar understanding of the institution in his accusation that Caracalla announced fictitious victories in order to rob and impoverish all mankind in his demands for *aurum coronarium.*[33] Suetonius, who was no more fond of Gaius than Dio was of Caracalla, intimated that everyone knew that the letters which that emperor sent to Rome with great ceremony advertised false victories in Britain.[34] But the fact of the matter was that no one in the provinces or at Rome was in any position to contradict the emperor: Dio described the honors voted to Trajan on the reception of his letters from the East in A.D. 116—indeed, their arrival is noted in the

---

29. On "victoriousness" as justification for, and eternal measure of, an emperor's reign, see Gagé 1933b, and Chapter 8, "Augustus and Victory."
30. See Chapter 8, "The Geography of the Roman Empire."
31. *Res gestae* 16.12.69 (quoted in Chapter 4 at n. 190).
32. John Chrysostom *Homil. in Matth.* 19.9 (*PG* 57.285).
33. Dio 77.9.1–2.
34. Suetonius *Gaius* 44.2.

fasti—and admitted that a long time passed before anyone realized that Trajan boasted of far more than he had, in fact, achieved.[35]

To illustrate the workings of this system in its lived reality, we can examine the documentary evidence for embassies sent to congratulate Septimius Severus during the first five years of his reign.[36] Severus was extraordinarily active during this time: from Pannonia, where he was acclaimed Augustus on 9 April 193, he marched on Rome, where he remained from the middle of June to the middle of July. From the start he had presented himself as the true heir to Pertinax: he consecrated his predecessor with great pomp and simultaneously advertised a dynastic link to him on his coins.[37] Recognizing that his claim was in some measure persuasive in proportion to his power to enforce it, he allied himself with Clodius Albinus, the governor of Britain and commander of three legions. The latter became Caesar and took Severus's nomen, Septimius.[38] Severus flattered his vanity and directed the mint at Rome to strike coins for Albinus, although the legends that appeared on the latter's coins are likely to have been more pleasing to Severus than to his Caesar.[39] Severus then rushed east to deal with Pescennius Niger and spent the winter of 193/194 in Perinthus; in early 194 he marched to Syria, where, having defeated the forces of Niger, he made preparations for a campaign against Parthia.

In the course of his war with Niger, Severus had been hailed as *imperator* by his army three times, the last such occasion coming in the fall of 194,

---

35. *Fasti Ostienses* (Smallwood, *Nerva* no. 23), A.D. 116; Dio 68.29.1–3. Trajan naturally wrote to bodies other than the Senate: an individual in Epidaurus could date the dedication of an altar "five years after the victory in Moesia of Nerva Trajan Caesar Augustus Germanicus" (*AÉ* 1991, 1450). Elsewhere in Asia Minor, in Sebastopolis, another individual dedicated a statue of the emperor, adding the new title *Dacicus* to his emperor's nomenclature (*AÉ* 1991, 1479; cf. Mitford 1991, 191).

36. Birley 1988, 89–128, provides a narrative. Rubin 1980, 201–214, analyzes the evolution of Severus's titulature. For his movement in these years see Halfmann 1986, 216–223. Mattingly's introduction to *BMC* V, lx–cxxviii, remains extremely helpful; cf. Soproni 1980, 41–43.

37. The consecration is described by Dio (74.4) and Herodian (4.2). On the dynastic claims embodied in *consecratio*, see Bickerman 1929, 16–17; *idem* 1972; and MacCormack 1981, 104–106. For the assumption of the name Pertinax, see *SHA Sev.* 7.9, and cf. *Pert.* 15.2 and Herodian 2.10.1. Severan coins advertising the connection to Pertinax: *BMC* V, Wars of Succession nos. 1–180 and 215–265; cf. *RIC* IV.1, pp. 92ff. Severus also tried to placate the Senate by compelling the passage of a *senatus consultum* forbidding the execution of a senator without the consent of the Senate (Herodian 2.14.3; Dio 74.2.1–2; *SHA Sev.* 7.5).

38. For his use of the name see *ILS* 414 (Rome) and 415 (Africa Proconsularis). Some dispute whether Severus officially adopted Albinus, but the use of the name and title would have been jarring without an official act (T. Mommsen 1887, 2.2.1147).

39. Herodian 2.15.3, 5. On the coinage of Albinus, see Mattingly, *BMC* V, lxxvii–lxxviii, lxxxv, and lxxxviii–xci.

after the battle of Issus.[40] The so-called First Parthian War, which began in the spring of 195, accomplished nothing; presumably it was mainly intended to allow Roman legions that had so recently fought each other to fight against a common enemy.[41] Indeed, there seems to have been little fighting—Herodian, for one, omits this campaign altogether—but Severus had to make a show of power against two vassals of Parthia who had supported Niger, the Arabians and Adiabeni. Some glorified the campaign by calling it a Parthian war, and Severus allowed his army to exult and to acclaim him *imperator* for the fifth, sixth, and seventh times during this campaign in the summer of 195, and an eighth time by the end of that year.[42] He presented himself more humbly before the Senate and worried lest he seem to glorify a victory in a civil war. When he returned to Rome in 196 the Senate voted him several titles and a triumph, but he refused the triumph.[43] Severus, however, did not wait for the Senate's approval before notifying the provinces about his victories:[44] his name starts to appear with the titles *Arabicus Adiabenicus,* or *Parthicus Arabicus Parthicus Adiabenicus,* in the summer of 195, a year before his return to Rome, on inscriptions from Africa, southern Italy, Rome, Cisalpine Gaul and Gallia Narbonensis, the Danubian provinces, and throughout the East.[45]

40. Rubin 1980, 202–223.

41. Birley 1988, 115.

42. Tiberius Claudius Candidus was a *dux exercitus* in *expeditione Asiana* (against Niger), *item Parthica* (the First Parthian War), *item Gallica* (against Albinus): *ILS* 1140. For Severus's titulature in 195 see Rubin 1980, 205–209.

43. *SHA Sev.* 9.9–11. He issued coins celebrating his acts in Rome (his arrival, a distribution to the public, and the celebration of games): *BMC* V, Severus nos. 595–598, 602–603; and *RIC* V.1, Severus nos. 73, 80, 81a–b, and 91. Severus began a propaganda campaign against Albinus, charging him, among other things, with having murdered Pertinax (Birley 1969, 266, and *idem* 1988, 118 n. 23). This campaign stands in contrast to his reception at Rome: the people in the Circus chanted against further warfare (Dio 75.4.1–6, on which see Birley 1988, 120).

44. In the first century, literary references suggest that the Senate assumed the task of awarding titles based on the names of conquered nations (Talbert 1984, 364 n. 27), and the *Historia Augusta* certainly implies that the Senate still felt such to be its right (*Sev.* 9.9–11). On the other hand, the army increasingly asserted control over the awarding of specifically military honors, which then obliged the emperor to reward the soldiers for their display of loyalty (Campbell 1984, 122–142).

45. Data compiled by Kneissl 1969, 135–136, with supplements: *(Parthicus) Arabicus (Parthicus) Adiabenicus* with *imperator* V: *ILS* 417 (Africa); *CIL* VIII 4364 (Africa); *CIL* X 7272 (Sicily); *IRT* 613 (Africa); Soproni 1980, 39 (Pannonia Inferior); *AÉ* 1984, no. 373 (Italy-Umbria). *Arabicus Adiabenicus* with *imperator* VI: *IGRR* IV 672 (Phrygia); *CIL* VIII 9317 (Africa). *Arabicus Adiabenicus* with *imperator* VII: *CIL* III 905 (Dacia); *CIL* V 4868 (Cisalpine Gaul); *CIL* VIII 1333, 24004 (Africa); *CIL* XII 56 (Gallia Narbonensis); *AÉ* 1946, no. 202 (Spain); *AÉ* 1984, no. 919 (Syria). *Arabicus Adiabenicus* with *imperator* VIII: *CIL* VIII 8835 (Africa); *IGRR* IV 566 (Phrygia). Definitely from 195 but without numeration of imperatorial acclamation is *CIL*

The spread of this titulature aptly illustrates the dynamics governing relations between an emperor and his various constituencies. Monopoly over the limited means of rapid communication in that day allowed Severus to act the *civilis princeps* before the Senate, which had once assumed control over the awarding of victory cognomina and which continued to assign that privilege to itself. At precisely the same time Severus could boast to the provinces about the same deeds with very different rhetoric: he needed their gold, and they would give it only to someone with clear and undisputed achievements in war. Finally, the immediate presence of his army constrained Severus to accept his soldiers' displays of loyalty—that is, their acclamations—even as both Severus and his army knew full well that such actions demanded from Severus a corresponding reward for his enthusiastic soldiery. This pattern in Severus's behavior, of distributing information selectively and modulating his self-presentation, continued to obtain for the next four years.

His quick success against Niger gave Severus the confidence to break with Albinus and to name his son Bassianus his official successor. To strengthen his claim as the only legitimate holder of imperial power, Severus also announced the adoption of himself and his family into the line of Marcus Aurelius and the deification of Commodus, and encouraged his army to declare Albinus an enemy of the state.[46] At roughly the same time—in this case we know the precise date, 14 April 195—Severus honored his wife, Julia Domna, with the title *mater castrorum*, a title held previously only by one woman, Faustina, the wife of Marcus Aurelius.[47] Severus probably also arranged that iconographically his official portrait and those of his family should closely resemble those of Marcus Aurelius, Faustina, and Commodus.[48] None of the legal actions relating to the adoption were constitutionally possible without the authorization of the Senate, and it is just possible that Severus chose to keep the Senate in the dark about his self-adoption for the time being. Certainly Cassius Dio, who was in Rome at this time, seems to have thought that Severus informed the Senate about his

---

III 14507 (cf. Lörincz 1979, 157, from Moesia Superior), and very likely also *AÉ* 1983, no. 830 (from Dacia). On the evidence from Egypt, see Bureth 1964, 94. Kneissl also lists *CIL* VI 1026 (from Rome), which contains the titles *Arabicus Adiabenicus* along with *imperator* IIII; the stone is, I believe, no longer extant, and it is very unlikely that Severus claimed these titles prior to the start of the Parthian campaign.

46. Severus first hinted at his connection to Marcus in his autobiography (Dio 74.3.1). On his use of Antonine nomenclature see below at nn. 54, 55. For Albinus as *hostis publicus,* see Herodian 3.6.8, before Severus departed for the West.

47. Soproni 1980, 41; Birley 1988, 115–116.

48. Baharal 1996, 20–33.

wishes for the first time only after the defeat of Albinus in 197.[49] Severus clearly informed his partisans and those under his control elsewhere: four inscriptions survive from different parts of the empire, all reflecting developments in Severus's self-presentation within 195. The earliest originates with the First Cohort of the Syrians, which was stationed at this time at Ulcisia Castra, located halfway along the road between Aquincum and Cirpi in Lower Pannonia, next to Severus's old province.[50] The precise impulse that occasioned the inscription is unknown—perhaps the happy coincidence of a Severan victory on the twentieth anniversary of the creation of the cohort—but its text is clear: "To Imperator Caesar Lucius Septimius Severus Pertinax Augustus, *pater patriae*, Arabicus Adiabenicus, *imperator* for the fifth time, consul for the second time, holding the tribunician power for the second year, pontifex maximus, and Marcus Aurelius Antoninus Caesar, the First Cohort of the Syrians, the Aurelian Antonine, makes this dedication, when Piso and Julianus are consuls."[51] The reference to Severus's fifth acclamation as *imperator* proves that Severus dispatched news to the army in Pannonia of his latest victory while still in the middle of the summer's campaign. The application of Antonine nomenclature to Caracalla alone merely suggests that the carver put as much on the stone as possible and that the document was of local origin, even if written in reaction to news sent from the imperial court.[52] Finally, the use of similar victory cognomina, again in conjunction with Severus's fifth acclamation, but without any reference to his self-adoption or to Caracalla, in an inscription from Umbria strengthens the possibility that Severus deliberately tailored his news bul-

49. Dio 75.7.4. See Mattingly, *BMC* V, xciii: "There is not a hint of any attempt by Septimius to win over the Senate. Even more than the people, it was secretly friendly to Albinus: had the fortune of Septimius shown any sign of wavering, it would have been quick to declare against him." Birley's claim (1988, 120 and again on 121), that the Senate declared Albinus a public enemy on 15 December 195, is incorrect: Dio does not even imply it at 75.4.1. On Dio's movements at this time, see Millar 1964, 16. The *Historia Augusta* insists that Severus announced the adoption during his return to the West in the spring of 196, during a stop at Viminacium on the border between Dacia and Moesia Superior (*Sev.* 10.3).

50. *Editio princeps* in Soproni 1980. Its implications are accepted by Halfmann 1986, 200, and Birley 1988, 120. Rubin 1980, 73 and 212, argued that the elevation of Bassianus should be dated after the battle of Issus, i.e., after Severus was declared *imperator* IV. That Julia Domna became *mater castrorum* prior to his acclamation as *imperator* V suggests that he may be right; the absence of any reference on this stone to *his* Antonine nomenclature is not conclusive either way. See below at nn. 57, 58.

51. Text translated from Soproni 1980, 39.

52. Compare the dedication from later in 195 by veterans of Legio VII Claudia, from Moesia Superior (*CIL* III 14507)—the text is heavily reconstructed but reasonably secure: [1][*Pro salute imp(eratoris) Caes(aris)*] | [2][*L(ucii) Septimi(i) Severi Pertin*]*a*[*cis*] | [3][*Aug(usti) Arab(ici) Adiab(enici) et M(arci)*] *Aurel(ii)* | [4][*Antonini Caes(aris) vet(erani) l*]*eg(ionis) VII Cl(audiae)*.

letins for particular audiences around the empire.[53] The Umbrian inscription, a public dedication, was very likely erected to commemorate the arrival of a victory bulletin from the war against Parthia.

Severus no doubt published another announcement after his next acclamation. The reception of that announcement is reflected in an inscription dedicated by the town magistrates of Castellum, between Tipasa and Caesarea in Mauretania Caesarensis. It is the earliest extant text to record what would become the common refrain of all those allying themselves with the Antonine monarchy:[54]

> To Imperator Caesar, son of the divine Marcus Antoninus Pius Sarmaticus Germanicus, brother of the divine Commodus, grandson of the divine Antoninus Pius, great-grandson of the divine Hadrian, descendant of the divine Trajan Parthicus, descendant of the divine Nerva, Lucius Septimius Severus Pius Pertinax Augustus, Arabicus Adiabenicus, pontifex maximus, holding the power for the third time, *imperator* for the sixth time, consul for the second time, proconsul, *pater patriae*, the bravest . . . unconquered general. Dedicated by C. Julius Januarius and L. Cassius Augustinus, *magistri quinquennales*.[55]

The nomenclature advertises Severus's fictive connection to the Antonine house, and the sixth acclamation as *imperator* points to a time later than the text from Ulcisia Castra. The text is quite lavish—abbreviations are kept to a minimum. Why then is Caracalla not mentioned? First, the inscription from Ulcisia Castra probably misrepresented the situation: Caracalla, only seven years old in 195, undoubtedly did not yet have a true share in his father's power. Rather, Severus had simply marked him out as his designated successor: the name Caesar, which Caracalla acquired at this time, therefore had no more and no less significance than the title *imperator destinatus*, which was attached to his name in some inscriptions until at least 197.[56] Second, even if Caracalla had been mentioned in the announcement that Januarius and Augustinus commemorated, they may not have known what his titulature signified. After all, Commodus had been the last child of an emperor to rule jointly with his father, and even he had not appeared at the head of an epistle until proclaimed Augustus in 177, when he was sixteen years old.[57]

It is, however, by no means clear that Severus attempted to claim that Caracalla was ruling jointly with him at this time before *every* audience. A fragmentary inscription from Prymnessus, in Phrygia in the province of

53. *AÉ* 1984, 373.
54. See Chapter 2 at nn. 86–95.
55. *CIL* VIII 9317.
56. Sasel 1983, publishing a text from Praetorium Latobicorum; Eck 1983, 291.
57. *ILS* 375; cf. Herrmann 1975, 152–153.

Asia, preserves the beginning of a letter from Severus to the town. Though only the beginnings of the lines are preserved, it is clear that the text dates from the second half of 195: Severus's connections to the Antonine house are specified, but he is still listed as consul for the second time. Most important, there is no space at all for any mention of Caracalla at the head of the letter.[58] Similarly, when Julius Pacatianus, the man installed by Severus as the first governor of Osrhoëne following the annexation of that territory in late summer of 195, surveyed the border between Osrhoëne and the kingdom of Abgar of Emesa, he cited the authority of Severus alone.[59]

The fragmentary state of Severus's letter to Prymnessus does not allow any clarity regarding its purpose. However, the likelihood that Severus was responding to an embassy sent by Prymnessus in response to some announcement about his victories and about the new status of Caracalla is greatly increased by the existence of a complete letter from Severus later in the same year, addressed to the city of Aezani, approximately a hundred kilometers from Prymnessus. In it Severus advertised his eighth acclamation as *imperator,* placing his response sometime after the fall of Byzantium in late 195, but before 10 December of that year. He thanked Aezani for its embassy:[60]

> The pleasure that you take in my success, and in the rise of my son Marcus Aurelius Antoninus with good fortune to the hopes of the empire and to a position alongside his father, I have seen most clearly in your decree. I am in addition pleased that you have conducted a public celebration and sacrificed thanks-offerings to the gods, since your city is famous and has long been useful to the Roman empire. Because I saw that a Victory had come to be a witness to my success, along with your decree, I have sent this letter to you to be placed among your local gods.

The Victory to which Severus refers is almost undoubtedly a golden statue of the sort that Tripolis, in the account provided by Ammianus, sent to Valentinian as its contribution of *aurum coronarium* on the occasion of his accession.[61] Though the Aezanitae had clearly been informed about the change in Caracalla's status and mentioned that change in their decree, Severus alone responded, indicating once again that Caracalla did not yet actively participate in the exercise of power.[62]

Severus waited to leave the East until he had certain news of the fall of

58. *IGRR* IV 672 (Oliver 1989, no. 214).

59. *AÉ* 1984, 919.

60. *ILS* 8805 (*IGRR* IV 566 = Oliver 1989, no. 213; trans. after Oliver and after Birley 1988, 119), ll. 12–25.

61. Ammianus 28.6.7. (See above at n. 17.)

62. *ILS* 8805, ll. 1–10.

Byzantium.[63] During this year the news of his self-adoption into the Antonine house spread further around the empire: awareness of the consecration of Commodus is abundantly attested in inscriptions during this year.[64] Though coins from the mint at Rome prove that Severus stopped in Rome in the winter of 196/197 before proceeding against Albinus in Gaul, that visit has left no trace in our literary sources. The history of Cassius Dio, whose narrative would no doubt have revealed much, is preserved only in fragments for this period, and both Herodian and the *Historia Augusta* depict Severus proceeding directly from the East to Gaul.[65] It is significant, in light of what was said before about Severus tailoring his self-presentation to conform to those constitutional niceties that would flatter the Roman Senate, that on the dedication to Nerva that Severus made in the fall of 196 at Rome he did not use nomenclature that claimed Antonine ancestry, so abundantly attested in other parts of the empire at this time: he called Nerva his "forefather," *atavus,* a term that staked a much less direct claim to ancestry than the official *abnepos,* "descendant," and he designated himself merely L. Septimius Severus Pius Pertinax Augustus.[66] The legislation for 196 preserved in the Code of Justinian that purportedly issues from "Severus and Antoninus, Augusti," can hardly be correct: Severus promoted Caracalla on the same day when he took the title Parthicus Maximus, which was, not coincidentally, Trajan's *dies imperii.*[67]

The situation had clearly changed once again in Severus's favor following the defeat of Albinus. Severus sent the head of Albinus to Rome to be displayed on a pole, along with a letter intimating the punishment of the friends of Albinus that was to come. It may be that he first informed the Senate officially of his adoption and his desires for Caracalla in this letter.[68] The

63. Dio 74.14.1–2; cf. Magie 1950, 1541–1542.

64. Hasebroek 1921, 89 n. 4.

65. Mattingly, *BMC* V, xcii–xciii; Birley 1988, 123.

66. *ILS* 418.

67. Fink, at Fink, Hoey, and Snyder 1940, 77–81. That the choice of 28 January was governed by propagandistic considerations and not by the actual events of the war, as suggested by Rubin 1975, 431–437, only strengthens (*pace* Rubin, 434) the *communis opinio* that Caracalla was elevated on this date. Rubin 1980, 210–211, was more hesitant, but his earlier suggestions about the dating of and motivation for the tenth imperatorial acclamation may stand; cf. Kienast 1990, 156 and 162. Trajan, too, had established his *natalis* on 18 September for propagandistic reasons: on that day Domitian had died, and Nerva had been promoted to the throne; "it would be a very remarkable coincidence, if Trajan's own birthday had actually fallen on that critical date" (H. Mattingly 1950, 183 n. 12). On local knowledge of *dies Augusti,* see Chapter 2 at n. 88. For efforts by Julio-Claudians to schedule events on days significant in the history of their dynasty, see Gagé 1968, chapter 1.

68. Herodian 3.8.1. Dio 75.5.3–8.4, alas, does not make it clear whether Severus's announcement of his self-adoption and desires for Caracalla were contained in the same speech

Senate, no doubt hoping to appease him prior to his return to the imperial city, sent an embassy both to him and to Antoninus Caesar, *imperator destinatus*.[69] The creation of a title for Caracalla, that of official successor to the throne, would be insulting if Caracalla already shared in the imperial power. Having declared Albinus an enemy of the state, if unconstitutionally,[70] Severus allowed his soldiers to rejoice in their victorious Gallic campaign.[71] The authority of Severus and the new position of Caracalla are firmly attested in a dedication from Lugdunum, the site of Albinus's final defeat on 19 February: on 4 May 197 a group of local priests and priestesses in the imperial cult vowed a *taurobolium* for the health and safety of Imperator L. Septimius Severus Pius Pertinax Augustus, M. Aurelius Antoninus *imperator destinatus*, Julia Augusta *mater castrorum*, and the whole *domus divina*, and for the condition of their colony.[72]

Finally, chance has preserved three further documents written in the context of Severus's Second Parthian War, in the latter half of 197 and lasting through early 198. Sometime in the late fall of 197 Severus was acclaimed *imperator* for the tenth time, probably following the fall of Ctesiphon.[73] News of this event then circulated. Severus subsequently chose to celebrate his victories in the East in grander style on the anniversary of the *dies imperii* of Trajan, the last man to conquer the Parthian empire. On 28 January, therefore, he was acclaimed again, and, in what was no doubt a splendid ceremony, he elevated Caracalla to Augustus and his younger son, Geta, to the rank of Caesar. In response to the initial message regarding Severus's tenth acclamation, the city of Aphrodisias in Caria issued a decree and dispatched an embassy to deliver it. The ability of such embassies—like that from Alexandria which reached Augustus in Gaul—to find the emperor in itself suggests something of the frequency and content of his dispatches to them. The Aphrodisian embassy reached Severus after the elevation of Caracalla, for the answer to it was issued jointly by Severus and

---

that he read out to the Senate in the summer of 197, in which he ridiculed the clemency of Pompey and Caesar and defended the memory of Commodus. Cf. Millar 1964, 142.

69. The embassy is recorded on a dedication which narrates the career of one of the ambassadors, P. Porcius Optatus (*ILS* 1143).

70. See at n. 47.

71. See the career inscription of Candidus (*ILS* 1140, quoted in n. 42), and compare *AÉ* 1914, 248 (*expeditio felicissima Gallica*), and *ILS* 3029: [1]*prestito Iovi s.* | [2][. . . . . . .] | [3]*tribunus coh. X* | [4]*praet., cultor nu-*|[5]*minis ipsius, profic-*|[6]*iscens ad opprimen-*|[7]*dam factionem* | [8]*Gallicanam iussu* | [9]*principis sui aram* | [10]*istam posuit.* Von Premerstein believed that he saw traces of Fulvius Plautianus in line 2; if so, his name would naturally have been erased following his downfall in January 205.

72. *ILS* 4134; the vow was completed on 7 May.

73. Rubin 1975, 436.

Caracalla, but it makes reference only to the joy of Aphrodisias at Severus's success against the barbarians.[74] The ceremony on 28 January 198 must have been widely publicized: Aphrodisias, either in response to news of that event, or because the earlier response from the Augusti revealed Caracalla's new status, wrote another decree and sent another embassy. This time the city specifically acknowledged the promotion of Caracalla, and it was he who ostensibly authored the reply: it was most fitting, he wrote, for a city that had already celebrated the victory over the barbarians, and the establishment of universal peace, now to congratulate him on his promotion.[75]

An embassy in response to the ceremony of 28 January also reached Severus from Nicopolis ad Istrum, in Moesia Inferior. That embassy thanked him for all his recent benefactions, to which Severus responded:[76]

> We see your good will toward us most clearly from your decree, for thus have you shown yourselves to be loyal and pious and anxious to better yourselves in our judgment, by rejoicing in the present conditions and by celebrating a public festival at the good news of our benefactions: an all-embracing peace existing for all mankind, created through the defeat of those barbarians who always harass the empire, and the joining of ourselves in this just partnership, because we have a Caesar who is from our house and legitimate. Therefore we have read your decree with appropriate respect and have accepted your contribution of 700,000 [denarii] as from loyal men.

The importance of Severus's claim to have established peace "for all mankind" will be discussed in chapter 8.[77] The more general importance of these Severan texts lies in their illustration of the continuing dialogue between emperor and provincials over his good deeds on their behalf and their corresponding displays of gratitude. More particularly, local governments had to respond to announcements with a decree that acknowledged a specific event, be it an anniversary or victory. Participants in those municipal councils cannot have failed to notice that the titulature at the head of any news bulletin evolved to reflect and record significant moments in the reign. This experience prepared the way for individuals to interpret the legends on coins and the ubiquitous milestones that they encountered in daily life.

THE SLOW JOURNEY OF EUTHERIUS

Modern histories of the empire frequently suggest that contests for the throne were waged and won on the field of battle, in the Senate, or in the

---

74. Oliver 1989, no. 218, was provisional; see now Reynolds 1982, no. 17.
75. Oliver 1989, no. 219 = Reynolds 1982, no. 18, ll. 2–3.
76. *IGBulg.* 659 (Oliver 1989, no. 217), ll. 21–35.
77. See Chapter 8 at n. 246 and cf. Chapter 3 at n. 33.

streets of Rome. Their authors have succumbed to the rhetoric of an earlier age, which depicted legitimate emperors sweeping through the provinces, city by city, to the universal joy and unanimous acclamation of the local populations. A considerable disjunction separates this picture from the realities of transportation technology in the ancient world. These conventional narratives existed precisely because would-be emperors required the support of provincial populations. Such men therefore advertised the displays of *consensus* that greeted them wherever they went, and contemporary rhetors and historians, whose thought-world drew a necessary connection between legitimacy and the consensual commitment of the populace, iterated the content of imperial propaganda. The conceptual links in this chain—success in claiming the throne, the *consensus* of the ruled, speedy progress through the empire—reinforced each other and forever shaped the historiographical tradition.

If historians and orators believed—or, at least, claimed—that emperors could move rapidly wheresoever they willed, the *viri militares* knew better. It *was* possible to move rapidly through the provinces, but only, as we shall see, for those who had carefully solicited the favor of the local populations well in advance. For if an emperor and his entourage—to say nothing of one accompanied by several legions—placed a heavy burden on the regions through which they passed, the converse is also true: in the face of concerted local resistance, travel in the ancient world was nearly impossible. When the rulership of the world hung in the balance, the volume of propaganda in the ancient world reached a crescendo. Such moments therefore offer an opportunity to examine in detail the creation of *consensus*, as well as the forms of its subsequent depiction.

Imperial epistles could take many different forms, depending in part on their audience. We have already seen that emperors used different means to address the Senate and the urban population at Rome.[78] They could also distribute leaflets to those not present to hear their words: thus Macrinus distributed pamphlets to soldiers in the East, arrogating to himself authority that required the sanction of the Senate—or so Cassius Dio claimed.[79] When the Senate demanded to know their contents, Macrinus forwarded some material, but the full extent of the discrepancy between his reports to the Senate and his actual activities became clear only after the ascendance of Elagabalus.[80] Macrinus's crime, however, lay in his deception, not merely

---

78. See Chapter 5 at nn. 8–10.

79. Dio 78.16.1–4. Compare the not definitely spurious letter of Marcus Aurelius to Cornelius Balbus quoted by the *Historia Augusta* (*Pesc. Nig.* 4.1–2). Even if fake, the letters presume an established practice of direct communication between an emperor and his *commilitones*.

80. The Senate's demand: Dio 78.21.1. The subsequent compliance by Elagabalus: Dio 79.2.1.

in the act of distributing the leaflets. Indeed, ancient historians often emphasized the importance of utilizing all avenues and opportunities for communication, and this was never more true than in an attempt on the throne.

For the aspiring emperor plotting an attempt on the throne, the prefect of Egypt constituted in many respects an audience unto himself. That official could, by ending grain shipments to Rome, precipitate a crisis in the capital, although he could not control the direction in which the population of that city cast the blame. In A.D. 66 Tiberius Julius Alexander entered the prefecture after two decades of service under Claudius and Nero. Alexander's actions over the next few years emerge from scattered sources that do not always yield an intelligible narrative. There can, however, be no mistaking his importance to the men who sought the throne between the summer of 68 and the winter of 69. On 6 July 68, Alexander issued a long edict touching on many administrative and legal issues. The preface to that edict delicately skirted around the recent accession of a new emperor, framing it as a moment of religious renewal.[81] It also acknowledged that stability in Egypt was necessary to ensure grain for Rome:[82]

> In order that you may more confidently hope for everything from our benefactor, Augustus Imperator Galba, who lights for us the path to the salvation of the human race—everything both for your salvation and for your pleasure—and in order that you may know that I have taken thought for matters relevant to your aid, I have responded with urgency concerning each of your requests, insofar as it lies within my power to judge and to act. Greater matters, requiring the power and majesty of the emperor, I will explain to him in all honesty, as the gods have preserved the safety of the entire world for this most sacred moment.

Although no text from Alexander's pen survives from the reigns of Otho and Vitellius, their titles are used in official dating formulas, suggesting very strongly that Alexander did not publicly act against the trend established in Rome as late as May of 69, when the armies of the empire most likely swore their last oath to Vitellius.[83] Vespasian, too, depicted himself as reluctant to break his oath to Vitellius and, therefore, as forced, in the end at swordpoint, to accept his proclamation as *imperator*.[84] Suetonius also followed that tradition, identifying Vespasian as the choice first of the armies of Moesia, then of Alexander and his legions—III Cyrenaïca and XXII Deiotariana—in Egypt on 1 July 69, and finally of Vespasian's own legions four days later.[85]

---

81. See Chalon 1964, 95–100. Alexander's career is summarized at *PIR*[2] I 139.

82. Text in Chalon 1964, 27, ll. 7–10.

83. For texts from the reigns of Otho and Vitellius see Bureth 1964, 36–37, but cf. Hanson 1982, publishing a roll of tax receipts collected under Nero, then Galba, then Vespasian.

84. Josephus *Bell. Iud.* 4.601–604.

85. Suetonius *Vespasian* 6.2–3.

Vespasian advertised widely the independence of judgment exercised by Alexander and his legions and assumed 1 July as his *dies imperii;* he subsequently traveled to Egypt to celebrate that province's loyalty.[86] Is that spontaneity credible? Tacitus thought not: he depicted Vespasian, Gaius Licinius Mucianus (the governor of Syria), and Alexander as allies already at the time Vespasian last (hypocritically) administered to his troops the oath of loyalty to Vitellius, in the spring of 69.[87] Vespasian thus must have begun courting the neighboring governor—Mucianus—and the prefect of Egypt long before their supposedly spontaneous demonstrations in his favor.[88]

Herodian's narrative of the war between Septimius Severus and Pescennius Niger in the last decade of the second century brings to the fore all the conventions of imperial rhetoric to and regarding provincial populations. Herodian drew a stark contrast between the two men: the former was all energy and activity; the latter, weakened by luxury and sloth. Herodian distinguished the two men in the first instance in the extent and effectiveness of their campaigns to win the allegiance of local populations, as well as of the officers and soldiers of nearby legions. For instance, once Niger had informed his commanders and tribunes of his decision to try for the throne, he then relied on rumor to bring this information to the attention of the rest of the East.[89] The initial reaction to his acclamation both locally and in Rome was favorable,[90] but this sloth cost him dearly. Niger should have departed immediately for Rome, argued Herodian. On his way to the capital he could have visited the Illyrian armies and been the first to cultivate their allegiance: "Instead he gave them no news of events and hoped that, if ever they did find out, the soldiers on that frontier would be in agreement with the wishes of the Romans and the sentiments of the armies of the East."[91]

With the behavior of Niger we may compare that of Septimius Severus: having induced his troops to proclaim him emperor, he sent out messages to the neighboring provinces and to the governors in the north: "Having paid court by correspondence to all the members of the Illyrian provinces and their governors, Severus won them over to his side."[92] Recognizing the necessity of flattering the Senate, Severus traveled first to Rome, where he cemented his authority over the western provinces by attaching himself to the family of his predecessor, making concessions to the Senate, and allying

---

86. For a commemoration of that event and the acclamations for Vespasian at that time, see *MW* no. 41 (*P. Fouad* 8 = Musurillo 1954, 30–31).

87. Tacitus *Hist.* 2.74.1.

88. On these events see Chilver 1979, 161–162, 233, and 238; cf. Wellesley 1989, 110–123.

89. Herodian 2.7.7.

90. Herodian 2.7.8 and 8.7–8.

91. Herodian 2.9–10.

92. Herodian 2.9.12, 10.1.

himself to the governor of Britain, Clodius Albinus. When Severus finally marched east to deal with Niger, Herodian describes a paradoxical journey through the Danubian provinces: Severus and his army moved with extraordinary speed, and yet stopped at every city, where he was warmly received and panegyrics were delivered.[93]

It is, of course, possible that Herodian's narrative does not accurately describe the activities of these two men in every detail, but that possibility need not trouble us here. For Herodian has in any event revealed a pair of interdependent presumptions about political life in the empire: first, that the *successful* claimant for the throne is he who best exploits the opportunities available to him for communicating with his different audiences—the army, the Senate, and the populations of Rome and of the provinces—and, second, that the legitimacy of that claimant manifests itself in his ability to move swiftly and unannounced through the provinces, while nevertheless receiving the adulation of his subjects.

The realities of marching several thousand men across the empire were, needless to say, far different from the narratives of historians and panegyrists. Scattered references in literary sources testify to the disturbance caused by imperial journeys even in times of peace.[94] For example, when describing Tiberius's oft-announced plans to tour the provinces, Suetonius noted that these announcements caused cities along his intended route to collect vehicles and supplies in preparation.[95] Philo complained in similar terms about the crowds and burdens that would accompany Gaius on his visit to Egypt: in addition to the emperor and his entourage, cities would have to feed and house both his soldiers and the sycophants from surrounding communities who would come to seek an audience.[96] An abundance of documentary papyri attests the preparations for imperial visits to Egypt, including a vast number of contracts with individuals to supply every conceivable foodstuff: barley and wheat, dates, suckling pigs and full-grown pigs, sheep, cattle, and camels, wine, olives, and olive oil. A person contracting to supply such provisions had to guarantee that he would fulfill the terms of the contract; one papyrus therefore preserves a contract by which one individual stood surety for another, who did not have sufficient collateral but had nevertheless undertaken to supply *garum*—fish sauce—for an upcoming visit by Caracalla. Such contracts appear as late as two months prior to the emperor's arrival, but some precede that event by as long as a year.[97]

93. Herodian 2.15.6.
94. Millar 1977, 28–41; Halfmann 1986, 65–89.
95. Suetonius *Tiberius* 38.
96. Philo *Leg.* 252–253.
97. *P. Got.* 3; *P. Panop. Beatty* 1; *PSI* 683; *P. Stras.* 245; cf. van Groningen 1956.

If we return now to political events, a large and varied body of evidence for the usurpation of Julian still survives, including historical narratives, panegyrics, and letters by contemporaries, as well as propagandistic tracts explicitly penned by the emperor, whose famous letter to the Athenians is but one of many letters published in the months between his elevation in Gaul in February 360 and his march against Constantius nine months later.[98] In point of fact, Julian had begun courting public favor as early as his first successful campaigns in Gaul: he wrote a pamphlet on his victory at Strasbourg that seems to have circulated throughout the East.[99] All these sources participate in, and may help us to close, the disjunction between rhetoric and reality in imperial usurpations.

Julian's campaign of disinformation certainly impressed his contemporaries. The ecclesiastical historian Socrates condemned his actions in no uncertain terms: "Julian neither negotiated with Constantius through ambassadors nor honored him as a benefactor;[100] he simply did everything as it seemed best to him. . . . He also slandered Constantius throughout the cities, by reciting publicly his letters to the barbarians."[101] This charge, that Constantius conciliated the barbarians and induced them to attack Julian, does appear in Julian's surviving letter to the Athenians.[102] Although Ammianus Marcellinus suggested that one should believe it only "if you feel compelled to place trust in rumor alone,"[103] others seem to have considered the accusation quite plausible: it is iterated, for example, by Claudius Mamertinus in his *gratiarum actio*, by Libanius, and by Sozomen.[104] Although these authors themselves reveal the influence of Julian's propa-

---

98. See Bowersock 1978, 60; Matthews 1989, 104–106; cf. Bidez and Cumont, *Imp. Iuliani fragmenta*, nos. 20–22, with testimonia.

99. Eunapius *Hist.* fr. 17. Cf. Ammianus 16.12.67, on the reports that Julian filed with Constantius.

100. Compare the response by the Senate to overtures from Julian at Ammianus 21.10.7: *quae cum Tertullo administrante adhuc praefecturam recitarentur in curia eminuit nobilitatis cum speciosa fiducia benignitas grata. exclamatum est enim in unum cunctorum sententia congruente "auctori tuo reverentiam rogamus."* On Constantius as Julian's *auctor* see also Ammianus 14.1.1, 14.11.10, 16.7.3, 20.5.3, 20.8.6, and 21.10.7 (cf. 26.4.3); Julian *Ep. ad Ath.* 285d; and Zosimus 3.9.2–5. Although Gregory of Nazianzus does not use a very precise translation for *auctor*, his condemnation of Julian's disrespect for Constantius clearly participates in this system of thought (*Or.* 4.38): γνωριμώτατον ἑαυτὸν ἐξ ἀσεβείας κατέστησε καὶ καινότερον τρόπον ἡμιλλήθη τῷ ἀναδείξαντι;

101. Socrates 3.1. It is probable that Socrates acquired this information from *Or.* 18 of Libanius, with which he was quite familiar.

102. *Ep. ad Ath.* 280b and 286a–b.

103. Ammianus 21.3.4.

104. See Libanius *Or.* 12.62; 13.35; 18.107 and esp. 113. See also Socrates 3.1, Sozomen 5.2.23, and Mamertinus at *Pan. Lat.* XI(3).6.1.

ganda, they do not explicitly connect that propaganda with his ultimate success against Constantius. And yet, when they describe Julian's eventual advance against his uncle, they would have us believe that he marched from Augusta Rauraca to Sirmium with such speed that his arrival in each town was completely unexpected.[105] As with Severus marching against Niger, Julian's sudden epiphanies did not prevent each city from formally receiving him and honoring him with panegyrics.[106] Could such receptions be truly spontaneous, or even possible, when the emperor was moving "like a shooting star or fiery dart?"[107]

On the contrary, the experience of Maximinus Thrax before the gates of Aquileia in the civil war of 238 urges that we take seriously the importance of procuring in advance the cooperation of local populations before leading an army through a province. Herodian once again provides our main narrative. Maximinus departed Sirmium for Italy with such haste, we are told, that his march was actually slower because of the lack of customary advance notice regarding the collection of supplies.[108] He encountered difficulty as soon as he reached Italy: the population of Emona had abandoned their city, and Maximinus's army went hungry.[109] Aquileia therefore assumed even greater importance for the provisioning of his army, but its population closed their gates against him.[110] Maximinus was then unwilling, or perhaps unable, to advance through hostile country—from which he could glean few if any supplies—while leaving a large, prosperous city at his back. After his besieging army began to starve, the soldiers, upset with their conditions, eventually murdered their commander and reconciled with Gordian and the Senate at Rome.[111]

If we accept the necessity of preparing the provinces for the passage of an emperor and his army, and if we believe that Julian did, in fact, speed from Gaul to Constantinople "like a fiery dart," then we must identify the moment when Julian published his charges against Constantius and, therefore, the means by which he prepared such a favorable reception for himself in the Illyrian provinces. The answer, I believe, lies in the letters from

---

105. Mamertinus at *Pan. Lat.* XI(3).6.2–7.3. For instructive parallels between the text of Mamertinus and that of Ammianus, as well as with other panegyrics, see Gutzwiller 1942, *ad loc.;* cf. MacCormack 1981, 48–49, and Halfmann 1986, 150–151.

106. Mamertinus at *Pan. Lat.* XI(3).6.3. See also Ammianus 21.10.1–2, together with Szidat 1996, 96–97, and esp. MacCormack 1981, 45–50.

107. Ammianus 21.9. The comparison between an emperor and a swift star had a long history; particularly instructive is Pliny *Pan.* 80.3.

108. Herodian 7.8.10–11.

109. Herodian 8.1.4–5; cf. *SHA Max.* 21.5.

110. Herodian 8.2; cf. *SHA Max.* 22.1.

111. Shortages in the army: Herodian 8.5.3, 6.4; *SHA Max.* 23.2. Death of Maximinus: Herodian 8.5.8–9.

Julian to Constantius, both public and private, and in the slow journey of Eutherius.

In the winter of 360/361, after his elevation to the rank of Augustus, Julian wrote a letter to Constantius urging that Constantius reconcile himself to Julian's new rank; Ammianus claims to reproduce the gist of this document.[112] Ammianus also claims that Julian simultaneously wrote Constantius an accusatory and insulting letter. That letter, Ammianus writes, was private, and he argues that it would not be appropriate to reveal its contents, even if he knew them.[113] It has been suggested that Ammianus has confused two separate incidents: on this theory, the second letter was sent after the first, more polite letter failed to achieve its goal.[114] This is possible but, as we shall see, unnecessary. Julian ordered two men to convey the letters to Constantius: Pentadius, his *magister officiorum*, who was actually a partisan of Constantius, and Eutherius, at that time Julian's *praepositus cubiculi* and trusted advisor.[115] Ammianus has described their journey in some detail: "The envoys followed with no less diligence, bearing with them the messages that I have mentioned and intent upon their journey; when, however, they fell in with higher officials, they were covertly detained. Having suffered long and aggravating delays throughout Italy and Illyricum, they finally crossed the Bosporus and, proceeding by slow stages, they found Constantius still tarrying at Cappadocian Caesarea."[116] It seems implausible that *iudices celsiores* could have detained high-ranking envoys bearing messages between the emperors in the midst of a crisis of such magnitude: after all, even according to Ammianus, the envoys continued to move in "slow stages" after they crossed the Bosporus. Ammianus has merely heard and related the explanation that the envoys offered to Constantius. In reality they were, I suggest, deliberately stopping at each major city on their route, in order to read aloud the letters of Julian to Constantius and, presumably, the letters purported to have passed between Constantius and the barbarians.

The journey of Eutherius thus interpreted appears consistent with Julian's other efforts to organize opinion and orchestrate his reception during his march to Constantius and the East. Fearing lest his advance to civil war provoke resistance, Julian attempted to impress the Danubian provinces with a show of power sufficient to imply legitimacy. He divided his forces in

112. Ammianus 20.8.4; the text quoted at 8.5–17.
113. Ammianus 20.8.18.
114. See den Boeft, den Hengst, and Teitler 1987 on Ammianus 20.8.18.
115. Ammianus 20.8.19. Pentadius did not swerve in his allegiance to Constantius and was tried at Chalcedon (Ammianus 22.3.5). It is frequently and plausibly maintained, on the basis of 16.7.5, that Eutherius was an important source for Ammianus. Cf. Thompson 1947, 20; Sabbah 1978, 228–230.
116. Ammianus 20.9.1 (trans. Rolfe, modified).

three, hoping to spur rumors of legions more numerous than those he actually controlled.[117] The plan was successful, and rumors spread: Julian's victories in Gaul implied the magnitude of his army and his own suitability for the throne.[118] Having reached the outskirts of Sirmium, Julian sent soldiers to conduct into his presence one Lucillianus, the master of the cavalry stationed in that city.[119] Those soldiers must also have instructed the city to prepare for Julian's arrival. The next day, "when Julian approached the suburbs, which sprawled far and wide, a throng of soldiers and civilians of every kind greeted him with many torches and flowers and happy prayers, acclaiming him Augustus and Lord, and led him to the palace."[120]

Julian was elated and . . . paused at Sirmium. Why? He had proceeded in haste and secrecy thus far. He had even avoided cities and camps along the way.[121] If he wished to avoid cities, why stop at Sirmium? But if he could organize Sirmium and stop there, why not elsewhere? Public receptions were a hazardous necessity. As much as Julian had worked to influence public opinion, he could not control it. Sirmium's reaction could not be taken for granted: such ceremonials were "a practiced fixedness founded on pure contingency."[122] The population at Rome had, after all, repudiated Severus's propaganda against Clodius Albinus, despite two years' effort to court that city's favor.[123] Sirmium may have behaved as Julian desired, and its acclamation will have then displayed the *consensus* of its populace, its recognition of Julian's legitimacy, and thus offered civilian ratification "of the military election at Paris. . . . Such ratifications were not regarded as mere ceremonial by-products of political events, but as political events in themselves."[124] Other traditions about his reception at Sirmium circulated in later years: above all that the city had thought it was Constantius approaching, or soldiers of Constantius.[125]

Whatever the truth of that day—whether Sirmium learned the night before or only upon Julian's appearance which emperor would grace their

117. Ammianus 21.8.2–3, with Szidat 1996, 72. Ammianus thought Julian aware that he was instigating a civil war (21.5.1), and this would not be inconsistent with the Senate's reaction to his overtures to that body. (See above, n. 100.) Note that Julian continued to feign Christianity until he had eliminated his rival, another attempt to adjust his deportment to public expectations (Ammianus 21.2.4–5).

118. Ammianus 21.9.3, with Szidat 1996, 85–91.

119. Ammianus 21.9.6.

120. Ammianus 21.10.1. On this episode see Fontaine 1996, 225–226, and Szidat 1996, 96–97.

121. Ammianus 21.9.2.

122. Schechner 1987, 10, on which see Chapter 5 at n. 14.

123. See above at nn. 43 and 49.

124. MacCormack 1981, 47.

125. Libanius *Or.* 18.111; Zosimus 3.10.3.

city—it was clearly in Julian's interest to spread rumors of a favorable reception accomplished without deceit. Julian therefore paused to allow the news of Sirmium's action to spread—a process he no doubt aided—"because, following the example of a populous and famous metropolis, he would be received in other cities, too, as a health-giving star."[126] In the event, he was successful. As Sabine MacCormack argues, Julian's final reception at Constantinople was, for all practical purposes, determined by the rumors of military success and favorable acclamations that had preceded that moment: "For it seemed closer to a dream that a man who was still young, of slender build but famed for great deeds, after the bloodstained destruction of kings and nations, should pass from city to city with unprecedented speed; that, moreover, his every arrival increased his wealth and strength, while he seized all things more easily than rumor flies; and, finally, that he should have taken up the throne with the assenting nod of heaven without any loss to the state whatsoever."[127]

We can thus create a degree of convergence between the historiographic convention and the realities of travel in the ancient world. It *was* possible for Severus and later for Julian to travel through the provinces with great speed, but only because each had carefully solicited the favor of all relevant audiences, from the governors and soldiers whose acclamations provided the impetus for Severus to the cities and towns through which Julian would have to move. The successful emperor had, however, to disguise that process of solicitation as much as possible. There was no flattery and no power in adulation if you admitted that you had arranged it three months ahead of time. It was precisely the apparent spontaneity and unanimity of local acclamations that legitimated the successful claimant to the throne, and so their panegyrists and biographers loyally wrote.

ACTING OUT *CONSENSUS*

Surviving evidence forces us to study expressions of *consensus* largely as moments in a stylized dialogue between local elites and the central government or through ideologically charged but elusive allusions within literary texts. We would be remiss, however, if we deduced from this material either the conclusion that the government of the empire sought only the approval of those elites or that *consensus* existed only as an ideal, to which rulers and ruled appealed but which could not be concretized through physical utterance or action. As the actions of the people of Sirmium reveal, the ancient

126. Ammianus 21.10.2. The panegyrist of 313 similarly invoked the *consensus* of Italy in support of Constantine against Maxentius (*Pan. Lat.* IX[12].7.3–4).
127. Ammianus 22.2.5.

world did possess a ritual expression of approval by a community, the acclamation (*acclamatio*):[128] the unisonal, rhythmic chanting of religious or political formulas. It was a common medium for communal expressions of piety in the East and in Greek religious life,[129] and had played a role in the relations between Hellenistic kings and their armies.[130] Under the empire this particular form of political behavior took on a profoundly greater significance: an acclamation was by definition an expression of *consensus*.[131] As such, acclamations were the primary vehicle through which the population of an entire city could ritually recognize the charisma of a particular ruler and the legitimacy of his government. In ancient terms, *consensus* as expressed through acclamation distinguished the *princeps* from the *tyrannus*.[132] In the words of John Chrysostom: "There are two types of royal power, the natural and the elected. Examples of natural monarchies are that of the lion over the beasts and that of the eagle over the birds. But the rule of the emperor among us is an elective monarchy. For our emperor does not wield power over slaves by some intrinsic right; therefore, too, emperors among us often lose their power."[133]

It may well be that acclamations were uncommon in Roman political life of the middle Republic precisely because they recognized a charisma that would have separated their honorand from his peers. Reports of acclamations thus became common in the last generation of the Republic, at precisely that time when individuals sought to outstrip the traditional strictures of aristocratic competition.[134] It was, not surprisingly, through acclamations that Caesar and his accomplices sought to legitimize his unique status and his claim to extraconstitutional leadership. During his unprecedented celebration of an *ovatio* during the *Feriae Latinae* on 26 January 44 B.C., "amidst

128. The best general survey of acclamations is that by Klauser in his *RAC* article (s.v. "Akklamation"); see also Peterson 1926, *passim*, but esp. 141–145; A. Alföldi 1934, 79–88; Kantorowicz 1946, 16–19; Roueché 1984; and Potter 1996c. On the metrical form of acclamations in the circus and in Byzantine ceremonial handbooks see Maas 1912 and A. D. E. Cameron 1976, 329–333.

129. Peterson 1926, 142–143; Klauser, *RAC* s.v. "Akklamation," cols. 217–221; and Dufraigne 1994, 95–147.

130. See Walbank at Polybius 10.40.2–9; Weinstock 1971, 107–109.

131. A point not often emphasized, but see Instinsky 1940, 271: the acclamation, as a sign of *consensus*, validates the *salutatio;* cf. MacCormack 1981, 22–23 and 80; and Dufraigne 1994, 21, 152, 160, and 169–176.

132. Cf. Béranger 1975, 165–190.

133. *Homil. ad populum Antiochenum* 7.2 (*PG* 49, col. 93): Τῶν γὰρ ἀρχῶν αἱ μέν εἰσι φυσικαί, αἱ δὲ χειροτονηταί· φυσικαὶ μέν, ὡς ἡ τοῦ λέοντος ἐπὶ τῶν τετραπόδων, ὡς ἐπὶ τῶν ὀρνίθων ἡ τοῦ ἀετοῦ· χειροτονηταὶ δέ, ὡς ἡ τοῦ βασιλέως τοῦ καθ᾽ ἡμᾶς· οὗτος γὰρ οὐχὶ φύσει κρατεῖ τῶν ὁμοδούλων· διὸ καὶ ἀποβάλλει πολλάκις τὴν ἀρχήν.

134. See, for example, Plutarch *Pompey* 57 and Caesar *BG* 8.51.

extravagant and unprecedented acclamations of the populace, someone from the crowd placed on Caesar's statue a laurel crown tied with a white fillet."[135] Roman emperors ever afterwards accepted the *consensus* of the population as expressed in their acclamations as one measure of their legitimacy. What is more, acclamations by the populace could balance and even suppress the disapproval of the Senate; they were the natural means of expressing gratitude for the *congiaria* and *frumentationes* that the *princeps* dispensed in his role as protector and patron of the plebs.[136] Recognition by the people as revealed through their acclamations remained indispensable in the late empire even in the selection of bishops, and for those processes Christians merely borrowed formulas familiar from imperial ceremonial. At the election of Ambrose, divine grace ensured that the divergent desires of catholics and Arians suddenly converged upon Ambrose, in a gesture of miraculous and incredible concord.[137] The demands made by Rutilius Pudens Crispinus and Tullius Menophilus, the commanders at Aquileia, after the death of Maximinus illustrate the currency of acclamation as a political gesture. Those men came before the army of Maximinus bearing statues of Maximus, Balbinus, and Gordian, crowned with laurel. The generals alone acclaimed the portraits, turned to the army, and demanded that it recognize by acclamation the emperors chosen by the Senate and people of Rome.[138]

Nero's introduction into Rome of a professional Alexandrian claque no doubt had an effect on the development of Roman acclamations,[139] not

135. Suetonius *Iulius* 79.1, and cf. Dio 54.9–10. On these events see Weinstock 1971, 318–331.

136. See Yavetz 1969. For acclamations in the Byzantine empire, see Baynes 1946a, 32, and Treitinger 1956; on popular election of emperors in early Byzantine political thought, see Dagron 1968, 135–144. The *De ceremoniis* preserves the acclamations chanted at the accessions of Leo, Anastasius, and Justin I (1.91–93).

137. Paulinus *Vita Ambrosii* 6.2: *itaque qui antea turbulentissime dissidebant—quia et Arriani sibi et catholici sibi episcopum cupiebant, superatis alterutris, ordinari—repente in hunc unum mirabili et incredibili concordia consenserunt.* Cf. Pontius *Vita Cypriani* 5.2; Sulpicius Severus *Vita Martini* 9.2–3; Possidius *Vita Augustini* 4.2 (*omnibus id uno consensu et desiderio fieri perficique petentibus*); and Augustine *Ep.* 213.1, 6: [1]*'presbyterum Eraclium mihi successorem volo.' a populo acclamatum est: 'Deo gratias, Christo laudes'—dictum est vicies terties—; 'exaudi, Christe, Augustino vita'—dictum est sexies decies—; 'te patrem, te episcopum'—dictum est octies. . . .* [6]*'video me de hac re, propter quam vos invitavi, omnia vobiscum egisse, quae debui. hoc ad ultimum rogo, ut gestis istis dignemini subscribere, qui potestis. hic responsione vestra opus est; teneam responsionem vestram, de hac assensione aliquid acclamate.' A populo acclamatum est: 'Fiat, fiat'—dictum vicies quinquies; 'dignum est, iustum est'—dictum vicies octies.* . . . The latter text is not a letter at all, but a transcript of the meeting. (See *Ep.* 213.2; cf. Teitler 1985.) In the East see Basil *Ep.* 161.1. See also Kantorowicz 1946, 119, and Peterson 1926, 176–180, on the ἄξιος acclamation.

138. Herodian 8.6.2. Cf. Dio 73.2.3 on the Roman mob's ability to manipulate its traditional chants.

139. Suetonius *Nero* 20.3 and Tacitus *Ann.* 14.15.5.

least in allowing speculation that acclamations could be the work of hired or otherwise compelled individuals.[140] It is altogether typical of the cynicism of Tacitus that he regarded the cheers at Rome for Otho as neither spontaneous nor compelled but rather symptomatic of the decline in self-respect that the Principate had wrought.[141] Whatever the influence of these Alexandrians at Rome, acclamation as a form of political behavior exercised its widest influence over the next few centuries as a Roman, Latin institution.[142] Roman formulas spread because acclamation as a form of expression within political ritual became—like *adoratio*[143]—embedded within the behaviors used to greet any representative or representation of the emperor, including texts authored by his hand.[144] This influence appears with particular clarity in the role played by acclamations in the procedures of corporate bodies. When Pliny boasted that the acclamations for Trajan in the Senate had been published in the *acta diurna,* he wished the Senate to stand before the world as a paradigm of political loyalty.[145] But the Senate's behavior undoubtedly influenced not only the spirit but also the form in which other corporate bodies throughout the Mediterranean world displayed their loyalty to king and country. They therefore copied the Senate's formulas because they wished to endow their own proceedings with similar legitimacy. We can observe such imitations in the acts of municipal senates, but they are most visible in the better-preserved proceedings of church councils.[146]

140. For example, Dio claims that the acclamations which senators showered upon Commodus after his performances in the arena were compelled (72.20.2). Constantine, who used acclamations to measure popular support for his subordinates, promised to investigate *si verae voces sunt nec ad libidinem per clientelas effusae* (*C. Th.* 1.16.6). For Themistius, the shallowness of the acclamations for Nero was paradigmatic: καὶ εὐφημοῦσι μὲν ἄνωθεν ἀπὸ τῆς γλώττης, τὰ δὲ εἴσω μεστὰ ὀδυρμῶν. οὕτω γὰρ τὸ μὲν Κύρου γῆρας εὐκτὸν ἦν τοῖς τὴν Ἀσίαν οἰκοῦσι, Νέρων δὲ ἐν ἀκμῇ τῆς ἡλικίας ἑαυτὸν ἀποσφάξας ὀψὲ λίαν ἐδόκει τεθνάναι (*Or.* 8.102c). Pliny even complained that men could be hired to cheer advocates at court (*Ep.* 2.14.4, 6), and in this he was not alone. Cf. Potter 1996c, 147–159.

141. Tacitus *Hist.* 1.90.3.

142. On bilingualism in circus acclamations in both East and West, see A. D. E. Cameron 1973, 77–80. For Latin in Byzantine acclamations, see Constantine *De ceremoniis* 1.73–74 and A. Toynbee 1973, 572–574.

143. On which see Chapter 4 at nn. 133–138, Chapter 7 at nn. 97 and 246–250, and Chapter 9 at nn. 244–245.

144. For the acclamations which close the Aphrodisias text of Diocletian's Price Edict, see Roueché 1984, 186 n. 51, and 1989, no. 231, chapter xxxv, l. 57. Compare the chants of the Senate at the reception of the Theodosian Code and the edict which promulgated it (*Gesta senatus Romani de Theodosiano publicando* 5).

145. See Chapter 5, "The Imposing Façade of Senatorial Support."

146. See Hirschfeld 1913, 693–695; J. Anderson 1913, 284–287; Batiffol 1913b; Peterson 1926, 146–152; A. Alföldi 1934, 86; Klauser, *RAC* s.v. "Akklamation," cols. 226–227; Colin 1965, chapter 4; Bowman 1971, 36, 104–107; and Roueché 1984, 182.

Although acclamations were, by definition, a momentary vocalization of communal feeling, an acclamation, like any other oral text, could be written down. In its written form, an acclamation became a portable expression of a community's loyalty toward its emperor. By the fourth century, inscribing acclamations had become common practice in the East, particularly in the empty spaces on milestones.[147] By this time acclamations had become the primary vehicle for the public's expression of its corporate will. Even in the late empire they continued to mediate a dialogue between the emperor and the plebs, through which those parties could circumvent or even discuss intermediary officials.[148] For example, late in his reign Constantine used acclamations to formalize an element of accountability in and popular supervision over the judicial duties of provincial governors. He ordained that governors must hold trials with their tribunals surrounded by people and forbade them to hear civil cases in private. His edict continued:[149]

> We grant to all the opportunity to praise by public acclamation the most just and most vigilant judges, so that we might offer them an increased flow of honor. Unjust evildoers, on the other hand, should be accused by cries of complaints, so that the strength of our censure might destroy them. For we shall investigate diligently whether acclamations were spontaneous or poured forth wantonly by clients. Let the praetorian prefect and the counts who are stationed throughout the provinces report to our wisdom the acclamations of our provincials.

By this legislation, acclamations became a tool through which to actualize a fundamental principle of imperial government, one stressed almost continuously in imperial propaganda. According to this principle, the emperor's personal concern for the well-being of his subjects outweighed any personal connection he might have with his subordinates. The members of the imperial administration were no more and no less subjects of the emperor than was the lowliest citizen.[150]

Constantine need not have been motivated solely by a desire to monitor his subordinates. Extant minutes of municipal proceedings reveal that ac-

147. Published milestones recording acclamations include Brünnow and Domaszewski 1905, 230 and 337; Robert 1954, nos. 123 and 124, republishing *MAMA* VI nos. 94, 95; and Welles 1938, nos. 345–348. On milestones and roads as media of propaganda see Chapter 8 at nn. 198–206. For the printing of acclamations on the coins of Ephesus in the third century, see Knibbe, Engelmann, and Iplikcioglu 1993, 147. For practice at Rome see Potter 1996c, 144–147.

148. See Browning 1952 on the role of acclamations in the riots at Antioch in 387. Note that those riots began when an official recited an imperial letter at the *dikasterion;* it is highly probable that the letter was announcing a victory and a corresponding request for *aurum coronarium.*

149. *C. Th.* 1.16.6.

150. See Chapter 9, "The Emperor and His Subordinates."

clamations for the emperor formed part of the acclamations at any official gathering. In about A.D. 300 the city of Oxyrhynchus gathered to greet two high-ranking officials, the governor of the district and the *catholicus,* the imperial procurator for all Egypt. The people chanted at the arrival: "Roman power forever! Lords Augusti! Good fortune, O governor; good fortune, *catholicus.*" In the middle of the meeting that followed, the people broke out again: "Lords Augusti! All victories for the Romans! Roman power forever. Good fortune, O governor; savior of honest men, *catholicus.*" The meeting ended with similar cries.[151] To this record we may compare the series of acclamations inscribed at Aphrodisias to honor a local benefactor, Albinus, for his renovation of a portico in the Aphrodisian agora sometime during the sixth century: "God is one, for the whole world! Many years for the emperors! Many years for the eparchs! Many years for the Senate! Many years for the metropolis! . . . Albinus—up with the builder of the stoa!"[152]

Later emperors evidently liked Constantine's legislation. In 371 Valentinian, Valens, and Gratian allowed the use of the public post to carry such texts to the court.[153] Nine years later Gratian, Valentinian II, and Theodosius reminded the prefect of Rome that the "customary acclamations" should be given to a variety of ex-magistrates "at every meeting and every assembly."[154] In the middle of the fifth century the praetorian prefects congratulated the proconsul of Asia on the favorable acclamations which had greeted him in Ephesus; these had presumably been recorded and sent to the capital.[155] Finally, Justinian excerpted and affirmed the validity of the last sentence of Constantine's law when he published his Code in 542.[156]

If all series of acclamations began with or at least contained invocations of the emperor, Constantine could use such texts to gauge both the performance of his appointees and the loyalty of his subjects.[157] In a way, these texts can reveal far more to us than they revealed to Constantine. The slow insinuation of prayers for the emperor into municipal ceremonies, like the gradual insinuation of the emperor into the multiple pantheons of Mediterranean paganism, suggested that the stability of local institutions and the mechanisms of daily life depended upon individual loyalty to the imperial

151. *P. Oxy.* I 41 (*Sel. pap.* 239, ll. 2–3, 20–22).
152. Roueché 1989, no. 83, nos. i–vi.
153. *C. Th.* 8.5.32.
154. *C. Th.* 6.9.2.
155. *I. Ephesus* no. 44, ll. 5–14. Some years later the *comes domesticorum* Phlegetius rendered a decision under the influence of the acclamations of "the splendid metropolis of the Ephesians" (*I. Ephesus* no. 1352).
156. *C. Iust.* 1.40.3.
157. Libanius presumes upon understanding municipal acclamations in these terms in his denunciation of Christian impiety and hypocrisy (*Or.* 56.16).

government. Conversely, they also placed the existence and the importance of those institutions in a continuum within the larger community of the empire. Through their acclamations people thus unconsciously iterated the binding links of imperial ideology, lending their tacit assent to Rome's control over the cultural script and to its right to enforce it. Through each smaller expression of *consensus,* they slowly found their place within a greater whole.

CHAPTER SEVEN

Images of Emperor and Empire

DECIUS AND THE *DIVI*

The strands of argument and systems of belief interwoven in this chapter find their nexus in the reign of Claudius Messius Quintus Decius Valerianus. Decius came to power in an era of instability. He himself seized the throne by killing his predecessor and patron, Philip the Arab, in a battle during the autumn of 249.[1] Decius then proceeded to Rome, where, at the urging of the Senate but through his own prompting, he added the name Trajan to his own.[2] Philip had celebrated the millennial anniversary of the city of Rome in 248, and there is some reason to believe that his action had aroused eschatological fears around the empire.[3] The honor of inaugurating a new *saeculum,* which Philip had desired for himself, fell to his challengers and therefore also to Decius.[4] Decius sought to reassure his subjects

---

1. For data on Decius and the chronology of his reign see H. Mattingly and Salisbury 1924b; Potter 1990, 40–45 and 258–283; and Peachin 1990, 30–32, 66–69, and 239–264.

2. See Alföldi at *CAH* XII 166 n. 1, and Syme 1971, 220. The common measure of the esteem in which Trajan's name was held is the acclamation reported by Eutropius, *felicior Augusto, melior Traiano* (8.5.3); and cf. Ammianus on Julian at 16.1.4. On the cheapening of the name Antoninus, see *SHA Elag.* 3.1, 34.6, and *Alex. Sev.* 9, and see Hartke 1951, 133–142, and Syme 1971, 79–80.

3. Potter 1990, 39, 258.

4. *RIC* IV.3, Philip I nos. 12–24 from Rome (rev.), SAECULARES AUGG.; cf., also from Rome, no. 25 (rev.), SAECULUM NOVUM; cf., from Antioch, no. 86 (rev.), SAECULUM NOVUM; etc. Cf. the coin of Pacatianus, *RIC* IV.3, Pacatianus no. 6 (rev.), ROMAE AETER. AN MILL. ET PRIMO, and those of Herennia Etruscilla, the wife of Decius, *RIC* IV.3, Decius no. 67, from Milan, SAECULUM NOVUM, and of Hostilianus, Decius's younger son, Decius no. 199, from Antioch, SAECULUM NOVUM (also no. 205).

of the health and stability of their empire, and the gods of their unanimous piety, by commanding a universal display of *consensus:* all citizens were to sacrifice to their ancestral gods for the safety of the empire.[5] Decius also gave expression to his piety—and to the sort of piety that he wished to foster—in a series of coins issued from the mint at Milan, devoted to the consecrated emperors: Augustus, Vespasian, Titus, Nerva, Trajan, Hadrian, Antoninus Pius, Marcus Aurelius, Commodus, Severus, and Alexander.[6]

What effect did these actions have in the urban centers of the empire? Let us attempt an imaginative reconstruction of the events that followed the battle of Verona. In October or November of 249 imperial messengers scatter throughout the provinces the empire, bringing word that a new emperor has ascended to the rulership of the world. The messengers enter each city in a formal procession, bearing the portrait of Decius himself. Local dignitaries receive them on the city's behalf and deliver speeches of thanksgiving, while the local populace signals its approval with rhythmic displays of its *consensus.* All present know full well that this announcement will require a formal response by the community, which will have to be accompanied by a congratulatory gift of gold.

Over the next few months new coins begin to circulate through the local economy. Suspicious individuals compare the portrait on the new coins with the official portraits now standing in the forum and throughout the city. A few coins, although new, bear the names of emperors from the past. Some of their names are familiar from the storehouse of historical knowledge that supplies anecdotes for local orators, and in many cases their busts survive, scattered in local temples, preserved if no longer honored. Late in 249 more officials arrive, summoning the local population to the reading of a new ordinance. Many attend, though a few will learn its content later from the posted text.

Decius has ordered all citizens of the empire to sacrifice on the empire's behalf.[7] For this purpose the officials bring forward an altar to the emperor,

---

5. On the Decian "persecution," see Alföldi at *CAH* XII 194, 202–204, who sees the command to sacrifice as directed against Christians. A more persuasive interpretation of his order views Decius as motivated by a desire to reinforce Rome's traditional relationship with her gods, and the persecution of Christians as an unfortunate but accidental consequence: for this theory see Baynes at *CAH* XII 656; Frend 1965, 405–407; and Potter 1990, 261–267.

6. *RIC* IV.3, Decius nos. 77–99. On the dating of the issue, see H. Mattingly and Salisbury 1924a, 235–237, and Mattingly at *RIC* IV.3.113.

7. What follows is one possible form for the ceremony, reconstructed on analogy with rituals adumbrated elsewhere in this book. Briefly put, individuals were expected in the first instance to bring favor upon the empire by worshiping those gods who protect the empire. (See the formulation in Eusebius *Hist. eccl.* 7.11.7: θεοὺς τοὺς σώζοντας αὐτῶν τὴν βασιλείαν προσκυνεῖν.) This meant, for all intents and purposes, all gods but the Christian one: see the

a vast collection of statues, a register of the local population, and a set of *fasces*, the symbolic equivalent of standards in civilian contexts.[8] In many cities in the West, the ceremony takes place at the local Capitolium, a religious complex designed to reproduce the central religious complex of Rome.[9] Though the request possesses a certain novelty, the ceremony itself resembles paying one's taxes or filing a census return or swearing the annual oath of loyalty. In other words, it draws on ceremonial forms long familiar. All must present a *libellus* in duplicate, a certificate attesting their performance of the required sacrifice; the text of the *libellus* is read aloud, to ensure that the illiterate understand the text that will bear their name. When petitioners have signed or verbally assented, they receive one copy of the *libellus* for their records.[10]

As each person steps up to the altar, he or she casts a glance over the portraits arrayed in an arc extending to the left and right of the centrally placed portrait of Decius himself. Among them the town's magistrates have placed statuettes of local deities.[11] But the display also includes names and faces of

---

confused response put to Pionius by the proconsul Julius Proculus Quintilianus: [Pionius] Οὔ· τῷ γὰρ θεῷ εὔχεσθαί με δεῖ. [Quintilianus] ὁ δὲ λέγει· Πάντες τοὺς θεοὺς σέβομεν καὶ τὸν οὐρανὸν καὶ τοὺς ὄντας ἐν τῷ οὐρανῷ θεούς (*Acta Pionii* 19.9–10). Many Christians "lapsed" because in the last instance local officials, like Polemon in Smyrna, dispensed a *libellus* for the minimal demonstration of loyalty of sacrificing to the emperor: Πολέμων εἶπεν· Ἐπίθυσον οὖν κἂν τῷ αὐτοκράτορι (8.4). On the minimal requirements, see also *Acta Cononis* 4.3–4, and cf. Robert 1994, 109–110. The place of the Decian persecution in the history of Roman and Christian political theologies is discussed in Chapter 9, "The Discovery of Roman Religion."

8. The use of census records is deduced from Eusebius *Hist. eccl.* 6.41.11, quoting Dionysius of Alexandria: Frend 1965, 407–408. On the fasces, see *Acta Pionii* 10.4 and Robert's note *ad locum*. For altars to the emperor in the Greek world see Benjamin and Raubitschek 1959, and cf. Gros 1988.

9. For the Capitolium at Carthage, see Tertullian *Coron.* 12.3; Cyprian *Laps.* 8 and 24, and *Ep.* 49.13.3. Vitruvius 1.7.1 assumes that cities will be under the protection of the Capitoline triad and will require a Capitol for their worship. Cf. canon 59 of the Council of Elvira, *prohibendum ne quis Christianus ut gentilis ad idolum Capitolii causa sacrificandi ascendat et videat*, as well as Pacian *Ep.* 2.3.1: *Numquid Cypriano sancto viro hoc obest quod populus eius apostaticum nomen habet, vel capitolinum, vel syndreum?* On Capitolia elsewhere see H. Leclercq, *Dictionnaire d'archéologie chrétienne et de liturgie* 2.2 (1925), s.v. "capitoles," cols. 2044–2048; and A. Hermann, *RAC* s.v. "Capitolium," cols. 852–855.

10. Knipfing 1923 reproduced and analyzed extant *libelli*; a few more have been published in the interim. Extant duplicates: Knipfing nos. 11 and 26, and cf. *P. Oxy.* XXXVIII 2855. On the reading of the text, see Cyprian *Ep.* 30.3.1; on the necessity of verbally assenting, see Cyprian *Ep.* 30.3.1 and 55.14.1.

11. See Tertullian *Nat.* 2.8.7 on the *deos decuriones cuiusque municipii* whose worship is circumscribed by their city's walls. On the participation of local officials see Knipfing 1923, 351. On the statuettes in the ceremony see Robert 1994, 61–62, 65–66, and 104, and cf. *idem* 1954, 119, *idem* 1960, *idem* 1987, 133–147, and *idem*, *OMS* 2:835, discussing the use of epithets for local deities in dedications to the emperor or the collocation of their images. For further evidence see Nock 1972, 202–204 and 223–236.

earlier emperors.[12] Like the strange coins of this new emperor, this display does not require an audience steeped in the details of imperial politics. On the contrary: one did not need to know specific dates or deeds of these emperors in order to understand their function in this ceremony. If their identities as idiosyncratic individuals were ambiguous, their collocation expressed a message wholly devoid of ambiguity.

Placed before such a gallery, individuals making their prayers for the eternity of the empire saw the current emperor as one in a series of uniquely capable individuals, whose succession encapsulated and expressed a narrative of stability and strength. Other currents in popular culture in these occasionally tumultuous times soothed momentary fears with talk of the eternity of Rome.[13] The sacrifice ordered by Decius, and the desire that it expressed, lent its voice to a chorus that included art and pageantry, rhetoric and religion. Toward this end, the coins of Decius had made a remarkable effort to enumerate only those gods held in common by all citizens of his empire.[14] All that was essential to the shared religion and history of the empire—and these were by now inextricably intertwined—was expressible through piety toward a pantheon of emperors whose succession would ensure peace now and for all time.

SYMBOLIC FORMS IN ROMAN LIFE

The script provided by Decius was enacted with different properties and altered stagecraft in every city of the empire. To appreciate its import we must look backwards and forward. On the one hand, we should ask how populations around the Mediterranean were taught to understand the language in which Decius addressed them, to say nothing of his message. Who looked at the portraits on coins? Why were coins bearing unfamiliar portraits not greeted with suspicion? What meaning, if any, did residents of Smyrna or Carthage or Ephesus attach to *fasces* or standards? At the same time, the empire under Decius stood at the threshold of a new era, but three generations

12. Cf. Mattingly at *RIC* IV.3.118: "The issue of the coins of *Divi* was a remarkable demonstration in favour of the religion of the State. It is doubly significant because it stands almost alone in the coinage of Decius, where armies, provinces, and imperial virtues have their part, but the great gods and goddesses of the pagan Pantheon—Jupiter, Juno, Minerva, Mars—are almost completely lacking."

13. See Friedlaender 1922, 1:32 n. 7; Nock 1972, 257–258, and Instinsky 1942, 334–345. Instinsky expresses concern about the lack of *aeternitas* issues during the reigns of Maximinus, Gordian, and Decius (343 n. 4), but I suspect that he focuses too closely on that particular legend: cf. *RIC* IV.3, Decius no. 47, ROMAE AETERNAE (also no. 66; cf. nos. 197, 198, 204, and 223, for Hostilianus), and no. 49, PAX AETERN.

14. Cf. Mitchell 1993, 1:113, discussing what was shared and what varied in local celebrations of imperial cult.

removed from seeing a Christian on its throne. Astonishingly, neither that emperor nor his successors, nor any meaningful number of their subjects, thought the ritual forms that Decius employed were tainted by the message Decius and later persecutors made them carry. It is not the replacement of a pagan *habitus* by a Christian one that marks the boundary of late antiquity. Rather, as Christianity was explained through comparison to familiar rituals, and the sentiments those inspired, it assimilated to their pace, their structures, and their logic. The presence of Christians on the throne is necessary but not sufficient to identify late antiquity; it is the Romanness of Theodosius that makes him the heir of Augustus and not the precursor of Charlemagne.

Decius addressed his audience in the first instance through its eyes. In an era of low literacy, this hardly surprises. Romans had long devoted special care to the use of visual imagery. We have already seen that Septimius Severus used large paintings with captions to inform the plebs regarding his recent victories. Similar practices obtained in the private sphere: like Aeneas wandering amidst the murals in the Temple of Juno at Carthage, Encolpius and his friends found in Trimalchio's forecourt a pictorial biography of the freedman, complete with captions.[15] Some symbols required no text but communicated their meaning through participation in the shared iconographic language of imperial art. Thus, according to Tacitus, twice in the reign of Galba groups expressed their solidarity with particular Roman legions by sending them figurines of right hands clasped in friendship. In one case, the legions of Syria urged common interest and shared experience with their brethren in the Praetorian Guard; in the other, the community of the Lingones, who had come under Roman rule only a century before, used a Mediterranean emblem to seek the good will of the legions of Upper Germany.[16] It is no accident that both Vitellius and Vespasian used this same image on their early issues, whether urging, advertising, or seeking desperately and hopelessly to maintain the *consensus* and loyalty of the armies (Fig. 2).[17] In many situations, the ambiguity of the nonverbal message had much to recommend it: the Lingones, for example, had neither need nor desire to express a preference for Galba or Vitellius, but wished only to maintain good relations with the local soldiery.

Artifacts are but the extant, static props of ceremonial dramas through which Romans—broadly construed—endlessly reenacted their roles in the

15. Petronius 29.4: *omnia diligenter curiosus pictor cum inscriptione reddiderat.*

16. Tacitus *Hist.* 1.54.1, *miserat civitas Lingonum vetere instituto dona legionibus dextras, hospitii insigne;* and 2.8.2, *dextras, concordiae insignia.*

17. *BMC* I, ccxxiii and Vitellius nos. 2 and 113–117, and II, Vespasian nos. 369 and 414–416; Brilliant 1963, 88–90. See also *MW* no. 38. On the evolution of *Concordia* in Roman thought, see Béranger 1975, 367–382, and Levick 1978.

Figure 2. Vitellius pleads for the solidarity of the legions.
Aureus from the mint of Lyons. *BMC* I, Vitellius no. 113.

cultural script. Though the lived realities of these dramas remain ever beyond our ken, surviving portrayals of them provide an entrance into the
conceptual framework that assigned roles and assessed the boundaries of
the possible in their rehearsal and interpretation. In other words, imperial
art became historically meaningful when its language enabled viewers to
place themselves within its world, and in this way produced authoritative,
timeless representations of diachronic experiences familiar in form and
tempo.[18] In thus appearing merely to record well-known tableaux, works of
art surreptitiously sanctioned the relations of domination formalized in the
rituals they distilled. Those experiences, their script and setting, properties
and dialogue, constitute what Clifford Geertz called "symbolic forms":[19]

> At the political center of any complexly organized society (to narrow our fo-
> cus now to that) there is both a governing elite and a set of symbolic forms ex-
> pressing the fact that it is in truth governing. No matter how democratically
> the members of the elite are chosen (usually not very) or how deeply divided
> among themselves they may be (usually much more than outsiders imagine),
> they justify their existence and order their actions in terms of a collection of
> stories, ceremonies, insignia, formalities, and appurtenances that they have
> inherited or, in more revolutionary situations, invented. It is these—crowns
> and coronations, limousines and conferences—that mark the center as cen-
> ter and give what goes on there its aura of being not merely important but in
> some odd fashion connected with the way the world is built. The gravity of
> high politics and the solemnity of high worship spring from liker impulses
> than might at first appear.

Art and architecture in the Roman empire did not, of course, function exclusively on an ideological plane, nor should we naively assume that ancient
aesthetics existed autonomously, apart from ideological considerations.
Nevertheless, comprehending imperial art on an ideological level requires

18. See MacCormack 1981, 22–31, discussing ancient attempts to reduce a familiar ceremony—an imperial *adventus*—to a fragmentary and concentrated image on a medallion or
coin, and cf. Bourdieu 1977, 188, and Pollini 1993, 273–279.

19. Geertz 1983, 124; cf. *idem* 1973, 33–54 and 87–125, and the criticisms of his formulation in Thompson 1990, 130–135.

our understanding that symbolic phenomena derive their ideological function from their sociohistorical context. We can achieve such comprehension only by examining both "the interplay of meaning and power" in ancient art and "the ways in which symbolic forms were employed, circulated, and understood" in the Roman world.[20]

In pursuit of that goal, this chapter examines three categories of imperial art: coins, imperial portraits, and the posters and standards familiar from martial contexts. Ultimately the importance of these artifacts rested on contemporaries' awareness and reception of them. Those processes were not mutually dependent: images do not require self-consciously interpretive viewers in order to exercise their influence. Nevertheless, popular consumption and imitation of Roman imagery suggest more complexly political conclusions if there existed a demonstrable popular belief that officials of the government or even the emperor himself oversaw the production and distribution of its images. Explications of coins in ancient sources indicate quite conclusively that residents of the empire held that conviction about imperial coinage. That conviction was undoubtedly far more important then, and should be now, than the elusive identities of those who actually selected the types.[21] What is more, literary sources suggest that contemporaries consciously identified coins and monuments as carriers of ideological meaning and as symbols of Rome and the legitimacy of her rule. The function of imperial images in daily life, from their supervision of markets and lawcourts to their cohabitation of temples and sanction of oaths, and their power in the popular imagination, in turn, both created and relied on a belief in some direct relationship between emperor and observers. To return to Althusser's term, those myriad personal links interpellated the residents of the empire as concrete subjects, subconsciously sundering their relations with each other and reconstituting them as the community of a benevolent Rome.[22] As the ideological stress of *aurum coronarium* universalized the benefit of particular victories into an ecumenical reward of imperial victoriousness, so imperial art worked at once to fragment and to unify the empire.[23]

In this task, imperial art and architecture proved not only an effective semantic system, but even a necessary one. Put simply, their iconographic language was more immediately intelligible to more people than was Latin or Greek. Indeed, its stylized simplicity was the key to its effectiveness. To use an example already adumbrated, emperors advertised their *congiaria* on

20. Thompson 1990, 56 and 138–139.
21. Cf. Howgego 1995, 70.
22. See Chapter 2 at n. 141; cf. Brilliant 1963, 64.
23. See Thompson 1990, 64–67.

Figure 3. Trajan supervises his second *congiarium*.
Aes from the mint of Rome. *BMC* III, Trajan no. 768.

their coins.[24] The distribution of a *congiarium* to the soldiers and local population, and to the city of Rome as soon as the new emperor reached Rome,
was one of the earliest acts of any reign. Performing the ceremony and advertising its correct performance became early benchmarks of the legitimacy of a reign. The need for intelligibility produced a swift resolution on
a type that ignored the contingent circumstances of any particular largesse
and that could therefore be reproduced in its essentials over and over again:
the emperor seated on a platform, presiding over an official distributing
grain or cash, usually with the figure of Liberalitas watching from the background (Figs. 3, 4).[25] Modern scholars have toiled to date those *congiaria*,
just as they have labored to identify the monuments depicted on particular
issues and artifacts.[26] But just as imperial victories and setbacks yielded
pride of place to an abstract and universal victoriousness, so the reductive
imagery of *congiaria* types directed attention away from the particular bene-
ficiary of one concrete act and toward the worldwide benefits of imperial
generosity.[27] This latter was a message particularly suited to iconographic

24. See Chapter 2 at n. 34.
25. Although the type remained constant, the legend went through a transformation.
Starting with Hadrian and throughout the second century, emperors ceased to enumerate
their *congiaria* and instead celebrated acts of generosity: LIBERALITAS I, II, etc. For the earliest
example of the latter legend, see *BMC* 3, Hadrian nos. 291–301 (plate 52, nos. 4 and 5, without the figure of Liberalitas, and nos. 6 and 7, with her). On the advertisement of cancellations
of taxes and debts, see Hanson 1981, 353. On the power of the *congiarium* legend to evoke a
complex set of images and ideas, see Charlesworth 1937, 114. On the history of such distributions, see van Berchem 1939, Mrozek 1987, Millar 1991, and, for the late empire, MacMullen
1962.
26. On the dating of *congiaria* see van Berchem 1939, 141–161. Ancient historians, too,
enumerated imperial acts of generosity: the *Chronicle of 354* lists each ruler's *congiaria* in second place in each biography, immediately following the length of his rule (*Chron. min.* 1:145–
148). On the representation of monuments, see J. Toynbee 1986, 213–224, or Hill 1989.
27. See Chapter 2 at n. 34, and cf. Hölscher 1987, 53, 69.

Figure 4. Hadrian provides a distribution through his Liberalitas. Aes from the mint of Rome. *BMC* III, Hadrian no. 1137.

representation.[28] The rapid diffusion of imperial imagery in this form created a visual language whose very simplicity rendered it almost universally intelligible and uniquely flexible.[29] Most important—and we will return to this issue in Chapter 8—as a semantic system imperial iconography was available to provincials, too. They adopted and manipulated its symbols to declare their loyalty to emperor and empire, anticipating official ideology by a century or more, even as their participation in the empire's language committed them to its normative structure.

The very preciosity of artifacts immeasurably magnifies the risk that their function in the ancient world will be misunderstood. Again, we must always move beyond Romans' theoretical reflections on the function of art to the context that generated and used, and was itself shaped by and interpreted through, coins, portraits, and standards. This is not to deny the role of aesthetics in the study of ancient artifacts: Romans, too, viewed these items as objets d'art. But they also knew that they carried messages. Chapter 4 investigated the evidence for and impact of widespread distribution of legal and administrative ordinances from center to periphery. Similarly, Chapter 5 investigated the documents through which emperors elicited expressions of *consensus* and thus implicated others in a culture of loyalism, while Chapter 6 examined the force of *consensus* as a theoretical underpinning to three radically different and recurrent events in ancient political life. All three chapters drew their conclusions about ancient mentalities by studying not only the content but the function of texts in ancient political life: it was, I argued, through insinuation into the immanent practices of daily life that Roman praxis came to occupy the functional position of ideology.[30] This chapter proceeds on similar assumptions. Provincials were more than sim-

28. Hölscher 1987, *passim,* but esp. 51–52; cf. Brilliant 1963, 56, 76, and 133.
29. Hölscher 1987; Zanker 1988, esp. 265–339.
30. See Jameson 1988, 2.54, and cf. Foucault 1972, 95–96.

ply cognizant that works of art carried meaning. Residents of the Roman empire—that is, users of Roman coins and viewers of Roman art—understood that these objects acquired their value not from their raw material but from their origin. That is to say, the legitimacy of the ruler of the world cloaked his portrait and its vehicles with some of his power, whether to offer protection to his children, to attest the honesty of his subordinates, or to guarantee the purity and weight of his coinage.

By acknowledging the efficacy of these artifacts, when it was guaranteed by the recognizable features of their emperor, provincials tacitly assented to the legitimacy of the system that selected their emperor and to his right to exercise power throughout his realm. The pacific passage of decades laid a foundation that moments of crisis and changes on the throne did not shake; the distinctly imperial quality of an emperor's visage derived as much from that emperor's unique qualities as from the unique office that he occupied. Each coin and every work of art similarly carried some message of immediate relevance, yet their most important achievement came about through their sheer variety and staggering numbers, in their creation of an audience prepared to interpret the next coin they received and to honor the next portrait they saw.

WHO WAS THOUGHT TO CONTROL THE MINTS?

There can be no question that the medium that reached the widest audience on the most continuous basis was the coinage.[31] Yet numismatists and historians have for decades argued over basic questions regarding the selection and reception of the types and legends of the imperial coinage. Did Roman emperors care about the appearance of their coins? Did the public understand the images or the abbreviations? Did the public even know to look at them? Was the primary audience for the coins not the public, but the emperor?[32] Logistical considerations must have constrained those emperors who did care: it would have been difficult to oversee issues of the imperial mint at Rome without being present in the city. On the other hand, during both major civil wars of the first and second centuries, imperial mints propagated simultaneously with claimants to the throne, as each would-be emperor asserted control over his regional mint. At the very least those men thought the coinage a useful medium through which to advertise the legitimacy and viability of their governments and deemed it profitable to pay

31. A point frequently stressed. See, for example, Charlesworth 1937, 114–115; Levick 1982, 104 n. 1; or Hannestad 1988, 11.

32. Ehrhardt 1984, and Howgego 1990 and 1995 cite earlier work.

their soldiers with coin bearing their names.[33] Plutarch's assessment of Lucullus's early career provides an ancient perspective on the circulation of such issues: Sulla so trusted Lucullus that he assigned him the most important tasks, among which was responsibility for striking coin: "Most of the money in the Peloponnese during the Mithridatic War was struck by him and was therefore called Lucullan. What is more, it continued to be used for a long time, since it received rapid circulation from military expenditures during the war."[34]

Yet today's sophisticated efforts to link particular issues to discrete historical events can reveal only so much. The mere existence of such connections does, of course, suggest that moneyers designed coins with one eye fixed on the current headlines. But often such research aids the reconstruction of historical narratives of the sort desired and designed by the modern historian, and it correspondingly neglects to appreciate the influence exerted by coins in their ancient context. Addressing that latter problem requires the collection and analysis of evidence for reactions to particular issues and for personal convictions regarding the supervision of mints and responsibility for the appearance of coins.[35] Historians have too often begun and ended their argument by citing Dio on the coins of Brutus: after killing Caesar, Brutus struck coins with his portrait on one side and a cap and two daggers on the other, "seeking through this image and through the legend to show that he, together with Cassius, had freed his fatherland."[36]

As it turns out, writers often attributed the conscious selection of types and legends to emperors and would-be emperors. What is more, their diction just as often indicates either that they regarded that responsibility as an imperial prerogative or, conversely, that they believed coins reflected the immediate political and propagandistic interests of the court. Suetonius, for example, wrote that Augustus was so pleased with his horoscope that he struck silver coins with the image of Capricorn, under which he was born, and that Nero, following the success of his performances in Greece, struck coins depicting himself as a lyre player.[37] Similarly, Eusebius insisted that Constantine himself had arranged for his mother, Helena, to receive the title *Augusta* and for her image to appear on an issue of gold coins.[38] Eusebius elsewhere argued that Constantine was directly responsible for his

33. See Mattingly, *BMC* I, xxi–xxii, and *BMC* V, xiv–xv. Cf. *RIC* I², 189–190, 197–202, and 216–221.

34. Plutarch *Lucullus* 2.1–2.

35. Price 1979, 277–278, collects a few passages, which Levick 1982, 107 n. 13, dismisses. Cf. Lendon 1990, 114–115, and Howgego 1995, 70–71.

36. Dio 47.25.3.

37. Suetonius *Augustus* 94.12 and *Nero* 25.2.

38. Eusebius *Vit. Const.* 3.47.2.

depiction in a posture of prayer on his coins.[39] Eusebius also described the *consecratio* coinage issued after Constantine's death. Although he did not attribute this set of images to Constantine's directive, it formed part of Eusebius's evidence that Constantine "shared in the imperial power after death, administering, as it were, the whole kingdom, and ruling the Roman empire in his own name, as Victor Maximus Augustus."[40]

A generation later Ephrem Syrus blamed Julian for the minting of coins whose reverse depicted a bull with two stars, a pagan image:[41]

> The circumcised saw the image that unexpectedly had become a bull; on his coins they saw the bull, a thing of shame. . . . The bull of paganism that was engraved in his heart, he imprinted on that [coin] face for the people who loved it. . . . The king, the king of Greece, suddenly became a bull and butted the churches and had to be led away. The circumcised saw the bull that was engraved on the stater, and they rejoiced that the calves of Jeroboam were reawakened.

The ecclesiastical historians Socrates and Sozomen also attacked Julian for the blatantly pagan symbolism of this issue; nor were they alone.[42] Although these writers can hardly have been aware of this fact, the likelihood that Julian himself ordered this particular issue is vastly increased by the simultaneous use of the same type with an identical legend by the mints at Lyons, Arles, Aquileia, Siscia, Sirmium, Thessalonica, Heraclea, Constantinople, Nicomedia, Cyzicus, and Antioch.[43] Socrates also recorded that the population of Antioch mocked Julian's beard and intimated that the bull on his coins symbolized his ruining of the world. Julian's satire to the Antiochenes confirms that narrative, and thus implicitly confirms that the Antiochenes noticed the images on his coins and attributed their selection to the emperor.[44]

Individuals also offered more generalized reflections in which they im-

---

39. Eusebius *Vit. Const.* 4.15.1–2.

40. Eusebius *Vit. Const.* 4.71.2, 73. On the events following the death of Constantine and contemporary interpretations of them, see MacCormack 1981, 118–121. On the *consecratio* issue for Constantine, see Koep 1958.

41. Ephrem Syrus *Hymni contra Iulianum* 1.16–18, trans. J. M. Lieu, in Lieu 1986, with modifications. On this episode see Szidat 1981, and Griffith 1987, 253–254.

42. Socrates 3.17 and Sozomen 5.19.2, and cf. Cassiodorus *Hist.* 6.40.2–4. Though he did not specifically mention these coins, Gregory of Nazianzus attacked Julian for associating his portrait with the figures of demons (*Or.* 4.80–81).

43. *RIC* VIII: Lyons nos. 236–238; Arles nos. 313–317 (cf. nos. 318–326); Aquileia nos. 242, 243; Siscia nos. 411–413, 417–419; Sirmium nos. 105–107; Thessalonica nos. 222–226; Heraclea nos. 101–104; Constantinople nos. 161–164; Nicomedia nos. 118–122; Cyzicus nos. 125–128; and Antioch nos. 210–218. It is probable the same type was issued from the other mints as well, but no specimens survive.

44. Socrates 3.17; Julian *Misopogon* 27 (355d).

puted to the emperor the desire and ability to control the mints, even though they did not all explicitly discuss the choice of types and legends. In Book 3 of his *Silvae*, published in the year 93 or 94, Statius enumerated the responsibilities of the emperor Domitian. Among them he counted the supervision of the coinage:[45]

> Watchful, too, is he, and shrewd of mind, and quick to reckon what the Roman arms beneath every sky demand, how much the tribes and the temples, how much the lofty aqueducts, and the fortress by the sea, or the far-flung lines of road. What wealth of gold gleams on the high ceilings of our prince, what weight of ore must be melted in the fire and shaped into the countenance of gods, how much shall ring when stamped in the fiery heat of Ausonia's mint?

Statius, of course, honored Domitian by revering the great burden associated with the guardianship of the world.[46] The anonymous fourth-century author of the reactionary pamphlet *De rebus bellicis* similarly regarded supervision of the mints as the special task of the emperors, but he regarded the emperors of his day as dilatory in that responsibility. He offered several reasons why they should display greater concern, foremost among them that awareness of the emperors' renewed interest would increase public confidence in coins as legal tender and therefore ease business transactions. The author also detailed reasons outside the economic sphere: since the coins carried the emperors' portraits, it diminished their prestige if people refused to accept their coins. The author closed this section by offering a set of types for the emperor's consideration.[47] Almost two centuries later Cassiodorus stressed precisely these same factors in arguing for greater supervision of the mints: the emperor's image was there impressed, and a legitimate currency was in the interest of general utility.[48]

Christian homilists and exegetes shared this understanding of coinage with the poets and historians of their day. Indeed, they assumed such an understanding on the part of their congregations, too, and based their explications of Scripture on that assumption. For example, at some point in the years after 410, Augustine delivered a sermon in Carthage on the parable of the wedding garment in Chapter 22 of the Gospel of Matthew. The last chapter of the sermon is not easy for a modern reader to understand: in his interpretation Augustine probably participated in a long tradition of reading the parables of that chapter together. He thus explicated the putting on

45. Statius *Silvae* 3.3.98–105. On this passage see Crawford 1970, 46. On imperial control over supplies of bullion, see Millar 1977, 144–153, and Howgego 1990, 4–7.

46. Cf. Béranger 1953, 169–217, and *idem* 1982.

47. *De rebus bellicis* 3.1 and 3.4.

48. Cassiodorus *Variae* 7.32.1.

of "the wedding garment" with a "reengraving" of the image of God. This in turn allowed him to establish an analogy between the anecdote that follows in that chapter, regarding the monies of Caesar, and the earlier reference to "the image of God":[49]

> By loving the truth, therefore, let that image, after which we were created, be reengraved, and let His coin be returned to our Caesar. For thus you have learned from the answer of the Lord to the Jews who were tempting him. "Why do you tempt me, hypocrites? Show me the tribute money!"—that is, He wished to be shown the engraving of the portrait and the legend. . . . They showed him a denarius. He asked whose portrait and legend it bore. They responded, Caesar's. That Caesar, too, sought his own image. Caesar does not want to lose that which he ordered [to be made], and God does not wish that which he made to perish. Caesar, my brothers, did not make the coin: the moneyers did; but Caesar commanded the artisans; he ordered his servants. A portrait was engraved on the coin; on the coin is the portrait of Caesar.

In Book 2 of *On Christian doctrine,* written some years before the sermon just quoted, Augustine listed a series of human institutions that facilitate the workings of earthly society as language does. Augustine there displayed much the same understanding of imperial coinage. Among conventions regarding dress, weights, and measures, he included the images and legends of the imperial coinage: he proved that these were human conventions by reminding his readers that they could be changed by a decision of each nation's *princeps*.[50]

Eastern Christians likewise numbered coinage among the universal institutions of earthly society and labeled it the responsibility of legitimate governments. Like Augustine, those Christians took it for granted that users of money would inspect the faces on their coins. In a work attributed to Athanasius of Alexandria, that bishop purportedly answered a series of questions from one Antiochus—presumably that Antiochus who, as *agens in rebus*, is mentioned in Chapter 10 of the genuine *Defense before Constantius*.[51] His interlocutor asked, "What should a man do if, on a holy day, he finds himself in a territory where orthodox rites of communion are not celebrated? Should he take communion with heretics, or remain without communion?" Athanasius supposedly made the following, somewhat incoherent response:[52]

> If the danger is very great that a man should commit adultery with his wife and have intercourse with her, or if a man happens to be in a foreign land, how

---

49. Augustine *Serm.* 90.10. For the date see Verbraken 1976, 75.

50. Augustine *Doct. Christ.* 2.25.38–39.

51. On that document and the interaction between Athanasius and Antiochus see Barnes 1993, 103.

52. [Athanasius] *Quaest. ad Antiochum* 112 (*PG* 28.665C).

much greater is the danger that one might betray orthodox belief through receiving communion with heretics? Just as those who wish to conduct business do not accept foreign currency in the place of currency stamped with the imperial seal for as long as they travel in foreign lands, so it is necessary to believe concerning the communion of Christ.

Two further, roughly contemporary homilies, long attributed to Macarius of Egypt but possibly authored by Simeon of Antioch, established an identical connection between the legitimacy of coins and the portrait they bore.[53] One homily compares the image of God as it existed in Adam after the Fall to the portrait of an emperor on a coin that has been illegally restamped: as the gold is destroyed and the portrait loses its value, such a fate also befell Adam.[54] The other seeks to describe the utter worthlessness of a soul that does not bear the image of the Holy Spirit: those souls resemble gold coins that have not been struck with the portrait of the emperor; those coins neither reach the market nor lie in the imperial treasury, but are worthless.[55]

The third-century jurist Paul explicitly connected the concerns of Augustine, Pseudo-Athanasius, and the *De rebus bellicis* in his narrative of the evolution of commerce from barter to money-based exchange. Systems of currency exchange worked, he insisted, because the authority of the state legitimated and guaranteed the value of its currency:[56]

> But since it did not always and easily happen that when you had something that I wanted, I, for my part, had something that you were willing to accept, a substance was chosen whose permanent value as legal tender could obviate the difficulties of barter by providing a constant medium of exchange. That substance, struck with a public seal, demonstrates its utility and value not so much from the inherent value of its raw material as from its quantity. The result is that items being exchanged are no longer both termed "wares," but one is called "the price."

Paul's fame was so great that a large body of spurious material came to circulate under his name in the second half of the third century. One such work represented Paul establishing an analogy between committing different types of fraud—suborning or giving false testimony, forgery, and counterfeiting—and rejecting as counterfeit a coin stamped with the portrait of the emperor: for all those crimes, upper-class individuals would be exiled and lower-class individuals sent to the mines or crucified.[57]

---

53. For the authorship of the homilies, see Dörries's introduction to the edition he prepared in cooperation with Klostermann and Kroeger (Berlin, 1964).

54. Macarius *Hom.* 12.1

55. Macarius *Hom.* 30.5.

56. Paul at *Dig.* 18.1.1 *pr.* (trans. Garnsey, with substantial changes).

57. *Sententiae Pauli* 25.1.

The belief that a coin was legitimated, indeed, rendered sacrosanct, by the portrait of the emperor that it carried had its origins in the Julio-Claudian era. Already in that period Romans had begun to apply the law of *maiestas* to acts that infringed on the dignity of the imperial portrait.[58] Suetonius associated this development with the reign of Tiberius: "Gradually charges of this kind proceeded so far that even the following became capital offenses: to strike a slave near a statue of Augustus, to change one's clothes near such a statue, to bring his portrait, whether stamped on a coin or ring, into a bathroom or a brothel, or to attack any word or deed of his with some opinion."[59] In point of fact, the two cases involving such charges that are known to us from the *Annales* of Tacitus both ended in acquittal: in A.D. 15 Marcus Granius Marcellus was accused of placing his statue in a loftier position than those of the Caesars, and of replacing the head of Augustus on a statue with that of Tiberius; and in A.D. 22 Lucius Ennius was accused of *maiestas* because he had melted a silver statue of Tiberius. Tiberius himself dismissed the charges.[60] Gnaeus Piso preempted the conclusion of his trial with his suicide, but the Senate numbered among the charges against him the suspicion that Piso "had violated the *numen* of the divine Augustus by disallowing all the honors that were maintained for his memory or for his portraits, which had previously been placed in the ranks of the gods."[61]

The beliefs that legitimate emperors ought to oversee the mints and that their faces ought to appear on their coins reinforced each other through long association. Indeed, it would be anachronistic to argue that Romans regarded these as concepts capable of separate and sustained articulation. On the contrary, they participated together in a system of beliefs and regulations that established direct and necessary correspondence between the legitimacy of an emperor and the sanctity and power of his image. In numismatic contexts these associations are expressed in the legislation that developed around the counterfeiting, altering, or melting of imperial coins.[62] For instance, in 317 Constantine instituted the death penalty for anyone who cut off the edge of a coin because the imperial portrait on it was smaller than its surface: Our face is the same on all solidi, and the same degree of veneration is due to it, Constantine wrote, and therefore all solidi carry the same value, even if the size of the image on them may vary.[63] A

---

58. Bauman 1974, 71–85. On *maiestas* and imperial portraits, see also below at nn. 127–136.

59. Suetonius *Tiberius* 58.

60. Tacitus *Ann.* 1.74.3 and 3.70.

61. *SC de Cn. Pisone patre* ll. 68–70.

62. *C. Th.* 9.21–23; *C. Iust.* 9.24 and 11.11.

63. *C. Th.* 9.22.1. The date is uncertain. The manuscripts unanimously assign the law to the consulate of Gallicanus and Bassus (A.D. 317), but the addressee, Leontius, was praetorian

generation later Constantius imposed a verdict of sacrilege and a penalty of death on those who melted money or transported it in order to sell it as bullion.[64] These laws on coins must be read in the context of a continual outpouring of legislation on the sanctity of the imperial portrait: for example, in A.D. 394 Theodosius, Arcadius, and Honorius informed the praetorian prefect Rufinus that it was forbidden to put up a poster of a pantomime in low costume, a charioteer in disorderly apparel, or a disgusting actor either in a public portico or in places where imperial images were customarily consecrated; the same law forbade mimes from dressing up like nuns.[65]

Although Roman imperial legislation tended to equate the acts of counterfeiting and of altering coins because both dishonored the emperor, they suggest a different conclusion within our argument. In perpetrating either crime, the criminal presumed upon the bankability of the imperial portrait. That is, someone who shaved the edge from a coin assumed that the smaller coin would still be accepted as legal tender because its appearance, its legends and its images, would be recognizable and, indeed, familiar. Similarly, the counterfeiter believed that his victims would accept coins stamped with a familiar portrait and legend, on the grounds that the imperial portrait in and of itself guaranteed the purity and weight of the metal. Ultimately it was the appearance of the coin, its message, broadly construed, that paved its way as a medium of exchange within the Roman world.

John Chrysostom drew on his congregation's familiarity with the rules protecting coins in order to explain Paul's Letter to the Galatians. Chrysostom maintained that Paul taught the Galatians about the unity of the Gospels: "The four Gospels are but one Gospel. Since the four say the same thing, they are not different texts because of their different authors, but they are one because of the harmony of the contents." To identify even the smallest difference between them is to pervert the whole: "Just as one who shaves the edge from the image on imperial coins renders the entire coin worthless, so that person who turns in the smallest way from proper faith is altogether corrupted, plunging headlong from that beginning into worse things."[66] A didactic passage from the biography of the Egyptian nun Syncletica draws a very similar analogy in a very different context. The author of this life remains unknown, although a late Byzantine tradition attributed it to Athanasius of Alexandria. Toward the end of the life, Syncletica lectures

---

prefect in the years 340–344 (*PLRE* I, Leontius 20). On the cutting or scraping of coins, see Tertullian *Paen.* 6.5 and Ulpian at *Dig.* 48.10.8.

64. *C. Th.* 9.23.1. Again, the date is disputed: the heading assigns the law to Constantius and Julian during their consulship of A.D. 356, but the putative addressee, Vulcacius Rufinus (*PLRE* I, Rufinus 25), ceased to be praetorian prefect in 352.

65. *C. Th.* 15.7.12

66. John Chrysostom *Comment. in Galat.* 1.6 (*PG* 61.622).

her young pupils about the relationship between youth and proper faith: "Examine carefully the imperial seal. For there are counterfeit seals, and though the nature of the gold is the same from coin to coin, they differ in their seals. Youth, self-control, and pity are like gold: the children of the Greeks [i.e., pagans] impress their own tyrannical image on them, and all heretics are famed for these qualities. You must watch for them, and flee from them as from counterfeiters."[67]

References by contemporaries to the effects of *damnatio memoriae* constitute another special category of evidence.[68] Removing coins from circulation if they bore the portrait of a condemned traitor is predicated on associating the image on a state's coinage, the sanctity of the state, and, in the case of an emperor, the legitimacy of that person's rule. Thus at Rome, just as the Senate claimed the right to award certain honors to emperors, so it asserted the power to condemn the memory of tyrants: it therefore ordered all bronze coins bearing the likeness of Gaius to be melted and recast, although Dio claims that Messallina used the bronze thus recovered as raw material for a statue of her lover Mnester the dancer.[69] Dio numbered it among Vitellius's good deeds that he did not order the recasting of all coins that displayed the images of Nero, Galba, and Otho, as he was untroubled by their portraits.[70] Caracalla, on the other hand, ordered all coins that bore the portrait of his murdered brother, Geta, to be melted; when Dio adds that Caracalla raged at the stones that supported Geta's portraits, he probably refers to the erasure of Geta's name from all documents, including both inscriptions and portrait bases, that followed on *damnatio memoriae*.[71] The circulation of coin did not always depend on the will of the Senate or *princeps:* though Epictetus voiced the truism that the coins of Caesar were legal tender and might not be refused, he also argued that coins that bore the portrait of Nero were unacceptable and rotten and should be shunned as one would shun men of poor character.[72] The genuineness and extent of this distrust or dislike of Neronian issues seems to be confirmed by the countermarks stamped on such coins by Greek cities, seeking to reassure the public of the legality of the currency.[73]

At no time were the stakes in legitimating the imperial power higher than

---

67. *Vita Sanctae Syncletycae* 100 (*PG* 28.1549B–C).

68. Official action against the memory of individuals presumably included removing from circulation coins bearing their portraits: see Tacitus *Ann.* 6.2.1 and 11.38.3, on Livilla and Messallina; Suetonius *Nero* 49.2 and *Domitian* 23.1.

69. Dio 60.22.3.

70. Dio 65.6.1.

71. Dio 77.12.6. The epigraphical evidence is vast; see, for example, *ILS* 458 and 459, together with Miller at *CAH* XII 43.

72. Epictetus 3.3.3, and cf. 4.5.15–17 and Martial 12.57.7–8.

73. Howgego 1985, 6.

during civil wars, and issuing currency with an appropriate legend and portrait played a large role both in attempted usurpations and in the historical accounts written about them. According to Herodian, the enemies of Perennius, the capable and unpopular praetorian prefect under Commodus, persuaded that emperor that this subordinate was plotting to usurp the throne for his son by producing coins with the latter's portrait on them.[74] According to Dio, Valerianus Paetus met his fate early in the reign of Elagabalus for similar reasons: when he stamped some pieces of gold with his own portrait as a present for his mistress, he was accused of minting coins in preparation for leading a revolt in Cappadocia.[75] On this topic no passage is more clear about both what the usurper was trying to achieve and what the emperor had at stake than the argument in the *Historia Augusta* concerning the status of one Firmus, who seems to have attempted to claim Egypt—perhaps for himself, perhaps for Zenobia—in conjunction with Palmyra's war against Aurelian in 272–274.[76] The author claims to have debated with others the question whether Firmus was an emperor or merely a brigand. In support of the former was adduced the evidence that Firmus had worn the purple and had titled himself Augustus on the coins that he struck and in the edicts that he published. In support of the latter there was only the testimony of Aurelian himself, who apparently claimed in an edict to have killed not a usurper but a brigand. The author himself inclined to the former position, on the grounds that emperors always labeled as brigands those whom they slew while seizing the throne—to do otherwise would have cast doubt on their legitimacy, by admitting that the charisma was attached to the office and only flowed thence to its unique occupant.[77]

The *Historia Augusta* appealed to the same issue in its account of the usurpation of one almost certainly fictitious Trebellianus—though others called him an "archpirate," he called himself *imperator,* ordered the striking of coins, and built himself a palace[78]—and again in its life of Victoria, the

---

74. Herodian 1.9.7. Dio also reported that Perennius was accused of attempting to elevate his son, but he did not mention the coins (72.9).

75. Dio 79.4.7.

76. The name Firmus is "known" only to the *Historia Augusta;* Zosimus 1.61.1, the only other ancient source to record Aurelian's trip to Egypt at this time, does not attach a name to the leader of this revolt. Surprisingly, the author of the *Historia Augusta* is probably correct to insist that he is right, and other authors are wrong, in differentiating between the many Firmi among Roman officials at this time (*SHA Quad. tyr.* 3.1; cf. *PLRE* I, Firmus 1, 3, and 7).

77. *SHA Quad. tyr.* 2.1–2. MacMullen 1963 locates the origin of such language in Stoic philosophy and not in efforts to create a uniquely charismatic occupant of a charismatic office. On the use of *tyrannus* to label usurpers see now Neri 1997; on the *Historia Augusta*'s obsession with *tyranni* see Paschoud 1997.

78. *SHA Tyr. trig.* 26.2–3.

mother of that Victorinus who ruled Gaul between 268 and 270: she legitimized herself by adopting the title *mater castrorum* and by minting coins in
her own name.[79] In like fashion, Claudian described Rufinus as plotting to
usurp the throne by similar means: among his many transgressions against
imperial prerogative are numbered his plot to address the army and to distribute a donative of coins stamped with his own image.[80]

Sufficient evidence survives for the attempted usurpation of Procopius,
cousin of Julian the Apostate, to reveal the importance placed on coins as a
medium of publication in the rapid events that followed his hazardous elevation in September 365.[81] Although Procopius was distantly related to Constantine and based his claim ultimately on that fact alone, he did not count
on that connection to dislodge the people's loyalty to the ruling emperors,
Valentinian and Valens.[82] Rather than put forward the less credible lie that
both Valentinian and his brother had died simultaneously in different parts
of the empire, Procopius announced by means of false emissaries only the
death of Valentinian. He clearly hoped that loyalty to the recently elevated
Valens would evaporate with the death of his *auctor*.[83] Procopius used a different trick on the armies of Illyricum. In order to convince them that he
was already ruling and was therefore not a brigand, he sent to them men
bearing coins struck with his likeness. The gesture clearly attempted to elevate his crime from an illegal usurping of another's throne to the claiming
of that same throne by its lawful occupant. In other words, Procopius presented himself as the legitimate emperor and provided as his only evidence
these coins.[84]

In the months that followed, Procopius advertised his connection to the
house of Constantine in many ways, above all on his coinage. He appears to
have devoted special care to his issues in bronze, perhaps because these

79. *SHA Tyr. trig.* 31.2–3. On the title see Chapter 6 at n. 47. Victoria is attested on perhaps a single inscription (*CIL* XIII 5868 = König 1981, no. 96 on 213). Of the coins of the
Gallic empire none can with certainty be attributed to her: Should we interpret VICTORIA
AUGUSTA as a reference to Augustan victory, or to the empress Victoria (cf. Chastagnol 1994,
857–858)?

80. Claudian *In Ruf.* 2.336–347 at 339–342. Other imperial prerogatives included giving
donatives in one's own name, addressing the troops, and presiding over games at Rome or
Constantinople from the imperial box: see Ammianus 15.6.2–3, 16.12.69, and 14.11.8–13,
respectively.

81. *Consularia Constant.* s.a. 365: *et ipso anno latro nocturnus hostisque publicus intra urbem Con-
stantinopolim apparuit die IIII kl. Oct.*

82. See Austin 1972, 189–191; Blockley 1975, 56; or Matthews 1989, 195–196.

83. For the term, see Chapter 6 n. 100, on Julian, and cf. *SHA Hadr.* 10.2 and *Ver.* 4.1–3.
See also Hartke 1951, 155–167; Martin 1997, 48–49; and Szidat 1997.

84. Ammianus 26.7.3 and 11. Cf. Socrates *Hist. eccl.* 5.13: Arians in Constantinople spread
false rumors that Theodosius had fallen in action against Maximus.

would circulate most quickly through the economy.[85] To begin with, Procopius used a portrait of himself sporting a beard, in imitation of Julian. This feature clearly and immediately distinguished his coins from those of Valentinian or Valens.[86] He also adopted a legend and its associated types that had first been used by the sons of Constantine in 348 and had appeared on their bronze coinage from every mint of the empire.[87]

His machinations proceeded far beyond the manipulation of words and images. Although the mints under his control initially struck coins in all metals at the same weights as did those controlled by Valens, they soon all reverted to the heavier *aes* that had been established by Julian. This was, needless to say, more expensive for the mint, and could have been done only at the command of Procopius, on the presumption that such a subtle change would be noticed. Finally, as Procopius had ordered men to feign that they brought news of Valentinian's death to Constantinople, so he directed at least one mint—very likely that of Constantinople—to strike a coin for himself using a mark of the mint at Arles and a reverse type and legend familiar from the reign of Julian, presumably in order to give a false display of support for himself in the West.[88]

The accounts of these usurpers, like the actions of the usurpers themselves, draw their force from the assumption that the accession of a new Caesar or new Augustus was accompanied, indeed, to an extent validated, by the minting of appropriate coins. We have already seen that Severus flattered his Caesar Clodius Albinus by allowing coins to be minted with his portrait.[89] The *Historia Augusta* suggests that Gallienus gave Odaenathus, the ruler of Palmyra, a share in the empire, bestowed upon him the title of

85. Procopius struck coin at all four mints over which he exercised even ephemeral control: Heraclea, Constantinople, Cyzicus, and Nicomedia: see Pearce, *RIC* IX, 189, 200–201, 237, and 248.

86. See *RIC* IX, plate XI, no. 6; or plate XII, nos. 5 and 6.

87. On the dating of the original issue FEL. TEMP. REPARATIO, and the event it was intended to commemorate (the 1,100th anniversary of Rome), see H. Mattingly 1933. Kent 1967 defends Mattingly's work against subsequent criticism. Compare the issues struck by Constantine after the elevation of Licinius, Crispus, and Constantine II at Serdica: they advertised the consecration of Claudius using types and legends from the series that had originally commemorated him—ones "with precedent or parallel elsewhere"—and rehabilitated Maximian (*RIC* VII, Trier nos. 200–207, Arles nos. 173–178, Rome nos. 104–128, Aquileia nos. 21–26, Siscia nos. 41–46, and Thessalonica nos. 24–26; cf. *RIC* V.1, Claudius nos. 293–296). Constantine even had the Senate vote to deify his former father-in-law (Athanasius *Contra gentes* 9). These issues laid the foundation for the dynastic superiority of Constantine's children, since they were henceforth descended from deified emperors on both sides of their family tree.

88. This is the very fine suggestion of Pearce, *RIC* IX, 215 n. 18, with plate XII, no. 5; cf. Kent, *RIC* VIII, Arles nos. 309–311.

89. Herodian 2.15.5.

Augustus, and further ordered that coins be struck in his name. In this the author of that work is guilty of anachronistic assumptions about the consequences of an emperor's assigning *imperium maius* to a subordinate.[90] The *Historia Augusta* also records that the first act following the acclamation of Antoninus Diadumenianus, the son of Macrinus, was the minting of coins in Antioch bearing his name.[91] Finally, among the acclamations for Severus Alexander preserved in the *Historia Augusta* and supposedly chanted by the Senate is "Let the name of Antoninus be returned to the coinage."[92]

When Epictetus argued that one should on moral grounds refuse to accept a coin bearing the portrait of Nero, he assumed that people both paid attention to coin types and could identify the individual whose image appeared on them, whether on iconographic grounds or from the legend.[93] Jesus, of course, challenged the Pharisees to do precisely that when they asked whether it was lawful to pay poll tax to Rome: "'Show me the coin for the poll tax.' They brought to him a denarius. And Jesus said to them, 'Whose portrait is this, and whose legend?' They said, 'Caesar's.'"[94] Similarly close attention to the legends on coins is said to have been paid by the men who first met the Seven Sleeping Martyrs at Ephesus. Entombed during the reign of Decius, they awoke under Theodosius II. They were physically unchanged and labored under the impression that they had slept for but one day. They selected one of their number, Malchus, gave him their money, and sent him to town. The coins, we are told, were minted under Decius. Malchus was probably no more surprised at the cross over the town gate and the church inside than were the men who received his money when he tried to buy food: "This man has discovered an ancient treasury; for behold, he offers money from the time of Decius."[95] In a later day John of Ephesus wrote a thorough and fascinating account of the accession of Tiberius II, first as Caesar to the mad emperor Justin II, and then to the rank of Augustus. On the latter occasion, wishing to make a very public profession of his Christianity, Tiberius ordered coins to be struck with a cross on the reverse. Justin, we are told, had put the figure of a woman on his coins— no doubt the personification of Constantinople, but it had commonly been interpreted as the portrait of Aphrodite. Tiberius ensured a wide audience

90. *SHA Gall.* 12.1. Relations between Gallienus and Odaenathus, like the latter's status within the Roman administration, remain matters of dispute: see Potter 1990, 381–394; Millar 1993a, 165–172; Swain 1993; and Potter 1996b.

91. *SHA Diad.* 2.6.

92. *SHA Alex. Sev.* 8.3.

93. See above at n. 56.

94. Matthew 22:18–21. The same story is told at Mark 12:14–17 and Luke 20:22–25; in both the latter versions Jesus explicitly asks to be shown a denarius.

95. Gregory of Tours *Passio septem dormientium* 7–8.

for this particular issue by distributing the coins at his "Augustaticum, or, as it is also called, 'Donative of the Romans.'"[96] The Coptic historian and bishop John of Nikiu falls outside the chronological limits of this book, so I simply note that when narrating the death of Heraclius, the successor to Tiberius II, he reported that contemporary gossip focused on his coinage: "And in accordance with the decree of God who takes away the souls of rulers, and of men of war as well as of kings, Heraclius fell ill with fever. . . . And some said, 'The death of Heraclius is due to his stamping the gold coinage with the figures of the three emperors—that is, his own and those of his two sons on the right and left—and so no room was found for inscribing the name of the Roman empire.'"[97]

THE DISTRIBUTION OF IMPERIAL PORTRAITS

Whence arose the portraits arrayed around Decius and his altar on the Capitolium at Carthage? Why would citizens have been confident that these were emperors? Any party to an exchange, suspicious of the change he had received, could ask a passerby to pull the coins from his purse, and they could compare their types and legends, for all knew that the government—and only the government—issued legal tender. But anyone could commission a portrait and inscribe the base as he willed. Could one person compare portraits in his town, or the portraits of his town with those in another town, and thus confirm their legitimacy? The use to which Decius put his and earlier imperial portraits suggests at the very least that he expected those portraits to inspire respect, even awe. Did other emperors share this expectation? What entitled them to have it and thence to act upon it?

Despite their implication in ideological beliefs about the nature and function of legitimate governments, coins lacked presence. Their size and utility rendered them commonplace. A patriotic and pious citizen probably could, in all sincerity, forget to empty his pockets before entering a brothel or going to the bathroom. For grandeur and permanence, for use in shrines and processions, for sheer visibility, emperors required portraits. Thus Constantine not only supervised his representation on coins in an attitude of prayer; he also caused the same likeness to be reproduced in monumental form over the entrance gates of palaces in several cities. He oversaw the pro-

---

96. John of Ephesus 3.11, 14. A. H. M. Jones 1974, 63, uses this story to prove that people were often unable to understand the types on coins. It may well prove two more important points: people knew that emperors used coins to communicate something, and they thought it worthwhile to figure out what that message was.

97. John of Nikiu 116.2–3 (trans. after R. H. Charles).

liferation of this image even in less permanent, painted forms.[98] In a famous aside in a literary letter ostensibly addressed to Hadrian but intended for a wider audience—his official reports to Hadrian were written in Latin—Arrian of Nicomedia describes his encounter with a statue of the emperor at Trapezus during a tour of his province: "A statue of you stands there, one quite suitable in its posture—for it points toward the sea—but as far as the execution goes, neither did it resemble you, nor was it very handsome. Send, therefore, a statue in the same posture, one truly worthy to carry your name, for the place is wholly suitable for an eternal memorial."[99] The passage is often cited as evidence for the wide diffusion of imperial portraits to the ends of the empire.[100] In a provocative essay, Paul Zanker turned this traditional reading on its head, by asking whether Arrian regarded the statue as a poor likeness because it was not of an official type.[101] In doing so he joined in a long-running debate over the production and distribution of imperial portraits. This debate had run its course for so long because, Zanker claimed, there were no literary sources to explain how an official portrait was selected, copied, and distributed.[102]

For the empire of the fourth century and beyond, Zanker is, in fact, incorrect: an abundance of literary evidence describes not only the sending out of portraits at the beginning of reigns, but also the reception of these portraits by local communities.[103] For a long time art historians were content to follow historians in positing imperial supervision over the distribution of imperial portraits because it seemed the easiest way to account for the remarkable "fixity and persistence of iconographic detail, observable throughout the whole course of imperial portraiture."[104] Although research continues to refine our understanding of the main types and especially of the variation tolerated in local copies, the basic methods and arguments have changed little since J. J. Bernoulli in the late nineteenth century. With-

98. Eusebius *Vit. Const.* 4.15.2–16, and cf. (*idem*) *Hist. eccl.* 9.9.10. On paintings in Constantinian propaganda, see also *Vit. Const.* 3.3. and 4.69.

99. Arrian *Periplus* 1.3–4; cf. Pomponius Mela 3.13. For the Latin reports (ἐν τοῖς Ῥωμαϊκοῖς γράμμασιν), see *Periplus* 6.2 and 10.1. On the date and genre of the *Periplus*, see Stadter 1980, 32–41.

100. For example, E. Swift 1923, 291; Pekáry 1985, 6 n. 31.

101. Zanker 1983, 7.

102. Zanker 1983, 8, and cf. the more limited claim in Smith 1996, 32. This issue therefore receives no separate treatment in Pekáry 1985, although he does touch on the topic occasionally (6, 24, and 43). Bibliography on this topic is limited to Friedlaender 1922, 3:61–63; E. Swift 1923; Stuart 1939; Bréhier 1949, 71–74; and Bruun 1976.

103. See Kruse 1934, 12–18, and below, "The Distribution of Imperial Portraits."

104. E. Swift 1923, 290. Stuart 1939 criticized Swift precisely for extrapolating the literary evidence to the earlier part of the empire.

out imperial supervision of the processes of distribution, it would be difficult to account for the speed and extent of the spread of official portrait types, or, indeed, for their longevity: the *Haupttypus* of Antoninus Pius remained unchanged for the twenty-three years of his reign.[105]

Over the last two decades it has become fashionable to be skeptical about the efficiency—indeed, almost about the very existence—of the Roman imperial bureaucracy, and this skepticism has urged that the bureaucracy would have been incapable of such a feat.[106] Even under the Julio-Claudians, however, it was necessary to distribute the portrait of a new emperor upon his accession in order that soldiers in legionary camps throughout the empire might swear the oath of loyalty to him: when Augustus was forced to allow Tiberius to succeed him, "Tiberius was taken up as son, colleague in office, and partner in the tribunician power, and was shown to all the legions."[107] The production of new types for coins with each new reign also required the selection and mass reproduction of an official portrait. Prior to Julius Caesar no portrait of a living person had appeared on Roman coins: this right was granted to Caesar by the Senate, presumably on analogy with Hellenistic practice, and was subsequently seized by Octavian and the triumvirs.[108] This innovation must have required the development of mechanisms to make, approve, and reproduce an official portrait, and the mechanisms in place for numismatic use in the early 30s B.C. could have served as a paradigm for mass production in other media.

At the very least, then, we must allow for the limited distribution of portraits derived from an official model as early as the first decade of the first century of this era. This concession then renders unproblematic the subsequent reliance on local workhouses to produce copies for local consumption.[109] We should not underestimate the eagerness of individuals to dem-

---

105. Bernoulli 1891, 1; Fries 1969, 23; Zanker 1979, 360–361, 364; Smith 1996.

106. Note Zanker's broad reference to Millar 1977 (at 1983, 47 n. 164).

107. Tacitus *Ann.* 1.3.3. See also A. Alföldi 1934, 71; Pekáry 1985, 24 and 43.

108. Dio 44.4.4, on which see Weinstock 1971, 274–275, and Rose 1997a, 58.

109. The existence of such local producers is fundamental even to proponents of the central distribution of plastic models, whether of plaster or of wax: see E. Swift 1923, 291; Pekáry 1985, 24. Hannestad 1988, 49, argues that the majority of surviving portraits—at least their heads—were probably produced in Rome. The most explicit ancient testimony on this practice is provided by Jerome's commentary on Habakkuk 3:14: *Deus itaque clementissimus qui miserat in capita iniquorum mortem, qui suscitaverat vincula usque ad collum, in finem dividit etiam capita potentium in stupore, ut primum principes separet a subiectis, et quasi corpus decollet a capite, et ubi caput pessimum fuerat, ibi caput optimum reponatur. Si quando tyrannus obtruncatur, imagines quoque eius deponuntur et statuae, et vultum tantummodo commutato ablatoque capite, eius qui vicerit facies superponitur, ut manente corpore capitibusque praecisis caput aliud commutetur.* For other evidence see Pekáry 1985, 39–40. Zanker's insistence, following Stuart 1939, that the private art trade could account for the spread of copies of an "official" portrait from Rome to provincial metropoleis, seems overly optimistic (1983, 8–9, 45; cf. 1988, 267). Pfanner 1992, 176–222,

onstrate loyalty, nor their ability to adopt and exploit Roman models to placate, persuade, or dupe their Roman overlords.[110] Even in the reign of Augustus, certain model portraits exercised such total dominance that all provincial portraits of Augustus may be classified as descending from one of their number.[111] Over the next two centuries, provincial copies imitated their models more and more closely, and the degree of variation between, for example, Spanish and Carian replicas grew smaller and smaller. This may have been a response to growing imperial intolerance for local preferences and techniques, but is much more likely due to changes in local aesthetics, which may easily have associated the persuasiveness of Roman taste and Roman power: "The result of the copying process was that, thanks to the abundance of honorific statues, a uniform conception of the emperor's appearance and that of his family prevailed."[112]

Toward the end of his first diatribe against Julian the Apostate, Gregory of Nazianzus wished to discuss Julian's manipulation of traditional ceremonial. In order to do so, he thought it necessary to reflect on the vanity of Roman emperors, so that he might distinguish between the customary honors of a sovereign and the element of idolatry that Julian had attempted to introduce:[113]

> It is a habit under monarchies that the ruler be honored with public portraits—I do not know whether among all men ruled by kings, but certainly the Romans observe it with considerable zeal. For neither the crowns nor the diadems, neither the brilliance of their purple robes nor the numbered bodyguards, nor even the multitude of their subjects suffices to strengthen their sovereignty; no, they require obeisance [προσκύνησις] in order to seem more august. Indeed, not only must they receive obeisance, but their images must do so as well, whether painted or sculpted, in order that their majesty be more insatiable and more complete. To these representations each emperor delights in adding different things: some depict the more distinguished cities bringing them gifts; some add Victories holding crowns over their heads, or magistrates offering obeisance and being honored with the tokens of their office; some depict the slaughter of beasts and feats of archery; and still others add diverse scenes of barbarians being defeated and trampled underfoot and slaughtered. For these men love not only the reality of those deeds on which they pride themselves, but also the representations of them.

---

provides the most thorough reconstruction of a system for mass-producing such portraits within the constraints of ancient technique. Cf. Smith 1996, 34.

110. As Rose 1997b, 109, emphasizes, "emperors did not set up portraits of themselves; provincial cities set up portraits of the emperor in gratitude for or in anticipation of imperial benefactions."

111. Boschung 1993; cf. Burnett and Walker 1981.

112. Zanker 1988, 301–302; Rose 1997a.

113. Gregory Naz. *Or.* 4.80; cf. Theodoret *Hist. Relig.* 26.12.

To select a portrait for public display and surround it with images evocative of particular achievements—this, according to Gregory, was imperial practice. To have one's portrait receive public veneration even as oneself did—this was imperial prerogative.[114] A large body of evidence corroborates Gregory's testimony that people commonly treated and were expected to treat imperial portraits with respect bordering on veneration. As a stand-in for the emperor's person, a portrait could witness an oath, receive cult acts, put the seal on diplomatic arrangements, or offer refuge to the oppressed. This correlation between loyalty to the emperor and veneration of his image could have become operative in the popular imagination only if individuals around the empire associated the accession of a new emperor with the arrival of his portrait.

THE POWER OF IMPERIAL PORTRAITS

Imperial portraits were ubiquitous.[115] As a symbol of loyalty to a political system that provided stability and order, they could be found "in every money-changer's bureau, booths, bookstalls, eaves, porches, windows: anywhere and everywhere the emperor's likenesses is exposed to view."[116] Insofar as the emperor also enjoyed a special relationship with the gods, his image could be found in temples throughout the empire. It was for that reason also carried in procession on local holidays, to celebrate the benefactions that he had brought to the empire and its citizens: this was true already of Augustus, though he would not allow the practice in Rome itself.[117] A pro-

---

114. It was likewise imperial prerogative to allow the portraits of an honored subordinate to be treated with public honors: see, for example, Suetonius *Tiberius* 65.1, on the statues of Sejanus (cf. Dio 58.4.4), *Gaius* 24.2; and Tacitus *Ann.* 4.23.1: as the emperor dispensed triumphal insignia, so he allowed the dedication of laureled statues. See also Eck 1972, 463: in A.D. 56 the Senate decreed nine statues for L. Volusius Saturninus *auctore Nerone Claudio Aug. Germanico.* From the fourth century see L. Swift and Oliver 1962, publishing a letter of Constantius inscribed at Ephesus, allowing *monumenta devotionis* and *statuas inauratas in opimis urbibus* to honor Flavius Philippus. See also *C. Th.* 9.40.17, ordering the destruction of all public and private portraits of Eutropius, both marble and bronze, as well as painted ones. On this topic see Friedlaender 1922, 3:65–68, or Kruse 1934, 18–22.

115. Friedlaender 1922, 3:58–59; Zanker 1979, 361; Price 1984b, 182–188; Pekáry 1985, 42–65. Pfanner 1989, 178–179, argues for the existence of between 25,000 and 50,000 portraits of Augustus in the empire, citing as analogous the mass-production of portraits of Napoleon between 1809 and 1812.

116. Fronto *Ep.* 4.12.6 (trans. Haines).

117. For example, from A.D. 1 see *AÉ* 1992, 1525, an honorific decree for Apollonios son of Apollonios, who organized "a magnificent and awe-inspiring procession and expensive games for Zeus and Augustus, ones worthy of the gods and his fatherland." See further Augustus *Res gestae* 24.2, Suetonius *Augustus* 52, and Dio 51.20.7–8, together with Nock 1972, 202–251, and Weinstock 1971, 188. On statues and processions in particular, see Tacitus *Ann.* 2.83.1, for the honors voted to Germanicus (*ludos circenses eburna effigies praeiret*), or *P. Lond.*

cession of statuary at Ephesus, funded in perpetuity by a benefactor's endowment, is paradigmatic of the integration of such rituals into the rhythms of civic life. By repeating the parade on both civic and imperial holidays, by running its course past monuments evocative of the city's Hellenic and imperial past, the Ephesians used cult acts involving imperial images to "negotiate their personal and social identities over space and time" and, ultimately, "to link [the city's] Roman, Hellenistic, and Ionian foundations." Even if the Ephesians' renewed commitment to Artemis truly reflected a desire to establish a "sacred identity" for the city, that desire arose because "by A.D. 104, some Ephesians . . . may have forgotten precisely what differentiated Ephesians from Romans socially, historically, and theologically."[118] For many, like C. Sextilius Pollio, who dedicated a temple jointly to Artemis, Augustus, Tiberius, and the *Demos* of Ephesus in the last decade of the reign of Augustus, such differentiation would have made no sense.[119] Ephesian and Roman were no longer mutually exclusive categories.

Portraits of the emperors also presided over Roman officials as they conducted their administrative and judicial tasks throughout the provinces: several statues of Antoninus Pius watched over the trial of Apuleius before the proconsul of Africa in 158, and we can imagine Pionius gesturing toward statues of the gods and an imperial portrait when he concluded his harangue in the agora of Smyrna: "Therefore we neither worship your so-called gods nor venerate this golden portrait."[120] Severianus, onetime bishop of Gabala in Syria and, following his move to Constantinople, alternately friend and opponent of John Chrysostom, played on popular awareness of the ubiquity and power of imperial portraits when trying to explain the invisibility of God to an audience in the capital:[121]

> You know how many are the magistrates throughout all the earth. Since the emperor cannot be present everywhere, it is necessary to set up a portrait of the emperor [τὸν χαρακτῆρα τοῦ βασιλέως] at tribunals, in marketplaces, at meetings, and in theaters. In fact, a portrait must be present in every place in which a magistrate acts, so that he might sanction whatever transpires [ἵνα βε-

---

1912 (*Sel. pap.* 212), ll. 34–40, together with Nock 1972, 653–675; and Robert, *OMS* 2:320 and 832–840.

118. Rogers 1991; the quotations are from 82, 114, and 142. Cf. Mitchell 1984, 130–132, and Swain 1996, 66–79.

119. *I. Ephesus* no. 404.

120. Apuleius *Apol.* 85, on which see Friedlaender 1922, 3:62–63, and *Acta Pionii* 4.24. On the interpretation of εἰκὼν χρυσῆ, see Robert's note *ad loc.* or his discussion in *OMS* 2:835 n. 1. Kruse 1934, 79–89, discusses the use of imperial portraits in the trials of Christians during the persecutions.

121. Severianus *In Cosmogoniam* 6.5 (*PG* 56.489). On Severianus's career and writings see Aubineau 1983, 11–24.

βαιῶται τὰ γινόμενα]. For the emperor, being a man, cannot be everywhere; God, being God, simply cannot be seen by men.

Severianus presumably did not recognize that his analogy validated precisely that correspondence between image and reality that the author of the Wisdom of Solomon had attacked. That author, writing in the first century under Roman rule, attributed the origin of idolatry to the grief of parents. Bereaved fathers fashioned images of their absent children, and over time and generations men came to worship as gods what were once dead human beings:[122]

> Then the ungodly custom, grown strong in time, was kept as a law, and at the command of monarchs graven images were worshiped [καὶ τυράννων ἐπιταγαῖς ἐθρησκεύετο τὰ γλυπτά]. When men could not honor monarchs in their presence, since they lived at a distance, they imagined their appearance far away, and made a visible image [ἐμφανῆ εἰκόνα] of the king whom they honored, so that by their zeal they might flatter the absent one as though present. Then the ambition of the craftsman impelled even those who did not know the king to intensify their worship [εἰς ἐπίτασιν θρησκείας]. For he, perhaps wishing to please his ruler, skillfully forced the likeness to take more beautiful form, and the multitude, attracted by the charm of his work, now regarded as an object of worship the one whom shortly before they had honored as a man. And this became a hidden trap for mankind, because men, in bondage to misfortune or royal authority, bestowed on objects of stone or wood the name that ought not to be shared.

In time, the iconoclasm of Wisdom would find an audience among Christians, both east and west. But the first four centuries of this era witnessed instead the gradual realization of a consensus on certain beliefs about the function and referential capacity of imperial portraits. That consensus in turn permitted an eastern Christian like Severianus to liken the omnipresence of his deity to that achieved by the emperor through the ubiquity of his animate image.

The portraits of select emperors achieved even greater importance when those emperors became objects of religious devotion in their own right: through him his subjects lived, through him they sailed, through him they enjoyed their liberty and their fortunes.[123] Individual piety could urge the

---

122. Wisdom 14:12–21 (RSV, slightly modified). For the date and origin of Wisdom, and particularly of its last nine chapters, see Robert 1938, 234–235. On this passage see Price 1984b, 200.

123. Suetonius *Augustus* 98.2: *Forte Puteolanum sinum praetervehenti vectores nautaeque de navi Alexandrina, quae tantum quod appulerat, candidati coronatique et tura libantes fausta omina et eximias laudes congesserant: per illum se vivere, per illum navigare, libertate atque fortunis per illum frui.* This passage would seem crucial to understanding popular feelings about imperial cult, but its evidentiary value was attacked repeatedly by Nock (1972, 355 and 840). The sentiments it records do not harmonize with political interpretations of imperial cult.

placement of an imperial portrait among a household's *penates:* at such a shrine Ovid offered incense "to the Caesars and the wife who is worthy of Caesar, true gods." When Marcus Aurelius Cotta Maximus sent silver portraits of the imperial family to Ovid, he enabled Ovid to "see gods and think them present, to speak, as it were, with a real deity." With an image of Augustus before him, what did Ovid's eyes lack, "save only the Palatine? And that place, if Caesar is removed, will be worthless. As I gaze on him, I seem to look on Rome, for he embodies the likeness of our *patria.*"[124]

The spread of imperial portraits to every conceivable public space within a community, as well as the range of powers widely believed to be resident in or accessible through them, is well described in the third-century rhetorical handbook whose author we call Menander Rhetor. In closing an "imperial oration," Menander suggested that orators "speak of the prosperity and good fortune of the cities: the markets are full of goods, the cities of feasts and festivals, the earth is tilled in peace, the sea sailed without danger, piety toward God is increased, honors are given to all in due fashion." Menander then switched to the first person, suggesting the very words that his reader might use:

> We fear neither barbarians nor enemies. The emperor's weapons are a safer fortress for us than our cities' walls. We acquire prisoners as slaves, not by going to war ourselves, but by receiving them from the emperor's victorious hand. What prayers ought cities to make to the power above, save always for the emperor? What greater blessing must one ask from the gods than the emperor's safety? Rains in season, abundance from the sea, unstinting harvests come happily to us because of the emperor's justice. In return, cities, nations, races, and tribes, all of us, garland him, sing of him, write of him. The cities are full of his images, some on painted tablets, some perhaps of more precious material [αἱ μὲν πινάκων γραπτῶν, αἱ δέ που καὶ τιμιωτέρας ὕλης].

Menander then returned to his didactic pose, addressing his reader once again: "After this, you must utter a prayer, beseeching God that the emperor's reign may endure long, and the throne be handed down to his children and his descendants."[125] Similarly evocative is the analogy drawn by the author of a late fourth-century Coptic homily on the Virgin, whose manuscript attributes the text to Theophilus, bishop of Alexandria from

---

124. Ovid *Pont.* 1.4.55–56; 2.8.9–10, 17–20; and cf. *Pont.* 4.9.105–112, on which see Millar 1993a, 16. Syme 1978, 166–167, doubts Ovid's sincerity—it is *adulatio*—but Zanker 1988, 265, is undoubtedly correct in arguing that Ovid's shrine was "no different from thousands of other house *aediculae.*" See, for example, Horace *Carm.* 4.5.29–36, Pliny *Ep.* 10.8, and *SHA Marc.* 18.5–6. Augustus boasted of having refused to allow himself to be worshiped with images in gold and silver, but his ostentatious melting of silver statues from Rome must have targeted public statues: *Res gestae* 24.2. See further Scott 1931b, esp. 111–113.

125. Menander Rhetor, Περὶ ἐπιδεικτικῶν 1–2, *Basilikos logos* (trans. Russell and Wilson).

385 until his death in 412: "For if the image of the emperor of this world, when painted and set up in the midst of the marketplace, becomes a protection to the whole city, and if violence is committed against anyone, and he goes and takes hold of the image of the emperor: then no man will be able to oppose him, even though the emperor is naught but a mortal man; and he is taken to a court of law. Let us, therefore, honor the image of our Lady the veritable Queen, the holy Theotokos."[126]

When reviewing the sacrosanctity of imperial portraits on coins we had occasion to review a pair of treason trials reported in the *Annales* of Tacitus. The charges against Granius Marcellus presumably concerned a private statue within his household, and the same was undoubtedly true in the case of L. Ennius.[127] Similarly, the attack on one Faianius early in the reign of Tiberius explicitly concerned a statue of Augustus that the *eques* had kept in his garden, like other *simulacra numinum*.[128] These passages are more famous as examples of the application of the law of *maiestas* to an increasing variety of acts that could be construed as disrespectful to the emperor. Despite a recent attempt to link this particular evolution to the consecration of some individual statues of the emperor, this would not have been possible in the first century.[129] The importance of such a "consecration" was a juristic fiction of the Antonine age and the early Severan period, when more sensible emperors and jurists attempted to restrain *delatores* by defining moments when one could not be prosecuted for involuntary insults to the imperial image. Although Venuleius Saturninus purportedly regarded as guilty of treason anyone who melted statues of the emperor that had already been consecrated (*imagines imperatoris iam consecratas*), the language of "consecration" almost undoubtedly represents a later interpolation into his text. Venuleius himself probably distinguished between intentional and accidental harm to portraits.[130] Among Antonine and Severan jurists, Quintus Cervidius Scaevola recorded only that the Senate acquitted a man who had melted down "rejected" statues of the emperor (*statuas imperatoris reprobatas*). Two generations later Aelius Marcianus reported that Severus and Caracalla had refused to allow trials for treason for accidentally striking an imperial portrait or for selling one prior to its consecration; Marcianus also insisted that repairing imperial portraits grown decrepit with age would not incur such a charge.[131]

---

126. Trans. after W. H. Worrell, *The Coptic manuscripts in the Freer collection*, University of Michigan, Humanistic Series, 10 (New York: MacMillan, 1923), 375.

127. See above at n. 60.

128. Tacitus *Ann.* 1.73.2–3. Dio 57.24.7 describes a similar episode in 24/25.

129. Pekáry 1985, 107–115.

130. Venuleius Saturninus, mid-first century A.D., at *Dig.* 48.4.6.

131. Scaevola at *Dig.* 48.4.4.1; Marcianus at *Dig.* 48.4.5.

Formal consecration would at least have justified charges of treason. Tacitus found the trials under Augustus and Tiberius so galling precisely because their invocation of *maiestas* had no legal foundation as such—it was not justified by reference to the emperor's tribunician sacrosanctity, nor by any consecration of his image—but rather was grounded in the presumed identity between the interests of the *res publica* and those of one man. As so often, his Tiberius can speak for them both: *principes mortales, rem publicam aeternam esse.*[132] In the absence of consecration, that putative identity of interest can have been the only justification for the Senate's voting a military guard for the statues of Gaius.[133] Earlier we reviewed the extension of this principle to cover performing lewd acts in the vicinity of an imperial portrait. Cassius Dio recorded two further examples of acts liable for prosecution: under Domitian a woman was prosecuted and killed for disrobing near a statue of that emperor, and under Caracalla men were still prosecuted for carrying coins with imperial portraits into brothels.[134] According to the *Historia Augusta,* Caracalla also convicted those who urinated near his statues or painted portraits.[135]

Men did not insist that identical veneration was due to the emperor and his portraits for the sake of mere casuistry. On the contrary, the ability of portraits to demand veneration, as it were, made them active forces within local affairs. They were instruments of power, and, in representing a unique mortal with superhuman power, they became powerful and animate in their own right. A law of Theodosius and Valentinian addressing public veneration of their portraits alludes to this belief, even as it reveals its authors' utter lack of reflection on the religious import of the traditional vocabulary of Roman legislation:[136]

> If at any time, whether on festal days, as is usual, or on ordinary days, statues or images of us are erected, let the magistrate be present without employing any overzealous element of worship, but so that he may show that his presence has graced the day, the place, and our memory. Likewise, if our images are shown at public spectacles, they shall demonstrate that our divinity [*numen*] and praises live only in the hearts and recesses of the minds of those who attend. A worship in excess of human dignity should be reserved for the divinity above [*superno numini*].

Christians like Severianus of Gabala thus drew on deep-seated currents in Mediterranean religious thought when they established analogies between

132. Tacitus *Ann.* 3.6.3. For Roman definitions of *maiestas* see Chapter 3 in n. 81.
133. Dio 59.26.3.
134. Dio 67.12.2 and 77.16.2².
135. *SHA Carac.* 5.7, and cf. Seneca *Ben.* 3.26.1–2.
136. *C. Th.* 15.4.1 (trans. Pharr, with adjustments).

the power latent in imperial portraits and the presence of Christ in religious icons.[137] Imperial portraits were not unique in containing some essence of the emperor's divinity, but they were the most common and least controversial such figures: hence their explanatory power. For example, both eastern and western theologians struggled to describe the role of the body after the Resurrection. Methodius, bishop of Lycian Olympus in the first decade of the fourth century, drew an analogy with imperial images: just as the body after the Resurrection was identical to the earlier body and yet not identical to it, so the images of the king receive honor even though they are not made of gold or silver or electrum or ivory:[138]

> For men attending to images not made from expensive material do not value them less than others, but they honor them all equally, whether they are made from gypsum or bronze. Furthermore, the one who blasphemes [δυσφημήσας] against either is not set free because he dishonored clay nor judged guilty because he valued gold, but is judged because he displayed impiety [ἀσεβήσας] toward the emperor and lord himself.

Basil of Caesarea appealed to another aspect of the essential identity between emperor and portrait when he sought to explain the unity of God, Christ, and Holy Spirit:[139]

> Just because the emperor and the image of the emperor are both addressed as "emperor" does not mean that there are two emperors. For his power is not

137. On pagan gods and statuary see Lane Fox 1986, 123–141 at 133–136. On Christian beliefs regarding imperial portraits see Setton 1941 and, briefly, Price 1984b, 198–204. Much of our evidence is preserved by John of Damascus, who closed each of his *Orationes de imaginibus* with quotations from earlier patristic writers that support his views.

138. Methodius *De resurrectione* 2.24.1 (quoted in an abbreviated form by John of Damascus *De imaginibus* 3.138). See also John Chrysostom, in a fragment from an otherwise unattested homily on Maccabees (John of Damascus 3.120): Καὶ ἡ διαφορὰ τῶν ὑλῶν οὐ λυμαίνεται τῷ ἀξιώματι τοῦ χαρακτῆρος ... ἀλλὰ πάσας ὁμοίως ὁ βασιλικὸς τύπος σεμνύνει καὶ οὐδὲν ἀπὸ τῆς ὕλης ἐλαττούμενος τιμιωτέραν τὴν δεχομένην ἐργάζεται. In a similar vein see Anastasius of Antioch on the Sabbath (John of Damascus 3.127): ῞Ωσπερ γὰρ ὁ παροινῶν εἰκόνι βασιλέως τιμωρίαν ὑφίσταται ὡς αὐτόχρημα βασιλέα ἀτιμάσας, καίτοι τῆς εἰκόνος οὐδὲν ἕτερον οὔσης ἢ ξύλον καὶ χρώματα κηρῷ μεμιγμένα καὶ κεκραμένα, τὸν αὐτὸν τρόπον ὁ τὸν τύπον τοῦδέ τινος ἀτιμάζων εἰς αὐτὸ ἐκεῖνο, οὗ τύπος ἐστίν, ἀναφέρει τὴν ὕβριν.

139. Basil *De spiritu sancto ad Amphilochium*, quoted by John of Damascus 1.35. Cf. Basil *Comm. in Is.* 13 (John of Damascus 3.58): ῞Ωσπερ γὰρ ὁ βασιλικὴν εἰκόνα καθυβρίσας ὡς εἰς αὐτὸν ἐξαμαρτήσας τὸν βασιλέα κρίνεται, οὕτω δηλονότι ὑπόδικός ἐστι τῇ ἁμαρτίᾳ ὁ τὸν κατ᾽εἰκόνα γεγενημένον καθυβρίζων. See also Gregory of Nyssa *De opif. hom.* 4 (John of Damascus 1.49): ῞Ωσπερ κατὰ τὴν ἀνθρωπίνην συνήθειαν οἱ τὰς εἰκόνας τῶν κρατούντων κατασκευάζοντες τόν τε χαρακτῆρα τῆς μορφῆς ἀναμάσσονται καὶ τῇ περιβολῇ τῆς πορφυρίδος τὴν βασιλικὴν ἀξίαν συμπαραγράφουσι καὶ λέγεται κατὰ τὴν συνήθειαν καὶ εἰκὼν καὶ βασιλεύς, οὕτω καὶ ἡ ἀνθρωπίνη φύσις, ἐπειδὴ πρὸς ἀρχὴν τῶν ἄλλων κατεσκευάζετο, οἷόν τις ἔμψυχος εἰκὼν ἀνεστάθη κοινωνοῦσα τῷ ἀρχετύπῳ καὶ τῆς ἀξίας καὶ τοῦ ὀνόματος.

divided, nor is his glory split in half. Indeed, just as the empire that governs us and its power are one, so it is with our doxology, one and not many, because the honor directed toward the image redounds to its prototype.

In constructing this explanation Basil drew on a long exegetic and homiletic tradition. The topic had been hotly debated for some time; after all, it had been the central issue in the Arian controversy.[140] In his treatment of this topic, indeed, in his use of this particular analogy, Basil undoubtedly followed Athanasius of Alexandria, who argued this point in the opening of his *Third oration against the Arians*. In an extraordinary passage, Athanasius pondered what an imperial statue might say to its audience: "The emperor and I are one. For I am in him, and he is in me. What you see in me, this you see in him. And what you have seen in him, you see now in me."[141]

IMPERIAL PORTRAITS AND THE FAILURE OF CHARISMA

In concentrating on the power of portraits of living emperors, we have begged several important questions about the reception and legitimation of new portraits, not least those of Decius, distributed in the months prior to the promulgation of his request for a universal sacrifice. What difference did it make whether the local commission enforcing the edict of Decius used a portrait of Decius or a portrait of Philip? After all, Philip had recently been emperor. In fact, what made either portrait recognizably imperial? And if law or custom required one to pay homage to the portraits of legitimate rulers, how did anyone know when that obligation began or ended? Extant evidence does not explicitly address these questions in this wording. Ancient historians were more interested in narrative than analysis, intent more upon action than mentalities. To find our answers, we must ask questions that Tacitus, Herodian, and Dio are prepared to answer. Did the heterogeneous populations of empire behave in ways that suggest they associated the power of a portrait with the legitimacy of the man it represented? That question opens two paths of inquiry: How did people behave when the portrait of a new emperor arrived, and what ceremonies or signs marked that portrait as imperial? And how did people behave when an emperor's falling fortunes revealed the failure of his unique charisma?

Fortune preserves evidence relevant to these questions in a systematically asymmetrical pattern. Many anecdotes from the first through the third centuries describe the destruction of portraits that followed the violent transfer of power or the death of an unpopular emperor.[142] Similarly, widespread

---

140. Hanson 1988 provides the best survey of this affair.

141. Athanasius *Contra Arianos* 3.5.

142. On this topic, see Friedlaender 1922, 3:59–60; A. Alföldi 1934, 71; and Pekáry 1985, 134–142.

testimony from the fourth and fifth centuries depicts the ceremonies enacted on the arrival of a new imperial portrait. We have already seen that emperors as early as the first century must have overseen the official and rapid distribution of their portraits at the start of their reigns: that remains the only hypothesis that can account for the many needs such portraits addressed early in any given reign.[143] Although I shall treat these two bodies of evidence separately, we must not forget that they speak to similar issues and reveal essentially the same assumptions in the minds of ancient actors.

The deaths of Augustus and Tiberius were neither unexpected nor controversial; nor did ill will toward Tiberius permeate the lower classes and army. Neither therefore aroused popular action against their portraits and inscriptions. At the death of Gaius, on the other hand, the people of Rome arose and spontaneously tore down his statues and images.[144] Some time later, the Senate considered formally condemning his memory. Although Claudius did not allow the measure to come to a vote, he voluntarily and quietly removed portraits of Caligula from public view and did not mention Gaius in the Senate's annual oath to uphold the acts of the previous emperors.[145] The Senate's reaction to the death of Domitian was no less symbolic: according to Suetonius, the senators formally passed a motion to condemn the memory of Domitian only after they had torn down all statues of that emperor in the Curia.[146]

In objecting to the position that imperial portraits were centrally distributed at the start of each new reign, Meriwether Stuart concentrated on the Julio-Claudian house and suggested that portraits of all members of that family were already widespread prior to any particular individual's accession to the throne.[147] If the inference is flawed, the premise, at least, is undoubtedly true.[148] If we turn, therefore, to the tumultuous year 68, do we find a population as yet unaware of the symbolic value of imperial portraits, of both tearing them down and putting them up?[149] Certainly the legions, accustomed to swearing an annual oath of loyalty before the portrait that resided among their standards, knew what such actions expressed. The troops at Rome removed the gold portrait of Galba from among their stan-

143. See above at n. 107.

144. Dio 59.30.1 [a].

145. Dio 60.4.5–6. On the senators' oath *in acta Caesarum*, see Sherwin-White 1966 on Pliny *Ep.* 10.35; the specific wording of this oath is not known, but Dio's information here seems confirmed by Tacitus *Ann.* 16.22.3: *eiusdem animi est Poppaeam divam non credere, cuius in acta divi Augusti et divi Iulii non iurare.*

146. Suetonius *Domitian* 23.1. See also Pliny *Pan.* 52.4–5 and Martial 1.70.6.

147. Stuart 1939, 602–603.

148. Rose 1997a.

149. A. Alföldi 1934, 71, proposed the "Vierkaiserjahre" as proof "daß die Gegenwart der Bildnisse zur Proklamation und zum Eidschwar der Legionen erforderlich gewesen ist."

dards to make room for Otho so that he might flatter them in a speech and offer them a bribe. Later, when they marched to the Forum, an officer in Galba's bodyguard tore his emperor's portrait from the standard: "By that signal the enthusiasm of all the soldiers toward Otho was made clear."[150] Similarly, when the legions in Lower Germany assembled to take the New Year's oath, the First and Fifth Legions signaled their change of allegiance by throwing stones at Galba's portrait, and in Upper Germany the Fourth and Twenty-second tore the portraits of Galba to pieces.[151] The population of Rome apparently felt quite differently about Otho. During the Festival of Ceres, "reliable informants" brought the news to the theater that Otho had died and that Flavius Sabinus, the urban prefect, had administered an oath to Vitellius to the Praetorian Guard; the people applauded and carried busts of Galba, adorned with laurel and flowers, in a parade around the temples.[152]

Later that year, when it appeared to commanders in northern Italy that the Flavian armies would soon emerge victorious, they heeded the suggestion of Antonius Primus that they should restore the portraits of Galba, which had been taken down "in every municipality"—it was no coincidence that Domitian in Rome was deploring the excesses of Otho and Vitellius and urging the restoration of honors to Galba's memory. Around the same time, Caecina Alienus, commanding the Vitellian camp at Hostilia that guarded the bridge over the Padus on the road between Mutina and Verona, assembled his officers and deplored the Vitellian position: his co-conspirators immediately swore an oath to Vespasian and in the same instant tore down the portraits of Vitellius and wrote up the name of Vespasian. Caecina's soldiers and some of his officers would not stand for his duplicity, and, taking him prisoner, they joined with other Vitellian forces and made a stand at Cremona. When they were routed by forces of Vespasian, the officers attempted to disguise their allegiance by tearing down every portrait of Vitellius and erasing all mention of his name.[153]

At the very end of the next century, early in the reign of Severus but after the deaths of Niger and Albinus, Tertullian wrote his *Apology*. He wished to defend the Christians from one attack in particular, namely that of disloyalty toward emperor and empire. God himself, Tertullian argued, had commanded the Christians to uphold mores consistent with the *pietas et religio et fides* that are rightfully owed the emperor of Rome.[154] At the climax

150. Tacitus *Hist.* 1.36.1.

151. Tacitus *Hist.* 1.55.2–3.

152. Tacitus *Hist.* 2.55.1.

153. Tacitus *Hist.* 3.7.2, 3.13.1, and 3.31.2.

154. On the use of *pietas* and *religio* as synonyms for *fides* at Tertullian *Apol.* 34.2, 35.5, and 36.2, see Chapter 9, "The Discovery of Roman Religion."

of his argument Tertullian mounted a twofold attack: he sarcastically conceded that "the other orders of society stand religiously for authority, as their loyalty requires. There is never a whiff of hostility from the Senate, from an *eques*, from the camps, or from the palace itself." He then asked his putative audience whence arose all those men who had claimed the throne over the last few years—he named Avidius Cassius, Pescennius Niger, and Clodius Albinus—or those who murdered Domitian: "From among Romans, unless I am mistaken; that is, from among non-Christians."[155] All these criminals, Tertullian added, sacrificed for the health of the emperor and swore by his *genius* until the very moment of their treason. Despite the many changes in leadership, however, the Christian never wavered in his loyalty: "If Nature drew over men's breasts some transparent material to let the light shine through, whose heart would not produce, engraved upon itself, one Caesar after another, presiding on a stage over the distribution of a *congiarium*, even in that hour when those same men are shouting, 'Jupiter take from our years to add to thine!'? A Christian knows no better how to utter those words than to wish for a new Caesar."[156] Tertullian clearly associated the accession of a new emperor both with the arrival of a new portrait on the coinage and with the advertisement of a particular ceremonial act.

Many emperors and several dynasties passed away during Tertullian's lifetime, not often peacefully. When Tertullian was in his early thirties, a widespread conspiracy at Rome arranged the murder of Commodus. Cassius Dio lived in Rome in these years, yet we may nevertheless suspect a senatorial bias in his report that the Senate and people wished to dismember the dead Commodus but were eventually satisfied with the destruction of his statues and portraits.[157] The biographer Marius Maximus, a contemporary of Dio, also recorded that the Senate formally condemned the memory of Commodus, and we have already examined the multiple strands in the campaign Caracalla waged against his brother's memory.[158] At the death of Caracalla, the Senate and the people were checked in their desire to censure his memory by the fondness that the troops still felt for him—and, one suspects, it was not terribly practical to annul all the *acta* of one who had held the throne so long. Nevertheless, even without the official act, the people expressed their hatred for him by disfiguring or melting down his statues within the city.[159]

155. Tertullian *Apol.* 35.8–9 (trans. Glover, modified).
156. Tertullian *Apol.* 35.7.
157. Dio's account of the plot and its completion seems otherwise quite reliable: Millar 1964, 133–134.
158. See Chapter 5 at n. 17 and above at n. 71.
159. Dio 78.9.2, 78.17.4–18.1, and 78.18.5.

Twenty years after Tertullian penned his *Apology*, early in the summer of 218, Elagabalus—or, rather, his ambitious mother—declared his candidacy for the purple. Within three weeks his forces had defeated those of Macrinus, who fled the field of battle and died shortly thereafter. Elagabalus immediately wrote to the Senate and people of Rome, disparaging the memory of Macrinus and adopting the titles of the imperial office before— so Dio observed—they had formally been voted to him. The Senate nevertheless responded with typical sycophancy and posthumously declared Macrinus a public enemy.[160] Though Elagabalus declared his desire to reach Rome as soon as possible, like Hadrian he found reasons to delay his arrival: Elagabalus arranged the execution of several senators and military men who had been close to Macrinus and saw no point in meeting the Senate so soon after thinning its ranks.[161] Herodian noted with revulsion that Elagabalus did, however, immediately order a full-length portrait of himself in his priestly garb, in the act of performing a sacrifice before his god. The painting was then hung from the ceiling of the Curia, directly above the Altar of Victory. Herodian conjectured that Elagabalus arranged this monstrosity in order to prepare Rome for his outlandish appearance.[162] But Elagabalus soon learned that manipulation of visual propaganda alone could not secure the loyalty of the troops. Two years after reaching Rome, Elagabalus adopted his cousin Alexander as his partner on the throne. Only one year later Elagabalus decided to dispose of Alexander. Wishing to show the Praetorians that he had formally withdrawn his support of his Caesar, Elagabalus sent them a letter to that effect and dispatched an agent to smear mud over his brother's name on the inscriptions that labeled the portraits in the Guard's camp.[163] Alexander proved more popular with the troops, and Elagabalus was soon executed, his memory condemned: Marius Maximus recorded with pleasure the erasure of his name from texts in Rome and throughout the provinces.[164]

As his observations on Elagabalus suggest, Herodian had a keen eye for the dynamics of popular opinion in the empire, including the means by which it was influenced and through which it was expressed. His narrative of the tumultuous events of 238 displays all his talents. Early in that year the population of Africa rose in revolt. According to Herodian, a particularly reprehensible procurator in the area of Carthage antagonized the young men of several wealthy families until, with only three days of planning, they

160. Dio 79.2. The chapter is mutilated; of what remains, see paragraphs 2 and 5–6.
161. For the senators and officers killed see Dio 79.3–7.
162. Herodian 5.5.6–7.
163. *SHA Heliogab.* 13.6–7.
164. *SHA Heliogab.* 17.4 and 18.1.

murdered him.[165] Mere contrition could not mitigate the murder of an imperial legate. The conspirators sought safety in a coup d'état. When the conspirators offered Gordian as a replacement for Maximinus, "the whole of Libya was immediately rocked by revolt: all the honorary dedications to Maximinus were torn down, and in their place the cities were adorned with portraits and statues of Gordian."[166] The fact that portraits of Gordian were ready for distribution and display suggests that Gordian had been consulted and the revolt planned for much longer than Herodian admits, although the Romans had long possessed the wherewithal to mass-produce portraits for such a demonstration.[167] In any event, Gordian's supporters were clearly aware of the need to advertise the name and legitimacy of their candidate and of the symbolic value of the means by which they chose to do so. The Senate, already angry with Maximinus, seized the opportunity. It named a board of consulars to direct efforts in support of Gordian and dispatched letters to the governors and populations of the provinces: they should ally themselves with those acting on behalf of the *communis patria* and its Senate.[168]

Within three weeks both Gordian and his son were dead.[169] Having declared themselves hostile to Maximinus, the senators at Rome had now to confront the angry emperor and his army alone. The Senate chose two of its own number to serve as joint emperors, M. Clodius Pupienus Maximus and D. Caelius Calvinus Balbinus.[170] A riot ensued, which Herodian attributes to popular feelings but which was probably instigated by the friends of Gordian I—precisely those men to whom Gordian had written for support when he was first acclaimed.[171] The Senate was able to quell the disturbance only by appointing Gordian's grandson, Gordian III, Caesar to the two Augusti.[172] A further struggle between senatorial forces and the legions stationed outside the city delayed preparations, but eventually the Senate sent men to the cities of northern Italy to prepare for the onslaught of Maximinus. Two men were sent to Aquileia, Rutilius Pudens Crispinus and Tullius Menophilus.[173] We have already examined the fate that befell Maximinus

165. Herodian 7.4; for the dating of these events see Kienast 1990, 188, or Potter 1990, 27–28.

166. Herodian 7.5.8 (trans. Whittaker).

167. See, for example, Plutarch *Caesar* 6.1.

168. Herodian 7.7.5. On the men chosen for the board see Syme 1971, 163–164.

169. *Chron. anni CCCLIIII* (*Chron. min.* 1.147, l. 28): *Duo Gordiani imper. dies xx. excesserunt Africae.* Zonaras 12.17 states that they ruled for 22 days.

170. Herodian 7.10.1–5.

171. Herodian 7.6.3.

172. Herodian 7.10.5–9.

173. For Crispinus, see *AÉ* 1929, 158; for Menophilus, *AÉ* 1962, 265.

before the gates of Aquileia.[174] We should remember in this context that when the soldiers in Second Parthian Legion decided to murder Maximinus, they first declared the abrogation of their allegiance by tearing his portrait off the standards that stood before his tent.[175] The leaders of the forces within Aquileia shared precisely the same understanding of the symbolic power of imperial portraits. Crispinus and Menophilus marched outside the gates, produced portraits of Pupienus, Balbinus, and Gordian III, and demanded that the army recognize them by acclamation.[176] The portraits in question must have been prepared within days of their accession and sent with Crispinus and Menophilus to Aquileia, as others were no doubt sent to every city in Italy. All parties evidently regarded these portraits as essential to this ceremony. The words of the oath were not enough: through the icons, the emperors were themselves somehow present to witness and to sanction the ceremony. No less than the citizens of Carthage and Aquileia, the soldiers in the legions wished to see their emperors, to know their faces and to feel their presence.

THE ARRIVAL OF ROMAN PORTRAITS IN A CHRISTIAN EMPIRE

The Tetrarchy raised many problems.[177] By providing for the systematic existence of multiple emperors, it created myriad new opportunities for claiming, awarding, and contesting a throne. In other words, to an extent hitherto unimaginable, Diocletian made the ceremonies and trappings of power available to multiple contestants. If the political realities of these years seemed fraught with new challenges and new potentialities, the Romans negotiated them with typical conservatism. The symbolic language through which legitimacy was expressed and assigned became more rigid. The insistence that Caesars should honor the Augustus responsible for their elevation, indeed, that their legitimacy depended wholly on that emperor's approval, merely expressed in new language a thoroughly familiar desire for dynastic continuity in the transmission of charismatic authority.[178] The

---

174. See Chapter 6 at nn. 108–111.

175. Herodian 8.5.9. For further discussion of imperial portraits and standards, see below, "*Signa* of Rome, *Signa* of Power."

176. Herodian 8.6.2; cf. *SHA Maxim.* 24.2.

177. The best introduction to imperial portraiture in the late empire is Engemann's article in *RAC* s.v. "Herrscherbild," which is particularly strong on portraits in media other than marble or bronze. Setton 1941 provides a disorganized but still helpful introduction to Christian attitudes toward the veneration of imperial portraits in the fourth and fifth centuries, on which see also Kruse 1934, 99–105, and Grigg 1979. For the honors paid to imperial portraits and the ceremonies through which that honor was expressed, see esp. Bréhier 1920, 59–65; *idem* 1949, 61–75; and Kruse 1934, 34–50.

178. For sources and bibliography on *auctores imperii,* see above in n. 83.

forms of ceremonial became subject to prescriptions from above rather than manipulation from below and, ultimately, may have lost their ability to shape and express social consensus.[179] In the immediate aftermath of the retirements of Diocletian and Maximian and the death of Constantius, men did not adopt such a long perspective. Would-be dynasts merely sought a mechanism through which to acquire the recognition of those who already occupied the thrones, and emperors accepted such overtures in order to acquire the power that accrued to the *auctor* of another's *imperium*. Both sides found that mechanism in the exchange of portraits.[180]

The efficacy of this economy depended on popular recognition of certain behaviors and actions as imperial prerogatives.[181] No one had contested the right of Severus or Gallienus to allow Albinus or Odaenathus to appear on imperial coins, nor had anyone misunderstood the significance of that act, precisely because all understood that right to be the emperor's, and the emperor's alone. Nothing else spoke so loudly to so many audiences. When Constantine sought recognition of his position as Augustus from Galerius in 306, he did not write him a letter—or, if he did, we know nothing about it. The extant ancient narratives describe only the symbolic forms through which each side articulated its claims. Constantine had already usurped the rank of Augustus—claiming it by right of inheritance and by acclamation of his troops, a clear violation of the system established by Diocletian. But Constantine needed the cooperation of the other emperors, and he could seek that cooperation only by exposing his own legitimacy to their scrutiny. Thus Constantine sent Galerius a laureate portrait of himself, and Galerius indicated his decision by accepting the statue and sending Constantine "the purple." Galerius outwitted Constantine, however, and acknowledged him only at the rank of Caesar. Although Zosimus's narrative for these events displays *condensation maladroite*, it nevertheless provides the additional detail that Constantine's portrait was subsequently exhibited at Rome, presumably with the knowledge and permission of Galerius.[182]

179. Cf. MacCormack 1981.

180. Bruun 1976.

181. For the testimony of Ammianus and Claudian on imperial prerogatives see above, n. 80.

182. Lactantius *Mort. pers.* 25.1, 3–5. Zosimus 2.9.2. On these events, see Barnes 1981, 28–43. Müller-Rettig 1990, 313–322, is particularly good on the competing claims for legitimacy of the principals in this drama; cf. Grünewald 1990, 13–61. Few have sought to identify the significant pagan sources behind the anti-Constantinian anecdotes preserved in Zosimus and elsewhere: Paschoud 1975; *idem* 1985, 244–253; Bleckmann 1991; and Fowden 1994 are exceptions. Bemarchius of Caesarea, author of a biography in ten books, deserves further scrutiny (*Suda* B 259).

It requires no imagination to appreciate that Constantine found his enforced demotion and subsequent subordination intolerable.[183] Nevertheless, his only course of action—barring the sudden demise of Galerius—was to find a source of legitimacy that possessed greater *auctoritas* than Galerius. When the other members of the imperial college quarreled amongst themselves in 306–307, Constantine agreed to an alliance with Maxentius and his father, Maximian, who had been the junior Augustus when Galerius was appointed as junior Caesar in 293.[184]

The events of the next three years are quite complicated, but suffice it to say that Maximian and his son fell out.[185] Infighting early in 308 had given the empire at least two sets of consuls and six emperors.[186] In November, Galerius brought Diocletian out of retirement for a conference at Carnuntum, in Pannonia Superior. Through Diocletian, who could legitimately claim to be the ultimate *auctor* of all concerned, Galerius sought a permanent settlement to the chaotic division of powers that then obtained. The only platforms of that settlement that need concern us are the promotion of still another Augustus, Licinius, the forced abdication of Maximian, for the second time, and a renewed assertion by the emperors of the East that Constantine was merely Caesar and not Augustus.

Relations between Constantine, Maxentius, and Galerius remained sour. Constantine's gambit with Maximian now became a liability. If there were to be any chance for a reconciliation with the eastern emperors, Constantine had to keep Maximian content in retirement. At the same time, he could not now abandon Maximian, his father-in-law and patron, without bringing aspersion on his own character and legitimacy. Maximian had not liked his first retirement and would not be satisfied now. He tried to steal Constantine's troops and throne, committing suicide when he failed. Without the presence of Maximian and still at odds with Galerius—who could claim to have promoted him in 306—Constantine required another source of le-

---

183. This does not mean, however, that Constantine did not play the role assigned to him: he advertised the *concordia* of the college, and labeled himself merely *nobilissimus Caesar* (Grünewald 1990, 15–16 with 16 n. 21, 43).

184. On the arrangements made on 1 March 293, see Barnes 1981, 8–9. In 307, Constantine cemented the alliance by marrying Fausta, the daughter of Maximian; the panegyric which celebrated the occasion survives (*Pan. Lat.* VI[7]). On its portrayal of the relationship between Constantine and Maximian, see Grünewald 1990, 26–34, and Nixon 1993, *passim*, but esp. 234 and 238.

185. See Galletier's introduction to *Pan. Lat.* VII(6), 34–46 and 51.

186. Lactantius *Mort. pers.* 29; Barnes 1981, 31–32. The chronological tables in the first chapter of Barnes 1982 are helpful, but he restricts the data there displayed to "legitimate" emperors, and removes "other emperors and usurpers" to chapter 2 (cf. Barnes 1997, 109). The resulting portrait is not a very useful guide to the political realities of these years.

gitimacy. He found it in a fictitious genealogy: he claimed descent through his father from the emperor Claudius II. Constantine again bypassed the strictures of Tetrarchic ideology and claimed legitimacy by birth, independent of any sanction from Diocletian or his successors.[187]

After Constantine terminated Maximian's final attempt to regain the throne, he ordered the destruction of all his portraits in every medium. That command made a profound impression on Constantine's partisans Lactantius and Eusebius. Lactantius understood that many works of art depicted Maximian and Diocletian together and that the disfiguring of Maximian would necessarily bring disgrace upon Diocletian: that fate had befallen no other emperor. Eusebius even maintained that Maximian was the very first to suffer this punishment.[188] The alliance that developed between Licinius and Constantine in the months that followed the death of Galerius scared Maximinus into seeking an alliance with Maxentius: his ambassadors brought portraits of their leader with them, and Maxentius signaled his acceptance of the offer by ordering their portraits to be displayed together.[189] Maxentius could arrange such displays only in the territories under his control. Constantine had, therefore, to deduce the existence of that alliance from the collocation of his enemies' portraits in Rome upon his defeat of Maxentius and entry into the capital. Licinius and Constantine subsequently punished the memory of their opponents following identical symbolic logic: they jointly declared Maximinus a public enemy and ordered the destruction of all his portraits. Eusebius, who recorded many of these actions, was so accustomed to the logic of Tetrarchic portrait groups that he interpreted images depicting Maximinus together with his children as proof that Maximinus had made them "partners with him in the imperial dignity"—a family portrait could not be just a family portrait.[190]

Half a century later a usurper confronted another emperor who temporarily lacked the resources to subdue the upstart. In 383 Magnus Maxi-

187. The "discovery" was announced in 310: see *Pan. Lat.* VII(6).2, esp. 2.5. Müller-Rettig 1990, 322–329, provides an excellent brief analysis of the issues raised in the panegyric. Cf. Grünewald 1990, 46–50. See also *Origo Constantini* 1.1, with König 1987, 55–57. Syme 1983, 63–79, surveys the whole topic.

188. Lactantius *Mort. pers.* 42.1–2; Eusebius *Hist. eccl.* 8.13.15, but cf. 9.11.2.

189. Lactantius *Mort. pers.* 43.2–3. Compare *Pan. Lat.* X(4).12.2–4, describing Maxentius's defacing of Constantine's portraits: *Aboleri vultus hic non potest. Universorum pectoribus infixus est, nec commendatione cerae ac pigmentorum fucis renitet sed desiderio efflorescit animorum.*

190. Eusebius *Hist. eccl.* 9.11.2 and 7; cf. Gregory Naz. *Or.* 4.96: μήτε Μαξιμῖνος, ὁ μετ' ἐκείνους καὶ ὑπὲρ ἐκείνους διώκτης, οὗ τὰ σύμβολα τῆς ἐπὶ τούτῳ πληγῆς αἱ εἰκόνες φέρουσιν ἔτι δημοσίᾳ προκείμεναι καὶ στηλιτεύουσαι τὴν λώβην τοῦ σώματος. See also *Origo Constantini* 5.15: *Cum Senicio auctor insidiarum posceretur ad poenam, negante Licinio, fracta concordia est, additis etiam causis quod apud Emonam Constantini imagines statuisque deiecerat. bellum deinde apertum convenit ambobus.*

mus, the commander of the legions in Britain, revolted and, in rapid succession, deprived the emperor Gratian of his army, captured him as he fled toward Italy, and deprived him of his life.[191] After the execution of Gratian, Maximus sent an embassy to Theodosius, leaving the choice of peace or civil war to him.[192] Theodosius may have attempted some action against Maximus in the next summer—certainly Themistius described his campaign of that year in those terms[193]— but over the next two years Theodosius clearly felt that the situation on the eastern frontier was more important than subduing Maximus. Finally, in 386, in response to several crises, Theodosius recognized the legitimacy of Maximus and his government, although there are reasons to believe that Theodosius had no intention of allowing this division of the empire to prevail any longer than necessary.[194] Theodosius advertised this new state of affairs in several ways: he accepted the man whom Maximus nominated as consul, Flavius Euodius, and therefore allowed his name to appear in the dating formulas of laws issued in the East during that year.[195] Both Theodosius and Maximus displayed other formal symbols of their joint rule: Theodosius allowed the mint at Constantinople to issue a bronze coin stamped with the name and portrait of Maximus, and Maximus struck a silver coin in the name of Theodosius and again in his own name, celebrating the "Concord of the Three Augusti." The reverse of that coin duplicated the type from another issue in the name of Theodosius from the years prior to Maximus's revolt.[196] Finally, we know from Zosimus that Theodosius ordered his praetorian prefect Cynegius to exhibit the portrait of Maximus in public in Alexandria and to announce to the people that this man had achieved a state of joint rule with him.[197]

The division between eastern and western empires became more rigid

191. The sources for Maximus are canvassed in *PLRE* I, Maximus 39. Matthews 1975, 173–182, and S. Williams and Friell 1995, 36–43 and 61–64, provide narratives of these events from different perspectives. Paschoud's notes to the relevant chapters of Zosimus are also exceptionally useful, although the narrative provided by Zosimus is once again overly compressed: for example, some three years pass between the embassy to Theodosius in 4.37.2 and Theodosius's recognition of Maximus in 4.37.3.

192. Zosimus 4.37.2.

193. Themistius *Or.* 18.220d, and see Dagron 1968, 23–24, or Matthews 1975, 178.

194. See Paschoud on Zosimus 4.37.

195. Matthews 1975, 179 n. 2; the alliance is also mentioned by Rufinus *Hist.* 11.15—who excuses the later execution of Maximus by insisting both that Valentinian and not Theodosius forged the alliance and that Valentinian had been deliberately insincere—and by Pacatus in his panegyric, *Pan. Lat.* XII(2).30.1–2.

196. The coin of Maximus: *RIC* IX, Constantinople no. 83(d). Coin of Theodosius: *RIC* IX, Trier no. 83(a); note that 83(b) and (c) have the same reverse with Maximus on the obverse. The earlier coin is Trier no. 55(a), which had also been issued with Gratian on the obverse (55[b]).

197. Zosimus 4.37.3.

and more formal throughout the fifth century. In response, the ceremony of recognizing a colleague by accepting his portrait became more regular and more highly stylized. For example, Constantine Porphyrogenitus preserved in his *Book of ceremonies* an account, no doubt taken from Peter Patricius, of the ceremony performed in 467 when the emperor Leo in Constantinople received the laureate portrait of Anthemius, the new emperor of Rome. The ambassador of Anthemius, Heliocrates, and the laureate image of Anthemius were introduced to the emperor's council chamber (*Consistorium*), where the *silentiarii* accepted the image. Next, Diapherentius, the prefect of Constantinople, and Dioscorius, the ex-prefect, each delivered a panegyric to both emperors. Then Leo signified his acceptance of his colleague and of his image: he gave the command for the laureate portrait of Anthemius to be sent to every city in the empire, and for their portraits to be exhibited together.[198] Finally, Leo himself gave a speech that advertised his sanction of the elevation of Anthemius as well as the unity of the empire:[199]

> Imperator Caesar blessed Leo, victor, perpetual Augustus, declares: The long-awaited portrait of the most merciful ruler Anthemius has now been sent forth and has brought us great joy. Therefore, by our divine assent, We ordain that his portrait should accompany our images in honor, to the delight of all the people, such that every city recognizes, in its happiness, that the ruling powers of each half are held in common and that we are united to his clemency.

Alas, all the good will and harmony of the eastern emperor could not save Anthemius from the displeasure of Ricimer but five years later.

Modern historians have tended to view references to a unified empire in fifth-century texts as ideological constructs, equally and patently as false to contemporaries as to us. Such arguments not infrequently offer the delivery of panegyrics to laureate statues as proof of the artificiality of court ceremonial in this period. It is not obvious that fifth-century viewers would have received such panegyrics thus. Rather, portraits that embodied the emperor's power to extend asylum or concretized his oversight of markets and lawcourts might well receive and propitiously acknowledge honors in the emperor's stead. Given that it had long been customary to perform *adoratio* before imperial epistles and other carriers of imperial dignity, we should be surprised that the earliest text recording the arrival of a new portrait is so late. In the middle of the third century the city of Termessus in Asia Minor celebrated the generosity of a visiting imperial official:[200]

---

198. Constantine *De ceremoniis* 1.87.
199. Constantine *De ceremoniis* 1.87.
200. Robert 1940, no. 113b (*IGRR* III 481 = *ILS* 8870). See also Robert, *OMS* 2:838–839. The statue reached Termessus on 7 November 253: Valerian had been acclaimed *imperator* during the summer of 253 but was able to return to Rome only in September. The earliest papyrus

The city and people and *gerousia* of Termessus near Oenoanda honor Valerius Statilius Castus, the most powerful *commiles* of the Augusti: he provided for peace on sea and land; he visited our beautiful city with every courtesy for nineteen days; he conducted games in the Lusorium on the seventh day before the Ides of November, on the same day that the sacred image of our new Augustus, Valerian, was introduced [into the city].

The use of the arrival of a portrait in a dating formula suggests that the event was a memorable one, similar in pomp, perhaps, to the arrival of the emperor himself—an event that not infrequently caused cities to restart their official calendars and that lingered long in local memories.[201] In the late empire, in addition to the description provided by Constantine Porphyrogenitus, we possess a considerable body of evidence about the ceremonies performed on such occasions: cities throughout the empire arranged to greet new portraits with pomp and panegyrics. Several such panegyrics survive, and it is notable that they all maintain the fiction that it is the emperor himself, rather than his portrait, whom they address, since they all speak to him in the second person.[202]

Imperial portraits could and did substitute for the emperor himself not simply at his arrival upon the throne but at any and every ceremony in civic life, whether at the regular rituals that orchestrated the rhythms of municipalities throughout the empire or on special occasions such as the announcement of a new imperial *beneficium*. In another homily from his stay in Constantinople, Severianus of Gabala drew again on his audience's fa-

---

that recognizes his reign is *P. Köln* IV 196, datable between 28 September and 27 October 253 (Rathbone 1986, 117). The distribution of official portraits therefore coincided with the dissemination of news of the accession itself or followed it very, very closely.

201. See the texts cited by Millar 1977, 36 nn. 60, 61. Oxyrhynchus, for example, continued to hold a festival on the day that Hadrian entered the city in the early third century (*P. Oxy.* XXXI 2553). For interactions between emperors and cities during visits see Halfmann 1986, 111–129.

202. The most famous and longest text is the panegyric of Procopius of Gaza to Anastasius. (See Kempen 1918 or Chauvot 1986, and cf. MacCormack 1981, 69–70.) Additional texts are preserved on papyrus and include a panegyric to Justin II by Dioscorus of Aphrodite (*P. Cair. Masp.* II 67183 = Heitsch 1961, XLII no. 1 = MacCoull 1984 = MacCoull 1988, 72–74); another panegyric, probably to Anastasius, probably by Christodorus of Coptus (*P. Vindob.* 29788A = Heitsch 1961, XXXV [Pamprepius]; on its date and the identity of its author, see Viljamaa 1968, 55–57 and 101–104, who does not contest the possibility of Pamprepian authorship of poems B and C, on which see A. D. E. Cameron 1965b, 486–487, and McCail 1978, assigning C to the reign of Zeno); and a panegyric to Heraclius (*PSI* 3 [1914], 253 = Heitsch 1961, XXXIV). On the use of the second person to address statues see Basil, *De spiritu sancto ad Amphilochium* (quoted by John of Damascus 1.35 and translated above at n. 139), and compare the Greek practice of referring to statues of (e.g.) Athena as "Athena" (Gordon 1979, 7–8).

miliarity with the emotive power of imperial portraits to explain the power of the cross as a visible symbol of an absent Deity:[203]

> For if the emperor is not present, a portrait takes the place of the emperor: magistrates venerate the portrait, the month's religious observances are performed, the magistrates come forward to greet the portrait, and the people venerate it, not as if they looked upon a painted board, but as if they looked upon the face of the emperor, even though he is not visible in the flesh but only displayed in a representation. How much greater is the power of the portrait of the immortal Emperor to break not simply stone, but also heaven and all the earth!

Severianus spoke primarily of day-to-day encounters with imperial portraits. In a law of 383 regulating the behavior of imperial messengers, Theodosius, Valentinian, and Gratian provided a catalogue of special occasions on which a portrait might enter a city in triumph or announce an imperial benefaction:[204]

> We sanction that whenever any of our auspicious achievements are announced, if wars should cease, or victories should arise, if the honor of the bestowal of consular vestments should be added to the calendar, if the tranquillity of arrangements for peace is to be published, if, by chance, we display to the eager public our sacred portraits, such occasions should be announced and received without price.

We have already seen how formally the arrival of a new imperial portrait was treated. The analogy of Severianus suggests that local dignitaries and populations had to observe ceremonial formalities toward any imperial portrait, on all occasions.

In a homily on the baptismal font, Severianus provides a salutary reminder not only that imperial images appeared in many forms other than portrait busts but also that people would have encountered them in, and associated them with, specific ceremonial acts: "When imperial portraits and statues are carried into a city and the magistrates and people process to greet them with acclamations and fear, they fear neither the wood nor the painted wax, but they venerate the portrait of the emperor."[205] As Gregory Nazianzus noted a generation earlier, such nonstatuary portraits would have resembled coins more than the disembodied busts we study today, in

---

203. Severianus *Oratio in Sanctam Crucem*, quoted by John of Damascus 3.123.

204. *C. Th.* 8.11.4, and cf. *C. Th.* 8.11.3.

205. Severianus *De lotione pedum* 9 (A. Wenger 1966), quoted by John of Damascus (3.122) under the title *In pelvim*. From a much later period, cf. Anastasius of Antioch on the Sabbath, quoted by John of Damascus 3.128: Ὥσπερ ἄν εἴ τις εἰκόνα βασιλέως διὰ τὸ καθῆκον τῆς περὶ τὸν βασιλέα προσκυνεῖ τιμῆς οὐδὲν οὖσαν ἢ κηρὸν καὶ χρώματα. On the use of imperial images in late-antique ceremonial see MacCormack 1981, 8–12, 70–73.

that they tended in and of themselves to depict the emperor in a context: with cities bringing them gifts, or accompanied by Victories; with magistrates offering obeisance, or with beasts being slaughtered or barbarians trampled.[206] Two of the passages from Herodian already cited specifically describe the context in which the artwork placed the emperor: the representations of Caracalla in sculpture and painting, set up "in every city," depicted him in the guise of Hercules, and the painted poster of Elagabalus, hung from the ceiling of the Senate House, had shown him in the garb of an Emesene priest.[207] Eusebius likewise recorded the precise attitude in which Constantine had ordered himself represented, whether humble in prayer or haughty in triumph. Finally, Sozomen recalled in his *Ecclesiastical history* that Julian had ordered public paintings of himself to show "either Jupiter reaching down from heaven and bestowing upon him the symbols of the imperial throne—the crown and the purple robe—or Mercury and Mars looking upon him, as if bearing witness with their gaze to his skill in rhetoric and in war."[208]

THE ART OF VICTORY

Although many people know Caesar's boast "I came, I saw, I conquered," few probably could identify its provenance: Caesar ordered these three words alone to be painted on the floats in his triumph. The phrase stuck in the memory, one presumes, because it was so unusual. Suetonius remarked, when relating the tale, that it was traditional for the captions to narrate the events of the war.[209] Readers today undoubtedly know the Romans' use of painted panels and floats best from their appearance in such triumphs. Ovid in his exile provided an elaborate description of the ceremony and customary artwork when he anticipated a triumph for Tiberius as the result of his campaigns in Germany:[210]

> All the populace will be able to see the triumph and, when each person sees the captured towns and the titles of their leaders, he will see kings bearing chains on their captive necks and marching before garlanded horses. . . . This lake, these mountains, all these forts, all these rivers were full of wild slaughter, full of blood. . . . Here, with broken horns and covered with sickly green

206. Gregory Naz. *Or.* 4.80.
207. Herodian 4.8.1–2 and 4.5.6–7.
208. Sozomen 5.17.3.
209. Suetonius *Caesar* 37.2: *Pontico triumpho inter pompae fercula trium verborum praetulit titulum VENI VIDI VICI non acta belli significantem sicut ceteris, sed celeriter confecti notam.* Note, however, that Appian claims that Caesar used the words in a letter to Rome (*Civ.* 2.384). Caesar presumably used them first in a letter to the Senate and again in his triumphal art.
210. Ovid *Tristia* 4.2.19–22, 37–38, 41–46 (trans. Goold, revised).

weeds, is the Rhine himself, discolored with his own blood. Behold! Germany, too, is borne along with streaming hair, sitting sadly at the feet of our invincible general; offering her proud neck to the Roman axe she bears chains on that hand in which she carried arms.

Tacitus provided a similar, if much briefer, catalogue of the visual displays in the triumph of Germanicus of A.D. 17: "Carried in the triumph were spoils, captives, and representations [*simulacra*] of mountains, rivers, and battles."[211]

We have already in another context had cause to mention the multimedia display that Severus designed to advertise at Rome his victory over the Parthians in the last decade of the second century.[212] Their familiarity and their pageantry rapidly made triumphs and triumphal art popular subjects for *ecphrasis* in poetry, oratory, and historiography. According to Pliny, painting for public consumption began at Rome when Appius Claudius hung portraits of his ancestors in the Temple of Bellona, together with captions that described their honors and achievements.[213] Large-scale painting for use in association with triumphs became popular later. According to Pliny, painting as an art form increased its public esteem, its *dignitatio,* from its association with triumphs. In 263 B.C., Manius Valerius Maximus Messalla triumphed for his victories in Syracuse and displayed a painting on the wall of the Curia Hostilia. The painting depicted his defeat of the Carthaginians and Hiero.[214] Pliny describes several subsequent paintings, although his narrative of such paintings lists only stationary works and not painted floats or portable panels.[215]

Pliny presumably did not comment on specific portable panels precisely because they were understood and intended to be topical, of purely ephemeral interest. Historians in antiquity similarly commented on the artwork in triumphs only when some circumstance rendered it unusual. Thus Quintilian mentioned the extravagance of the wooden and ivory models used in the triumphs of Fabius Maximus and Julius Caesar, respectively.[216] Herodian described the letters and posters of Maximinus Thrax not least because he genuinely believed that Maximinus had participated in the fighting, but also because the Senate would soon break its ties to that emperor and order

211. Tacitus *Ann.* 2.41.2.

212. See Chapter 5 at n. 19.

213. Pliny *Nat.* 35.12.

214. Pliny *Nat.* 35.22. The date transmitted there is incorrect, but Pliny elsewhere cites Varro on the booty that Valerius Maximus brought back from Syracuse and there uses the proper date, A.U.C. 491 (*Nat.* 7.214).

215. Pliny *Nat.* 35.22–23.

216. Quintilian *Inst.* 6.3.61.

all his artwork destroyed.[217] What Herodian does not reveal, but his narrative suggests, is that he derived his information from Maximinus's report and posters and organized his own narrative into scenes that iterated their content.[218] Romans came to expect triumphs to supply information at this level of detail: Pliny observed that writers reported the conquests of Cornelius Balbus in precisely the order in which they were depicted on the tableaux in his triumph, while Pomponius Mela predicted that geographic and ethnographic information about Britain would be transmitted in the triumph of Claudius.[219] The *Historia Augusta* described the triumph of Aurelian in 273 at great length—noting in particular the use of placards to identify the captives and the cities that had contributed *aurum coronarium*— presumably because so much time had passed since an emperor had visited Rome in triumph, and more still would pass before the capital welcomed another.[220]

Eunapius, like Suetonius, once drew attention to a victory celebration's violation of its genre. Virtually every aspect of the relevant fragment of his *Histories* has been hotly contested.[221] But the precise event described matters little here. Regardless of whether he described a display at Rome or at Constantinople, Eunapius was angry because the painted panels had not shown or even alluded to the bravery of the emperor and the armies. On the contrary, they had merely depicted a hand coming down from the clouds with the caption "The hand of God driving off the barbarians" and, on the other side, "The barbarians fleeing God." These expectations regarding the narrative function of triumphal art remained largely constant. In an aside on Justinian's triumph over the Vandals in 534, Corippus explained matter-of-factly that Justinian "had ordered that the history of his triumphs be recorded on individual vessels cast from barbarian gold, at the time when in triumph he cast chains on captured tyrants, when in his fourth consulship the emperor trod the high Capitol in his triumphal procession."[222] The pictures on the vessels presumably duplicated the scenes

217. Herodian 7.2.8, largely repeated by *SHA Maxim.* 12.10.

218. Whittaker 1970, 166 n. 1.

219. Pliny *Nat.* 5.36–37 (the tableaux comprise *nomina et simulacra*, while the *Mons Gyri* is preceded by a *titulus*); Pomponius Mela 3.49. Pomponius was not disappointed: Suetonius *Claudius* 21.6. See also *Nero* 25.1: Nero triumphed on his return from Greece, displaying his crowns with *tituli* that explained their origin.

220. Aurelian's triumph and subsequent activity at Rome have therefore left a disproportional mark in our sources: see *Chron. anni CCCLIIII* on Aurelianus (*Chron. min.* 1:148), Festus 24.1, Aurelius Victor 35.1–7, Eutropius 9.13, and *SHA Aurel.* 33–34, but esp. 34.1–3.

221. Eunapius *Hist.* fr. 68 (*Excerpta de sententiis* fr. 72). See MacCormack 1981, 11; Blockley 1981, 161–162; Holum 1982, 67–69; McCormick 1986, 96–118; Sivan 1991; and A. D. E. Cameron, Long, and Sherry 1993, 218–223.

222. Corippus *In laudem Iustini minoris* 3.121–125 (trans. Cameron, revised).

depicted in his triumphal art. We may safely assume that Justinian also arranged the depiction of this triumph in mosaic form at the Bronze Gate to his palace.[223] We can acquire some feeling for the intimacy with which ancients associated triumphs and triumphal art by comparing Ovid's use of triumphs to set the scene for seductions, in which some familiar reality forms the backdrop for a literary conceit, to the panegyrics of Eusebius and Symmachus three centuries later, in which both authors praised real imperial ceremonies by suggesting that they were as pretty as pictures.[224]

Thus far we have concentrated on the uses of triumphal art at Rome and Constantinople, the capitals of the empire. That emphasis corresponds to the biases of our data and to the genuine importance those cities possessed within Roman political life. Not for naught had Severus and Maximinus arranged pictorial displays of their military victories even when they were unable to celebrate their triumphs at Rome in person.[225] Indeed, the most celebrated description of such artwork may be found in another account of a triumph at Rome, namely Josephus's narrative of the magnificent triumph of Vespasian in June of 71:[226]

> Nothing in the procession excited so much astonishment as the moving scaffolds. Because of their size there was fear regarding the stability of their structures, for many were three stories tall, and some were four stories. One could not see the richness of the material covering them without astonishment. . . . The war was depicted piecemeal through many representations, one after another, in the most vivid fashion: here one saw rich farmland being burned, here the ranks of the enemy being slaughtered. . . . The skill and the workmanship of these structures displayed all these things to those who had not witnessed them, as if they were actually present.

The fame of this narrative has perhaps obscured the significance of an earlier passage in that same book of *The Jewish War*. After the close of the war in September, A.D. 70, Titus returned to Italy only after visiting the eastern provinces, passing through Caesarea, Berytus, and Antioch before turning south toward Alexandria, whence he would depart for Italy in May of 71. At Caesarea and Berytus, Titus held games to celebrate the birthdays of his brother and father, respectively.[227] Of his route after departing Berytus Josephus wrote: "Departing thence, he exhibited costly spectacles in all the

223. Procopius *Aed.* 1.10.10–20 at 15–19.

224. Ovid *Ars* 1.209–228, and cf. *Pont.* 2.1 and 3.4.83–112. Eusebius *Vit. Const.* 4.7: ὥσπερ ἐν πίνακος γραφῇ. Symmachus *Or.* 3.5: *Turmas supplices, cuneos ambientes, digna tabula saeculis, digna pictura temporibus, quibus magis utiles videmus eligi quam volentes!*

225. On Severus see Chapter 5 at n. 19; on Maximinus see above at n. 217.

226. Josephus *Bell. Iud.* 7.139–140, 142–143, 146 (trans. Thackery, adapted).

227. Josephus *Bell. Iud.* 7.37–40.

cities of Syria through which he passed, making his Jewish captives serve to display their own destruction."[228]

Josephus may have intended merely that Titus held gladiatorial games with Jewish victims in all the cities of Syria. Yet Titus was doing more than touring the eastern provinces. He had just won a war and was returning to Rome in triumph. He must have made a formal *adventus* into each city. But what was the formal *adventus* of a victorious *imperator,* when leading thousands of captives, if not a triumph? In other words, Titus was teaching the cities of the East that characteristically Roman variation on the arrival that was the triumph, with its pageantry and ideologically charged images of conqueror and conquered.[229] They certainly knew how to respond: they offered him a crown.[230] We have already seen that receipt of *aurum coronarium* depended on the dissemination of news and that emperors dispatched painted panels for viewers at Rome; we must then admit the possibility that some pictorial representations accompanied the bulletins that brought the news of imperial victories to provincial municipalities. It is highly probable that the largest cities received such artwork on occasions of particular importance. Menander Rhetor included among the benefits of empire the fact that he and his fellows acquired "prisoners as slaves, not by going to war ourselves, but by receiving them from the emperor's victorious hand."[231] King Agrippa had also relied on the familiar imagery of imperial captives in his admonition of the Jews: "Which of you has not heard tell of the horde of Germans? Nay, you have surely often seen their stalwart and burly figures, for the Romans have captives from that nation everywhere."[232] By the end of the first century, provincials not only had experienced Roman conquest; they had learned the forms and ceremonies through which Romans described, narrated, and celebrated their victories.

Victory celebrations were but one of the many contexts in which people encountered painted panels of the emperor. In addition to describing the portraits depicting Constantine at prayer, Eusebius also recorded that Constantine ordered a panel set up before his palace, "so that it might be visible to all," representing himself with a cross over his head and Licinius in the form of a slain dragon at his feet, an image that appeared in condensed

---

228. Josephus *Bell. Iud.* 7.96 (trans. Thackery).

229. This is not to say that the Roman triumph did not have important eastern antecedents (on which see Versnel 1970), but rather that eastern populations rapidly learned to associate one form of this behavior with the culture of those who ruled them—a culture many of them wished to join.

230. Philostratus *Vit. Apollonii* 6.29.

231. See above at n. 125.

232. Josephus *Bell. Iud.* 2.376 (trans. Thackery). Cf. *Bell. Iud.* 7.118: When Titus sent the best-looking Jews from Egypt to Italy for his triumph, what did he do with the rest?

form on Constantine's coins.[233] Such works of art before the palace were intended for a wide audience. Art within the palace could be brought to the public's attention through public oratory: thus the rhetor who celebrated the marriage of Constantine and Fausta described for his audience a painting of the happy couple in the palace at Aquileia, even though he had not himself seen the painting, and Corippus alluded to the *pietas* of Justin II by mentioning that portraits of Justinian were everywhere in the palace.[234] Panegyrists undoubtedly welcomed the chance to display their talent for *ecphrasis*. Doing so also provided them the relative safety of merely describing the content of another ideological display that had already received imperial sanction.

We would be remiss if we thought posters and floats media that the Romans exploited only during triumphs. Their ease of manufacture made them suitable for many occasions and innumerable subjects. Eunapius, for example, placed the Christian artwork that he despised in the circus, an obvious location through which to address the widest possible audience. Writing at a time when Christians were still subject to legal sanction, Tertullian described similar artwork, this time mocking the Christian God. That display can be connected with the events that culminated in the death of Perpetua on the birthday of Geta in 203. That poster, too, must have addressed its audience at a public spectacle.[235]

Painted panels exhibited in forums had the additional advantage that they remained visible to those who could not be present for triumphs or recitations of victory bulletins. This had been the justification of Lucius Aemilius Rectus, the prefect of Egypt in A.D 41, when he publicly displayed a letter from Claudius to the Alexandrians after it had already been read aloud.[236] The Senate exploited all the advantages and accessibility of posters in the Forum when it displayed its piety toward the memory of Constantine by commissioning paintings of that emperor residing in a heavenly palace. The Senate announced this display in a letter that also requested that Constantine be buried at Rome, a clear attempt to renew the power of the imperial city. Constantius demurred and buried his father in the city which bore his name.[237] The law of 394 that made it illegal to put up posters for public entertainers "in the places where imperial portraits are customarily

233. Eusebius *Vit. Const.* 3.3, esp. paragraph 1. On the relationship between the painting and the coins see Gagé 1933a, 399.

234. *Pan. Lat.* VI(7).6.2–3. Corippus *In laudem Iustini minoris* 3.111–115.

235. Tertullian *Apol.* 16.12, and cf. *Nat.* 1.14.1–2; the latter text has been poorly transmitted. Determining the site of these events depends on whether Tertullian used the phrase "that city" (*ista civitas*) to refer to Rome.

236. *Sel. pap.* 212, ll. 1–13.

237. Eusebius *Vit. Const.* 4.69.2.

consecrated" reveals how accessible this medium was, even as it suggests that such ephemeral portraits were continually produced, consecrated, and displayed.[238] All the influences of this artwork, both on contemporaries and on later historians, are thus revealed in John of Ephesus's description of the accession of Tiberius II to the rank of Caesar. Having described the ceremony and the words of the angel who spoke through Justin II, John then reported that posters depicting the ceremony in precisely his terms had been displayed afterward, and that many *notarii* had been present, taking down the speeches word for word.[239]

SIGNA OF ROME, *SIGNA* OF POWER

Like his rival Severianus, John Chrysostom spoke before a congregation always already implicated in the associative network and ceremonies of Roman power. Like Severianus, John presumed upon that fact in constructing analogies to explain the unfamiliar. So, for example, when John needed to explain the importance of the apostolate of Paul, he turned to the well-known ceremony set in motion by the arrival of soldiers, who, as everyone knew, bore portraits of the emperor on their standards:[240]

> Whenever men bearing imperial standards come to cities, preceded by a mass of soldiers and with a trumpeter sounding before them, the whole population is accustomed to come together, in order to hear the noise and to see the standards held on high, and to admire the strength of the men who hold them. When, therefore, Paul enters on this day, not into a city but into the world, let us all run together. For he, too, bears a standard, not that of the emperor, but the cross of Christ; and men do not precede him, but angels do, for the honor of the one borne aloft and for the safety of the one who bears him.

It is, of course, true that Chrysostom's analogy could stand solely on its invocation of the power wielded by the imperial portrait borne on standards, as it is true that standards derived some of their power from that portrait. This was, after all, true of the portrait-bearing rectangles that distinguished and ordered magistrates and men of rank in the late empire: the rectangles without portraits may have been legally sufficient to designate rank, but the higher magistrates were clearly honored and empowered by carrying an imperial portrait on their cloth.[241] And yet, standards had been the ubiquitous companions of the Roman army under the Republic, too, and were thus al-

---

238. *C. Th.* 15.7.12.

239. John of Ephesus 3.5. John transcribed σημεῖα to describe the shorthand used by νοτάριοι, a word he also transcribed. On John's language see Margoliouth 1909, 104–105.

240. John Chrysoston *Homiliae de laudibus S. Pauli* 7 (*PG* 50.507–508).

241. Grigg 1979.

ready and everywhere familiar. Likewise, John's analogy relies not simply on its audience's construing "standard-bearer" as "portrait-bearer," but on its knowing the shape of the standard itself. These complications urge us to examine standards and the meanings they carried more closely.[242]

We should first be clear about the precise appearance of a standard.[243] Each could have four parts, and the technical word for any of these parts could stand in metonymy for the whole. At the very least a *signum* consisted of a tall cross of wood, crowned by a statuette of an eagle (an *aquila*) or a statuette of Victory.[244] From the crossbar hung a cloth banner, the *vexillum*, on which appeared the name of the legion and, in imperial times, that of the emperor whom it served.[245] The *vexillum* therefore also identified the face depicted on the *imagines*, the small reliefs attached to the long vertical pole of the *signum*. These could also include images relevant to particular legions; their most common subjects after imperial portraits were animals.[246] The placement of a person's portrait among the standards was a signal honor and normally an imperial prerogative. According to Tacitus, Sejanus attempted to incite Tiberius against Agrippina and Nero by suggesting "that the people would soon choose new leaders and emperors, whose portraits they would follow like standards."[247]

Even before the foundation of the Principate, standards maintained a powerful hold on the loyalty of soldiers in the Roman army. Each man swore an oath not to leave them behind. Significantly, they swore the oath to the "military gods," whose power was manifested in those standards: Livy argued that soldiers who swore a false oath to the standards endangered not simply their lives but the standards, the eagles, and the religious scruple of their oath.[248] The legions honored the divine power in these symbols at

242. Seston provides the best introduction by far to all aspects of this subject at *RAC* s.v. "Feldzeichen." Von Domaszewski 1895 and 1909, 1–15 and 86–89, retain value; cf. A. Alföldi 1934, 68–69. Kruse 1934, 51–64, largely summarizes those essays. For standards in Byzantine ceremonial, see Gagé 1933a.

243. Seston, *RAC* s.v. "Feldzeichen," fig. 2; Bishop and Coulston 1993, fig. 8, no. 1. Standards appear with emperors on the reverses of coins from the beginning of the Principate and become extremely common in the Severan period. I believe that emperors are first depicted as actually holding the standards only in the fourth century; significantly the first members of the imperial family thus represented are the children of Constantine rather than Constantine himself. (See Bruun, *RIC* VII, index II, s.v. "principi iuventutis.")

244. Eagles: see Livy 26.48.12, *ILS* 2295, Vegetius 2.6. Victory: see Tertullian *Nat.* 1.12.14–16 or *Apol.* 16.7–8. See Rostovtzeff 1942, 95.

245. Suetonius *Vespasian* 6.3, Dio 40.18.3, and Vegetius 2.6 and 2.13.

246. Von Domaszewski 1909, 1–15.

247. Tacitus *Ann.* 5.4.4.

248. Livy 26.48.12; cf. Dionysius Hal. *Ant. Rom.* 6.45. On oaths, see the analogy that Ammianus draws to explain the behavior of the Quadi: since they swear oaths on their swords, they must believe them to be divine (*eductisque mucronibus, quos pro numinibus colunt, iurauere se per-*

a shrine in the center of every legionary camp, and the honor of maintaining the shrine fell to the first cohort of the legion.[249] Augustus paid homage to the power of standards in his endless celebrations of the "recovery" of the standards lost by Crassus near Carrhae.[250] When, for example, Munatius Plancus felt threatened by hostile legionaries during the mutiny among the Rhine armies in A.D. 15, he fled to the shrine and the standards at the middle of the camp. In describing that incident, Tacitus presumed upon his audience's familiarity with the traditional presence of *altaria deum* in the camps.[251]

Legions expressed their devotion to their standards not only by displaying and decorating them on dates of religious significance or at moments of military significance, but also by celebrating several special holidays dedicated to them. These holidays included an armywide crowning of the standards with roses in both May and June, and each legion's celebration of the birthday of its particular standards.[252] We can gauge the soldiers' affection for the standards by drawing an analogy between their attitude toward the standards and a common practice in civilian life. The army allowed the soldiers to deposit part of their pay *ad signa,* "at the standards": Vegetius believed that this had long been required, and papyrological records of military pay prove that this was common practice as early as the first century A.D.[253] Residents of Rome, on the other hand, commonly deposited cash at the Temple of Castor and Pollux or at the Temple of Peace, under the assumption that religious scruple would prevent theft from a place of worship.[254]

---

mansuros in fide, 17.12.21). Pomponius Mela 2.15 appears to employ similar logic to understand the religion of the Scythians.

249. Dio 40.18. Compare Herodian 4.4.5 and 5.8.5, as well as Vegetius 2.6 and *SHA Pesc. Nig.* 4.1. On this issue see von Domaszewski 1895, 11, and 1909, 86–89.

250. Augustus *Res gestae* 29.2; cf. *BMC* I, Augustus nos. 332, 410–423, and 679–681, or *RIC* I², nos. 41, 58, 60, 80–87, 287–289, 304, 305, 314, 315, 508, and 521–526. On the importance of this episode in Augustan propaganda see Picard 1957, 274–285, or Kienast 1982a, 283–286.

251. Tacitus *Ann.* 1.39.4; cf. *Ann.* 1.18.2 and *Hist.* 3.10.7.

252. See Hoey 1937, 16–20; and Fink, Hoey, and Snyder 1940, 115–120. For the treatment of standards on holidays, see Pliny *Nat.* 13.23: *aquilae certe ac signa, pulverulenta illa et cuspidibus horrida, unguuntur festis diebus.* For the birthdays of legions, see, for example, *ILS* 9125, from Asturica, *I. O. M. pro salute M. Aureli Antonini et L. Aureli Veri Augustorum ob natale aquilae;* cf. *ILS* 9126, from the same date but inscribed by a different cohort, and *ILS* 9127, likewise from Spain, but from a different date. Compare *ILS* 2295, from Moesia, a dedication to *dis militaribus, Genio, Virtuti, Aquilae sanc., signisque leg. I. Ital. Severianae,* from A.D. 224.

253. Vegetius 2.20. For the records of military pay, see *RMR* 68–74.

254. For the temple of Castor, see Juvenal 14.259–262, with helpful comments *ad loc.* in the *Scholia vetustiora.* For the Temple of Peace see Herodian 1.14.2–3. On the practice of depositing goods in temples in general see Cicero *Leg.* 2.41.

The association of imperial portraits with the standards only reinforced the influence that they wielded; it also allowed them to function as representatives of Rome and her ruler. Some have expressed hesitation regarding the honors paid to standards after a military victory: Didn't that act contradict the ideology that victories were won under the auspices of the emperor and through his *felicitas?*[255] Since the *signa* commonly carried imperial portraits, the question is academic. The reaction of soldiers to a recent success when fighting in Judaea under Titus illustrates the complex interaction between these supposedly conflicting loyalties: "After the rebels fled into the city, while the temple itself and its environs burned, the Romans carried their standards into the sacred precinct and placed them opposite the eastern gate; there they sacrificed to them and hailed Titus as *imperator* with loud acclamations."[256] Tacitus described a similar celebration of the emperor's role in a victory during the campaigns of Germanicus in A.D. 16: during a battle with the Cherusci, the prince saw eight eagles in flight overhead. "March on!" he exhorted his men: "Follow the birds of Rome, the special divinities of the legions!" The Roman forces routed the Cherusci and immediately acclaimed Tiberius *imperator.* They also celebrated by erecting a mound on which, in the fashion of a trophy, they hung the arms of the tribes they had defeated, labeled with their names.[257] Suetonius's diction when describing events after the death of Sejanus also alluded to the religious power of the standards and the portrait that hung on them: Tiberius distributed a reward to the legions in Syria because they alone had not worshiped the portrait of Sejanus among the standards.[258]

As representatives of Roman military authority and stand-ins for the emperor, standards bearing his portrait could witness a formal surrender or the conclusion of treaty negotiations. For such episodes we can compare behavior during similar ceremonies when the emperor was present or absent. The ceremonies were, in fact, much the same. For example, in 359 Constantius attempted to arrange a diplomatic settlement to Rome's long series of skirmishes with the Limigantes. He met them near the shores of the Danube. He set the stage for the meeting by building a mound in the shape of a tribunal, from which position he could look down on the submissive barbarians. Ammianus specifies in this passage only that Constantius sat on a throne with a golden cushion, but other passages in his narrative describing Constantius delivering speeches to the army or defeated foes suggest strongly that the emperor appeared on the tribunal surrounded by stan-

255. Hoey 1937, 21.
256. Josephus *Bell. Iud.* 6.316.
257. Tacitus *Ann.* 2.17.2 and 18.2.
258. Suetonius *Tiberius* 48.2.

dards and eagles. This setting was already widely familiar as a coin type.[259] No earlier reference to such a ceremony conveys the same level of detail as the narrative of Ammianus, but the essence of the ceremony—the veneration of the standards and portrait of the emperor—was clearly fixed at a much earlier date. For example, in A.D. 37 Artabanus, the king of Parthia, made peace with Rome. Though he negotiated the details of the treaty and the ceremony with Lucius Vitellius, the father of the emperor, he signified his submission by greeting and paying homage to the Roman standards and to the portraits of the Caesars. Suetonius described the ceremony twice, and Dio once; their narratives hint at the ready conceptual association of imperial portraits and imperial standards by describing the object of Artabanus's veneration as the eagles and standards and portraits, the portraits alone, or the standards alone.[260] Later in the first century Zorsines, leader of a tribe near the Black Sea, Tiridates, king of Armenia, and various hostile Germanic kings acknowledged the supremacy of Rome through identical acts of veneration before the standards and statues of the emperor.[261]

The third-century Athenian historian Dexippus provided in his *Scythica* a fairly thorough description of such a diplomatic encounter between an emperor and the leaders of a barbarian tribe, in this case between Aurelian and the Juthungi.[262] Having been defeated in battle, the Juthungi sued for peace. Wishing to impress upon them that he was free to grant or withhold that peace, Aurelian made their embassy wait. On the appointed day, the emperor ordered the legions to assemble as if for battle, to terrify the enemy. When the arrangement of the army satisfied him, he put on his purple robes and mounted a lofty tribunal, ordering the army to form a crescent on either side of him. Behind the emperor were arranged the standards of his select army: these standards included the golden eagles, the portraits of earlier emperors, and the names of the legions written in gold letters. Aurelian's preparations were successful: the Juthungi, we are told, were stunned and remained silent for a long time. They finally spoke only when the emperor granted them permission to do so.[263]

Dexippus described the setting of Aurelian's drama using a mixture of technical and purely descriptive vocabulary. To refer to standards he used

259. Ammianus 19.11.8, 10, 12, and cf. 17.13.25.

260. Suetonius *Gaius* 14.3, and cf. (*idem*) *Vitellius* 2.4, as well as Dio 59.27.3. Josephus alone attributed the impetus for negotiations with Parthia to Tiberius. If the ceremony took place in the summer of 37, he must be correct (*Ant. Iud.* 18.96).

261. See Tacitus *Ann.* 12.17.2 and 15.24.2, and *ILS* 986, an inscription honoring Ti. Plautius Aelianus, propraetorian legate of Moesia, ll. 16–18: *ignotos ante aut infensos p. R. reges signa Romana adoraturos in ripam, quam tuebatur, perduxit.*

262. On Dexippus see Millar 1969, Alföldy 1974, or Potter 1990, 74–90.

263. *Excerpta de legationibus,* Dexippus 1 de Boor (*FHG* fr. 24 = Dindorf, *HGM* fr. 22).

τὰ σήματα, a word that designates standards in appropriate contexts but otherwise means "signs," broadly construed. Some speakers of Greek apparently found the broad semantic field of "sign" unsatisfactory: by the third century we start to find the Latin *signum* transliterated into Greek, τὸ σίγνον.[264] The most extended and self-conscious allusion to this practice springs, however, from the end of the fourth century. During John Chrysostom's occupancy of the see of Constantinople he delivered fifty-five homilies on the Acts of the Apostles. In his *Homily* 46 John dealt with Paul's confrontation of the hostile mob in Jerusalem. The soldiers had actually been required to protect Paul from the mob, which shouted, "Take him away!" "What does this mean, 'Take him away!'?" John asked his audience:[265]

> It was a custom among the Jews to say this against those whom they condemned, as in the time of Christ they appear to do this against him, saying, "Away with him!" meaning, "Remove him from among the living." But some say that the Jews meant that which men among us signify by saying, according to the Roman custom, "Cast him among the standards!"

Chrysostom has two explanations, one that establishes an analogy with another situation in the New Testament, and one that establishes an analogy with language and behavior familiar in his own day. To construct the latter comparison, he not only reminded his audience that they deliver criminals unto the Roman justice system; he also did so in language that constructed "us" *as* "Roman."

Chrysostom discussed standards in this homily because they were familiar symbols of Roman rule. But standards had always held a particular fascination for Christians. The reason is not far to seek: the basic wooden frame of a standard was shaped like a cross. Tertullian alluded to this fact in his *Apology* when he suggested that the Roman army was, in fact, a Christian institution, and the *castrensis religio* merely the worship of crosses:[266]

> You also worship Victories, since crosses are the skeletons of trophies. The whole religion of your army is the worship, the adoration of standards: the army swears by standards and prefers them to all other gods. All those collections of portraits on the standards are but jewelry on crosses; the cloth of the banners and pennants are cloaks for crosses. I praise your diligence: you did not wish to worship unadorned and naked crosses!

---

264. See *LSJ* s.v., citing *IG* 14.971 and *P. Lond.* 2.413 and *P. Lond.* inv. 2487. Cf. Robert 1954, 181, on οὐήξιλλος for *vexillus.* On the transcription of Latin terms on inscriptions of Asia Minor see A. Cameron 1931.
265. John Chrysostom *Homil. in Acta Apost.* 46.1 (*PG* 60.323).
266. Tertullian *Apol.* 16.7–8 and *Nat.* 1.12.14–16. Cf. Minucius Felix 29.6–8.

The standards could thus appeal to pagans and Christians alike, and to each on their own terms.[267]

Indeed, it was presumably the power of the symbol to speak to both pagan and Christian that provided Constantine with one of his most brilliant inspirations. Constantine had already shown himself favorably disposed toward Christians in the early years of his rule in Gaul, but he could not afford to alienate the pagan majority while he was still extending his power to the heart of the empire in his war with Maxentius. Prior to his assault on Rome on 28 October 312, Constantine ordered his soldiers to paint an emblem on their shields; the precise nature of that sign and the source of Constantine's inspiration remain a mystery.[268] Lactantius, who may already have joined the court of Constantine, alone recorded those details, and in matters of religion he was not unbiased.[269] In a roughly contemporary narrative, Eusebius, writing at the opposite end of the empire from the events he describes, suggested that Constantine ordered that a cross be placed in the hand of his statue in Rome, to commemorate his victory. A pagan might have seen only a standard. Constantine himself wrote a text to accompany his statue, but it studiously avoided imputing any religious significance to the object in his hand.[270]

As late as 25 July 336, when Eusebius delivered a panegyric for the thirtieth anniversary of Constantine's accession, he still failed to impose any restrictive religious significance on Constantine's chosen symbol. Indeed, his language on that occasion mirrored the ambiguities inherent in the shape of the standards themselves. The speech overall concentrated on the virtues

267. That is not to say that such symbols were not controversial: on controversies in Byzantium over the religious associations of public art see Mango 1963, or Dagron 1984, 369–377.

268. See Baynes 1931, 9 and 60–65; and DiMaio, Zeuge, and Zotov 1988.

269. The precise movements of Lactantius in these years remain a matter of dispute: see Barnes 1973, who argues for a relatively early date for *Mort. pers.* and for the independence of Lactantius from the court; his main opponent is Piganiol 1932. Until Moreau publishes the new edition of his text and commentary, the clearest introduction to Lactantius's life and works is that by Wlosok, *NHLL* §570. See *Mort. pers.* 44.5.

270. Eusebius *Hist. eccl.* 9.9.10–11, as well as *Triak.* 9.8. The panegyric to Constantine delivered in 313 refers to this statue in a passage that is unfortunately corrupt: *Pan. Lat.* IX(12).25.4; cf. Aurelius Victor 40.28. The reader must decide two things: Whom did the statue depict, and what was it holding in its hand? I follow the interpretation of Gagé 1933a, 385–386, who argued that the subject was Constantine and that he held a standard in his hand. M. Alföldi 1961 presents a strong case for a statue of Victory, suggesting that *signum dee* at *Pan. Lat.* IX(12).25.4 should be restored as *signum deae* rather than *signum dei*. But Victories in Constantinian coinage hold a trophy or a shield, not a *vexillum* (Bruun, *RIC* VII, index II, 754–756). Constantine erected a similar statue of himself in his capital; on its probable appearance see Mango 1993. For religious ambiguities in Constantinian art and iconography, see Downey 1940; *idem* 1941; and MacMullen 1990, 107–116.

of Constantine as a religious figure; that it did so without explicit references to Christianity has in itself aroused considerable interest.[271] Eusebius referred several times to the "sign" adopted by Constantine prior to the battle of the Milvian Bridge, but the word he uses, σημεῖον, also means "military standard." Nowhere did Eusebius employ language to suggest that the "sign" was anything other than a standard, however much personal significance he attributed to it.[272]

It was thus at the end of his life that Constantine apparently "revealed" to Eusebius the events that had led up to his adoption of the labarum; Eusebius recorded that Constantine spoke to him at great remove from the events themselves.[273] In the biography that he started after Constantine's death in 337, Eusebius described anew and thus reinterpreted what would henceforth be viewed as the central event in Constantine's rise to power. According to Eusebius, Constantine affixed a perpendicular bar to a spear, forming a cross, and at the center he affixed a wreath, and within the wreath attached two overlapping letters, chi and rho. The entire decoration—wreath and monogram—occupied the place normally held by the *imagines,* the portraits and distinctive emblems of the legions. Subsequent generations referred to this particular combination of standard and decoration as the "labarum."[274] What is more, Eusebius described the labarum in precisely these terms, as a standard that bore the idiosyncratic device of its emperor, referring to the symbol as "the victorious trophy, that is, the salutary standard," and continued to describe the item that Constantine added to his statue in Rome as "the salutary sign . . . a long spear in the shape of a cross."[275]

Of course Constantine did far more than adopt a bastardized standard as a personal ensign and advertise that fact on his coins and in other media. He also controlled the full geographic span of the empire for fourteen years. As a result, people appear to have associated the standard with impe-

271. Drake 1976, 46–60.

272. See the diction at Eusebius *Triak.* 9.8, τὸ σωτήριον καὶ ζωοποιὸν σημεῖον, τὸ νικοποιὸν σημεῖον, διαρρήδην τε ἀνεξάλειπτον σωτήριον τουτὶ σημεῖον τῆς Ῥωμαίων ἀρχῆς καὶ τῆς καθόλου βασιλείας φυλακτήριον; or at 9.12, τὸ νικοποιὸν σημεῖον; or at 9.14, τὸ σωτήριον τρόπαιον.

273. Eusebius *Vit. Const.* 1.28–31 (esp. 1.28.1: μακροῖς ὕστερον χρόνοις).

274. On subsequent allusions to the iconography established by Constantine see Grigg 1977, 470 and 475.

275. Eusebius *Vit. Const.* 1.37 (τὸ νικητικὸν τρόπαιον τὸ δὴ σωτήριον σημεῖον), 1.40.1 (τὸ σωτήριον σημεῖον), and 40.2 (ὑψηλὸν δόρυ σταυροῦ σχήματι). Compare Prudentius *Symm.* 1.464–469: Theodosius bids Rome acknowledge his *signa,* on which gleams an *effigies crucis;* it was by *hoc signo* that Constantine dissolved the servitude imposed by Maxentius. On Constantine's idiosyncratic use of Christian and pagan symbols, see Rufinus *Hist.* 10.8: Constantine used the nails from Christ's cross to make a bridle for his horse and a helmet for himself.

rial prerogative and imperial power more closely than ever before. Christians in particular came to regard the labarum as the special symbol of their emperor and their Christian empire, but, for obvious reasons, they also extended their proprietary feelings to the mere crosses that were the regular standards of the Roman legions. In this way imperial usage began to have an influence on Christian art. Tertullian wrote sarcastically when he suggested that Romans did not wish to worship naked crosses, but Christians after Constantine began to paint their crosses with imperial *paludamenta,* the purple victory cloak that hung on trophies and standards during triumphs.[276] This arrogation of the standard explains Gregory's reaction to Julian's perversion of the cross. According to Sozomen, Julian had attached images of Jupiter, Mars, and Mercury to his standards.[277] Gregory was incensed because he believed that Julian had desecrated the Christians' proprietary symbol:[278]

> He has already committed outrage against the great standard that marches together with the cross and that, carried on high, leads the army. It gives relief to burdens, is renowned among the Romans, and rules, so to speak, over the other standards, such as are adorned by imperial portraits and woven banners of different colors and different writing, or by the forms of dragons, their fearsome, gaping mouths filled by the wind when hung on spears. The scales woven onto their coiled bodies flash and present to the eyes a sight at once pleasing and awe-inspiring.[279]

The dragons to which Gregory referred were special banners, like wind socks, introduced to the Roman army by eastern auxiliaries in the early second century. Lucian, writing in 166, knew them only as features of the Parthian army, but by the fourth century they had become one of the most familiar symbols of the Roman army, and the literary references to them constitute a special, and remarkably extensive, category of evidence for the impact made by official art.[280]

Although it had been possible for Christians before Constantine to use standards as symbols of leadership and legitimate power—for instance, Tertullian wrote of "standards of Christ" and "standards of the Devil"[281]—once again it was Constantine's power and appeal that established this metaphor

---

276. Kantorowicz 1965, 18. On changes in the iconography of Christ and his association with the cross, before and after Constantine, see G. Snyder 1985, 56 and 165.

277. Sozomen 5.17.2 and 5.17.3.

278. See Gagé 1933a, 387–391 and *passim.*

279. Gregory Naz. *Or.* 4.66.

280. Lucian *Hist. conscr.* 29. For the date of that work see C. Jones 1986, 59–67. For later references, see Fiebiger, *RE* s.v. *Draco* (2); Seston, *RAC* s.v. "Feldzeichen," cols. 697–698; MacMullen 1990, 93–94; or Levy 1971, on Claudian *Ruf.* 2.177.

281. *Idol.* 19.

on sound footing.[282] Around the year 321, Constantine wrote to the orthodox bishops of Africa to urge tolerance toward the Donatists: if they simply
ignore the Donatists, then the men "who put themselves forward as the
standard-bearers of that most pathetic strife" would soon see the error of
their ways.[283] Indeed, as soon as Christians gained control over the secular
power of the state, they began urging the emperor to "raise the standard of
the Faith" against the pagans:[284]

> Raise the standard of the Faith: the divinity has assigned it to you. By the favor
> of the supreme God you are victorious over all your enemies, whose activities
> disfigured the Roman empire. Raise the standard of the reverend Law, sanc-
> tify it, and promulgate what will be beneficial. Let it be a holy blessing for the
> state that among the throngs of slain sacrifices you have laid low an army of
> the enemy.

By "the enemy" Firmicus intended Constantius to understand "the pagan";
this usage is in itself a remarkable assertion that the pagan majority that had
ruled the empire a generation earlier had now, by choice of religion, become enemies of the *res publica*.

When writing early in the next century of the continuing struggle against
the Donatists in Africa, Augustine adopted a usage similar to that of Constantine, whose writings on the Donatists Augustine knew intimately: "A religious and pious emperor should prefer to correct the error of this impiety
by most pious laws and to compel to Catholic unity by terror and coercion
those who bear the standards of Christ against Christ."[285] Prior to Constantinian coinage it would have been impossible to describe an emperor bearing standards: that was a task for a distinguished legionary, not for a general.
In the fourth century, however, as the language of Chrysostom suggests, the
bearing of standards became a badge of leadership and the mark of sovereign power. Appealing to this conceptual framework, Chrysostom called
both Paul and the emperor "standard-bearers of Christ," usage that enjoyed
a long popularity in East and West.[286] Perhaps even more fascinating, and
even more indicative of the depth to which this imagery penetrated, is the
appearance of standards in representations of local divinities both on the

---

282. On Christian references to *vexillum fidei, vexillum crucis, vexillum veritatis,* etc., see Seston, *RAC* s.v. "Feldzeichen," cols. 707–710.
283. Constantine at Optatus, appendix 9 Ziwsa (von Soden no. 31).
284. Firmicus Maternus *Err.* 20.7.
285. Augustine *Ep.* 185.7.28.
286. Chrysostom *Homil. de laudibus S. Pauli* 7 (*PG* 50.507–508). In Latin literature, see
Paulinus *Carm.* 19.650–655, Leo *Serm.* 59.4 (*PL* 54.339C–340A), and Dracontius *Laud. Dei*
2.504–508 (at 506) and 3.222–224.

coinage of Syrian cities and in the artwork of local temples.[287] This phenomenon is mirrored in the Danubian provinces by dedications displaying
a renewed interest in native gods during the third century—but these native gods are clearly honored with characteristically Roman expressions of
piety, and their aid is invoked in the preservation of Roman vows for the Roman empire.[288] What is more, the specific banners and insignia that appear
in the Syrian and Punic shrines do not belong to any particular legion with
which the temples could be associated. On the contrary, their appearance
requires the explanation that local artists, in their efforts to make their gods
look powerful, adapted an imagery associated with the most visible deity
they knew.[289]

CONCORDIA IN CHURCH AND STATE

In matters of peace and war, in both church and state, the turn of the century was full of turmoil.[290] The death of Theodosius on 18 January 395 left
the empire to his two sons, Arcadius and Honorius, both minors in experience and ability if not in age.[291] The formal regency of Stilicho over Honorius in the West created pressure and opportunity for officials in the East to
claim similar powers over Arcadius. The result was a practical division of the

287. See Rostovtzeff 1942 and Kantorowicz's remarkable "Gods in uniform" (1965, 7–24).
See also Gichon 1972, discussing a Syrian lamp decorated with the plan of a legionary camp,
and Alföldy 1989, 81 and 92, on Roman forms used to worship both Roman and native gods
in the Danubian provinces.

288. Alföldy 1989, 79–81, 86–87, 92, and 99.

289. On the adoption and evolution of "presentness," or visibility (expressed with ἐπι-
φανής and ἐπιφανέστατος), as an imperial attribute, see Grant 1946, 356–367, and Mitthof
1993. Cf. Pliny Pan. 80.3. Nock 1972, 42, argued against interpreting the association of the ep-
ithet with local deities as assimilating qualities from the emperor to the divine, but it seems
hard to rule out that possibility.

290. A. D. E. Cameron, Long, and Sherry 1993 provide full analysis of political events in
these years.

291. Arcadius, born in 377, was seven years older than Honorius and not legally a minor,
but he lacked strength of mind or character. See, for example, Marcus Diaconus Vita Porph. 49:
Arcadius wanted to celebrate his infant son's baptism by arranging for him to issue his first
edict. Viewing Arcadius and Honorius as a pair encouraged viewing them as equal in age. See,
for example, Severianus In theophaniam pr. (A. Wenger 1952, 48), delivered soon after 395:
[When I say these things in praise of the empire] τὴν δυάδα τῶν ἀδελφῶν καὶ τὴν συμφωνίαν
ᾄδω τῆς βασιλείας, ἢ καὶ τὸ θεῖον ἐπαληθεύει λόγιον τὸ "Ἀδελφὸς ὑπὸ ἀδελφοῦ βοηθούμενος
ὡς πόλις ὀχυρὰ καὶ ὡς τεθεμελιωμένον βασίλειον [Prov. 18:19]." Severianus next quotes
Zech. 4:14 and continues τὸν μακάριον βασιλέα βλέπω λάμποντα μετὰ τῶν τέκνων, surely a
reference to a contemporary portrait group. Of course, this and subsequent references to the
princes as τέκνα were rhetorically easy—among other things, they made imagining their concord easy—but distorted the difference in their ages.

empire, expressed most publicly in the formal concession that the eastern and western courts should each nominate one of the year's consuls. The multiplication of courts in the past had admittedly led to the occasional multiplication of consuls, but those occasions had generated an excess of eponymous officials, as would-be emperors claimed the right to name the year. It was only in the years after 395 that miscommunication could so disable the system that the East would promulgate a law in the year "when the consuls were Theodosius, for the fourth time, and whoever shall have been named [by the West]."[292]

At the same time, the empire had often seen colleagues on the throne, and we would err greatly if we drew any conclusions about popular beliefs from subtle alterations in the mechanics of government.[293] It is, for example, a virtual certainty that the law whose final dating formula we just construed as evidence of crippling bureaucratic punctiliousness had been formally promulgated by the *Imperatores Honorius et Theodosius Augusti,* namely by the harmonious corulers of a unified empire.[294] The agents of the government and the people of the empire jointly conspired to believe their empire a notional and necessary unity, and that belief remained fundamental to imperial ideology in art and ceremony in the years to come. Indeed, it lent to official works of art, with their endless images of paired emperors, soldiers, or angels, a formal balance in theme and composition that must have rendered their messages as immediately intelligible as they were pleasing.[295]

Ecclesiastical politics in Constantinople in these years would have been fractious even without their entanglement in the affairs of the court.[296] In the spring of 400, one Eusebius, bishop of Valentinopolis, attempted to read a series of charges against Antoninus, bishop of Ephesus, in a minor synod presided over by John Chrysostom, the extraordinary preacher and bishop of Constantinople. John tried to persuade Eusebius to be quiet: many make accusations out of passion but are unable to prove them. "After your indictment of Eusebius has been formally recited and come to the hearing of all, and after the minutes have been recorded, it will no longer

292. *C. Th.* 5.16.33; the *Consularia Constantinopolitana* lists Theodosius alone for this year. On the consuls for 401, see Bagnall et al. 1987, 16–17, 356–357, and 667–668. But cf. Gregory Naz. *De vita sua* 1002, referring to Theodosius as βασιλεὺς ἑῷος.

293. Cf. A. D. E. Cameron, Long, and Sherry 1993, 304.

294. The page containing the text of 5.16.33 is badly damaged, but cf. *C. Th.* 7.4.32 (from the East), 7.13.20, and 15.1.48; and *Const. Sirm.* 11 (from the West). The last text is erroneously attributed to 411 in Mommsen and Krueger's edition, a casualty of the same confusion that produced *C. Th.* 5.16.33.

295. On images of imperial harmony in art and texts from this period see Grigg 1977, a justly famous essay.

296. J. Kelly 1995 provides the most recent narrative.

be possible for you, though you are a bishop, to request an *abolitio* [a formal dismissal of the charges]."[297] Eusebius pressed on, and John rashly announced that he would personally investigate the charges in situ. The court immediately forbade this: Gaïnas, the disgruntled *magister militum,* was effectively besieging the capital, and John was required to mediate between the helpless imperial officials within the city and Gaïnas and his compatriots without.

When Eusebius first publicized his charges, no one could have predicted the events of the following months: the population of Constantinople conducting a pogrom against the Goths; Gaïnas slowly losing a battle of will with his opponents and withdrawing to Thrace, there to die at the close of the year; Eusebius failing to produce witnesses and suffering excommunication; and Antoninus, seemingly on the verge of vindication, falling sick and dying.[298] When the church at Ephesus asked John to right its affairs after the death of Antoninus, the court allowed his departure. He divided his duties between his archdeacon, Serapion, and his Syrian protégé, Severianus, bishop of Gabala, and departed for a tour of Asia. His two assistants quarreled almost from the start, but it was naturally Severianus, the preacher, who attracted the favorable attention of the court and, therefore, the jealousy of his former patron.

When John returned from Asia in the spring of 402, the court intervened to restore harmony between the warring factions of the church, much as it had tried to use John to mediate between factions in the military and civil bureaucracy two summers earlier.[299] The empress Eudoxia in particular saw an opportunity to make peace as never before in her reign. The instability that had produced Gaïnas had provoked Stilicho in the West to humiliate the eastern court by repeatedly contesting its authority, most pointedly in its nomination of consuls; order in that matter had been restored late in 401, when Rome received and accepted the nomination of Fravitta for that year, and the imperial brothers advertised their renewed harmony, and that of their putative subordinates, by assuming a joint consulate for 402. Their relationship, symbolized by their physical collocation, was then celebrated on coins and monuments throughout the empire.

Eudoxia now brokered a peace between Severianus and John, which was celebrated over two days, John speaking on the first and Severianus on the

---

297. Palladius *Dialogus* 14.44–46: μετὰ γὰρ τὸ ἀναγνωσθῆναι καὶ εἰς ἀκοὰς πάντων ἐλθεῖν, πραττομένων ὑπομνημάτων, οὐκέτι σοι ἔξεστιν, ἐπισκόπῳ ὄντι, ζητεῖν ἀβολιτίωνα.

298. The massacre of the Goths: 12 July 400. The retreat of Gaïnas: late summer, 400. The death of Gaïnas: December or January 400. Eusebius and his witnesses: June–August 400. The death of Antoninus: before winter 401.

299. For the role of Eudoxia see Socrates 6.11.

second. The event sparked interest around the Mediterranean; both homilies soon circulated in abbreviated Latin translations.[300] John's homily, alas, survives only in that form. Severianus's homily has survived in its original Greek, by the slimmest of threads.[301] He began by invoking the appearance of the Heavenly Host before the shepherds: "We, too, bring you news of great joy: today the church is at peace." Severianus built to an initial crescendo comparing present repose with former perturbation, present joy with former despair. Then he returned to the theme of peace:[302]

And what can we say that is worthy of Peace, which is the name of Christ? For concerning Christ Paul spoke, saying, "He is our Peace, Who has made us both one" [Eph. 2:14]. The two were not divided in thought, they were not estranged in faith, but they were torn asunder by the envy of the Devil. Just as before an imperial arrival the streets are cleaned and the colonnades are crowned with beautiful decorations, so that nothing may appear unworthy of the imperial gaze, so at the approach of Christ, the King of Peace, everything distressful has departed from our path. The truth shines forth, and falsehood has fled! Harmony shines forth, and discord has fled![303] Just as often the best of painters, wishing to illustrate unity of spirit [βουλόμενοι τῆς ψυχῆς τὴν ἕνωσιν δεῖξαι], place behind kings or brothers who are magistrates Concord, in the form of a woman [ἐν σχήματι γυναικὸς . . . τὴν ὁμόνοιαν], embracing with both her arms those who are unified—in order to show that those divided in body are united in thought—so the peace of Christ unifies by its embrace those who stand apart, and thus the saying of the prophet is fulfilled in us, "And there will be a council of peace between them" [Zech. 6:13].

The movement of the passage carefully observes and thus reveals the boundaries of the lifeworld inhabited by Severianus and his audience. He turned naturally to Scripture, easily applying Paul's vision for the Christian community to the church at the moment of the ceremony: as Christ dissolved the antipathy of Jew and Gentile, so His grace would now end the mutual antagonism of John and Severianus. But Severianus then elicited from his audience solemnity appropriate to the occasion by turning away from Scripture to imperial ceremonial: the arrival of Christ that had brought peace could best be understood by recalling an imperial arrival. And if Severianus first lamented his ability to explain the peace of Christ,

300. John: *PG* 52.423–426. Severianus: *PG* 52.425–428.
301. The only edition is the first, in A. Papadopoulos-Keremeus, Ἀνάλεκτα Ἱεροσολυμιτικῆς Σταχυολογίας (St. Petersburg, 1891 [reprint Brussels: Culture et Civilisation, 1961]) 1: 15–26.
302. Severianus *De pace* 1.
303. I read διχόνοια, Papadopoulos-Keremeus's correction for the paradosis, διχόνια. Since it rhymes with ὁμόνοια, it is clearly preferable to the διαφώνια of A. D. E. Cameron, Long, and Sherry, who in any event report the contents of the manuscript incorrectly (1993, 408 n. 13).

he discovered a heuristic device in the iconography of a tableau at once grandiose and everyday, the immediately topical harmony of emperors who were brothers. He closed the hermeneutic circle, seemingly without violence or contradiction, by likening the benevolent influence of Concordia to the fulfillment of a prophecy first delivered a thousand years before. Zechariah now lived amidst the stagecraft and properties of Decius, and he wore a toga.

PART THREE

From *Imperium* to *Patria*

CHAPTER EIGHT

Orbis Terrarum and *Orbis Romanus*

Imperialism possesses its own logic and requires a particular geography. It divides the peoples of the world: some are conquerors; all others are already or yet to be conquered. Neither Roman nor Gaul is likely soon to have forgotten the campaigns of Caesar. A substantial difference in legal rank and a vast emotive gulf will have separated them; nor will Roman attempts to collapse the former necessarily have had any effect on the latter. The integration of the empire presupposed a different geography, a different division of the world.

Yet imperialism would seem essential to the Roman self-image and to Roman political life. It was through victory in war that Caesar had established his preeminence, and it was through warfare once again that Augustus had staked his own claim to charismatic appeal. If success in warfare had remained essential to legitimate the candidacy of would-be emperors, neither Roman nor provincial would have been likely to recognize his stake in their shared community. After all, victories had to come at someone's expense. On an emotive level, the celebration of recent victories could have stirred up bitterness among the subject populations of the provinces; on an intellectual and ideological level, the rhetoric and iconography of such celebrations presumed and must have partially articulated a vision of the geography of the empire and the world. So long as emperors fought wars to add territory and peoples to the empire, they implicitly recognized a system of status distinctions that situated noncitizen residents somewhere between citizens and barbarians. If some provincials had earned seats in the Curia, many were regarded with scorn and condescension little different from that heaped on those outside the empire.

The theology of victory that developed under Augustus issued in a rather different outcome. The incarnation of Augustan victoriousness as Augustan

Victory attached such charisma as flowed from military achievement to the office that Augustus had endowed, and it remained there for his successors to bank or to lose.[1] Augustus did not intend that Romans should not esteem martial glory, nor did his actions cause such a change. Vespasian succeeded to the throne because he defeated others in war; Nerva needed Trajan, or a Trajan. But Augustan Victory made the cessation of warfare possible, and it was that potentiality that Hadrian actualized when he renounced imperialism and forever altered the geography of the empire.

This change of attitude within the governing class unfolded with the passage of generations, nor was it ever complete. But Hadrian did more than set policy for his subordinates and precedents for his successors. He participated in an ongoing discourse among provincials on the project and goal of empire. Recipients of propaganda that constructed them in Roman terms, provincials adopted and adapted the language and iconography of those messages toward a very different end. When Hadrian aligned imperial policy with provincial sentiment, he shifted the meaning of imperial victoriousness. The universalizing rhetoric of *aurum coronarium* now became unifying, as well. Identifying the beneficiaries of imperial victories now meant dividing the world between resident beneficiaries and barbarian victims, uniting in the former category citizen and noncitizen as jointly privileged participants in a single community.

AUGUSTUS AND VICTORY

Victory did not have an altar or temple at Rome until the third century B.C. According to Livy, Lucius Postumius Megellus dedicated an altar to Victory as consul in 294, fulfilling a vow that he had made some years earlier. Livy, alas, did not record the circumstances of that vow.[2] Two centuries passed before the cult achieved a special place within the ritual life of the Roman army. Marius seems to have been responsible for having placed the figure of Victory on the standards of the legions.[3] Extant evidence does not permit us to gauge the affection that soldiers of the Republic felt for their goddess, since the overwhelming majority of inscriptions by legionaries date from the Principate and beyond, but it is certainly clear from dedications in that period that Victory had a special place in the hearts of Roman soldiers.[4]

---

1. Cf. Nock 1972, 621: "For the emperor [Victory] was adjunct as well as attribute."

2. Livy 10.33.9. See Axtell 1907, 15; Wissowa 1912, 139–141; Weinstock 1957, 215; or *idem, RE* s.v. "Victoria," cols. 2504–2507.

3. Von Domaszewski 1895, 4 and 118, discussing Pliny *Nat.* 10.16, who attributes the reform of the standards to Marius but there writes that Marius added only the eagle.

4. See the collection of dedications in von Domaszewski 1895, 37–40, or Weinstock, *RE* s.v. "Victoria," cols. 2529–2531.

A particular representation of Victory received official sanction when Augustus took a statue of Victory from Tarentum and dedicated it on 28 August 29 B.C. in the Senate House that Julius Caesar had begun but not finished.[5] Imitations of it appeared thereafter in every medium of imperial art throughout the empire.[6]

To anticipate the effects of the actions discussed below: the collocation of emperor and Victory quickly became familiar to provincial populations. Those who honored her did so because Victory had brought them peace and continued to bring safety from those beyond the borders of their empire. As early as the first century Aphrodisias had two dedications to Victory of the Augusti, the plural referring to the emperors of the Julio-Claudian dynasty.[7] Subsequently temples to Victory are found apart from military installations in cities throughout Italy, in Gallia Cisalpina, in the provinces along the Danube, and in Germany and Africa.[8]

But Victory did not require her own temple to receive homage. She could also receive honor in association with the emperor whom she accompanied and protected. Just as cities and individuals could associate imperial portraits with statuettes of local deities, so many local groups paid homage to Victory in celebrations of the imperial cult. Organizers of such events could have learned this practice by observing the rituals of the army—after all, Tertullian and John Chrysostom both presumed upon their audiences' familiarity with the appearance of a legion.[9] Cassius Dio even explained a prodigy in such terms: among the portents and prodigies of 42 B.C. he included a notice that "a boy carrying a Victory fell down while marching in a procession, such as the soldiers lead."[10] Three papyri from Oxyrhynchus attest to the association of Victory and the emperor in cult acts from that city, from the second to the fourth century. Two of those describe Victory as "advancing before [the portrait busts of the emperors]," no doubt referring simultaneously to the concrete acts performed in impe-

---

5. The date is noted in the *fasti Maffeiani* and *Vaticani* (*EJ* p. 51); see Weinstock, *RE* s.v. "Victoria," or *idem* 1971, 111. For the statue, see Dio 51.22.2.

6. Weinstock, *RE* s.v. "Victoria," cols. 2522–2529; Hölscher 1967, 6–12 and *passim*. Gurval 1995, 50 and 62, doubts that the Tarentine statue was represented on Roman coins as early as the early 20s, but any statue so dedicated must have been an obvious model for any moneyer in that period.

7. Reynolds 1981, 323; cf. *CIG* 2310.

8. Weinstock, *RE* s.v. "Victoria," cols. 2531–2532.

9. See Chapter 7 at nn. 240 and 266.

10. Dio 47.40.8. For processions of soldiers bearing Victories before the emperor, see Nock 1972, 669–671, or Weinstock, *RE* s.v. "Victoria," cols. 2523–2524, 2529. For images from the Column of Trajan and the arches of Titus, Trajan, and Constantine, see Hölscher 1967, plates 7 and 10.

rial cult and to the common belief that Victory accompanied the emperor on his military expeditions.[11] Very similar must have been the statues dedicated in the reign of Gordian by a *flamen perpetuus* in Africa Proconsularis: he vowed and built a temple of the Victories, adorned with "three statues of the Victories of our emperor." At the dedication of the building he provided a public banquet for the population of his city.[12] Themistius asserted the close companionship of emperor and Victories when he sought to explain the special significance of the emperor's arrival in the capital city: "The Victories, rising up with Helios, run brightly to the west and, together with the emperor, come to earth in the metropolis of trophies."[13]

In the first instance Augustus undoubtedly presented his dedication of the statue of Victory in the Curia as the completion of his adoptive father's plans; after all, he allowed the Festival of Victoria Caesaris to continue throughout his reign, and he persisted in naming the building the Curia Julia.[14] The statue did not serve, however, merely as a reminder of past successes. Victory stood over an altar.[15] It had been customary under the Republic for a magistrate to take auspices before opening a meeting of the Senate.[16] We do not know whether that custom fell into abeyance, but Suetonius and Dio both record that Augustus, desirous of promoting piety, ordered that every senator offer incense and wine at the altar of the god in whose temple the Senate was meeting.[17] Although several authors subsequently refer to the religious rituals that preceded the formal start of a meeting, Herodian provides the first clear reference to senators burning incense to Victory when they met in the Curia Julia: Elagabalus ordered that his painted portrait should hang over the statue of Victory, "where each senator pours a libation of wine and burns incense as he enters the Curia."[18]

11. See *P. Oxy.* X 1265, ll. 9–11 (from A.D. 336), κωμαστοῦ θίων προτομῶν καὶ νίκης αὐτῶν προα(γ)ούσης, and *P. Oxy.* XII 1449, col. 1, fr. 1, l. 2 (A.D. 213–217), κωμαστῶν προ[τομῶν τοῦ] κυρί[ο]υ Σεβαστοῦ καὶ νίκ[ης αὐτοῦ προαγούσης. Cf. *P. Oslo* III 94, from the second or third century. From another region altogether, see *Pan. Lat.* VII(6).5.4: *Nam quid ego de receptione Britanniae loquar ad quam ita quieto mari navigavit ut Oceanus ille tanto vectore stupefactus caruisse suis motibus videretur, ita pervectus ut non comitata illum sit, sed praestolata Victoria?*

12. *AÉ* 1895, 71.

13. Themistius *Or.* 3.42b. On the circumstances of this speech, see Dagron 1968, 205–212, or Wirth 1979, 302–304.

14. For the Festival of Victoria Caesaris, see *ILS* 9349 (from A.D. 15); for its date, see *ILS* 8744 (the *fasti Maffeiani*) at 20 July, with Wissowa 1912, 140 and 293.

15. Herodian 5.5.7 and 7.11.3.

16. Gellius 14.7.9, quoting Varro.

17. Suetonius *Augustus* 35.3; Dio 54.30.1.

18. Herodian 5.5.7. On prayers to Victory in the Senate, see Weinstock 1957, 219 n. 39 and 240 n. 162, or *idem, RE* s.v. "Victoria," cols. 2507 and 2521. Cf. Prudentius *Psych.* 840–844, discussing the altar in the *curia* of the soul.

The actions of Augustus necessarily identified Victory as a tutelary deity of the Roman Senate.[19]

But Victory meant much more. Senators surely did not burn incense to her for their sake alone. Although the evidence is late and controversial, there is some reason to believe that the Senate addressed prayers to Victory even when not meeting in the Curia. The author of the *Historia Augusta,* who possessed a keen eye for official protocol, recorded that the Senate met in the Temple of Concord to consider the elevation of Probus. According to the *Life of Probus,* Manlius Statianus had the right of *sententia prima* at that time. In making his motion he invoked the Gods of the Capitol (Jupiter Optimus Maximus, Juno, and Minerva), Concord, in whose temple the Senate was meeting, and Victory.[20] In the eyes of one author, then, Victory achieved a status of equivalency with the Capitoline Triad, and, certainly, as the goddess of the Curia she could lay claim to preeminence as a goddess of the Roman state. Although not directly connected with the Senate, the Arval Brethren had certainly begun to number Victory among the gods of the Roman state as early as 69, and she figured in their prayers for emperors ever after.[21]

The insinuation of Victory into the central pantheon of the Roman state succeeded, in all likelihood, beyond even Augustus's wildest expectations. To understand more precisely what Augustus wished to achieve, and to clarify the ramifications of his ambitions, we must recall that the completion of the Curia formed a small part of an ongoing effort by Augustus both to dominate political life at Rome and to construct an ideological apparatus to disguise the fact of that dominance. In this task nothing proved so astonishingly brilliant as the adoption of the name Augustus. Suetonius described the evolution of Augustus's nomenclature in an early chapter of his biography:[22]

> Afterwards [Octavian] took the names Gaius Caesar and then Augustus, the one by the will of his great-uncle, the other on the motion of Munatius Plan-

19. See, for example, *ILS* 495, from Africa, perhaps dated from the reign of Gordian: an altar to, or simply statue of, *Victoria sen. Rom.*

20. *SHA Prob.* 11.5, 12.7.

21. In 69, when praying *ob comitia tribuniciae potestatis imperatoris,* the Brethren invoked *Iuppiter, Iuno, Minerva, Salus (rei publicae), Victoria,* and *Genius populi Romani.* In the prayers for Trajan in 101, we find *Iuppiter Optimus Maximus, Iuno regina, Minerva, Iuppiter victor, Salus rei publicae populi Romani, Mars pater, Mars victor,* and *Victoria.* See *Acta fratrum Arvalium,* s.a. 69, ll. 60–61, and s.a. 101, ll. 25, 32, 36, 40, 43, 47, 51, and 55. Roughly the same gods appear when Hadrian returned to Rome in 118 (s.a. 118, col. II ll. 53–56). On Victory's place among the gods invoked by the Brethren, see Scheid 1990, 392 and 406–407.

22. Suetonius *Augustus* 7.2; see also Ovid *Fasti* 1.607–616: Augustus shares his name with Jupiter and temples. From a vast bibliography see most usefully Gagé 1930a and *idem* 1931b, 84–85 and 106–107.

cus. For when some had proposed that he should be called Romulus, as if he were a second founder of the city, Plancus carried the proposal that he should instead be called Augustus, not only because the name was new, but also because it was more impressive, insofar as places—whether sacred [*religiosa*] in their own right or consecrated by augury—are called "august."

In the words of Florus: "The Senate also debated whether he should be called Romulus because he had founded the empire. But the name Augustus seemed more holy and reverent, insofar as even while alive he might be worshiped under that name and title."[23]

Cassius Dio's analysis of this title holds special value because he tried to explain to Greeks the significance of *Augustus* to Romans. He did so by connecting the import of *Augustus* with the semantic field of its standard Greek translation:[24]

> When he had completed these matters of detail, the name Augustus was awarded to him by the Senate and the people. They desired to address him in a fashion both unique and appropriate—some proposed one name, and others chose another—while Caesar desired strongly to be called Romulus. When he saw that because of this he was suspected of desiring the kingship, he ceased to claim it and called himself Augustus instead, as if he were something more than human. For everything that is greatly honored and sacred is termed "august." Because of this, speakers of Greek address him as σεβαστός, meaning someone worthy of veneration, from the word σεβάζεσθαι [to venerate, worship].

It is entirely typical of their respective attitudes toward Augustus that Suetonius recorded the name of the senator whose motion awarded the name, while Dio preferred to see the mind and will of Augustus behind all the developments of these years. In doing so he underestimated the peculiar creativity of the sycophant.[25]

Dio also interpreted the placement of the statue of Victory in the Curia as the ideologically charged act of a master propagandist: "When [Augustus] had completed these things, he dedicated the temple to Athena—the one called the Chalcidicum—and the Curia Julia, which existed to honor his father. He set up in it the statue of Victory that is there even now, in order to show, as it seems, that he had established his rule by her dispensation."[26] Dio thus understood that the dedication made a symbolic point

---

23. Florus 2.34(66).
24. Dio 53.16.6–8.
25. For example, in the case of Munatius Plancus, compare Suetonius *Augustus* 7.2 with Velleius 2.83.1: *Inter hunc apparatum belli Plancus, non iudicio recta legendi neque amore rei publicae nec Caesaris (quippe haec semper impugnabat) sed morbo proditor, cum fuisset humillimus adsentator reginae et infra servos cliens.*
26. Dio 51.22.1–2.

about the legitimacy of Augustus and only indirectly honored his father.[27] Dio's narrative raises many questions for modern readers. How could a tribute to Victory be read as an implicit claim to superhuman status? And in the case of Augustus, how could his contemporaries not be shocked when such a claim sprang from an individual with such modest accomplishments in war?

For example, Augustus had not distinguished himself at the battle of Philippi. Sympathetic accounts, echoing the defense advanced in the *Autobiography*, urged that Augustus had left his camp in response to an ominous dream—albeit one that had visited his doctor.[28] But hostility or honesty could fashion a different narrative, even from facts reported by Agrippa and Maecenas: Augustus fled danger and the scene of battle and hid in a marsh for three days.[29] Similarly, Augustus himself made much of the peace achieved under his rule, and even Tacitus did not deny its reality, yet Augustus could not prevent the judgment that his peace had been purchased with much blood.[30] The claim to have brought peace to Rome, moreover, was itself implicitly a claim to martial prowess. Romans understood peace to be a condition created through military action. When Augustus boasted that the Gates of Janus had been closed more times under his rule than during all recorded history before him, he was nominating himself the most successful general in Roman history.[31] Presented in this fashion, the evidence requires that we argue that most Romans either somehow ignored, or possibly did not see, what seems to us an obvious disjunction between Augustan propaganda and the reality of Augustan mediocrity.

In fact, for a Roman the disjunction simply did not exist. Romans had always understood that human action and the idiosyncratic qualities of any particular general could not in themselves guarantee victory: "You rule, Roman, because you hold yourself inferior to the gods; from them all things begin; to them ascribe every outcome."[32] Republican formulas for registering responsibility for a military success did so by reference to three factors: a general's power to command (*imperium*), his responsibility for taking aus-

27. Compare Pliny *Nat.* 2.94 on the comet that appeared during the first Games for Venus Genetrix: *haec ille in publicum: interiore gaudio sibi illum natum seque in eo nasci interpretatus est; et, si verum fatemur, salutare id terris fuit.*

28. Valerius Maximus 1.7.1, Velleius 2.70.1, Suetonius *Augustus* 91.1, Florus 2.17.9–10, and Dio 47.41.3–4. For the *Autobiography* as the common source see Blumenthal 1913, 281.

29. Pliny *Nat.* 7.148. For surviving traces of anti-Augustan rhetoric and historiography, see Gabba 1984, 78 and 82–85.

30. Augustus *Res gestae* 13; Tacitus *Ann.* 1.10: *pacem sine dubio post haec, verum cruentam.*

31. See Ovid *Fasti* 1.279–288, and cf. Weinstock 1960, 45; Brunt and Moore on *Res gestae* 13; Gurval 1995, 135; Gruen at *CAH*[2] X 188–194; and Lott 1996.

32. Horace *Carm.* 3.6.5–6. Cf. Sallust *Cat.* 12.4–5; Livy 5.51–52, with a climax at 51.5 (*Intuemini enim horum deinceps annorum vel secundas res vel adversas; invenietis omnia prospera evenisse sequentibus deos, adversa spernentibus*), and Tertullian *Apol.* 25.2.

pices (*auspicium*), and his blessedness (*felicitas*)—a measure of his relationship with the divine.[33] Livy transcribed two inscriptions from the second century B.C. that recorded military successes, attributing agency in these terms.[34] For example, a Roman fleet under Lucius Aemilius Regulus routed the fleet of Antiochus in 194 B.C. Livy both narrated and explained that success by writing that it had occurred through Regulus's *auspicio, imperio, felicitate ductuque,* and this formula appears with slight variations throughout Republican literature.

As a matter of religious principle, then, Romans believed that military success resulted not from the leadership of any commander whatsoever, nor from the actions of any individual or group on the battlefield itself, but from the special relationship established between the gods and the relevant holder of *imperium et auspicium.* They expressed their allegiance to this principle most publicly and politically when they awarded triumphs only to such men and not to those subordinates whose leadership might seem responsible for the victory.[35] Romans handled the defeat of a Roman army in similar terms: failure in war resulted from inadvertent errors during the religious rituals that had measured the gods' disposition toward the undertaking. If such an error had been discovered during the taking of the auspices, the action would have been abandoned or postponed, or the presiding magistrate could have undertaken an expiatory ritual. But many errors revealed themselves only through the fact of a military disaster. Romans sadly followed such disasters with expiation, all the while seeking to understand the contingent circumstances of the disaster in order to increase their storehouse of knowledge concerning *res divinae.* Nevertheless, the nature of such errors in and of itself mitigated any human failings of the general in charge.[36] In victory or defeat, the position and responsibility of a Roman general within his province was unique.

Elasticity in Roman attributions of agency and responsibility in military affairs ultimately generated pressure on the semantic range of *victoria* itself. For example, some described the *dominatio* of Sulla as the result of his "use" or "exploitation" of his victory. In that context *victoria* denoted the political situation that had resulted from a military engagement.[37] In awarding the name Augustus, the Senate acknowledged Augustus's unique stature, his charisma, on several levels, each comprehensible in scope, if not in scale, in

33. See Gagé 1930b, 8–9 and 12–13; Charlesworth 1943, 1; Weinstock 1957, 231 and 236; Wistrand 1987.
34. Livy 40.52.6; cf. 41.28.8–9, and see Wistrand 1987, 16–18.
35. Wissowa 1912, 386–387; Gagé 1933b, 2–4.
36. Rosenstein 1990, 7, 54–91.
37. Weinstock 1957, 220–221; *idem, RE* s.v. "Victoria," col. 2509.

purely traditional terms.[38] For Romans looking to Augustus throughout the 20s and beyond, the most important evidence by far of his special relationship with the gods—of his *felicitas*—was simply the fact of Roman success under his rule.

Several important consequences followed from the honors voted to Augustus and from the settlements of 27 and 23 B.C., though it would be a mistake to assume that the practical implications of those settlements had been worked out in advance.[39] First, at a legal level, few if any commanders of Roman forces subsequently fought under their own auspices and *imperium*. The last two senators to win triumphs or acclamations as *imperatores* were, naturally, proconsular governors of the public province of Africa, L. Cornelius Balbus in 19 B.C. and Junius Blaesus in A.D. 23. In recording the latter's award, Tacitus exposed its latent hypocrisy: armies were supposed to acclaim their generals spontaneously, and now were merely permitted to do so by the emperor; nor was an acclamation supposed to render a general unique—until, that is, Augustus made *imperator* a personal name.[40] Dio traced the source of this imperial prerogative to the refusal of a triumph by Agrippa in 14 B.C.:[41]

> For these successes, sacrifices were made in the name of Agrippa, but he did not celebrate the triumph that was voted to him. Indeed, he did not even write to the Senate concerning his accomplishments; because of this those after him, observing his practice as if it were law, neither wrote anything to the Senate nor accepted the award of a triumphal procession. Because of Agrippa's refusal, triumphs were not granted to any of his contemporaries, at least as I understand it; rather, they merely celebrated with triumphal honors [*ornamenta triumphalia*].

In this Dio is undoubtedly wrong, though the unselfish and unswerving loyalty of so fine a general as Agrippa must have made the accomplishments and, therefore, the ambitions of his contemporaries seem quite foolish.[42]

Augustus's role as an intermediary between Rome and her gods can only have increased with his assumption of the office of pontifex maximus on

---

38. See Picard 1957, which must be used with caution.

39. A point emphasized by von Premerstein 1937 and by Syme, *RP* 1.181–196 and *RP* 3.1198–1219.

40. On Balbus see *fasti triumphales Capitolini* (*EJ* p. 36). On Blaesus, see Tacitus *Ann.* 3.74.4. On *imperator* and Augustus's nomenclature, see Chapter 2 at n. 45.

41. Dio 54.24.7–8. Suetonius *Tiberius* 9.2 seems erroneously to date the origin of *ornamenta triumphalia* to the successes of Tiberius in 9–7 B.C.

42. See Servius on *Aen.* 8.682, *VENTIS ET DIS AGRIPPA SECUNDIS 'secundis' ergo dixit Augusti comparatione: nam hoc dicit: Augustus nimio ventorum et numinum utebatur favore, Agrippa sequenti, hoc est, ille habuit primum favorem, hic secundum.* Cf. Syme 1986, 78.

6 March 12 B.C.: "Over the eternal fire presides the eternal divinity of Caesar: you see the pledges of empire mutually conjoined."[43] Why should anyone have wanted to risk personal failure and consequent harm to the state when evidence of the *felicitas* of Augustus was so near to hand? We tend to scoff at crediting the successes of generals on the Rhine to Augustus in Rome, but this was no constitutional or theological pretense for Romans. The practical effects of their beliefs are visible across several types of evidence even during the lifetime of Augustus. In Book 4 of his *Odes,* written around 12 B.C., Horace celebrated the Augustan principate, and in *carmen* 14 of that collection he reviewed for Augustus the military successes of his adopted sons, Drusus and Tiberius. "With your soldiery" Drusus defeated the Genauni; "under your favorable auspices" Tiberius drove back the Raeti; "you supplied his forces, his plan, and the favor of the gods."[44] Horace elsewhere made Augustus responsible for the general welfare of the state: he was "the guardian of human affairs" (*custos rerum*). Slightly more than a decade earlier, in Book 1 of his *Odes,* Horace had reassured Jupiter that though his task were mighty, Augustus stood by, capable of assuming his mantle and his role as "father and guardian of the human race."[45] Fourteen years later the town of Pisa referred to Augustus in precisely these terms when it drafted its decree responding to the death of Gaius Caesar: Augustus was "the guardian of the Roman empire and the protector of the entire world."[46]

Augustus himself exploited with economy and elegance the system that gave him credit for his legates' victories. Early in the *Res gestae* he asserted that he had "waged many civil and foreign wars on land and sea throughout the world." When he later described specific deeds, he wrote that they were accomplished "by [his] command and under [his] auspices" or "beneath [his] standards," identifying in asides the humans who had served as agents: Augustus settled Armenia "through [his] son Gaius" and conquered Pannonia "through [his] stepson and legate Tiberius Nero."[47]

43. Ovid *Fasti* 3.415–428 at 421–422.

44. Horace *Carm.* 4.14, esp. 9, 16, and 33–34.

45. Horace *Carm.* 1.12.49–52 and 4.15.17; cf. Ovid *Fasti* 1.607–612 and 2.129–132. The title may have had official sanction: the *Feriale Cumanum,* as supplemented by Mommsen, records on 30 January a *supplicatio Imperio Caesaris Augusti cust*[*odis imperii Romani pacisque orbis terrar*]*um.* Dessau and Weinstock approved this text (*ILS* 108; Weinstock 1960, 49 n. 59). Other suggestions have been offered (see, for example, *EJ* p. 46). In reading *Carm.* 1.12 as indicating limits on the power of Augustus, Putnam 1990, 214–215, neglects the effect achieved by addressing Jupiter in 49–52.

46. *ILS* 140 (*EJ* no. 69), ll. 6–8: [6]*Augusti patris patri-*|[7]*ae* [*po*] *ntif. maxsumi custodis imperi Romani totiusque orbis terrarum prae-*|[8]*si*[*dis.*

47. For the assigning of credit, see *Res gestae* 3.1, 25.3, 26.5, and 30.2; for the attribution of agency, see 27.2 or 30.1.

Artists of the period also developed a pictorial language to give this ideology monumental form. Although few public monuments survive in recognizable form from the last fifteen years of Augustus's reign, it was popular to copy in miniature—on gems, in engravings, and through wall paintings—the grandiose displays built by Augustus or sponsored by others to honor him.[48] None of these miniatures can reproduce for us the precise impression conveyed by the original works: not only were the originals undoubtedly accompanied by inscribed or painted captions of some kind, but the patron who commissioned the miniature or the artist who realized the commission could select a particular panel or a particular motif for emphasis. Nevertheless, the scenes imitated in these works must have been intimately familiar to residents of Rome and, in all likelihood, to people in large cities throughout the empire. The loss of the original works, and of the texts that accompanied and explained them, complicates the interpretation of the surviving artifacts, but—insofar as we understand the basic form of the triumph—some generalizations are possible and reasonably secure. We may consider first the so-called Gemma Augustea, an engraved piece of sardonyx now housed in Vienna.[49] It contains two pictures: on the bottom, several soldiers erect a trophy in the presence of surrendering barbarians; on the top, Augustus watches a young prince—almost undoubtedly Tiberius—descend from a chariot, presumably at the climax of a triumph. Several gods surround Augustus, including Ocean, Earth, and Oecumene, who crowns him, while Rome sits to his right and Victory drives the triumphal chariot. All the gods look toward Augustus and not at the prince; they have extended a degree of blessedness to the young conqueror only because of their special relationship with his adoptive father.

Similar scenes appear on the Boscoreale Cups: one panel depicts Tiberius riding alone in triumph; its model almost undoubtedly dates from his reign. The other contains two scenes that mirror those on the Gemma Augustea: in one Augustus receives the surrender of some northern barbarians. Such scenes were familiar to Romans of all periods from the painted artwork that accompanied triumphs.[50] Personifications of geographic landmarks and ethnic groups had, of course, figured in Greek and Hellenistic art, but Greeks had identified these as abstracts and therefore represented them as idealized female figures. The realistic portrait, in which the artist attempts to convey by symbolic means not only the abject state of the figure

48. Zanker 1988, 265–295.
49. On its interpretation, see Bernoulli 1886, 262–274 and plate XXIX; Furtwängler 1900, 1 plate 56 and 2.257–258; Gagé 1930b, 28–29; Picard 1957, 304–310; Richter 1971, no. 501; Megow 1987, no. A10 on 155–163; Hannestad 1988, 78–80, with an excellent photograph (fig. 51 on p. 79); Zanker 1988, 230–232, with fig. 182 on p. 231; and Pollini 1993.
50. See Chapter 7, "The Art of Victory."

but also its nationality, developed at Rome and in the context of triumphal art. Such surrendering figures appeared not only in triumphal art and in miniature representations of monuments and painted panels, but also regularly on imperial coins at the conclusion of a campaign.[51]

The other cup from Boscoreale depicts an enthroned Augustus receiving a statuette of Victory from Venus.[52] Once again, his unique relationship with the gods has brought him success, and, the viewer may easily conclude, it is uniquely through him that Rome may hope for continued successes. Though we do not have the monuments that supplied the images reflected in these works, we do possess through Suetonius a description of the triumph celebrated by Tiberius in A.D. 12, which also formed the subject of an issue of imperial coinage: "After two years Tiberius returned to the city from Germany and celebrated the triumph that he had postponed; his legates, for whom he had demanded *ornamenta triumphalia*, followed him in that procession. Before he turned into the Capitol, he dismounted from his chariot and fell to his knees before his father, who was presiding over the ceremonies."[53] We could interpret the description of Augustus in this passage as if Augustus played a wholly traditional role: as *princeps senatus* he met the *triumphator* and accompanied him to the Capitol. The programs of the Boscoreale Cups and Gemma Augustea suggest that Augustus acted, and contemporaries saw him, in a very different light. The humility of Tiberius, like the gaze of the gods on the Gemma Augustea, directed credit to Augustus first, and only indirectly to his adoptive heirs.[54] This concentration of attention on Augustus began with the receipt of bulletins from the front; it continued with a ceremonial action integrating populace and rulers; and it achieved long-lasting relevance by passing from concrete detail to more abstract representation on the jewels, coins, and tableware that kept the emperor and his benefactions ever before one's eyes.[55]

Constitutional niceties surely eased the transfer of power from Augustus to Tiberius, but close attention to them can easily efface an important question: How did Tiberius come to possess a *felicitas* in any way comparable to

51. On *simulacra gentium*, their use at Rome, and their Greek antecedents, see J. Toynbee 1934, 7–23; Picard 1957, *passim;* and Ostrowski 1990 and 1996.

52. On the Boscoreale Cups, see Hölscher 1967, plate 3 no. 1 and plate 10 no. 2; Hannestad 1988, 95; Zanker 1988, 227–230. Kuttner 1996 has excellent new plates. On Augustus's exploitation of the cult of Venus Genetrix see Pliny *Nat.* 2.93–94, and Servius on *Aen.* 8.681, together with Weinstock 1971, 80–90.

53. Suetonius *Tiberius* 20. See *BMC* I, Augustus nos. 508–512, and Hannestad 1988, 79 n. 132.

54. Cf. Pollini 1993, 267–269.

55. E.g., *BMC* I, Augustus nos. 443–449: Augustus sits on a stool on a platform, while two men dressed in military garb—perhaps Tiberius and Drusus—offer him olive branches, the fruits of the victories won under his auspices.

that of Augustus, and, by extension, how did that *felicitas* pass to the other Julio-Claudians? Tiberius had had, to be sure, an extremely distinguished career in the field under Augustus; he alone of the Julio-Claudians possessed military distinction in his own right. On the other hand, he had served his entire life under another's auspices; he had acknowledged, by his behavior in his triumph, his debt for those successes to his adoptive father. Augustus himself seems to have envisioned passing his name, the imprimatur par excellence of his blessedness, to his son and heir; Tiberius's refusal of the name did not make his accession any easier.[56]

At the same time, Tiberius's difficult relations with the Senate need not have occluded his importance as the singular holder of *imperium et auspicium*. How was Tiberius the sole ruler represented in the iconography of Augustan Victory? For an answer we turn to the Great Cameo of France, a decorated jewel similar in form to the Gemma Augustea, which dates to the early years of Tiberius's reign. Its program still eludes full explication, but the main figures in its three tiers can be identified easily enough.[57] The main scene depicts not a triumph, but rather the departure of a member of the royal house; the now traditional interpretation assigns the scene to the departure of Germanicus for the East in A.D. 17.[58] Tiberius occupies the center of the gem. Before him stand Germanicus, Agrippina, and the young Gaius. On Tiberius's left sits an older woman who cannot be firmly identified: we would expect the goddess Roma, but her characteristic attributes are not clearly present. Perhaps this woman is Livia.[59] Behind their chair stands a young man, smaller than the prince and therefore likely to be the younger Drusus, gesturing toward the upper tier. In the lower tier appear barbarians in many modes of dress, symbolizing the different nations conquered by the departing prince on his previous expedition. In the upper register—that is, in heaven—sits the divine Augustus. On either side of Augustus appear the elder Drusus and the young Marcellus; in front of and

56. See Chapter 2 at n. 67.

57. See Bernoulli 1886, 275–299 with plate XXX; Furtwängler 1900, 1 plate 60 and 2.268–271; Gagé 1930b, 18–21; Richter 1971, no. 502; Megow 1987, no. A85 on 202–206. Megow reports the *communis opinio* on this gem and then advances a striking theory, dating the gem late in the reign of Claudius. He seeks to explain thereby the artist's selection of individuals from the *domus divina*. He realizes, however, that his theory also raises an important question: Why is the not-deified Tiberius rather than the reigning Claudius so centrally placed (206)? His answer, establishing an analogy between the events of 17 and 50, does not suffice.

58. Scholars have not been unanimous in supporting this interpretation. Some have identified the elder prince before Tiberius as Gaius, dating the scene to A.D. 37; others have named him Nero and dated the gem later still. Neither reading would change the emphasis of the overall image on the divine origin and sanction for the *domus Augusta*.

59. Megow 1987, 203, pronounces firmly for Livia, noting Livia's importance for Tiberius in the early years of his reign. Dea Roma appears beside Augustus on the Gemma Augustea and beside Gaius on the Vienna Fragment (Megow nos. A10 and A60).

slightly below Augustus appears Aeneas in Phrygian costume. Aeneas holds in his hands a globe, symbolizing the worldwide domination that Jupiter promised to his descendants and thus to Augustus and his *domus divina*, who continue by their oversight to bless the rule of Tiberius.[60]

The role ascribed to the divine Augustus in the Great Cameo adds new complexity to the developing theology of imperial victory, a new level of mediation between *imperator* and the gods. Augustus had been the unique agent of divine favor toward Rome, and his legates had been his instruments. His continued presence would subtly qualify the claims of his successors to an independent charismatic authority. These various strands of thought, both Augustan and post-Augustan, find concrete expression on the engraved scabbard of the so-called Sword of Tiberius, discovered in 1848 in Germany and now preserved in the British Museum.[61] The engraving represents Tiberius in much the same posture as the Gemma Augustea depicts Augustus, though, naturally, the space on the scabbard allows for less detail than appears on the magnificent gem. On either side of the seated Tiberius stand Mars Ultor and Victory—both gazing at Tiberius— while a young man, almost undoubtedly the prince Germanicus, gives him a small statuette of Victory. A shield leans against the throne on which Tiberius sits; the legend on the shield reads *Felicitas Tiberii*, "The Blessedness of Tiberius." The gods of war who attend Tiberius do so because of that blessedness, and thus it is through him that Germanicus has achieved his victory. The iconography rendered this fact apparent even to those who did not know, or did not care, that Tiberius held the relevant *imperium* and *aus-*

---

60. Cf. Gagé 1932, 68–69. The middle and upper registers of the French cameo are repeated with slight variations in the smaller Hawkins cameo; the smaller size of the engraving evidently did not permit duplication of the lower register. I have been unable to locate a modern plate of this gem or even to discover its present location. Since Furtwängler condemned it as a modern copy it has been little discussed, though he did so on the basis of a photograph, and though Bernoulli, no less an authority, accepted it as genuine on the basis of the same photograph (Bernoulli 1886, 276–277 and 294–295; Furtwängler 1900, 2.268–269). I offer that information as a caution, with the following observation: if it is a fake based on the French cameo, I fail to see wherein lay the inspiration for the variations between it and its model. Even if it is a later copy of an earlier gem that was itself modeled on the same monument as the French cameo, it can still be useful to us. The variations in the earthly sphere are slight indeed: Antonia looks toward Tiberius and not Germanicus, and the young Drusus wears a more Roman, less divine costume, and he no longer props up a standard. In heaven the changes are several, though the totality of those changes little affects the ideological import of the scene. Augustus has been replaced by Venus Genetrix, the founder of his line. Another woman, perhaps the goddess Roma, holds the globe over the head of Tiberius. Finally, a winged Victory appears in the corner made vacant by the disappearance of the *vexillum* behind the head of Drusus. For discussion of this gem see Gagé 1930b, 23.

61. See von Domaszewski 1895, 11. See also the comments by Mommsen, Hirschfeld, and Zangemeister at *CIL* XIII 6796; Gagé 1930b, 8–10; and Zanker 1988, fig. 183a–b.

picium. The sword simply reveals that Tiberius has somehow acquired the special relationship with the gods that Augustus had displayed in his early successes, and thus guarantees in his person the victoriousness of those under his command.

But there is more. The careful viewer will have found on the sword a thoroughly extraconstitutional explanation for the *Felicitas Tiberii.* The Victory that flanks Tiberius on his left holds a shield bearing the legend *Vic. Aug.* In another reign we would not know whether to expand the abbreviation to "Augustan Victory" (*Victoria Augusta*)—that is, "Victory of the (reigning) Augustus"—or to "Victory of (the first) Augustus" (*Victoria Augusti*). Since Tiberius never took the name Augustus, we can be fairly certain that this figure represents not his patron goddess, but rather that of his father. As on the Great Cameo, the divinity of Augustus sanctions the legitimacy of Tiberius, in this case through the presence of the deified abstraction whose favor earlier identified Augustus himself as uniquely entitled to rule.[62] Such appeals to Victoria Augusti helped to negotiate the complex pitfalls inherent in any attempt to transfer charismatic authority from one leader to the next, pitfalls that were perhaps especially precarious in an ideological system that elsewhere advertised an anachronistic adherence to constitutional forms.

In his relations with his subordinates Tiberius proceeded on much the same terms as had Augustus.[63] In describing the campaigns of Germanicus in A.D. 15–16, for example, Tacitus repeatedly observed the formal distinction between Tiberius as holder of *auspicium* and Germanicus as agent in the field. He also suggested that legionaries and their commanders understood this difference: when Manlius Ennius, commander of a legionary camp in Upper Germany, condemned the mutinous behavior of his soldiers, he reminded them that their actions reflected not upon him as commander, but upon Germanicus their general (*dux*) and upon Tiberius their emperor (*imperator*).[64] In such contexts, *imperator* had specific, legal reference: Tiberius was the formal holder of *imperium* and, therefore, responsible for the auspices, too. Similarly, after the Romans under Germanicus had defeated the Cherusci early in A.D. 16, Tacitus recorded—without any aside that someone had prompted them—that the soldiers acclaimed Tiberius as *imperator* on the field of battle and built a mound, after the fashion of trophies, on which they put the arms of the slaughtered tribes, with their names written underneath (*subscriptis victarum gentium nominibus*).[65] Germanicus

62. Gagé 1932, 64 and 68. Cf. Nock 1925, 43 n. 81.

63. See Picard 1957, 315–342.

64. Tacitus *Ann.* 1.38.2. See also *Ann.* 1.58.5: Germanicus receives an imperatorial acclamation *auctore Tiberio.*

65. Tacitus *Ann.* 2.18.2.

himself later supervised the construction of a trophy whose inscription effaced his own existence: "Having conquered the tribes between the Rhine and the Elbe, the army of Tiberius Caesar dedicates this monument to Mars, Jupiter, and Augustus."[66] And when the year 16 closed, the Senate dedicated an arch near the Temple of Saturn to celebrate the recovery of the standards lost with Varus, a deed accomplished "under the leadership of Germanicus, under the auspices of Tiberius."[67]

No subsequent Julio-Claudian emperor operated so long in the public eye and at the pinnacle of power as had Tiberius. It should therefore come as no surprise that, where Tiberius had refused to place excessive ideological weight on the divine foundations of his position, Gaius, Claudius, and Nero all minted coins with the legend VICTORIA AUGUSTI, with Nero starting in the second year of his reign and continuing every year thereafter. *Felicitas*, blessedness, thus became a permanent quality of the emperor, and, through it, so did victoriousness. Although this attribute was late finding expression in imperial titulature, emperors from Claudius on boasted of this quality ceremonially in their adoption of the clothing of the *triumphator* for everyday use.[68] It is very likely that Claudius established this custom precisely because he had never earned independent military credentials.

TRIUMPHATOR PERPETUUS

The later Julio-Claudian emperors lacked military experience and distinction. Their invocations of Victoria Augusti might seem hollow and therefore suggest Victory and victoriousness had diminished in importance as signs of that *felicitas* through which the Romans identified their charismatic leaders. Nothing could be further from the truth. Rather, the incarnation in Victoria Augusti of the special relationship between Augustus and Victory attached the favor of that goddess to the position Augustus had established. This had important political consequences. Aspirants to that position no longer had necessarily to found their claim on prior military success. Imperialist action was no longer a sine qua non of an emperor's or a would-be emperor's career. Many did so advance their careers—it was a quintessentially Roman path to political eminence—but it was not necessary. And, insofar as the emperor alone held *imperium et auspicium,* he was both constitutionally and religiously unique, and the *felicitas* associated with him in his tenure in office was his to lose. If true legitimacy and charismatic power did not automatically accrue from the mere occupation of the imperial office, that oc-

---

66. Tacitus *Ann.* 2.22.1.
67. Tacitus *Ann.* 1.41.1.
68. Weinstock 1957; A. Alföldi 1935, 9–68, esp. 25–28 and 36–38.

cupation at least guaranteed that the emperor should be the only person campaigning for them. When it worked, the system provided for greater stability than Augustus could have anticipated.

To the extent that Augustus did search the future, he planned a dynasty. He could not have foreseen Nero. That emperor's failure and death were both test and proof of the Augustan system. How did Nero lose the legitimacy that Augustus had bequeathed to his degenerate heirs? Neither the murder of Agrippina, nor the fire in Rome in 64, nor the suppression of the Pisonian conspiracy in 65, nor even his tour of Greece in 66 had kindled a successful coup. Events after Nero's death suggest that interest groups throughout the empire had begun to focus their loyalties on the imperial office and the administrative structure of which it was the head, rather than on the figure of Nero himself. This subconscious shift was made possible, in part, by the dissociation of martial charisma from particular *principes* and its embodiment in Augustan Victory. At the very least, these constituencies— the army, the population of Rome, the Senate, provincial populations—discovered their stake in the system as a whole and learned to control their dissatisfaction with its details.

We may call *Augustus* a title. At the start of 68 it was a family name. Beyond the claims of blood, no one knew how to earn the favor of the Victory that had smiled so long on the House of Augustus. What rules governed claims to charismatic authority "in armed competition for the purple? Men lacking the benefit of birth and renown could not have risen against Nero."[69] In the immediate aftermath of Nero's death, individuals advertised and sought to render manifest their own felicitous victoriousness. Under those circumstances, the rules would be simple. The field of candidates had to be reduced to one before the contest ended: in practical terms the proof of the legitimacy of any claim to charismatic authority lay solely in its ultimate uniqueness.

VICTORIA therefore appeared conspicuously on the coins of Galba, Otho, and Vitellius. Galba signaled his independent stature as a blessed leader with a reverse legend of "Victory of Galba Augustus," but, in keeping with his Republican propaganda, he also adopted the legends "Victory of the Roman People" and "Victory of the Roman Empire."[70] Otho, on the other hand, showed no hesitation in advertising himself as a guarantor of the empire's fate: holders of coin were expected to see that "Victory of Otho" had brought "peace throughout the world."[71] Vitellius tolerated the display of

---

69. Syme 1958, x–xi.

70. *RIC* I², Galba nos. 10, 11, and 48 (Spain); 98–101 and 110–116 (Gaul); 131–133, 148, 173–175, 215–217, 233, and 234 (Rome); and 519 and 520 (Africa).

71. *RIC* I², Otho nos. 3–6 (PAX ORBIS TERRARUM) and 13–17 (VICTORIA OTHONIS).

his predecessors' portraits, seeking legitimacy for himself by advertising the stability of the system that he wished to lead; he thus reverted to the more neutral "Victory of the Augustus."[72]

The swiftness of events in 69 did not allow much time for reflection, but Vitellius's reversion to VICTORIA AUGUSTI, even more than Galba's or Otho's personal Victories, at once acknowledged and legitimated the transfer of charismatic power from Augustus and his family to the office that he had created. In this process the use of *Augustus* as a title and the ambiguity inherent in Latin abbreviations can only have smoothed the way.[73] Once a clear winner emerged in the person of Vespasian, he could draw on the same theology of imperial victory that had propped up the descendants of Augustus: indeed, the Flavians largely reestablished the familiar forms and rituals of Augustan victory.[74]

The passage of time and dynasties caused some people to reflect self-consciously on attributing agency in martial endeavors uniquely to the emperors, wherever they might be. In a panegyric to Constantius delivered in 297 or 298, following that emperor's successful expedition to Britain, one orator contrasted his task in praising the deeds of Constantius with the fulsome rhetoric of Fronto, who could praise Antoninus Pius only for completing wars while residing at Rome.[75] But elsewhere appeals to the theology of Augustan Victory remained as potent as ever. In a panegyric delivered to Maximian in 289, a Gallic rhetor congratulated the emperor on the recent accomplishments of his generals: "At last, under the leadership [*ductu*] of such men, taking advantage of your most blessed auspices [*felicissimis vestris auspiciis*], that treacherous and deceitful race of barbarians received the treatment it deserved. This praise is yours, my emperor, yours: for all that is achieved through others begins with you. . . . Your good luck, I say, your blessedness, my emperor, has brought your soldiers victoriously to the

---

72. *RIC* I², Vitellius nos. 13, 14, and 46 (Spain); 61–63 (Gaul); 84, 111, 112, 123, 124, 142, 143, 151, 152, 165, 169, and 176 (Rome).

73. On the expansion of the abbreviation *V. Aug.*, see Gagé 1932, 63–65, and Weinstock, *RE* s.v. "Victoria," cols. 2518–2521. For example, the people who dedicated *CIL* VIII 15576 or *AÉ* 1895, 71, seem to be giving thanks for specific victories, but texts that use the same grammatical constructions, yet which are known to have been attached to altars, must have advertised a dedication to the goddess (e.g., *CIL* X 3816). Gellius 10.1.7–9 preserves a story from Tiro, in which Cicero advises Pompey to use an abbreviation *ut verbo non perscripto res quidem demonstraretur, sed dictio tamen ambigua verbi lateret.*

74. See Gagé 1933b, 11–13, or Picard 1957, 344–366. Vespasian restored some temples of Victory. The terms in which he advertised that deed lamented that his predecessors had tarnished the military reputation of their empire: see, for example, *ILS* 3813: *imp. Caesar Vespasianus Aug. pontifex maximus, trib. potestatis, censor aedem Victoriae vetustate dilapsam sua impensa restituit.*

75. *Pan. Lat.* IV(8).14.1–2. But note that Fronto himself could play with this convention: *Ep. ad Verum* 2.1.2 and 5.

shores of the ocean."[76] Another speaker, addressing Maximian two years later on the occasion of his birthday, touched on the same theme in a different fashion, describing the benefits brought to remote provinces by the mere existence of so great a pair of emperors as Diocletian and Maximian: "For no part of the earth lacks the presence of your majesties [*maiestatis vestrae praesentia*], even when you yourselves seem to be absent." Indeed, just as Jupiter fills all the world while reigning from heaven, so "I now dare to clam concerning each of you: wherever you are, even if you both rest in a single palace, your divinity reaches everywhere, and all lands and all seas are filled with you. If the world can be full of Jupiter, what is so miraculous about it being full of Hercules?"[77]

At some level these orators simply followed the precedent established by Horace in Book 1 of his *Odes*. This tradition did not simply view the governments of heaven and earth as analogous; on the contrary, the emperor's sole rule on earth elevated him to near equivalence with God in heaven. The author of a panegyric to Maximian and Constantine in 307 alluded to the same equality of role between Jupiter and the senior emperor at the close of his speech: "It is proper for you, Father, to oversee the world you share from the very height of empire and with a celestial nod to decide the outcome for human affairs, to give the auspices when wars must be waged, and to fix the rules for making peace."[78] Jupiter's "celestial nod" probably owed much to earlier poetry, and in particular to Vergil's Jupiter, whose nod shook all Olympus.[79] But the nod was also a symbol for the exercise of will by a sovereign power. Under Augustus, Livy could speak of the "nod" of the Roman people. Likewise, when Cicero lamented that the Senate obeyed the nod of the veterans, or Nero in the *Octavia* boasted that the corrupt mob had learned to obey the nod of its *princeps,* the nod was symbolic of a perversion of legitimate authority.[80] In a similar fashion, the orators of 289 and 307 referred to the emperor's auspices in part because their emperors conducted military actions through subordinates much as Augustus had done and were, therefore, responsible for safeguarding relations between the empire and the gods, in times of failure as of success. But both orators no doubt also participated in a much more complex development within popular belief, perhaps originating in this official discourse on imperial victoriousness, which saw the emperor as capable of acting across the vast geographic extent of the empire without concern for time and space.[81] The

76. *Pan. Lat.* II(10).11.4–5, 7.
77. *Pan. Lat.* III(11).13.5, 14.2–4.
78. *Pan. Lat.* VI(7).14.1.
79. *Aeneid* 9.106.
80. Cicero *Phil.* 10.19; [Seneca] *Octavia* 843; cf. Athenagoras *Legatio* 37.
81. For further expressions of this belief see Chapter 9, "The Discovery of Roman Religion."

power to conquer Pannonia through Tiberius while resident in Rome was not simply an exercise of constitutional theory, nor did it simply render Augustus unique. It made him more than human.

The divorce of Victory from the idiosyncratic occupant of the throne never became complete—an emperor could still have a personal Victory—and in any event took place gradually. Nevertheless, this process allowed Victory to become a patron deity of the *imperium Romanum* independent of her relationship with a given *princeps*. By the fourth century, invocations of Victory could operate on many levels simultaneously. In this era several official inscriptions named Victory the "companion" of the emperor. If the term implies that the passage of time had elevated the status of the emperor, it also suggests the independence of Rome's victoriousness from that of her emperor.[82] What is more, Roman victoriousness and the goddess who ensured its continuance carried too much ideological weight to disappear in the Christianization of the empire: Ammianus's description of the payment of *aurum coronarium* to Valentinian in the form of Victory statuettes proves this. As Julian had exploited the appeal of military standards to both pagans and Christians, so at least one pagan author in the fourth century may have sensed the hypocrisy in Christians' expressing their gratitude for imperial victories by fashioning and honoring statuettes of a goddess: "Here we are, the Victories, the laughing maidens, bringing victories to the city that loves Christ. Those who love the city painted us, giving us shapes appropriate to Victories." The author of this poem, Palladas of Alexandria, described "the city" as φιλόχριστος, "Christ-loving," as a play on the metrically equivalent φιλόχρηστος, "loving righteousness."[83] The lament of Palladas notwithstanding, Augustan Victory lived on, altered but essential to the Christian empire of late antiquity.

EX SANGUINE ROMANO TRIUMPHATOR

Statues of Victory were only the most abstract form through which Romans memorialized success in war.[84] Augustus and later *principes* also built more

---

82. See *ILS* 3811, from Lambaesus in North Africa: *Victoriae divinae, Virtutis comiti Auggg., r(es) p(ublica) c(oloniae) L(ambaesitanae)*. See also *CIL* VI 31402–31404, all of which were dedicated by Symmachus as urban prefect: 31402 is a dedication to *Imperator Caesar Dominus noster Flavius Valens Maximus pius felix victor ac triumfator semper Augustus;* 31403 and 31404 are separate dedications to *Victoria Augusta, comes dominorum principumque nostrorum.* Though often invoked in this context, I do not see that the invocation by Himerius *Or.* 65(19).3 of Νίκη χρυσοπτέρυγε, Νίκη Διὸς τοῦ μεγάλου παῖ, εὐπατέρεια καὶ φιλόγελως, has anything to do with Νίκη Σεβαστή.

83. *Anth. Pal.* 16.282, on which see A. D. E. Cameron 1965a, 17. For a contemporary parallel, see Gregory Naz. *Or.* 42.27: Χαῖρε, ὦ μεγαλόπολι καὶ φιλόχριστε.

84. The title of this section alludes to Ammianus 16.10.1: *Constantius quasi cluso Iani templo stratisque hostibus cunctis Romam visere gestiebat post Magnenti exitium absque nomine ex sanguine Ro-*

traditional monuments that commemorated specific victories after the fashion of triumphal art, by representing and narrating the defeat and surrender of a specific enemy. Such representations in their traditional form were proudly imperialist: a defeated barbarian in native garb crouched before the Roman conqueror or fell beneath the wheels of the *triumphator*'s chariot. They also had the potential to arouse considerable discontent among provincial populations, even, perhaps especially, among those not depicted but nevertheless recently conquered. Did Augustus expect Greeks to rejoice when he advertised the conquest of Spain? Were Spaniards asked to rejoice at the recovery of the standards lost by Varus? Could the traditional iconography of victory monuments be altered to evoke not the experience but the benefits of conquest? How did provincials interpret such monuments, quite apart from the meaning they were intended to carry?

Augustus had no one to offend at Rome. In the capital city he was free to boast of the conquests with which he had adorned and enriched the empire. To this end he constructed a portico in his forum that contained representations at the very least of the peoples he had conquered or, perhaps, of all nations subject to Rome at the time of its construction. Much is uncertain; references to it in literature are few. In his description of the shield presented to Aeneas, Vergil described Augustus sitting before the Temple of Apollo acknowledging gifts of *aurum coronarium*.[85] Servius responded to these lines with two comments: first, an explanation of *aurum coronarium*, and, second, a description of the place where Augustus displayed these "gifts":[86]

> *He acknowledged the gifts of the nations:* Vergil refers to *aurum coronarium*, which even today is given to victors by conquered peoples. Generals impose this burden when extending an exemption from tribute. For this reason he writes "gifts"; if he were not referring to *aurum coronarium*, he would have written "spoils."
>
> *He attaches them to the lofty portals:* Augustus built a portico in which he placed representations of all races [*simulacra omnium gentium*]: this portico is called "the Portico to the Nations."

The elder Pliny used the same name for this gallery, "the Portico to the Nations," to situate for his readers a statue of Hercules.[87]

We cannot be certain that these "representations" were Roman *simulacra gentium*, as opposed to Greek abstractions. But that likelihood is greatly in-

---

mano triumphaturus. Cf. 21.16.15, describing the same emperor's *triumphales arcus ex clade provinciarum.*

85. *Aeneid* 8.720–723.
86. Servius on *Aen.* 8.721.
87. Pliny *Nat.* 36.39.

creased by connecting these references to an aside by Velleius Paterculus. According to that historian, "in addition to the Spains and the other nations whose names adorn his forum," Augustus also added Egypt to the empire.[88] Velleius clearly associated the portico with depictions of those regions and races conquered by Augustus. That fact, which alone established their relevance to the Forum of Augustus, would have determined the manner of their depiction. What is more, in the format of this display Augustus had—as so often—a precedent in the boasting of Pompey, who had decorated his theater with fourteen labeled images of nations that he had conquered.[89]

Augustus provided a literary and supremely public complement to these Roman monuments in his *Res gestae;* the litany of names in that document "affirms and proves the direct or indirect completion of the conquest of the *orbis terrarum* in geographical terms."[90] He also left instructions regarding the form of his funeral, to which, if Tacitus reports events correctly, certain amendments may have been made:[91]

> Then there was debate concerning his funeral honors, during which the most notable [proposals] seemed the motion of Asinius Gallus, that the funeral procession should be led through a triumphal arch, and that of Lucius Arruntius, that the titles of the laws that he had passed and the names of the races that he conquered should be borne before him. . . . The senators shouted together that his body should be carried on the shoulders of senators, but Tiberius excused them with arrogant moderation.

While Tacitus concentrates on the debate in the Senate, Cassius Dio provides a description of the ceremony as it was actually performed:[92]

> There was a couch made of ivory and gold, decorated with cloth of purple and gold; his body was hidden within and underneath it, in some sort of box, while a wax image of him in triumphal costume was displayed publicly. This image was brought from the Palatine by the consuls for the next year. Another, of

88. Velleius 2.39.2.

89. Pliny *Nat.* 36.4, and see Suetonius *Nero* 46.1. Pliny elsewhere makes it clear that Pompey did not restrict the decorations solely to items that reflected upon his own achievements (*Nat.* 7.34). On other Pompeian monuments as precedents for Caesar and Augustus, see Weinstock 1971 and Nicolet 1991, 29–56. On Pompey's trophy in the Pyrenees, see below at n. 100.

90. Nicolet 1991, 29; Gruen at *CAH*² X 190.

91. See Suetonius *Augustus* 101 and Tacitus *Ann.* 1.8.3, 5.

92. Dio 56.34.1–3. Dio also mentions that bronze likenesses of the subject *gentes* were carried in the funeral of Pertinax (74.4.5: τὰ ἔθνη πάντα τὰ ὑπήκοα ἐν εἰκόσι χαλκαῖς, ἐπιχωρίως σφίσιν ἐσταλμένα), and these passages are often cited as analogous. I do not see the parallel: Dio specifies that the funeral of Augustus displayed only the images of those nations which Augustus had conquered. Pertinax, on the other hand, had conquered no one; his funeral display boasted rather the diversity of the empire.

gold, was brought from the Curia, and still another was brought on a triumphal chariot. After these images followed those of his ancestors and of his dead relatives—except for that of Caesar, because he had been enrolled among the heroes—as well as images of other Romans who were famous for whatever reason, beginning with Romulus himself: even a likeness of Pompey the Great was seen. All the nations followed, as many as he had acquired, each one represented in some characteristic native fashion.

The procession's use of triumphal art and its passage through a triumphal arch continued to emphasize a strictly Roman imperialist attitude toward those provinces added to the empire in the Augustan age, in a martial fashion befitting the man who, in his own words, "had extended the borders of all those provinces of the Roman people adjacent to which were nations that did not obey our empire."[93] Indeed, the procession was the natural style in which to honor in death a man who in life had been voted the privilege of decorating his house with laurel and oak, as "one who was always conquering the enemies of Rome and saving her citizens."[94]

The format of the funeral did more, however, than merely name Augustus the greatest general in Roman history. Romans customarily displayed the wax images of their famous ancestors in their funerals. Indeed, Romans inculcated the prestige and honor of public service not least by effacing the identities of the living: only those counted whom posterity had judged worthy of commemoration. But these displays, like the funerals themselves, had been memorials for individual families.[95] By displaying images of famous Romans of all families, both here and in his forum, Augustus gave expression to his own vision of Roman history and claimed the culminating position not simply in the history of his family, but in the history of the Roman people as a whole. Nothing less would have been appropriate for the Father of His Country.[96]

We can move a long way toward confirming that Augustus intended his Roman audience to read these monuments with precisely such a narrowly Roman perspective if we return to the advice given by Augustus "to Tiberius

93. Augustus *Res gestae* 26.1 (translation by Brunt and Moore, adapted): *Omnium provinciarum populi Romani quibus finitimae fuerunt gentes quae non parerent imperio nostro fines auxi.* Compare Ovid *Fasti* 1.599–600: *si petat a victis, tot sumet nomina Caesar, quot numero gentes maximus orbis habet.*

94. Dio 53.16.4. Dio wrote merely "enemies," but the juxtaposition of "conquering enemies" and "saving citizens" justifies, I believe, the translation above.

95. Polybius 6.53–54.5. See, for example, the reports of the funeral of Caesar's aunt Julia at Suetonius *Iulius* 6.1 and Plutarch *Caesar* 5.2–5.

96. On the portrait galleries in the Augustan forum see Suetonius *Augustus* 31.5, together with Frier 1979, 196–200; Syme 1986, 79; and Luce 1990. On the power of the title *pater patriae*, see Chapter 9, "The Father of the Human Race."

and the populace" among his final papers.[97] He urged "especially that they should not free too many slaves, lest they fill the city with an indiscriminate mob, and that they not enroll a great many to citizenship, in order that there be a substantial difference between themselves and their subjects." By "fill the city" Augustus intended "fill the city with citizens descended from slaves," since the children of freedmen were automatically enrolled among the citizen body. He therefore lumped slaves and foreign subjects together as a class of humanity that existed to be exploited for the profit and comfort of the citizens of Rome. He had made his priorities clear early in the *Res gestae* when he described his clemency in foreign wars: "When foreign races could safely be spared, I preferred to preserve rather than exterminate them."[98] The safety in question is that of the *res publica populi Romani;* the decision to spare or slaughter came only after considering the safety of one's own kind. Nor does the verb "prefer" suggest that Augustus recognized his decision as a moral one: sparing the vanquished may have been an active good, and therefore deserving of commensurate gifts of *aurum coronarium,* but extermination had always been an option.[99]

Even if Rome had vastly greater armed forces at her disposal than any of her conquered provinces—and this situation surely obtained in the age of Augustus—it seems incredible that the government should advertise such arrogance to its subjects. Rulers at Rome surely possessed the ability, given the practical constraints on interprovincial communication of that day, to address Rome in one fashion and the provinces in another. What do we know of Julio-Claudian monuments in the provinces?

Once again Pompey had set an important precedent. After sweeping through the West "from the Alps to the borders of Further Spain," he built trophies in the Pyrenees on which he listed the names of the 876 communities that he had compelled to surrender.[100] Unlike Pompey, who conducted the war against Sertorius in person, Augustus "pacified the Alps from the region near the Adriatic to that near the Tuscan Sea" in a series of campaigns fought entirely through his legates.[101] When Suetonius wished to

97. Dio 56.33.3, quoted in Chapter 5 at n. 85.

98. Augustus *Res gestae* 3.2 (trans. Brunt and Moore).

99. Indeed, "extermination" was the easy path to a triumph. Since men were seeking triumphs for easy victories, a law was passed requiring five thousand dead in a single battle to earn a triumph. After all, it was not the number but the glory of the triumphs that would distinguish the city. Similarly, generals upon their return had to swear that the numbers reported in their dispatches to the Senate had been accurate (Valerius Maximus 2.8.1).

100. Pliny *Nat.* 3.18, on which see Picard 1957, 183–186. Cf. *Nat* 7.96 and Servius on *Aen.* 11.6 (Sallust *Hist.* 3.89): *CONSTITUIT TUMULO in colle, quia tropaea non figebantur nisi in eminentioribus locis. Sallustius de Pompeio ait, 'de victis Hispanis tropaea in Pyrenaei iugis constituit.'*

101. Augustus *Res gestae* 26.3.

boast that Augustus conducted wars "sometimes by his own leadership and sometimes by his own auspices," he had to qualify this assertion with an admission that Augustus traveled only as far as northern Italy.[102] Nevertheless, to commemorate this deed the Senate and people built a trophy in the Alps; the inscription on that arch survives in the Castello della Turbia and was recorded by the elder Pliny: "To Imperator Caesar Augustus, the son of a god, pontifex maximus, fourteen times acclaimed *imperator,* in the seventeenth year of his tribunician power the Senate and people of Rome dedicate this monument, because under his leadership and auspices [*eius ductu auspiciisque*] all the Alpine nations which extend from the Upper Sea to the Lower were brought under the *imperium* of the Roman people. Alpine nations conquered were: [forty-six names follow]."[103] Although Suetonius describes Augustus's role in the conquest of this territory in the same terms as the monument, he need not have read, or even seen, the arch in the Alps himself. He could have read about it in Pliny's work, or, what is more likely, he could have learned of it from the decree of the Senate that ordered the construction of the arch, whose text undoubtedly circulated widely in Rome at that time.[104] Indeed, insofar as the phrase is entirely formulaic, it may simply have recommended itself as the most obvious and accurate way for a Roman to describe the role of Augustus in the conquest.

The operations of Germanicus in the West under Tiberius provide invaluable information regarding the forces that produced monumental art at Rome and in the provinces during this period, because the *Annales* of Tacitus and a plethora of epigraphical evidence narrate and describe the placement and aspect of the artworks that commemorated the victories on those campaigns. It lay within the prerogative of an army and its commander to erect a trophy on the site of a particularly important or bloody victory: the forces under Germanicus did so twice in the same series of battles in the year 16, after defeating the Cherusci and Arminius.[105] Such a trophy could take many forms, but they were traditionally decorated with the weapons and names of the defeated armies. In gauging the longevity of such trophies, we should not underestimate what several hundred men, trained to build camps, roads, and other structures as well as to fight, could achieve

102. Suetonius *Augustus* 20–21 at 21.1.

103. The text may be found in *EJ* as no. 40 or at Pliny *Nat.* 3.136–137, but is best read with the invaluable and concise commentary by Mommsen at *CIL* V 7817. See also Pomponius Mela 3.11, referring to a victory monument erected in Spain following Augustus's campaigns there.

104. Cf. Horace *Carm.* 4.14.1–6: the Senate and people will honor Augustus with inscriptions and memorials wherever the sun illuminates settled lands.

105. Tacitus *Ann.* 2.18.2 and 22.1, discussed above at nn. 65–66. On those passages and the events they describe see also Picard 1957, 317–328.

when motivated by self-interest.[106] When Ammianus marched through Iraq on Julian's expedition, he encountered physical evidence of Roman attacks on Persia over the previous two and a half centuries, from the invasions of Trajan, Severus, Gordian, and Carus.[107]

Equally important and even more visible to provincial viewers were the triumphal arches built at public expense in Rome and elsewhere on the initiative of the Senate, especially insofar as surviving decrees ordering their construction do not suggest that the artwork on each should be adjusted to reflect their respective local audiences. During the year 19 the Senate voted two arches at Rome, one for Drusus and one for Germanicus, following their successes in A.D. 18 in Europe and Armenia, respectively.[108] By 10 October 19 Germanicus lay dead in Syria. The news reached Rome in early December. To commemorate the young prince, the Senate voted a series of honors. Two different catalogues of those honors have been preserved: a fragmentary copy of the *senatus consultum* that proposed the specific honors, and an account by Tacitus of the motions considered in the Senate during its deliberations. According to Tacitus:[109]

> Honors were devised and decreed to the extent that each man possessed love for Germanicus or talent for flattery: . . . that an ivory statue of him should lead parades at circus games. Added [to these proposals] were arches, to be built at Rome, on the banks of the Rhine, and on Mt. Amanus in Syria, with an inscription recording his accomplishments and the fact that he died in the service of his country. Proposed as well were a sepulchre in Antioch, where he was cremated, and a tribunal at Epidaphne, where he ended his life. It would be difficult for anyone even to count the statues and sites in which he was to be worshiped.

The corresponding sections of the Senate's decree, which survived on bronze in the Spanish province of Baetica, list all these honors in a vastly more wordy fashion. They also preserve the Senate's instructions regarding the decoration and commemorative function of these arches:[110]

> It has pleased the Senate that a marble archway be constructed in the Circus Flaminius . . . with representations of the nations that he conquered, and that

---

106. On the use of the army in imperial and local construction projects, see MacMullen 1959, 214–217; for technical training in the army, see, e.g., *ILS* 7741, a monument to one L. Marius Vitalis, who joined the army to learn a craft, or *ILS* 5795, a famous text on a tunneling project gone awry: the army's engineer ultimately saved the project by encouraging a friendly rivalry between soldiers from the navy and the locally recruited auxiliaries.

107. Ammianus 23.5.7, 24.2.3, 24.5.3, and 24.6.1; cf. 25.8.5 and 21.16.15, on the monuments of Constantius.

108. Tacitus *Ann.* 2.64.

109. Tacitus *Ann.* 2.83.1–2.

110. *Tabula Siarensis,* frag. a (*RS* 37), retaining the reconstruction of line 26 offered by Lebek 1987, 147. On the monuments on the Rhine see Suetonius *Claudius* 1.3 and Dio 55.2.3.

it be inscribed on the front of the arch that the Senate and people of Rome dedicated the monument to the memory of Germanicus Caesar because he defeated the Germans in war. . . . Let there be a third, especially magnificent arch by the Rhine near that tomb which the grieving army of the Roman people started to build for Drusus, the brother of Tiberius Caesar Augustus, our *princeps*, and then finished by permission of the divine Augustus; and on it should be placed a statue of Germanicus Caesar, showing him receiving the standards recovered from the Germans; and let an order be given to those Gauls and Germans who live beyond the Rhine, whose communities were commanded by the divine Augustus to perform religious rites at the tomb of Drusus, to the effect that they should perform a similar sacrifice every year on that day on which Germanicus died; and, as often as an army of the Roman people is in that region on the very day of the sacrifice or on the birthday of Germanicus Caesar, let it pass through the arch that is built in accordance with this decree of the Senate.

It would be difficult to imagine a decree better suited to remind provincials of the "great gulf" with which Augustus had wished to separate citizen and subject. Although the tribes ordered to perform sacrifices before the statues of Drusus and Germanicus are not themselves subjects, the ritual, resembling so closely the veneration given to standards and imperial portraits in diplomatic meetings, must have reminded those who were subjects of the moment when they had capitulated and, as thanks for being given the option to surrender, had been assigned to pay a gift to the Roman *dux*.

THE RECEPTION OF IMPERIAL ARTWORK IN THE PROVINCES

The search for provincial responses to imperial artwork is fraught with danger. Excitement at apparent replicas of imperial commissions is tempered by ignorance: we can be fairly confident that people saw public statuary, but a statue without a base yields no information about its donor. Was the individual a Roman citizen living in the provinces? Or was it a provincial aristocrat paving his way into the corridors of power? Was it commissioned by a town's council, its dedication a partial payment on an imperial benefaction? We should also distinguish between provinces conquered long ago and those recently seized. Aggregate data on the evolution of urban space and public art in the early empire are now readily available, but we should be cautious of attempts to explain the spread of Roman forms on aesthetic grounds.[111] Why should a Roman aesthetic have appealed to so many different populations? The answer that "the leading families in each city . . . were those who

---

111. MacDonald 1982 and 1986 and Zanker 1988 provide exemplary, complementary surveys.

contributed most to the ruler cult and also profited most from it" is insufficient.[112] Among other things, it presupposes a largely political role for ruler cult. Even then, that conclusion is possible only because our evidence for individual participation in the cult springs from that class of men who could afford to erect enduring memorials. What is required instead is a clearer understanding of the ideological complex in which imperial artwork was produced, viewed, and imitated. For example, the martial imagery of much Roman art undoubtedly aroused some resentment among provincials, but that resentment will have been substantially tempered among those who ceded to Rome the right to govern themselves and their world.

Among the iconographic repertoire of imperial art, *simulacra gentium* might seem most unlikely candidates for imitation in the provinces. And yet, they would have become familiar to audiences throughout the provinces very early in their contact with Rome. Furthermore, the victory monuments that carried this imagery spoke precisely of prowess that no provincial could question, that formed the basis of Roman claims to divine favor. Triumphal art was on those grounds uniquely suited to widespread reception and manipulation from below.

Let us start with Italy. The decree of Pisa in response to the death of Gaius Caesar in A.D. 4 did more than identify local with Roman interests. The city also consciously decided to honor the dead prince with Roman monuments. This fact emerges from the discrepancies between the honors voted to Gaius and those voted two years earlier to Lucius Caesar. At that time the city had decreed that an altar be built at public expense and that its magistrates, dressed in the Gabine manner, should sacrifice a black bull and ram on that altar every year.[113] In A.D. 4, however, Pisa proceeded in a very different fashion: the decurions and colonists designated the day of Gaius's death unfit for public activity, using the same language extant in later, Flavian municipal laws, and they agreed "that an arch should be erected in the most public place of our colony, decorated with the spoils of those races whom he conquered or who surrendered unconditionally to him [*spoleis devictarum aut in fidem receptarum ab eo gentium*]; above the arch shall stand a statue of him on foot in triumphal dress [*triumphali ornatu*], and on either side shall stand statues of Gaius and Lucius Caesar on horseback, gilt with gold."[114] Pisa clearly wrote this document in reaction to an announcement of honors voted at Rome, honors closely resembling those voted to Germanicus fifteen years later. The reference in this decree to "races whom he conquered or who surrendered unconditionally to him," in the distinc-

---

112. Zanker 1988, 332.

113. *EJ* no. 68 (*ILS* 139), ll. 15–26. On the use of Gabine dress to signify a rite's putative foreign origin see Valerius Maximus 1.1.11 and Wissowa 1912, 417, and cf. Scheid 1995.

114. *EJ* no. 69 (*ILS* 140), ll. 34–37.

tive language of Roman politics, must also have been influenced by such a document.

Where would Pisa acquire spoils from earlier campaigns with which to decorate its arch? It is possible, of course, that "spoils" here stands for "representations of spoils." But Latin was perfectly capable of expressing that idea. The collocation of the reference to spoils and the insistence that Gaius be depicted in triumphal garb strongly suggests that Pisa had received an official announcement of Gaius's victories in Gaul in 8 B.C. or of his imperatorial acclamations in A.D. 1 and 3, or both.[115] It also suggests the possibility that those announcements had been accompanied by select images copied from panels in the capital and perhaps even by objects seized from the enemies of Rome.[116]

These sentiments among the elite at Pisa mirror similar trends throughout Italy. On the opposite coast from Pisa, at Potentia in Picenum, someone or some group of people dedicated a duplicate of the famous Tarentine Victory at Rome. The people of Potentia carefully recorded that the statue had been given by the Senate and people, and its shield, like its model, catalogued the virtues of their *princeps*.[117] Other towns reproduced Roman monuments that suggested an identification with Rome at an even deeper level: the city of Salvia reproduced the *fasti triumphales*, and Arretium, in eastern Etruria, must have devoted fantastic efforts to reproducing the statues and biographies of noble Romans from the portrait gallery in the Forum of Augustus.[118] These latter cities sought to create a history of themselves as communities that was in harmony with the peculiar version of the Roman past that Augustus was promulgating at Rome. Indeed, to some extent they simply adopted Roman history as their history, and Roman victories as their victories. It may well be that it was the revisionist nature of the Augustan narrative that allowed these communities to discover, as it were, the aspects that they shared.[119] If it is correct to say that a large measure of the internal pressure on the Republican system came about because the oligarchic government at Rome failed to satisfy either the basic demands of the rural populations of Italy, from which the army was by then primarily recruited, or the ambitions of aristocrats from Italian municipalities, from whose stock Octavian himself had sprung, then a large measure of the

115. An acclamation for Drusus in A.D. 3 is well attested; for the possibility of another in A.D. 1 see Syme, *RP* 3.1205.

116. See further Chapter 7, "The Art of Victory."

117. *ILS* 82: the name or names of the dedicator or dedicators is or are lost. On the shield, see Augustus *Res gestae* 34.2.

118. On Salvia, see *AÉ* 1926, 121. On Arretium, see *ILS* 50–60, with Dessau's notes and introduction.

119. On Augustus's forum as historical museum, see Zanker 1988, 211–215, and Luce 1990.

credit for the success of the Augustan principate must surely lie in its culti-
vation of those two constituencies, beginning already with Octavian's mobi-
lization of public opinion against Antony in the years before Actium.[120] The
enthusiasm of Italian communities for Augustus and his vision of their role
in Roman history may then be readily understood.

Italy was not the provinces, some will counter. They would do well to remember that Italy had risen in revolt in Caesar's lifetime. Indeed, its gradual unification must have provided many lessons for Romans seeking to
pacify the provinces.[121] When, therefore, we turn to the provincials and
their artistic commissions, there are reasons to think their loyalism sincere,
and reasons to hold it suspect. Obviously we should not discount the role
that self-interest must have played in public displays of patriotism in every
region of the empire. And yet, the advent of the Principate had radically
changed the nature of Roman administration, and there is every reason to
believe that the change was both noticed and welcomed.[122] For example,
despite Augustus's revealing to Cyrene and all the provinces "how much
care he and the Senate took that none of their subjects suffers any wrong or
exaction," the prosecution of Roman officials for extortion continued during the first century, although it is worth noting that governors of public
provinces were indicted proportionately more often than were imperial
legates.[123] In spite of this, literary reflections on the nature of Roman government suggest that provincial administration became substantially less
corrupt and the provinces correspondingly more affluent in the first centuries of this era. The discrepancy between those reflections and the reality
of the extortion courts may simply confirm that the reorganization of
provincial administration under a professional hierarchy, supervised by the
princeps, produced greater efficiency and increased honesty, at least in the
imperial provinces. But the discrepancy can surely also be explained by sus-
ceptibility to the promises of the Cyrene Edict.[124]

In addition, beginning with the principate of Augustus, local communities desirous of improving their material infrastructure frequently were able
to acquire assistance in such tasks from the imperial government. In exchange for a suitably phrased request, accompanied by an appropriate display of flattery—putting portraits of the emperor's family on local coinage
was the most popular choice, followed by renaming months in the local calendar or similar acts, while renaming one's city was far more assertive, or

120. See Syme 1939 and Brunt 1988.
121. On Italy see David 1996, esp. 99–181, and Tarpin in *Integration* 2.1–70.
122. See Chapter 5, "Augustus as Augustan Author," on the so-called Fifth Cyrene Edict.
123. For the data see Brunt 1990, 153–195, and Millar 1977, 443–445.
124. On the public perception of the emperor as policeman over his officials, see Chapter 9, "The Emperor and His Subordinates."

sycophantic—the emperor would help to finance the cost of building projects, usually by issuing temporary exemptions from taxation, and might aid in the construction by supplying Roman technical support staff.[125] In this way "the wealth of Rome's subjects was in part, and sometimes very magnificently, restored to them."[126] Within such a system of exchange, the line between sycophancy and gratitude cannot be drawn so easily; indeed, when the rewards for the former could be immediate and generous, it may not be profitable to draw the line all.

Pisa's decree attributes the dedication of its arch and establishing of its holidays to the municipality as a whole. But many such monuments, in both Italy and the provinces, were built through the initiative of individuals who were attempting to further their own careers.[127] Knowing this, or suspecting this, should not overly determine our appreciation of them; allowing it to do so would confuse cause with effect. Even a cynical reading of motives must admit the continuing importance and subtle alteration of classical euergetism, which now demanded that people of wealth display their influence and power by directing imperial benefactions toward their community.[128] A special category of such individuals were imperial officials, who now more than ever tended to hold their posts in a particular area for many years. Not a few settled down in the communities that had flattered them while they held power.[129] Pliny's request to Trajan for permission to build a gallery of imperial portraits illustrates some of these trends:[130]

125. For the renaming of cities as Juliopolis see Hanson 1980b. For alterations to the local calendar see Scott 1931a and esp. Hanson 1984a.

126. For general studies see MacMullen 1959, 207; Millar 1977, 420–434; and Zanker 1988, 323–333. Mitchell 1987a catalogues and analyzes imperial building projects in the eastern provinces, asking of each project what it received from the emperor, whether money, raw materials, or expertise.

127. See Hanson 1989 on "the apparent vigor with which Nemesion," a relatively well-to-do resident of Egyptian Philadelphia in the first century A.D., "identified his own interests with collecting the tax levies for Rome and the advantage he took of the prerogative of his office," and cf. Hanson 1992 on the privileges extended by Romans to dwellers in large cities. Nemesion, alas, seems to have done little to benefit Philadelphia. Cf. Strabo 14.5.14 on Boethius of Tarsus, with Lassère 1982, 876–877.

128. C. Jones 1978, 104–114, is an exemplary treatment of Dio Chrysostom's benefactions. For the scale and economic impact of civic euergetism in the first two centuries A.D., see Duncan-Jones 1974; Sartre 1991, 147–166; Mitchell 1993, 1:206–211; and Jacques at *Integration* 1.324–330.

129. See Robert, *Hellenica* 4.60–76; Reynolds 1982, 156–164; Mitchell 1993, 1:66; and cf. Cicero *Ep. ad Q. fratrem* 1.1.31. On donations in Spain, see Mangas 1971, breaking down known benefactors by legal rank. For benefactions by procurators in Africa, see Duncan-Jones 1974, 81 n. 24, and cf. 1982, 63–119. Haensch 1997 collects honorific texts thanking imperial officials for benefactions to local communities, province by province: see "Dokumentation," B III 4.

130. Pliny *Ep.* 10.8.1.

> Since your divine father, Lord, encouraged euergetism among all citizens in
> his beautiful speech and by his honorable example, I asked of him that I
> be permitted to transfer to the local municipality a set of imperial portraits
> that I inherited through several bequests and have kept, as I received them,
> on a far-off estate. I also asked permission to include a statue of himself
> among them.

Trajan assented, and Pliny arranged with the town that it should provide a
site on which he would construct a temple to house the portraits. Although
Pliny directed his benefaction toward an Italian *municipium*, he appealed to
the example and encouragement of Nerva, just as Paullus Fabius Persicus
cited the example of Claudius when declaring his devotion to the welfare of
Ephesus: [131]

> At the urging of Tiberius Claudius Caesar Augustus Germanicus, Paullus
> Fabius Persicus has declared this edict beneficial to the city of the Ephesians
> and to the whole province; he published it in Ephesus and ordered that it be
> inscribed on a column on the fifth day before the Kalends of April: Being my-
> self of the opinion that, above all, magistrates in charge of provinces should
> perform the duties of the office entrusted to them with all care and honesty,
> in such a way that they take thought for the perpetual and lifelong advantage
> of the province as a whole and of each city, and not merely for the year in which
> they hold office, I nevertheless acknowledge that I have been drawn to this be-
> lief by the example of the most powerful and most truly just *imperator*, who has
> received the entire human race into his personal care.

In Pliny's case, the specific act he envisioned—the creation of a temple to
past and present emperors—reveals the complex dynamic that allowed the
emperor, at no cost to himself, to encourage the generosity of others and so
to foster the culture of loyalism that supported his rule: those benefactors
could modestly allow that they were simply following his lead and through
displays of loyalty seek to further their own careers.

Once erected, portrait galleries and arches affected their viewers in ways
not necessarily related to the motives and aspirations of their donors. Pliny
and Persicus may have hoped to earn the favor of Trajan and Claudius, but
the ultimate beneficiaries of their actions were the cities and people who received and enjoyed the buildings, temples, and works of art that they endowed. What is more, many contingencies may have governed the sentiments in municipalities toward both benefactor and benefaction in the
immediate aftermath of the donation. Yet it is almost inevitable that local
residents would slowly have relinquished their feelings of the moment and,
through happenstance gazing on Pliny's museum, have replaced those feel-

---

131. Smallwood, *Gaius* no. 380 (*SEG* IV 516), col. 2, ll. 1–15.

ings with a mildly heightened awareness of the history of their empire and of their place in it.

In the long-conquered province of Africa, for example, we know of no local protest aroused by the erection of a series of altars modeled on the Ara Pacis at Rome; one of those altars was devoted to the local cult of the *gens Augusta* and was established by an imperial freedman, one P. Perelius Hedulus.[132] We do not know whether the city of Arelate or an individual funded the local placement of a copy of the statue of Victory and the Shield of Augustus—along with a copy of the text that the Senate attached to the original—but its dedication passed without incident.[133] The Augustan age witnessed an explosion of construction throughout the empire; the influence of all this building on civic centers in Gaul and Spain was particularly acute, since those areas lacked indigenous traditions of urban architecture on a Roman scale.[134] For example, as Jonathan Edmondson has shown, native urban centers in Lusitania did not immediately wither under Roman rule. Rather, the Romans promoted an ambitious program of monumentalization in colonies like Augusta Emerita, whose forum and temples mirrored those at Rome itself, and those colonies then served as models for urban projects elsewhere in their provinces.[135]

Roman influence in Greece must be measured differently. On one estimation, Rome's major contributions to Greek architecture were the aqueduct and Roman cement, and, to be sure, it would be difficult to underestimate the positive impression that the introduction of a stable, clean water supply could have made on living conditions in urban areas throughout the East.[136] But such analyses, predicated upon simplistic views of cross-cultural contact, were dismissed two thousand years ago by Strabo: Greeks and Romans in his day lived in their respective cities differently, and he proudly noted that some Romans found Greek urbanism to their taste.[137] Rome contributed to already developed urban centers not so much through the sudden construction of new buildings, but through a slow transformation of

132. See the report in *CRAI* 1913, no. 680; the text is reproduced as *EJ* no. 135. Cf. Strong at *CAH* X 552, or Zanker 1988, 313–315.

133. *EJ* no. 22.

134. Gros 1976 provides an exemplary analysis of what was Augustan in Augustan temple architecture. On general trends in the West in the reign of Augustus see Gros 1981, 42, and Mierse 1990.

135. Edmondson 1990; cf. Woolf 1998, 106–141.

136. Waelkens 1989. See also Macready and Thompson 1987 and Dodge 1990.

137. See Strabo 5.4.7 on Roman fondness for τὴν ἐν Νεαπόλει διαγωγὴν τὴν Ἑλληνικήν. He continues, with revealing diction: καὶ τῶν Ῥωμαίων δ᾽ ἔνιοι χαίροντες τῷ βίῳ τούτῳ, θεωροῦντες τὸ πλῆθος τῶν ἀπὸ τῆς αὐτῆς ἀγωγῆς ἐπιδημούντων ἀνδρῶν, ἄσμενοι φιλοχωροῦσι καὶ ζῶσιν αὐτόθι.

the nature of urban life in general and, above all, through a gradual reorientation in popular conceptions of the role and functioning of cities and smaller urban centers.[138] The government, in the form of specific emperors endowing specific buildings, aided that process by creating a new style of urban planning, whose features were clearly laid in the Augustan age but came to fruition over a period of centuries.[139]

Gallia Narbonensis stood out among the western provinces for the length of its contact with Rome and for the favor it received from Augustus and his house.[140] Augustus signaled his satisfaction with its loyalty and stability in 22 B.C. when he transferred control of Narbonensis and Cyprus to the Senate "because they no longer required his soldiers."[141] Augustus himself took charge of the census of Narbonensis at this time, and during his visits to the province over the next two decades first Agrippa and then Augustus himself received credit for laying roads, designing aqueducts, and paying for city walls.[142] In this process Augustus must have finalized boundaries of every sort, both between the territories of individual cities and between Narbonensis and its neighbors.[143] To mark these boundaries Augustus and his subordinates deployed a series of monuments, triumphal arches within the province and trophies on its frontiers.[144] The arches undoubtedly commemorated some unique feature of the relationship between a given community and Augustus; alas, most of the arches in Narbonensis no longer preserve their dedicatory texts. Their decorative figures do, however, preserve the imagery of captives and conquest that marked Augustan monuments at Rome.[145] The arches must have sent a mixed message, arousing memories of the process of Roman conquest while providing material evidence of Rome's willingness to recognize and reward loyalty. The trophies, furthermore, addressed people on both sides of the border: this province has been and will continue to be protected by the might of Roman arms. Provincials and others could make of that message what they willed.

Is it possible to move beyond purely negative evidence for the impact made by Roman triumphal art in the provinces—that no one vandalized

138. See MacDonald 1986, 248–273; Rogers 1991, 80–135; Mitchell 1993, 1:198–199 and 216–217; Gros 1996; and Walker 1997.

139. MacDonald 1986, Mitchell 1987b.

140. On Gaul under Roman rule see Raepsaet-Charlier in *Integration* 143–195.

141. Dio 54.4.1: ὡς μηδὲν τῶν ὅπλων αὐτοῦ δεομένας.

142. Goudineau at *CAH*² X 474–487.

143. Cf. Edmondson 1992/93, 26–30.

144. Gros 1979, 83; Küpper-Böhm 1996.

145. See Mierse 1990, 318–322, and Küpper-Böhm 1996, 19–20 and 121–128, with plate 22 no. 2 and plate 23 nos. 2–4. Cf. Gros 1979, 83, expressing dissatisfaction with then existing explanations for the iconographic programs of the Narbonnensian arches, on the grounds that their programs seem too likely to have caused resentment among the Gauls.

the ubiquitous arches and trophies, or tore them down in protest—to find evidence of a willingness among provincials to view such art from a Roman perspective? In a sense we have already done so. The seeming significance of the truism that no Greek or Latin author of the empire save Marcus Aurelius was born at Rome has distracted attention from its corollary, that all literature of the empire save the *Meditations* was written by provincials, who came to view the history of their conquerors as their own and who viewed the distribution of political power in the Roman world as participants in the dominant ideology of its ruling power. The success of Augustus in demilitarizing Gallia Narbonensis raised the hope that the distribution of the trophies and arches along the Rhine could eventually appeal to the residents of Germania as the trophy near Lugdunum Convenarum appealed to the citizens of Narbonensis to its east.

Three very different monuments of the Augustan age reveal the sophisticated ways in which residents of the provinces adapted the iconography of the Roman triumph to justify and to display their faith in the imperial government. First, in A.D. 17 an earthquake shook the cities of Lydia: in gratitude for Roman aid, the cities dedicated a statue group in the Forum of Julius Caesar at Rome. The group contained personifications of each of the cities, surrounding a colossal statue of Tiberius himself. Two more statues, those of Phrygian Cibyra and Ephesus, were added later, as those cities, too, received imperial aid. The portrait group was probably destroyed when the forum burned in A.D. 80, but already in the reign of Tiberius the Augustales at Puteoli had arranged to copy the entire group of personifications on the base of a statue of Tiberius.[146] They are presumed to have done so because Puteoli had strong commercial ties to the cities in question. These cities had well-developed iconographies for their own representation, and it is probable that they sent terracotta models to Rome when they commissioned the statue group.[147] Their use of personifications is not, therefore, in itself surprising. It is, however, notable that when the mint at Rome struck a coin to celebrate the restoration of the cities of Asia, it depicted Tiberius as he appeared in the cities' dedication, as a god, laureate rather than radiate, just as the Augustales with their statue worshiped rather than honored their emperor.[148]

Second, sometime early in the Julio-Claudian period one family at

---

146. The earthquakes and the Roman response are described most fully by Tacitus *Ann.* 2.47 and 4.13.1; but see also Strabo 13.4.8, Velleius 2.126.4, Seneca *Nat.* 6.1.13, Pliny *Nat.* 2.200, Suetonius *Tiberius* 48.2, and Dio 47.17.7. On the portrait base from Puteoli see *ILS* 156 and J. Toynbee 1934, 122–123.

147. Vermeule 1981.

148. *BMC* I, Tiberius nos. 70–73. On the interpretation of the datives in *ILS* 156 see Veyne 1962, 68.

Aphrodisias made itself known to members of the imperial house; the exchange of flattery for pleasantries eventually resulted in a grant of citizenship from Claudius to a member of that family. Perhaps through the efforts of its best-attested member, one Tiberius Claudius Diogenes, that family built an elaborate temple complex in honor of Augustus and the royal house. It included two distinctly different types of statuary: first, a portrait gallery of members of the *domus divina,* and, second, a remarkable set of representations of provinces and peoples, depicted in precisely the sort of identifying ethnic garb that featured so prominently in triumphal art.[149] The first publications on the *simulacra gentium* and their accompanying bases already compared them to Roman triumphal art and suggested that the particular items chosen for inclusion had all featured in victories under Augustus.[150] The selection must therefore have drawn upon information distributed from Rome. The use of Roman personifications must likewise have been influenced by Roman images. Nor need anyone have traveled to Rome to view triumphal art: painted panels might well have accompanied the bulletins that allowed Aphrodisians to compile a list of Augustan campaigns.

But the artists at Aphrodisias did not mindlessly replicate Roman originals. In his publication of the statuary R. R. R. Smith made the important observation that the "iconography of the surviving *ethnos* and island reliefs . . . [does] not stress the iconography of defeat."[151] Yet the people of Aphrodisias and the artists who crafted the Sebasteum knew full well the appearance of Roman *simulacra:* a triumphal relief celebrating the conquest of Britain depicts Claudius in heroic garb, weapon raised, threatening to strike a suppliant native.[152] The artist of the *ethnos* gallery and his patron evidently divided the world into two categories. The Britons, then the object of Roman campaigns, were not yet members of the civilized world. But the other reliefs clearly indicate a choice not to celebrate Augustan conquest as such, but rather to depict the other members of the political universe of which Aphrodisias and all the East were now one part.

The third monument is the altar from a temple to Augustus founded at Lugdunum late in the second decade B.C.[153] Neither the temple nor the al-

---

149. On the portrait gallery see Reynolds 1980; *idem* 1986; and Smith 1987. On the *simulacra gentium* see Reynolds 1981, 323–327, Erim 1982, and Smith 1988. See also Rose 1997a, 163–169, whose work places the Aphrodisian Sebasteum in an empirewide context of vastly greater scope and accuracy than before. On the family of Tiberius Claudius Diogenes, see Reynolds 1981, 317–322.

150. Reynolds 1981, 327, discusses not the statues as such, but only the statue bases.

151. Smith 1987, 59.

152. Erim 1982, 279–280.

153. Crook at *CAH²* X 98 has advanced the theory that the *Ara Galliarum* was dedicated in 10 B.C., rather than the traditional date of 12, for which see Gruen, Goudineau, and Rüger at *CAH²* X 181, 493, and 524, respectively. The ancient evidence may be briefly quoted. See Livy

tar is extant, but Strabo wrote about the latter in his report on Lugdunum in Book 4 of his *Geography*: "The Temple to Caesar Augustus that was built by all of Gaul cooperatively stands before the city [of Lugdunum] at the confluence of the rivers [the Rhône and Arar]. There is in addition a remarkable altar, which has an inscription with the names of the *ethne*, sixty in number, as well as images of them, one for each *ethnos;* there is also a large statue of Augustus."[154] We can be fairly confident that these tribes did not have a tradition of differentiating themselves within their larger corporate identity using statues that distinguished each tribe by its idiosyncratic garb, craft, or crop. Indeed, their corporate identity was itself an artificial imposition of their Roman overlords. The people who designed the altar must have looked to Rome for an appropriate vehicle through which to express their loyalty toward Augustus. They settled on an altar and cult to his *genius*. But they also wished to declare their allegiance both as members of a province and as individual ethnic groups. They found the means to achieve that end within Roman triumphal art, scarcely two generations after Julius Caesar had swept through Gaul. Even if the altar was erected by a wealthy elite in order to flatter their Roman overlords, the provincials' ability to transform an image intimately informed by the iconography of defeat into one celebrating unification speaks volumes about the depth to which Roman idealism about relations between individual political groups and the *imperium Romanum* had already penetrated. It was, sadly, an idealism that in their lifetime found a readier audience in Gaul than in Rome.

HOW TO APPEAL TO A PROVINCE

Some eighty years passed before an official artwork of the Roman government adopted this revolutionary use of geographical personifications, and its use at that time reflected a temporary fluctuation in the relationship between governors, armies, and local populations. Although it is axiomatic that the government desired the good will of the provincials, the governors and generals who revolted against Nero in 68 and fought with each other throughout 69 desired that good will with an altogether new sense of urgency. They recognized, even if modern historians have not, the impor-

---

Per. 139 (*ara dei Caesaris ad confluentem Araris et Rhodani dedicata, sacerdote creato C. Iulio Vercondaridubno Aeduo*), Suetonius *Claudius* 2.1 (*Claudius natus est Iullo Antonio Fabio Africano coss. Kal. Aug. Luguduni eo ipso die quo primum ara ibi Augusto dedicata est*), and cf. Dio 54.32.1.

154. Strabo 4.3.2. The translation above follows Tyrwhitt's emendation to καὶ ἄλλος ⟨Καίσαρος⟩ μέγας. W. Aly's (Bonn, 1972) may be even more attractive: καὶ ναὸς μέγας, "there is also a large temple." Lassère (Paris, 1966) and Sbordone (Rome, 1970) retain the paradosis, which seems to me unacceptable. For the history of the imperial cult of *Tres Galliae,* see Fishwick 1970 and 1978.

tance of obtaining the cooperation of local populations when campaigning within the borders of the empire. Many of the usurpers in that long year used their coinage to address their troops; the army received vast donatives during this period, and it was through the army that most coin must initially have circulated. But some usurpers spoke to their provincials, too, and for that they adopted a symbolic language that provincials would understand and appreciate.

Galba was acclaimed by his troops on 2 April, A.D. 68. He had only one legion under his control. He rapidly raised another, the Seventh, which was named the "Spanish" and nicknamed "Galbian" until it was reconstituted in 70 by Vespasian, who gave it formal status and consecrated its standards on 10 June.[155] At approximately the same time Clodius Macer, legate of the Third Legion in North Africa, broke with Nero. He, too, recruited a new legion, which he called I Macriana Liberatrix. Macer struck coins at Carthage with which to pay his two legions. Of his most common reverse types, one advertised his control over the sea and resultant control over the grain supply of Rome. Others honored his legions: an eagle paired with two standards, with the legends LEGIO I MACRIANA and LEGIO III AUGUSTA. Galba likewise exploited military themes, early, often, and throughout his brief reign. He did so, however, by reference to the renaissance of Roman military might and without specific reference to individual legions.[156] Later writers credited Galba with old-fashioned severity or with impolitic parsimony. In practical terms, this described his unwillingness to flatter the legions, and his consequent loss of their loyalty.

Yet neither Clodius Macer nor Galba controlled overwhelming military force. Neither could afford the disapprobation of the provinces whence they drew their strength. They both must have issued coin to pay for supplies: forced exactions at too high a level could have induced cities to shut their gates as Aquileia would before Maximinus Thrax two centuries later. Clodius Macer therefore issued two coins with his familiar legionary reverses and obverses depicting not himself, but Africa—a draped bust wearing an elephantskin headdress.[157] Macer also occupied Carthage, but he seems to have done so peacefully. In any event, he issued a further coin associating his person with that city: its reverse carried a bust of Carthage before a cornucopia, with a legend dedicated to L. Clodius Macer at Carthage.[158] Rome had already been suffering a shortage of grain prior to

---

155. For its later name, see *AÉ* 1972, 203. For its earlier nickname, see Tacitus *Hist.* 2.86.2.
156. *BMC* I, Clodius Macer nos. 1–4. *BMC* I, Galba nos. 25–28 (Rome), 77–84 and 87–108 (Rome and Gaul), 178–189 (Spain).
157. *BMC* I, Clodius Macer class 2(a) and (b), with Mattingly's notes on 286.
158. *BMC* I, Clodius Macer no. 5.

Nero's death, and its populace turned their anger toward Macer. As cooperation with Galba became less and less likely, Macer may have struck a coin seeking to earn support for himself in Spain: the mint at Carthage struck a denarius in 68 carrying a bust of Spain, with the legend HISPANIA. No mark identifies its association with Macer, and its inspiration and audience must remain a mystery.[159]

Galba, too, asked for the loyalty and support of his province. Among his earliest issues are numbered coins with a personification of Hispania, not kneeling before a conqueror but alone, with sheaves of grain, two javelins, and the round shield characteristic of the Spanish auxiliaries.[160] Even earlier the Spanish mint had issued a coin advertising solidarity with Gaul, bearing a legend boasting of the "Concord of the Spanish and Gallic Provinces," together with busts of Hispania and Gallia, separated by that eminently imperial symbol, a Victory standing on a globe.[161] It remains unclear whether Galba intended to support the candidacy of Vindex, whether Vindex sought Galba's support by suggesting his candidacy, or whether they merely agreed on a mutual hatred of Nero. The lack of a name on the Spanish coins of early 68 could have signaled anachronistic Republicanism to an audience at Rome. Nameless coins certainly could not offend either Spain or Gaul by putting forward either Vindex or Galba and thereby precluding the other.[162] The death of Nero on 9 June and the subsequent humility of the Praetorians gave the Senate the courage to claim its prerogative.[163] Their vote for Galba gave the courage and initiative he had lacked. He now issued coins boasting of the joint support of Gaul and Spain, with his own name and title proudly on the obverse.[164] He also began to strike coins honoring Spain, Gaul, and the Three Gauls, from all the mints under his control.[165]

The motivation for Galba's Hispania coins arose under a specific nexus of forces. Vespasian's triumph over Judaea suggested that little if anything had changed in the Roman elite's attitudes toward the provinces, at least insofar as they presented themselves in the capital city. And, indeed, nothing about Vespasianic propaganda elsewhere suggested a change in mentality at the top. We have already reviewed the triumphs staged by Titus in the cities of the East, following his final victory over the Jews in A.D. 70, and consid-

159. *BMC* I, Civil Wars no. 15.
160. *BMC* I, Galba nos. 161–163.
161. Smallwood, *Gaius* no. 72c = *MW* no. 26.
162. For Galba and Vindex, see Syme, *RP* 4.124–125.
163. Griffin 1984, 182.
164. *BMC* I, Galba nos. 170 and 171 (Spain) and 228 (Gaul); and cf. 1, 2, 164, and 216, CONCORDIA PROVINCIARUM.
165. *BMC* I, Galba nos. 14–18, 172–175, 206, 207, 211–214, and 228.

ered the reaction it drew from the citizens in Antioch. Titus may have expected the cities in the East to rejoice with him in his triumphal display; on the other hand, he may simply have been delivering a lecture on the consequences of disobedience. In any event, a triumph over disobedient subjects was hardly an appropriate vehicle with which to unify the provinces. Thus the people of Antioch studied the symbolism of Titus's *adventus* and drew the obvious conclusion that the Romans would soon punish the Jews everywhere. Their request for immediate sanctions against the Jews at Antioch forced Titus to reject a petition that harmonized with the ideological implications of his own ceremony. At Rome, Domitian continued to employ traditional *simulacra gentium* in his double triumph over the Chatti and the Dacians in A.D. 89, after which Dacia became a client kingdom. Even forty years after the revolutionary coins of 68, the Spaniard Trajan so thoroughly absorbed an anachronistic sense of imperialist grandeur that he would likely have used a similar means of representing his foes on his column had that monument celebrated a victory over rebellious provincials instead of commemorating his victories in the Dacian wars.[166]

Much changed in the forty years that followed the death of Domitian. In the course of his long reign Hadrian changed the nature of imperial ideology on several fronts: the roots of his actions lie deep within the character of this most inscrutable emperor. Trajan, too, had been born in Spain, but not without reason was he called "the last of the Romans."[167] Hadrian had served a long and exemplary career in the army: legate of three different legions under Domitian, he served as quaestor to Trajan in Dacia in 101, after which he returned to Rome to act as secretary for the Senate, then tribune of the plebs, then praetor, in a three-year span. Returning to the army immediately thereafter, he served as legate of still a different legion before taking up the governorship of Pannonia Inferior. He returned to Rome to hold a suffect consulate in 108 before traveling east with Trajan for that emperor's Parthian expedition, at which time he also served as legate of Syria.[168] Hadrian's experience with the folly of Trajan's Parthian campaign left him profoundly ambivalent toward military conquest and the acquisition of new territories: he allowed himself to be acclaimed *imperator* only at the end of the Jewish War in 134, an abrupt change from Trajan's thirteen

166. On artwork from the triumphs of Domitian and Trajan, see J. Toynbee 1934, 9 and 22–23, and Brilliant 1963, 110–117. Cf. Trajan's strict reasoning at Pliny *Ep.* 10.50: *nec te moveat, quod lex dedicationis nulla reperitur, cum solum peregrinae civitatis capax non sit dedicationis, quae fit nostro iure.*

167. Cf. Syme 1958, 248–249, and *RP* 6.157–191.

168. Biographical information reconstructed from his career inscription in Athens (*ILS* 308, for which Dessau's notes are invaluable). See also Syme, *RP* 2.617–628 and 4.310, as well as Kienast 1990, 128–131.

acclamations. According to that measure of achievement, Hadrian in more than two decades merely equaled the record of the civilian Nerva's sixteen months on the throne.

Hadrian signaled his *ungeheure Umwälzung* most memorably when he refused to keep the territories acquired by Trajan on that last campaign.[169] For this he came under heavy criticism: realizing his own shortcomings, some said, he masked as policy a poisonous jealousy for his predecessor.[170] His long and successful career in the army and continued interest in military discipline give the lie to such accusations. The truth is quite different. Here, as elsewhere, the anonymous fourth-century author of the *Libellus de vita et moribus imperatorum* shows a fascinating independence of judgment: he marvels at the fantastic energy required to tour the provinces on foot, to inspect the legions, and to restore the cities: "Varied of mood, complex in personality, with a many-faceted intellect, he was born a ruler over the virtues and vices that plague other men. Ruling the impulse of his mind by some talent, unaccustomed to praise, he artfully concealed a character at once grudging, sad, and mischievous; putting on a mask of modesty, facility, and clemency, he concealed a passion for glory with which he burned."[171]

Hadrian reached Rome on 9 July 118.[172] After cohabiting with the Senate for three years, he left for a tour of the western provinces. Over the next thirteen years he visited much of the empire, inspecting and organizing its resources, surveying its frontiers, and devising economical means for its defense.[173] These travels made a profound impression on contemporaries—the hostile Fronto suggested that Hadrian on his travels had littered the cities of Europe and Asia with the gravestones of his victims[174]—and his vis-

---

169. See Stadter 1980, 135–144, reconstructing Arrian's reactions to and history of the Parthian expedition. More generally, see Syme, *RP* 3.1436–1446; Brunt 1990a, 473–474; Potter 1990, 288–289; and *idem* 1996a, 54.

170. Fronto *Princ. hist.* 8–9. See also Festus 14.3 (*Sed Hadrianus qui successit Traiano, invidens Traiani gloriae, sponte sua Armeniam, Mesopotamiam, Assyriam reddidit ac medium inter Persas et Romanos Euphraten esse voluit*) and 20.4, as well as Eutropius 8.6 and *SHA Hadr.* 5.1–4 and 9.1. Aurelius Victor 14.1–6 reads like an accusation: *Igitur Aelius Hadrianus . . . pace ad orientem composita Romam regreditur. Ibi Graecorum more . . . Deinde, uti solet tranquillis rebus, remissior rus proprium Tibur secessit permissa urbe Lucio Aelio Caesari.* On Hadrian's arrangements in the East upon his accession see Syme, *RP* 3.1436–1446.

171. *Anonymi Libellus de vita et moribus imperatorum* 14.6: *Varius multiplex multiformis; ad vitia atque virtutes quasi arbiter genitus, impetum mentis quodam artificio regens, ingenium invidum triste lascivum et ad ostentationem sui insolens callide tegebat; continentiam facilitatem clementiam simulans contraque dissimulans ardorem gloriae, quo flagrabat.*

172. Syme, *RP* 6.347.

173. Cf. Syme 1958, 247.

174. Fronto *Princ. hist.* 8, and cf. (*idem*) *De Feriis Alsienibus* 5. For further literary evidence on Hadrian's peregrinations, see J. Toynbee 1934, 2 n. 2, or Halfmann 1986, 188–210 *passim*.

its to small communities created a lasting sense of loyalty to the emperor who honored them with his presence.[175]

After his last tour of the East, Hadrian returned to Rome in the spring of 134, there to stay until his death.[176] He there arranged a series of imperial issues that celebrated the *consensus* of the diverse populations and legions of the empire.[177] The most famous of these consisted of coins in bronze, silver, and gold whose types portrayed personifications of twenty-six provinces, though some provinces fail to appear and two cities are included.[178] The rather eclectic nature of the selections suggests all the more strongly Hadrian's personal involvement in their design. The *exercitus* series depicted Hadrian addressing the legions of each province. As preserved, that series, too, has gaps—the armies of Judaea, Egypt, and Africa are not represented. Again, if deliberate, the omissions argue in favor of Hadrianic selection or guidance.[179] Some have expressed surprise that "the garrisons of the different parts of the Empire [were] encouraged by such separate honour under distinctive local names, to cherish a special local pride," but this concern arises from knowledge of the divisive loyalties that pitted army against army in the third and fourth centuries.[180] We might note in response that Hadrian's particular attention to inspecting the armies of the empire won him

175. Hadrian's temple in Oxyrhynchus continued to be active into the fourth century (*P. Oxy.* XVII 2154); offerings were made to celebrate the day on which he entered the city (*P. Oxy.* XXXI 2153, from the late second or early third century; cf. *P. Oxy.* VIII 1113). See also *BCH* 9 (1885), 124–125, from Nysa, which continued to celebrate Hadrian's birthday during the reign of Antoninus Pius. Weinstock 1971, 184, notes that Hadrian "was called outside Rome κτίστης and 'conditor' more often than anyone before or after him."

176. Hadrian had returned to Rome by 5 May of that year (*IGRR* I 149). Hadrian's movements between spring 132 and May 134 are the subject of some dispute: the sources are canvassed by Halfmann 1986, 208–210, and Syme, *RP* 6.353–356. Syme, who is almost certainly correct, delays Hadrian in the East to oversee the war in Palestine during the winter of 132/133.

177. For the dating of the so-called *adventus, exercitus,* and provincial series and other related issues, see Mattingly, *BMC* III, cxlii–cxliv and clxxi–clxxv. The coins are reproduced on plates 91–97 of that volume or as *RIC* II, Hadrian nos. 296–329.

178. Mattingly, *BMC* III, clxxiv–clxxv. For an analysis of the images, see J. Toynbee 1934, 24–130, or Kantorowicz 1965, 46–49, who also compares later *adventus* types. The series includes Achaea, Aegyptus, Africa, Alexandria, Arabia, Asia, Bithynia, Britannia, Cappadocia, Cilicia, Dacia, Gallia, Germania, Hispania, Italia, Judaea, Libya, Macedonia, Mauretania, Moesia, Nicomedia, Nilus, Noricum, Phrygia, Sicilia, Thracia, and Tiberis.

179. Mattingly, *BMC* III, clxxii–clxxiii. Halfmann 1986, 195, explains the presence or absence of an army by determining whether Hadrian had inspected the army in question during his second or third tour of the empire; Syme, *RP* 6.356, cautions against such an easy explanation. Appearing are: Exercitus Britannicus, Cappadocicus, Dacicus, Germanicus, Hispanicus, Mauretanicus, Moesiacus, Noricus, Raeticus, Syriacus, as well as the Cohortes Praetoriae.

180. Mattingly, *BMC* III, clxxiii.

the admiration of the troops: soldiers boasted on their tombstones of having performed well under his gaze.[181]

Very similar to these was a series that celebrated his arrival in the various provinces in the course of his travels throughout the empire.[182] Finally, just as Hadrian had honored the armies in the military provinces of the empire, so he celebrated the more settled provinces in their own series: its coins bear a legend dedicating them "to the restorer [*restitutor*] of [the province]."[183] Only the province of Hadrian's birth, Hispania, receives commemoration in both the *exercitus* and the *restitutor* series. The particular image used for any given province sought to distill and evoke its distinctive features; in the language used by Cassius Dio of the *simulacra gentium* displayed during the funeral of Augustus, "each one was represented in some characteristic native fashion." That these images resonated with local spirit and remained in some way vital is suggested by their occasional repetition in later, local issues.[184]

The rest of this chapter analyzes the conceptual geographies of intellectuals under the empire. The reign of Hadrian marked a turning point in their history. Yet regarding Hadrian himself, his motives and his aims, we must be satisfied with speculation. Service around the empire had taught Hadrian what good might be achieved within the borders of the empire by resources that would be wasted in civilizing Armenia and Parthia. He put that lesson into practice upon his accession, risking the scorn of senators who had been deluded by Trajan's exaggerated letters from the front. Living at Rome as magistrate and then emperor revealed the precious and anachronistic pretensions of the Italian aristocracy. Hadrian now directed benefits toward the provinces, of which his cancellation of nine hundred million sesterces of overdue debts to the government was only the most ostentatious.[185] The Senate and people celebrated that act in a famous relief among the Anaglypha Traiani and on an inscription which may reveal

---

181. *ILS* 2558 (Smallwood, *Nerva* no. 336). Dio specifically recalls this feat but attributes this skill to all Batavian cavalry (69.9.6). A speech that Hadrian delivered after inspecting Legio III Augusta at Lambaesis survives in substantial fragments (*ILS* 2487, on which see Campbell 1984, 77–80). Dio described Hadrian as inspecting and reforming every aspect of military life: his military reputation ensured that barbarians were afraid to attack the empire (69.9; cf. *SHA Hadr.* 10.2–11.1).

182. For a list of the surviving types, see Mattingly, *BMC* III, clxxi–clxxii: Africa, Arabia, Asia, Bithynia, Britannia, Cilicia, Gallia, Hispania, Italia, Judaea, Macedonia, Mauretania, Moesia, Noricum, Phrygia, Sicilia, Thracia.

183. Mattingly, *BMC* III, clxxiii–clxxiv. The series comprises Achaea, Africa, Arabia, Asia, Bithynia, Gallia, Hispania, Italia, Libya, Macedonia, Nicomedia, Phrygia, and Sicilia, as well as Orbis Terrarum.

184. See, for example, MacCormack 1981, 30 n. 67, on the coinage of Carthage.

185. *SHA Hadr.* 7.6–7; cf. Dio 69.8.1².

something of Hadrian's mind: "By this generosity he rendered safe not only his present citizens but also their posterity."[186] His celebration of the provinces had its counterpart in his reduction of Italy to the level of a province, if not in name, then in point of fact: he appointed four consular legates to hold assize courts in "the nurse and mother" of the world.[187]

THE GEOGRAPHY OF THE ROMAN EMPIRE

In his advice on extending the franchise, Augustus necessarily recognized the division of the residents of the empire into two categories, an act that stood uneasily next to his boasting of the benefactions that he had extended to the empire at large. His advice to his successors not to extend the borders of the empire contradicted far more directly his own claims to have "brought the entire world [*orbis terrarum*] under the empire of the Roman people."[188] The conflict between dreams of world conquest and the practical limitations of ancient technology had, of course, existed ever since Alexander brought those dreams to life: it was his accomplishments that made world conquest seem possible, but his campaigns had simultaneously made Greek geographers aware of how far short he had fallen.[189] At the level of public discourse this conflict mattered little: Augustus and Rome controlled more of the world than most could even imagine, and honors voted to Augustus throughout the empire iterated and thus sustained his claim to world conquest. Cities throughout Asia addressed Augustus as "the father of his country and of the entire human race," and thanked him because "the land and sea are at peace, and the cities flourish with good will, harmony, and prosperity."[190] The Sebasteum at Aphrodisias included a personification of Earth reaching out to the goddess Rome, expressing visually

---

186. *ILS* 309: *s. p. q. R. imp. Caesari, divi Traiani Parthici f. divi Nervae nepoti Traiano Hadriano Aug. pont. max. trib. pot. II, cos. II, qui primus omnium principum et solus, remittendo sestertium novies milies centena milia n. debitum fiscis, non praesentes tantum cives suos sed et posteros eorum praestitit hac liberalitate securos.* On the relief see Boatwright 1987, 182–187, with her fig. 41.

187. Syme, *RP* 4.322, and Tarpin, *Integration* 2.21–29.

188. The heading to the *Res gestae: Rerum gestarum divi Augusti, quibus orbem terrarum imperio populi Romani subiecit (EJ,* p. 2, ll. 1–2). That Augustus himself made this claim is strongly suggested by the language of Livy *Per.* 134: *C. Caesar rebus conpositis et omnibus provincis in certam formam redactis Augustus quoque cognominatus est.*

189. On the intellectual ferment provoked by Alexander's conquests, see Tarn 1948, 2.378–449, or Dion 1977, 175–222.

190. Texts from Asia Minor are collected in Buckler 1935. *IBM* 894 (*EJ* no. 98a = Buckler 1935, no. 6) is representative of their wording: Αὐτοκράτωρ Καῖσαρ θεοῦ υἱὸς Σεβαστός, ἀρχιερεὺς μέγιστος καὶ πάτηρ τῆς πατρίδος καὶ τοῦ σύμπαντος τῶν ἀνθρώπων γένους. On Greek manipulations and interpretations of the title *pater patriae,* see Chapter 9, "The Father of the Human Race."

the dominance that other cities honored in their public documents.[191] We have already seen that Horace in his *Odes* and Pisa in its municipal decree celebrated Augustus as the "protector of the human race."[192] Likewise, when the city of Narbo established the rules governing its cult of Augustus in A.D. 12–13, it ordained a sacrifice on 7 January, because on that day "Augustus had inaugurated his rule over the *orbis terrarum.*" The city also scheduled a sacrifice on 23 September, Augustus's birthday, because "on that day the blessedness of the age had given Augustus as ruler to the *orbis terrarum.*"[193]

No one knew the falsity of such claims to world conquest better than officials of the empire. At an administrative level Rome had a profound interest in defining geographic space. The fantastic efforts poured into the census fixed the gaze of every inhabitant of the empire upon the extent of his property and, by implication, on the ability of Rome to measure and to map its world.[194] The servants of the emperor also marked the land. They maintained a special interest in the boundaries between the Roman empire and the territory of foreign powers, especially when customs could be collected from the trade along those borders.[195] Within the empire their interest was often no less acute. In 216, for example, Caracalla ordered a survey of the land around Pessinus; the centurion who carried out the survey left an elaborate tribute to the emperor in whose name he had toiled:[196]

Good Fortune! Imperator Caesar Marcus Aurelius Antoninus, the unconquered, pious, and blessed Augustus, pontifex maximus, Parthicus Maximus, Britannicus Maximus, Germanicus Maximus, holding tribunician power for the nineteenth year, four times consul, proconsul, father of his country, or-

191. See Reynolds 1981, nos. 6 and 7.

192. See above at n. 45.

193. *ILS* 112 (*EJ* no. 100), ll. 14–16 and 23–25: [14]*VIIII k. Octobr. qua die* | [15]*eum saeculi felicitas orbi terrarum* | [16]*rectorem edidit;* and [23]*VIIquoq.* | [24]*idus Ianuar. qua die primum imperium* | [25]*orbis terrarum auspicatus est.*

194. Nicolet 1991, 123–147. See also Chapter 5 at nn. 82–96 and Chapter 9, "The Ritual Life of the Roman Citizen."

195. See, for example, the Severan boundary stone discussed in Chapter 6 at n. 59. On surveyors in the imperial service, see Dilke 1971 and Sherk 1974. See Potter 1996a, 57, on Procopius *Aed.* 3.3.9–11: "The important point . . . is not that the border was no obstacle to movement, but that, even though it was no obstacle, people knew it was there." Compare the terms of the treaty established between Justinian and Chosroes, preserved in a fragment of the *History* of Menander Protector: the "Persians" are responsible for preventing access to the Roman empire at certain mountain passes, while commerce between citizens of the empires must be conducted at "specified customs posts" (fr. 6.1). Each side knew the the border to be a legal fiction.

196. The text edited in Devreker 1971; I have silently corrected an error in the dating formula.

dered that the lands of the whole territory of the famous city of the Pessinun-
tians be surveyed with the sacred measuring rod. Caesius Felicissimus, centurion, supervised the work in the consulates of Catius Sabinus—for the second
time—and Cornelius Anulinus.

Hadrian, too, was called upon to settle land disputes around the empire.
From Aezani in Anatolia survives a dossier of letters that passed between
Hadrian, the proconsul of Asia Avidius Quietus, and the local imperial
procurator, one Hesperus. In the end Hesperus arranged a survey and set
up boundary stones in Latin and Greek, but even Avidius Quietus justified
the legitimacy of this project and its outcome by appeal to the authority of
the emperor.[197]
The inhabitants of large cities might have been able to avoid seeing a
boundary stone in a field. Every inhabitant of the empire must have used its
roads: "They united the subjects of the most distant provinces by an easy
and familiar intercourse; but their primary object had been to facilitate the
marches of the legions; nor was any country considered as completely subdued, till it had been rendered, in all its parts, pervious to the arms and authority of the conqueror."[198] The men who supervised the construction of
those roads marked every mile with a monument to the emperor of whom
the road itself was, in some way, a testament.[199] No mere sample of milestones can do justice to the experience of walking a Roman road: a series of
such inscriptions, recording the emperor who built and the emperors who
repaved the road, their titulature boasting their ancestry and their conquests, constituted in itself a lesson in the history of one's empire.[200]
Emperors sometimes ordered roads built at their expense, and sometimes they freed up money so that communities could pay for roads themselves.[201] However funded, their construction remained an essential concern, expressive of the stability of the empire and the interest that the
emperor took in his subjects.[202] Given his interest in promoting an image of

197. *MAMA* IX, xxxvi–xliii. For the emperor's role in fixing boundaries between cities see
Millar 1977, 435–436.

198. Gibbon chapter 1 (1.77).

199. There exists no brief introduction to milestones—where they were placed, who
funded them, what they measured—to rival Hirschfeld 1913, 703–743. For a more thorough
treatment of Roman roads see Pekáry 1968; briefer and more contemporary is Halfmann
1986, 85–89.

200. Readers can acquire some feel for the content of milestones from the sample provided in *ILS* 5801–5904. For a description of the milestones along the roads in Arabia, see
Brünnow and von Domaszewski 1905, chapter 7. Cf. *MAMA* X, xxiii–xxvii, or French 1981 and
1988.

201. Obviously a generalization. For the details see Pékary 1968, 91–117.

202. Cf. Plutarch *Gaius Gracchus* 7.1: Gaius built roads with an eye on utility, grace, and
beauty; the product of his efforts had ὁμαλὴν καὶ καλὴν ὄψιν. On road building and other
marks on the landscape as displaying imperial power see Purcell 1990.

continuity at the heart of the empire, it is no surprise that Decius engaged in a massive program of repaving roads in his brief stay on the throne.[203] What is more, just as wealthy individuals sought lasting fame by providing large public buildings for their cities, they similarly chose to devote their monies to constructing roads, clearly believing that the audiences for their buildings would read milestones, too.[204] One imperial official made such a donation to Amastris in Pontus, under the emperor Claudius, and left a record in Greek and Latin: "As thanks for Augustan peace, in honor of Tiberius Claudius Germanicus Augustus, Gaius Julius Aquila, priest for life of the divine Augustus, twice prefect of engineers, having been transferred to serve in the treasury by the consuls Aulus Gabinius Secundus and Taurus Statilius Corvinus, cut this mountain and at his own expense laid the bed and built this road."[205] Over time provincials learned to view milestones, dedicated to the emperor by the procurators and engineers who built the roads, as testaments of personal and communal loyalty, and they began to refurbish milestones with civic funds, recording on them civic acclamations or honorary decrees. They were still milestones, of course, but they had become a means to engender and a vehicle to express a wider sense of belonging in those who read and used them.[206]

The Greeks had marveled when the Persian king ordered a channel dug through Mt. Athos. Roman emperors took such power over the landscape for granted: just as they brought water to cities no matter what the obstacles, so Roman engineers, on the orders of their emperor, led roads over bridges and cut or tunneled through mountains.[207] Provincials certainly understood that the agency of the emperor lay behind such achievements: the city of Ephesus, for example, thanked Hadrian because "he provided shipments of grain from Egypt, rendered the harbors navigable, and turned aside the river Caÿster, which had been harming the harbors."[208] Strabo had earlier insisted that it was the responsibility of good rulers to try to control the waterways of the world.[209]

---

203. See the catalogue of milestones in H. Mattingly and Salisbury 1924b.

204. See *ILS* 5878, from Aeclanum: Gaminia Sabine paved three miles of road in honor of her son, Tiberius Claudius Corus Maximus, son of Tiberius, grandson of Tiberius, who died at the age of twenty.

205. *ILS* 5883.

206. Pékary 1968, 16–22, and esp. 16–18. Pékary's suggestion that imperial officials approved texts on dedicatory milestones prior to their inscription has met with some criticism.

207. On tunneling, see *ILS* 5795, discussed above in n. 110. For another mountain cut away, see *ILS* 5863 (from Orsova): *imp. Caesar divi Nervae f. Nerva Traianus Aug. Germ. pontif. maximus trib. pot. IIII pater patriae, cos. III, montibus excisis anconibus sublatis viam fecit.* Statius *Silvae* 4.3.40–58 reflects on the nature of road building and provides a proverbial comparison to Xerxes: *O quantae pariter manus laborant! . . . hae possent et Athon cauare dextrae.*

208. *SIG* 839, ll. 12–16.

209. Strabo 16.1.9–11 at 10.

When Vitruvius announced, shortly after Actium, that Caesar's "divine mind and godhead" had acquired control over the *orbis terrarum,* he participated in a tradition of late Republican political rhetoric that attributed such control to one dynast after another.[210] He could afford to: nowhere in a work on architecture would he have to report new conquests after having dedicated his work to the ruler of the world. To a certain extent Roman imperialist thought had already developed an answer to the existence of forests and deserts beyond the borders of the empire: they just weren't worth conquering. Cicero implicitly questioned the wisdom of having conquered Africa, Spain, and Gaul when he reminded his brother that he would still have had to consider the best interests of his subjects even if he had been sent to govern savage, barbarous tribes in those lands.[211]

The varied strands of Augustan propaganda, emphasizing peace at home and victories in far-off lands, conditioned the mental geographies of contemporaries. Horace, for example, insisted on the empire's internal stability and peace, a condition brought about by the relegation of warfare to its borders.[212] Strabo went still further, viewing warfare as an evil necessity, motivated by defensive concerns rather than imperialist aggression. Thus he admired Augustus for not allowing his legions to move beyond the Rhine and argued that the occupation of Britain was pointless: it would be easy to tax those trading with the Continent, but the cost of occupation would far outweigh the additional money brought in as tribute.[213] This vision of Augustan imperialism—whatever its relation to Augustan policy—allowed Horace and especially Strabo to view the empire as a unity. Like the men who commissioned and built the Sebasteum at Aphrodisias, Strabo recognized the existence of recent victims of Roman arms, but he did not see them as similar in kind to the Greeks or Gauls or Africans who constituted the limbs of the unitary body of his empire. This vision of the empire even shaped Strabo's perception of Roman administration: although he paid brief lip service to the division of provinces between emperor and Senate, he otherwise viewed the provinces as the single and unified responsibility of Augustus and his heir.[214]

Strabo's remarks, together with the advice of Augustus to Tiberius and

---

210. Vitruvius 1 *pr.* 1. On world conquest in Republican rhetoric, see Nicolet 1991, 29–56. On the use of *divina mens et numen,* see Janson 1964, 100–106.

211. Cicero *Ep. ad Q. fratrem* 1.1.27.

212. Oliensis 1998, 107–127.

213. For Strabo on Germany see Chapter 5 n. 85. On Britain see 4.5.3, and cf. 6.4.2 and 17.3.24.

214. On Tiberius as continuator of the work of Augustus see Strabo 6.4.2; on the formal division of the provinces see 17.3.25. The best treatment of Strabo's political geography probably remains Lassère 1982. Otherwise see Vogt 1960, 193–194, or Bowersock 1965, 127–131.

the people of Rome, have been subjected to intense scrutiny in debates on Roman imperialism of the first and second centuries.[215] Assessing essentially the same data from very different perspectives, scholars have reached radically different conclusions about the aims and rationality of the Roman government in this period.[216] It may be that our data, consisting of scattered remarks by men who frequently lived and wrote far from the corridors of power, and archaeological evidence from Europe, the Near East, and Africa, will not yield a pattern of consistent explanatory power. What those remarks can reveal, however, are the conceptual and ideological frameworks through which residents conceived of the empire as a geographical and political entity.[217] If we must concede that we cannot know whether Tiberius or Hadrian consciously decided to restrict the expansion of the empire, we should also concede that many of Hadrian's contemporaries knew his thoughts no better than we do. Residents of the empire did, however, believe that their government was rational, that emperors and their advisers made calculated decisions based on the best information available to them.[218] Contemporaries' beliefs about the policies of their rulers may, therefore, tell us little about their government, but a great deal about themselves.[219]

Later writers on Augustan imperialism shared Strabo's point of view. Velleius Paterculus, writing under Tiberius, questioned whether the military achievements of Pompey had won as much of glory as they had cost in toil.[220] Writing under Claudius, Seneca asked his audience to "consider all the races to whom Roman peace [*Romana pax*] does not extend—the Germans, for example, and whatever nomadic races harass us along the Danube. Eternal winter and a gloomy sky smother them; barren ground ill sustains them; they fend off rain with thatch or leaves; they wander marshes hardened by ice; and they capture wild animals for food."[221] Early in the second century the historian Florus, who was born in Africa and lived in Spain before moving to Rome when middle-aged, wrote a history of Roman imperialism through the reign of Augustus, "by which time Roman arms had pacified the entire world."[222] If Strabo thought little of Britain, Florus

215. Luttwak 1976 marked a watershed. The bibliography since then has been enormous. Whittaker 1994 and 1996 and Kennedy 1996 provide thorough bibliographies, and each includes a helpful bibliographic excursus.

216. Wheeler 1993 provides a rigorous survey of recent work.

217. See Brunt 1990, 288–323 and 433–480; Gruen at *CAH*[2] X 188–197; and Potter 1996a.

218. Whittaker 1994, 62–70.

219. Cf. Syme 1958, 249–252, and *RP* 4.45.

220. Velleius 2.40.1.

221. Seneca *Dial.* 1.4.14.

222. Florus 1 *pr.* 7. On Florus see Brunt 1990, 475–476.

thought less of the Sarmatians, conquered by Lentulus in 12 B.C.: "They have nothing except snow, frost, and trees. Their barbarism is such that they don't even understand peace."[223] The history of the remaining wars under Augustus depressed Florus still further: "Would that Augustus had not thought so highly of conquering Germany. Our losses there have been more shameful by far than our acquisitions glorious."[224] Florus closed by recognizing that there remained people beyond the borders of the empire: they were *inmunes imperii*—by which he intended not that they were invincible, but that they, like the Sarmatians, were not advanced enough to know good government when it was imposed on them. Nevertheless Florus was confident that, in spite of their innate shortcomings, these people recognized the greatness of the Roman people and respected them as the conqueror of nations.[225]

Strabo did not make the same racial judgments that Florus would a century later. Nevertheless, both men accommodated Roman claims to world rule by dividing humanity much as Augustus had divided the residents of the empire: some were worth conquering, and some were not.[226] Strabo and Florus merely drew the line in a profoundly different place. For example, Strabo judged the Armenians and those beyond Colchis to be good subjects for client kings, since they required only leaders, whereas the Nomads were intractable toward all because of their lack of contact with other men. For that reason, Strabo continued, the Nomads posed no threat to Rome and needed only to be monitored.[227] In concluding his work, Strabo happily reaffirmed this Romanocentric point of view: "This is how the parts of the world that we inhabit lie."[228] Strabo qualified his remarks still further: the Romans inhabited the best and best-known portions of the world. They did not have all of Libya: some of that country was uninhabited or suited only for a wretched and nomadic lifestyle. Nor did they govern the Heniochi, who lived in nomadic fashion in barren and sterile lands.[229]

Strabo's judgment was echoed by other Greek authors under Augustus. Dionysius of Halicarnassus, who wrote his antiquarian history of Roman institutions while living in Rome under Augustus, justified the topic of his history by reference to the unprecedented size of the Roman empire: "The city

223. Florus 2.29: *Nihil praeter nives pruinasque et silvas habent. Tanta barbaria est, ut nec intellegant pacem.*

224. Florus 2.30.21.

225. Florus 2.34.61. See also Statius *Silvae* 3.3.167–171: Domitian did not want to honor the Marcomanni and Sarmatians by celebrating a triumph over them.

226. For this problem in the late empire see Vogt 1967 and Dagron 1987.

227. Strabo 6.4.2.

228. Strabo 17.3.24.

229. Strabo 17.3.24.

of the Romans rules the entire earth, as much of it as is not inaccessible but rather inhabited by men; and she rules all the sea, not only that within the Pillars of Hercules but also the Ocean, as much as is navigable; she is the first and only city in all history that limits her power at the rising and setting of the sun."[230] All the qualifications hint at an unease that prevented Dionysius from making an explicit claim of world rule for Rome. That unease did not extend so far that Dionysius admitted the existence of any rival to Rome's claim to universal hegemony.[231] The elder Pliny showed no such hesitation, calling Rome the "conqueror of lands and ruler of the entire world, . . . which sends its commands to foreign peoples."[232] Clearly a Roman saw no contradiction between ruling "the entire world" and the existence of "foreign peoples" to whom one sent commands.[233]

Latin diction in the Augustan period and later reflected these ambiguities in the concept "world." *Orbis* had frequently signified the entire world even when not accompanied by *terrarum*. But in the Augustan period Vergil and Ovid at times denoted by *orbis* simply a "region," whether contrasting Europe and Asia or simply referring to a particular territory.[234] Late in the reign of Augustus and writing from the Black Sea, Ovid thanked Fama for bringing him word of the victories of Germanicus: "By thy evidence I learned that recently countless races assembled to see their leader's face; and Rome, which embraces the measureless world within her vast walls [*quaeque capit vastis inmensum moenibus orbem*], scarce had room for her guests."[235] At a concrete level Ovid referred only to the city of Rome, whose population would witness the triumph of Germanicus; at an abstract level, Rome here stands for her "measureless" empire, whose "world" she somehow manages to fix within the circuit of a wall. The poets Manilius under Tiberius and Lucan under Nero used *orbis* frequently with this meaning. They, however, attached the adjective "Roman" to it, in order to designate that portion of the globe occupied by the empire. But the phrase *orbis Romanus* did more than substitute for *imperium Romanum*. The latter indicated the sphere of Roman political power. *Orbis Romanus* did, too, by labeling that sphere the world.

From the middle of the first century prose authors began to adopt this

---

230. Dionysius Hal. *Ant. Rom.* 1.3.3.

231. Dionysius Hal. *Ant. Rom.* 1.3.4–5.

232. Pliny *Nat.* 36.118; cf. 2.189–190 and Vegetius 1.2, prefacing his remarks with the assertion that he ought not pass over *ea, quae a doctissimis hominibus comprobata sunt.*

233. Cf. Plutarch *Fort. Rom.* 317B–C: the Romans brought peace to the world by controlling not simply the races and peoples within their empire but also the foreign and overseas territories of kings (ἀλλοφύλους καὶ διαποντίους βασιλέων ἡγεμονίας).

234. Vogt 1960, 165–166; *OLD* s.v. "orbis," 13a.

235. Ovid *Pont.* 2.1.21–24 (trans. Wheeler; rev. Goold); cf. *Fasti* 1.85–86: *Iuppiter arce suo totum cum spectat in orbem, nil nisi Romanum, quod tueatur, habet.*

usage. They often spoke not of "the Roman world," but of "our world." The practice of the elder Pliny is altogether typical of later authors. Pliny wrote of a spice that he called Daphnis's casia that "it even grows in our *orbis*— indeed, I have seen it at the edge of the empire, where the Rhine flows, planted among the beehives—but the characteristic color produced by the sun is absent, and because of this its scent is likewise missing."[236] Pliny regarded as known those facts confirmed by autopsy; he therefore distinguished the proper subjects for scientific inquiry by their location within his "world." Strabo displayed a similar understanding of the function of knowledge: the purpose of geographical inquiry was, for him, the pursuit of honest and efficient government. "Scholars in our day cannot speak of anything beyond Ierne, which lies just north of Britain. It is home to complete savages who lead a miserable existence because of the cold. I therefore believe that the northern boundary of the world [τὸ τῆς οἰκουμένης πέρας] should be placed there."[237] Strabo has done more than label accurate knowledge of Britain and Ireland unnecessary; he has placed them beyond the limits of the world.

Of course, the outside world did not simply bristle with men who didn't understand peace. Strabo had been forced to acknowledge this fact whenever his gaze turned to the eastern border of the empire, and whenever he defined the scope of scientific geography. The Parthians were powerful, indeed, almost rivals of Rome, but they also acknowledged Roman superiority to such an extent that they sent back the standards which they had taken from Crassus, provided the Romans with hostages, and turned to Rome when it came time to crown their king.[238] Writing some forty years later, Philo of Alexandria attempted to set the fall of Gaius in perspective. According to him, Gaius had inherited from Tiberius a prosperous empire, one at peace with itself and with its neighbors. Nor was the Roman empire like other empires:[239]

> [It was] not simply an empire that contained most of the most essential parts of the world—although, of course, one might legitimately describe those parts as a world, albeit one bounded by the Euphrates and the Rhine, the latter forming a frontier with Germany and the more barbarous tribes, while the Euphrates forms a frontier with Parthia and the Sarmatian and Scythian

236. Pliny *Nat.* 12.98; cf. *Nat.* 2.242: *Pars nostra terrarum, de qua memoro.*
237. Strabo 2.5.8.
238. Strabo 6.4.2; see also 11.9.2 and 17.3.24. Among later authors see Pomponius Mela 1.34 and Dio 40.14.3–4: the Parthians have had so much success against the Romans ὥστε . . . καὶ δεῦρο ἀεὶ ἀντίπαλοι νομίζεσθαι.
239. Philo *Leg.* 10 (trans. Smallwood, modified).

tribes, which are no less savage than the Germans—but, as I have already said, it was an empire stretching from the sunrise to the sunset and comprising lands both within and beyond the Ocean.

Elsewhere in that same treatise, employing precisely the same words as Strabo, Philo gives Gaius's predecessors credit for bringing back a golden age "to the world that we inhabit."[240] If it be a "world" that Rome ruled— and Philo did not hesitate to say that it could be one—then, Philo acknowledged, that world contained both savages not worth conquering and the Parthians.

Emperors after Tiberius were unable to resist the imperialist impulse: each one, almost in direct proportion to his unpopularity, mounted campaigns to extend the boundaries of the empire.[241] Parthia's weakness throughout the Julio-Claudian period allowed emperors of the first century to direct their energies and resources elsewhere, but Parthia remained by virtue of its size and coherence the only serious rival to Roman power. Wars mounted for conquest necessarily suggested the relative equality of past and recent victims of Roman aggrandizement. Whether Trajan genuinely sought to rival Alexander the Great or not, contemporary and later historians interpreted his campaign in the East in those terms. Parthia was in the air in the early second century, and Florus therefore felt the need to account for its continued existence. He did not mention Trajan's campaign, but he was happy to number the Parthians among those who "recognize the greatness of the Roman people and respect them as the conqueror of nations" because "they returned of their own accord the standards stolen in the defeat of Crassus, as if repentant of their victory. Thus the entire human race possessed everywhere a secure and continual peace, achieved through war or treaty."[242] Florus strikes us as oddly myopic: How could he continue to base his arrogance toward Parthia on events a century earlier? Yet that practice would continue for centuries into the future, interrupted only by the brief periods in which the power in the East waxed and turned aggressive. The conservatism of Roman ethnographers aided greatly in maintaining this anachronistic illusion. By refusing to acknowledge the profound changes in power in the East—from Persian to Parthian to Sassanid—they could claim that the king of that country was a direct descendant of those men who had knelt to be crowned by a Roman emperor and bowed before his standards.

240. Philo *Leg.* 49: εἰς τὴν καθ' ἡμᾶς οἰκουμένην.
241. Brunt 1990, 471.
242. Florus 2.34.63–64. Contrast Fronto *Princ. hist.* 3: the Parthians alone of all men have been worthy adversaries of the Roman people, as is shown by their victories over Crassus and Antony and the cost of the triumph that Trajan exacted from them.

HADRIAN AND THE LIMITS OF EMPIRE

Hadrian's retreat from the new provinces that Trajan had annexed represented the first institutional recognition of the "limits of empire" since Tiberius, heeding the advice of Augustus, had restrained the martial ardor of the young Germanicus.[243] In so doing, Hadrian implicitly retreated from an imperialist mentality that divided the world into peoples already and not yet conquered. Rather, by announcing, as it were, that all those who had the capacity to appreciate the benefits of empire now lived within its borders, he brought imperial ideology into line with the worldview espoused by provincial intellectuals. His coins thus celebrated the provinces not by reverting to the idealized women of Greek art, but by lending dignity to figures still fitted with characteristic native dress and ornaments. To some Hadrian lent an additional air of *Romanitas*. For example, Trajan had celebrated the conquest of Dacia with a coin advertising the addition of *Dacicus* to his titulature and depicting either a Dacian man in various postures of submission—hands tied, sitting before a trophy, kneeling before the goddess Peace or Trajan or the Senate—or Dacia herself, either kneeling or prostrate beneath the foot of Trajan or the goddess Peace. Hadrian's Dacia, on the other hand, held a standard (Figs. 5, 6).[244] His coinage and his universal cancellation of delinquent taxes seem ever more in harmony in their ideological thrust. Hadrian thus also created an environment in which the ideological justification for *aurum coronarium* made sense: if Rome disavowed further conquests, she must be fighting to protect those whom she now embraced. When, therefore, Severus and Caracalla advertised that peace had been established "throughout the entire world" or "for all men, everywhere," they spoke to provincial populations eager to identify themselves as coextensive with the beneficiaries of empire—that is, as Romans.[245]

Optimistic provincials delighted in viewing Hadrian's actions as a policy that assimilated imperial ideology to the position they had maintained since Augustus. Because Hadrian had moved toward them, his policy, however innovative, did not substantially alter provincial thought on the division of humanity. Yet the racial language of Florus did develop from an important shift in the nature of that divide. A set of categories based on technological sophistication or cultural progress allowed for ethnic divisions within the Roman community; a racial division like that espoused by Florus did not.

---

243. See Potter 1996a, 51, on Tacitus *Ann.* 2.26.2.

244. Hadrianic DACIA issues: *BMC* III, Hadrian nos. 1616, 1735–1746.

245. For the letters of Severus and Caracalla, see *IGBulg.* 659 (quoted in Chapter 6 at n. 76) and Reynolds 1982, no. 18 (quoted in Chapter 6 at n. 75). Cf. Robert, *OMS* 5:654, on thanks offered to Gordian by Ephesus because he had restored peace "to his cosmos" (τῷ ἰδίῳ κόσμῳ), and Mitford 1991, nos. 5 and 6 on 190–191 = *AÉ* 1991, 1478–1479.

Figure 5. Trajan threatens a defeated Dacian. Aes from the
mint of Rome. *BMC* III, Trajan no. 902.

Figure 6. Dacia takes her place among Hadrian's provinces.
Aes from the mint of Rome. *BMC* III, Hadrian no. 1739.

Greek orators and historians continued, like Strabo, to divide the human
race between those inside and outside the borders of the empire. But they
began in this period more and more often to speak of the empire and its institutions using first-person possessives. The Roman empire was now their
empire.[246]

This new mental geography found expression in the language exploited
to describe the borders of the empire. The *Historia Augusta,* drawing on
Marius Maximus, narrated Hadrian's efforts to defend the frontier as though
those beyond that frontier were of a single type: "During this period and on
many other occasions also, in many regions where the barbarians are held
back not by rivers but by artificially designated boundaries, Hadrian shut
them off by means of high stakes planted deep in the ground and fastened
together in the manner of a palisade."[247] We have already seen that Aelius
Aristides used the same image as a metaphor to describe the borders of the
empire, even though he understood that there was, in fact, no wall surrounding the whole of its territory.[248]

246. See Palm 1959, 56–62, 75–76, 82–83. For the period beyond Palm's study see Vogt
1967.
247. *SHA Hadr.* 12.6 (trans. Magie, adapted); see also 5.1, 5.3, and 11.2.
248. See Chapter 3 at n. 68.

Some years after Florus wrote his history, Appian, an Alexandrian Greek, retired from his service in the imperial bureaucracy and his career as an advocate at Rome. He devoted his retirement to writing a military history of Rome. Like Dionysius of Halicarnassus many years earlier, Appian justified his history by boasting of the greatness of the empire:[249]

> The time from those kings [Caesar and his heirs] to the present has been approximately two hundred years, during which the city has been adorned, its revenues greatly increased, and everything has advanced in great peace and security toward an undisturbed happiness. The emperors have added some nations to those formerly conquered and have overpowered others when they revolted. On the whole, already possessing the best parts of the land and sea, they desire to preserve their empire through good counsel rather than to extend their rule endlessly over impoverished and unprofitable barbarian races [ἐπὶ βάρβαρα ἔθνη πενιχρὰ καὶ ἀκερδῆ]. Some of these I myself have seen in Rome, when they came in embassy to offer themselves as subjects, but the emperor did not accept them, because they were of no use to him. To other races, most of them ignorant, the emperors merely give kings, since they need nothing from them for the empire. On some of these client kingdoms they waste money, being ashamed to release them even though they frequently require expenditure of some kind. The emperors also surround the empire in a circle with great armies, and they guard the whole expanse of land and sea like some small plot of land.

If Appian praised Rome as fervently as had Dionysius, he defined the empire in very different terms. In his view, Roman imperialism has already reached its natural limits, and efforts to influence the politics of barbarian kingdoms are almost overextending Roman power. In contrast to that costly indulgence, however, the emperor has quite rightly used his military to separate his people from the rest of humanity. Thus Appian's history of Rome's expansion and civil wars could close with a *rationarium imperii*.[250] Nor, on this reasoning, was there any need to write beyond the civil wars. The state of the empire was not one of temporary slumber, but one of complete and natural perfection.

Of the Greek historians of the Severan period, Herodian displayed little interest in foreign wars—his account of the Parthian campaigns of Septimius Severus is woefully terse—but Cassius Dio regarded both the Parthian campaigns of Severus and that of Trajan as outrageous burdens on the empire, undertaken to soothe the vanity of foolish men.[251] An early third-century panegyrist whose work was transmitted in the corpus of Aelius Aris-

---

249. Appian *pr.* 24–28.
250. Appian *pr.* 61.
251. Dio 68.29.1–3, 33.1; 75.3.2–3.

tides thought it natural to praise his emperor because he had trained the races beyond the borders to acknowledge their place in the order of things. "For when the Celts, who are the most physically imposing and murderous of all men beneath the sun and have committed many outrages, now make obeisance to their lord, knowing that it is better to live in peace than to make war . . . , when all dwelling beyond the Euphrates and Tigris to the east have been shaken, constrained, and taught to know their betters, when every continent is at peace, and land and sea crown their protector, and Greeks and barbarians speak in harmony, and the empire, like a ship or a wall, has been repaired and fortified and safely harvests its goods—what virtue could be better than this? Or what better or more profitable condition than this could there be?"[252]

In the fourth century the title "lord of the entire world" (expressed as *dominus totius orbis* or *dominus orbis terrarum*) became a regular part of imperial titulature, and writers of nonfiction in this period happily quoted the title even as they displayed an awareness that *totius orbis* merely equaled *orbis Romanus*. The historian Ammianus, for example, described a conversation between Theodosius and the barbarian king Igmazen in which the latter asked, "What rank are you, and what have you come here to do?" The latter responded, "I am the *comes* of Valentinian, lord of the entire world [*orbis terrarum dominus*]."[253] Theodosius saw no contradiction between that titulature and the fact that he addressed an independent king. Elsewhere Ammianus revealed that he, at least, knew better: in describing negotiations between Rome and the Limigantes, he recorded a request by that people to take up residence in far-off lands, so long as they lay within the confines of the *orbis Romanus*.[254] He similarly regarded as arrogant Valentinian's behavior toward the Quadi. That emperor built a fortress on the other side of the Danube, in their territory, as if they were subject to Rome.[255]

The author of the fourth-century geographical tract known as the *Descriptio totius mundi* also referred to the emperor as *dominus orbis terrarum*

---

252. [Aristides] *Or.* 35.35–36. The date and authorship of this work have been contested, largely because the author mentioned few concrete details about his subject. I follow Groag 1918, L. Swift 1966, and Oliver 1978, in assigning the work to the reign of Philip the Arab, but its precise date is of little import in my argument. For bibliography on this issue see Behr 1981, 399–400.

253. Ammianus 29.5.46; cf. Rufinus *Hist.* 10.8: Helena is *regina orbis ac mater imperii*. For one reflection of imperial usage in his period, see Grégoire 1922, no. 332 *bis:* Constantine and his three sons are τοὺς γῆς καὶ θαλάσσης καὶ παντὸς ἀνθρώπων ἔθνους δεσπότας.

254. Ammianus 19.11.6: the Limigantes were prepared *intra spatia orbis Romani, si id placuerit, terras suscipere longe discretas.*

255. Ammianus 29.6.2: *Valentinianus . . . flagrans trans flumen Histrum in ipsis Quadorum terris quasi Romano iuri iam vindicatis aedificari praesidiaria castra mandavit.*

and nevertheless began his work by describing, first, the lands beyond Persia, then the Persians and Saracens, and then at last Rome.[256] The author unconsciously produced similar inconcinnities when he set forth the plan of his work: "I ought first to describe how the races are distributed from east to west, after that how many are the races of barbarians, then the whole land of the Romans, as many provinces as there are in all the world [*quot sint in omni mundo provinciae*], and the wealth and power of each; what cities exist in each province, and what is most notable in each province or city."[257] We find a far more rational accounting of geography in the schoolboy's handbook compiled by Lucius Ampelius. We know nothing about Ampelius; even his dates cannot be fixed, though his text is often dated on stylistic grounds to the fourth century.[258] In the first chapter of his marvelous encyclopedia Ampelius defined the term *mundus* as the universe: "It has four parts: fire, from which comes heaven; water, from which comes the ocean; air, from come the winds and storms, and earth [*terra*], which, because of its shape, we call the *orbis terrarum.*"[259] When Ampelius returned to "earth" in the sixth chapter, he made a further distinction between the *orbis terrarum* that is beneath heaven, and the *orbis terrarum* that we inhabit.[260]

When the emperors Theodosius II and Valentinian II promulgated their collection of imperial legislation, they opened Book 1 with a selection of earlier pronouncements on the universal validity of imperial edicts. One of their own had urged that "if in the future it should please us to publish a law in one half of this most united empire," that law would be valid in the other half, provided that it had been properly transmitted.[261] The same emperors continued to produce legislation after the publication of their Code. At the heading of a law limiting the prerogatives and exemptions of imperial officials, the emperors complimented themselves for their eternal vigilance on behalf of their subjects: "By the majesty of that foresight by which Roman control has proceeded, bit by bit, to empire over the entire world [*totius orbis terrarum imperium*], we always take thought for the best interests of one and all."[262] Of course, the first law suggested by its very content that the em-

---

256. *Descriptio* 1–21 = *Expositio* 5–20. There is no need to enter here into the thorny question of priority between two texts that clearly reproduce the same source. Rougé's introduction only complicates the problem by referring to that source as the *Expositio.*

257. *Descriptio* 2.

258. *NHLL* §530. M. Arnaud-Lindet is far more circumspect about the linguistic arguments in the introduction to her edition. Her argument, however, that the dedicatee must be the future emperor Macrinus does not persuade. But the work must be dated after Trajan, with whose wars Ampelius was familiar.

259. Ampelius 1.2.

260. Ampelius 6.1–2.

261. *C. Th.* 1.1.5.

262. *N. Th.* 7.3.

pire was not "most unified," and Theodosius and Valentinian undoubtedly realized that they did not rule the world.

In fact, in the year before the second law was issued, the emperors wrote an edict on wills. This document, like all in its genre, preceded its legal content with an elaborate justification for both the content of the law and the authority of those who issued it: "It will profit barbarian races to be delivered to the sovereignty of our divinity, our victories will seem fruitful to our subjects, only if the advantages of peace are established by the regulations of the laws."[263] In referring to the settlement of barbarians within the empire, this law did not allude to a problem restricted to the late empire, as historiography on the subject has long suggested. Rather, such settlements, which had begun under Augustus, acquired new ideological purport after the government renounced its right and intent of eventually seizing their territory. Barbarians had now to knock on the door, so to speak, and be judged worthy of admission. Yet this law did far more than admit the existence of barbarian races beyond the limits of the empire. It submitted the legitimacy of the government to the judgment of its subjects; in so doing, the emperors acknowledged that obedience to their authority was predicated upon the rationality of their administration. Finally, the law qualified imperial victoriousness: the charisma that in an earlier age had demanded *consensus* now humbly bowed before it, no longer offering its victories as goals in and of themselves. The end of Victory was now peace.[264]

---

263. *N. Th.* 16.1 (trans. Pharr).

264. Cf. Josephus *Bell. Iud.* 7.158, construing the building of the Temple of Peace as the final act of Vespasian's triumph, and *Pan. Lat.* IX(12).10.5: Constantine is *in proeliis ferocissimus et parta securitate mitissimus.*

CHAPTER NINE

The King Is a Body Politick . . . for that a Body Politique Never Dieth

HOW DID ONE JOIN THE ROMAN COMMUNITY?

The emperor of the Roman world did not seize the imagination and then hold the allegiance of his subjects merely by asserting his invincibility in war, however divinely ordained.[1] Awareness of the engendering of loyalty as a process, indeed, one that came to fruition over generations, should not diminish our estimation of the cumulative effect of Rome's six centuries of undisputed hegemony over the Mediterranean world. "Dazzled with the extensive sway, the irresistible strength, and the real or affected moderation of the emperors, [the ancients] permitted themselves to despise, and sometimes to forget, the outlying countries which had been left in the enjoyment of a barbarous independence; and they gradually usurped the license of confounding the Roman monarchy with the globe of the earth."[2] Already in the late Republic, Romans could despair that flight beyond the empire was impossible, through a parochial unwillingness to contemplate life beyond the bounds of civilization. As Cicero remarked to Marcellus, on the subject of Caesar: "You ought to think of this: wherever you are, you will be in the

---

1. The title of this chapter is quoted from John Marsh, *An argument or debate in law: Of the great question concerning the militia; as it is now settled by ordinance of both the Houses of Parliament* (London: Underhill, 1642), 27: "For there is such a reciprocall and dependent relation, betwixt the King and his Kingdom, that the one cannot subsist without the other, for if they permit the kingdom to be destroyed, the King must of necessitie be ruined also. If the Master die, the relation of a servant must needs cease: for that relatives cannot subsist, the one, without the other. And if the kingdom fail, the King and Scepter must needs fall to the ground. And this is, in part the reason of that policy of Law, in the 7. *Rep. Calvins* case, that the King is a body politick, lest there should be an *interregnum;* for that a body politique never dieth."
2. Gibbon chapter 1 (1.55).

power of him whom you seek to flee. . . . The power of him whom we fear stretches so far that it embraces the entire world."[3] King Agrippa would like-wise caution the Jews: "For in the habitable world all are Romans, unless, maybe, the hopes of some of you soar beyond the Euphrates and you count on obtaining aid from your kinsmen in Adiabene."[4] Likewise, the congru-ence between provincial visions of the empire under Augustus and imperial artwork under Hadrian should not deceive us into thinking that a group of wealthy men, gathered to celebrate the imperial cult throughout the *koinon* of Asia, spoke for their province or that rhetoric directed at a province spoke to the consciousness of its residents. Reconciliation to Roman rule took place at the level of the individual, as each person incorporated the Roman emperor into his personal pantheon and accommodated himself to the bureaucratic rituals and ceremonial forms that endowed membership in the Roman community with meaning.

Many victims of Roman aggression agreed with the Romans themselves that success in war was proof of divine favor toward Rome. Polybius sub-scribed to that belief, but he had also insisted that it remained important to judge whether the Romans managed their δυναστεία for well or ill.[5] The Romans accepted the challenge implicit in that judgment: they prided themselves on their special skill in government as much as on their ability in war. In rhetoric addressed to audiences both at Rome and abroad, they claimed to govern for the simultaneous advantage of ruler and ruled.[6] It be-came possible for provincials to take this claim seriously—meaning, among other things, that they could cite this ideal against Romans who failed to live up to it—only with the advent of the Principate.[7]

The Romans continued to be victorious in war. Their requests that provincials display gratitude first for the expansion and then for the defense of the empire could have been received with bitterness. But many provin-cials chose to receive the announcement of Roman victories at face value. It is not now, nor is it likely to have been then, possible to determine whether their motives were genuine or self-interested. Over time that distinction be-came academic. A perceived change in Roman policy toward expansion al-lowed provincials to view the ideals and aims of their government as their own: all could now share a vision of humanity that bound residents of the

3. Cicero *Ep. ad fam.* 4.7.4; cf. Gibbon chapter 3 (1.106–107). But cf. Tacitus *Ann.* 6.14.2: *At Rubrio Fabato, tamquam desperatis rebus Romanis Parthorum ad misericordiam fugeret, custodes additi.*

4. Josephus *Bell. Iud.* 2.388 (trans. Thackeray).

5. Polybius 3.4.3–11.

6. See Chapter 3 at nn. 43–44.

7. See Chapter 4 at nn. 32–33, Chapter 5 at n. 64, and Chapter 8 at nn. 122–124; and cf. below, "The Emperor and His Subordinates."

empire together in opposition to those outside. The universalizing tendencies of *aurum coronarium* became one means toward unification.[8]

A similar gradual coalescence took place in the ideology of governance. The publications of the imperial bureaucracy must have given to many an impression of unprecedented activity and rationality. Provincials displayed their faith in the truth value of those documents when they constructed personal and institutional histories based on their contents and chronology.[9] That rationality was not merely one of equitable and systematic exploitation. Rather, the rulers of the empire perpetually sought to found their actions on the *consensus* of their subjects, making them active participants in their own subjugation by urging them to iterate the principles of the ruling order.[10] Many provincials were also eager to see an all-powerful emperor as superintendent over the empire's administration and guarantor of its fairness. As we have seen, imperial artwork went far to confirm that desire.[11]

This chapter explores how these intertwined perspectives shaped interactions between residents and the imperial administration. How could provincials conduct their business with the imperial administration through local functionaries and scribes and yet view their empire as ruled personally by the unique inhabitant of a charismatic office? How did agents of the government position themselves between emperor and subjects? To suggest two extremes: Did procurators present themselves as partners of the emperor in ruling over others, or as equivalent to civilians in subordination to an all-powerful ruler? Popular conceptions of the structure of society within the borders of the empire were linked to popular understanding of the nature and function of those borders, in ways both obvious and subtle. The rituals that marked passage into the Roman community are likely to have mirrored the ideological associations of the rituals through which members symbolically reenacted their commitment to that community.

Those rituals were necessary not least because the Roman community was constituted on premises atypical in the ancient world. The Romans' disinterest in defining themselves as a race and, therefore, in limiting their franchise to the children of citizens stood in stark contrast to practice elsewhere around the Mediterranean. Accordingly, when the conceptual geographies that ordered the Roman world acknowledged the realities of its political frontiers, they had above all to acknowledge that its boundaries were permeable. People knew that the citizen body, like the empire itself, had grown. They also recognized the existence of peoples who could not

---

8. See Chapters 3, 6, and 8.
9. Chapter 4.
10. Chapters 5 and 6.
11. Chapter 7.

or would not be added to their empire. Widely publicized events like the crowning of kings for Armenia and the recovery of standards lost by Crassus and Varus had, in different ways, established limits for Roman arms and signaled the flexibility of Roman foreign policy, even if one believed those limits temporary or voluntary or both.

If Romans did not regard the mere fact of conquest as sufficient reason to annex territory, nor annexation as necessary for the exercise of influence, how did their government define entry into the Roman community? Romans characterized membership in their community through participation in political and religious rituals that were variously open to or required of people of differing legal ranks.[12] Like the iconography of imperial victories, the rituals that concretized the ideology of governance proved susceptible to alternative interpretations. Provincials so inclined could manipulate their meaning to render them more inclusive, using them to erase the border between citizen and alien and to reposition it between resident and nonresident. As with histories constructed from documentary texts, or ethnic identities fashioned from triumphal iconography, so here Roman concepts and Roman rituals provided the raw material from which others could forge new, more inclusive definitions of emperor and empire.

Let us consider initially the official language of the state. In the process of annexation a territory had to be reduced *in formam provinciae*. This process produced a legal document called a *formula,* which described the relations between Rome and the political institutions of that province.[13] Like the government that he served, Velleius Paterculus regarded the process of annexation as separate from military history: only after recounting the history of Roman colonization, and then the history of Roman wars, did he announce his intent "to run through which races and nations were reduced *in formulam provinciae* and made tributary, and by what generals."[14] Others described Roman conquest in similar fashion: the Vindelici had been ignorant

---

12. Hopkins 1991b treats the Roman Republic, concluding that Augustus "degutted the central political rituals of the city of Rome" and that "the empire as a whole had no effective rituals to give all the inhabitants of the empire a single collective identity" (497, 498). I disagree.

13. On this process see Lintott 1993, 28–32, or Nicolet 1996, 22–23. This process and its Latin terminology were alike incomprehensible to those subjected to them. When Menippus succeeded in obtaining autonomy from the province for his city, Clarus thanked him awkwardly because it did not know what to thank him for: τῆς ἐπαρχείας ἀπὸ τῆς αὐτονομίας χωρισθείσης, in Robert and Robert 1989, ll. 37–39. Later Greeks translated *forma* quite literally as τύπος. (Cf. Reynolds 1982, no. 14, l. 3, or no. 15, ll. 12–14.) Mason 1974 does not treat *formula* and *forma* in these meanings. *Forma* was also the word used to designate maps, and these, too, had a specific bureaucratic form and function: see Nicolet 1991, 149–169, and Moatti 1993.

14. Velleius 2.38.1. Cf. Livy *Per.* 134, quoted in Chapter 8, no. 188.

of Latin law before being conquered by the princes of Augustus, just as the emperor's campaigns would cause the Tigris and Euphrates to flow beneath Roman laws.[15] Florus drew on the same distinction in the gnomic generalization he offered while describing the pacification of Germany: "It is more difficult to govern a province than to acquire one: for they are conquered by force, but they must be retained by law."[16]

In defining Roman governance of a province by the application of the rule of law, Florus showed himself in harmony with the laws of Theodosius and Valentinian quoted at the end of Chapter 8. Writing three centuries later than Florus, those emperors had used the uniformity and rationality of Roman law to express their vision of what united the empire, and of what distinguished life inside the empire from life outside. Roman authors from both East and West in that period thought in the same terms. For example, Ammianus wrote of the conquest and annexation of Arabia that "having imposed the title of 'province' and assigned a governor, the emperor Trajan compelled [Arabia] to obey our laws, after having often crushed the arrogance of its inhabitants while he pressed Media and the Parthians in war."[17] The author of the *Historia Augusta,* a contemporary of Ammianus, inserted a fictitious prophecy of the *haruspices* into his biography of the emperor Tacitus:[18]

> From the family of Florian and Tacitus will come an emperor of Rome . . . who will give judges to the Parthians and Persians, who will govern the Franks and Alamanni under Roman laws, who will remove every barbarian from Africa, who will impose a governor on the Taprobani, who will send a proconsul to the island of Juverna, who will act as judge over all the Sarmatians, who will make all the land surrounded by Ocean his own by conquering all nations.

The prophecy as a whole reveals a detailed awareness of the people who lived beyond the borders of the empire. In his choice of verbs and metaphors for conquest—"give judges to," "govern under Roman laws," "act as judge"—the author reveals himself in accord with the dominant paradigm of his culture.

Somewhat removed from these men, both in time and in subject matter, the historian Zosimus wrote a history of the decline of Rome under her Christian emperors. In his Book 4 Zosimus turned to the years between the accession of Valentinian I and the death of Theodosius I. His narrative of

---

15. Horace *Carm.* 4.14.7–9; Propertius 3.4.1–6. See also Pomponius Mela 1.41–42.
16. Florus 2.30.29.
17. Ammianus 14.8.13.
18. *SHA Tac.* 14.2.

these years relied primarily but not exclusively on the history of Eunapius of Sardis, who lived contemporaneously with the events that he described.[19] The history of the first half of Theodosius's reign concentrates on his efforts to reach a stable *modus vivendi* with the various barbarian tribes on either side of the Danube near Thessalonica.[20] In Chapter 30, Zosimus describes the attempt by Theodosius to introduce some "Scythian" recruits into the army. Rather than allow several legions of foreign troops to operate in the same area, Theodosius sent some of the new troops to Egypt and ordered troops from that province to join him on the Danube. When these two groups passed each other at Lydian Philadelphia, a fight broke out. A barbarian soldier had taken something from a merchant in a market and refused to pay, whereas the Egyptian soldiers showed great politeness to local civilians. When the barbarian soldier injured several merchants, the Egyptian soldiers, "being moved by what had happened, mildly advised the barbarians to refrain from such offenses, on the grounds that such a deed did not befit men who desired to live according to Roman laws [κατὰ ʽΡωμαίων νόμους]."[21] Regardless of the actual words spoken on that day, Zosimus, and perhaps Eunapius, presumed that reasonable barbarians would want to enter the empire for the privilege of living under Roman laws, that other people—in this case the Egyptian soldiers—labored under the same presumption, and that the rules governing civilian life also applied to representatives of the government, including the army.

This Roman model for the unification of a community infiltrated different modes of discourse in different populations. For example, Plutarch wrote an essay in two books on the fortune of Alexander the Great. He attributed to Alexander a desire to unite the world under a single *logos* and a single form of government and to join all men in a single *demos,* as constituent parts of a united political collectivity. Plutarch distinguished him in this respect from soldiers who, like brigands, plundered their conquests for booty—like Hannibal in Italy, or Treres in Ionia, or the Scythians in Media: "If the deity that sent down Alexander's soul had not called him back so swiftly, one law would govern all men, and they would look toward a single system of justice as toward a common light."[22] Although some impute to Alexander a desire to unite the world, supposing the influence of Stoic cosmopolitanism, that aspect of Stoic thought itself developed late in Zeno's work, and only in response to Alexander's conquests. Others see in this tra-

19. The precise period covered by the *History* of Eunapius is a matter of considerable dispute: see Barnes 1978, 114–123; Goulet 1980; Blockley 1981, 1–26; and Paschoud 1985.
20. Heather 1991, 147–156.
21. Zosimus 4.30.4.
22. Plutarch *Fort. Alex.* 330D–E.

dition the influence of Isocratean political rhetoric, which assigned to kings the duty to promote *homonoia,* or harmony in the state.[23] Neither theory seems to me necessary or sufficient to explain Plutarch's emphasis on law as the binding force within a *politeia.* On the other hand, Plutarch knew a great deal about Roman history and was, above all, well acquainted with Roman writings on Roman imperialism. Plutarch may here as elsewhere be indicted of rewriting Hellenistic history through Roman eyes.

Since Plutarch elsewhere credited the Romans with bringing their vast empire "within an orderly and single cycle of peace," we can feel relatively confident that he understood the import that Romans assigned to their legal and administrative expertise and was himself influenced by their beliefs.[24] Scattered evidence from the western provinces suggests that some there accepted Roman superiority on Roman terms, while others simply exploited Romans' correlation of the use of Roman legal forms with the attainment of civilization. In the first quarter of the first century B.C. two villages in the territory of Contrebia brought a dispute to the senate of that city. The senate referred the dispute to the Roman governor, C. Valerius Flaccus, who gave right of judgment in this matter back to it. The text that records these details describes the case in the technical language of Roman law, noting that the senate adopted in the course of its deliberations the necessary fiction, the *fictio,* that the rules of one community applied to both.[25] Although the senate of Contrebia did not use Roman laws as such, it clearly and deliberately learned and adopted Roman methods of legal argument, as well as the verbal formalities that endowed the legal process with its legitimacy. Finally, the inscription of the text on bronze, in Latin, suggests that the rituals of Roman government had already left a profound impression on this community.[26]

Roman arms did not inspire universal awe; nor was every race willing to concede Roman superiority in the customs of peace. Roman willingness to assume that such was the case could have disastrous consequences: this was the error of Quintilius Varus, governor of Germany under Augustus, who lost his life, his army, and their standards in the Teutoburg Forest in A.D. 9. Although Velleius Paterculus laid the blame squarely on Varus, he did so in part by arguing that Varus attempted to deal with the Germans as though they could be civilized. Velleius served under Tiberius in Germany and Dal-

---

23. For a powerful critique of such theories see Tarn 1948, 402–404 and 417–426.

24. See Chapter 3 at n. 26. Cf. Aelian *Hist.* 2.38: τί δὲ οὐκ ἂν ἔποιμι καὶ τὸν Ῥωμαίων νόμον; καὶ πῶς οὐκ ὀφλήσω δικαίως ἀλογίαν, εἰ τὰ μὲν Λοκρῶν καὶ Μασσαλιωτῶν καὶ τὰ Μιλησίων διὰ μνήμης ἐθέμην, τὰ δὲ τῆς ἐμαυτοῦ πατρίδος ἀλόγως ἐάσω;

25. Richardson 1983 and Lintott 1993, 155.

26. Other texts of this period on bronze are written in Celtiberian: Richardson 1983, 40.

THE KING IS A BODY POLITICK *343*

matia in precisely this period,[27] and this extraordinary narrative probably represents his rendering of the official explanation for the *Variana clades:*[28]

> When Varus took charge of the army in Germany, he decided that the Germans could be pacified by the law—even though they bear no resemblance to men beyond their possession of voices and limbs, and they cannot be subdued by the sword. Having entered Germany under this assumption, as though he were among men who rejoiced in the pleasures of peace, he dragged out the campaigning season with regular judicial activities. But the Germans are highly cunning despite their extreme wildness; indeed, theirs is a race of born liars to an extent scarcely credible to one who has no experience with them. So, by trumping up a series of fictitious lawsuits and issuing summonses to each other, then giving thanks that Roman justice was settling their disputes and that their wildness was being tamed by the novelty of this unknown discipline and that matters that they had been accustomed to decide by arms were now being resolved by law, they seduced Varus to such a state of torpor that he thought of himself as an urban praetor administering the law in the Roman Forum and not as the commander of an army in the wilds of Germany.

Velleius must have been fully aware that this narrative demanded the somewhat ironical concession that the Germans had been clever enough to exploit Roman pride in the superiority of their legal system, but he diverted this compliment by arguing that this deed simply revealed the perversity that rendered the Germans unsuitable for inclusion within the Roman state. We cannot, of course, trust Velleius to have known or even to have reported accurately the deeds, perceptions, and motivations of the Germans, but even as a commentary on Roman attitudes the passage reveals much.

A generation after Plutarch, the Christian apologist Tatian wrote his address to the pagans. He composed that treatise after traveling across the empire from his birthplace in Assyria to the city of Rome; he later claimed to have carefully examined monumental art and sculpture on those journeys.[29] In a central section of that work, Tatian criticized Greek science for relying on rhetorical argument rather than a genuine search for the truth. He also criticized its exponents for "making laws for themselves out of their own opinions."[30] Tatian connected Greek political thought and practice with other branches of learning and found no good in those disciplines, either:

---

27. Sumner 1970 remains the best introduction to the career and literary ambitions of Velleius, emphasizing his diligence and desire for accuracy. Cf. Gabba 1984, 80–81.

28. Velleius 2.117.3–118.1. Compare Suetonius *Iulius* 30.1: Caesar held assizes while waiting to cross the Rubicon.

29. Tatian *Ad Gr.* 33–35.

30. Tatian *Ad Gr.* 27.3.

"For this reason I also despise the code of law among you. For although there ought to be a single form of government for all men, at present there are as many codes of law as there are types of cities, with the result that practices shameful among some men are honorable among others."[31] Although Tatian directed his accusations about Greek philosophy exclusively against classical writers—Anaxagoras, Epicurus, and Herodotus, among others— he turned his eyes toward Rome and contemporary life when he wrote on political affairs. In those contexts he revealed the influence of Roman claims to have united the world under a single form of government and a single code of law, however much he wished to deny that Rome had succeeded in this aim.

In positing the Christian community as an alternative political structure to contemporary municipalities and even to the Roman empire, Tatian became one of the earliest participants within a debate that would divide Christians internally as much as it divided Christians from pagans.[32] Although others have emphasized the novelty of this willingness to stand outside the Roman community—and the Romans would discover how genuinely subversive this stance could be—Tatian's aspiration to unite the world reveals a powerful debt to Roman conceptions of political space and to Roman definitions of community. Indeed, positing the Roman empire as the only serious rival to Christianity's ambitions explicitly acknowledged that debt.

At the very end of Book 8 of his response to the pagan Celsus's exposition of *True doctrine,* Origen considered Celsus's argument that the desire to unite the entire world under a single "law" was idiotic:[33]

> After these things he pronounced some sort of wish: "Would that the Greeks and barbarians inhabiting Asia, Europe, and Libya, even to the ends of the earth, could agree to follow a single law!" Regarding this as impossible, he added, "Whoever thinks that, knows nothing." If I must say something, let me say a few words on this topic—although it requires much investigation and analysis—in order to reveal that his wish is not merely capable of realization, but will in fact be realized: all that is rational [$\pi\tilde{\alpha}\nu\ \tau\grave{o}\ \lambda o\gamma\iota\varkappa\acute{o}\nu$] will agree to follow a single law.

Writing under Marcus Aurelius, Celsus had probably rejected the possibility of uniting mankind on the grounds that some barbarians were not worthy to join the empire because they were *immunes imperii.* Origen did not contest the contemporary relevance of Celsus's remark, that such unity nei-

---

31. Tatian *Ad Gr.* 28.

32. On the history of this debate among early Christians see Peterson 1959, and cf. Momigliano 1986, and *idem* 1987, 142–158.

33. Origen *Cels.* 8.72.

ther obtained nor could be attained under the Roman empire. Rather, Origen argued, the Christian believed that the Logos would bring about such unity at some future date, all the while admitting that that date was probably far off: "it is probably true that such a condition is impossible for those who are still in the body; but it is certainly not impossible after they have been delivered from it."[34]

Over the next three chapters Origen argued a related and even more contentious point, namely how the Christian stood in relation to the Roman state. Origen took a position on this topic very much in harmony with that adopted by Tatian:[35]

> Celsus exhorts us also to "accept public office in our *patria* if it is necessary to do this for the sake of piety and the preservation of the laws" [ἕνεκεν σωτηρίας νόμων καὶ εὐσεβείας]. But we know of the existence in each city of another form of *patria*, created by the Logos of God [ἄλλο σύστημα πατρίδος κτισθὲν λόγῳ θεοῦ]. And we call upon those who are competent to take office, who are sound in doctrine and life, to rule over the churches.

Superficially Origen here has propounded a radically new definition of "community" and of the relationship that ought to obtain between an individual and the secular or non-Christian government. Like Tatian, however, Origen has accepted from the culture of Celsus many basic assumptions about the structure and governance of political collectivities. In particular, he embraces without question a nexus binding public service, piety, a normative legal code, and the notion of fatherland.

This insistence on divorcing the governance of a religious community from the political community in which and with which it coexisted, curiously enough, found its most politically powerful exponent in the emperor Constantine. In his biography of that emperor, Eusebius quoted a letter from Constantine to Sapor II, ruler of the Sassanid empire. Eusebius believed that Constantine wanted to place the Christians of Persia under his own care and regarded this as one expression of Constantine's desire to take thought for all men.[36] But Constantine did not question the legitimacy of Sapor's governance over Persia, nor even his rulership over his Christian subjects—so long as Sapor's piety toward them remained unquestioned.[37]

---

34. Origen *Cels.* 8.72.

35. Origen *Cels.* 8.75.

36. Eusebius *Vit. Const.* 4.8. On the text of the letter see Dörries 1954, 125–127.

37. Constantine at Eusebius *Vit. Const.* 4.13. If I am correct on the ideological thrust of Constantine's letter, then Barnes 1985, 131–132, misunderstands Constantine's claims regarding the Christians of Persia, though either way the effect seems to have been to incite Sapor against the Christians in his empire (ibid., 136). On Constantine's understanding of his governance over Christians and relations with the church see Seston 1947, Bréhier 1948, and Straub 1967; on Constantine's legacy in these matters, see Vittinghoff 1987 or Dagron 1996.

In general a very different picture of Christianity's relationship to Rome dominated Christian political thought. Most Christians argued that God himself had favored the foundation of a world empire by Augustus in order that Christianity might spread more easily through its homogeneous population. In adopting the reign of Augustus as the start of the empire, proponents of this view reveal the power exercised by Augustan ideology in reshaping popular narratives of Roman history.[38] Augustus had attempted to erase memories of the Triumvirate at Rome and of Republican corruption in the provinces, and his success issued in a peculiar myopia in ancient attempts to periodize their history. The Christians' argument also presumed the universal extent of the empire and, as such, was premised on a very traditional, Roman view of the extent of the empire. Christians tended to express this belief in two different fashions: by looking to the past, to the role of divine providence in the foundation of the empire, or forward, when the end of Rome—the fourth kingdom—would herald the end of the world. Already at the end of the second century, Tertullian seems to have inherited this theme as a standard response to charges of treason: Christians prayed for the emperor, and thus for the universal orbit and condition of the empire, as they did for Rome's affairs generally, because they knew that the great force that threatened the end of the entire world with hideous sufferings was held back by the respite provided by the Roman empire.[39] He combined that theme with the traditional tropes of imperial panegyric in his book *On the pallium:*[40]

> How much of this world has this age reformed! How many cities has the triple virtue of the present empire founded or augmented or restored! With God favoring so many emperors uniformly, how many censuses have been taken? How many peoples defeated? How many orders restored? How many barbarians shut out? Truly the world is the well-tilled field of this empire.

A century later Lactantius, another African Christian, but one who had very different relations with the imperial power, wrote in similar terms in the last book of his *Divine institutes:*[41]

> Indeed, the matter itself declares the collapse and ruin of the world will happen soon, except that it seems unnecessary to fear anything of the sort while the city of Rome is safe. But when that capital of the world [*caput illud orbis*] falls and begins to be a street, as the Sibyls say will happen, who doubts but that the end will have come for human affairs and for the entire world? Rome is the city that still sustains everything.

38. Cf. Vittinghoff 1964, 564–565, touching on related issues.
39. Tertullian *Apol.* 32.1, and cf. *Scap.* 2.6–7.
40. Tertullian *De pallio* 2.7.
41. Lactantius *Div. inst.* 7.25.6–8, and cf. 7.15.10.

"Lactantius is not only a Christian, he is a Roman who shrinks in terror from the thought that one day according to the scriptures of his religion the Empire of Rome would pass, as had already passed the empires of Babylon and of Alexander."[42]

Western Christians most openly praised the role of divine providence in the foundation of the empire after Christianity had become its official religion, when contemporary reality seemed to fulfill their *post eventum* prophecies. The Spaniard Prudentius, who abandoned an official career in order to honor his God in verse, invoked divine favor to prove Symmachus wrong in the desire to credit Victory with Rome's military glories: God rather than Victory had been instrumental in the empire's continued successes, for he had wished to join "people of discordant languages and kingdoms with different cultures under a single empire" to prepare the way for Christ.[43] The historian Orosius likewise hailed from Spain, though he traveled to Africa and Syria and back again before embarking on the history that would establish his fame. Again and again Orosius praised the empire as the preeminent sign of God's work on earth. On God's command Augustus had established the truest and most secure peace throughout the world, closing the Temple of Janus in the year when Christ was born. Augustus had likewise declined the title *Dominus* at precisely that time when the true Lord of the entire human race was born among men. The Roman empire was thus the fourth and final kingdom, and it would endure under the kingship of Christ until the end. Again, it was because the empire was founded through divine will that it unified the world. It had, for example, allowed Orosius to travel easily between provinces, identifying himself as both Roman and Christian throughout the world, with all the benefits that the former name brought him in matters of law and that the latter brought in matters of religion. Orosius took special pleasure in the benefits ensured by the presence of Christian emperors: Arcadius could avert earthquakes by his prayers.[44]

The West also brought forth the most famous successor to Tatian's hostility to Rome, namely Augustine. We should note in this context that despite his rejection of the terrestrial *civitas*, Augustine did give a privileged place to Rome. It was Rome whose foundation through fratricide mirrored the foundation of the earthly city.[45] The kingdom of the Jews remained unconquered until God allowed the Romans to make it tributary.[46] Augustine's readings in Sallust even prepared him to concede that the early citizens of Rome had founded their empire through a certain innate integrity: God

42. Baynes at *CAH* XII 661.
43. Prudentius *Symm.* 2.583–592 and 619–648.
44. Orosius 2.1.5–3.7, 3.3.2–3, 5.1.11–2.8, 6.1.5–9, and 6.22.4–11.
45. Augustine *Civ.* 15.5.
46. Augustine *Civ.* 17.23.

had thus shown "in the exceedingly wealthy and famous empire of the Romans how much civic virtues could achieve even without true religion."[47]

In his *Apology* Melito of Sardis insisted that divine providence had arranged the foundation of the empire to coincide with the birth of Christ, and thus the full growth and splendor of the empire dated from that era.[48] As in the West, this understanding of the relationship between the Roman state and the Christian church became especially widespread with the advent of a Christian emperor. But where Melito argued only that Augustus had not persecuted the church, Eusebius could, as Constantine's Christian apologist, attribute all evils of that day to polytheistic error (τῇπολυθέῳ πλάνῳ).[49] He developed this theme most fully in his panegyric *On the Church of the Holy Sepulchre,* delivered before Constantine himself in Jerusalem in September 335. Eusebius explained on that occasion that with the advent of Christ had come an end to regional and local governments, monarchies and democracies alike, "as the single empire of the Romans overcame them all and the eternally implacable and irreconcilable enmity of nations was completely resolved."[50] Just as the teaching of Christ would eventually create a universal kingdom of God, so the Roman empire aspired to bring the entire human race together in unity and concord. It had already succeeded in this aim with most nations, and was destined to reach to the edges of the world.[51] As the whole world came to resemble a single harmonious and united household, it became possible for anyone who pleased to make a journey and to leave home for wherever he might wish, and thus for all to travel from East to West and back again, as if traveling to their native lands.[52]

Among the next generation of Greek intellectuals Diodorus, bishop of Tarsus and friend of Basil, has been rather neglected, especially in light of the influence he wielded in the battle against Arianism, culminating in the Council at Constantinople in 381. This undoubtedly results from the almost total loss of his voluminous writings, which may itself be due to his occasional periods of exile.[53] Diodorus spent the early part of his career around the coast in Antioch, where he taught John Chrysostom and Theodorus of

47. Augustine *Ep.* 138.3.17. Augustine responded to the still widespread belief among pagans that only proper worship of the gods of the state could save the empire. The evidence for that belief is elegantly summarized in Baynes 1946a, 176–177.

48. Melito, at Eusebius *Hist. eccl.* 4.26.7.

49. Eusebius *Triak.* 16.3.

50. Eusebius *Triak.* 16.3–4 (translation indebted to Drake 1976).

51. Eusebius *Triak.* 16.5–6.

52. Eusebius *Triak.* 16.7.

53. For a list of his works, see *Suda* Δ 1149 (and cf. *CPG* 2:3815–3822). As the *Suda* attributes its list to one Theodorus, it seems a safe assumption that the works of Diodorus did not survive to its day. The editing of the fragments of Diodorus has only just begun.

Mopsuestia, among others. He wrote an astonishing number of books for his students, among which were a set of corrections to the *Chronicle* of Eusebius and many commentaries, including one on Paul's Letter to the Romans. In response to Romans 13:1 Diodorus wrote:[54]

> The Roman empire acquired its stewardship of the world from God. For, as the Savior was about to appear among men, God, anticipating his arrival, sent forth the Roman empire in His service, so that through it He might establish a calm and more peaceful life for men. Thus he delivered men from warring upon each other, and gave them the leisure to make His acquaintance.

Diodorus's enthusiasm for the benefits of empire seems all the more remarkable because the emperor Valens, his enthusiasm for Arianism waxing late in life, had used the secular power of the government to exile many orthodox, including Diodorus.

Deposition and exile were occupational hazards in that schismatic age. John Chrysostom proved no more able at avoiding controversy than his teacher, although his posthumous reputation and the condition of his corpus have not suffered for that fact. John shared Diodorus's views on the role of divine providence in the foundation of the empire. He expressed this belief in both the forms discussed above. For example, in a sermon on the Second Letter to the Thessalonians, John explained to his flock when the Son of Perdition would arrive and what was currently holding him back:[55]

> What is it that keeps him back? Some say the grace of the Holy Spirit, and others the Roman empire; I place myself among the latter. . . . When the Roman empire is completely overthrown, then he will come. And that is fitting. For as long as fear of this empire lasts, no one will submit swiftly. But when it is destroyed, he will seize upon the resultant anarchy and will attempt to steal the government of God and men.

Why does John speak of people "submitting" to the rule of Satan? Nothing in the text on which he comments suggests that the arrival of Satan will require active submission or active resistance. Rather, John believed that confidence in the strength and providentiality of the empire imbued its citizens with an extra degree of moral rectitude. Such a view was entirely in keeping with John's faith that the Roman empire was governed by an elected monarch. It was ultimately the *consensus* of the people, as expressed in their

---

54. Diodorus *Comm. in Ep. ad Rom.* 13:1: ἡ δὲ τῶν Ῥωμαίων ἀρχὴ καὶ οἰκονομίας ἐξαιρέτου παρὰ τοῦ θεοῦ τετύχηκεν. μέλλοντος γὰρ τοῦ σωτῆρος ἐπιφαίνεσθαι τοῖς ἀνθρώποις, μικρὸν προλαβὼν ὁ θεὸς εἰς ὑπηρεσίαν ἑαυτοῦ τὴν Ῥωμαϊκὴν προσεβάλλετο, δι᾽ ἧς ἥμερον καὶ εἰρηνικώτερον τῶν ἀνθρώπων τὸν βίον κατέστησεν, τῶν μὲν ἐπ᾽ ἀλλήλων πολέμων ἀπαλλάξας αὐτούς, τοσαύτην δὲ σχολὴν δοὺς τῆς ἑαυτοῦ ἐπιγνώσεως.

55. *Homil. in Epist. II ad Thessal.* 4.1 (*PG* 62.485–486).

choice of monarch and support for the state, that created the bulwark slowing the Final Judgment, even as it invested the emperor with his power.[56]

From John's early career as a priest in Antioch few sermons survive. In 386 or 387 he delivered a sermon on Christmas in which he explained at some length what evidence supported the dating of Christ's birth. Having referred briefly to the patent truth of the prophecies, John quoted Luke 2:1–7, which describes the journey undertaken by Mary and Joseph from Nazareth to Bethlehem when Augustus ordered a census:[57]

> From these verses it is clear that he was born at the time of the first census. From the ancient records in the *tabularia publica* at Rome, it is possible, for one who desires to know accurately, to learn the precise time of the census. . . . For Augustus did not publish his edict on the census of his own accord, but God aroused his spirit to do so, so that even unwittingly he might minister to the birth of Christ. And just how did Augustus contribute to the plans of God? . . . Christ was supposed to be born in Bethlehem: therefore the edict came forth, on God's urging, that compelled them, even unwillingly, to that city. For the law, which ordered all to register their names in their native cities, compelled Joseph and Mary to travel from Nazareth to Bethlehem in order to file their census declaration there.

On this occasion John did not explicitly insist that God had given rule of the world to the Romans in order to prepare the way for Christ; that belief, however, is implicit in the suggestion that divine providence ordered Augustus to take a census of all the world. John's confidence in the existence and accuracy of public records at Rome, silent testimonials to the rigor of Roman bureaucracy, is equally apparent.

John returned on other occasions to the prophecies that foretold the circumstances of Christ's birth. His sermons on the Jews, for example, often focused on the failings of the Jews that led God to transfer his favor to the Christians. In one such sermon he spoke of the prophecy of Jacob in Genesis 49 and concentrated on the verses concerning Judah, who, in his interpretation, stood for the Jewish nation:[58]

> Behold how this prophecy is fulfilled. For it happened at that time, when Jewish leaders were failing and the Jews came under the scepter of the Romans. And thus was fulfilled the prophecy that says, "Nor will a ruler leave Judaea, nor a leader from its feet, before he should come to whom it will bow down," meaning Christ. For just as Christ was born, the very first census was held,

56. See John Chrysostom *Homil. ad populum Antiochenum* 7.2, quoted at Chapter 6 n. 133.

57. *Homil. in diem natalem d. n. Jesu Christi* 2 (PG 49.353–354). See also his *Homiliae in Sanctum Matthaeum Evangelistam* 8.4 (PG 57.87).

58. John Chrysostom *Homil. contra Iudaeos et Gentiles* 3 (PG 48.817).

when the Romans ruled the race of the Jews and led them beneath the yoke of their empire.

Divine providence again stands in the background, present and potent insofar as God is responsible for the fulfillment of every prophecy. Much more fascinating here is the metonymy that John employs to describe the Roman conquest of the Jewish nation. The ritual of the census, so John insisted, in itself staked an ideological claim to ownership of the world. It was the functional equivalent of forcing one's enemies beneath the yoke, and it was all the more effective because it affected, indeed, could potentially uproot, the entire population of a conquered territory, and not just its army.

THE RITUAL LIFE OF THE ROMAN CITIZEN

Although John displayed great insight in acknowledging that an administrative act could perform ideological work, he recognized that achievement only in the imposition of the first census. We know, on the other hand, that the imperial government ordered a census every fourteen years. (This system changed in the early fourth century, when the government began to levy taxes in kind on the basis of assessments made every fifteen years. The fourteen-year periods between censuses in the early empire are often anachronistically called "indictions," after the official term for the fifteen-year assessments of late antiquity.) Indeed, Tertullian associated the multiple takings of the census with victories over barbarians as the activities of legitimate emperors and governments.[59] Although later censuses neither took so much time to perform nor required direct imperial supervision, they undoubtedly constituted a well-known and regular invasion into one's daily life. We have already considered the nature of that victoriousness for which *aurum coronarium* constituted such important evidence. But military victories could not be scheduled, and, in any event, anyone could flatter himself that the empire that had conquered him was truly warlike, indeed. We have also seen how a city might celebrate for years the day on which it received an imperial epiphany, but, once again, no one in the ancient world outside the city of Rome held his breath waiting for the arrival of his ruler.[60]

---

59. See *De pallio* 2.7, quoted above at n. 40.

60. See Chapter 7 in n. 201 for Hadrian at Oxyrhynchus, and cf. Sijpesteijn 1969. See also *IG* II² 3190, from Athens (a dating formula: τὸ Γ′ ἀπὸ τῆς Καίσαρος Ἀδριανοῦ ἐπιδημίας); *I. Didyma* I 254, honoring an individual for providing oil τῆι τηε νομιζομένηι ἱερᾶι ἡμέραι τῆς ἐπιδημίας τοῦ Αὐτοκράτορος Τραιανοῦ Ἀδριανοῦ Καίσαρος; *IG* IV² 383 and 384 (*SIG* 842), both from Epidaurus, registering the date from Trajan's visit to the city (and cf. *SEG* XXVI 826 and XXXIX 358, from Cyrene and Epidaurus, respectively); *IG* V.2 50–52, from Tegea, all dating around Hadrian's journeys (50, ἔτους ΜΒ′ ἀπὸ τῆς θεοῦ Ἀδριανοῦ εἰς τὴν Ἑλλάδα

Administrative rituals, on the other hand, ideally operated in harmony with, even as they helped to constitute, the rhythms of daily life. They therefore provided a field in which people could "practice the rituals of ideological recognition."[61] As we have seen, the Romans themselves defined membership in their community through participation in its bureaucratic procedures and not simply by coincidental habitation within the boundaries of the empire. What were the rituals of Roman citizenship? What brought about regular contact between provincials and the representatives of Rome? And how did these rituals help individuals to construct new identities within their familiar surroundings and within the larger community of their empire?

Although this section concentrates on regularly performed bureaucratic procedures, we should emphasize, in support of John Chrysostom, the extraordinary novelty of the Roman census.[62] The Romans themselves admitted that the census was a burden, and they knew it to be especially hard upon those for whom it was new. When the emperor Claudius urged the Senate to favor his grant of senatorial status to nobles of Gaul, he illustrated the law-abiding nature of the Gauls by reminding the Senate that they had not revolted during the taking of the first census in their province: "It was at that time a new and unaccustomed burden for the Gauls. We all know from intimate personal experience how laborious that chore is for us, now more than ever, although nothing is required beyond a public reckoning of our resources."[63] The Gauls may well have deserved these thanks: the tax rebellion in Egypt during the prefecture of Cornelius Gallus was probably associated with the initial imposition of the Roman tax system and, therefore, with the census. So, too, the Cappadocian Cieti revolted against their king Archelaus and took to the mountains when he attempted to impose a Roman-style census.[64] Reasons both practical and ideological thus recommended that a member of the *domus divina* personally supervise the first census in the provinces of the West.[65]

παρουσίας; 51, ἔτους δὲ ΚΖ' ἀπὸ τῆς θεοῦ Ἀδριανοῦ εἰς τὴν Ἑλλάδα τὸ πρῶτον ἐπιδημίας; and 52: ἔτους ΞΟ' ἀπὸ τῆς θεοῦ Ἀδριανοῦ τὸ πρῶτον εἰς τὴν Ἑλλάδα παρουσίας).

61. Cf. Jameson 1988, 2.54.

62. See Brunt 1990, 325; Edmondson 1990, 160–162; and Bowman and Rathbone 1992, 112–113.

63. *ILS* 212, col. 2, ll. 35–41.

64. On Egypt see Strabo 12.53; on the Cieti see Tacitus *Ann.* 6.41.1; and cf. Acts 5.37. Dyson 1971 and 1975 analyze revolts under the empire and argue that most revolts occurred during the organization of recently conquered territories, as local populations were pressured to meet Roman administrative demands. Tacitus seems to have agreed (*Ann.* 13.54.1).

65. In 27 B.C. Augustus held a *conventus* in Narbo and conducted a census of the three Gauls (Dio 53.22.5 and Livy *Per.* 134). Drusus supervised another census fourteen year later, a process connected, perhaps causally, with unrest in the region (*ILS* 212; Livy *Per.* 138–139; Dio 54.32). It seems almost certain that Augustus supervised the first census of Spain during his

Beyond the sheer physical disruption that excited Chrysostom's interest, the census demanded a detailed reckoning of one's position in the world: Where do I live? How many people live in my household, and how are they to be identified? How much habitable property do I have, and where is it? Individuals had to locate their household in a particular *civitas* and *pagus,* and name their closest neighbors.[66] The required information went far beyond that necessary for the assessment of capitation taxes or the compilation of land registers, though separate lists of that sort could be extracted from the rolls of collected census returns.[67] The initial impression created by the census must have been the arrogation by Rome of ultimate ownership of the land: after all, the power to adjudicate property disputes like those in Aezani and Pessinus implied the right also to deprive both parties of the land in question. Obviously Rome did not as a general rule take land away from provincials but simply reserved the right to tax it and, to this end, insisted upon detailed records of both ownership and changes in ownership of land throughout the empire.[68]

In asking that individuals claim property, know its boundaries, and mentally attach it to particular administrative entities, Romans forced permanent changes in the perception of local landscapes throughout the em-

---

organizational tour between 16 and 13 B.C.; the taking of the census would then have been associated with the first major wave of surveying and roadbuilding throughout the peninsula (Alföldy at *CAH*[2] X 454–455).

66. See Ulpian at *Dig.* 50.15.4.1, and cf. Bagnall and Frier 1994, 20–26. Brunt 1990, 329–335 and 345–346, considers the possibility that different information was collected in different provinces according to local needs. Census returns survive in reasonable abundance; for relatively complete examples see *Sel. pap.* 312 and 313, or *P. Mich.* VI 370, with signatures detailing the men who received copies for examination. Census returns required only a general description of the location of habitable property. Provincials had to file separate documents regarding other property, from which—as distinct from the census—a "map" of a community could be drawn: see Hanson 1994.

67. *P. Lond.* II 257–259 extracts lists of free males subject to the capitation tax, and *P. Mich.* XI 603 preserves a contract between a body of scribes and a metropolis for the former to extract from the census returns, among other things, a list of those *not* subject to taxation. From the Diocletianic census, which was not quattuordecennial, *P. Cair. Isid.* 7 extracts information about the landholdings of two brothers, separated into tax categories; though the information ultimately came to the authorities by way of the census, it is not clear whether the immediate source of this extract was the roll of census returns or the village land register. Several detailed land registers have survived; on them and the information in them see Hanson 1979, 1992, and 1994; Bowman 1985; and Bagnall 1992.

68. For examples of declarations of arable land, see *P. Mich.* VI 366–369. For Roman interest in real-estate transactions outside Egypt see *P. Yadin* 16, Wörrle 1975; Nicolet 1991, 149–169; Edmondson 1992/93, 27–28; and Moatti 1993. Note that Babatha obtained her "verified" copy from an imperial official; another copy was posted in the local basilica (ll. 1–5). The original text may have been in Greek, but the prefect's signature on the original was in Latin (l. 36).

pire.[69] Florus recorded the efforts of Augustus to induce Spaniards to abandon the hills for life in new cities on the plains.[70] He did not notice that the Romans imposed new ethnic categories on the Spaniards. In Gaul, names as familiar as "Narbonensis" appear to have become standard and legally correct only under Augustus, when the emperor himself supervised the first census of that region.[71] Strabo, on the other hand, did notice that the Roman administrative map of Asia Minor took little account of previously existing political or ethnic boundaries.[72] The Romans caused similar disruption in Gaul: in A.D. 46 Claudius attempted to resolve a problem that had arisen some decades before. The Romans had imposed names, groupings, and differing legal statuses on tribes around Tridentum, without regard for their existing ties to each other. Some of those people, through deceit or confusion, had claimed citizenship when it was awarded to the Tridentini, and their enthusiasm for Rome had extended so far that some from those tribes had served in the army and Praetorian Guard. Some had even served on juries at Rome. Claudius took the only reasonable way out and awarded citizenship to the Anauni, Tulliasses, and Sinduni alike.[73]

The initial census thus created wrinkles in the social fabric that were both greater and longer-lasting than simple physical disruption. But the Romans went further still. Long before the Roman administration decided to compile a new census every fourteen years, Rome began to administer the census in Egypt in 11/10 B.C., in conjunction with the imposition of the poll tax.[74] Those early censuses did more than register persons and property: they recorded, and initially they must have determined, the status of all Egyptians in their relations with their government. The assignment of new legal ranks must also have reconstructed individuals' roles in their local municipalities and, therefore, their relations with each other.[75]

The fourteen-year cycle took shape under Tiberius.[76] In its stable form, the most recent census did not include children born since the last census.[77] Such children might easily, on the death of their parents, require confir-

---

69. On this process in Lusitania see Edmondson 1992/93, 26–30.

70. See Chapter 3 at n. 9 on Florus 2.33.59–60.

71. See C. Goudineau at *CAH²* X 471 on Dio 53.22.5.

72. See Chapter 3 in n. 61 on Strabo 13.4.12.

73. *ILS* 206.

74. Bagnall 1991, esp. 264–265, argues for a seven-year census cycle in Egypt beginning as early as 11/10 B.C. Rathbone 1993 agrees and adds further evidence.

75. See Nelson 1979; Bagnall and Frier 1994, 28–30; and Hanson 1997, 417–421.

76. Bagnall 1992, 255–256 and 264, denies this for lack of explicit evidence for a census in 19/20, fourteen years before the attested census of 33/34.

77. There did exist, as early as the reign of Tiberius, a supplementary registration of minors not yet liable for *laographia:* see Hanson 1979 on *P. XV Congr.* 13, l. 6.

mation of their status under Roman law. The *Tabula Banasitana* provides ample evidence of the value that Rome placed on accuracy in recording grants of citizenship. Imperial Rome did far more than that, however. As one consequence of his marriage legislation, Augustus ordered the registration of all births of legitimate children to Roman citizens. Although birth certificates have survived only in Egypt, literary references to such registrations prove that the system operated throughout the empire.[78] By the end of the first century citizen parents had begun to register their illegitimate children, and by the end of the second century it seems that noncitizens also informed authorities of additions to their families.[79] To complete their own records and to provide for their children, parents could request a personal copy of the official record:[80]

> When C. Bellicius Calpurnius Torquatus and P. Salvius Julianus were consuls [A.D. 148] on 11 November in the twelfth year of Imperator Caesar T. Aelius Hadrian Antoninus Augustus Pius, on the seventh day in the month Hathyr, in Egyptian Alexandria, this copy was made and certified from the white board of registrations of freeborn children that is posted in the Atrium Magnum, on which was written what is written below:
>
>> When C. Bellicius Calpurnius Torquatus and P. Salvius Julianus were consuls, in the twelfth year of Imperator Caesar T. Aelius Hadrian Antoninus Augustus Pius, when M. Petronius Honoratus was the prefect of Egypt, registrations of children were received without official investigation.[81] From tablet 5, after page 3: on 14 September Tiberius Julius Discorides HSS V has declared his daughter, Julia Ammonus, born to him by the woman Julia Ammonarius on 20 August of that year,[82] to be a Roman citizen, according to the record book.

78. On birth certificates in general see Schulz 1942 and 1943. For registrations outside Egypt see Apuleius *Apol.* 89, Juvenal 9.84–85, together with *Scholia vetera in Iuvenalem* (*ad loc.*). See also *SHA Marc.* 9.7–8, and Servius on Vergil *G.* 2.502, quoting and commenting on Juvenal 9.84. See also Dessau on the *Tabula alimentaria Ligurum Baebianorum* and the *Tabula alimentaria Veleias, ILS* 6509 and 6675, respectively.

79. See *P. Petaus* 2, from A.D. 185, and cf. *P. Oxy.* X 1267, from A.D. 209, which may preserve the registration of a legitimate noncitizen child: the parents do not specify their citizenship, either directly or indirectly, nor do they record the possession of priestly rank.

80. *CPL* 156. *CPL* contains several other declarations, for legitimate and illegitimate children, some with Greek summaries. (See, for example, 157 l. 13: *tabula IIII pagina V* 158–160 record births to soldiers.) For the expansion of the abbreviations, see Schulz 1943, 56–57. For registrations in Greek, see *P. Hamburg* 31, *P. Oxy.* X 1267 and XXXI 2565, *P. Tebt.* II 299, and *Sel. pap.* 309 and 311.

81. In the present context this phrase (*citra causarum cognitionem*) refers to the lack of an investigation of each parent's claim to citizenship: Schulz 1942, 87.

82. The combination of high infant mortality and no tax liability until age fourteen seems to have caused many to wait some time before registering children: the parents in *P. Oxy.* X 1267 registered their son at age three years and five months.

The extraordinary fullness of the administrative details testifies to the value that the Roman government and parents alike placed on providing their children with accurate and official records of their status. Over time, as the franchise extended, more and more people would have become eligible to obtain such powerful artifacts from their government. In the meantime, noncitizens could have seen in such texts not only the privileges that accrued to Roman citizens, but also the profound interest the government took in knowing the precise legal status of everyone under its care.

The Roman imperial administration intruded into its subjects' lives to mark several other milestones of life. Just as newborn Roman citizens received certificates documenting their status, so military veterans received diplomas documenting the award of citizenship to them and their posterity on completion of their military service. The army presented the award as a specific grant by the emperor himself and gave to each soldier a personal copy of the emperor's edict, called a *diploma*. The diploma consisted of two copies of the imperial grant on two separate sheets of bronze, tied together so that one copy faced out and one was protected inside.[83] As scribes did with birth certificates, the copyists of these documents placed a premium on exact duplication of the official text:[84]

> Imperator Caesar Vespasian Augustus, pontifex maximus, holding the tribunician power for the sixth time, fourteen times acclaimed *imperator*, father of his country, censor, consul six times and consul-designate seven times: to the footsoldiers and cavalry who served in the Tenth Cohorts, which are called the First Antiochene and Sugambrian . . . , who served twenty-five or more years and whose names are written below, and to their children and their posterity, Vespasian grants citizenship, and to the soldiers he gives the right of lawful marriage. . . . On 28 April, in the consulship of Caesar Domitian son of Augustus [for the third time], and of L. Pasidienus Firmus.
>
> From the First Rhaetian Cohort, under the command of C. Quintius Laberius Tutor Sabinianus, to footsoldier Hera son of Serapion, from Antioch. Copied and verified from the bronze tablet that hangs on the Capitolium at Rome, by the public fishpond on the Tribunal of the Gods.

83. Texts and drawings of extant diplomata are edited with invaluable introductory material in *CIL* XVI. On the role of diplomas in aiding veterans and their families to identify with the empire's dominant culture see Vittinghoff 1986.

84. Roxan 1978, no. 2. The inside copy reads *descriptum et recognitum ex tabula aenea quae fixa est Romae in Capitolio*. The outside copy adds *pos. piscinam in tribunal. deorum*, as well as the names of the witnesses to the authentication of this copy. Diplomas from Egypt frequently refer to an original posted on the Caesareum (Σεβαστεῖον) in Alexandria: *recognitum fecisse ex tabula aenea, quae est fixa in Caesareo Magno escendentium scalas secundas sub porticum dexteriorem secus aedem Veneris Marmoreae in pariete, in qua scriptum est id quod infra scriptum est* (*CPL* 104, exerior col. II, ll. 6–9).

In the case of the military diplomas, the men producing copies for the individual soldiers reproduced the entire heading of the original grant precisely, including the reference to the plural "names written below," even though only one name followed on personal copies. The senate of Contrebia had well understood the nature of Roman legal forms: it was not merely what was written, but how it was written, that endowed a document with its legal power.

Since the census could update the tax lists only every fourteen years, the government allowed individuals to file information related to their tax liability at any time in the intervening years. Since males became liable for the poll tax only at age fourteen, there was no administrative need to register the births of noncitizens: they would be caught, as it were, in the next census.[85] In theory the law required parents to present boys to local officials at age fourteen in order to record their eligibility for the poll tax; they had an incentive to do so if they believed that the result of the examination would be partial or full exemption from the tax. Of course, proving eligibility for such an exemption required the family to present corroborating documents relevant to its status. Self-interest thus demanded that families keep personal archives of all official documents, and the sands of Egypt have yielded abundant proof that families did just that.[86] Hence there is every reason to believe that Egyptians rapidly came to understand the respect that Roman officials paid to official documents: residents of Oxyrhynchus in the middle of the third century continued to establish their legal status by referring to their families' *epikriseis* of A.D. 4/5.[87]

Taxpayers in every age have sought to avoid their obligations and reduce their liability. The Roman system had a loophole: families could conceal their male children for an extra fourteen-year cycle by underreporting their ages at the first census after their birth. If a sufficient number of males sought to understand the law well enough to circumvent it, this system could have effected a permanent shift in the way men spoke of their age. Extant Egyptian census returns suggest an underreporting of male children con-

85. But see above in n. 77 on the process of supplementary registrations. The government also recorded arrears for taxpayers delinquent because they were away from their *idia* at the time of the *laographia:* Hanson 1980b, 242.

86. See, for example, *Sel. pap.* 314 (*P. Ryl.* 103): the young man registering his brother is able to cite his father's registration documents, his immediate family's previous two census returns, his mother's birth registration, and his mother's parents' census return, as well as the records of his own examination and the records of his property holdings. For the importance of such personal archives, see below, "The Faith of Fifty Million People." Priestly rank, which exempted some individuals from the poll tax, was hereditary and proved by presenting documentation of one's father's rank: see *P. Oxy.* X 1265.

87. Hanson 1997, 419 n. 19.

sistent with this practice.[88] Families were, of course, not liable for relatives who died. If people had incentive to underreport male births, they had every reason to report deaths.[89] There was, of course, a form for this, too:[90]

> [In a professional hand:] . . . My grandson Sarapion, registered in the afore-mentioned quarter of Dionysius's District, subject to the poll tax, died in the month Mecheir of this present thirteenth year of Hadrian Caesar our emperor. I therefore request that he be put on the list of the deceased. . . . [Signed in the hand of Sabinus, the declarant:] I swear by the fortune of Imperator Caesar Trajan Hadrian Augustus that the foregoing is true. [In a third, scribal hand:] To the scribes of the metropolis: if the aforementioned is truly dead, take appropriate action. [In a fourth hand:] Signed by me, Philoxenus, scribe. [In a fifth hand, registering its receipt:] Dionysius's District.

Just as the census required information far beyond that necessary for the tax rolls, so we find death registrations of people not subject to poll tax. Such texts uniformly contain the notable admonition that the relevant name should be struck from the lists of persons with similar legal status.[91]

Individuals also had to inform the administration of changes in their property holdings. Papyri thus preserve submissions to the authorities regarding the birth and death of slaves, as well as records of land use, transactions involving land, and agricultural and livestock production.[92] Declarations regarding the fertility of farmland were particularly important: Rome did not wish to tax land merely because someone owned it. As Ulpian wrote in Book 3 of his *On censuses:* [93]

> The census taker must allow for fairness, insofar as it is appropriate to his office for a man to be relieved of his tax burden if, for just cause, he is not able to enjoy the extent of land declared in the public records. If some of his land has fallen into an abyss, he should be relieved of liability for it by the census taker. If his vines are dead or his trees have withered, it would be unfair for their number to be counted in the census. If, on the other hand, he has cut down his trees or vines, he is ordered to declare their number as it was at the time of the census, unless he can show cause to the census taker for having cut them down.

88. Bagnall and Frier 1994, 27, 97–98.

89. On death registrations see Montevecchi 1946.

90. *Sel. pap.* 310.

91. See, for example, *P. Tebt.* II 300 and 301, from A.D. 151 and 190, respectively, both submitting news of the deaths of priests exempt from the poll tax.

92. Slave births: *Sel. pap.* 311. Slave deaths: *P. Oxy.* XXXI 2564. Land use: *P. Mich.* VI 366–369. Real-estate transactions: *Sel. pap.* 325 (*P. Oxy.* II 245). Agricultural production: *Sel. pap.* 321, 322, and 331. Cf. *P. Amh.* II 73, a declaration of sheep and goats, comparing present stock with the previous year's.

93. Ulpian at *Dig.* 50.15.4.1.

The intrusiveness of the government thus had its complement in the government's widely advertised and rigorously observed desire that the tax burden should be distributed and administered fairly.

The detailed geographical knowledge compiled through the Roman census was exploited most eloquently by Agrippa in the pages of Josephus. In the famous speech in which Agrippa sought to dissuade the Jews from revolting, he asked them to consider the strength of their foe. Starting with the provinces north of Judaea, he surveyed the empire: the five hundred cities of Asia observed Roman rule without garrisons. The tribes and regions along the Danube were once fiercely independent but now submitted; likewise the Gauls and Iberians. Germany and Britain had more reason to feel confident than did the Jews, yet they dared less than the Jews were contemplating. When, at length, Agrippa turned to the subject of Egypt, he was satisfied to recount its history and present condition: "It has seven and a half million men, excluding those dwelling in Alexandria, as can be seen from the returns for the poll tax." Josephus did more than depict Agrippa as familiar with the extent and arms of the empire. He also found it credible that Agrippa should know the figures yielded by the census of Egypt, and he certainly thought that the institution of the census and its accuracy would be familiar to all.[94]

The annual oaths sworn to the emperor seem to stand apart from the administrative rituals discussed thus far. Neither filing a census return nor registering the birth of a baby required an obvious emotional commitment to Rome. In point of fact, filing any official declaration with the imperial bureaucracy required swearing an oath regarding its truth value, and that oath was sworn by the *genius* of the current emperor.[95] That act in itself had religious implications, which will be discussed below.[96] But provincials had also to swear an oath of loyalty to the emperor each year, quite apart from their necessary interactions with his representatives. The loyalty oaths have attracted attention from distinguished scholars in the past, and regarding their form and frequency I have nothing new to contribute.[97] All later oaths fall into two categories, both of which have antecedents in the reign of Augustus: prayers for the health of the reigning emperor (*vota pro valetudine* or

---

94. Josephus *Bell. Iud.* 2.365–387 at 385.

95. For the form and uses of the θεῖος ὅρχος see Packman 1991, 1992a, 1992b, and 1994, citing earlier bibliography. For the later period see Worp 1982.

96. See below at n. 240, and Chapter 6 at n. 235.

97. See in particular Cumont's commentary on *Studia Pontica* III, no. 66. That text is reproduced as *ILS* 8781 and as *EJ* no. 315. See also von Premerstein 1937, *passim*, but esp. 32–73. Among later works see Weinstock 1962, Sherwin-White 1966 on Pliny *Epp.* 10.35–36 and 100–101, Herrmann 1968, González 1988 (publishing *AÉ* 1988, 723), and Mitchell 1993, 1.92 and 100–102.

pro salute principis) and oaths to obey his commands (*iurare in verba principis*).[98] These oaths had developed in a series of experiments between the final years of Caesar and the early 20s B.C. In form and content they duplicated and came to replace the Republican prayers for the health of the state (*vota pro rei publicae salute*). As such they participated in a gradual transference of focus in both popular and official religious acts, from concern for the commonwealth to concern for the individual in whose care the commonwealth now resided.[99] After the death of Augustus, the latter oaths evolved into oaths to uphold the deeds of the divine Augustus or of all the *divi* (*iurare in acta divi Augusti* or *in acta divorum principum*). In their fully developed form, the oaths were sworn on two separate occasions: on 3 January all undertook prayers for the health of the reigning emperor and for the eternity of the Roman empire.[100] Joyce Reynolds has shown that the wording of the *vota* undertaken in Cyrenaïca in the first century followed a pattern identical to that observed by the Arval Brethren at Rome. Reynolds modestly suggests that it is "perhaps of some significance also to the study of Rome's relations with the provinces to establish that, in what [was] almost certainly a civilian context, and in a Greek-speaking province, these ceremonies followed a characteristically Roman pattern, and that the prayers were both made and recorded in Latin."[101] Individuals then repeated their prayers for the emperor's safety and renewed their oaths of loyalty on the reigning emperor's *dies imperii*. Some cities sent annual embassies to congratulate the emperor on that day, no doubt mentioning their own displays of *pietas* loudly and often in their messages.[102]

The wording of the oaths is uncontroversial and will not detain us here. The specific form of the ceremony in which the prayers were made and the oaths administered, on the other hand, requires some investigation. Al-

98. See Augustus *Res gestae* 9.1–2 and 25.2.

99. Versnel 1980, esp. 562–577. Cf. below at nn. 264–268.

100. Plutarch *Cicero* 2.1; Gaius at *Dig.* 50.16.233.1; cf. Tertullian *Apol.* 35.4.

101. Reynolds 1962, 33. For the Flavian period, see *Acta fratrum Arvalium*, s.a. 75 (p. xcix Henzen = *ILS* 5033), s.a. 81 (p. cvii Henzen), and s.a. 87 (p. cxvi Henzen = *ILS* 5034). See also Pliny, *Epp.* 10.35–36 and 100–101, under Trajan, and *Feriale Duranum* on 3 Jan. (Fink, Hoey, and Snyder 1940, 52–73).

102. For oaths on the *dies imperii* of Vitellius see *Acta fratrum Arvalium*, s.a. 69 (*ILS* 241 is preferable for these events to the text in Henzen's edition); on the *dies imperii* of Vespasian see Tacitus *Hist.* 2.79 (*Initium ferendi ad Vespasianum imperii Alexandriae coeptum, festinante Tiberio Alexandro, qui kalendis Iuliis sacramento eius legiones adegit. isque primus principatus dies in posterum celebratus, quamvis Iudaicus exercitus V nonas Iulias apud ipsum iurasset*). For the oath to Trajan on 28 Jan., see Pliny *Ep.* 10.52–53. On annual embassies see Pliny *Ep.* 10.53.1–2; with Sherwin-White 1966, *ad loc.*; and Millar 1977, 375–385. Severus advertised his relationship with Trajan not least in his maintenance of prayers at that emperor's *dies imperii* (Fink, Hoey, and Snyder 1940, 77–79; cf. Chapter 6 at n. 67).

though Pliny reported to Trajan the prayers that he made during his first January in Bithynia, his wording on that occasion reveals little about exactly who made them: "We have undertaken our solemn prayers for your safety, by which the public safety is maintained, Lord."[103] Pliny generally wrote of himself and his staff in the first person singular. To whom does the plural "we" on these occasions refer? Trajan responded by revealing his pleasure that Pliny together with "the provincials" had "freely" renewed the prayers.[104] Pliny's letter regarding the oath on Trajan's *dies imperii* mentioned that soldiers and provincials alike undertook that oath. Praying for Trajan on behalf of the human race, whose safety and security depended on his health, the soldiers swore "in solemn fashion," while the provincials swore the same oath, vying with the soldiers in their display of piety.[105] In his letters from the next year, on 3 and 28 January, Pliny named both soldiers and provincials as participating in both sets of prayers and oaths. Since Pliny, as a senator, would have undertaken these same vows in the Senate at Rome, we must presume that he both presided over and participated in the ceremonies.[106] Though extant epigraphic records of oaths take different approaches to describing the ceremony itself, many identify other participants in the ceremony, beyond the residents of the municipality swearing the oath. Some, for example, name the legate who presided, and others include "the Roman citizens among us" as participants.[107] Pliny's letters make it clear that all residents in a given area took part in the ceremony, with each other as witnesses to their piety, regardless of their respective legal ranks.

Registering one's children could guarantee privileges in the future, and prompt filing upon a relative's death could lower one's tax burden; neither the census nor property returns, however, promised anything beyond the assumption of some fiscal liability to the government. Rome's further requests for seemingly pointless information could easily have created suspi-

---

103. Pliny *Ep.* 10.35.

104. Pliny *Ep.* 10.36.

105. Pliny *Ep.* 10.52.

106. Compare *ILS* 4907, from Salona: the pontifex read the text to the duovir, who repeated after him. Note, too, that the the colonists explicitly follow Roman practice (*ceterae leges huic arae eaedem sunto, quae arae Dianae sunt in Aventino monte dictae*). Other colonies used similar language to declare their allegiance to paradigms established at Rome. (Cf. *ILS* 112 and *CIL* XI 361.)

107. See *ILS* 190, from Aritius in Lusitania; *ILS* 8781 (*EJ* no. 315), from Gangra, near Neapolis in Paphlagonia; and *IGRR* IV 251 (Smallwood, *Gaius* no. 33), from Assus in the Troad. On *AÉ* 1988, no. 723, see González 1988, 115. Compare *AÉ* 1955, 210, which, despite its date (A.D. 220), some have interpreted as indicating that citizens in Gaul celebrated the imperial cult separately from the Council of the Three Gauls (Beard, North, and Price 1998, 1.353 n. 116). I incline to treat its mention of citizenship as the proud boast of those who now possessed it.

cion toward an intrusive and exploitative government. What did the average provincial receive for working hard and playing by the rules? Trajan's first response to Pliny provides one clue. The oath ceremony at one level required "free" participation from the provincials: their universal consent to Roman rule generally, and to a specific emperor in any given year, actively legitimated their submission to his governance. Each family's copy of its most recent census return thus gave physical form and bureaucratic permanence to an abstract relationship that existed between individuals and their emperor. Each regular ritual interaction with the imperial bureaucracy thus interpellated provincials as individual subjects, an impression reinforced by the government's retention and distribution of copies of its records. Latent behind the entire ritual of the census was the possibility that Hadrian, for example, could potentially know as much about residents of the empire as they knew about him, and that he could extract a list of all the residents from the assembled returns. How better to identify, define, and unite the members of his community?

THE EMPEROR AND HIS SUBORDINATES

The imperial government flooded the provinces with legislation and administrative acts. Those documents insisted on the internal rationality of the system that generated them: just as the rewards of imperial victories fell upon all residents of the empire equally, so, too, did its burdens and regulations. The dramatic clauses regulating both the legibility of texts and the probationary periods before they took effect were directed toward a similar end. Yet all the rules and regulations in the empire availed naught if the imperial officials administering those rules were corrupt. Given the difficulty of asking any bureaucracy to police itself, emperors could do little more than advertise their desire that their administration of the empire be as fair and honest as possible. The mere publication of these advertisements must have created some impression. Emperors did far more than that, however, and the ideological import of the oath and prayer ceremonies directs our attention in a profitable direction. Provincials cannot have failed to notice that the soldiers and imperial procurators swore the same oath and made the same vows as they did: the ceremony paraded the equivalency of all its participants as subjects of a higher power. The Roman government had, of course, more than the two levels of governor and emperor. On the one hand, imperial propaganda to the provinces asserted the rationality of its bureaucracy. It was in theory possible to appeal the decisions of an official at one level to an official at the next.[108] On the other, the emperor adver-

---

108. Cf. Ulpian at *Dig.* 1.16.6.2: Legates ought not consult the emperor, but rather their proconsul, and he is obliged to respond to the inquiries of his legates.

tised himself as the ultimate arbiter over the rulings of his subordinates. His unique, charismatic power thus guaranteed the regular operation of his formally hierarchic administration.

We have already seen that Augustus promised provincial populations that his concern on their behalf would reform and oversee the administration of both the provinces under his control and those under the authority of the Roman people.[109] Strabo's *Geography* includes the only extant description of Augustan provincial administration by a contemporary. Although he admitted the division of the provinces between "those of Caesar" and "those of the people," Strabo also wished to see Augustus as final arbiter over the people's provinces: it was Augustus who "in the beginning organized the people's provinces, making two of them consular . . . and ten praetorian."[110] Writing at a considerable remove from that period, Cassius Dio applauded this promise not for its immediate realization, but for the restrictions it imposed on senatorial governors in particular.[111] Josephus had similarly depicted King Agrippa urging the Jews to exploit such promises for their own benefit: "'We ought to conciliate the powers that be, not rouse them to anger."[112] It would be both unwise and unfair to risk war with Rome for the evils of a single governor: "Granted that the agents of Rome are intolerably harsh, it does not follow that all the Romans are unjust to you any more than is Caesar. Yet it is against them that you are going to war. It is not by their orders that some oppressive governor comes from them to us, and they cannot see in the West their officers in the East. . . . How absurd it were, because of one man to make war with many, for trifling grievances to take up arms against so mighty a power, which does not know even the nature of our complaints!"[113]

Romans had always sought to govern their far-flung empire through local aristocracies, because their personnel were few and because they consciously sought to create social structures committed to the maintenance of the status quo.[114] But the emperors of Rome did not treat the use of civilian rather than imperial officials as an opportunity to abdicate responsibility in matters of justice. When governor of Asia, Antoninus Pius published a provincial edict setting forth the *formulae* through which he would administer jus-

---

109. See Chapter 4 at nn. 32–33, Chapter 5 at n. 64, and Chapter 8 at nn. 122–124 on the Fifth Cyrene Edict. On Greek perceptions of the division between imperial and senatorial provinces see Millar 1984, 46–48.

110. Strabo 17.3.25.

111. Dio 54.7.4–5.

112. Josephus *Bell. Iud.* 2.350.

113. Josephus *Bell. Iud.* 2.352–353 (trans. Thackeray, with minor revisions). Cf. Cicero *Planc.* 63, who expresses the sentiment in very different terms: *Sed ita multa Romae geruntur ut vix ea quae fiunt in provinciis audiantur.*

114. See Chapter 3 at nn. 46–50.

tice. That edict also quoted the *mandata* given to Antoninus by the emperor. The jurist Marcianus later quoted a chapter of that edict, in which Antoninus had insisted that local policemen have stenographers present when they interrogated a suspect. When they sent a suspect to a magistrate for further investigation, they had to send with him a sealed transcript of their interrogation. They also had to be prepared to answer questions regarding that transcript. Antoninus carefully concluded that any Roman magistrate finding that an interrogation was malicious or a transcript was falsified should make an example of the policeman, lest anything similar be attempted thereafter.[115] Almost two centuries later Constantine wrote to Felix, the *praeses Corsicae,* reminding him that his subordinates should transcribe their records every six months and forward copies to the prefect, so that the judges themselves might be judged; simultaneously, he reminded Felix that provincials had the right to approach him regarding the negligence or greed of his subordinates.[116]

The advice given by Agrippa to the Jews did not exist in isolation. An entire branch of rhetorical theory developed in antiquity around the "art of safe criticism," an essentially deconstructive practice through which orators exploited the tropes of imperial propaganda to manipulate the actions of imperial agents.[117] When, therefore, imperial officials iterated the rhetoric of the Cyrene Edict—whether Strabo Libuscidianus, or Paullus Fabius Persicus, or Avidius Quietus—they provided leverage that provincials could exploit for their own benefit, much as the villagers of Beth Phouraia learned to use authenticated texts and to interpret official deportment in order to control the actions of local procurators. There exists abundant evidence suggesting that individuals and collectivities knew this ideology on the supervision of local magistrates well. First, papyri preserve copious public and private copies of records of interrogations and related proceedings in direct speech.[118] Among examples of this type of document are journals of the daily activities of local magistrates: these had to be posted for public inspection on a regular basis before being formally entered into the local record

115. *Dig.* 48.3.6.1; cf. Ulpian at *Dig.* 1.16.6.1. Marcian also observed that Hadrian had issued rescripts on this topic, too (48.3.6 *pr.*). The acts of the Christian martyrs supply abundant evidence for and references to the taking and later recitation of minutes and to later use of those texts by historians: see *Acta Apollonii* 11 (Ἀναγνωσθήτω τὰ ἄκτα Ἀπολλώ) and *Acta Pionii* 19, with Robert's note *ad loc.*, as well as Eusebius, *Hist. eccl.* 5.18.9, quoting Apollonius of Ephesus on Alexander the Montanist: καὶ οἱ θέλοντες μαθεῖν τὰ κατ' αὐτὸν ἔχουσιν τὸ τῆς Ἀσίας δημόσιον ἀρχεῖον. For the use of such transcripts in contexts internal to the bureaucracy, see *P. Panop. Beatty* 1.100–101, with Skeat's note *ad locum.*
116. *C. Th.* 1.16.3.
117. See Mesk 1912, Maguiness 1932, Ahl 1984, and Sabbah 1984.
118. The most recent catalogue provided in the appendix to Coles 1966.

office.[119] Despite occasional and vague references in classical Greek literature to the use of shorthand, it was probably the Romans who introduced
the use of *oratio recta* in recording the minutes of judicial proceedings.[120] It
was in any event Roman practice that made a deep impression on popular
thought and that crafted a ready association between the impartiality of
recording proceedings and the impressive formality of Roman law. Greeks
signaled their awareness of the Roma origin of this genre, as it were, when
they named such records ἄϰτα. Imperial and local stenographers through
the eastern provinces further declared their indebtedness to imperial ideology when they used Latin for the formal headings and phrases that endowed these processes with legitimacy and Greek for the text of speakers'
comments.[121]

Next, imperial governors often publicly threatened to punish local
officials who did not enforce or obey the law. The prefect of Egypt in A.D.
198, for example, ordained that local magistrates who knowingly failed to
prosecute those engaged in illegal magical practices would be subject to the
same punishment as the magicians themselves.[122] Finally, some provincials
demonstrated a full awareness of the distinction between imperial and local officials and of the power that the former wielded over the latter. After
having imprisoned Pionius on charges of being a Christian, the local priest
Polemon and the local magistrate Theophilus brought him forth and demanded that he sacrifice at the Temple of Nemesis. Pionius responded:
"Those sent to prison ought to await the proconsul. Why are you usurping
his authority?" Polemon and Theophilus became angry but, in the end, had
to await the assize of the proconsul.[123]

An edict issued by Alexander Severus at the start of his reign preserves
an official formulation of this ideology with particular clarity. Alexander
published the edict on his accession to excuse contributions of *aurum coronarium* for that occasion. He also used its publication as an opportunity to
stress the benefits his rule would bring to the provinces:[124]

---

119. See, for example, *Sel. pap.* 242.
120. On the history and development of stenography in the Roman world see Milne 1934.
On its uses within the Roman administration see Coles 1966, and for a prosopography of
stenographers and related personnel see Teitler 1985.
121. See Roussel and de Visscher 1942/43, on an inscription from Dmeir (*SEG* XVII 759);
Frend 1956, publishing a text from Phrygia; *P. Oxy.* VIII 1114, XVI 1876, 1877, 1888, 1889,
and XLII 3016; and *Sel. pap.* 263.
122. Rea 1977 (*P. Coll. Youtie* 30), ll. 18–23.
123. Robert's commentary is essential to understanding the vocabulary of this text. See
15.1–5 at 3: Πιόνιος εἶπεν· Τοὺς βληθέντας εἰς τὴν φυλακὴν ἀκόλουθόν ἐστι περιμένειν τὸν
ἀνθύπατον· τί ἑαυτοῖς τὰ ἐκείνου μέρη ἐπιτρέπετε;
124. *Sel. pap.* 216, ll. 15–23, trans. Hunt and Edgar.

For it was not my aim to amass money by every means, but rather by liberality and kindnesses to increase the welfare of this empire, in order that the governors whom I have sent abroad to occupy charges, and whom I tested and selected with utmost care before dispatching, should likewise make it their purpose to behave with the utmost moderation. For the governors of provinces will learn more and more how zealously it behooves them to spare and be considerate of the peoples over whom they have been placed, when they are able to see the emperor also conducting the business of his realm with so much propriety and moderation and self-restraint. Let the magistrates in each city see to it that copies of this my edict are set up in public in full view of those who wish to read.

Alexander resided in Rome at this time; the extant copy was written in Egypt several decades later. At least one copy must, therefore, have traveled from Rome to Egypt. There a conscientious local magistrate posted a copy, even though it contained explicit admonitions regarding the behavior of men in his position. Later in the same year Alexander issued a separate rescript to the *koinon* of the Greeks in Bithynia, in response to a complaint that an imperial official had attempted to block their appeal of his ruling to the emperor. Despite its immediate concern, this text, like the edict on *aurum coronarium,* achieved wide circulation: the compilers of Justinian's *Digest* preserved a quotation of it by the jurist Paul. Two separate copies of it also exist on papyrus.[125] In that rescript Alexander professed some confusion at the action of his subordinate: "I do not see how anyone may be prevented by his judges from appealing their ruling, since it is permissible for him to make use of another route to the same end and to reach me more quickly. But we forbid procurators and provincial governors . . . to obstruct provincials' approach to us. They shall obey this my command in the knowledge that I care as much for the liberty of my subjects as for their good will and obedience."[126]

Many texts from the reign of Diocletian have survived outside the Theodosian and Justinianic corpora and therefore preserve the rhetorical frames that justified their purely legal or administrative content. In one such text, whose unfortunate state of preservation precludes assigning it a certain date, Diocletian addressed abuses and illegal confiscations by imperial officials. He closed by exhorting individuals affected by such wrongs to demand restitution of their property and by ordering that his ruling be published for all to see: "In order that this be clear to one and all, we have ordered subjoined to this edict a copy of the instructions that we issue to all our prefects and all governors of the provinces, to officials of the state and privy purses,

125. For the copies, see Chapter 4 at n. 144.
126. *Dig.* 49.1.25.

so that, with them being familiar to all, our provincials might rejoice that their best interest has been provided for by our benevolence."[127] In other legislation Diocletian adopted a similar tone: he ascribed the motivation for the Edict on Maximum Prices to the tetrarchs' concern for the "common fortune" and "common good," a natural outgrowth of their role as "parents of the human race." Just as the emperors thought about the "public happiness," so they exhorted "the devotion of all, in order that this rule, established for the common good, be maintained with good-willed obedience and proper scruple, especially since in a statute of this sort provision seems to be made not for individual cities or peoples or provinces, but for the whole world, toward whose harm a tiny minority is known to have raged, whose greed neither length of time nor the very wealth for which they are thought to strive can assuage or sate."[128]

Alexander Severus implied and Diocletian explicitly suggested that provincials should come forward with any complaints they might have about imperial officials. Constantine took this theme a step further in two laws now preserved in abridged form in the Theodosian Code. We have had cause to mention one of these already, which provided for the recording and transmission of public acclamations for imperial judges: if the acclamations praised the judges, Constantine promised to reward them; if the public accused them, the strength of Constantine's censure would destroy them.[129] In another law of precisely the same date, Constantine catalogued the potential crimes of regional judges and their staffs: selling verdicts to the highest bidder, charging litigants for admission to a hearing, and selling transcripts for a price. In every case Constantine directed the governors of provinces to punish the guilty parties with execution. If, moreover, governors refused to investigate such extortion, Constantine granted to everyone the right to complain about such conduct to higher officials, whether to the *comes provinciarum* or to the praetorian prefects, so that, on their information, Constantine himself could hand out the appropriate punishment to such brigands.[130]

This strand of imperial propaganda proved useful to imperial officials in settling local and regional disputes. When Agrippa informed the Jews that most provinces remained quiescent despite the paltry number of Roman troops actually resident in them, he urged them to consider why agents of Rome exercised power far beyond the coercive force at their disposal. He

---

127. *CIL* III 13569, ll. 42–46.
128. Diocletian *Edictum de pretiis* 20; cf. chapters 6 (*fortunae communes*), 7 (*communis necessitudinis, parentes . . . generis humani*), and 12 (*publicae felicitatis, communis humanitatis ratio*).
129. *C. Th.* 1.16.6, quoted in Chapter 6 at nn. 140 and 149.
130. *C. Th.* 1.16.7.

offered two obvious answers: others were grateful for the personal security that accrued from Roman peace, or else they were prudent enough to fear the overwhelming force at the disposal of the emperor, to whom the Jews would ultimately have to answer. The charismatic authority of the emperor thus did far more than regulate his representatives; it also animated them as agents of his power. Imperial officials echoed this formulation of the emperor's power when they assigned credit for their actions to the emperor. In so doing, they lent his sanction to their own words. In his edict on illegal exactions, Strabo Libuscidianus claimed to do no more than provide written confirmation of the rules already laid down by "the Augusti, one the greatest of gods, the other the greatest of emperors."[131]

In Egypt in July 68, the prefect Tiberius Julius Alexander published an edict establishing his policies on myriad issues, not least regarding the criminal behavior of officials under his authority. Copies of that text were sent to *strategi* throughout Egypt, and Julius Demetrius, *strategus* of the Thebaid oasis, forwarded a copy to the Temple of Hibis, in the modern oasis of Khargeh, where it was inscribed on stone on the northern gate of the temple.[132] Despite the edict's focus on matters of concern only in Alexander's province, the prefect nevertheless claimed that he acted merely in order to show what all might expect from "the common benefactor of the human race, the emperor Galba, who lights for us all the path to salvation."[133] Like Pliny swearing his oath in Bithynia, Alexander has identified himself with his provincials, claiming to seek salvation through the guidance of Galba. We can witness the iteration of this ideology in dialogues between provincials and officials not only in the Syrian village of Beth Phouraia, but also in North Africa. There a set of inscriptions records the interactions between two procurators in charge of several imperial estates, the tenants who farmed those estates, and other officials of the equestrian order. In a letter addressed to the procurators, the tenants asked them to act "with that providence which they exercise in the name of Caesar." In their response, the procurators claimed to actualize the express will of "our Caesar, [in keeping with] the tireless care through which he continuously takes thought for the utility of the human race."[134]

How did a solitary individual exercise tireless care in taking thought for the entire human race? The easy answer is, quite simply, by being present

---

131. See Chapter 4 at n. 178.

132. For prefectural edicts from Egypt, preserved in the form of copies forwarded by nome strategi to lower officials, see Katzoff 1980, 821 n. 45, listing *WC* 13, *OGIS* 665 (*SEG* VIII 794 = *SB* V 8248), *P. Yale* inv. 1593, *OGIS* 669 (that of Tiberius Julius Alexander), *P. Iand.* VII 140, *BGU* II 646 (*WC* 490), *P. Oxy.* VIII 1100, and *P. Oxy.* XII 1408.

133. See Chapter 6 at nn. 81–82.

134. *CIL* VIII 25943 and 26416, edited and translated in Kehoe 1988, 56–59.

everywhere. Roman law's insistence on the sacrosanctity of the imperial portrait had its counterpart in the popular belief that imperial portraits were numinous, that they somehow shared in and were animated by that "double in another sphere of being" that connected the emperor to forms of existence beyond the human and to regions beyond himself.[135] It is well known that individuals could appeal decisions up the ladder to the emperor simply by informing the relevant magistrate of their desire to do so.[136] Indeed, Lucius the Ass at one time sought aid by invoking "the holy name of the emperor." He therefore attempted to shout the "august name of Caesar" amidst a crowd of native Greeks on market day. Alas, he proved incapable of enunciating any more than "O!"[137] But this notional right of appeal took its most characteristically ancient form in the granting of protection to those who fled to the emperor's statue.[138] Already in the first century A.D., jurists recognized the right of slaves to seek asylum "by fleeing to a statue of Caesar." Although it is possible to find antecedents for this practice in the worship of Julius Caesar prior to and immediately after his death, it became widespread and achieved lasting legal recognition during the reign of Augustus.[139]

In the eastern provinces, Greeks had a long tradition of granting asylum to temples of Hellenistic kings.[140] They easily applied the same practices to Augustus: the Cretans sought permission from the Senate to grant right of asylum to a temple of Augustus in A.D. 22.[141] Over the decades and centuries that followed, Greeks began to credit statues inside and outside temples with more ill-defined and untraditional powers, in a fashion at once discontinuous with Roman legal theory and yet consonant with the referential and functional capacity they attributed to such icons in everyday discourse. Thus not only did Greeks honor rights of asylum at imperial statues outside temples, but they also credited those statues with the power to represent the emperor as arbiter over local authorities in judicial contexts. In his *Life of Apollonius,* Philostratus described an episode connecting many of these issues. In his youth Apollonius passed some years in Cilicia and Pamphylia.

---

135. MacCormack 1975b remains, to my mind, a uniquely successful attempt to articulate the nature of the *genius* in the terms and concepts of ancient theology. On imperial portraits see Chapter 7, esp. "The Power of Imperial Portraits."

136. On appeals to the emperor see A. H. M. Jones 1960, 51–65, or Millar 1977, 507–516.

137. Apuleius *Met.* 3.29.

138. On this issue see Hopkins 1978, 222–224, or Price 1984b, 191–192.

139. For the Caesarian antecedents see Weinstock 1971, 395–397. On the legal aspects at Rome see Bauman 1974, 85–92. See esp. Ulpian at *Dig.* 1.12.1.8 and 21.1.17.12 and the cases described at Tacitus *Ann.* 3.36.1 (intimating widespread practice) and 4.67.4, and at Suetonius *Tiberius* 53.2 and 58.

140. Robert, *Hellenica* 6.33–42.

141. Tacitus *Ann.* 3.63.4.

Upon arriving in Aspendus, he discovered a crowd attempting to kill the governor in their anger over a shortage of grain. They were doing so "although he was clinging to the imperial images, which were more dreaded and more inviolate at that time than were the statues of Zeus at Olympia. For they were statues of Tiberius, in whose reign someone is said to have been judged guilty of impiety for striking his own slave when the slave was carrying a silver drachma struck with the image of Tiberius."[142] Elsewhere Greeks paid judicial fines at the feet of imperial images.[143]

Some went further still. In A.D. 267 a senator from Antinoë, one Aurelius Serapion, found himself nominated for a liturgy from which he thought himself exempt. Frustrated in his appeals to local officials, he deposited another appeal "in our local Sebasteum, at the divine feet of our Lord Imperator Gallienus Augustus." The appeal was, notably, addressed not to Gallienus but to the prefect of Egypt. Serapion clearly believed that respect for the power of Gallienus would induce the same local officials who had already rejected his appeal now to forward it to their superior. Nor was Serapion alone: a petitioner at Hermopolis had recourse to the same device some years earlier, and one Colluthus likewise laid his petition in the most holy Hadrianeum, also addressed to the prefect.[144] All these individuals counted on respect for their shared status as subjects to outweigh the discrepant power of the official whose judgment they appealed, at least in asserting their right to make such an appeal.

The interactions between Flaccus and the Jews of Alexandria required of the latter almost superhuman faith in precisely this ideology. Philo described in detail the efforts of the Jews to send letters to Gaius. They always had to rely on Flaccus, even though that prefect repeatedly failed to forward such documents to the emperor's attention.[145] Only the arrival of King Agrippa allowed the Jews to escape the power exercised by Flaccus within his province and to display their "piety toward the beneficent house."[146] Introducing the subsequent disgrace that befell Flaccus, Philo wrote:[147]

> Some, indeed, of those who held governorships in the time of Tiberius and his father, Caesar, had perverted their office of guardian and protector into domination and tyranny. . . . But these people, on their return to Rome, after the termination of their time of office, had been required by the emperor to render an account and submit to scrutiny of their doings, particularly when

142. Philostratus *Vit. Apoll.* 1.15. Cf. Pliny *Ep.* 10.74, with Sherwin-White 1966, *ad locum*.
143. See Price 1984b, 192, on *IGRR* IV 353 and 807.
144. See *P. Oxy.* XVII 2130, with the note on l. 18; *CPR* 20; and *P. Amh.* II 80. On these texts see Kunderewicz 1961, 127–128.
145. E.g. Philo *Flacc.* 97.
146. Philo *Flacc.* 103: εὐσεβεῖν εἰς τὸν εὐεργέτην οἶκον.
147. Philo *Flacc.* 105 (trans. Colson).

the aggrieved cities sent ambassadors. For on these occasions the emperors showed themselves impartial judges; they listened equally to both the accuser and the defender.

Like King Agrippa's in the narrative of Josephus, Philo's faith in the impartial justice of the emperor, who valued truth far above any partiality toward subordinate or provincial, commended in retrospect the Jews' compliance with the "tyranny" of Flaccus. They had suffered while waiting for Gaius to act, but that had been their only reasonable course of action.

Like Roman propaganda regarding imperial victoriousness, assigning the right of asylum to imperial statues had unintended consequences. In the fertile field of the provincial imagination, granting credit to the emperor for victories everywhere came to make sense not because he alone held *imperium* and took the auspices. Rather, provincials naturally associated the emperor's victoriousness with his role as an intermediary between themselves and the divine. His victoriousness thus became one expression of his superhuman capacity to act beyond the scope of mortal men. The individuals who sought asylum from persecution and relief from corruption through the emperor did so out of a manifold faith in the imperial system. They earnestly trusted the emperor to esteem justice above favoritism; they relied on the emperor's prefect to actuate his patron's values and to abide by his patron's laws; and they believed that the emperor's portraits potentially, substantively, indeed actually and actively manifested the emperor's personal concern for their well-being in every corner of the empire.

Panegyrists and historians echoed these beliefs in ways both simple and complex. Aelius Aristides exploited the universality of the emperor's concern to explain the uniformity of Roman administration that obtained across the empire in both surface and substance. He first deplored the infighting among the satraps of the Great King of Persia and contrasted it with the harmony and industry of imperial procurators:[148]

> The governors sent out to the city-states and ethnic groups are each of them rulers of those under them, but in what concerns themselves and their relations to each other they are equally among the ruled, and in particular they differ from those under their rule in that it is they—one might assert—who first show how to be the right kind of subject. So much respect has been instilled in all men for him who is the great governor, who obtains for them their all.

Aristides subsequently referred specifically to the civil and criminal jurisdiction of governors and to their frequent and humble recourse to the superior knowledge of their emperor. The emperor of Rome has, therefore, "no need to wear himself out traveling around the whole empire. . . . It is

---

148. Aristides *Or.* 26.31 (trans. Oliver).

very easy for him to stay where he is and manage the entire civilized world by letters, which arrive almost as soon as they are written, as if they were carried by winged messengers."[149] In the Roman empire, Aristides iterated, there were no conflicts between governors, since the emperor ruled the entire world as if it were a single city-state: "Appeals from one court to another are made with no greater menace for those who make them than for those who simply accept the local verdict."[150] The vast distance separating the emperor from his subjects and governors alike, and his profound interest in their welfare, thus created a world in which there existed a judicial equality between the humble and the great, the obscure and the famous, the poor and the rich, and the low- and the well-born.[151]

Panegyrists in the Latin tradition concentrated on similar themes. On 21 April 289, a Gallic orator delivered a speech before Maximian in Trier. Although Maximian had been elevated to Augustus at least three years earlier,[152] the orator followed a traditional opening—on Maximian's character and love of Rome—with a catalogue of the duties imposed on Maximian when he agreed to take on the burden of empire:[153]

> To admit into your heart the care of so great a state, to support the fate of the entire world, to live for the people while forgetting yourself, so to speak, to stand at the lofty summit of human affairs from which you can look down over all lands and seas and scan with your eyes and mind where peace is secure and where it is threatened by storms, which governors emulate your justice and which military leaders preserve the glory of your virtue, to receive countless messengers from everywhere and to send forth as many commands, to take thought for so many cities and races and provinces, to pass every night and every day in perpetual concern for the safety of all.

Following this tradition left the Gallic orator Pacatus in something of a bind: having come to Rome to deliver a panegyric in the presence of Theodosius in the early fall of 389, he could not avoid commenting on the war that had brought Theodosius to Rome, namely the revolt by Magnus Maximus, an officer in the imperial army who had served with Theodosius in Britain and Africa under the latter's father and had been promoted to the command of Britain by Theodosius's colleague in the imperial power. As might be expected, Pacatus had his cake and ate it, too: he praised the discretion shown by Theodosius in his appointments and then cast all blame for the recent

---

149. Aristides *Or.* 26.33.

150. Aristides *Or.* 26.36–37.

151. Aristides *Or.* 26.39.

152. The only explicit ancient testimony survives in the *Consularia Constantinopolitana*, s.a. 286. See Barnes 1982, 4 nn. 5 and 6; and Chastagnol 1984, 255–256.

153. *Pan. Lat.* II(10).3.3–4.

revolt onto the perfidy of Maximus. Maximus, in this narrative, continued throughout his revolt to boast of his close relationship with Theodosius; Pacatus's strategy thus had the additional effect of excusing those who followed Maximus by suggesting that they might have done so out of confused loyalty to Theodosius.[154]

In his youth the future emperor Julian had to deliver several panegyrics before his relatives. Julian's panegyrics tend to diverge much further from the formulas established in handbooks like that of Menander Rhetor than do the Latin panegyrics of the fourth century. Nevertheless, in a speech devoted to comparisons between Constantius and an ideal monarch, Julian discussed the virtues of appointing honest men and then watching over them: "While the good and pious king himself oversees and directs everything and governs those who govern, he must also ensure that the people placed in charge of the greatest projects and provinces share his concern for the common welfare and that they are good men and that they emulate himself as far as possible."[155] The corollary to these praises, which none of these panegyrists save Pacatus had to confront, is that bad subordinates reflect badly upon the glory of their patron. Pacatus, as we have seen, attempted to escape that seemingly inevitable conclusion. Maximus, however, lasted several years on the throne, and Theodosius had consented to the distribution of propaganda that advertised their joint rule.[156] Theodosius faced a no-win situation: civil wars redounded to no one's credit. Writing under Theodosius about events some forty years earlier, the historian Ammianus Marcellinus recounted the activities of a notorious member of the imperial secret police, one Paul the Chain, who framed several honest officials and ruined their careers. Ammianus generally wrote with an open mind about Constantius, but he could not forgive him his continued patronage of Paul, "from whose deeds came an impious crime, which marked the reign of Constantius with an eternal blemish."[157]

THE FAITH OF FIFTY MILLION PEOPLE

In its fully developed form, the imperial government thus presented itself as fulfilling two fundamental tenets of legal or rational domination: first,

154. For praise of Theodosian appointments, see *Pan. Lat.* XII(2).15. On Maximus see XII(2).23. For his claims to friendship with Theodosius, see 24.1. (Cf. *PLRE* I, Maximus 39.) Delmaire 1997 analyzes the support enjoyed by usurpers in the fourth century and locates it generally in the middle echelons of the administration. Compare Ammianus 28.3.6: punishing a legion after a revolt is best accomplished through scapegoats.

155. Julian *Or.* 3(2).31 (Spanheim 91B).

156. See Chapter 7 at nn. 191–197.

157. Ammianus 14.5.6, and cf. 27.6.15 and 30.5.9–10.

administrative acts, decisions, and proceedings were formulated and re-corded in writing—the imperial government, as we have seen, also imposed this requirement on its local representatives—and, second, its bureaucracy was organized hierarchically, with, in principle, a universal right to appeal the decision of a lower office to a higher one. The principles of legitimation to which a regime subscribes do not, however, determine the motivation for obedience in individual subjects. Submission to magistrates with access to coercive force need not be motivated by faith in a regime's legitimacy. Loy-alism, like all behaviors, can be simulated, by individuals or groups, from opportunism, calculated self-interest, or sheer helplessness.[158] Certainly Roman efforts to impose new systems of stratification onto local societies must have impeded individuals from discovering common anti-Roman in-terests. Although we cannot determine why residents of the empire com-plied in their subjugation, the scarcity of revolts among those residents pro-vides the best measure of that compliance. Furthermore, even if we concede the possibility that every subject acted purely from a rational calculation of utility, we can nevertheless see in surviving documentary texts the profound impression left by the government's claim to rationality: residents demon-strated their faith in the system when they played by its rules and especially when they attempted to exploit them.

The fantastic catalogue of previous emperors in the *Tabula Banasitana* placed a huge, if theoretical, constraint on the actions of a Roman emperor. Romans had a profound respect for precedent, especially in the issuing and interpretation of law. They conveyed that attitude to provincials in myriad ways, and provincials responded by citing and manipulating precedents of every kind. Tiberius did not even have to cite the deeds of his father: his titulature advertised at once the source of his power and the man whose memory he was bound to respect. When the city of Gytheum approached Tiberius proposing to honor Augustus and himself with a festival including a procession of the images of Augustus, Livia, and Tiberius, he responded with a letter that announced him as "Tiberius Caesar Augustus, son of the god Augustus" and expressed the emperor's pleasure that Gytheum dis-played piety toward Augustus but merely paid honor to himself. It is no sur-prise that Gytheum then dedicated the first day of its festival to Augustus, the second to Tiberius, and the rest to other divinities, heroes, and mem-bers of the *domus divina*. The city attempted, albeit with awkward result, to design its festival in accordance with the Romans' desire to suppress honors for the living. The citizens' attempt should have issued in a festival that hon-ored Tiberius by worshiping his father. In the event, they merely gave Au-gustus pride of place.[159]

---

158. Weber 1978, 214.
159. *EJ* nos. 102a, 102b (*SEG* XI 922, 923).

Temples and portrait galleries were an obvious and traditional means to honor an emperor and dynasty. But documents like the *Tabula Banasitana,* or the repetitive letters on the Aphrodisian archive wall, responded to an altogether more practical and far-reaching respect for the past. This did not escape the notice of Rome's provincial subjects, nor were they slow to explore the leverage it gave to them. Provincials arguing their cases before an imperial magistrate—under the Principate, before a governor at his *conventus*[160]—thus cited a fantastic number and variety of earlier decisions in formulating their cases. Before examining the documents they submitted, however, let us review briefly how they acquired information about earlier cases.[161]

Imperial governors spent a lot of their time presiding over civil and criminal judicial proceedings, and the proper performance of this function appears prominently in the honors awarded to them by their provincial subjects.[162] Although the route traveled by a governor in tours of his province followed an established pattern, the governor or some subordinate nevertheless advertised his route ahead of time.[163] Although it seems likely that rules regarding the functioning of an assize were published with the governor's *mandata* or provincial edict, several papyri preserve rules for the running of the *conventus* that evidently circulated independently.[164] In A.D. 111, for example, the prefect Sulpicius Similis announced, among other rules, "that those wishing to defer their case [would] have no excuse, having known long ago the time fixed for the *conventus.*" He added that "if anyone of those whose names were posted at the termination of the *conventus* [had] not already obtained a hearing, he [would] be able to be judged before the nome's *strategus.*"[165] Both rules clearly operated on the premise that, prior to the *conventus* itself, individuals would submit petitions asking that their case be heard and would receive a response. Other texts prove that assizes operated thus: in A.D. 175–176 the prefect Titus Pactumeius Magnus issued a warning to those who received answers to their petitions, saying, "Submit the case to me before the tribunal." Titus clearly intended that petitioners

160. On the assize system see Haensch 1997.

161. Cf. Hobson 1993, 195–196 and 202–203, contrasting knowledge of prefectural edicts in Oxyrhynchus and Soknopaiou Nesos. Hobson concludes that villagers in Soknopaiou Nesos had little knowledge of law, especially when compared with residents of Oxyrhynchus. "Knowledge of the law" was, however, "not a prerequisite for appealing to a legal official" (215).

162. Haensch 1997 collects, province by province, texts honoring Roman officials (documentation type B III 4b). See also Robert, *Hellenica* 4; Nock 1972, 731–734; and Kantorowicz 1965, 1–6.

163. See *P. Oxy.* IV 709, or *P. Ryl.* II 74.

164. On the formalities of the *conventus* see N. Lewis 1981.

165. *P. Oxy.* XXXVI 2754.

appreciate his desire for efficiency: once notified of their opportunity, they would not be granted any delay of the hearing.[166] Other papyri seem to preserve the petition requesting a hearing because a scribal hand, belonging neither to the writer of the petition nor to its plaintiff, signed them with a date and the words "To the administration: let him be heard."[167]

The governor's assize attracted a large audience from the surrounding area and brought no little prestige and economic benefit to those cities designated to host it.[168] In a speech probably delivered in Apamea under Nerva, Dio Chrysostom expounded on the glory and wealth brought to that city by the *conventus:* "And what is more, the courts are in session every year among you and they bring together an unnumbered throng of people: litigants, jurymen, orators, princes, attendants, slaves, pimps, muleteers, hucksters, harlots, and artisans. Consequently not only can those who have goods to sell obtain the highest prices, but also nothing in the city is out of work, neither the teams nor the houses nor the women. And this contributes not a little to prosperity; for wherever the greatest throng of people comes together, there necessarily we find money in greatest abundance, and it stands to reason that the place should thrive."[169]

At the actual hearing a stenographer took down the statements of plaintiffs and defendants, but the governor did not issue a ruling immediately.[170] Instead, he listened to a bewildering number of cases very rapidly and then retreated to consult with his advisors before posting his decisions. Two famous Severan texts testify to the number of cases heard at a *conventus* and to the system in place for announcing decisions. In the first, Serapion, *strategus* of two divisions of the Arsinoïte nome, announced that the prefect had just posted in Alexandria his decisions in the 1,804 cases he had heard in Arsinoë on days 26–28 of the month Phamenoth. Serapion assured his charges that their answers would be posted in Arsinoë as well. He added that they could submit requests to have personal copies made of the decisions in their cases, although they would have to travel to Arsinoë to fetch them.[171] The second text preserves an authenticated copy of a petition with

---

166. *P. Oxy.* XLII 3017. Cf. Skeat on *P. Panop. Beatty* 1.100–101.

167. *P. Oxy.* VII 1032; cf. Feissel and Gascou 1995, 101, on *P. Euphr.* 3–4.

168. See Haensch 1997.

169. Dio *Or.* 35.15–16 (trans. after Crosby).

170. Several papyri preserve the minutes of such hearings. For examples see *P. Oxy.* XXXVI 2757 and XLII 3015, and *P. Stras.* 179. On the fate of individuals' petitions during and after the hearing see Feissel and Gascou 1995, 77–80 and 105.

171. *P. Yale* I 61. Compare *BGU* III 970 (*WC* 242), a copy of a decision by Titus Pactumues Magnus, prefect of Egypt, from A.D. 177; the heading notes that the prefect heard this case at a *conventus* in Juliopolis, which information would hardly be necessary if this text had been copied from a set officially posted in the city in which the case had been heard. J. Thomas 1983,

its rescript: the heading records the original location in which the decision was posted and its place in the official records of that *conventus*. It had been petition number 1009.[172]

While the individual petitioner retained the right to request a copy of the decision in his or her case from the records, it is unclear whether others could do so.[173] An interested party could, obviously, scan the wall of the local temple of the imperial cult after an assize and find hundreds of decisions on innumerable topics: records of trials in Rabbinic literature generally mention the basilica as the site in which the trial took place.[174] This could easily account for the many papyri that preserve collections of rescripts with minimal information regarding the original case.[175] These collections fall into two categories. First, there exist several papyri containing collections of rescripts in cases on similar issues: these collections could have been made by lawyers, or by individuals or organizations with special interest in a particular topic.[176] Second, other papyri preserve collections of decisions that seem to have little to do with each other: these were probably collected by lawyers.[177] We have already seen that cities obtained and then inscribed not only imperial epistles addressed to themselves but also epistles addressed to

---

377–381, argues cautiously that prefects either posted or returned petitions, but the evidence does not require us to make that choice.

172. *P. Oxy.* XVII 2131; see also *BL* VI 204 and VII 282. Haensch 1994, 544–546, lists further texts testifying to their position within the archives of a particular assize, either a number alone or a number within a specified roll. Other papyri preserve the formulas for authentication and the signatures and seals of witnesses in varying states of completeness: see Hanson 1984b, publishing *P. Mich.* inv. 6554. The published decision generally did not quote the original petition in full; for an exception, see *P. Corn.* inv. I 76, published by Lewis in *BASP* 6 (1969), 17–19, and reedited as *SB* 10537; cf. N. Lewis 1981. On the rolls, files, and item numbers used for and in these documents see J. Thomas 1983, 381–382, and Feissel and Gascou 1995, 68 and 77. On the accessibility of archives see *P. Fam. Tebt.* 15 and 24, *P. Hamburg* 31, and the texts in *P. Mich.* V.2. Haensch 1992 surveys much of the evidence, but he concentrates on the storage and use of information by officeholders.

173. See von Premerstein, *RE* s.v. *libellus* col. 42, and Lukaszewicz 1981, publishing *P. Berlin* inv. 16546. Multiple parties to a particular dispute frequently possessed and quoted copies of the relevant documents, though we cannot say with certainty whence those copies were obtained (Hanson 1997, 417).

174. On the locations in which decisions were posted see Kunderewicz 1961; on Roman trials in Rabbinic literature, see Lieberman 1944, 13–14. See also Chapter 4 nn. 108–110.

175. See Katzoff 1980, 838–841.

176. See *P. Flor.* III 382 (on local liturgies), *P. Mich.* inv. 148 verso, *P. Oxy.* VII 1020 (on *restitutio in integrum*), XXVII 2475–2477 (on Dionysiac artists), XLII 3015 (several citations on testamentary disposition), and 3018 (two items, one Hadrianic and one Severan, on *Paeanistae*), *P. Phil.* 1 (on the exemption of weavers from liturgies), *PSI* IV 281 (on the limitation of actions), *SB* 5225 (*BGU* IV 1074, on Dionysiac artists).

177. See *P. Columbia* 123 (*P. Apokrimata*), edited in Westermann and Schiller 1954, and cf. Youtie and Schiller 1955, and N. Lewis 1995, 224–241. For the text, see now *SB* 9526; on its

other cities that affected their own status.[178] Private organizations (e.g., groups of Dionysiac artists) and wealthy individuals did the same.[179]

Roman legal textbooks cannot readily explain the importance that precedents assumed in Roman law and administration: even as late as the sixth century, Justinian could argue that decisions should be based on statutes and not precedent.[180] In fact, the word often translated as "precedent" or "example," *exemplum,* should usually be translated as "analogy." There did exist a body of thought within classical jurisprudence on the force of *res similiter iudicatae.* Callistratus, for example, preserved a rescript of Severus urging that ambiguities between statutes be resolved through the authority of a succession of similar judicial decisions. The jurists, however, often did ascribe to precedents statutory force.[181] Nevertheless, by citing a rescript of Severus to justify case law, Callistratus identified the wild card that had raised precedents to the force of statute within the daily practice of Roman law in the provinces: the emperor, whose every deliberative utterance *was* law.[182] Many petitioners and litigants cited precedents after quoting an imperial edict or constitution. It is unlikely, however, that they distinguished between constitutions as sources of law and precedents as mere proof that the law was in force. In forming provincials' "authoritative source of their knowledge of the law," precedents became, for them at least, authoritative as sources of law.[183]

Judges clearly recognized that a properly cited text of the emperor's could settle an issue. A papyrus from Tebtunis written sometime after the death of Hadrian explicitly preserves an extract from one of his rescripts; the text actually contains a proceeding in which Hadrian's rescript is quoted. Julius Theon, the *hypomnematographus* hearing the case, simply acknowledged the power of that rescript: "There is no need to inquire into the issue of possession, since we must venerate the rescripts of the deified Trajan and our Lord Hadrian Caesar Augustus."[184] Marcus Sempronius Liberalis, prefect for some years under Antoninus, used equally strong, if less overtly reli-

---

origin and purpose see Katzoff 1981, reviewing earlier literature. For further examples see *P. Amh.* II 63, P. *Oxy.* XII 1407 and XLII 3015, and *P. Stras.* IV 224.

178. See Chapter 4 at nn. 71–79.

179. *IGRR* IV 1399 (*SIG* 851 = Oliver 1989, nos. 157, 158); Oliver 1989, nos. 96A-C and 142–153; cf. Hanson 1989, 431 n. 8.

180. *C. Iust.* 7.45.13; cf. Katzoff 1972, 256, and *idem* 1980.

181. Callistratus at *Dig.* 1.3.38.

182. See Ulpian at *Dig.* 1.4.1 *pr.,* quoted in Chapter 2 at n. 55.

183. This argument breaks down the distinction maintained by Katzoff 1980, 842–843.

184. *P. Tebt.* II 286, ll. 21–24: [21]περὶ γὰρ τῆς νομῆς οὐδὲν ζητεῖν | [22] δεόμεθα προσκυνεῖν ὀφείλοντες τὰς ἀνα | [23] γνωσθείσας τοῦ θεοῦ Τραιανοῦ καὶ τοῦ κυρίου ἡμῶν | [24] Ἀδριανοῦ Καίσαρος Σεβαστοῦ ἀποφάσεις. On this case see Katzoff 1972, 273–274.

gious, language when speaking about imperial precedents: "For the edicts stand firm and are unshakable, and I suppose that this principle is observed by all: to transgress the edicts is equivalent to committing outrage or homicide."[185] Decisions by earlier prefects did not carry similar weight, nor did prefects themselves necessarily seek out earlier precedents.[186] The sheer body of case law could lead to conflicts. Occasionally litigants presented judges with conflicting prefectural precedents. In one such case the judge deliberately singled out one as influential on his decision; in another, a litigant offered the advice that a former prefect had adopted the rule that one should follow the majority of precedents in making a decision.[187] Some plaintiffs resorted to abstract appeals to a consensus of earlier decisions, all based on an imperial constitution. In A.D. 250 Appius Sabinus heard a case regarding liturgies at Arsinoë. The plaintiff's lawyer quoted an edict issued by Severus in the spring of A.D. 200—it proved popular with villagers seeking to avoid metropolitan liturgies and was often quoted—and then concluded with the flourish that "all prefects after Severus have ruled thus."[188]

It being incumbent upon the litigant to cite the relevant edict or case law, individuals sought out the texts of edicts and earlier proceedings and transcribed them with a particular purpose in mind. As with inscribed texts of imperial epistles, the resulting texts observe a fantastic variety of conventions for recording their origin and relationship to their original. Ann Hanson has now demonstrated that *P. Mich.* inv. 6060 and *BGU* I 163 are two copies of the same record of a proceeding.[189] As she notes, the differences in those texts confirm the suggestion made years ago by R. Coles that private individuals produced copies of proceedings that reflected their particular interest in the original.[190] The owner of *P. Oxy.* X 1204, for example, had no interest in the full text of the document he quoted but simply gave what he regarded as "the essential part of the proceedings and the judgment."[191] Fragmentary copies of later imperial proceedings, many of which

---

185. *P. Mich.* inv. 2964 verso; ll. 25–28, published in Pearl 1970.

186. On the weight carried by previous prefectural decisions see Katzoff 1972, 262–263, 266, and 274. In his examples *all* evidence of prior decisions and all citations of statutes and edicts are provided by the litigants.

187. Youtie 1977, publishing *P. Mich.* inv. 148 verso: see col. iv, ll. 3–9, and col. v, ll. 13–16.

188. *SB* V 7696, on which see N. Lewis 1996, 109.

189. Hanson 1996.

190. Cf. Coles 1966, 16–18. See also Lewis on the two copies of a response of Caracalla preserved by *P. Mich.* IX 529 and *P. Berlin* 7216: N. Lewis 1995, 201–223. *P. Mich.* IX 529 contains two further texts: a petition to the prefect Maevius Honoratianus and the text of a Severan edict on restricting responsibility for taxes and requisitions to single individuals and not assigning unfulfilled burdens to other family members.

191. *P. Oxy.* X 1204, l. 11: ὧν τὸ διαφέρον μέρος καὶ τῶν ἀποφάσεων οὕτως ἔχει.

betray their Latin origin, seem to prove that, at some level, the Latin text of the imperial *commentarii* was widely available, even as each fragment also betrays the idiosyncratic interest of its excerptor.[192] In his visit to Egypt in A.D. 200, Severus issued an edict on *cessio bonorum* that is preserved by two petitions filed in subsequent decades, though one assigns the edict to January/February and another to March/April.[193]

The survival of private copies of official documents, as of personal archives, testifies to a deeper-seated trend, in which the symbolic power of Latin played only a small role. Individuals kept such documents because they had faith in the rationality of Roman administration. They believed that it would abide by its established rules, whether they liked those rules or not. In this, provincials displayed an intuitive sense of the natural consequences of imperial dynastic ideology, even though their "sense" did not accord with a strict view of the role of precedent in Roman law. As J. F. Gilliam remarked regarding a birth certificate for illegitimate twins: "It reminds one that Roman law and status had real significance for tens of thousands of persons in Egypt at this time, even for an illiterate woman, new-born illegitimate children, and a *tutor* who wrote his *subscriptio* in Greek. Such important matters as marriage, testaments, and inheritances were involved, and in some cases a sense of identity, one may assume."[194]

The private collections of documents bore fruit in the remarkable array of surviving petitions that cite such precedents in formulating their own case.[195] The most famous such petition was submitted by a woman named Dionysia, in a complaint against her father, Chaeremon, in A.D. 186.[196] She cited the prefectural edict of Mettius Rufus, letters that passed between local officials regarding a petition that her father filed with the prefect Longaeus Rufus, and her own petition to that prefect. After one decision she appealed, citing a decision of the prefect Flavius Sulpicius Similis that supported her interpretation of the edict of Mettius Rufus. Finally, she quoted a new array of evidence, including minutes of a hearing before the prefect

192. See, for example, *P. Oxy.* XLII 3019 and 3023. On the original language of imperial rescripts, Naphtali Lewis has long followed Ulrich Wilcken (1935, 235; 1936, 112–117) in arguing that Latin originals must lie behind these private copies. His articles confirm the suggestion by Schiller that imperial rescripts were first posted in Latin. Lewis discusses the language of publication in his articles on *P. Mich.* IX 529 and *P. Berlin* 7216. The relevant pages in his collected papers (N. Lewis 1995) are 201–211, 213–214, 222–223, 224–229, 315–327, and 335–336. See also Westermann and Schiller 1954, on *P. Apokrimata* 11–14 and 39–42, and Youtie and Schiller 1955, 334–335 and 343–345.

193. *P. Oxy.* XII 1405 (mid-third century) and *P. Oxy.* XLIII 3105 (between 229 and 236). See N. Lewis 1996, 109, who compares *BGU* II 473, which quotes an edict referred to but not quoted by *PSI* IV 292.

194. Gilliam 1978, 123; cf. *idem* 1975, 771.

195. See Katzoff 1980, 834–841, and *idem* 1981, 570 n. 41.

196. *P. Oxy.* II 237, with invaluable introduction by the editors; cf. Katzoff 1972, 257–268.

Flavius Titianus, a hearing six years later before an *epistrategus,* a trial forty years prior to that before a *iuridicus,* and finally the opinion rendered by a jurist, Ulpius Dionysodorus, when consulted by a military officer some years earlier. The list continues. In one of the great tragedies of textual transmission, the end of the petition, which may have recorded the ultimate decision of the prefect, is lost. Though Dionysia displayed exceptional diligence and almost undoubtedly hired legal advisors, the mere fact of formally citing precedents to impress the governor was not unusual. It was practiced by soldiers, doctors, parents, women, and men, as well as organizations and municipalities.[197]

If, in citing precedents, petitioners display their faith in the regular operation of the Roman administration, successful petitioners show their confidence in the power of the bureaucracy by posting their decisions in some permanent medium.[198] Those dissatisfied with the decision show faith of the same sort when they appeal to higher officials. Such petitions could take two forms. We have already examined the route alluded to by Alexander Severus, that of laying a petition at the foot of an imperial portrait in the local Sebasteum. As a general rule, however, people started the process by going up the ladder: it helped to cite the decisions of the lower official and explain as reasonably as possible why he might have been wrong.[199] Of course, the appeal did not always turn out favorably; not infrequently, an appeal received the answer that the local official should hear the case again, a process which could lead to bitter disappointment.[200] We should nevertheless remember that we usually possess the record of a failed appeal because people continued to keep documentation of their interactions with the authorities, even if they were disappointing. Family archives, or dossiers, in themselves attest to an everyday familiarity with the rationality of Roman rule.[201] The Greek texts in the dossier of Babatha reveal a woman eager to exploit Roman law and Roman authorities in order to settle a host of long-standing legal disputes, even at a time when Arabia was just being reduced *in formam provinciae.*[202]

---

197. See *CPL* 103; *P. Corn.* inv. I 76; *P. Hamburg* 31; *P. Oxy.* VII 1032, XII 1045, XLII 3018, XLIII 3093; *Sel. pap.* 260 (*JEA* XVIII 70), 284 (*BGU* II 648), and 294 (*P. Oxy.* IX 1204); *P. Würz.* 9.

198. Cf. Morris 1981. Herrmann 1990 cites the posting of rescripts in the third century as evidence that the government was breaking down. The *issuing* of rescripts on bureaucratic corruption might point in that direction; inscribing the rescript on bronze suggests a belief, or at least a desire to believe, in the efficacy of that document. On illegal exactions, see N. Lewis 1995, 47–52; Mitchell 1976; *Sel. pap.* 221 (*PSI* 446); and *AJ* no. 113.

199. See *P. Oxy.* VII 1032 and XXXI 2563.

200. E.g., *P. Oxy.* XLIII 3094.

201. Cf. Schubert 1990, on the archive of Marcus Lucretius Diogenes.

202. The Greek texts in the dossier of Babatha have been published as *P. Babatha.* On her archive see Goodman 1991a; Cotton 1993; *idem* 1994; and Millar 1993b, 95–98.

Perhaps no other documents can testify so eloquently to the desire to take advantage of the Roman administration as spurious ones can. In another context we mentioned Pliny's request that Trajan have someone verify that a rescript quoted in a petition was both genuine and accurately quoted.[203] The *Acta Alexandrinorum* and the imperial letters attached to the corpus of Justin were clearly written by people intimately familiar with the phrasing and formulas of imperial documents, as also, obviously, was the letter from Vespasian to Apollonius of Tyana quoted in the biography of Philostratus.[204] The author of the *Sentences of Paul* envisioned forgery of documents as well as of money: according to him, the same punishment befell those who forged birth certificates and wills and those who stamped counterfeit coin. It was, according to that author, precisely to prevent forgeries, in fact, that Romans developed the complex system of binding treble-pierced diptychs with seals of wax and the marks of witnesses.[205] The Theodosian Code contains repeated injunctions that regional magistrates and judges should beware of forged legislation; indeed, one purpose of the codification of law had been to prevent forgery by eliminating the need for new legislation.[206]

Beyond the direct exploitation of Roman administrative institutions, provincials displayed their knowledge of and respect for those institutions when they altered their local institutions in order to imitate Roman ones, or when they used metaphors in literature that drew on their audience's familiarity with them. For example, an inscription from North Africa in the middle of the third century records the formulation by a town council of a decree to redress recent incursions on the town's territory. The council arrived at its decision by citing an imperial rescript, but not one addressed to the village. Rather, they had in good Roman fashion sought an *exemplum,* an inscribed rescript on an analogous topic. They then formulated their decision according to the best senatorial protocol, which they no doubt learned from long acquaintance with published *consulta* of the Roman Senate.[207] The great learning and wide travels of Apuleius make it difficult to determine the import of the realia in his novel. Nevertheless, we should note that the procession of Isis, which purportedly took place near Cenchreae, included

---

203. See Chapter 4 at nn. 81–83.

204. Philostratus *Vit. Apol.* 8.7.3. On spurious documents in general see L. Wenger 1953, 431, and Bickerman 1986, 152–153, and cf. Bisbee 1988.

205. *Sententiae Pauli* 5.25.5–6.

206. See *C. Th.* 1.1.5 (cf. 7.18.11, 11.1.2, 11.39.4, 6, and 7, and esp. 9.35.1), and *N. Th.* 1.6.

207. *AJ* no. 146 (*AÉ* 1903, 202). The imperial rescript is quoted at ll. 9–15. The town dates its text with consular dating and begins the formal text of its resolution with *quit fieri placeret de ea re universi censuere* (ll. 15–16).

someone "playing at being a magistrate, with rods and a purple toga."[208] Likewise hailing from North Africa but two generations later, Tertullian defended the legality of Christian assemblies by comparing them to a certain Roman assembly: "When decent people, when good men, gather, when the pious and the chaste assemble, that is not to be called a faction. It is a senate."[209] Tertullian's claim had a basis in fact: the minutes of synods of African bishops in the middle of the third century reveal that their meetings observed precisely the protocol of the Roman Senate.[210] The city of Oxyrhynchus may have imitated Rome in a far more subtle and curious fashion by modeling its alimentary program on that of Rome.[211]

From Asia Minor comes evidence of a similar fascination with the forms and protocols of Roman political life. For example, I suspect that Carian Apollonia changed the name of its local senate from βουλή to σύγκλητος in imitation of Rome, just as, according to Cyprian, African cities worshiped the deities of Rome in their own Capitolia.[212] At Ephesus, various influences—the dedications of senators resident in the city, ostentatiously inscribed texts of *senatus consulta*, and cultic images of the Roman Senate and local council—encouraged the populace "to focus reflection upon the body which was at the center of political and legal authority at Rome" and to view their own council as "a provincial mirror of the Roman Senate."[213] At some point in the middle of the third century, the city of Tymandus, in Pisidia on the road between Antioch and Ephesus, petitioned the emperor for the right to become a *civitas:* with that award they acquired the right to meet in a *curia* and to elect aediles and quaestors.[214] A few years later the city of Orcistus, in northern Phrygia, petitioned the emperor Constantine for the same privilege: they had flourished for so long, the citizen body said, that they deserved the adornment of annual magistrates escorted by fasces. In granting their request, Constantine wrote to his prefect Ablabius, commending the city's "forum, which is decorated with statues of the earlier emperors."[215] Although somewhat later, this request mirrors the trickle of

208. Apuleius *Met.* 11.8 (trans. Hanson). Cf. *Met.* 6.4 and 6.22, playing on the universal application of Roman law.

209. Tertullian *Apol.* 39.20–21 (trans. Glover): *non est factio dicenda, sed curia.* Cf. Prudentius *Psych.* 838–839.

210. Batiffol 1913b; cf. Dvornik 1951, 4.

211. E. Turner 1975.

212. The city's coinage observes the change: see Robert 1954, 267. On Capitolia see Chapter 7 at n. 9.

213. Rogers 1991, 92.

214. *ILS* 6090. Mimicking Roman elections required the use of the Roman calendar, and helped to spread Roman celebrations for the New Year in the East, on which see Meslin 1970.

215. *ILS* 6091, on which see Chastagnol 1981a and 1981b.

petitions from western cities, which rose to a flood in the second century, asking for permission to be constituted as either *civitates* or Roman colonies.[216] Eastern cities also petitioned for this privilege. When drafting their petitions, Greeks simply transliterated Latin *colonia*. They did so even though they possessed a word meaning "colony," ἀποιϰία. Their recourse to transliteration therefore reveals an awareness, perhaps never consciously articulated, that the semantic field of ἀποιϰία did not match the purely emotive relationship that their request was intended to convey. In choosing thus to express their allegiance to Rome, they opened the doors of their beloved language to the vocabulary of their rulers and the conceptual framework that it reified, even as they sought to join the community of their metropolis, "the nurse and mother of all the world."

It is no surprise that regional dynasts just beyond the borders of the empire, and the Gallic emperors within them, imitated the structure and ceremonial of the Roman imperial court. What other paradigm did they have?[217] After all, already in the reign of Augustus, Claudius Cogidumnus aspired to no greater title than *legatus Augusti*,[218] and Augustus had earned the loyalty of Cottius, the son of one Donnus, a former client king of Rome, by granting him citizenship, giving him three names, and making him prefect over his father's former subjects. Cottius proudly wrote his new name and filiation in the best Roman form.[219] In Chapter 2 we noted the spread of imagery in Greek and Latin theological texts which drew on the organization of the imperial court. These influences are also apparent in texts whose provenance is more difficult to determine, namely the Apocalypse of John and the Heikhalot corpus.[220] The ceremonies observed at imperial arrivals also helped to shape liturgical rituals in both East and West.[221]

When discussing imperial standards, we had cause to observe the appearance of standards in representations of deities in local temples in the Syrian countryside. Syriac theological literature also abounds with imagery in which the titles and the garb of Roman officials were applied to Christ. Such texts often also describe Christ's kingdom on analogy with the gover-

216. See Ando 1999, and cf. Beard, North, and Price 1998, 329–330 and 333–337.

217. On the Gallic emperors, see König 1981, with a useful catalogue of relevant inscriptions, and Drinkwater 1987. For the Roman pretensions of the dynasts of Palmyra, see Seyrig 1934, 1937, 1963, and 1966, and cf. Chapter 7 n. 90. On the titulature of the kings of Edessa, see Teixidor 1989 and Ross 1993. For an ancient perspective on foreign governments see Ammianus 18.5.3 and 19.2.6.

218. *RIB* 91.

219. *EJ* no. 166 (*ILS* 94): *M. Iulius regis Donni f. Cottius praefectus ceivitatium quae subscriptae sunt.*

220. Aune 1983 and P. Alexander 1991.

221. La Piana 1912 and 1936; Grabar 1968, 44–45; and Fontaine 1971.

nance of the world that God gave to the Romans.[222] The Syrian bishop Theodoret, who wrote in both Greek and Syriac, presumed that the Persian king Sapor II knew what the Roman emperor looked like: according to him, when Sapor laid siege to Nisibis in A.D. 337, the monk Jacob prayed in the church. Sapor then had a vision of a man standing on the city's wall, with imperial carriage and wearing the glow of purple robe and diadem: supposing this man to be the emperor of Rome, Sapor threatened to kill the men who had failed to bring the news of his presence.[223] Theodoret made the assumption that Sapor, like everyone else, knew that certain adornments, like certain behaviors, fell within imperial prerogative. The bishop Paul of Samosata knew better than to cross that boundary: when he wished to look important, he dressed himself up and marched about town in the fashion of an imperial procurator—or so his detractors maintained. He even modeled his church after the basilica at which a procurator held court: he built himself a tribunal and retreated occasionally to a *secretum*.[224] In Chapter 6 we considered the widespread familiarity of residents of the empire with the ritual of the imperial donative: in the recension of the *Acts of St. Demetrius of Thessalonica* attributed to one John, later archbishop of that city, St. Demetrius appeared in a time of famine and proceeded to distribute a *congiarium*, "like a consul after he has received the insignia of office from the emperor."[225]

THE DISCOVERY OF ROMAN RELIGION

Many different men, from very disparate backgrounds, occupied the throne of the empire in its first four centuries. For a hundred reasons and in a thousand ways, the imperial office dominated them more than they dominated it. They all justified their rule in similar terms; they even expressed their desire to renew the state in wholly traditional terms.[226] Did the revolving door on the imperial office imply that anyone could fulfill its qualifications, or that the emperor was no different than any other man? Phrased in that fashion, the question misses the point. The incarnation of the charismatic power of Augustus within the imperial office was completed successfully when Tiberius assumed the throne. The Romans themselves had sev-

222. Murray 1975, 192–193, 241–242; Brock 1982.

223. Theodoret *Hist. eccl.* 2.30.9. He tells the same story somewhat differently at *Hist. Religiosa* 1.12.

224. Eusebius *Hist. eccl.* 7.30.8–9. On reflections in Rabbinic literature of the physical space in which procurators held court see Lieberman 1944, 18–19. On Paul of Samosata see Millar 1971 and Potter 1996b, 283–284.

225. *Miracula St. Demetrii* 42. See Chapter 7 at n. 96 on John of Ephesus.

226. Cf. Baynes 1935, 82.

eral explanations for this: Tiberius had held appropriate *imperium* from A.D. 4; Victoria Augusti or the *numen* of Augustus or both now watched over him and through him preserved the state; by adopting him, Augustus himself had recognized Tiberius as the best man for the job. Any particular individual might assent to one or all of these propositions. Endowed with legitimacy by a century of stability, the imperial office withstood the final years of Nero and the long year A.D. 69.

When dynasties passed or emperors adopted heirs outside their *domus,* people could have shaken their heads with disgust: "Valentinian who?" Among the military men *consensus* tended to fall upon individuals outside the highest echelons of power: jealousy cautioned against selecting a true peer for elevation to divinity. How did those outside the corridors of power receive the sudden epiphany of a new emperor? How could the common man, even a literate member of the upper class, describe the power of such an individual, and do so in a fashion that justified obedience and loyalty?

Augustus established an economy of flattery that did not permit emperors to claim divinity, especially not at Rome. Provincials could offer, and emperors could accept, all manner of honors. Emperors could also reject the most extravagant of those offered to them and thus parade a Roman *modestia* that provincials must have found very strange, indeed. *Civiles principes* after Augustus largely followed his lead and advertised not their qualities or attributes but their concrete acts: specific victories, *congiaria,* money to build theaters and forums, and temporary tax relief.[227]

Of course, people could be grateful to the emperor for benefactions or potentialities quite separate from those he advertised. Though the distribution of news of imperial victories ensured a steady flow of income into the imperial coffers and ultimately may have encouraged a popular mind-set that divided the world into Roman and barbarian, its most important contribution to provincial internalization of imperial ideology may have been far more subtle. As we have seen, "the fact that subordinates fought under [the emperor's] *auspicia,* not their own, may well have implied from early in the principate that the ruler was credited with potentialities operating beyond the range of his presence and even of his directives."[228] The people of Rome recognized the extraordinary powers at Augustus's disposal in areas other than military action. When the food supply in the city of Rome failed in 23 B.C. after Augustus ceased his continuous occupation of the consulate, the people rioted and demanded that he assume the dictatorship. He re-

227. Cf. Fishwick 1990a, 273, noting "that the advice Maecenas gives to Augustus on the ruler cult had been common policy for two hundred years or more."

228. Nock 1972, 671–672, although I have cautioned against his emphasis on the emperor's auspices as an important component in provincial belief.

fused, but nevertheless restored the grain supply in a matter of days.[229] In commenting on the behavior of Gallus in Antioch three and a half centuries later, Ammianus suggested that the ability to stop a famine was embodied in and specific to the imperial office: when supplicated by the populace, Gallus "did not, as is the custom with emperors whose widespread power [*diffusa potestas*] sometimes cures local hardships, order that anything be done, such as bringing grain from neighboring provinces."[230]

In a brilliant early essay, Arthur Darby Nock explored this ancient capacity to distinguish between divine powers and divine personalities.[231] Nock argued that from "this interest in ἡ τοῦ θεοῦ δύναμις" we could understand the habit "of investing one deity with the attributes of others": "By so representing the god you invested him with an accumulation of powers."[232] Throughout his career Nock resisted taking the next step, which was to use this framework to understand how emperors were assimilated to gods. Thus he interpreted the prayer that the Alexandrian sailors at Puteoli made to Augustus, that "through him they lived, through him they sailed, through him they enjoyed their liberty and their fortune," as an acclamation "of the concrete blessings of the Pax Augusta, and of all that it had been given to a unique individual to achieve—by genius and tact and industry, not by calming the waves or moving in three strides from Thrace to Troy."[233] But emperors *did* move like fire or lightning through the provinces.[234] In exercising such powers they forced all their subjects to confront unanswerable, inseparable, and largely unspeakable questions: Is the current emperor actually divine? And what role does he play in mediating between us and the gods and thus in insuring our well-being? And what do we owe him in return? The answer to the first question simply revealed itself in the manner of a given emperor's death: after all, "the souls of all men are immortal, but those of brave and good men are divine."[235] To the second two, Romans

229. Dio 54.1.1–4; Augustus, *Res gestae* 5.2.

230. Ammianus 14.7.5.

231. Nock 1972, 33–48.

232. Nock 1972, 39.

233. Nock 1972, 840. Cf. Friesen 1993, 146–152, making an important attempt to discuss imperial cult without discussing the ontological status of the emperor.

234. Cf. Ammianus 22.2.3–5, on Julian's *inopina velocitas* and Claudius Mamertinus, *Pan. Lat.* XI(3).6–7, describing Julian's passage from Paris to Constantinople, by way of Sirmium.

235. Cicero *Leg.* 2.28: *Quod autem ex hominum genere consecratos, sicut Herculem et ceteros, coli lex iubet, indicat omnium quidem animos inmortalis esse, sed fortium bonorumque divinos.* Cf. Augustine *Serm. Dolbeau* 26.13 discussing Acts 14:11: Paul and Barnabas performed miracles that surpassed *humanum modum*, so the pagans named Barnabas "Jove" and Paul "Mercury," *secundum consuetudinem suam.* Athenagoras *Leg.* 30 makes it abundantly clear that Christian critique of imperial cult proceeded on very different theological assumptions.

and provincials ultimately crafted an answer that of necessity bound them together.

Uniting the empire through piety toward the emperor required, on this understanding, a set of shared beliefs about the nature and extent of the emperor's power. In point of fact, mere faith in the existence of such beliefs would have been sufficient. Although we cannot conclusively demonstrate whether either condition obtained, we can begin by observing that the beneficent powers attributed to the emperor did not in and of themselves favor citizens over subjects. The plebs at Rome may have felt that Augustus smoothed the seas to bring grain to them and them alone, but the Alexandrian sailors at Puteoli did not feel themselves excluded from enjoyment of his benefactions. In some formulations the emperor's victoriousness favored "Romans" over all others, but we have already seen that an emperor might invite provincials to view themselves as equal recipients of his care and concern in matters of war. Provincials likewise read texts like the Fifth Cyrene Edict as promising imperial impartiality in disputes between provincials and Roman officials. Discharging these responsibilities—eternal vigilance in war and peace—required the emperor to exercise influence far beyond his person.[236]

Emperors received praise for other divine qualities and deeds, and, again, enjoyment of their fruits did not depend on an individual's legal status. Pacatus, the panegyrist of Theodosius, wondered aloud whether the emperor's divine soul chose a body to inhabit on the basis of its outstanding beauty or whether the fact of the soul's habitation made the emperor's body beautiful. His opening description of the emperor's virtues rose to a rhetorical climax: "To you alone, Emperor, along with your companion deity, let that secret be revealed. I will say only what it is right for a man to understand and to speak: such ought to be the man who receives the reverence of nations, to whom private and public prayers are addressed through the world, from whom those setting sail seek a calm sea; those about to travel, a safe return; and those about to fight, the favor of the gods."[237] Like the Alexandrian sailors arriving in Italy or soldiers saluting their standards, Pacatus viewed Theodosius as responsible for the well-being of his world.

Other writers throughout the length and history of the empire expressed similar gratitude for the ability to travel that the *pax Romana* afforded, for the empire's lack of piracy, of strife, and even of shipwrecks. As the elder Pliny set the limits of the knowable at the boundaries of the empire, so he acknowledged that the benefits of Roman rule reached only to the limits of Roman power. To the people they ruled, the Romans had been given by the

236. See Chapter 8 at nn. 78–81 and Chapter 9 at nn. 135–144.
237. *Pan. Lat.* XII(2).6.4.

gods as a second sun. Luke and Aelius Aristides, Eusebius and Orosius, Florus and Epictetus, Pacatus and Claudian, Horace and Themistius wrote in similar terms. When they thanked the emperor for his oversight of travel and commerce, they acknowledged that emperors exercised divine power to achieve those ends only for the portion of the world that mattered. "Is there not every opportunity for all to travel wheresoever they will? Are not all harbors active? Do not mountains offer the same security to travelers as cities offer to their inhabitants? Does not grace cover the fields? Has not all fear of all things departed? Of river fords that forbid crossing, or of straits that close the sea? Now assemblies are more joyous, and feasts more dear to the gods. Now the fire of Demeter burns brighter and more purely."[238]

Already under Augustus, Philo of Alexandria had stopped just short of attributing to the Roman emperors control over the weather itself: "We owe to the art of government that all the fertile, deep land on plains and hills is farmed, and that merchant ships safely navigate every sea to exchange the goods that countries offer to each other in their desire to associate, receiving in turn what they need and sending their surplus products away in return. . . . For the family of the Augusti has banished all the evils that used to flourish and be found in our midst over the frontiers to the ends of the earth and depths of Tartarus, while it has brought back to the world that we inhabit all those benefits and blessings that had been, as it were, in exile from the limits of earth and sea."[239] The entire human race would have been destroyed through internecine strife had not Augustus ended all wars, chased away all pirates, and preserved the peace. It was therefore fitting, according to Philo, that it was the Temple of Augustus at Alexandria that "gave hope of safety to sailors when they set out to sea and when they returned."[240] In the same era Horace and Valerius Maximus easily made the leap that Philo avoided, as later did the rhetorical handbook attributed to Menander. According to its author, "rains in season, abundance from the sea, unstinting harvests come happily to us because of the emperor's justice."[241]

The format of imperial oaths likewise suggested that the emperor possessed powers beyond those of mortal men. The inclusion of the emperor

---

238. [Aristides] *Or.* 35.37. See Pliny *Nat.* 14.2 and 27.2–3, and cf. Chapter 8 at n. 236. On Aristides see *Or.* 26.100, together with Chapter 3 n. 25. On Orosius and Eusebius see above at nn. 44 and 52, respectively. Cf. Horace *Carm.* 4.5.19–20, Florus *Verg.* 1–3, Epictetus 3.13.9–10, Claudian *De cons. Stilich.* 3.154–159; and Themistius *Or.* 6.75b–c. Much ancient prose fiction presumed a united Mediterranean: see Millar 1981b, 66, on Apuleius; Robbins 1991 on Luke; and Woolf 1997, 11, on Acts and Philostratus *Vita Apollonii.*

239. Philo *Leg.* 47, 49 (trans. Smallwood, with minor revisions).

240. Philo *Leg.* 141–151 at 151. Cf. Nock 1972, 841.

241. Menander Rhetor, Περὶ ἐπιδεικτικῶν 1–2, *Basilikos logos.* See also Horace *Carm.* 4.5.17–24; Valerius Maximus *pr.*, naming Tiberius *regimen maris;* and *Pan. Lat.* III(11).9.2.

himself or his *genius* or *numen* among the divinities sanctioning an oath clearly attributed to him, or to the divine potentiality within him, omniscience in knowing if that oath should be broken and omnipotence in his power to punish the perjurer.[242] Again, even if no one believed that all emperors possessed such power, some people clearly believed that some emperors did.[243] But it was ultimately the emperor's superhuman acts— manifested above all in his unique ability to be a "benefactor and savior of the entire human race"—that made people attribute superhuman powers and superhuman status to him and identified him as "the god of all mankind."[244] The second-century sophist Artemidorus twice quoted an "old saying": "To rule is to have the power of a god."[245] A second-century papyrus, following a format traditional in magical texts for the answering of commonplace questions with commonplace answers, answered the question "What is a god?" with "To rule." It then asked, "What is an emperor?" To that the answer was, "Equal to a god."[246] Other second-century Greeks wrote in similar terms. According to Arrian, Epictetus argued that "we perform obeisance before the emperors as before gods, because we consider that which has the power to confer the greatest advantage to be divine."[247] Lucian likewise insisted that the emperors' greatest reward was "praise, universal fame, receiving obeisance for their benefactions [τὸ ἐπὶ ταῖς εὐεργεσίαις προσκυνεῖσθαι], and the statues and temples and shrines such as exist among subjects: all these are payments for the care and foresight that these men exercise in always watching over the *res publica* [τὰ κοινά] and making it better."[248]

Traditional Mediterranean paganism in general, and Roman state religion in particular, happily acknowledged the existence of divinities as yet unknown.[249] Judaeo-Christian scholars have maintained that Christian theology has no word with which to translate *numen*, the *divinus animus* that separated the emperor from mortal men: it was the emperor's *numen* that answered prayers and that survived in the heavens after an emperor's

242. See Chapter 7 in n. 235, and cf. Tertullian *Apol.* 32.2 and *Nat.* 1.17.2–3; Vegetius 2.5; and Gregory Naz. *De vita sua* 1101–1107.

243. See, for example, Suetonius *Iulius* 85; Tacitus *Ann.* 1.73.4 and 2.50; and Tertullian *Apol.* 28.2–3.

244. Philostratus *Vit. Apoll.* 8.4: τὸν ἀπάντων ἀνθρώπων θεόν.

245. Artemidorus 2.36 (cf. 2.69): ὀρθῶς γὰρ καὶ τοῦτο τὸ παλαιὸν ἔχει 'τὸ κρατοῦν δύναμιν ἔχει θεοῦ.'

246. *P. Heidelberg* inv. 1716 verso, published in Bilabel 1924/25. Ingekamp 1969 discusses the question-and-answer format, and Nock 1972, 135, and Price 1984a, 95, discuss its relationship to the language of imperial cult.

247. Epictetus 4.1.60 (trans. Oldfather, with revisions).

248. Lucian *Apol.* 13 (trans. Kilburn, with revisions).

249. See Wissowa 1912, 43–52; cf. Nock 1972, 145–146.

death.[250] But we must acknowledge that Christians of the fourth century had an answer: *numen* could designate the god that was the emperor as easily as it designated the Christian God.[251] Four centuries earlier Velleius Paterculus ended his brief history with a prayer to Jupiter Capitolinus, Mars Gradivus, Vesta, and any other *numen* that had raised the expanse of the Roman empire to its broad hold on the *orbis terrarum:* they were to guard and protect the present condition, the present peace, as well as the reigning emperor and all successors to his station.[252] Unwillingness to countenance a scale of divine potentialities that included both Augustus and Christ can only impede attempts to understand the foreign thoughtworld of the ancient Mediterranean: we must understand how Vitruvius could believe that both Augustus and God had "divine minds."[253] As with any traditional deity, the emperor's divinity implied neither moral perfection nor true omnipotence, and, with Vergil, many probably understood that an emperor's *animus* was in many ways constrained by the mortality of his body. Menander did not suggest, ultimately, that the emperor himself controlled the weather; rather, men should pray to the gods for the emperor's safety because his special blessedness positioned him to mediate between the divine and the mortal. When Aelius Aristides wrote that the "mere mention of the emperor's name" caused men to rise and in a single breath "pray to the gods on the emperor's behalf, and to the emperor for his own affairs," he participated in the same theological position: the emperor's exalted position allowed him to exercise godlike power among mortal men, even as it prevented him from receiving aid, save from the gods.[254]

Long before Menander, Dio Chrysostom acknowledged a special relationship between Zeus and Trajan and argued for parallels between the governance of heaven and of earth.[255] At roughly the same time Plutarch wrote even more explicitly: "One could more truly say that rulers serve god for the care and salvation of men, so that of the beautiful and good things that god gives to men, they share out some and safeguard others."[256] Quite apart from the official religious tenets of the Roman state, then, individuals around the empire could accommodate the emperor within their personal

250. Fishwick 1990c and 1994 provide excellent surveys of ancient attitudes toward the *numen* of the living emperor and the *numina* of the *divi.* On modern difficulties in articulating ancient modes of thought see MacCormack 1975b.

251. See *C. Th.* 15.4.1, quoted in Chapter 7 at n. 136.

252. Velleius 2.131.1–2.

253. Vitruvius 1 *pr.* 1 and 8 *pr.* 3; cf. Cicero *Leg.* 2.10 and Ovid *Fasti* 1.531–534.

254. Aristides *Or.* 26.32.

255. Dio *Or.* 1.9–41; cf. Beaujeu 1955, 71–87.

256. Plutarch *Ad. princ. inerud.* 780D.

theologies as a worldly representative of whatever local or personal deity they worshiped.[257] Communities and individuals did just this in their acts of worship, whether they called their god "Augustan" or "Lover of Caesar," housed the imperial image with that of other gods, or simply asked their god to be the emperor's special protector.[258] According to Tertullian, even though every province and every city had its own gods, those gods were not necessarily worshiped at Rome. Rome, on the other hand, exported to the provinces the "god of the Romans," the deity of "Roman religion," namely the emperor.[259] It had not been possible to export the Capitoline Triad in this fashion, for example: people simply identified them as different incarnations of local deities.[260] Augustus, on the other hand, revealed his divine nature to the whole world at once, and thus endowed the Roman empire with its only universally shared deity.

The Roman state flourished when it enjoyed the favor of the gods. That favor came about above all through the universal piety of the Roman people: Roman legislation expressed the necessity of *consensus* in religious matters when it adopted medical imagery to express the "infection" of the Roman body politic by some foreign "poison."[261] The earliest use of this imagery comes in the law of Cornelius Hispalus of 139 B.C. banishing the Chaldaeans and Jews from Rome.[262] The metaphor of the people as a single homogeneous body nicely expressed the necessity of *consensus,* but it was even more appropriate under the Principate, when the body of the people had

257. This argument tends to break down the traditional division between "civic" and personal religions. North 1992 provides a sophisticated argument for that division. Proponents of this model seek to explain a genuine problem, but arguing that individuals turned to so-called personal religions because they wanted "choice" presupposes a profound shift in individuals' attachment to their communities. I agree that such a shift took place, although I would place it much later than most, but even on their terms such scholars should admit that religion is a symptom rather than a cause, evidence rather than explanation for an as yet unarticulated problem.

258. See Chapter 7 at n. 14. For φιλόχαισαϱ used of gods see *LSJ* s.v. For further evidence see esp. Nock 1972, 41–45, 202–251, and 653–675, and cf. Latte 1960, 315–316 and 324–325. See also Josephus *Ant. Iud.* 16.162–165 and Philo *Flacc.* 49–50. On inscriptions to Zeus Patroös in Asia Minor see Buckler 1935 and Reynolds 1986, 110.

259. Tertullian *Apol.* 24; cf. (*idem*) *Nat.* 1.17.2 on the *religio Caesarianae maiestatis,* together with *Acta Cypriani* 1 (*Sanctissimi imperatores Valerianus et Gallienus litteras ad me dare dignati sunt quibus praeceperunt eos, qui Romanam religionem non colunt, debere Romanas cerimonias recognoscere*) and 3.4 (*inimicum the diis Romanis et sacris religionibus constituisti*). On the assimilation of the emperor within the varied civic cults of Asia Minor see Robert 1994, 104.

260. But cf. Beaujeu 1976, and Alföldy 1989, a remarkable essay.

261. Cicero *Har. resp.* 9.19; cf. Tertullian *Apol.* 25.2.

262. Valerius Maximus 1.3.3, preserved in the epitome of Julius Paris: *Cn. Cornelius Hispalus . . . Iudaeos, qui Sabazi Iovis cultu Romanos inficere mores conati erant, repetere domos suas coegit.* See also Cicero *Sest.* 98 and *Rab. Post.* 33.

and required a single head.[263] If the Roman people transferred their *imperium et potestas* to the emperor, if Ovid could look at Augustus and see Rome, if the emperor's *felicitas* made him a mediator between the gods of the state and the state itself, then, just as surely, attacks on the emperor could constitute treason (*maiestas*) against the Roman people, and piety toward the gods who ensured the well-being of the state could and should be expressed in piety toward the emperor. As early as the reign of Augustus, the emperor could react to the Senate's condemnation of Gallus by praising "the piety of those who were so indignant on his behalf."[264] Even Tertullian, a Christian with an avowed hostility to *religio Romanorum*, conceded that all men owed the emperor "their piety and religious devotion and loyalty"—a set of synonyms that reveals much about the overlap of religion and patriotism in the Roman world.[265] A figure in the Roman pantheon deserved no less: Augustus had, after all, watched the races in the Circus Maximus while enshrined before an altar.[266] Modern translations and dictionaries rob texts from this era of much of their power when they render the words "sacred" and "divine" as "imperial," as though Augustus had been merely a man.[267]

263. On Roman use of this metaphor, with full collections of evidence, see Béranger 1953, 218–239, and Kienast 1982b. Both are particularly sensitive to language and metaphors associated with this root through analogical extension. Velleius 2.89–90 is particularly suggestive for its collocation of imagery. Not cited by either are Valerius Maximus 4.3.3; [Aristides] 35.13; *Pan. Lat.* IV(8).10.1; and [Aurelius Victor] *De viris illustribus* 18.

264. See, for example, Suetonius *Augustus* 66.2: *Sed Gallo quoque et accusatorum denuntiationibus et senatus consultis ad necem compulso laudavit quidem pietatem tanto opere pro se indignantium.* Cf. Charlesworth 1943, 1.

265. Tertullian *Apol.* 36.2. The process of transferring "piety" from the state to an individual was not as "natural" as Charlesworth 1943, 1, seems to think, and certainly not for a Christian.

266. See Augustus *Res gestae* 19.1–2:. *pulvinar ad circum maximum . . . feci,* which the Greek renders ναὸν πρὸς τῷ μεγάλῳ ἱπποδρόμῳ, on which see A. Alföldi 1934, 31–33; *idem* 1935, 41–42; Nock, 1972, 841, acknowledging that this language must at least have received the approval of Augustus; Weinstock 1971, 282–284; and Fishwick 1990b, 481. Both Alföldi and Weinstock discuss the Caesarian precedents, Alföldi arguing that Augustus's *pulvinar* was Caesar's gilded *sella curulis,* and Weinstock suggesting that the imperial seats "were attached to this construction." Although he does not cite Nock, Fishwick agrees that "the use of the word in connection with the emperor surely hints at his sacralization or superhumanization." Suetonius proves that the reference was *not* to a real altar: *Ipse circenses ex amicorum fere libertorumque cenaculis spectabat, interdum ex pulvinari et quidem cum coniuge ac liberis sedens* (*Augustus* 45.1). Suetonius also proves, *pace* A. Alföldi 1934, 32, that Augustan usage neither rendered this an unquestioned imperial prerogative nor made its language acceptable as *adulatio:* it was evidence of Domitian's arrogance that he called his seat *pulvinar suum* (*Domitian* 13.1).

267. See *LSJ* s.v. θεῖος I.4, and Robert, *OMS* 2:833 n. 2. The editors of *OLD* show a similar lack of sensitivity to ancient religious sentiment when they separate uses of *sacer* in "religious" contexts from those applied to members of the imperial house. The texts from the ancient world that explicitly describe cult acts as honorific are few, indeed: see Nock 1972, 355 n. 27,

Indeed, the insinuation of the emperor into loyalty oaths was but merely one front by which Augustus encroached upon or, perhaps, cloaked his person in the dignity of the Roman state. Of course, many writers gradually directed toward the emperor the expressions of patriotism that they had once spoken of the state; the subtle ways in which they insinuated traditional formulas in those expressions suggest a complex interplay of conscious and subconscious forces at work.[268] But in religious acts at every level, Augustus took his place beside Rome or came to overshadow her. Images of Augustus resided in temples once reserved for Dea Roma, just as they appeared together on the imperial coinage.[269] The college of the Arval Brethren was resuscitated to earn the favor of Dea Dia for the state, but its prayers clearly indicate that the person of the emperor was the conduit through which Dea Dia would aid the world. It was only natural that the Brothers should then celebrate auspicious events in the life of the emperor and *domus divina.*[270] At a more prestigious and visible level, the Senate and other organs of government rapidly learned to direct expressions of thanks to the gods, as well as prayers for their favor, in connection with health of their *princeps.*[271] The deaths of princes, soldiers, and imperial favorites could likewise be interpreted as self-sacrifices, *devotiones* for the emperor analogous to that performed by Decius Mus *pro salute omnium.*[272]

It was thus wholly understandable that the imperial cult should come to be called "the religion of the Romans," as Tertullian referred to it in his *Apology.* It was during his lifetime that agents of the Roman government came to appreciate, if they never quite understood, the danger represented by Christianity. Unlike other religious minorities, the Christians were unwilling to accommodate the divinity of the empire within their theology, and in the second century their numbers brought them to the attention of the authorities. During Tertullian's youth, the proconsul of Africa, Vigellius Saturninus, prosecuted Christians at Madaura and Carthage. In the preserved *acta* of his interrogation of Christians from Scilli, Saturninus denounced the Christians' claim to special piety. "We, too, are religious," Saturninus announced. "Our religion is a simple one: we swear by the *genius* of our lord

---

although I would contest his interpretation of his evidence, and add *OGIS* 456, ll. 35–48. Readers of dedications should remember the distinction drawn by Veyne 1962, 68: a name in the accusative indicates that the donor honors the named individual; a name in the dative indicates that the donor dedicates something to the named individual, who can receive it without being physically present. Thus dedications to emperors named in the dative are divine honors.

268. Among many studies see Knoche 1952.
269. Latte 1960, 312–313 and 316–317; Mellor 1975, 200–201.
270. Scheid 1975.
271. Latte 1960, 313–315; Freyburger 1978.
272. Cf. Versnel 1980, 562–577.

the emperor and we offer prayers for his health, something that you, too, should do." It was in all likelihood Christianity that brought Saturninus and others of his age to view one cult as the defining *religio* of the Romans, and it was Christian *obstinacia* that created the binarism between living *aut Christianorum aut Romanorum more*.[273]

It is within this framework that we must read Caracalla's edict extending citizenship to all residents of the empire. Caracalla attributed his action to piety: the gods had saved him from an attack, and to them he owed his gratitude. Wishing to lead the people of the empire in a unanimous display of consensual piety, and believing that the *populus* of the empire was most properly constituted by its citizen body, Caracalla granted citizenship to all its residents.[274] In other words, the *consensus* of the empire's population would speak more loudly if all were citizens.[275] To choose an unlikely parallel, Caracalla shared with Cicero the belief that only the *consensus universorum* could ensure the continued favor of the gods. Caracalla simply applied that principle to the giving of thanks. As Cicero had done when defining *maiestas*, Caracalla assumed that only citizens properly belonged within that "universal and harmonious body" of the state.

Even if we lack the apparatus to understand ancient belief and the terminology to describe it, we should not underestimate its power. As early as the reign of Augustus, Greek-speaking subjects of the Roman empire indicated their understanding of his relationship with the gods when they rendered *maiestas* as θειότης and described treason as impiety.[276] Decius's decision to acknowledge a crisis in the condition of the empire determined his

273. *Passio S. Scillitanorum* 3, and cf. 14: *Saturninus proconsul decretum ex tabella recitavit: Speratum . . . et ceteros ritu Christiano se vivere confessos, quoniam oblata sibi facultate ad Romanorum morem redeundi obstinanter perseveraverunt, gladio animadverti placet.* Compare Tertullian *Apol.* 24.9: *Sed nos soli arcemur a religionis proprietate! Laedimus Romanos nec Romani habemur, quia nec Romanorum deum colimus.* Elsewhere in Africa in the same period, Publius Flavius Pudens, a man most pious toward the *numina* of Caracalla and his mother, dedicated an altar *et cultui publicae religionis et honestamento dignae civitatis* (*AÉ* 1987, 1078). Cicero *De natura deorum* 3.5–6 claims to discuss "the whole of Roman religion" (*Cumque omnis populi Romani religio in sacra et in auspicia devisa sit, tertium adiunctum sit si quid praedictionis causa ex portentis et monstris Sibyllae interpretes haruspicesve monuerunt*), but in fact concentrates on precisely those aspects of Roman civic religion that were specific to Rome as a city-state and which were ultimately not exported to the empire. The history of that problem is enormous and complex, but only tangential to the problem under investigation here. Gods were easier to export than rites, with their accompanying theological presumptions

274. *P. Giss.* 40, col. I, ll. 4–8. This paraphrase avoids confronting the real difficulties in the preservation of this text. Among editions after its *princeps*, see *MC* 377; *AJ* no. 192; and Oliver 1989, no. 260.

275. His motivation simply cannot have been financial, as though he lacked the power to tax noncitizen residents. Dio's authority as a contemporary witness has blinded many to the extreme idiocy of his argument (at 77.9.5).

276. See Reynolds 1980, 73.

next action: Rome must have temporarily lost the favor of the gods that it had won *pietate ac religione*. That favor could be regained only by a renewal of *consensus*.[277] As Tertullian knew long before the first Decian *libellus* was written, the Romans would recognize the validity of an individual's choices in worship so long as he also recognized the gods of the state.[278] Christians, it will be recalled, prayed for the empire because its survival postponed the Day of Judgment: we may therefore presume that Dionysius of Alexandria, when asked to worship "the gods that preserve the empire," answered sincerely when he said, "We worship and venerate the one God, the creator of all, who has entrusted the empire to the Augusti Valerian and Gallienus, whom he loves greatly, and to him we pray continuously on behalf of their empire, that it should remain unshaken."[279]

Diocletian was a pious man. Fired, as Decius had been, by a desire to renew the Roman state, he knew what had turned the gods aside from Rome and what would win them back. In 295 he issued a law to restore the sanctity of marriage: "motivated by personal piety and religious scruple," he and Maximian sought in this law to exhort all to adhere to "the discipline of our age." "For it is certain that all immortal gods [*cuncta numina*] will continue to be favorable and well disposed to the Roman name, as they have always been in the past, only if we see to it that everyone living under our empire leads a pious and religious and peaceful and chaste life in every way."[280] Diocletian emphasized both the necessity of *consensus* and his own personal responsibility for ensuring that relations between the "gods who preserve their empire" and the citizens of that empire were on a sound footing. Two years later, in Alexandria, Diocletian learned of the influx of Manichaeans in Africa and of their attempts to introduce "new and unknown revelations": "He was consumed by an overwhelming desire to punish the stubbornness of the depraved minds of those most dissolute men." That the Manichaeans came from Persia made them more despicable: Diocletian feared lest "they should try, out of innate malevolence, to infect these men of more innocent nature, the modest and peaceful Roman race, and indeed our entire world, with the hateful customs and scandalous laws of the Persian, as if with poison."[281]

In light of these beliefs, Diocletian's initial courtesy toward Christians

---

277. Though Augustus turned down the title of *curator legum et morum*, he clearly believed himself responsible for reestablishing the moral rectitude of the Roman people. The refusal of that unprecedented office (*nullum magistratum contra morem maiorum delatum recepi*) was wholly in keeping with a man who held seven other time-hallowed priesthoods: *Res gestae* 6.1 and 7.3.

278. See Tertullian *Apol.* 24. Cf. Celsus, at Origen *Cels.* 8.62: Κἂν λέγῃ οὖν Κέλσος "τούτοις ἀφοσιωτέον, ἐφ᾽ ὅσον συμφέρει, πάντῃ γὰρ τοῦτο ποιεῖν οὐχ αἱρεῖ λόγος." On the Decian renewal see Chapter 7, "Decius and the *Divi*."

279. Eusebius *Hist. eccl.* 7.11.7–8.

280. *Collatio* 6.4.1, and cf. 6.4.6.

281. *Collatio* 15.3.3–4.

cannot be easily explained. Perhaps he unconsciously yielded to the arguments of Tertullian and Origen, that Christians were devout patriots at heart. A series of omens rapidly changed his mind.[282] Pagans readily interpreted these messages to suggest that the *concordia* of gods and men had been broken: in 299, in the presence of Diocletian and Galerius, the *haruspices* failed to obtain an appropriate reading from some entrails. A lack of *consensus* therefore threatened the well-being of the emperors and their endeavors, so all members of their staffs and army were ordered to display their unanimous support for the ancestral religion.[283] Three years later, in the winter of 302/303, the Oracle of Apollo at Didyma refused to respond to an imperial embassy. Diocletian summoned a council of civilian and military officials, who, in the words of Lactantius, spoke out against the "enemies of the gods and traitors to the state religion [*inimicos deorum et hostes religionum publicarum*]."[284] "It may be presumed, that [the courtiers present at that meeting] insisted on every topic which might interest the pride, the piety, or the fears, of their sovereign in the destruction of Christianity. Perhaps they represented that the glorious work of the deliverance of the empire was left imperfect, as long as an independent people was permitted to subsist and multiply in the heart of the provinces. The Christians (it might speciously be alleged), renouncing the gods and the institutions of Rome, had constituted a distinct republic, which might yet be suppressed."[285]

During the time when he achieved sole control of the West, and for the rest of his reign, Constantine faced constant schisms among the Christians within his empire. He found that intolerable. Like Cicero and Caracalla, Constantine knew that only the *consensus* of the people could earn and keep the favor of his God. Like Decius and Diocletian, Constantine was divinely appointed to the rulership of the world; like them, he acknowledged his personal responsibility for creating that *consensus*. But Constantine's exposure to Christianity provided him with additional motivation for stamping out dissension: he feared for his own immortal soul. Where Diocletian had stressed his duty to think only of the common good, Constantine stressed his fears for his personal welfare.[286] As he wrote to Aelafius, *vicarius* of Africa:[287]

---

282. Davies 1989.

283. Delehaye 1921.

284. Lactantius *Mort. pers.* 11.6.

285. Gibbon chapter 16 (1.563).

286. See, for example, *C. Th.* 9.1.4: Constantine closes a law by praying, *Ita mihi summa divinitas semper propitia sit et me incolumem praestet, ut cupio, felicissima et florente re publica.* The *res publica* sits in an ablative absolute, as an afterthought.

287. Constantine to Aelafius, vicarius of Africa = Optatus, appendix III. On Constantine's fears see Baynes 1946b, 136–137.

I consider it a matter of religious scruple that such contentions and altercations not be hidden from me, by which perchance the highest divinity might be aroused not only against the human race but also against me, into whose care by his divine assent he has entrusted all the world to be governed, and thus angered, decree something worse than hitherto. For I will be able to feel truly and completely safe, and to hope always for the best and most prosperous gifts from the ever-ready kindness of the most powerful god, only when I sense that all men worship the most sacred god with the proper worship of the catholic religion in a harmonious fraternity of religious observance.

He touched on these themes in other letters, using far stronger language: he promised "to destroy and strike asunder" those not worshiping his God with the veneration that He deserved: "I will see to it without any hesitation that they suffer a fitting ruin for their madness and rash obstinacy."[288] Constantine knew that uniting "the representations of all nations concerning the divine into a single and settled condition" would repair "the harmony of the body of the whole world [τὸ τῆς κοινῆς οἰκουμένης σῶμα], as it was then struggling with some serious wound."[289] He therefore outlawed heretical beliefs, ordered the burning of heretical books, and confiscated heretical houses of worship for the use of the catholic church. The introduction of this demand of *consensus,* the use of secular power in religious persecution, and labeling religious dissidents as members of another "nation" constituted only the most harmful of the many ways in which Constantine transformed Christianity into a Roman religion.[290]

THE FATHER OF THE HUMAN RACE

A Roman prince could neither compel the gratitude of his provincials nor even determine the origins of the respect they gave him. Provincials' acquiescence to the government's normative authority should not seduce us into equating the themes of imperial propaganda with an imperial ideology, as though the government always spoke with one voice and ideology were static. An ideology as a lived system is dynamic, determined and defined through the evolution and manipulation, no less than the internalization and iteration, of the ruling order's normative script. I close with a test of the model adumbrated in this book.

As imperial propaganda informed but did not control provincial expressions of gratitude to their emperor and his empire, so imperial titulature

---

288. Constantine to Celsus, vicarius of Africa = Optatus, appendix VII.

289. Constantine to Alexander, bishop of Alexandria, and Arius, at Eusebius *Vit. Const.* 2.65.1. Cf. Eusebius *Vit. Const.* 1.26: Εἶθ᾽ ὥσπερ μέγα σῶμα τὸ πᾶν τῆς ἐννοήσας στοιχεῖον.

290. Of course, Scripture had provided ample ammunition to earlier Christians arguing for *consensus.* See Cyprian *Ep.* 11.3.1–2, citing Ps. 67:7, Matthew 18:19, John 15:7, and Acts 4:32.

could not fix the terms in which provincials addressed and spoke of the emperor in affective contexts. In official decrees or administrative texts, to be sure, municipalities as well as individuals used that official titulature and, in doing so, kept abreast of their emperor's most recent titles and military successes.[291] But even as their faith in the Roman system found expression in their exploitation of its rationality rather than in continual celebrations of imperial victories, so they gave voice to their appreciation of the emperor by calling him not "general," *imperator,* but "father."

Like provincial manipulations of Roman triumphal iconography, this use of *pater* was both a development of and a departure from official usage. "Father" as such was sanctioned by neither official writ nor tradition. Romans under the Republic had adopted the title *pater patriae,* "father of his country," as a reward for a specific type of achievement: for saving the city from invaders or conspirators, or for saving the lives of many citizens.[292] They associated that appellation with Romulus, whose name they also considered using as an honorific title: he had been the founder of the city, and someone who saved the city could be regarded as having founded it a second time.[293] In 27 B.C., after considerable debate, the Senate awarded Octavian the name Augustus, rather than Romulus, and twenty-five years later they gave him in addition the title *pater patriae.*[294] Thereafter it was rapidly numbered among the titles and honors voted upon an individual's accession.

But Augustus had done far more than save his country from a military disaster, and the attempt to name him *curator legum et morum* hints at the special qualities Augustus was believed to embody. The expectations regarding his role as arbiter of Roman mores had existed long before he accepted the title *pater patriae,* and they were manifest whenever writers suggested that Augustus be regarded as a "father." Of course, *pater* could be used as an abbreviation for *pater patriae,* not least by writers suggesting that Augustus should have that title in the years before he assumed it.[295] At times,

291. See *Pan. Lat.* IV(8).5 and 14.1: The author first rapidly lists recent imperial victories but passes over others, leaving it to "messengers even now arriving" to announce the devastation of the Moors. Later he contrasts the martial conduct of Constantius with the indolence of earlier emperors, who sat at Rome while their generals acquired for them "the *cognomina* of conquered races."

292. A. Alföldi 1970b, 40–101; cf. Weinstock 1971, 175–184, 200–205. Note that Cicero *Rab. perd.* 27 (*C. Marium, quem vere patrem patriae, parentem, inquam, vestrae libertatis atque huiusce rei publicae possumus dicere*) does not develop "father" as a biological metaphor, but rather construes *pater* as *parens* in the sense of *auctor.*

293. See Livy 5.49.7 on Camillus, and cf. Weinstock 1971, 184 n. 2.

294. On this event see Chapter 5 at n. 70.

295. For example, Horace *Carm.* 1.2.49–52 (*hic ames dici pater atque princeps*), where the emphasis on Octavian's military achievements suggests that Horace speaks of Octavian's official titles.

however, the context suggests that *pater* was being used not simply as a title, but was rather a role that Augustus was expected to fulfill. When Horace addressed Jupiter as "father and guardian of the human race," "with Caesar next in power," he both honored Augustus and assigned him a heavy burden.[296] The distinction is fundamental: *pater patriae* had been an honorific title, not an office: it put the seal of official gratitude on past achievements.[297]

Augustus transformed it into something more than a title and something less than an office. Augustus exercised his supreme *auctoritas* as *pater patriae* for sixteen years, a span of time that induced men to describe him wielding quasi-official, quasi-paternal authority over his children.[298] To put it briefly, by demonstrating the moral rectitude and earning the *auctoritas* necessary to become, if only potentially, *curator legum et morum*, Augustus incarnated the qualities of Numa as well as Romulus.[299] As we have seen, Horace was already willing to place such demands on Augustus in the mid-20s:[300]

> Whoever desires to banish
>   impious slaughter and civil war,
> if he should seek that "Father of Cities"
>   be inscribed beneath his portraits,
> let him dare to restrain our lawless license.

Later in that same ode Horace asked Augustus to employ his *auctoritas* to restore moral rectitude to a people whose disrespect for tradition had emasculated their laws.[301] Over the next two decades, this experiment issued in

---

296. See Horace *Carm.* 1.12.49–60 at 49–52, and cf. *Carm.* 3.5.1. See also Ovid *Met.* 15.858–860 (Jupiter and Augustus are *pater . . . et rector uterque*), *Fast.* 2.130 (*pater orbis*), and *Trist.* 2.215–218. At Statius *Silvae* 4.1.17 Janus addresses Domitian as *magne parens mundi*, but Statius most clearly expands on Horace *Carm.* 1.12.49–60 at *Silvae* 4.3.128–129: *En! hic est deus, hunc iubet beatis pro se Iuppiter imperare terris.* See also *Silvae* 3.4.48 and 4.2.14–15. Elsewhere see Martial 7.7.5, addressing Domitian as *summe mundi rector et parens orbis*, and 9.5.1, addressing the same emperor as *summi Rheni domitor et parens orbis, pudice princeps.*

297. Several writers of the late Republic and Augustan age assign the origin of *patres* as a title for senators to their exercise of paternal authority (e.g., Cicero *Rep.* 2.14, Sallust *Cat.* 6.6, and Livy 1.8.7). Although the influence wielded by Augustus was altogether different in scope and scale, such passages establish a ready context for Romans' willingness to graft the terminology of the family and *patria potestas* onto the institutions and workings of political life.

298. But cf. Weinstock 1971, 200–205, noting that Cicero's acclamation as *pater patriae* had not "invested him with special status," whereas Caesar "was the first for whom the title meant more than glory." Yet Weinstock regards the subsequent development of *principes'* paternal authority as "unexceptionable" (201). See also A. Alföldi 1970b, 118–124.

299. For characteristically insightful treatments of Augustan manipulations of religious offices and scruples see Gagé 1930a, 158–171, and *idem* 1931b. Cf. Eisenhut 1982, ostensibly on Propertius but with substantially wider range.

300. Horace *Carm.* 3.24.25–29.

301. Horace *Carm.* 3.24.35–36.

the wholesale association of the language and conceptual apparatus of fatherhood with the figure of Augustus: in tacit opposition to an absent deity, Horace named Augustus as the "present guardian of Italy and Mistress Rome." An apocryphal story likewise circulated about Quintus Catulus and two dreams he had after dedicating the Capitol in the early 60s B.C.: in one, Jupiter Optimus Maximus entrusted an image of Roma to a boy, and in the other Jupiter declared that the same boy was being raised for the guardianship of the state. The next day Catulus saw the young Augustus and recognized him as the boy in his dreams.[302]

A generation later, at the end of Augustus's life, Ovid begged the emperor's pardon by invoking "our fatherland, which is safe and secure with you as its parent," later naming Augustus "father of our country."[303] That their *patria* remained secure because Augustus was its *parens* suggests, once again, that fatherhood was now a role rather than a title. Just a few years later, Valerius Maximus explicitly drew the connection between the *auctoritas* of the Augustan house and this titulature. In his preface he invoked Tiberius as his muse: to him the *consensus* of gods and men had entrusted the guidance of land and sea; he was the certain health of their *patria*. Tiberius possessed the heavenly providence that nurtured virtue and censured vice.[304] In an anecdote under the rubric "Disregard for religious scruple," Valerius argued that Augustus had showed himself "an efficacious avenger of spurned religious scruple" when he ordered the execution of Antony's sacrilegious lieutenant Turullius. Placed in a succession of stories about divine vengeance, the anecdote depicted Augustus as the earthly agent of the gods.[305] Similarly, the piety of Drusus, "the ornament of our age and the glory of the Julian line," ensured the favor of Jupiter, "that most faithful guardian of the Roman empire."[306]

No Republican author could have discussed the piety due toward one's *patria* by drawing an analogy between its *maiestas* and the *auctoritas parentium*. "As a *domus*"—Would any reader not have understood that Valerius referred to the *domus divina?*—"is overthrown [by a lack of *pietas* toward one's parents], how can the *status* of the *res publica* remain [when *pietas* toward it is lacking]?" "The ruin of the city must needs drag down with it the *penates* of all."[307] Thus, when Valerius turned to the issue of dissension within fam-

---

302. Horace Carm. 4.14.43–44: *o tutela praesens / Italiae dominaeque Romae*. Suetonius *Augustus* 94.8: *is ad tutelam rei publicae educaretur*. On these themes see Béranger 1953, 256–261 and 267–268.

303. Ovid *Tristia* 2.157 and 181.

304. Valerius Maximus 1.*pr.*

305. Valerius Maximus 1.1.19: *efficax ultor contemptae religionis*.

306. Valerius Maximus 5.5.3.

307. Valerius Maximus 5.6 *praefatio*.

ilies over the inheritance of property, he concluded the narration of one case by relating Augustus's verdict upon it. He attributed the fairness of Augustus's decision to his "exercise of the spirit of a *pater patriae*" (*patris patriae animo usus*).[308]

Later Latin writers followed in these footsteps. Seneca wrote of the duty of a good *princeps* that it resembled that of good parents, who should not disinherit a son at his first offense: "A parent must follow this course of action, and also a *princeps*, whom we call father of his country, though not through empty flattery." Romans, Seneca added, had given other titles as honors—he listed "Great," "Blessed," and "August"—"but we have given the name *pater patriae* [to our *princeps*] so that he should know that a father's power has been given to him, constraining him to think of his children's interests and placing his after theirs."[309] Seneca clearly did not realize, or did not wish to say, that this interpretation of that name had been an innovation of the Augustan age. Seneca wrote *On clemency* in part as an exhortation to the young Nero and so did not dwell on the characteristics of a bad prince. In his panegyric to Trajan, however, Pliny felt free to draw that distinction clearly, since the end of the Flavian dynasty had rendered Domitian's memory easy prey. There was no need, Pliny argued, to flatter Trajan as though he were a god: he was not a tyrant but a fellow citizen, a father and not a master (*non de tyranno sed de cive, non de domino sed de parente*).[310] The more cynical Tacitus depicted Tiberius adopting this terminology with cold condescension on the occasion of that emperor's accession. Tiberius told the Senate that, though he was not equal to the burden of the state, he would undertake the guardianship of whatever part was entrusted to him.[311] Closer in temper to Tacitus than to Pliny, though he knew both their writings, Tertullian also discussed the use of "Lord" as a title for the emperor: "Augustus, the founder of the empire, did not wish to be called *dominus*, for that is the name of God. I will openly call the emperor *dominus*, but only in a mundane fashion, and only when I am not compelled to call him *dominus* as if he were *deus*. . . . He who is *pater patriae*, how is he its *dominus*? Surely the name suggesting piety and not power is the more pleasurable. Even the fathers of families are called *patres* rather than *domini*."[312]

Although Homer occasionally referred to Odysseus as a "king" and "father," the latter name and the qualities it implied did not become part of

308. Valerius Maximus 7.7.3.
309. Seneca *Clem.* 1.14.2.
310. Pliny *Pan.* 2.3. Cf. 7.4: *Adscivit enim the filium non vitricus sed princeps, eodemque animo divus Nerva pater tuus factus est, quo erat omnium.*
311. Tacitus *Ann.* 1.12.1.
312. Tertullian *Apol.* 34.1–2.

Hellenistic titulature.³¹³ Indeed, one study has suggested that *pater patriae* "was intended as something distinct from the kinds of epithets by which Hellenistic kings were known."³¹⁴ A series of inscriptions from Asia Minor, all dating after Augustus's assumption of the title *pater patriae* in 2 B.C., reflects that addition to Augustan titulature from a Greek perspective. Although some translate the title directly as πατὴρ τῆς πατρίδος ("father of his country"), that title could imply a distinction between Augustus's role at Rome and his role in the provinces. Some clearly wished to obscure this difference, which claimed Augustus as the property of Rome alone, and thus rendered the title as πατὴρ τῆς πατρίδος καὶ τοῦ σύμπαντος τῶν ἀνθρώπων γένους: "father of his fatherland and of the entire human race." This translation appears first in decrees of the *koinon* of Asia.³¹⁵ At one level, this represents a perfectly natural adaptation of royal honors from the Hellenistic period: kings at that time were always benefactors or saviors of the human race. And yet the intrusion of that phrase into several lines of Latin nomenclature must have been intended, at least in part, to claim Augustus as their father, too. Greeks began to share the empire by first sharing the emperor.³¹⁶

The geographer Strabo, writing contemporaneously with Valerius Maximus, ended Book 6 of his *Geography* with a summary of the history of Roman imperialism. He closed by noting that the Italians had tended to fight among themselves until they had passed under the sway of the Romans. In the end, the task of governing so large an empire proved too great even for the Roman Republic, and so the Romans turned their empire over "to a single man, as though to a father." From the moment when Augustus assumed total power, "Rome and her allies" had enjoyed peace and prosperity; and those conditions continued under his son Tiberius, "who succeeded him and who has made Augustus his model in all things."³¹⁷ Like the *koinon* of Asia, Strabo could regard Augustus as the "father" of all because, in naming Rome's subjects her "allies," Strabo had effected a unification of the empire beyond anything imagined by his emperors.

This conceptual transformation of *pater patriae* into *pater* became stan-

<hr>

313. For example, Mentor at Homer *Od.* 2.231–234, uses both βασιλεύς and πατήρ in reference to Odysseus. Powerful benefactors were, however, described as fathers in Greek literary texts, but the usage was not restricted to kings: A. Alföldi 1970b, 49, 119–121, and Stevenson 1992, 430.

314. Stevenson 1992, 430.

315. Texts collected in Buckler 1935, 177–188: see *IGRR* IV 1410.6–7; *IGRR* IV 1611 (*OGIS* 470), tablet B.6–8; *IGRR* IV 1756, section X, ll. 101–102; and *IBM* 894.

316. See also *IG* XII.2. 206, from Mytilene, describing Tiberius as κοινὸν μὲν τᾶς οἰκημένας εὐεργέταν, τὰς δὲ ἄμμας πόλιος ἐπιφανέστατον καὶ κτίσταν.

317. Strabo 6.4.2.

dard among Greek and Latin writers of the empire. Herodian, for example, repeatedly referred to Pertinax as a father figure to the Senate and people of Rome: he was a "constitutional ruler" and "gentle guardian" and "father," and not an "emperor."[318] Cassius Dio had so completely absorbed this interpretation that he regarded the title awarded to Augustus (and thus to all subsequent emperors) as simply *pater,* and not *pater patriae:* "The name 'father' gives to them a certain power over us all, like that which fathers have over their children, although it did not originate for this purpose, but as an honor and an admonition, that they should love their subjects as their children, just as their subjects would respect them like their fathers."[319] While Dio clearly misrepresented the precise wording of Augustan titulature, he nevertheless understood the function of the title in terms startlingly close to those offered by Seneca in *On clemency.*

Despite continually being referred to as "father," Roman emperors retained the traditional wording of the title *pater patriae* and, with the extension of the franchise and the emphasis on universalization in imperial propaganda, it must have become easier and easier for all to see themselves as equal members of that *patria.* Diocletian was the first emperor, to my knowledge, to refer explicitly to his responsibility as a "parent of the human race."[320] When Aurelius Victor, writing some sixty years after Diocletian, began to narrate the reign of that emperor, he returned in good classicizing fashion to the political topoi that had preoccupied Pliny and Tertullian: Diocletian's vices, he wrote, were obscured by his good qualities, for "although he allowed himself to be addressed as *dominus,* he acted like a parent."[321]

Some two decades after Victor laid down his pen, the senator Quintus Aurelius Symmachus, the most famous orator of his day, gave a speech before the Senate at Rome, giving thanks for the nomination of his father to the consulate for the next year. In that speech he brought together in a single paragraph the varied tropes that have seized our attention. Symmachus reminded the Senate how rarely the *res publica* had known *principes*

318. Herodian 2.4.1 and 2.6.2, contrasting σεμνὸς καὶ ἤπιος ἄρχων καὶ πατήρ and πατήρ τηε ἤπιος καὶ χρηστὸς προστάτης with βασιλεύς. Cf. Herodian 1.4.8 and 2.2.8, on Marcus Aurelius and Pertinax, respectively.

319. Dio 53.18.3. Compare the words attributed to Augustus by Dio in his speeches on marriage and procreation at the start of Book 56: Augustus addresses the men as πατέρες, καὶ γὰρ ταύτην ἄξιοι τὴν ἐπωνυμίαν ὁμοίως ἐμοὶ ἔχειν ἐστέ (56.3.8, and cf. 9.1 and 9.3). See also Herodian 2.2.9, on the titles awarded to Pertinax: μὴ κατασχὼν ἑαυτοῦ ὁ δῆμος μελλόντων καὶ ὀκνούντων ἔτι τῶν στρατιωτῶν Σεβαστόν τηε ἀναγορεύει καὶ πατέρα καλεῖ πάσαις τηε γεραίρει εὐφημιαῖς.

320. Diocletian *Edictum de pretiis, praefatio* 7: *convenit prospicientibus nobis, qui parentes sumus generis humani.*

321. Aurelius Victor 39.8: *Verum haec in Valerio obducta ceteris bonis; eoque ipso, quod dominum dici passus, parentem egit.*

who desired what the Senate wanted. That was deplorable, since the authority of the imperial office was such that public mores were corrupted by the reigns of wicked men. Under such rulers good men either were oppressed by the plots of the wicked or were themselves corrupted. Yet now, like an inheritance, the guardianship of the state had passed to Gratian: "Now our emperors desire what the senators want. The whole body of the *res publica* flourishes so mightily because the vigorous health of its head is protected by the strength of its limbs." Although "good magistrates desire to be chosen by all and not by a single person," his father had no reason to feel diminished at being nominated by the emperor and not elected by the Senate or people of Rome. For the emperors understood the desire to be chosen by unanimous consent. Nevertheless, as "parents of the human race," they also knew that the voting tribes were polluted by lawless and plebeian dregs and were therefore subject to the influence of venal bribery. Symmachus could easily have used the language of Horace or Ulpian or Cassius Dio, describing the emperors' nominations as an exercise of their guardianship of the state, or of that *imperium ac potestas* that the people had surrendered to them, or even of their fatherly care. The result was the same: "For who does not equate the judgment of our emperors with that of the entire world?"[322]

322. Symmachus *Or.* 4.5–7. For similar sentiments see Ausonius *Gratiarum actio* 13 and Claudius Mamertinus at *Pan. Lat.* XI(3).16 and 19; on these passages see Gibbon chapter 17 (1.605).

CHAPTER TEN

Conclusion

Singulare et Unicum Imperium

Legum denique idcirco omnes servi sumus ut liberi esse possimus.
CICERO *Clu.* 146

If more of Cicero's *De legibus* survived, this Conclusion would be easier to write.[1] Ancient political theorists started with noble assumptions—for example, that the state, formed by a primitive social contract, existed to benefit the common good. To be fair, one must admit that these assumptions shaped Cicero's beliefs that a republic could not truly exist unless founded on the *consensus* of the political orders and that such concord must itself be founded upon the highest degree of justice.[2] These theorists also assumed, however, that true political power ought to reside in men of their class; much of their "political theory" simply exhorted their peers to a career in the service of a state whose actual constitution they outlined in the barest of terms. The *De legibus* promised more: whatever Cicero intended, it had the potential to reveal one exceptional intellectual's vision of the bond that held the social fabric together. In that work Cicero provided a constitution for the ideal state that he had described in his *De re publica* some years before. He also supplied an extensive commentary on each section of that ideal law code, in which he set forth the objective good toward which each clause of that code was directed. Insofar as Cicero displayed an equal concern for the quality of a citizen's obedience, we can see, behind the perspective of the commentary, a particular understanding of the Roman citizen's adherence to his society's normative order.

---

1. The only extant work comparable in scope and topic to *Leg.* is Cicero *Off.* 3, on which see Dyck 1996. The Latin title of this chapter is quoted from Tertullian *Adv. Praxean* 3.2; for the context, see Chapter 2 at n. 123.

2. Cicero *Rep.* 2.69–70. See also Cicero *Rep.* 6.13.2, with Macrobius *Comm.* 1.8.13, discussed in Chapter 1 at nn. 20–21.

Cicero's exposition began with the rules governing the state religion, its priesthoods, and their function. While Cicero allowed for private worship of ancestral deities, he also insisted on the universal acceptance of an approved state pantheon and the universal observance of state-sanctioned holidays.[3] The Principate made it possible for this ideal *consensus* to be realized: quite independent from the steady extension of the franchise, the position of Augustus atop the empire allowed the Mediterranean world to share a deity for the first time. It did so by providing, in the first instance, the reality of a shared calendar. The only remotely comparable phenomena prior to Augustus were those formed within diplomatic negotiations, when city-states recognized commonalities between their respective mythological traditions or identified Jupiter Capitolinus with a local Zeus, for example.[4] The comparison cannot bear much scrutiny, though; cities neither changed the names of their own deities nor instituted new festivals on appropriate days in response to such identifications. In point of fact, the sheer absence of uniformity in civic calendars made the attempt pointless. A century after Augustus that situation had changed entirely. A traveler could recognize at least one temple in every city he visited and would know the prayers for one divinity in every ritual he witnessed; he could identify the dates of imperial holidays in any civic calendar as shared with every municipality in the empire. When Aulus Gellius sought in the second century to explain why cities would petition to acquire the status of a colony and so give up the traditionally privileged status of *municipium*, he could suggest only the desire to achieve precisely this identity with the larger community of empire:[5]

> But the relationship of "colonies" is a different one. For they do not come into citizenship from without nor grow from roots of their own, but they are, as it were, transplanted from the citizen body and have all the laws and institutions of the Roman people, not those of their own devising. This condition, although it is more exposed to control and less free, is nevertheless thought preferable and more prestigious because of the greatness and majesty of the Roman people, of whom the colonies seem to be miniature images and, as it were, duplicates.

3. Cicero *Leg.* 2.19; cf. 2.27 and 29.
4. See Ando 1999 at nn. 30 and 35–37, citing earlier bibliography.
5. Gellius 16.13, esp. 8–9 (trans. Rolfe, with minor changes); cf. Tacitus *Ann.* 14.27.1–3. Cf. *C. Iust.* 1.17.10: *Sed et si quae leges in veteribus libris positae iam in desuetudinem abierunt, nullo modo vobis easdem ponere permittimus, cum haec tantummodo obtinere volumus, quae vel iudiciorum frequentissimus ordo exercuit vel longa consuetudo huius almae urbis comprobavit, secundum Salvii Iuliani scripturam, quae indicat debere omnes civitates consuetudinem Romae sequi, quae caput est orbis terrarum, non ipsam alias civitates.*

It goes without saying that the "laws and institutions" received from Rome would have included the Roman calendar.[6] Cicero may not have envisioned a community of such magnitude, but imperial cult and imperial anniversaries began to shift conceptions of the *res publica* away from the neatly geographic *pomerium* of Rome and toward coextension with her *imperium*.

Imperial cult existed not as a system of belief, although it presupposed one, but as a set of ritual observances. Africans greeting Gordian, or Antiochenes welcoming Niger, or Constantinopolitans honoring Procopius did so using largely identical ceremonies, because they, like the citizens at Oxyrhynchus and Athens, had practiced that ritual throughout their lives before imperial portraits.[7] Even those who never left the city of their birth could realistically imagine, when swearing their annual oath and making the concomitant prayers for the health of their ruler, that every other citizen of the empire was performing the same act at precisely the same time. The ceremonies that ordered political life under the empire thus continually brought the existence of both emperor and empire before the mind of the individual provincial. In doing so, they enabled him to see himself as a member of a larger, regularly reconstituted community.

Cicero turned next to secular legislation, which he introduced with an exhortation on the preeminence of law:[8]

> Just as the laws preside over the magistrates, so the magistrates preside over the people, and truly it is possible to say that a magistrate is a speaking law, while the law is a silent magistrate. For nothing is so completely suited to justice and the rightful ordering of nature—when I say that, I wish to be understood as saying the Law—than the legitimate exercise of power [*imperium*]. Without it neither a home, nor a city, nor a nation, nor the human race, nor nature itself, nor even the world can long endure.

Cicero's scheme did not simply ordain the legitimacy of magistrates: the law circumscribed their power of command in specific ways, even as it urged the citizen to obey that power in its legitimate domain.[9] The mechanics of that relationship would not always satisfy both parties, and for that reason the ideal state provided the citizen with the right of appeal to equal or higher magistrates and provided in general for the preservation and accessibility of a written record of all laws and administrative acts.[10] Whatever the sad realities of political life from the Gracchi to Actium, Romans imagined that

---

6. Cf. Nock 1972, 741.

7. Cf. Momigliano 1987, 101.

8. Cicero *Leg.* 3.2–3. On the nexus of *ius, condicio naturae,* and *leges* see also *Off.* 3.23, with Dyck 1996 *ad locum.*

9. Cicero *Leg.* 3.5, and cf. *Off.* 1.124.

10. Cicero *Leg.* 3.6 and 11.

their constitution, like their legal system, operated through a constructed harmony of domination and obedience.

The dramatic expansion of the body of Roman citizens in Italy in the last century of the Roman Republic provided a crucial impetus in the evolution of the Roman legal system from a purely philosophical appreciation of autonomous law toward its practical realization under the classical jurists.[11] Nothing could have been more natural, it may seem, than extending such rationality beyond the citizen body in Italy to the administration of the empire's provincial subjects. In fact, Romans of the Republic did regard such rationality in the governance of the provinces as an ideal, though it was seldom realized; nothing could have struck provincials as so shockingly innovative as Augustan promises to make this ideal concrete. To the cynic, Augustan propaganda simply informed provincials that Augustus would spread the burden of his exploitation as evenly as possible; in practice Augustus revolutionized ancient imperialism. First, Augustus insisted that he was *not* νόμος ἔμψυχος—"law animate"—but that he himself was subject to the law, while all other agents of the government were answerable to him.[12] Second, he claimed responsibility for initiating, however imperfectly, the extension of Roman law and its principles to the outer edges of his empire. In this he lied, but lied truthfully, for if Republican governors had occasionally made some token gestures toward the honest administration of their provinces, it was Augustan propaganda that made provincials believe or even want to believe in such gestures.

Roman bureaucratic niceties do not excite modern scholars.[13] They were, however, the lived testimonials that suggested the truthfulness of Augustan propaganda. As such they seized the imagination of the ancient world. People from the Euphrates to the Tyne could recognize the formalities of a decree of the Roman Senate. Assuming two parties to each suit, and only one suit per litigant, 902 litigants passed before the prefect's tribunal in Arsinoë on those two and a half days in the month Phamenoth seventeen centuries ago. It is very likely that all lived in Egypt, and virtually all in the Arsinoïte nome. Yet few would have doubted that, if transported to Bithynia or Baetica, the same procedural rules would obtain, or that all relevant legal formulas could be learned from the local procurator's *mandata* or from the governor's edict, which could be found either in the regional *tabularium*

---

11. Frier 1985, 252–287 and esp. 273–280.

12. On this feature of the Principate and its evolution as factors in establishing a periodization of imperial history see Bleicken 1978, 22–24.

13. See Momigliano 1987, 100: "Again, the emperor was known to make laws and regulations and to answer petitions of various kinds. The great amount of paperwork passing from center to periphery and vice versa (about which we have now the learned work by Fergus Millar) was not the kind that would strike the imagination and create widespread loyalty."

or at the local Sebasteum. It does not matter that most provincials probably never left the province in which they were born. Rather, their appreciation of the empire grew from the belief they shared with Orosius, that they *could* travel the length of the empire and still know precisely what benefits accrued from their membership in the Roman community. For that Aristides thanked Rome profusely: "It is you again who best proved the general assertion that Earth is the mother of all and our common *patria*. Now indeed it is possible for Greek or barbarian, with or without his property, to travel wherever he wills, easily, as simply as if passing from country to country. . . . For safety it suffices to be a Roman or, rather, one of your subjects."[14]

The imperial office sat atop a pyramid formed by the several and aggregate claims to authority implicit in the Augustan system. This book argues that the charismatic power of the imperial office guaranteed the orderly functioning of the Roman bureaucracy. In his *Panegyric* Pliny explicitly assimilated Trajan's oversight of his administration to his semidivine status: "This is indeed the care of a true *princeps*, or even of a god, to reconcile competing cities, to pacify angry peoples less by exercise of power than by reason, to intercede against the injustices of magistrates, to undo what should not have been done: in short, like the swiftest star to see everything, to hear everything, and to be present at once with aid wherever your help is sought."[15] It is no less true that the continued functioning of that bureaucracy strengthened people's faith in the imperial office when its occupants appeared less than superhuman. Just as imperial cult was well established under the Julio-Claudians, so provincial exploitation of the Roman administration began long before Roman citizenship became universal. Even before Hadrian restored the world by raising the provinces from their knees, the work of Romanization—of establishing a new paradigm for the political community, of creating new definitions of "us" and "them," of endowing literary and everyday language with new metaphors for the state— had begun (Fig. 7). Hadrian made the completion of that task inevitable, long before Caracalla formalized expressions of *consensus universorum (civium)*.

After two centuries of universal citizenship, John Chrysostom had to explain to his congregation why Paul in Jerusalem had identified himself as an ἄνθρωπος Ῥωμαῖος: "Those worthy to be called that name possessed a certain privilege, but not all obtained that right. For they say that everyone was labeled 'Roman' by Hadrian, but earlier that was not the case."[16] John has

---

14. Aristides *Or.* 26.100.

15. Pliny *Pan.* 80.3 (trans. Radice, with alterations).

16. John Chrysostom *Homil. in Acta Apostolorum* 48.1 (*PG* 60.333): Μεγάλην εἶχον ταύτην τότε προνομίαν οἱ ἀξιούμενοι οὕτω καλεῖσθαι· καὶ οὐ πάντες τούτου ἐτύγχανον· ἀπὸ γὰρ Ἀδριανοῦ φασι πάντας Ῥωμαίους ὀνομασθῆναι, τὸ δὲ παλαιὸν οὐχ οὕτως ἦν.

Figure 7. Hadrian as *Restitutor Orbis*. Aes from
the mint of Rome. *BMC* III, Hadrian no. 1213.

clearly confused Hadrian's extraconstitutional revolution with the *Constitutio Antoniniana;* in one sense, however, he, like Aelius Aristides, has merely
identified all recipients of the benefits of empire as Roman. In fact, the language used by the Senate to thank Hadrian for his cancellation of debts alluded to the universalization he set in motion: by that act of generosity he
provided for the safety of "*his* citizens and their posterity." Others thus attributed to Hadrian a personal relationship with the residents of his empire
a century before Caracalla termed the admission of barbarians "their undertaking to enter into *my* people."[17]

The extraordinary efficiency of the Roman imperial bureaucracy made
all this possible. Someone, somewhere, may, in fact, have determined what
the provinces should and should not know of the emperor's deeds. No one
ever questioned, however, that a continual stream of information about the
emperor's benefactions to his people would prepare them to receive favorably his requests for information, for money, and for obedience. Rome did
not rely on the inertia or the awe of her subjects to compel their quietude;
her guardians instead defined, distributed, and ultimately decorated the
landscape of their *imperium,* while their images stood in every square, their
names marked every road, and their coins jingled in every market in the
empire.

Political historians, obsessed with personality, may suggest that the imperial office evolved with the accession of each new emperor. Rather, the
charisma of the office ultimately dominated them: neither the madness of
Gaius nor the despotism of Domitian, neither the capture of Valerian at
Edessa nor the death and loss of Valens at Adrianople, noticeably weakened
the authority of their successors. The civic temper with which Augustus had
forged his *dominatio* continued to tame the license with which divine elec-

17. On Hadrian see *ILS* 309. On Caracalla see *P. Giss.* 40, col. I, ll. 6: ὁσάκις ἂν ὑπει-
σέλθωσιν εἰς τοὺς ἐμοὺς ἀνθρώπους.

tion crowned the Christian emperors of Byzantium. The promises of the emperor Majorian, who undertook the "principate" not of his own will, but through obedience to the common good, are the distant but recognizable descendants of those made by Alexander Severus two and a half centuries earlier.[18] An English translation, sadly, could not possibly do justice to the rhetoric with which Constantius launched Julian on his career of public service and rulership "over a pacified world." As rendered by Ammianus, the close of that speech brought together all the terms and concepts that have bound this work together: *Ad summam i, i, propera sociis omnium votis, velut assignatam tibi ab ipsa re publica stationem cura pervigili defensurus.*

In closing, I quote from the jurist Callistratus, by birth a Greek and by profession a Roman jurist, whose career probably fell during the reign of Alexander Severus. In his volumes devoted to judicial examinations, Callistratus touched on the constraints implicit in a punishment of exile; the topic attracted attention under the empire because a person exiled from one province by its governor could satisfy his sentence while causing trouble in another province or even, as it seems, in Rome. Callistratus thought this wrong: "A relegated person cannot stay in Rome, even if this condition was not included in his sentence, because Rome is the *patria* of us all; nor can a relegated person stay in the city in which the emperor stays or through which the emperor passes; for only those allowed to enter Rome may look upon the emperor, for the emperor is the *pater patriae.*"[19] On this topic Callistratus and his colleagues faced the central ideological boundaries that separated them from their Republican forebears. A judge could not easily exile someone when Rome ruled the entire world, nor could a governor easily move someone outside his territory when exercising influence on the affairs of another province so clearly infringed upon the prerogative of the most manifest god. Though Rome herself still demanded and received special consideration in formulating administrative and criminal legislation, Callistratus had now simultaneously to account for the not quite conflicting loyalties focused on her tireless servant.

18. *N. Maioriani* 1. Cf. [Aristides] *Or.* 35.12, saying of the emperor that ἦν ... μέγα ὄφελος τῇ βασιλείᾳ καὶ πρὶν εἰς ταύτην καταστῆναι. On the ideological constraints on Byzantine monarchs and their expression in ceremonial see Charanis 1940 and Henry 1967.

19. *Dig.* 48.22.18.

WORKS CITED

Ahl, F. 1984. "The art of safe criticism in Greece and Rome." *AJP* 105:174–208.

Alcock, S. E. 1993. *Graecia capta: The landscapes of Roman Greece.* Cambridge: Cambridge University Press.

————, ed. 1997. *The early Roman empire in the East.* Oxbow Monographs, 95. Oxford: Oxbow.

Alexander, J. 1991. "Habermas and critical theory: Beyond the Marxian dilemma?" Honneth and Joas 1991, 49–73.

Alexander, L., ed. 1991. *Images of Empire.* Journal for the Study of the Old Testament, Supplement 122. Sheffield: Sheffield Academic Press.

Alexander, P. S. 1991. "The family of Caesar and the family of God: The image of the emperor in the Heikhalot literature." L. Alexander 1991, 276–297.

Alföldi, A. 1934. "Die Ausgestaltung des monarchischen Zeremoniells am römischen Kaiserhofe." *MDAI(R)* 49:1–118.

————. 1935. "Insignien und Tracht der römischen Kaiser." *MDAI(R)* 50:1–171.

————. 1947. "On the foundation of Constantinople: A few notes." *JRS* 37: 10–16.

————. 1970a. *Die monarchische Repräsentation im römischen Kaiserreiche.* Darmstadt: Wissenschaftliche Buchgesellschaft. (Reprint of Alföldi 1934 and 1935, with new indexes and a new introduction.)

————. 1970b. *Der Vater des Vaterlandes im römischen Denken.* Darmstadt: Wissenschaftliche Buchgesellschaft.

Alföldi, M. R. 1961. "Signum Deae: Die kaiserzeitlichen Vorgänger des Reichsapfels." *JNG* 11:19–32.

Alföldy, G. 1974. "The crisis of the third century as seen by contemporaries." *GRBS* 15:89–111.

————. 1989. "Die Krise des Imperium Romanum und die Religion Roms." In *Religion und Gesellschaft in der römischen Kaiserzeit: Kolloquium zu Ehren von Friedrich Vittinghoff,* edited by W. Eck, 53–102. Köln: Bohlau.

Althusser, L. 1970. "Ideology and ideological state apparatuses." In *Lenin and phi-*

losophy and other essays, translated by B. Brewster, 127–186. New York: Monthly Review Press.

Amory, P. 1997. *People and identity in Ostrogothic Italy, 489–554.* Cambridge: Cambridge University Press.

Anderson, B. 1983. *Imagined communities: Reflections on the origin and spread of nationalism.* New York: Verso.

Anderson, J. G. C. 1913. "Festivals of Mên Askaênos in the Roman colonia at Antioch of Pisidia." *JRS* 3:267–300.

Ando, C. 1993. Review of H. W. Bird, *Eutropius:* Breviarium (Liverpool: 1993). *BMCR* 4:420–422.

———. 1996. "Pagan apologetics and Christian intolerance in the ages of Themistius and Augustine." *JECS* 4:171–207.

———. 1997. "Tacitus, *Annales* VI: Beginning and end." *AJP* 118:285–303.

———. 1999. "Was Rome a *polis?*" *ClassAnt* 18:5–34.

Arnaud-Lindet, M.-P. *L. Ampelius: Aide-mémoire (Liber memorialis).* Paris: Les Belles Lettres.

Aubineau, M. 1983. *Un traité inédit de christologie de Sévérien de Gabala* In centurionem *et* Contra Manichaeos et Apollinaristas. Geneva: P. Cramer.

Aune, D. E. 1983. "The influence of Roman imperial court ceremonial on the Apocalypse of John." *Biblical Research* 28:5–26.

Austin, N. J. E. 1972. "A usurper's claim to legitimacy." *Rivista Storica dell'Antichità* 2:77–83.

Avenarius, G. 1956. *Lukians Schrift zur Geschichtsschreibung.* Meisenheim am Glan: Anton Hain.

Avery, W. T. 1940. "The *adoratio purpurae* and the importance of the imperial purple in the fourth century of the Christian era." *MAAR* 17:66–80.

Axtell, H. L. 1907. *The deification of abstract ideas in Roman literature and inscriptions.* Chicago: University of Chicago Press.

Badian, E. 1989. "The *scribae* of the Roman Republic." *Klio* 71:582–603.

Bagnall, R. 1991. "The beginnings of the Roman census in Egypt." *GRBS* 32:255–265.

———. 1992. "Landholding in late Roman Egypt: The distribution of wealth." *JRS* 82:128–149.

Bagnall, R., A. Cameron, S. R. Schwartz, and K. A. Worp. 1987. *Consuls of the later Roman empire.* Atlanta: Scholars Press.

Bagnall, R., and B. W. Frier. 1994. *The demography of Roman Egypt.* Cambridge: Cambridge University Press.

Baharal, D. 1996. *Victory of propaganda: The dynastic aspect of the imperial propaganda of the Severi—The literary and archaeological evidence, A.D. 193–225.* BAR International Series, 657. Oxford: Tempus Reparatum.

Baldwin, B. 1979. "The *acta diurna.*" *Chiron* 9:189–203.

———. 1981. "Acclamations in the *Historia Augusta.*" *Athenaeum* 69:138–149.

Barnes, T. D. 1973. "Lactantius and Constantine." *JRS* 63:29–46.

———. 1974. "The victories of Augustus." *JRS* 64:21–26.

———. 1978. *The sources of the* Historia Augusta. Collection Latomus, 155. Brussels: Revue d'Études Latines.

————. 1981. *Constantine and Eusebius.* Cambridge, Mass.: Harvard University Press.

————. 1982. *The new empire of Diocletian and Constantine.* Cambridge, Mass.: Harvard University Press.

————. 1985. "Constantine and the Christians of Persia." *JRS* 75:126–136.

————. 1989. "Panegyric, history and hagiography in Eusebius' *Life of Constantine.*" In *The making of orthodoxy*, edited by R. Williams, 94–123. Cambridge: Cambridge University Press.

————. 1993. *Athanasius and Constantius: Theology and politics in the Constantinian empire.* Cambridge, Mass.: Harvard University Press.

————. 1997. "Christentum und dynastische Politik (300–325)." Paschoud and Szidat 1997, 99–109.

Barrett, M. 1991. *The politics of truth from Marx to Foucault.* Stanford: Stanford University Press.

Batiffol, P. 1913a. "La conversion de Constantin et la tendance au monothéisme dans la religion romaine." *Bulletin d'Ancienne Littérature et d'Archéologie Chrétiennes* 3:132–141.

————. 1913b. "Le règlement des premiers conciles africains et le règlement du sénat romain." *Bulletin d'Ancienne Littérature et d'Archéologie Chrétiennes* 3:3–19.

————. 1920. "L'église et les survivances du culte impérial." In *Les survivances du culte impérial romain*, 5–34. Paris: Picard.

Bats, M. 1994. "Les débuts de l'information politique officielle à Rome au premier siècle avant J.-C." Demougin 1994, 19–43.

Bauckham, R. 1991. "The economic critique of Rome in Revelation 18." L. Alexander 1991, 47–90.

Bauman, R. 1974. *Impietas in principem: A study of treason against the Roman emperor with special reference to the first century A.D.* Münchener Beiträge zur Papyrusforschung und Antiken Rechtsgeschichte, 67. Munich: Beck.

Bay, A. 1972. "The letters *SC* on Augustan *aes* coinage." *JRS* 62:111–122.

Baynes, N. H. 1931. "Constantine the Great and the Christian church." *PBA* 15:341–442. (Reprinted as a monograph with a new preface by H. Chadwick [Oxford: Clarendon Press, 1972]).

————. 1933. "Eusebius and the Christian empire." In *Mélanges Bidez*, Annuaire de l'Institut de Philologie et d'Histoire Orientales, no. 2, 13–18. Brussels: Secrétariat de l'Institut.

————. 1935. Review of J. Vogt and E. Kornemann, *Römische Geschichte* (Leipzig: Teubner, 1933). *JRS* 25:81–87.

————. 1946a. Review of McGeachy, "Quintus Aurelius Symmachus and the senatorial aristocracy of the West" (dissertation, University of Chicago, 1942). *JRS* 36:173–177.

————. 1946b. Review of Setton 1941. *JRS* 36:135–140.

Beard, M., J. North, and S. Price. 1998. *Religions of Rome.* Volume 1, *A history.* Cambridge: Cambridge University Press.

Beaujeu, J. 1955. *La religion romaine à l'apogée de l'empire: La politique religieuse des Antonins (96–192).* Paris: Les Belles Lettres.

————. 1976. "Cultes locaux et cultes d'empire dans les provinces d'occident aux trois premiers siècles de notre ère." In *Assimilations et résistance à la culture gréco-romaine dans le monde ancien: Travaux du VIᵉ congrès international d'études classiques* (Madrid, 1974), 433–443. Paris: Les Belles Lettres.

Beck, H.-G. 1980. "Constantinople: The rise of a new capital in the East." In *Age of spirituality*, edited by K. Weitzmann, 29–37. New York: Metropolitan Museum of Art.

Behr, C. A. 1981. *P. Aelius Aristides: The complete works.* Volume 2, *Orations XVII-LIII*. Leiden: Brill.

Bellinger, A. R., and M. A. Berlincourt. 1962. *Victory as a coin type.* Numismatic Notes and Monographs, 149. New York: American Numismatic Society.

Bendix, R. 1960. *Max Weber.* New York: Doubleday.

Benjamin, A., and A. E. Raubitschek. 1959. "Arae Augusti." *Hesperia* 28:65–85.

Benner, M. 1975. *The emperor says: Studies in the rhetorical style in edicts of the early empire.* StudGoth 33. Göteborg: Acta Universitatis Gothoburgensis.

Béranger, J. 1953. *Recherches sur l'aspect idéologique du principat.* Schweizerische Beiträge zur Altertumswissenschaft, 6. Basel: Reinhardt.

———. 1975. *Principatus.* Publications de la Faculté des Lettres de l'Université de Lausanne, 20. Geneva: Droz.

———. 1977. "*Imperium*, expression et conception du pouvoir impérial." *RÉL* 55:325–344.

———. 1982. "SHA Alex. Sev. 48,1 et la *cura rei publicae*." Wirth 1982, 308–323.

van Berchem, D. 1939. *Les distributions de blé et d'argent à la plèbe romaine sous l'empire.* Geneva: Faculté des Lettres, Université de Genève.

Bernoulli, J. J. 1886. *Römische Ikonographie, zweiter Teil: Die Bildnisse der römischen Kaiser.* Volume 1. Berlin: Spemann.

Beskow, P. 1962. *Res gloriae: The kingship of Christ in the early church.* Stockholm: Almqvist & Wiksell.

Bickermann, E. 1929. "Die römische Kaiserapotheose." *Archiv für Religionswissenschaft* 27:1–34.

———. 1952. "*Origines gentium*." *CP* 47:65–81.

———. 1972. "*Consecratio*." *EntrHardt* 19:3–37.

———. 1986. *Studies in Jewish and Christian history.* Volume 3. Leiden: Brill.

Bidez, J., and F. Cumont, eds. 1922. *Imperatoris Caesaris Flavii Claudii Iuliani epistulae leges poemata fragmenta varia.* Paris: Les Belles Lettres.

Bilabel, F. 1924/25. "Fragmente aus der heidelberger Papyrussammlung." *Philologus* 80:331–341.

Birley, A. R. 1969. "The coups d'état of the year 193." *Bonner Jahrbücher* 169:247–280.

———. 1988. *The African emperor Septimius Severus.* 2d edition. London: Batsford.

———. 1997. *Hadrian: The restless emperor.* London: Routledge.

Bisbee, G. A. 1988. *Pre-Decian acts of martyrs and commentarii.* Harvard Dissertations in Religion, 22. Philadelphia: Fortress Press.

Bishop, M. C., and J. C. N. Coulston. 1993. *Roman military equipment: From the Punic Wars to the fall of Rome.* London: Batsford.

Blagg, T., and M. Millett, eds. 1990. *The early Roman empire in the West.* Oxford: Oxbow.

Bleckmann, B. 1991. "Die Chronik des Johannes Zonaras und eine pagane Quelle zur Geschichte Konstantins." *Historia* 40:343–365.

Bleicken, J. 1966. *Der Preis des Aelius Aristides auf das römische Weltreich (Or. 26 Keil).* Nachrichten der Akademie der Wissenschaften in Göttingen, Philosophisch-historische Klasse, Nr. 7.

———. 1978. *Prinzipat und Dominat: Gedanken zur Periodisierung der römischen Kaiserzeit.* Frankfurter Historische Vorträge, 6. Wiesbaden: F. Steiner.

Blockley, R. C. 1975. *Ammianus Marcellinus: A study of his historiography and political thought.* Collection Latomus, 141. Brussels: Revue d'Études Latines.

———. 1980. "Was the first book of Zosimus' New History based on more than two sources?" *Byzantion* 50:393–402.

———. 1981. *The fragmentary classicising historians of the later Roman empire.* Volume 1. Liverpool: Francis Cairns.

———. 1983. *The fragmentary classicising historians of the later Roman empire.* Volume 2. Liverpool: Francis Cairns.

Blumenthal, F. 1913. "Die Autobiographie des Augustus, I." *WS* 35:113–130 and 267–288.

———. 1914. "Die Autobiographie des Augustus, II." *WS* 36:84–103.

Boatwright, M. T. 1987. *Hadrian and the city of Rome.* Princeton: Princeton University Press.

den Boeft, J., D. den Hengst, and H. C. Teitler. 1987. *Philological and historical commentary on Ammianus Marcellinus XX.* Groningen: Egbert Forsten.

den Boer, W. 1975. "Trajan's Deification." In *Proceedings of the XIVth international congress of papyrologists* (Oxford, 1974), E.E.S. Graeco-Roman Memoirs, no. 61, 85–90. London: Egypt Exploration Society.

Bollansée, J. 1994. "*P. Fay.* 19, Hadrian's memoirs, and imperial epistolary autobiography." *Ancient Society* 25:279–302.

Bonjour, M. 1975. *Terre natale: Études sur une composante affective du patriotisme romain.* Paris: Les Belles Lettres.

Bonnefond-Coudry, M. 1989. *Le sénat de la République romaine de la guerre d'Hannibal à Auguste: Pratiques délibératives et prise de décision.* BÉFAR 263. Rome: École Française de Rome.

Boschung, D. 1993. *Die Bildnisse des Augustus.* Das Römische Herrscherbild 1.2. Berlin: Gebr. Mann.

Bourdieu, P. 1977. *Outline of a theory of practice.* Translated by R. Nice. Cambridge: Cambridge University Press.

———. 1990. *The logic of practice.* Translated by R. Nice. Stanford: Stanford University Press.

Bowersock, G. W. 1965. *Augustus and the Greek world.* Oxford: Clarendon Press.

———. 1973. "Syria under Vespasian." *JRS* 63:133–140.

———. 1978. *Julian the Apostate.* Cambridge, Mass.: Harvard University Press.

———. 1982. "The imperial cult: Perceptions and persistence." In *Jewish and Christian self-definition,* edited by B. F. Meyer and E. P. Sanders, 171–182. London: SCM.

———. 1984. "Augustus and the East: The problem of the succession." Millar and Segal 1984, 169–188.

————. 1986. "From emperor to bishop: The self-conscious transformation of political power in the fourth century A.D." *CP* 81:298–307.

————. 1990. "The pontificate of Augustus." Raaflaub and Toher 1990, 380–394.

————. 1991. "The Babatha papyri, Masada, and Rome." *JRA* 4:336–344.

Bowie, E. L. 1970. Review of Levick 1967. *JRS* 60:202–207.

Bowman, A. K., 1967. "The crown-tax in Roman Egypt." *BASP* 4:59–74.

————. 1971. *The town councils of Roman Egypt.* ASP, 11. Toronto: Hakkert.

————. 1985. "Landholding in the Hermopolite nome in the fourth century A.D." *JRS* 75:137–163.

————. 1991. "Literacy in the Roman empire: Mass and mode." Humphrey 1991, 119–131.

Bowman, A. K., and D. Rathbone. 1992. "Cities and administration in Roman Egypt." *JRS* 82:107–127.

Box, H. 1939. *Philonis Alexandrini In Flaccum: Edited with an introduction, translation, and commentary.* London: Oxford University Press.

Branigan, K. 1991. "Images—or mirages—of empire? An archaeological approach to the problem." L. Alexander 1991, 91–105.

Bréhier, L. 1915. "Constantin et la fondation de Constantinople." *RevHist* 119:241–272.

————. 1920. "Les survivances du culte impérial romain à Byzance." In *Les survivances du culte impérial romain,* 35–73. Paris: Picard.

————. 1948. "ΙΕΡΕΥΣ ΚΑΙ ΒΑΣΙΛΕΥΣ." In *Mémorial Louis Petit,* 41–45. Bucharest: Institut Français d'Études Byzantines.

————. 1949. *Les institutions de l'empire byzantin.* Paris: Albin Michel.

Brilliant, R. 1963. *Gesture and rank in Roman art.* Memoirs of the Connecticut Academy of Arts and Sciences, 14. New Haven: The Academy.

Brock, S. 1982. "Clothing metaphors as a means of theological expression in Syriac tradition." In *Typus, Symbol, Allegorie bei den östlichen Vätern und ihren Parallelen im Mittelalter,* edited by M. Schmidt, 11–38. Regensburg: Pustet.

Browne, G. M. 1975. "A panegyrist from Panopolis." *Proceedings of the XIVth international congress of papyrologists,* E.E.S. Graeco-Roman Memoirs, no. 61, 39–33. London: Egypt Exploration Society.

————. 1977. "Harpocration panegyrista." *ICS* 2:184–195.

Browning, R. 1952. "The riot of A.D. 387 in Antioch: The role of the theatrical claques in the later empire." *JRS* 42:13–20.

Brünnow, R. E., and A. von Domaszewski. 1905. *Die Provincia Arabia.* Strassburg: Karl J. Trübner.

Brunt, P. A. 1971. *Italian manpower 225 B.C.–A.D. 14.* Oxford: Clarendon Press.

————. 1977. "Lex de imperio Vespasiani." *JRS* 67:95–116.

————. 1982. "The legal issue in Cicero, *Pro Balbo.*" *CQ* 32:136–147.

————. 1984. "The role of the Senate in the Augustan regime." *CQ* 34:423–444.

————. 1988. *The fall of the Roman Republic and related essays.* Oxford: Clarendon Press.

————. 1990. *Roman imperial themes.* Oxford: Clarendon Press.

Brunt, P. A., and J. M. Moore. 1967. *Res gestae Divi Augusti.* Oxford: Oxford University Press.

Bruun, P. 1976. "Notes on the transmission of imperial images in late antiquity." In *Studia Romana in honorem Petri Krarup septuagenarii,* edited by K. Ascani et al., 122–131. Odense: Odense University Press.

Buckler, W. H. 1935. "Auguste, Zeus Patroos." *RPhil,* 3d series, 9:177–188.

Bureth, P. 1964. *Les titulatures impériales dans les papyrus, les ostraca, et les inscriptions d'Égypte (30 a.C.–284 p.C.).* Papyrologica Bruxellensia, 2. Brussels: Fondation Égyptologique Reine Élisabeth.

Burnett, A., and S. Walker. 1981. *The image of Augustus.* London: The British Museum.

Burton, G. P. 1976. "The issuing of mandata to proconsuls and a new inscription from Cos." *ZPE* 21:63–68.

———. 1993. "Provincial procurators and the public provinces." *Chiron* 23:13–28.

Callu, J.-P. 1960. *GENIO POPULI ROMANI (295–316): Contribution à une histoire numismatique de la Tétrarchie.* Paris: Champion.

Cameron, A. 1931. "Latin words in the Greek inscriptions of Asia Minor." *AJP* 52:232–262.

Cameron, A. D. E. 1965a. "Palladas and Christian polemic." *JRS* 55:17–30.

———. 1965b. "Wandering poets: A literary movement in Byzantine Egypt." *Historia* 14:470–509.

———. 1967. "Rutilius Namatianus, St. Augustine, and the date of the *De reditu.*" *JRS* 57:31–39.

———. 1970. *Claudian: Poetry and propaganda in the court of Honorius.* Oxford: Clarendon Press.

———. 1973. *Porphyrius the charioteer.* Oxford: Clarendon Press.

———. 1976. *Circus factions.* Oxford: Clarendon Press.

Cameron, A. D. E., J. Long, and L. Sherry. 1993. *Barbarians and politics at the court of Arcadius.* Berkeley and Los Angeles: University of California Press.

Cameron, Av. 1983. "Eusebius of Caesarea and the rethinking of history." In *Tria corda: Scritti in onore di Arnaldo Momigliano,* edited by E. Gabba, 71–88. Como: Edizioni. New Press.

Campbell, J. B. 1984. *The emperor and the Roman army, 31 B.C.–A.D. 235.* Oxford: Clarendon Press.

Cerfaux, L., and J. Tondriau. 1956. *Un concurrent du christianisme: Le culte des souverains dans la civilisation gréco-romaine.* Tournai: Desclée & Cie.

Chalon, G. 1964. *L'édit de Tiberius Julius Alexander: Étude historique et exégétique.* Bibliotheca Helvetica Romana, 5. Lausanne: Graf.

Chaniotis, A., and G. Preuss. 1990. "Neue Fragmente des Preisedikts von Diokletian und weitere lateinische Inschriften aus Kreta." *ZPE* 80:189–202.

Charanis, F. 1940. "Coronation and its constitutional significance in the later Roman empire." *Byzantion* 15:49–66.

Charlesworth, M. P. 1935. "Some observations on ruler-cult, especially at Rome." *HThR* 28:5–44.

———. 1936. "Providentia and aeternitas." *HThR* 29:107–132.

———. 1937. "The virtues of a Roman emperor: Propaganda and the creation of belief." *PBA* 23:105–133.

———. 1943. "*Pietas* and *victoria:* The emperor and the citizen." *JRS* 33:1–10.

Chastagnol, A. 1960. *La préfecture urbaine à Rome sous le bas-empire.* Paris: Presses Universitaires de France.

———. 1981a. "L'inscription constantinienne d'Orcistus." *MÉFR* 93:381–416.

———. 1981b. "Les *realia* d'une cité d'après l'inscription constantinienne d'Orkistos." *Ktema* 6:373–379.

———. 1984. Review of Barnes 1981 and 1982. *CP* 79:253–259.

———, ed. 1994. *Histoire Auguste: Les empereurs romains des IIe et IIIe siècles.* Paris: Robert Laffont.

Chauvot, A. 1986. *Procope de Gaza, Priscien de Césarée: Panégyriques de l'empereur Anastase Ier.* Antiquitas, Reihe 1, Band 35. Bonn: Habelt.

Chestnut, G. F. 1986. *The first Christian histories.* 2d edition. Macon: Mercer University Press.

Chilver, G. E. F. 1979. *A historical commentary on Tacitus' Histories I and II.* Oxford: Clarendon Press.

Chilver, G. E. F., and G. B. Townend. 1985. *A historical commentary on Tacitus' Histories IV and V.* Oxford: Clarendon Press.

Christ, F. 1938. *Die römische Weltherrschaft in der antiken Dichtung.* Tübinger Beiträge zur Altertumswissenschaft, 31. Stuttgart: Kohlhammer.

Christol, M. 1994. "Pline l'Ancien et la *formula* de la province narbonnaise." Demougin 1994. 45–63.

Cockle, W. E. H. 1984. "State archives in Graeco-Roman Egypt from 30 B.C. to the reign of Septimius Severus." *JEA* 70:106–122.

Coles, R. 1966. *Reports of proceedings in papyri.* Papyrologica Bruxellensia, 4. Brussels: Fondation Égyptologique Reine Élisabeth.

Colin, J. 1965. *Les villes libres de l'orient greco-romain et l'envoi du supplice par acclamations populaires.* Collection Latomus, 82. Brussels: Revue d'Études Latines.

Corbier, M. 1974. *L'aerarium Saturni et l'aerarium militare: Administration et prosopographie sénatoriale.* CÉFR 24. Rome: École Française de Rome.

———. 1987. "L'écriture dans l'espace public romain." In *L'urbs: Espace urbain et histoire (Ier siècle av. J.-C.–IIIe siècle ap. J.-C.),* CÉFR 98, 27–60. Rome.

Corcoran, S. 1996. *The empire of the Tetrarchs.* Oxford: Clarendon Press.

Cornell, T. J. 1991. "Rome: The history of an anachronism." In Molho, Raaflaub, and Emlen 1991, 53–69.

Cotton, H. 1993. "The guardianship of Jesus son of Babatha: Roman and local law in the province of Arabia." *JRS* 83:94–108.

———. 1994. "A cancelled marriage contract from the Judaean desert?" *JRS* 84:64–86.

Coudry, M. 1994. "Sénatus-consultes et *acta senatus:* Rédaction, conservation et archivage des documents émanant du sénat, de l'époque de César à celle des Sévères." Demougin 1994, 65–102.

Courcelle, P. P. 1964. *Histoire littéraire des grandes invasions germaniques.* 3d edition. Paris: Études Augustiniennes.

Craddock, P. B. *Edward Gibbon, luminous historian, 1772–1794.* Baltimore: The Johns Hopkins University Press.

Crawford, M. 1970. "Money and exchange in the Roman world." *JRS* 60:40–48.

———. 1988. "The laws of the Romans: Knowledge and diffusion." González and Arce 1988, 127–139.

Curty, O. 1995. *Les parentés légendaires entre les cités grècques.* Hautes Études du Monde Greco-Romain, 20. Geneva: Droz.

Dagron, G. 1968. "L'empire romain d'orient au IVe siècle et les traditions politiques de l'hellénisme: Le témoignage de Thémistios." *Travaux et Mémoires* 3:1–242.

———. 1984. *Naissance d'une capitale: Constantinople et ses institutions de 330 à 451.* 2d edition. Bibliothèque Byzantine, Études, 7. Paris: Presses Universitaires de France.

———. 1987. "'Ceux d'en face': Les peuples étrangers dans les traités militaires byzantins." *Travaux et Mémoires* 10:207–228.

———. 1996. *Empereur et prêtre: Étude sur le 'césaropapisme' byzantin.* Paris: Gallimard.

D'Arms, J. H. 1981. *Commerce and social standing in ancient Rome.* Cambridge, Mass.: Harvard University Press.

David, J.-M. *The Roman conquest of Italy.* Translated by A. Nevill. Oxford: Blackwell.

Davies, P. S. 1989. "The origin and purpose of the persecution of A.D. 303." *JThS* 40:66–94.

Delatte, L. 1942. *Les traités de la royauté d'Ecphante, Diotogène, et Sthénidas.* Bibliothèque de la Faculté de Philosophie et Lettres de l'Université de Liége, fasc. 97.

Delehaye, H. 1921. "La persécution dans l'armée sous Dioclétien." In *Bulletins de la classe des lettres et des sciences morales et politiques,* 150–166. Brussels: Académie Royale de Belgique.

Delmaire, R. 1997. "Les usurpateurs du bas-empire et le recrutement des fonctionnaires (Essai de reflexion sur les assises du pouvoir et leurs limites)." Paschoud and Szidat 1997, 111–126.

Demougin, S., ed. 1994. *La mémoire perdue: À la recherche des archives oubliées, publiques et privées, de la Rome antique.* CNRS, Série Histoire Ancienne et Médiévale, 30. Paris: Sorbonne.

Devreker, J. 1971. "Une inscription inédite de Caracalla à Pessinonte." Latomus 30:352–362.

Dilke, O. A. W. 1971. *The Roman land surveyors: An introduction to the* Agrimensores. New York: Barnes & Noble.

DiMaio III, M., J. Zeuge, and N. Zotov. 1988. "*Ambiguitas Constantiniana:* The *caeleste signum Dei* of Constantine the Great." *Byzantion* 58:333–360.

Dion, R. 1977. *Aspects politiques de la géographie antique.* Paris: Les Belles Lettres.

Dodge, H. 1990. "The architectural impact of Rome in the East." In *Architecture and architectural sculpture in the Roman empire,* edited by M. Henig, Oxford University Committee for Archaeology Monographs, no. 29, 108–120. Oxford: Institute of Archaeology.

Dölger, F. J. 1932. "Zur antiken und frühchristlichen Auffassung der Herrschergewalt von Gottes Gnaden." *Antike und Christentum* 3:117–127.

———. 1937. "Rom in der Gedankenwelt der Byzantiner." *ZKG* 56:1–42.

von Domaszewski, A. 1895. *Die Religion des römischen Heeres.* Westdeutsche Zeitschrift für Geschichte und Kunst, 14. Trier: Lintz.

———. 1909. *Abhandlungen zur römischen Religion.* Leipzig: Teubner.

Dörries, H. 1954. *Das Selbstzeugnis Kaiser Konstantins.* AbhGött, Heft 34. Göttingen: Vandenhoeck & Ruprecht.

Downey, G. 1940. "The pilgrim's progress of the Byzantine emperor." *Church History* 9:207–217.

————. 1941. "Ethical themes in the Antioch mosaics." *Church History* 10:367–376.

Drake, H. A. 1976. *In praise of Constantine: A historical study and new translation of Eusebius'* Tricennial orations. University of California Publications in Classical Studies, 15. Berkeley and Los Angeles: University of California Press.

Drinkwater, J. F. 1987. *The Gallic empire.* Historia Einzelschriften, 52. Stuttgart: Steiner.

Dufraigne, P. 1994. *Adventus Augusti, adventus Christi: Recherche sur l'exploitation idéologique et littéraire d'un cérémonial dans l'antiquité tardive.* Collection des Études Augustiniennes, Série Antiquité, 141. Paris.

Duncan-Jones, R. P. 1974. "The procurator as civic benefactor." *JRS* 64:79–85.

————. 1982. *The economy of the Roman empire: Quantitative studies.* 2d edition. Cambridge: Cambridge University Press.

————. 1990. *Structure and scale in the Roman economy.* Cambridge: Cambridge University Press.

Dvornik, F. 1934. "The authority of the state in the oecumenical councils." *The Christian East* 14:95–108.

————. 1951. "Emperors, popes, and councils." *DOP* 6:3–23.

————. 1966. *Early Christian and Byzantine political philosophy.* Washington, D.C.: Dumbarton Oaks.

Dyck, A. R. 1996. *A commentary on Cicero, De officiis.* Ann Arbor: University of Michigan Press.

Dyson, S. 1971. "Native revolts in the Roman empire." *Historia* 20:239–274.

————. 1975. "Native revolt patterns in the Roman empire." *ANRW* 2.3.138–175.

Eck, W. 1979. *Die staatliche Organisation Italiens in der hohen Kaiserzeit.* Vestigia, 28. Munich: Beck.

————. 1980. "Die Präsenz senatorischer Familien in den Städten des Imperium Romanum bis zum späten 3. Jahrhundert." In *Studien zur antiken Sozialgeschichte: Festschrift F. Vittinghoff,* edited by W. Eck, H. Galsterer, and H. Wolff, 283–322. Cologne: Böhlau.

————. 1993. "Das *s.c. de Cn. Pisone patre* und seine Publikation in der Baetica." *Cahiers Glotz* 4:189–208.

————. 1995. "Plebs und Princeps nach dem Tod des Germanicus." Malkin and Rubinsohn 1995, 1–10.

Eck, W., A. Caballos, and F. Fernández. 1996. *Das senatus consultum de Cn. Pisone patre.* Vestigia, 48. Munich: Beck.

Eckstein, A. M. 1985. "Polybius, Syracuse, and the politics of accommodation." *GRBS* 26:265–282.

————. 1990. "Josephus and Polybius: A reconsideration." *ClassAnt* 9:175–208.

————. 1995. *Moral vision in the* Histories *of Polybius.* Hellenistic Culture and Society, 16. Berkeley and Los Angeles: University of California Press.

Eder, W. 1990. "Augustus and the power of tradition: The Augustan principate as binding link between Republic and empire." Raaflaub and Toher 1990, 71–122.

Edmondson, J. C. 1990. "Romanization and urban development in Lusitania." Blagg and Millett 1990, 151–178.

———. 1992/93. "Creating a provincial landscape: Roman imperialism and rural change in Lusitania." *Historia Antigua* 10/11:13–30.

———. 1996. "Roman power and the emergence of provincial administration in Lusitania during the Republic." In *Pouvoir et imperium,* edited by E. Hermon, 163–211. Naples: Jovene.

———. 1997. "Two dedications to *Divus Augustus* and *Diva Augusta* from Augusta Emerita and the early development of the imperial cult in Lusitania reexamined." *MDAI(M)* 38:89–105.

Ehrhardt, C. T. H. R. 1984. "Roman coin types and the Roman public." *JNG* 34:41–54.

Eisenhut, W. 1982. "*Deus Caesar:* Augustus in den Gedichten des Properz." Wirth 1982, 98–108.

Enßlin, W. 1943. "Gottkaiser und Kaiser von Gottes Gnaden." *SitzBay* 1943, no. 6, 53–83.

———. 1954. "Der Kaiser in der Spätantike." *HZ* 177:449–468.

Erim, K. T. 1982. "A new relief showing Claudius and Britannia from Aphrodisias." *Britannia* 13:277–281.

Erskine, A. 1988. "Rhodes and Augustus." *ZPE* 88:271–275.

———. 1990. *The Hellenistic Stoa: Political thought and action.* Ithaca: Cornell University Press.

———. 1997. "Greekness and uniqueness: The cult of the Senate in the Greek East." *Phoenix* 51:25–37.

Fears, J. R. 1977. Princeps a diis electus: *The divine election of the emperor as a political concept at Rome.* Papers and Monographs of the American Academy at Rome, 26.

Feissel, D., and J. Gascou. 1989. "Documents d'archives romains inédits du moyen Euphrate (IIIe siècle après J.-C.)." *CRAI* 1989:535–561.

———. 1995. "Documents d'archives romains inédits du moyen Euphrate (IIIe s. après J.-C.)." *Journal des Savants,* 65–119.

Feldman, L. H. 1993. *Jew and gentile in the ancient world.* Princeton: Princeton University Press.

Fink, R. O., A. S. Hoey, and W. F. Snyder. 1940. "The *Feriale Duranum.*" *YCS* 7: 1–222.

Finkelstein, M. 1934. "Mandata principum." *Tijdschrift voor Rechtsgeschiedenis* 13:150–169.

Fishwick, D. 1970. "*Flamen Augustorum.*" *HSCP* 74:299–312.

———. 1978. "The federal cult of the Three Gauls." In *Les martyrs de Lyon (177),* edited by J. Rougé and R. Turcan, Colloques Internationaux du CNRS, no. 575, 33–45. Paris: Éditions du CNRS.

———. 1990a. "Dio and Maecenas: The emperor and the ruler cult." *Phoenix* 44:267–275.

———. 1990b. "Prudentius and the cult of Divus Augustus." *Historia* 39:475–486.

———. 1990c. "Votive offerings to the emperor?" *ZPE* 80:121–130.

———. 1994. "Numinibus Aug(ustorum)." *Britannia* 25:127–141.

Fontaine, J. 1971. "Vienne, carrefour du paganisme et du christianisme dans la Gaule du IVe siècle." *Bulletin de la Société des Amis de Vienne* 67:17–36.

————. 1996. *Ammien Marcellin, Histoire.* Tome III, *Livres XX-XXII.* Paris: Les Belles Lettres.

Fornara, C. 1983. *The nature of history in ancient Greece and Rome.* Berkeley and Los Angeles: University of California Press.

————. 1989. "Eunapius' epidemia in Athens." *CQ* 39:517–523.

Foucault, M. 1972. *The archaeology of knowledge.* Translated by A. M. Sheridan Smith. New York: Pantheon Books.

————. 1980. *Power/knowledge.* Translated by C. Gordon. New York: Pantheon Books.

Fowden, G. 1994. "The last days of Constantine: Oppositional versions and their influence." *JRS* 84:146–170.

Frederiksen, M. W. 1965. "The Republican municipal laws: Errors and drafts." *JRS* 55:183–198.

Freeman, P. W. M. 1993. "'Romanisation' and Roman material culture." *JRA* 6:438–445.

French, D. 1981. *Roman roads and milestones of Asia Minor.* Fasc. 1, *The Pilgrim's Road.* BAR International Series, 105. Oxford: Tempus Reparatum.

————. 1988. *Roman roads and milestones of Asia Minor.* Fasc. 2, *An interim catalogue of milestones.* 2 parts. BAR International Series, 392. Oxford: Tempus Reparatum.

Frend, W. H. C. 1956. "A third-century inscription relating to *angareia* in Phrygia." *JRS* 46:46–56.

————. 1965. *Martyrdom and persecution in the early church.* Oxford: Blackwell.

Freyburger, G. 1978. "La supplication d'action de grâces sous le haut-empire." *ANRW* 2.16.2.1418–1439.

Friedlaender, L. 1922. *Darstellung aus der Sittengeschichte Roms in der Zeit von Augustus bis zum Ausgang der Antonine.* 10th edition, prepared by G. Wissowa. Leipzig: S. Hirzel.

Frier, B. W. 1979. *Libri annales pontificum maximorum: The origins of the annalistic tradition.* Papers and Monographs of the American Academy in Rome, 27.

————. 1985. *The rise of the Roman jurists.* Princeton: Princeton University Press.

Fries, G. 1969. "Das römische Porträt der Kaiserzeit als politisches Programm." *Altsprachliche Unterricht* 12:5–29.

Friesen, S. J. 1993. *Twice neokoros: Ephesus, Asia, and the cult of the Flavian imperial family.* Leiden: Brill.

Fuhrmann, M. 1968. "Die Romidee der Spätantike." *HZ* 207:529–561.

Furtwängler, A. 1900. *Die antiken Gemmen: Geschichte der Steinschneidekunst im klassischen Altertum.* Leipzig: Giesecke.

Gabba, E. 1982. "Political and cultural aspects of the classicistic revival in the Augustan age." *ClassAnt* 1:43–65.

————. 1984. "The historians and Augustus." Millar and Segal 1984, 61–88.

————. 1991. *Dionysius and the history of archaic Rome.* Berkeley and Los Angeles: University of California Press.

Gagé, J. 1930a. "Romulus-Augustus." *MÉFR* 47:138–181.

————. 1930b. "La Victoria Augusti et les auspices de Tibère." *RevArch,* 5th series, 32:1–35.

————. 1931a. "Divus Augustus: L'idée dynastique chez les empereurs Julio-Claudiens." *RevArch,* 5th series, 34:11–41.

———. 1931b. "Les sacerdoces d'Auguste et ses réformes religieuses." *MÉFR* 48:75–108.

———. 1932. "Un thème de l'art impérial romain: La Victoire d'Auguste." *MÉFR* 49:61–92.

———. 1933a. "Σταυρὸς νικοποιός: La Victoire impériale dans l'empire chrétien." *Revue d'Histoire et de Philosophie Religieuses* 13:370–400.

———. 1933b. "La théologie de la Victoire impériale." *RevHist* 171:1–43.

———. 1936. "De César à Auguste: Où en est le problème des origines du principat? À propos du *César* de M. J. Carcopino." *RevHist* 177:279–342.

———. 1968. *"Basiléia": Les Césars, les rois d'orient, et les "mages."* Paris: Les Belles Lettres.

———. 1982. "Auguste écrivain." *ANRW* 2.30.1.611–623.

Galinsky, K. 1996. *Augustan culture: An interpretive introduction.* Princeton: Princeton University Press.

Geertz, C. 1973. *The interpretation of cultures: Selected essays.* New York: Basic Books.

———. 1983. *Local knowledge: Further essays in interpretive anthropology.* New York: Basic Books.

Geffcken, J. 1906. "Die Stenographie in den Akten der Märtyrer." *Archiv für Stenographie* 57:81–89.

———. 1910. "Die christlichen Martyrien." *Hermes* 40:481–505.

Georgacas, J. G. 1947. "The names of Constantinople." *TAPA* 78:347–367.

Gernentz, W. 1918. *Laudes Romae.* Rostock: Adler.

Gibbon, E. 1972. *The English essays of Edward Gibbon.* Edited by P. B. Craddock. Oxford: Clarendon Press.

Gichon, M. 1972. "The plan of a Roman camp depicted upon a lamp from Samaria." *PEQ* 104:38–58.

Giddens, A. 1983. "Four theses on ideology." *Canadian Journal of Political and Social Theory* 7:18–21.

———. 1984. *The constitution of society.* Berkeley and Los Angeles: University of California Press.

Gilliam, J. F. 1969. "On *Divi* under the Severi." In *Hommages à Marcel Renard,* edited by E. J. Bibauw, Collection Latomus, no. 102, 2:284–289. Brussels.

———. 1975. "Notes on Latin texts from Egypt." In *Le monde grec: Hommages à Claire Préaux,* edited by J. Bingen, G. Cambier, and G. Nachtergael, 766–774. Brussels: Éditions de l'Université de Bruxelles.

———. 1978. "Some Roman elements in Roman Egypt." *ICS* 3:115–131.

González, J. 1986. "The *lex Irnitana:* A new Flavian municipal law." *JRS* 76:147–243.

———. 1988. "The first oath pro salute Augusti found in Baetica." *ZPE* 72:113–127.

González, J., and J. Arce, eds. 1988. *Estudios sobre la Tabula Siarensis.* Anejos de Archivo Español de Arqueologia, 9. Madrid: CSIC.

Goodman, M. 1991a. "Babatha's story." Review of Y. Yadin, *The documents from the Bar Kokhba period . . . : Greek papyri* (Jerusalem: Israel Exploration Society, 1989). *JRS* 81:169–175.

———. 1991b. "Opponents of Rome: Jews and others." L. Alexander 1991, 222–238.

————. 1994. *Mission and conversion: Proselytizing in the religious history of the Roman empire*. Oxford: Clarendon Press.

Gordon, R. L. 1979. "Production and religion in the Graeco-Roman world." *Art History* 2:5–34.

Goulet, R. 1980. "Sur la chronologie de la vie et des oeuvres d'Eunape de Sardes." *JHS* 100:60–72.

Grabar, A. 1968. *Christian iconography: A study of its origins.* Princeton: Princeton University Press.

Grant, M. 1946. *From* imperium *to* auctoritas: *A historical study of* aes *coinage in the Roman empire 49 B.C.–A.D. 14.* Cambridge: Cambridge University Press.

————. 1950. *Roman anniversary issues: An exploratory study of the numismatic and medallic commemoration of anniversary years, 49 B.C.–A.D. 375.* Cambridge: Cambridge University Press.

Grégoire, H. 1922. *Recueil des inscriptions grecques chrétiennes d'Asia Mineure.* Paris: Leroux.

Griffin, M. 1991. "*Urbs Roma, plebs,* and *princeps.*" L. Alexander 1991, 19–46.

Griffith, S. H. 1987. "Ephraem the Syrian's hymns 'Against Julian': Meditations on history and imperial power." *Vigiliae Christianae* 41:238–266.

Grigg, R. 1977. "'Symphonian aeido tes basileias': An image of imperial harmony on the base of the Column of Arcadius." *Art Bulletin* 59:469–482.

————. 1979. "Portrait-bearing codicils in the illustrations of the *Notitia dignitatum?*" *JRS* 69:107–124.

Groag, E. 1918. "Die Kaiserrede des Pseudo-Aristides." *WS* 40:20–45.

van Groningen, B. A. 1956. "Preparatives to Hadrian's visit to Egypt." In *Studi in onore di Aristide Calderini e Roberto Paribeni*, vol. 2, *Studi di papirologia e antichità orientali,* 253–256. Milan: Ceschina.

Gros, P. 1976. *Aurea templa: Recherches sur l'architecture religieuse de Rome à l'époque d'Auguste.* BÉFAR 231. Rome: École Française de Rome.

————. 1979. "Pour une chronologie des arcs de triomphe de Gaule narbonnaise (À propos de l'arc de *Glanum*)." *Gallia* 37:55–83.

————. 1981. "Qui était l'architect de la Maison Carrée?" *Histoire et Archéologie* (Dijon) 55:37–43.

————. 1988. "Les autels des Caesares et leur signification dans l'espace urbain des villes Julio-Claudiennes." In *L'espace sacrificiel dans les civilisations méditerranéennes de l'antiquité: Actes du colloque tenu à la Maison de l'Orient, Lyon, 4–7 juin 1988,* edited by R. Etienne and M.-T. Le Dinahet, Publications de la Bibliothèque Salomon Reinach, no. 5, 179–186. Lyon: Bibliothèque Salomon Reinach.

————. 1996. "Les nouveaux espaces civiques du début de l'empire en Asie Mineure: Les exemples d'Ephèse, Iasos et Aphrodisias." In *Aphrodisias Papers,* edited by C. Roueché and R. R. R. Smith, no. 3, 111–120. *JRA,* Supplementary Series, no. 20. Ann Arbor: Journal of Roman Archaeology.

Gruen, E. S. 1992. *Culture and national identity in Republican Rome.* Ithaca: Cornell University Press.

Grünewald, T. 1990. *Constantinus Maximus Augustus: Herrschaftspropaganda in der zeitgenössischen Überlieferung.* Historia Einzelschriften, 64. Stuttgart: Steiner.

Gurval, R. A. 1995. *Actium and Augustus: The politics and emotions of civil war.* Ann Arbor: University of Michigan Press.

Gutzwiller, H. 1942. *Die Neujahrsrede des Konsuls Claudius Mamertinus vor dem Kaiser Julian.* Freiburg: Paulus.

Habermas, J. 1979. *Communication and the evolution of society.* Translated by T. McCarthy. Boston: Beacon Press.

———. 1984. *The theory of communicative action.* Vol. 1, *Reason and the rationalization of society.* Translated by T. McCarthy. Boston: Beacon Press.

———. 1987. *The theory of communicative action.* Vol. 2, *Lifeworld and system: A critique of functionalist reason.* Translated by T. McCarthy. Boston: Beacon Press.

———. 1991. "A reply." Honneth and Joas 1991, 214–264.

Habicht, C. 1970. *Gottmenschentum und griechische Städte.* 2d edition. Zetemata, 14. Munich: Beck.

———. 1975. "New evidence on the province of Asia." *JRS* 65:64–91.

———. 1985. *Pausanias' Guide to Ancient Greece.* Berkeley and Los Angeles: University of California Press.

Habicht, C., and P. Kussmaul. 1986. "Ein neues Fragment des Edictum de Accusationibus." *MH* 43:135–144.

Haensch, R. 1992. "Das Statthalterarchiv." *ZSavRom* 109:209–317.

———. 1994. "Die Bearbeitungsweisen von Petitionen in der Provinz Aegyptus." *ZPE* 100:487–546.

———. 1997. Capita provinciarum: *Statthaltersitze und Provinzialverwaltung in der römischen Kaiserzeit.* Mainz: von Zabern.

Halfmann, H. 1979. *Die Senatoren aus dem östlichen Teil des* Imperium Romanum *bis zum Ende des 2. Jahrhunderts n. Chr.* Hypomnemata, 58. Göttingen: Vandenhoeck & Ruprecht.

———. 1986. Itinera principum: *Geschichte und Typologie der Kaiserreisen im römischen Reich.* Heidelberger Althistorische Beiträge und Epigraphische Studien, 2. Stuttgart: Steiner.

Hammer, R., trans. 1986. *Sifre: A Tannaitic commentary on the Book of Deuteronomy.* New Haven: Yale University Press.

Hammond, M. 1938. "Curatores tabularum publicarum." In *Classical and mediaeval studies in honor of E. K. Rand,* edited by L. W. Jones, 123–131. New York: n.p.

———. 1948. "Ancient imperialism: Contemporary justifications." *HSCP* 58–59: 105–161.

———. 1951. "Germana patria." *HSCP* 60:147–174.

———. 1957. "Composition of the Senate, A.D. 68–235." *JRS* 47:74–81.

Hannestad, N. 1988. *Roman art and imperial policy.* Aarhus: Aarhus University Press.

Hanson, A. E. 1979. "Documents from Philadelphia drawn from the census register (P. XV Congr. 13–14)." In *Actes du XVᵉ congrès international de papyrologie,* Papyrologica Bruxellensia, no. 17, 60–74. Brussels: Fondation Égyptologique Reine Élisabeth.

———. 1980a. "Juliopolis, Nicopolis, and the Roman camp." *ZPE* 37:249–254.

———. 1980b. "P. Princeton I 11 and P. Cornell 21v." *ZPE* 37:241–248.

———. 1981. "Evidence for a reduction in laographia at Philadelphia in Gaius' second year." In *Proceedings of the XVIth international congress of papyrology,* ASP, no. 23, 345–355. Chico: Scholars Press.

———. 1982. "P. Mich. inv. 1434: Receipts for syntaximon and beer tax." *BASP* 19:47–60.

————. 1984a. "Caligulan month-names at Philadelphia and related matters." In *Atti del XVII congresso internazionale di papirologia*, 3.1107–1118. Naples: Centro Internazionale per lo Studio dei Papiri Ercolanesi.

————. 1984b. "P. Mich. inv. 6554: An expanded affidavit formula for an authenticated copy of a prefectural *subscriptio*." *ZPE* 55:191–199.

————. 1989. "Village officials at Philadelphia: A model of Romanization in the Julio-Claudian period." In *Egitto e storia antica dall'ellenismo all'età araba*, edited by L. Criscuolo and G. Geraci, 429–440. Bologna: CLUEB.

————. 1991. "Ancient illiteracy." Humphrey 1991, 159–197.

————. 1992. "Egyptians, Greeks, Romans, *Arabes*, and *Ioudaioi* in the first century A.D. tax archive from Philadelphia: *P. Mich.* inv. 880 recto and *P. Princ.* III 152 revised." In *Life in a multi-cultural society: Egypt from Cambyses to Constantine and beyond*, edited by J. J. Johnson, Studies in Ancient Oriental Civilization, no. 51, 133–145. Chicago: Oriental Institute of the University of Chicago.

————. 1994. "Topographical arrangement of tax documents in the Philadelphia tax archive." In *Proceedings of the 20th international congress of papyrologists*, edited by A. Bälno-Jacobsen, 210–218. Copenhagen: Museum Tusculanum Press.

————. 1996. "A petition and court proceedings: P. Mich. inv. 6060." *ZPE* 111: 175–182.

————. 1997. "Isodorus of Psophthis, Augustan cultivator: An update." In *Akten der 21. internationalen Papyrologenkongresses (Berlin, 13.–19.8.1995)*, edited by B. Kramer et al., 1:413–429. Leipzig: Teubner.

Hariman, R. 1995. *Political style: The artistry of power*. Chicago: University of Chicago Press.

Harl, K. 1987. *Civic coins and civic politics in the Roman East, A.D. 180–275*. The Transformation of the Classical Heritage, 12. Berkeley and Los Angeles: University of California Press.

Harris, W. V. 1989. *Ancient literacy*. Cambridge, Mass.: Harvard University Press.

Hartke, W. 1951. *Römische Kinderkaiser: Eine Strukturanalyse römischen Denkens und Daseins*. Berlin: Akademie-Verlag.

Hasebroek, J. 1921. *Untersuchungen zur Geschichte des Kaisers Septimius Severus*. Heidelberg: Winter.

Hassall, M., M. Crawford, and J. Reynolds. 1974. "Rome and the eastern provinces at the end of the second century B.C.: The so-called 'Piracy Law' and a new inscription from Cnidos." *JRS* 64:195–220.

Heather, P. 1991. *Goths and Romans 332–489*. Oxford: Clarendon Press.

Heitsch, E. 1961. *Die griechischen Dichterfragmente der römischen Kaiserzeit*. AbhGött, 3d series, no. 49.

Henry III, P. 1967. "A mirror for Justinian: The *Ekthesis* of Agapetus Diaconus." *GRBS* 8:281–308.

Herrmann, P. 1968. *Der römische Kaisereid*. Hypomnemata, 20. Göttingen: Vandenhoeck & Ruprecht.

————. 1975. "Eine Kaiserurkunde der Zeit Marc Aurels aus Milet." *MDAI(I)* 25: 149–166.

————. 1990. *Hilferufe aus römischen Provinzen*. Göttingen: Vandenhoeck & Ruprecht.

Hidber, T. 1996. *Das klassizistische Manifest des Dionys von Halikarnass: Die Praefatio zu* De oratoribus veteribus. Stuttgart: Steiner.

Hill, P. V. 1989. *The monuments of ancient Rome as coin types.* London. B. A. Seaby.

Hirschfeld, O. 1913. *Kleine Schriften.* Berlin: Weidmann.

Hobson, D. W. 1993. "The impact of law on village life in Roman Egypt." In *Law, politics and society in the ancient Mediterranean world,* edited by B. Halpern and D. W. Hobson, 193–219. Sheffield: Sheffield Academic Press.

Hodot, R. 1982. "Décret de Kymè en l'honneur du prytane Kléanax." *J. Paul Getty Museum Journal* 10:165–180.

Hoey, A. S. 1937. "*Rosaliae signorum.*" *HThR* 30:15–35.

Hoff, M. C., and S. I. Rotroff, eds. 1997. *The Romanization of Athens.* Oxbow Monographs, 94. Oxford: Oxbow.

Hölscher, T. 1967. *Victoria Romana.* Mainz: von Zabern.

———. 1987. *Römische Bildsprache als semantisches System.* AbhHeid, 1987, no. 2. Heidelberg: Winter.

Holum, K. G. 1982. *Theodosian empresses.* Berkeley and Los Angeles: University of California Press.

Holum, K. G., and G. Vikan. 1979. "The Trier Ivory, *adventus* ceremonial and the relics of Saint Stephen." *DOP* 33:113–133.

Honneth, A. 1991. *The critique of power: Reflective stages in a critical social theory.* Translated by K. Baynes. Cambridge, Mass.: MIT Press.

Honneth, A., and H. Joas, eds. 1991. *Communicative action: Essays on Jürgen Habermas' The Theory of Communicative Action.* Translated by J. Gaines and D. L. Jones. Cambridge, Mass.: MIT Press.

Honoré, T. 1979. "'Imperial' rescripts A.D. 193–305: Authorship and authenticity." *JRS* 69:51–64.

———. 1986. "The making of the Theodosian Code." *ZSavRom* 103:133–222.

Hopkins, K. 1978. *Conquerors and slaves: Sociological studies in Roman history.* Volume I. Cambridge: Cambridge University Press.

———. 1980. "Taxes and trade in the Roman empire (200 B.C.–A.D. 400)." *JRS* 70:101–125.

———. 1991a. "Conquest by book." Humphrey 1991, 133–158.

———. 1991b. "From violence to blessing: Symbols and rituals in ancient Rome." In Molho, Raaflaub, and Emlen 1991, 479–498.

Howgego, C. J. 1985. *Greek imperial countermarks.* Royal Numismatic Society, Special Publication no. 17. London.

———. 1990. "Why did ancient states strike coins?" *NumChron* 150:1–25.

———. 1995. *Ancient history from coins.* London: Routledge.

Huchthausen, L. 1974a. "Herkunft und ökonomische Stellung weiblicher Adressaten von Reskripten des *Codex Iustinianus* (2. und 3. Jh. u. Z.)." *Klio* 56:199–228.

———. 1974b. "Kaiserliche Rechtsauskünfte an Sklaven und in ihrer Freiheit angefochtene Personen aus dem Codex Iustinianus." *WZRostock* 23, Gesellschafts- und Sprachwissenschaftliche Reihe, Heft 3, 251–257.

———. 1975. "Kaiserliche Reskripte an Frauen aus den Jahren 117 bis 217 u. Z." In *Actes de la XIIᵉ conférence internationale d'études classiques "Eirene,"* 479–488. Bucharest: Editura Academiei.

————. 1976. "Zu kaiserlichen Reskripten an weibliche Adressaten aus der Zeit Diokletians (284–305 u. Z.)." *Klio* 58:55–85.

Humphrey, J. H., ed. 1991. *Literacy in the Roman world.* JRA Supplement 3. Ann Arbor: Journal of Roman Archaeology.

Ingenkamp, H. G. 1969. "Τὸ ἅμα? Zu einem Papyrus mit Fragen und Antworten." *RhM* 112:48–53.

Instinsky, H. U. 1940. "Consensus universorum." *Hermes* 75:265–278.

————. 1942. "Kaiser und Ewigkeit." *Hermes* 77:313–355.

Isaac, B. 1996. "Eusebius and the geography of the Roman provinces." Kennedy 1996, 153–167.

Jameson, F. 1981. *The political unconscious: Narrative as a socially symbolic act.* Ithaca: Cornell University Press.

————. 1988. *The ideologies of theory: Essays 1971–1986.* Minneapolis: University of Minnesota Press.

Janson, T. 1964. *Latin prose prefaces: Studies in literary conventions.* Acta Universitatis Stockholmiensis, Studia Latina Stockholmiensia, 13. Stockholm: Almqvist & Wiksell.

Jones, A. H. M. 1960. *Studies in Roman government and law.* Oxford: Blackwell and Mott.

————. 1964. *The later Roman empire.* Oxford: Blackwell.

————. 1971. *The cities of the eastern Roman provinces.* 2d edition. Oxford: Clarendon Press.

————. 1974. *The Roman Economy.* Oxford: Blackwell.

Jones, C. P. 1971. *Plutarch and Rome.* Oxford: Clarendon Press.

————. 1978. *The Roman world of Dio Chrysostom.* Cambridge, Mass.: Harvard University Press.

————. 1984. "The Sacrae Litterae of 204: Two colonial copies." *Chiron* 14:93–99.

————. 1986. *Culture and society in Lucian.* Cambridge. Mass.: Harvard University Press.

————. 1996. "The Panhellenion." *Chiron* 26:28–56.

Judge, E. A. 1974. "'Res publica restituta': A modern illusion?" In *Polis and imperium: Studies in honour of Edward Togo Salmon,* ed. J. A. S. Evans, 279–311. Toronto: Hakkert.

Jussen, B. 1998. "Liturgie und Legitimation, oder: Wie die Gallo-Romanen das römische Reich beendeten." In *Institutionen und Ereignis: Über historische Praktiken und Vorstellungen gesellschaftlichen Ordnens,* edited by R. Blänker and B. Jussen, 75–136. Göttingen: Vandenhoeck & Ruprecht.

Kantorowicz, E. 1946. Laudes regiae: *A study in liturgical acclamations and mediaeval ruler worship.* University of California Publications in History, 33. Berkeley and Los Angeles: University of California Press.

————. 1963. "*Oriens Augusti—Lever du roi.*" *DOP* 17:119–177.

————. 1965. *Selected studies.* Locust Valley: Augustin.

Karayannopulos, I. 1956. "Konstantin der Grosse und der Kaiserkult." *Historia* 5:341–357.

Katzoff, R. 1972. "Precedents in the courts of Roman Egypt." *ZSavRom* 89:256–292.

————. 1980. "Sources of law in Roman Egypt: The role of the prefect." *ANRW* 2.13.807–844.

————. 1981. "On the intended use of P. Col. 123." In *Proceedings of the XVIth International congress of papyrology*, ASP, no. 23, 559–573. Chico: Scholars Press.

Kehoe, D. P. 1988. *The economics of agriculture on Roman imperial estates in North Africa*. Hypomnemata, 89. Göttingen: Vandenhoeck & Ruprecht.

Kelly, C. M. 1994. "Later Roman bureaucracy: Going through the files." In *Literacy and power in the ancient world*, edited by A. K. Bowman and G. Woolf, 161–176. Cambridge: Cambridge University Press.

Kelly, J. N. D. 1975. *Jerome: His life, writings and controversies*. London: Duckworth.

————. 1995. *Golden mouth: The story of John Chrysostom, ascetic, preacher, bishop*. Ithaca: Cornell University Press.

Kempen, K. 1918. *Procopii Gazaei in imperatorem Anastasium panegyricus*. Bonn: Typis Caroli Georgi Typographi Academici.

Kennedy, D. L., ed. 1996. *The Roman army in the East*. JRA Supplement 18. Ann Arbor: JRA.

Kent, J. P. C. 1967. "FEL. TEMP. REPARATIO." *NumChron*, 83–90.

Kienast, D. 1982a. *Augustus: Prinzeps und Monarch*. Darmstadt: Wissenschaftliche Buchgesellschaft.

————. 1982b. "*Corpus imperii:* Überlegungen zum Reichsgedanken der Römer." Wirth 1982, 1–17.

————. 1990. *Römische Kaisertabelle*. Darmstadt: Wissenschaftliche Buchgesellschaft.

Klauser, T. 1944. "Aurum coronarium." *MDAI(R)* 59:129–153.

Klein, R. 1981. *Die Romrede des Aelius Aristides*. Darmstadt: Wissenschaftliche Buchgesellschaft.

————. 1986. "Die Romidee bei Symmachus, Claudian und Prudentius." In *Colloque genevois sur Summaque*, edited by F. Paschoud, 119–144. Paris: Les Belles Lettres.

Klingner, F. 1927. "Rom als Idee." *Das Antike* 3:17–34.

Kneissl, P. 1969. *Die Siegestitulatur der römischen Kaiser*. Hypomnemata, 23. Göttingen: Vandenhoeck & Ruprecht.

Knibbe, D., H. Engelmann, and B. Iplikcioglu. 1993. "Neue Inschriften aus Ephesos, XII." *JÖAI* 62:113–150.

Knipfing, J. R. 1923. "The libelli of the Decian persecution." *HThR* 16:345–390.

Knoche, U. 1952. "Die augusteische Ausprägung der Dea Roma." *Gymnasium* 59:324–349.

Koenen, L. 1993. "The Ptolemaic king as a religious figure." In *Images and ideologies: Self-definition in the Hellenistic world*, edited by A. Bulloch et al., Hellenistic Culture and Society, no. 12, 25–115. Berkeley and Los Angeles: University of California Press.

Koenen, L., and D. B. Thompson. 1984. "Gallus as Triptolemos on the Tazza Farnese." *BASP* 21:111–156.

Koep, L. 1958. "Die Konsekrationsmünzen Kaiser Konstantins und ihre religionspolitische Bedeutung." *JbAC* 1:94–101.

Kögler, H.-H. 1990. "Fröhliche Subjektivität: Historische Ethik und dreifache Ontologie beim späten Foucault." In *Ethos der Moderne: Foucaults Kritik der Aufklärung*, edited by E. Erdmann, 202–226. Frankfurt: Campus.

Kolendo, J. 1981. "La répartition des places aux spectacles et la stratification sociale dans l'empire romain: À propos des inscriptions sur les gradins des amphithéâtres et théâtres." *Ktema* 6: 301–315.

König, I. 1981. *Die gallischen Usurpatoren von Postumus bis Tetricus*. Vestigia, 31. Munich: Beck.

————. 1987. *Origo Constantini, Anonymus Valesianus, Teil 1: Text und Kommentar*. Trierer Historische Forschungen, 11. Trier: Trierer Historische Forschungen.

Kraft, K. 1962. "S(enatus) C(onsulto)." *JNG* 12: 7–49.

Kroll, J. H. 1997. "Coinage as an index of Romanization." Hoff and Rotroff 1997, 135–150.

Kronman, A. 1983. *Max Weber*. Stanford: Stanford University Press.

Kruse, H. 1934. *Studien zur offiziellen Geltung des Kaiserbildes im römischen Reich*. Studien zur Geschichte und Kultur des Altertums, Band 19, Heft 3. Paderborn: F. Schoningh.

Kunderewicz, C. 1961. "Quelques remarques sur le rôle des ΚΑΙΣΑΡΕΙΑ dans la vie juridique de l'Égypte romaine." *JJP* 13: 123–129.

Küpper-Böhm, A. 1996. *Die römischen Bogenmonumente der Gallia Narbonensis in ihrem urbanen Kontext*. Kölner Studien zur Archäologie der Römischen Provinzen, 3. Espelkamp: Leidorf.

Kuttner, A. 1995. *Dynasty and empire in the age of Augustus: The case of the Boscoreale Cups*. Berkeley and Los Angeles: University of California Press.

Lane Fox, R. 1986. *Pagans and Christians*. New York: Knopf.

de Lange, N. R. M. 1978. "Jewish attitudes to the Roman empire." In *Imperialism in the ancient world*, edited by P. D. Garnsey and C. R. Whittaker, 255–281. Cambridge: Cambridge University Press.

La Piana, G. 1912. *Le rappresentazioni sacre nella letteratura bizantina dalle origini al sec. IX, con rapporti al teatro sacro d'occidente*. Grottaferrata: S. Nilo.

————. 1936. "The Byzantine theater." *Speculum* 11: 171–211.

Larrain, J. 1979. *The concept of ideology*. London: Hutchinson & Co.

Lassèrre, F. 1982. "Strabon devant l'empire romain." *ANRW* 2.30.1.867–896.

Latte, K. 1960. *Römische Religionsgeschichte*. Munich: Beck.

Lauffer, S. 1971. *Diokletians Preisedikt*. Berlin: de Gruyter.

Lebek, W. D. 1987. "Die drei Ehrenbögen für Germanicus: Tab. Siar. frg. I 9–34; CIL VI 31199a 2–17." *ZPE* 67: 129–148.

Lendon, J. E. 1990. "The face on the coins and inflation in Roman Egypt." *Klio* 72: 106–134.

————. 1997. *Empire of honour: The art of government in the Roman world*. Oxford: Clarendon Press.

Levick, B. 1967. *Roman colonies in southern Asia Minor*. Oxford: Clarendon Press.

————. 1978. "Concordia at Rome." In *Scripta nummaria Romana: Essays presented to Humphrey Sutherland*, edited by R. A. G. Carson and C. M. Kraay, 217–233. London: Spink and Son.

————. 1982. "Propaganda and the imperial coinage." *Antichthon* 16: 104–116.

————. 1983. "The *senatus consultum* from Larinum." *JRS* 73: 97–115.

————. 1986. "'Caesar omnia habet': Property and politics under the Principate." *EntrHardt* 33:187–218.

————. 1990. *Claudius.* New Haven: Yale University Press.

Levy, H. L. 1971. *Claudian's* In Rufinum: *An exegetical commentary.* APA Monographs, 30. Cleveland: The Press of Case Western Reserve University.

Lewis, N. 1981. "The prefect's *conventus:* Proceedings and procedures." *BASP* 18: 119–129.

————. 1995. *On government and law in Roman Egypt.* Edited by A. E. Hanson. ASP, 33. Atlanta: Scholars Press.

————. 1996. "The humane legislation of Septimius Severus." *Historia* 45:104–113.

Lewis, R. G. 1993. "Imperial autobiography, Augustus to Hadrian." *ANRW* 2.34.1.629–706.

Lieberman, S. 1944. "Roman legal institutions in early Rabbinics and in the *Acta martyrum." JQR* 35:1–57.

————. 1946a. "Palestine in the third and fourth centuries, I–II." *JQR* 36:329–370.

————. 1946b. "Palestine in the third and fourth centuries, III." *JQR* 37:31–54.

————. 1962. *Hellenism in Jewish Palestine.* 2d edition. Texts and Studies of the Jewish Theological Seminary of America, 18. New York.

Lieu, S. N. C. 1986. *The emperor Julian: Panegyric and polemic.* Liverpool: Liverpool University Press.

Lintott, A. 1982. "The Roman judiciary law from Tarentum." *ZPE* 45:127–138.

————. 1993. *Imperium Romanum.* London: Routledge.

Lippold, A. 1968. "Herrscherideal und Traditionsverbundenheit im Panegyricus des Pacatus." *Historia* 17:228–250.

L'Orange, H. P. 1955. "The *adventus* ceremony and the slaying of Pentheus as represented in two mosaics of about A.D. 300." In *Late classical and mediaeval studies in honor of A. M. Friend, Jr.,* edited by K. Weitzmann, 7–14. Princeton: Princeton University Press.

Lörincz, B. 1979. "C. Gabinius Barbarus Pompeianus, Statthalter von Moesia Superior." *ZPE* 33:157–160.

Lott, J. B. 1996. "An Augustan sculpture of August Justice." *ZPE* 113:263–270.

Luce, T. J. 1990. "Livy, Augustus, and the Forum Augustum." Raaflaub and Toher 1990, 123–138.

Lukaszewicz, A. 1981. "A petition from priests to Hadrian with his subscription." In *Proceedings of the XVIth international congress of papyrology* (New York, 1980), ASP, 23, 357–361. Chico: Scholars Press.

Luttwak, E. 1976. *The grand strategy of the Roman empire from the first century A.D. to the third.* Baltimore: The Johns Hopkins University Press.

Maas, P. 1912. "Metrische Akklamationen der Byzantiner." *BZ* 21:28–51.

MacCormack, S. 1975a. "Latin prose panegyrics." In *Empire and aftermath,* edited by T. A. Dorey, 143–205. London: RKP.

————. 1975b. "Roma, Constantinopolis, the emperor, and his genius." *CQ* 25:131–150.

————. 1981. *Art and ceremony in late antiquity.* The Transformation of the Classical Heritage, 1. Berkeley and Los Angeles: University of California Press.

MacCoull, L. S. B. 1984. "The panegyric on Justin II by Dioscorus of Aphrodito." *Byzantion* 54:575–585.

———. 1988. *Dioscorus of Aphrodito: His work and his world.* The Transformation of the Classical Heritage, 16. Berkeley and Los Angeles: University of California Press.

MacDonald, W. L. 1982. *The architecture of the Roman empire.* Vol. 1, *An introductory study.* 2d edition. New Haven: Yale University Press.

———. 1986. *The architecture of the Roman empire.* Vol. 2, *An urban appraisal.* New Haven: Yale University Press.

MacMullen, R. 1959. "Roman imperial building in the provinces." *HSCP* 64:207–235.

———. 1962. "The emperor's largesses." *Latomus* 21:159–166.

———. 1963. "The Roman concept robber-pretender." *RIDA*, 3d series, 10:221–225.

———. 1982. "The epigraphic habit in the Roman empire." *AJP* 103:233–246.

———. 1990. *Changes in the Roman empire.* Princeton: Princeton University Press.

Macready, S., and F. H. Thompson, eds. 1987. *Roman architecture in the Greek world.* Society of Antiquaries of London, Occasional Papers, n.s., 10.

Magie, D. 1950. *Roman rule in Asia Minor to the end of the third century after Christ.* Princeton: Princeton University Press.

Maguiness, W. S. 1932. "Some methods of the Latin panegyrists." *Hermathena* 47:42–61.

Malkin, I., and Z. W. Rubinsohn, eds. 1995. *Leaders and masses in the Roman world: Studies in honor of Z. Yavetz.* Leiden: Brill.

Mangas, J. 1971. "Un capítulo de los gastos en el municipio romano de Hispania a través de las informaciones de la epigrafía latina." *Hispania Antiqua* 1:105–146.

Mango, C. 1963. "Antique statuary and the Byzantine beholder." *DOP* 17:55–75.

———. 1993. "Constantine's column." In *Studies on Constantinople,* III. 1–6. Brookfield, Vermont: Variorum.

Margoliouth, J. P. 1909. *Extracts from the Ecclesiastical History of John, bishop of Ephesus.* Semitic Studies Series, 13. Leiden: Brill.

Martin, J. 1997. "Das Kaisertum in der Spätantike." Paschoud and Szidat 1997, 47–62.

Mason, H. J. 1974. *Greek terms for Roman institutions: A lexicon and analysis.* ASP, 13. Toronto: Hakkert.

Matthews, J. F. 1974. "The letters of Symmachus." In *Latin literature of the fourth century,* edited by J. W. Binns, 58–99. London: RKP.

———. 1975. *Western aristocracies and imperial court, A.D. 364–425.* Oxford: Clarendon Press.

———. 1989. *The Roman empire of Ammianus Marcellinus.* Baltimore: The Johns Hopkins University Press.

———. 1993. "The making of the text." In *The Theodosian Code: Studies in the imperial law of late antiquity,* edited by J. Harries and I. Wood, 19–44. London: Duckworth.

Mattingly, D. J., ed. 1997. *Dialogues in Roman imperialism: Power, discourse, and discrepant experience in the Roman empire.* JRA Supplement 23. Portsmouth: JRA.

Mattingly, H. 1933. "FEL. TEMP. REPARATIO." *NumChron*, 182–202.

———. 1950. "The imperial 'vota.'" *PBA* 36:155–195.

Mattingly, H., and F. S. Salisbury. 1924a. "A find of Roman coins from Plevna in Bulgaria." *NumChron*, 5th series, 4:210–238.

———. 1924b. "The reign of Trajan Decius." *JRS* 14:1–23.

McCail, R. C. 1978. "P. Gr. Vindob. 29788C: Hexameter encomium on an unnamed emperor." *JHS* 98:38–63.

McCarney, J. 1980. *The real world of ideology*. Atlantic Highlands: Humanities Press.

McCarthy, T. 1993. *Ideals and illusions: On reconstruction and deconstruction in contemporary critical theory*. Cambridge, Mass.: MIT Press.

McCormick, M. 1986. *Eternal victory*. Cambridge: Cambridge University Press.

Megow, W.-R. 1987. *Kameen von Augustus bis Alexander Severus*. DAI, Antike Münzen und Geschnittene Steine, 11. Berlin: de Gruyter.

Mellor, R. 1975. Θεὰ Ῥώμη: *The worship of the goddess Roma in the Greek world*. Hypomnemata, 42. Göttingen: Vandenhoeck & Ruprecht.

Mesk, J. 1912. "Zur technik der lateinischen Panegyriker." *RhM* 67:569–590.

Meslin, M. 1970. *La fête des kalendes de janvier dans l'empire romain*. Collection Latomus, 115. Brussels: Revue d'Études Latines.

Mierse, W. 1990. "Augustan building programs in the western provinces." Raaflaub and Toher 1990, 308–333.

Millar, F. G. B. 1964. *A study of Cassius Dio*. Oxford: Clarendon Press.

———. 1969. "P. Herennius Dexippus: The Greek world and the third-century invasions." *JRS* 59:12–29.

———. 1971. "Paul of Samosata, Zenobia, and Aurelian: The church, local culture, and political allegiance in third-century Syria." *JRS* 61:1–17.

———. 1977. *The emperor in the Roman world*. Ithaca: Cornell University Press. (Reprinted 1992 with original pagination and a new afterword.)

———. 1981a. *The Roman empire and its neighbours*. 2d edition. New York: Holmes and Meier.

———. 1981b. "The world of *The Golden Ass.*" *JRS* 71:63–75.

———. 1984. "State and subject: The impact of monarchy." Millar and Segal 1984, 37–60.

———. 1988. "Imperial ideology in the Tabula Siarensis." González and Arce 1988, 11–19.

———. 1989. "'Senatorial' provinces: An institutionalized ghost." *Ancient World* 20:93–97.

———. 1991. "Les congiaires à Rome et la monnaie." In *Nourrir la plèbe: Actes du colloque tenu a Genève . . . en hommage à Denis van Berchem*, edited by A. Giovannini, 143–159. Basel: Freidrich Reinhardt.

———. 1993a. "Ovid and the *domus Augusta:* Rome seen from Tomoi." *JRS* 83:1–17.

———. 1993b. *The Roman Near East 31 B.C.–A.D. 337*. Cambridge, Mass.: Harvard University Press.

Millar, F., and E. Segal, eds. 1984. *Caesar Augustus: Seven aspects*. Oxford: Clarendon Press.

Millett, M. 1990. "Romanization: Historical issues and archaeological interpretation." Blagg and Millett 1990, 35–41.

Milne, H. J. M. 1934. *Greek shorthand manuals: Syllabary and commentary*. London: Egypt Exploration Society.

Mitchell, S. 1976. "Requisitioned transport in the Roman empire: A new inscription from Pisidia." *JRS* 66:106–131.

———. 1984. "The Greek city in the Roman world—The case of Pontus and Bithynia." In *Acts of the 8th international congress of Greek and Latin epigraphy, Athens, 1982*, 1:120–133. Athens: Hypourgeio Politismou kai Epistemon.

———. 1987a. "Imperial building in the eastern provinces." *HSCP* 91:333–365.

———. 1987b. "Imperial building in the eastern Roman provinces." Macready and Thompson 1987, 18–25.

———. 1988. "Maximinus and the Christians in A.D. 312: A new Latin inscription." *JRS* 78:105–124.

———. 1993. *Anatolia: Land, men, and gods in Asia Minor*. Oxford: Clarendon Press.

Mitford, T. B. 1991. "Inscriptiones Ponticae—Sebastopolis." *ZPE* 87:181–243.

Mitteis, L. 1891. *Reichsrecht und Volksrecht in den östlichen Provinzen des römischen Kaiserreichs*. Leipzig: Teubner.

Mitthof, F. 1993. "Vom ἱερώτατος Καῖσαρ zum ἐπιφανέστατος Καῖσαρ: Die Ehrenprädikate in der Titulatur der Thronfolger des 3. Jh. n. Chr. nach den Papyri." *ZPE* 99:97–111.

Moatti, C. 1993. *Archives et partage de la terre dans le monde romain (IIᵉ siècle avant– Iᵉʳ siècle après J.-C.)*. CÉFR 173. Rome: École Française de Rome.

———. 1994. "Les archives des terres publiques à Rome (Iᵉʳ siècle av.–Iᵉʳ siècle ap. J.-C.): Les cas des assignations." Demougin 1994, 103–119.

Mocsy, A. 1970. *Gesellschaft und Romanisation in der römischen Provinz Moesia Superior*. Amsterdam: Hakkert.

Mohrmann, C. 1946. "Quelques traits caractéristiques du Latin des chrétiens." In *Miscellanea Giovanni Mercati*, Studi e Testi, no. 121, 1:437–466. Vatican City: Biblioteca Apostolica Vaticana.

Molho, A., K. Raaflaub, and J. Emlen, eds. 1991. *City-states in classical antiquity and medieval Italy*. Ann Arbor: University of Michigan Press.

Momigliano, A. 1963. "Pagan and Christian historiography in the fourth century A.D." In *The conflict between paganism and christianity in the fourth century*, edited by A. Momigliano, 79–99. Oxford: Clarendon Press.

———. 1986. "Some preliminary remarks on the 'religious opposition' to the Roman empire." *EntrHardt* 33:103–133.

———. 1987. *On pagans, Jews, and Christians*. Middletown: Wesleyan University Press.

Mommsen, T. 1887. *Römisches Staatsrecht*. 3d edition. Leipzig: S. Hirzel.

Mommsen, T. E. 1959. "Orosius and Augustine." In *Medieval and renaissance studies*, edited by E. F. Rice, Jr., 325–348. Ithaca: Cornell University Press.

Montevecchi, O. 1946. "Ricerche di sociologia nei documenti dell'Egitto greco-romano." *Aegyptus* 26:111–129.

Moreau, P. 1994. "La mémoire fragile: Falsification et destruction des documents publics au Iᵉʳ siècle av. J.-C." Demougin 1994, 121–147.

Morris, R. L. B. 1981. "Reflections of citizen attitudes in petitions from Roman

Oxyrhynchus." In *Proceedings of the XVIth international congress of papyrology (New York, 1980)*, ASP, 23, 363–370. Chico: Scholars Press.

Mrozek, S. 1987. *Les distributions d'argent et de nourriture dans les villes italiennes du haut-empire romain*. Collection Latomus, 198. Brussels: Revue d'Études Latines.

Müller-Rettig, B. 1990. *Der Panegyricus des Jahres 310 auf Konstantin den Grossen*. Palingenesia, 31. Stuttgart: Steiner.

Murray, R. 1975. *Symbols of church and kingdom: A study in early Syriac tradition*. Cambridge: Cambridge University Press.

Musurillo, H. 1954. *The acts of the pagan martyrs*. 2d edition. Oxford: Clarendon Press.

Nelson, C. A. 1979. *Status declarations in Roman Egypt*. ASP, 19. Amsterdam: Hakkert.

Neri, V. 1997. "L'usurpatore come tiranno nel lessico politico della tarda antichità." Paschoud and Szidat 1997, 71–86.

Nicolet, C. 1991. *Space, geography and politics in the early Roman empire*. Ann Arbor: University of Michigan Press.

———. 1994. "Documents fiscaux et géographie de la Rome ancienne." Demougin 1994, 149–172.

———. 1995. "La Tabula Siarensis, la plèbe urbaine et les statues de Germanicus." Malkin and Rubinsohn 1995, 115–127.

———. 1996. *Financial documents and geographical knowledge in the Roman world*. Oxford: Leopard's Head Press. (An expanded translation of Nicolet 1994.)

Nixon, C. E. V. 1983. "Latin panegyric in the Tetrarchic and Constantinian period." In *History and historians in late antiquity*, edited by B. Croke and A. Emmett, 88–99. Sydney: Pergamon Press.

———. 1993. "Constantinus Oriens Imperator: Propaganda and panegyric: On reading Panegyric 7 (307)." *Historia* 24:229–246.

Nixon, C. E. V., and B. S. Rodgers. 1994. *In praise of later Roman emperors: The Panegyrici Latini*. Transformation of the Classical Heritage, 21. Berkeley and Los Angeles: University of California Press.

Nock, A. D. 1972. *Essays on religion and the ancient world*. Edited by Z. Stewart. Oxford: Clarendon Press.

North, J. 1992. "The development of religious pluralism." In *The Jews among pagans and Christians in the Roman empire*, edited by J. Lieu et al., 174–193. London: Routledge.

Ober, J. 1982. "Tiberius and the political testament of Augustus." *Historia* 31:306–328.

Oliensis, E. 1998. *Horace and the rhetoric of authority*. Cambridge: Cambridge University Press.

Oliver, J. H. 1949. "The Divi of the Hadrianic period." *HThR* 42:35–40.

———. 1953. *The ruling power: A study of the Roman empire in the second century after Christ through the Roman oration of Aelius Aristides*. TAPhS, n.s., 43, no. 4, 871–1003. Philadelphia: American Philosophical Society.

———. 1978. "The piety of Commodus and Caracalla and the Εἰς Βασιλέα." *GRBS* 19:375–388.

———. 1979. "Greek applications for Roman trials." *AJP* 100:543–558.

———. 1989. *Greek constitutions of early Roman emperors from inscriptions and papyri.* Memoirs of the American Philosophical Society, 178. Philadelphia.

Oliver, J. H., and R. E. A. Palmer. 1955. "Minutes of an act of the Roman Senate." *Hesperia* 24:329–349.

Olmstead, A. T. 1942. "The mid-third century of the Christian era." *CP* 37:241–262 and 398–420.

Ostrow, S. E. 1990. "The *Augustales* in the Augustan scheme." Raaflaub and Toher 1990, 364–379.

Ostrowski, J. A. 1990. "*Simulacra barbarorum:* Some questions of Roman personifications." In *Akten des XIII. internationalen Kongresses für klassische Archäologie, Berlin, 1988,* 566–567. Mainz: von Zabern.

———. 1996. "Personifications of countries and cities as a symbol of victory in Greek and Roman art." In *Griechenland und Rom,* edited by E. G. Schmidt, 264–272. Jena: Palm & Enke.

Packman, Z. M. 1991. "Notes on papyrus texts with the Roman imperial oath." *ZPE* 89:91–102.

———. 1992a. "Epithets with the title *Despotes* in regnal formulas, in document dates, and in the imperial oath." *ZPE* 90:251–257.

———. 1992b. "Further notes on texts with the imperial oath." *ZPE* 90:258.

———. 1994. "Still further notes on papyrus documents with the imperial oath." *ZPE* 100:207–210.

Palazzolo, N. 1977. "Le modalità di trasmissione dei provvedimenti imperiali nelle province (II–III sec. d. C)." *Iura* 28:40–94.

Palm, J. 1959. *Rom, Römertum und Imperium in der griechischen Literatur der Kaiserzeit.* Acta Regiae Societatis Humaniorum Litterarum Lundensis, 57. Lund: Gleerup.

Panciera, S. 1991. "Gli 'Elogia' del mausoleo di Augusto." In *Epigrafia: Actes du colloque international d'épigraphie latine en mémoire de Attilio Degrassi,* CÉFR 143, 133–152. Rome: École Française de Rome.

Parker, R. W. 1991. "Potamon of Mytilene and his family." *ZPE* 85:115–129.

Parsons, T. 1971. *The system of modern societies.* Englewood Cliffs: Prentice-Hall.

Paschoud, F. 1967. *Roma aeterna: Études sur le patriotisme romain dans l'occident latin à l'époque des grandes invasions.* Bibliotheca Helvetica Romana, 7. Rome: Institut Suisse de Rome.

———. 1975. *Cinq études sur Zosime.* Paris: Les Belles Lettres.

———. 1985. "Eunapiana." *BHAC,* 1982/83, 239–303.

———. 1989. "La préface de l'ouvrage historique d'Eunape." *Historia* 38:198–223.

———. 1997. "Le tyran fantasmé: Variations de l'*Histoire Auguste* sur le thème de l'usurpation." Paschoud and Szidat 1997, 87–98.

Paschoud, F., and J. Szidat, eds. 1997. *Usurpationen in der Spätantike.* Historia Einzelschriften, 111. Stuttgart: Steiner.

Peachin, M. 1990. *Roman imperial titulature and chronology, A.D. 235–284.* Amsterdam: Gieben.

———. 1996. Iudex vice Caesaris: *Deputy emperors and the administration of justice during the Principate.* Stuttgart: Steiner.

Pearl, O. M. 1970. "Excerpts from the minutes of judicial proceedings." *ZPE* 6:271–277.

Pekáry, T. 1968. *Untersuchungen zu den römischen Reichsstrassen.* Antiquitas, Reihe 1, Band 17. Bonn: Habelt.

———. 1985. *Das römische Kaiserbildnis in Staat, Kult und Gesellschaft: Dargestellt Anhand der Schriftquellen.* Das Römische Herrscherbild, 3. Abteilung, Band 5. Berlin: Mann.

———. 1987. "*Seditio:* Unruhen und Revolten im römischen Reich von Augustus bis Commodus." *Ancient Society* 18:133–150.

Peter, H. 1897. *Die geschichtliche Literatur über die römische Kaiserzeit bis Theodosius I.* Leipzig: Teubner.

Peterson, E. 1926. Εἷς Θεός: *Epigraphische, formgeschichtliche und religiongeschichtliche Untersuchungen.* Forschungen zur Religion und Literatur des Alten und Neuen Testaments, n.F., 24. Göttingen: Vandenhoeck & Ruprecht.

———. 1935. *Der Monotheismus als politisches Problem.* Leipzig: Hegner.

———. 1959. "Das Problem des Nationalismus im alten Christentum." In *Frühkirche, Judentum und Gnosis,* 51–63. Freiburg: Herder.

Pfanner, M. 1989. "Über das Herstellen von Porträts: Ein Beitrag zu Rationalisierungsmaßnahmen und Produktionsmechanismen von Massenware im späten Hellenismus und in der römischen Kaiserzeit." *JDAI* 104:157–257.

Picard, G.-C. 1957. *Les trophées romains: Contribution à l'histoire de la religion et de l'art triomphal de Rome.* BÉFAR, 187. Paris: Boccard.

Pierce, R. H. 1968. "*Grapheion,* catalogue, and library in Roman Egypt." *SO* 43:68–83.

Piganiol, A. 1932. *L'empereur Constantin.* Paris: Rieder.

Pighi, G. B. 1965. *De ludis saecularibus populi Romani quiritium libri sex.* 2d edition. Amsterdam: Schippers.

Portmann, W. 1988. *Geschichte in der spätantiken Panegyrik.* Frankfurt: Peter Lang.

Potter, D. S. 1990. *Prophecy and history in the crisis of the Roman empire.* Oxford: Clarendon Press.

———. 1996a. "Emperors, their borders and their neighbours: The scope of imperial *mandata.*" Kennedy 1996, 49–66.

———. 1996b. "Palmyra and Rome: Odaenathus' titulature and the use of the *imperium maius.*" ZPE 113:271–285.

———. 1996c. "Performance, power, and justice in the high empire." In *Roman theater and society,* edited by W. J. Slater, 129–159. Ann Arbor: University of Michigan Press.

Preisigke, F. 1917. *Die Inschrift von Skaptoparene in ihrer Beziehung zur kaiserlichen Kanlei in Rom.* Schriften der Wissenschaftlichen Gesellschaft in Strassburg, 30. Strassburg: K. J. Trubner.

von Premerstein, A. 1937. *Vom Werden und Wesen des Prinzipats.* AbhBay, 15. Munich.

Price, S. R. F. 1979. Review of Fears 1977. *CR* 29:277–279.

———. 1984a. "Gods and emperors: The Greek language of the Roman imperial cult." *JHS* 104:79–95.

———. 1984b. *Rituals and power: The Roman imperial cult in Asia Minor.* Cambridge: Cambridge University Press.

Purcell, N. 1983. "The *apparitores:* A study in social mobility." *PBSR* 51:127–173.

————. 1990. "The creation of provincial landscape: The Roman impact on Cisalpine Gaul." Blagg and Millett 1990, 6–29.

Putnam, M. C. J. 1990. "Horace *Car.* 2.9: Augustus and the ambiguities of encomium." Raaflaub and Toher 1990, 212–238.

Raaflaub, K. A., and L. J. Samons II. 1990. "Opposition to Augustus." Raaflaub and Toher 1990, 417–454.

Raaflaub, K. A., and M. Toher, eds. 1990. *Between republic and empire: Interpretations of Augustus and his principate.* Berkeley and Los Angeles: University of California Press.

Rathbone, D. W. 1986. "The dates of the recognition in Egypt of the emperors from Caracalla to Diocletianus." *ZPE* 62:101–131.

————. 1993. "Egypt, Augustus, and Roman taxation." *Cahiers Glotz* 4:81–112.

Raven, S. 1993. *Rome in Africa.* 3d edition. London: Routledge.

Rawson, E. 1985. *Intellectual life in the late Roman Republic.* Baltimore: The Johns Hopkins University Press.

————. 1991. *Roman culture and society.* Oxford: Clarendon Press.

Rea, J. 1977. "A new version of P. Yale inv. 299." *ZPE* 27:151–156.

Reynolds, J. 1962. "Vota pro salute principis." *PBSR* 30:33–36.

————. 1978. "Hadrian, Antoninus Pius, and the Cyrenaïcan cities." *JRS* 68:111–121.

————. 1980. "The origins and beginning of imperial cult at Aphrodisias." *PCPhS* 26:70–84.

————. 1981. "New evidence for the imperial cult in Julio-Claudian Aphrodisias." *ZPE* 43:317–327.

————. 1982. *Aphrodisias and Rome.* JRS Monograph 1. London: Society for the Promotion of Roman Studies.

————. 1986. "Further information on the imperial cult at Aphrodisias." *StCl* 24:109–117.

Reynolds, J., M. Beard, and C. Roueché. 1986. "Roman inscriptions 1981–85." *JRS* 76:124–146.

Richard, J.-C. 1966a. "Incinération et inhumation aux funérailles impériales: Histoire du rituel de l'apothéose pendant le haut-empire." *Latomus* 25:784–804.

————. 1966b. "Tombeaux des empereurs et temples des *Divi:* Notes sur la signification religieuse des sépultures impériales à Rome." *Revue de l'Histoire des Religions* 170:127–142.

————. 1978. "Recherches sur certains aspects du culte impérial: Les funérailles des empereurs romains aux deux premiers siècles de notre ère." *ANRW* 2.16.2.1121–1134.

Richardson, J. S. 1983. "The *Tabula Contrebiensis:* Roman law in Spain in the early first century B.C." *JRS* 73:33–41.

Richter, G. M. A. 1971. *The engraved gems of the Greeks, Etruscans and Romans.* Part 2, *Engraved gems of the Romans.* London: Phaidon.

Riepl, W. 1913. *Das Nachrichtenwesen des Altertums.* Leipzig: Teubner.

Robbins, V. K. 1991. "Luke-Acts: A mixed population seeks a home in the Roman empire." L. Alexander 1991, 202–221.

Robert, L. 1938. *Études épigraphiques et philologiques.* Bibliotheque de l'École des

Hautes Études, Sciences Historiques et Philologiques, 272. Paris: Champion, 1938.

———. 1954. *La Carie*. Tome 2, *Le plateau de Tabai et ses environs*. Paris: Librairie d'Amérique et d'Orient.

———. 1977. "La titulature de Nicée et de Nicomédie: La gloire et la haine." *HSCP* 81:1–39.

———. 1987. *Documents d'Asie Mineure*. BÉFAR 239 *bis*. Paris: Boccard. (Articles from *BCH*, 1977–85.)

———. 1994. *Le martyre de Pionios, prêtre de Smyrne*. Edited by G. W. Bowersock and C. P. Jones. Washington, D.C.: Dumbarton Oaks.

Robert, L., and J. Robert. 1989. *Claros*. Volume 1, *Décrets hellénistiques*. Paris: Recherche sur les Civilisations.

Rogers, G. M. 1991. *The sacred identity of Ephesos*. London: Routledge.

Rösch, G. 1978. ONOMA ΒΑΣΙΛΕΙΑΣ: *Studien zum offiziellen Gebrach der Kaisertitel in spätantiker und frühbyzantinischer Zeit*. Byzantina Vindobonensia, 10. Vienna: Verlag der Österreichischen Akademie.

Rose, C. B. 1997a. *Dynastic commemoration and imperial portraiture in the Julio-Claudian period*. Cambridge: Cambridge University Press.

———. 1997b. "The imperial image in the eastern Mediterranean." Alcock 1997, 108–120.

Rosenstein, N. 1990. *Imperatores victi: Military defeat and aristocratic competition in the middle and late Republic*. Berkeley and Los Angeles: University of California Press.

Ross, S. K. 1993. "The last king of Edessa: New evidence from the middle Euphrates." *ZPE* 97:187–206.

Rossi-Landi, F. 1990. *Marxism and ideology*. Translated by R. Griffin. Oxford: Clarendon Press.

Rostovtzeff, M. 1942. "*Vexillum* and Victory." *JRS* 32:92–106.

Roueché, C. 1984. "Acclamations in the later Roman empire: New evidence from Aphrodisias." *JRS* 74:181–199.

———. 1989. *Aphrodisias in late antiquity*. JRS Monograph 5. London: Society for the Promotion of Roman Studies.

Roussel, P., and F. de Visscher. 1942/43. "Les inscriptions du temple de Dmeir." *Syria* 23:173–200.

Rowe, G. 1997. "*Omnis spes futura paternae stationis:* Public responses to the Roman imperial succession." D.Phil. thesis. The Queen's College, Oxford.

Roxan, M. M. 1978. *Roman military diplomas 1954–1977*. Institute of Archaeology, University of London, Occasional Publications, 2. London.

———. 1985. *Roman military diplomas 1978–1984*. Institute of Archaeology, University of London, Occasional Publications, 9. London.

Rubin, Z. 1975. "Dio, Herodian, and Severus' second Parthian war." *Chiron* 5: 419–441.

———. 1980. *Civil-war propaganda and historiography*. Collection Latomus, 173. Brussels: Revue d'Études Latines.

Ruggini, L. C. 1976. "La vita associativa nelle città dell'oriente greco: Tradizioni locali e influenze romane." In *Assimilations et résistance à la culture gréco-romaine dans le monde ancien: Travaux du VIe congrès international d'études classiques* (Madrid, 1974), 463–491. Paris: Les Belles Lettres.

Sabbah, G. 1978. *La méthode d'Ammien Marcellin.* Paris: Les Belles Lettres.

———. 1984. "De la rhétorique à la communication politique: Les Panégyriques latins." *BAGB* 1984:363–388.

de Ste. Croix, G. E. M. 1981. *The class struggle in the ancient Greek world.* Ithaca: Cornell University Press.

Sansterre, J.-M. 1972. "Eusèbe de Césarée et la naissance de la théorie 'césaropapiste.'" *Byzantion* 42:131–195 and 532–594.

Saria, B. 1950. "Noricum und Pannonien." *Historia* 1:436–486.

Sartre, M. 1991. *L'orient romain: Provinces et sociétés provinciales en Méditerranée orientale d'Auguste aux Sévères.* Paris: Éditions du Seuil.

———. 1995. *L'Asie Mineure et l'Anatolie d'Alexandre à Dioclétien, IVe siècle av. J.-C./IIIe siècle ap. J.-C.* Paris: Colin.

Sasel, J. 1983. "Dolichenus-Heiligtum in Praetorium Latobicorum (Caracalla, Caesar, Imperator Destinatus)." *ZPE* 50:203–208.

Schechner, R. 1987. "Preface." V. Turner 1987, 7–20.

Scheid, J. 1975. *Les frères arvales: Recrutement et origine sociale sous les empereurs julioclaudiens.* Bibliothèque de l'École des Hautes Études, Sciences Religieuses, 77. Paris: Presses Universitaires de France.

———. 1990. *Romulus et ses frères: Le collège des frères arvales, modèle du culte public dans la Rome des empereurs.* BÉFAR 275. Rome: École Française de Rome.

———. 1994. "Les archives de la piété." Demougin 1994, 173–185.

———. 1995. "*Graeco ritu:* A typically Roman way of honoring the gods." *HSCP* 97:15–31.

Schubert, F., ed. 1990. *Les archives de Marcus Lucretius Diogenes et textes apparentés.* Papyrologische Texte und Abhandlungen, 39. Bonn: Habelt.

Schulz, F. 1942. "Roman registers of births and birth certificates." *JRS* 32:78–91.

———. 1943. "Roman registers of births and birth certificates, Part II." *JRS* 33:55–64.

von Schwind, F. F. 1940. *Zur Frage der Publikation im römischen Recht.* Münchener Beiträge zur Papyrusforschung und Antiken Rechtsgeschichte, 31. Munich: Beck.

Scott, K. 1931a. "Greek and Roman honorific months." *YCS* 2:201–278.

———. 1931b. "The significance of statues in precious metals in emperor worship." *TAPA* 62:101–123.

Seeck, O. 1906. *Die Briefe des Libanius.* Leipzig.

———. 1919. *Regesten der Kaiser und Päpste.* Stuttgart: Metzler.

Seston, W. 1947. "Constantine as a 'bishop.'" *JRS* 37:127–131.

———. 1962. "Les chevaliers romains et le *iustitium* de Germanicus." *RHDFE* 30:159–177.

Seston, W., and M. Euzennat. 1971. "Un dossier de la chancellerie romain: La *Tabula Banasitana,* étude de diplomatique." *CRAI* 1971:468–490.

Setton, K. M. 1941. *Christian attitude towards the emperor in the fourth century.* New York: Columbia University Press.

Seyrig, H. 1934. "Antiquités syriennes." *Syria* 15:155–186.

———. 1937. "Antiquités syriennes." *Syria* 18:1–4.

————. 1963. "Les fils du roi Odainat." *Annales Archéologiques de Syrie* 13:159–172.

————. 1966. "Vhabalathus Augustus." In *Mélanges offerts à Kazimierz Michalowski,* edited by M. L. Bernhard, 659–662. Warsaw: Panstwowe Wydawnictwo Naukowe.

Shaw, B. 1981. "The elder Pliny's African geography." *Historia* 30:424–471.

————. 1995. "Josephus: Roman power and responses to it." *Athenaeum* 83:357–390.

Sherk, R. K. 1974. "Roman geographical exploration and military maps." *ANRW* 2.1.534–562.

Sherwin-White, A. N. 1966. *The letters of Pliny: A historical and social commentary.* Oxford: Clarendon Press.

————. 1973a. *The Roman citizenship.* 2d edition. Oxford: Oxford University Press.

————. 1973b. "The *tabula* of Banasa and the *Constitutio Antoniniana.*" *JRS* 63:86–98.

————. 1982. "The *lex repetundarum* and the political ideas of Gaius Gracchus." *JRS* 72:18–31.

————. 1984. *Roman foreign policy in the East, 168 B.C. to A.D. 1.* Norman: University of Oklahoma Press.

Sijpesteijn, P. J. 1969. "A new document concerning Hadrian's visit to Egypt." *Historia* 18:109–118.

Simon, D. 1994. "Legislation as both a world order and a legal order." In *Law and society in Byzantium: Ninth–twelfth centuries,* edited by A. E. Laiou and D. Simon, 1–25. Washington, D.C.: Dumbarton Oaks.

Sivan, H. 1991. "Eunapius and the West: Remarks on frg. 78 (Müller)." *Historia* 40:95–104.

Smallwood, E. M. 1970. *Philonis Alexandrini* Legatio ad Gaium: *Edited with an introduction, translation, and commentary.* 2d edition. Leiden: Brill.

Smith, R. R. R. 1987. "The imperial reliefs from the Sebasteion at Aphrodisias." *JRS* 77:88–138.

————. 1988. "*Simulacra gentium:* The *ethne* from the Sebasteion at Aphrodisias." *JRS* 78:50–77.

————. 1996. "Typology and diversity in the portraits of Augustus." *JRA* 9:30–47.

Snyder, G. F. 1985. Ante pacem: *Archaeological evidence of church life before Constantine.* Mercer: Mercer University Press.

Snyder, W. F. 1940. "Public anniversaries in the Roman empire." *YCS* 7:223–317.

von Soden, H. 1913. *Urkunden zur Entstehungsgeschichte des Donatismus.* Kleine Texte für Vorlesungen und Übungen, 122. Bonn: Marcus und Weber.

Soproni, S. 1980. "Die Caesarwürde Caracallas und die syrische Kohorte von Szentendre." *Alba Regia* 18:39–51.

Spawforth, A. J., and S. Walker. 1985. "The world of the Panhellenion, I: Athens and Eleusis." *JRS* 75:78–104.

————. 1986. "The world of the Panhellenion, II: Three Dorian cities." *JRS* 76:88–105.

Stadter, P. A. 1980. *Arrian of Nicomedia.* Chapel Hill: University of North Carolina Press.

Staehelin, F. 1944. "Felicior Augusto, melior Traiano!" *MH* 1:179–180.

Stahl, M. 1978. *Imperiale Herrschaft und provinziale Stadt: Strukturprobleme der rö-*

mischen Reichsorganisation im 1.–3. Jh. der Kaiserzeit. Hypomnemata, 52. Göttingen: Vandenhoeck & Ruprecht.

Stein, A. 1930a. "Römische Inschriften in der antiken Literatur, 1. Teil." *Bericht der Lese- und Redehalle der Deutschen Studenten in Prag* 78:5–41.

———. 1930b. "Römische Inschriften in der antiken Literatur, 2. Teil." *Bericht der Lese- und Redehalle der Deutschen Studenten in Prag* 79:5–49.

Stemberger, G. *Introduction to the Talmud and Midrash*. Translated by M. Bockmuehl. 2d edition. Edinburgh: T&T Clark.

Stern, M. 1987. "Josephus and the Roman empire as reflected in *The Jewish War*." In *Josephus, Judaism, and Christianity*, edited by L. H. Feldman and G. Hata, 71–80. Detroit: Wayne State University Press.

Stevenson, T. R. 1992. "The ideal benefactor and the father analogy in Greek and Roman thought." *CQ* 42: 421–436.

Straub, J. 1939. *Vom Herrscherideal in der Spätantike*. Forschungen zur Kirchen- und Geistesgeschichte, 18. Stuttgart: Kohlhammer.

———. 1967. "Constantine as ΚΟΙΝΟΣ ΕΠΙΣΚΟΠΟΣ." *DOP* 21:37–55.

Stuart, M. 1939. "How were imperial portraits distributed throughout the Roman empire?" *AJA* 43:601–617.

Sumner, G. V. 1970. "The truth about Velleius Paterculus: Prolegomena." *HSCP* 74:257–297.

———. 1978. "Varrones Murenae." *HSCP* 82:187–195.

Sutherland, C. H. V. 1976. *The emperor and the coinage: Julio-Claudian studies*. London: Spink.

———. 1987. *Roman history and coinage, 44 B.C.–A.D. 69*. Oxford: Clarendon Press.

Swain, S. 1993. "Greek into Palmyrene: Odaenathus as 'Corrector Totius Orientis'?" *ZPE* 99:157–164.

Swan, M. 1966. "The consular *fasti* of 23 B.C. and the conspiracy of Varro Murena." *HSCP* 71:235–247.

Swift, E. H. 1923. "*Imagines* in imperial portraiture." *AJA* 27:286–301.

Swift, L. J., 1966. "The anonymous encomium of Philip the Arab." *GRBS* 7:267–289.

Swift, L. J., and J. H. Oliver. 1962. "Constantius II on Flavius Philippus." *AJP* 83:247–264.

Syme, R. 1939. *The Roman revolution*. Oxford: Clarendon Press.

———. 1958. *Tacitus*. Oxford: Clarendon Press.

———. 1971. *Emperors and biography*. Oxford: Clarendon Press.

———. 1978. *History in Ovid*. Oxford: Clarendon Press.

———. 1983. *Historia Augusta papers*. Oxford: Clarendon Press.

———. 1986. *The Augustan aristocracy*. Oxford: Clarendon Press.

Szidat, J. 1981. "Zur Wirkung und Aufnahme der Münzpropaganda (Iul. Misop. 355d)." *MH* 38:22–33.

———. 1996. *Historischer Kommentar zu Ammianus Marcellinus Buch XX-XXI*. Teil III, *Die Konfrontationen*. Historia Einzelschriften, 89. Stuttgart: Steiner.

———. 1997. "Die Usurpation Julians: Ein Sonderfall?" Paschoud and Szidat 1997, 63–70.

Taeger, F. 1960. *Charisma: Studien zur Geschichte des antiken Herrscherkultes*. Band 2. Stuttgart: Kohlhammer.

Talbert, R. J. A. 1984. *The Senate of imperial Rome*. Princeton: Princeton University Press.

———. 1988. "Commodus as diplomat in an extract from the *acta senatus*." *ZPE* 71:137–147.

Tarn, W. W. 1948. *Alexander the Great*. Vol. 2, *Sources and studies*. Cambridge: Cambridge University Press.

Teitler, H. C. 1985. Notarii *and* Exceptores. Dutch Monographs on Ancient History and Archaeology, 1. Amsterdam: Gieben.

Teixidor, J. 1989. "Les derniers rois d'Édesse d'après deux nouveaux documents syriaques." *ZPE* 76:219–222.

Thomas, J. D. 1983. "*Subscriptiones* to petitions of officials in Roman Egypt." In *Egypt and the Hellenistic World*, edited by E. Van't Dack et al., 369–382. Leuven: Orientaliste.

Thomas, Y. 1996. *"Origine" et "commune patrie": Étude de droit public romain (89 av. J.-C.–212 ap. J.-C.)*. CÉFR 221. Rome: École Française de Rome.

Thompson, J. B. 1990. *Ideology and modern culture: Critical social theory in the era of mass communication*. Stanford: Stanford University Press.

Toll, K. 1991. "The *Aeneid* as an epic of national identity: *Italiam laeto socii clamore salutant*." *Helios* 18:3–14.

———. 1997. "Making Roman-ness and the *Aeneid*." *ClassAnt* 16:34–56.

Topping, E. C. 1977. "Romanos on the entry into Jerusalem: A *basilikos logos*." *Byzantion* 47:65–91.

Townend, G. B. 1964. "Some rhetorical battle-pictures in Dio." *Hermes* 92:467–481.

Toynbee, A. J. 1973. *Constantine Porphyrogenitus and his world*. Oxford: Oxford University Press.

Toynbee, J. M. C. 1934. *The Hadrianic school*. Cambridge: Cambridge University Press.

———. 1947. "*Roma* and *Constantinopolis* in late-antique art from 312 to 365." *JRS* 37:135–144.

———. 1953. "*Roma* and *Constantinopolis* in late-antique art from 365 to Justin II." In *Studies presented to D. M. Robinson*, edited by G. E. Mylonas, 2:261–277. St. Louis: Washington University Press.

———. [1944] 1986. *Roman medallions*. Numismatic Studies, 5. New York: American Numismatic Society. (Reprint, with bibliographic addenda by W. E. Metcalf.)

Treitinger, O. 1938. Remarks on P. Charanis, "The imperial crown *modiolus* once more" (*Byzantion* 13 [1938]: 377–381). *BZ* 39:194–202.

Turner, E. G. 1975. "Oxyrhynchus and Rome." *HSCP* 79:1–24.

Turner, V. 1974. *Dramas, fields, and metaphors*. Ithaca: Cornell University Press.

———. 1987. *The anthropology of performance*. New York: PAJ Publications.

Vandorpe, K. 1995. *Breaking the seal of secrecy: Sealing-practices in Graeco-Roman and Byzantine Egypt, based on Greek, Demotic, and Latin papyrological evidence*. Leiden: Papyrologish Instituut.

Verbraken, P.-P. 1976. *Études critiques sur les sermons authentiques de S. Augustin*. Instrumenta Patristica, 12. Steenbergen: Abbatia S. Petri.

Vernay, E. 1913. "Note sur le changement de style dans les constitutions impériales de Dioclétien à Constantin." In *Études d'histoire juridique offertes à Paul Frederic Girard par ses élèves*, 2:263–274. Paris: Paul Geuthner.

Versnel, H. S. 1970. *Triumphus*. Leiden: Brill.

———. 1980. "Destruction, *devotio* and despair in a situation of anomy: The mourning for Germanicus in triple perspective." In *Perennitas: Studi in onore di A. Brelich*, 541–618. Rome: Ateneo.

Veyne, P. 1962. "Les honneurs posthumes de Flavia Domitilla et les dédicaces grecques et latines." *Latomus* 21:49–98.

Vidén, G. 1984. *The Roman chancery tradition: Studies in the language of the* Codex Theodosianus *and Cassiodorus'* Variae. StudGoth 46. Göteborg: Acta Universitatis Gothoburgensis.

Viljamaa, T. 1968. *Studies in Greek encomiastic poetry of the early Byzantine period*. Commentationes Humanarum Litterarum, 42, no. 4. Helsinki: Societas Scientiarum Fennica.

Vittinghoff, F. 1964. "Zum geschichtlichen Selbstverständnis der Spätantike." *HZ* 198:529–574.

———. 1986. "Militärdiplome, römische Bürgerrechts- und Integrationspolitik der hohen Kaiserzeit." In *Heer und Integrationspolitik: Der römische Militärdiplome als historische Quelle*, edited by W. Eck and H. Wolff, Passauer Historische Forschungen, no. 2, 535–555. Cologne: Böhlau.

———. 1987. "Staat, Kirche und Dynastie beim Tode Konstantins." *EntrHardt* 34:1–34.

Vogt, J. 1960. *Orbis: Ausgewählte Schriften zur Geschichte des Altertums*. Freiburg: Herder.

———. 1967. "Kulturwelt und Barbaren: Zum Menschheitsbild der spätantiken Gesellschaft." AbhMainz, 1967, no. 1.

Waelkens, M. 1989. "Hellenistic and Roman influence in the imperial architecture of Asia Minor." In *The Greek renaissance in the Roman empire*, edited by S. Walker and A. Cameron, BICS Supplement 55, 77–88. London: Institute of Classical Studies.

Walbank, F. 1948. "The geography of Polybius." *Classica et Mediaevalia* 9:155–182.

———. 1972. *Polybius*. Berkeley and Los Angeles: University of California Press.

Walker, S. 1997. "Athens under Augustus." Hoff and Rotroff 1997, 67–80.

Wallace-Hadrill, A. 1990. "Roman arches and Greek honours: The language of power at Rome." *PCPhS* 36:143–181.

———. 1997. "*Mutatio morum:* The idea of a cultural revolution." In *The Roman cultural revolution*, edited by T. Habinek and A. Schiesaro, 3–22. Cambridge: Cambridge University Press.

Warmington, B. H. 1974. "Aspects of Constantinian propaganda in the Panegyrici Latini." *TAPA* 104:371–384.

Waters, K. A. 1969. "Traianus Domitiani Continuator." *AJP* 90:385–405.

Weber, M. 1968. *On charisma and institution building*. Edited by S. N. Eisenstadt. Chicago: University of Chicago Press.

———. 1978. *Economy and society*. Edited by G. Roth and C. Wittich. Berkeley and Los Angeles: University of California Press.

Webster, J., and N. Cooper, eds. 1996. *Roman imperialism: Post-colonial perspectives*. Leicester Archaeology Monographs, 3. Leicester: School of Archaeological Studies.

Weinstock, S. 1957. "Victor and invictus." *HThR* 50:211–247.

———. 1960. "Pax and the 'Ara Pacis.'" *JRS* 50:44–58.

———. 1962. "Treueid und Kaiserkult." *MDAI(A)* 77:306–327.

———. 1971. *Divus Julius*. Oxford: Clarendon Press.

Welles, C. B. 1938. "The inscriptions." In *Gerasa: City of the Decapolis*, edited by C. H. Kraeling, 355–616. New Haven: American Schools of Oriental Research.

Wellesley, K. 1989. *The long year* A.D. *69*. 2d edition. Bristol: Bristol Classical Press.

Wenger, A. 1952. "Notes inédits sur les empereurs Théodose I, Arcadius, Théodose II, Léon I." *RÉByz* 10:47–59.

———. 1966. "Une homélie inédite de Sévérien de Gabala sur le lavement des pieds." *RÉByz* 24:219–234.

Wenger, L. 1942. Review of F. de Visscher, *Les édits d'Auguste découverts à Cyrène* (Louvain: Bibliothèque de l'Université de Belgique, 1940). *ZSavRom* 62:425–436.

———. 1953. *Die Quellen des römischen Rechts*. Denkschriften der Österreichischen Akademie der Wissenschaften, 2. Vienna: Holzhausens.

West, A. B. 1931. *Corinth*. Vol. 8, part 2, *Latin inscriptions (1896–1926)*. Cambridge, Mass.: Harvard University Press.

Westermann, W., and A. Schiller. 1954. *Apokrimata: Decisions of Septimius Severus on legal matters*. New York: Columbia University Press.

Wheeler, E. L. 1993. "Methodological limits and the mirage of Roman strategy." *The Journal of Military History* 57:7–41 and 215–240.

White, P. 1993. *Promised verse: Poets in the society of Augustan Rome*. Cambridge, Mass: Harvard University Press.

———. 1997. "Julius Caesar and the publication of *acta* in late Republican Rome." *Chiron* 27:73–84.

Whittaker, C. R., ed. 1970. *Herodian*. Cambridge, Mass.: Harvard University Press.

———. 1994. *Frontiers of the Roman empire: A social and economic study*. Baltimore: The Johns Hopkins University Press.

———. 1996. "Where are the frontiers now?" Kennedy 1996, 24–41.

Wieacker, F. 1955. *Vulgarismus und Klassizismus im Recht der Spätantike*. SitzHeid 1955, no. 3. Heidelberg: Winter.

Wifstrand, A. 1939. "Autokrator, Kaisar, Basileus: Bemerkungen zu den griechischen Benennungen der römischen Kaiser." In *DRAGMA Martino P. Nilsson . . . dedicatum*. Skrifter Utgivna av Svenska Institutet i Rom, no. 1, 529–539. Lund: Ohlssons.

Wilcken, U. 1894. "Ὑπομνηματισμοί." *Philologus* 53:80–126.

———. 1920. "Zu den Kaiserreskripten." *Hermes* 55:1–42.

———. 1930. "Zur *propositio libellorum*." *Archiv* 9:15–23.

———. 1935. "Urkunden-Referate, VII: P. Harr." *Archiv* 12:234–236.

———. 1936. "Ueber den Nutzen der lateinischen Papyri." In *Atti del IV Congresso internazionale di papirologia Firenze, 28 aprile–2 maggio 1935*, 101–122. Milan: Aegyptus.

Williams, S., and G. Friell. 1995. *Theodosius: The empire at bay.* New Haven: Yale University Press.

Williams, W. 1975. "Formal and historical aspects of two new documents of Marcus Aurelius." *ZPE* 17:37–78.

———. 1980. "The publication of imperial subscripts." *ZPE* 40:283–294.

———. 1986. "Epigraphic texts of imperial subscripts: A survey." *ZPE* 66:181–207.

Williamson, C. 1987. "Monuments of bronze: Roman legal documents on bronze tablets." *ClassAnt* 6:160–183.

Wirth, G. 1979. "Themistios und Constantius." *ByzF* 6:293–317.

———, ed. 1982. *Romanitas-Christianitas: Untersuchungen zur Geschichte und Literatur der römischen Kaiserzeit, J. Straub zum 70. Geburtstag gewidmet.* Berlin: de Gruyter.

Wiseman, T. P. 1995. *Remus: A Roman myth.* Cambridge: Cambridge University Press.

Wissowa, G. 1912. *Religion und Kultus der Römer.* 2d edition. Munich: Beck.

Wistrand, E. 1987. *Felicitas imperatoria.* StudGoth 48. Göteborg: Acta Universitatis Gothoburgensis.

Woodman, A. J. 1977. *Velleius Paterculus: The Tiberian narrative (2.94–131).* Cambridge Classical Texts and Commentaries, 19. Cambridge: Cambridge University Press.

———. 1983. *Velleius Paterculus: The Caesarian and Augustan narrative (2.41–93).* Cambridge Classical Texts and Commentaries, 25. Cambridge: Cambridge University Press.

———. 1993. "Amateur dramatics at the court of Nero: *Annals* 15:48–74." In *Tacitus and the Tacitean tradition,* edited by T. J. Luce and A. J. Woodman, 104–128. Princeton: Princeton University Press.

Woolf, G. 1997. "The Roman urbanization of the East." Alcock 1997, 1–14.

———. 1998. *Becoming Roman: The origins of provincial civilization in Gaul.* Cambridge: Cambridge University Press.

Worp, K. A. 1982. "Byzantine imperial titulature in the Greek documentary papyri: The oath formulas." *ZPE* 45:199–223.

Wörrle, M. 1975. "Zwei neue Inschriften aus Myra zur Verwaltung Lykiens in der Kaiserzeit." In *Myra: Eine lykische Metropole in antiker und byzantinischer Zeit,* edited by J. Borchhardt, Istanbuler Forschungen von der Abteilung Istanbuls der DAI, 254–300. Berlin: Mann.

Yavetz, Z. 1969. *Plebs and princeps.* Oxford: Clarendon Press.

Youtie, H. C. 1971a. "ΑΓΡΑΜΜΑΤΟΣ: An aspect of Greek society in Egypt." *HSCP* 75:161–176.

———. 1971b. "Βραδέως γράφων: Between literacy and illiteracy." *GRBS* 12:239–261.

———. 1975a. "'Because they do not know letters.'" *ZPE* 19:101–108.

———. 1975b. "ΥΠΟΓΡΑΦΕΥΣ: The social impact of illiteracy in Graeco-Roman Egypt." *ZPE* 17:201–221.

———. 1976. "P. Mich. III 203." *ZPE* 20:288–292.

———. 1977. "P. Mich. inv. 148, verso: The rule of precedent." *ZPE* 27:124–137.

Youtie, H. C., and A. A. Schiller. 1955. "Second thoughts on the Columbia *apokri-mata* (P. Col. 123)." *Chronique d'Égypte* 60:327–345.

Zanker, P. 1979. "Prinzipat und Herrscherbild." *Gymnasium* 86:353–368.

———. 1983. *Provinzielle Kaiserporträts: Zur Rezeption der Selbstdarstellung des Princeps.* AbhBay 90. Munich.

———. 1988. *The power of images in the age of Augustus.* Ann Arbor: University of Michigan Press.

de Zulueta, F. 1953. *The Institutes of Gaius.* Part 2, *Commentary.* Oxford: Clarendon Press.

GENERAL INDEX

INDEX LOCORUM

Text:	10/12 Baskerville
Display:	Baskerville
Composition:	G & S Typesetters, Inc.
Printing and binding:	Thomson-Shore, Inc.

CPSIA information can be obtained
at www.ICGtesting.com
Printed in the USA
JSHW061557030822
28854JS00001B/3